NEW PERSPECTIVES
ON COMPUTER CONCEPTS

COMPLETE EDITION

JUNE JAMRICH PARSONS
University of the Virgin Islands

DAN OJA
GuildWare, Inc.

A Susan Solomon Book

Course
TECHNOLOGY

Course Technology, Inc. *One Main Street, Cambridge, MA 02142*
An International Thomson Publishing Company

I T P

New Perspectives on Computer Concepts, Complete Edition, is published by Course Technology, Inc.

Director of Production	MYRNA D'ADDARIO
Product Manager	SUSAN SOLOMON COMMUNICATIONS
Production Supervisor	KATHRYN DINOVO
Desktop Publishers	KIM MUNSELL
	ANDREA GREITZER
Production Specialist	ERIN C. BRIDGEFORD
Copyeditor/Labs Tester	JENNIFER HOOPER
Proofreaders	JOAN WILCOX
	NANCY KRUSE HANNIGAN
Indexer	ALEXANDRA NICKERSON
Product Testing and Support Supervisor	JEFF GODING
Prepress Production	GEX, INC.
Manufacturing Manager	ELIZABETH MARTINEZ
Photo Researcher	SARAH BENDERSKY
Art Director	DAVID REED
Illustrators	ILLUSTRIOUS, INC.
	STANLEY ROBERTS
Cover and Text Designer	DAVID REED

ISBN 1-56527-164-5

Printed in the United States of America
10   9   8   7   6   5   4   3   2

FROM THE PUBLISHER

At Course Technology, Inc., we believe that technology will transform the way that people teach and learn. We are excited about bringing you, college professors and students, the most practical and affordable technology-related products available.

The Course Technology Development Process

Our development process is unparalleled in the higher education publishing industry. Every product we create goes through an exacting process of design, development, review, and testing.

Reviewers give us direction and insight that shape our manuscripts and bring them up to the latest standards. Every manuscript is quality tested. Students whose backgrounds match the intended audience work through every page, carefully checking for clarity. Together with our own technical reviewers, these testers help us ensure that everything that carries our name is error-free and easy to use.

Course Technology Products

We show both how and why technology is critical to solving problems in college and in whatever field you choose to teach or pursue. Examples and applications are chosen and crafted to motivate students. Interactivity and active learning are our watchwords.

The Course Technology Team

This book will suit your needs because it was delivered quickly, efficiently, and affordably. Every employee contributes to this process. The names of all our employees are listed below:

Tim Ashe, David Backer, Stephen M. Bayle, Josh Bernoff, Michelle Brown, Ann Marie Buconjic, Jody Buttafoco, Kerry Cannell, Jim Chrysikos, Barbara Clemens, Susan Collins, John M. Connolly, Kim Crowley, Myrna D'Addario, Lisa D'Alessandro, Howard S. Diamond, Kathryn Dinovo, Joseph B. Dougherty, MaryJane Dwyer, Chris Elkhill, Don Fabricant, Kate Gallagher, Jeff Goding, Laurie Gomes, Eileen Gorham, Andrea Greitzer, Catherine Griffin, Tim Hale, Roslyn Hooley, Nicole Jones, Matt Kenslea, Susannah Lean, Suzanne Licht, Laurie Lindgren, Kim Mai, Elizabeth Martinez, Debbie Masi, Don Maynard, Dan Mayo, Kathleen McCann, Jay McNamara, Mac Mendelsohn, Laurie Michelangelo, Kim Munsell, Amy Oliver, Michael Ormsby, Kristine Otto, Debbie Parlee, Kristin Patrick, Charlie Patsios, Jodi Paulus, Darren Perl, Kevin Phaneuf, George J. Pilla, Cathy Prindle, Nancy Ray, Marjorie Schlaikjer, Christine Spillett, Michelle Tucker, David Upton, Mark Valentine, Karen Wadsworth, Anne Marie Walker, Renee Walkup, Tracy Wells, Donna Whiting, Janet Wilson, Lisa Yameen.

PREFACE

The Genesis of New Perspectives

About a year ago our editor asked us to write a textbook for the introductory computer concepts course. We agreed, but recognized that a new paradigm was needed, that topic coverage should reflect changes in the rapidly developing computer industry, and that pedagogy should reflect the learning styles of today's students.

We wrote *New Perspectives on Computer Concepts* to empower students to be self-sufficient computer users. To achieve this goal we have presented new ways to look at computer concepts—ways that students can apply immediately when they use computers at home, at work, or in school labs.

You hold in your hands a text that is unique in many respects. This text emphasizes the practical aspects of today's computing environment—the basics of installing software, expanding a computer system, and defragmenting a disk, for example. This text integrates liberal studies with technical concepts and skills; it introduces data representation using the lanterns that signaled Paul Revere from Old North Church; it ties a discussion of user interfaces to the film *2001: A Space Odyssey*; and it presents the philosophic controversy "Can computers think?" This text delves into how things work—how a CD-ROM drive reads data from the CD, how an object-oriented database deals with objects and methods, how cables, computers, network cards, and software connect to form a local area network. And we have made every effort to weave this material together in a clear, interesting, and entertaining style.

The New Perspectives

What are the "new perspectives" that make this text more realistic for today's computing environments? Here is a short list of some; others you will discover as you read through the text.

- The place to start learning about computers is with the user interface.
- Learning how to *learn* about computing is an essential skill for computer users.
- Computer users should have a clear understanding of copyright regulations.
- The term "file" is used in many different ways, and it is important to distinguish among them to understand computer manuals, articles, and conversations.
- The microcomputer is the dominant architecture in today's computing environment.
- Understanding how computers represent and store data is important as a foundation for understanding how data, sound, and video files are stored and how files are compressed.
- Networks can no longer be explained simply as ring, bus, or star; now it is necessary to understand Ethernet, Token Ring, ARCnet, peer-to-peer, hierarchical, and client server protocols.
- Systems analysis and design are a joint venture between users and systems professionals.

- Understanding some of the trends in the computer *industry*—companies, market channels, products, and services—to make informed purchasing decisions is more important than learning the history of computer *machines*.

- Computer languages have outgrown rigid categories and now can be best described by the degree to which they exhibit characteristics such as declarative, procedural, object-oriented, event-driven, high-level, and low-level.

A Student-Centered Approach

New Perspectives on Computer Concepts encourages a student-centered and interactive approach to learning that returns the responsibility and rewards of learning to the students. Many of the features of this text are designed to encourage students' natural curiosity and drive to learn. At the beginning of each chapter, the Chapter Preview asks questions rather than states traditional objectives; this encourages students to take an active, inquisitive approach to learning. At the end of each chapter, the Chapter Review helps students think back over the material they've read, learn the terminology, and devise charts, outlines, or hierarchies to organize concepts.

Similarly, the Chapter Quizzes provide students the opportunity to test their understanding of the significant concepts presented in the chapter. In keeping with the active learning approach, the answers to these quizzes are included at the back of the book, so students can check their work.

The Projects are designed to help students review and extend their understanding of the chapter concepts. A Project might require individual written work, use of library reference materials, or collaboration with other students. Suggestions for administering the Projects are included in the Instructor's Resource Manual.

Finally, the Resources section at the end of each chapter is an eclectic list of books, articles, films, and other media designed to interest a diverse student population. It demonstrates that computers and computing are legitimate academic disciplines, each with a broad foundation of research and theory. Tips for incorporating the Resources in class discussions, assignments, or extra-credit activities are included in the Instructor's Resource Manual.

The Labs

The *New Perspectives on Computer Concepts* text articulates with the computer lab in a way never before available. Twenty-two innovative hands-on computer Labs combine illustrations, animations, digital images, and simulations to illustrate concepts and provide students with an environment for exploration and problem solving. For example, concepts such as defragmentation, physical file storage, and clusters, which are difficult to convey in lecture using traditional explanations, are communicated quickly and dramatically in the Defragmentation Lab. The simulation of an electronic bulletin board in the Data Communications Lab shows students what it's like to send and receive electronic mail. The Multimedia Lab allows students to experience this exciting new dimension of computing. In short, *the Labs show students what textbooks can only talk about.*

Lab Assignments are included at the end of each chapter in the text. Instructors can use these written assignments to verify that students have successfully completed the Labs. You are licensed to use *all* of the Labs whether you are using the Complete Edition or the Brief Edition.

See pages xiv-xv for a complete list and brief description of each Lab.

A Book for All Learning Styles

We've made illustrations an integral part of *New Perspectives on Computer Concepts*. For example, we introduced spreadsheet software with a two-page illustration of screens and printouts that show how formulas work, how spreadsheet models are made, and how graphs are created from spreadsheets. This "superfigure" employs the well-known fact that people always look at the pictures first. As students look at the figures, they will also read the associated text, thereby merging the graphic with the concept.

Supplements

An Instructor's Resource Kit is available upon adoption of this text. It contains the following items:

- Instructor's Resource Manual — For each chapter, we have included a Lesson Plan with Chapter Outline, Answers to the Preview Questions, Lecture Notes, Suggestions for Integrating the Labs, Word Puzzles using key terms, Answers to the Chapter Review and Chapter Quiz, and Solutions for the Projects and the Labs.

- Test Bank — For each Chapter, the Test Bank contains 50 multiple choice, 50 true/false, and 50 short-answer questions.

- Electronic Test Bank — The Electronic Test Bank allows instructors to edit individual test questions, select questions individually or at random, and print out scrambled versions of the same test to any supported printer.

- Electronic Transparencies — Electronic Transparencies present a selection of key illustrations from the textbook available in electronic format.

Interact with the Authors

We developed this textbook and the accompanying Labs in response to our classroom experience and to reviewers' comments. We expect this textbook and the Labs to evolve through the process of revision. Your experiences with *New Perspectives on Computer Concepts* are a valuable aid to us in this process. So please share your comments, questions, and suggestions with us. Our Internet address is jparsons@uvi.edu.

Acknowledgments

We are indebted to the reviewers who believed in our new perspectives: Joe Adamski, Grand Valley State University; Anthony Baxter, University of Kentucky; Chris Carter, Indiana Vocational Technical College; Stephanie Low Chenault, College of Charleston; Charles Hommel, University of Puget Sound; John Shepherd, Duquesne University; and Sandra Stalker, North Shore Community College. We are also indebted to Jeff Goding and his quality assurance team of student and professional testers.

Greg Gagnon, MGH Communications Cabling Wizard, and Ramachandran Bharath of Northern Michigan University made invaluable contributions to the Labs. Many thanks to Lynn Rosenthal and John Munro of the University of the Virgin Islands for their input on the illustrations.

The Course Technology, Inc. production staff worked miracles to showcase our work. We are grateful to Myrna D'Addario, Kim Munsell, Jennifer Hooper, and especially, Kathryn Dinovo.

Many thanks to Eileen Gorham, who produced some very creative marketing and truly believed in our project from the start. Thanks also to all of the sales representatives for their enthusiasm.

To Joe Dougherty goes our unceasing gratitude for his flexibility and persistent efforts to ensure that *New Perspectives* became a text we are all proud of. Our thanks to John Connolly, president of Course Technology, for supporting our vision. And finally, our thanks to Susan Solomon—through thick and thin, every bit the best editor in the business.

June Jamrich Parsons
Dan Oja

BRIEF CONTENTS

Brief Edition Only goes thru chapter 7 does not contain 8 - 11

CHAPTER ONE

USING COMPUTERS: ESSENTIAL CONCEPTS	NP 3
Computers: Mind Tools	NP 4
The Basics of Computer Hardware	NP 6
Interacting with the Computer	NP 13
Learning to Use Computers	NP 23

CHAPTER TWO

SOFTWARE AND MULTIMEDIA APPLICATIONS	NP 35
Computer Programs and Computer Software	NP 36
System Software	NP 39
Application Software	NP 44
Software Compatibility	NP 54
Installing and Using Software	NP 56
Multimedia Computing	NP 63

CHAPTER THREE

COMPUTER FILES	NP 77
Data and Information	NP 78
Computer Files	NP 78
Storage Media and Devices	NP 86
Using Files	NP 101

CHAPTER FOUR

COMPUTER ARCHITECTURE	NP 113
Digital Electronics	NP 114
The Main Board	NP 116
Bus	NP 117
Memory	NP 118
Processors	NP 123
The Boot Process	NP 130
Expanding the System	NP 135

CHAPTER FIVE

DATA COMMUNICATIONS	NP 151
Transmitting and Receiving Information	NP 152
Encoding Information	NP 152
Data Compression	NP 168
Communications Channels	NP 172
Communications Protocols	NP 176
Modems	NP 181

CHAPTER SIX

COMPUTER NETWORKS AND INFORMATION SERVICES	NP 191
Using a Computer Network	NP 192
Network Configuration	NP 198
Network Interactions	NP 205
Electronic Mail	NP 206
Bulletin Boards	NP 208
Commercial Information Services	NP 209
The Internet	NP 211

CHAPTER SEVEN

SECURITY, CONTROL, AND CONFIDENTIALITY	NP 225
Lost or Invalid Data	NP 226
Operator Error	NP 226
Power Problems	NP 230
Hardware Failure	NP 230
Trojan Horses, Time Bombs, Worms, and Logic Bombs	NP 232
Computer Viruses	NP 234
Computer Crime	NP 237
Restricting Access to Your Computer System	NP 239
Backup	NP 241
Confidentiality	NP 246

CHAPTER EIGHT

DEVELOPING EFFECTIVE INFORMATION SYSTEMS	NP 259
Information Systems	NP 260
System Development Life Cycle	NP 268
Analyze Needs	NP 269
Design the New System	NP 275
Construct the System	NP 279
Implement the New System	NP 282
Maintain the System	NP 284

CHAPTER NINE

MANAGING THE DATA IN FILES AND DATABASES	NP 295
File and Database Concepts	NP 296
Approaches to File and Database Management	NP 308
File and Database Management Tasks	NP 313

CHAPTER TEN

COMPUTER PROGRAMMING	NP 339
Software Engineering	NP 340
Problems and Algorithms	NP 340
Coding Computer Programs	NP 348
Program Testing	NP 352
Program Documentation	NP 353
Programming Language Characteristics	NP 354
Programming Languages	NP 362

CHAPTER ELEVEN

PERSPECTIVES ON THE COMPUTER INDUSTRY	NP 375
Historical Threads in the Computer Industry	NP 376
The Computer Marketplace	NP 395
Buying Computer Equipment and Software	NP 403

TABLE OF CONTENTS

CHAPTER ONE

USING COMPUTERS: ESSENTIAL CONCEPTS   **NP 3**

Computers: Mind Tools   **NP 4**
Von Neumann's Definition   NP 4
The User Interface   NP 5

The Basics of Computer Hardware   **NP 6**
Categories of Computers   NP 6
Computer System Configurations:
Microcomputer Examples   NP 7
Computer System Components   NP 7
Microcomputer Compatibility   NP 8
The Computer Keyboard   NP 9
The Mouse   NP 9
Peripheral Devices   NP 11

Interacting with the Computer   **NP 13**
Command-Line User Interfaces   NP 13
Menu-Driven User Interfaces   NP 15
Prompted User Interfaces   NP 19
Graphical User Interfaces   NP 21

Learning to Use Computers   **NP 23**
Tutorials   NP 24
Reference Manuals   NP 25
On-line Help   NP 26
Other Sources of Information   NP 26

CHAPTER REVIEW   **NP 28**
CHAPTER QUIZ   **NP 28**
PROJECTS   **NP 29**
LABS   **NP 30**
   Keyboard Lab   NP 31
   Mouse Lab   NP 32
   User Interfaces Lab   NP 32
   Peripheral Devices Lab   NP 32
RESOURCES   **NP 33**

CHAPTER TWO

SOFTWARE AND MULTIMEDIA APPLICATIONS   **NP 35**

Computer Programs and Computer Software   **NP 36**

System Software   **NP 39**
Operating Systems   NP 39
   Control Basic Input and Output   NP 39
   Allocate System Resources   NP 40
   Manage Storage Space   NP 40
   Maintain Security   NP 40
   Detect Equipment Failure   NP 41
Microcomputer Operating Systems   NP 41
Device Drivers   NP 44
Utilities   NP 44

Application Software   **NP 44**
Productivity Software   NP 46
Business Software   NP 47
Entertainment Software   NP 54
Education and Reference Software   NP 54

Software Compatibility   **NP 54**

Installing and Using Software   **NP 56**
Software Copyrights   NP 58
Software Licenses   NP 59
Public Domain Software   NP 61
Shareware   NP 62

Multimedia Computing   **NP 63**
Multimedia Applications   NP 64
Multimedia Equipment   NP 66

CHAPTER REVIEW   **NP 68**
CHAPTER QUIZ   **NP 68**
PROJECTS   **NP 69**
LABS   **NP 71**
   Word Processing Tour   NP 71
   Spreadsheet Tour   NP 72
   Database Tour   NP 72
   Multimedia Tour   NP 73
RESOURCES   **NP 74**

CHAPTER THREE

COMPUTER FILES   **NP 77**

Data and Information   **NP 78**

Computer Files   **NP 78**
Data Files   NP 79
Program Files   NP 80
File-naming Conventions   NP 80
Logical File Storage   NP 83

Storage Media and Devices   **NP 86**
Magnetic Storage   NP 87
   Floppy Disk Storage   NP 87
   Hard Disk Storage   NP 91
   Tape Storage   NP 94

Bernoulli Storage NP 95

Optical Storage NP 96
CD-ROM Storage NP 96
Other Optical Storage NP 98

Physical File Storage NP 98

Using Files **NP 101**
Running an Application NP 102
Retrieving a Data File NP 102
Saving a Data File NP 103
Other File Operations: Copy and Delete NP 103

CHAPTER REVIEW **NP 105**
CHAPTER QUIZ **NP 106**
PROJECTS **NP 107**
LABS **NP 110**
Defragmentation Lab NP 110
File Operations Lab NP 110
RESOURCES **NP 111**

CHAPTER FOUR

COMPUTER ARCHITECTURE **NP 113**
Digital Electronics **NP 114**
The Main Board **NP 116**
Bus **NP 117**
Memory **NP 118**
Random Access Memory NP 119
RAM Capacity NP 121
RAM Technology NP 121
CMOS Memory NP 122
Read Only Memory NP 123

Processors **NP 123**
Microprocessors NP 126
Clock Rate NP 127
Word Size NP 127
Data Bus Width NP 128
Math Coprocessor NP 128
Cache Memory NP 129
Instruction Set NP 129

The Boot Process **NP 130**
Power Up NP 131
Boot Program NP 132
Diagnostic Tests NP 133

Load the Operating System NP 133
Check Configuration Data NP 134
Display the Operating System Prompt NP 134

Expanding the System **NP 135**
Expansion Buses, Slots, and Cards NP 135
PCMCIA Slots and Cards NP 137
Floppy Disk and Hard Disk Controllers NP 138
Video Display Adapters NP 138
Parallel Ports NP 140
SCSI Ports NP 142
Serial Ports NP 142
Mouse Ports NP 142

CHAPTER REVIEW **NP 144**
CHAPTER QUIZ **NP 145**
PROJECTS **NP 146**
LABS **NP 147**
Computer Architecture Lab NP 147
Troubleshooting Lab NP 147
RESOURCES **NP 148**

CHAPTER FIVE

DATA COMMUNICATIONS **NP 151**
Transmitting and Receiving Information **NP 152**
Encoding Information **NP 152**
Representing Numbers NP 157
Representing Characters NP 159
ASCII NP 160
ANSI NP 161
EBCDIC NP 161
Unicode NP 161
Representing Graphics NP 162
Bitmap Graphics NP 162
Vector Graphics NP 164
Representing Video NP 166
Representing Sound NP 166
Waveform Audio NP 166
MIDI Music NP 168

Data Compression **NP 168**
Text Compression NP 170
Graphics Compression NP 171
Video Compression NP 171

Communications Channels   **NP 172**
Twisted Pair Cable   NP 173
Coaxial Cable   NP 174
Fiber Optic Cable   NP 175
Wireless Communications   NP 176

Communications Protocols   **NP 176**
Parallel and Serial Communications   NP 177
Synchronous and Asynchronous Protocols   NP 177
Parity   NP 178
From Simplex to Echoplex   NP 179
Transmission Speed   NP 180

Modems   **NP 181**
Configuring a Modem   NP 182

CHAPTER REVIEW   NP 184
CHAPTER QUIZ   NP 185
PROJECTS   NP 185
LABS   NP 187
  Data Representation Lab   NP 187
  Data Communications Lab   NP 188
RESOURCES   NP 188

CHAPTER SIX

COMPUTER NETWORKS AND
INFORMATION SERVICES   NP 191

Using a Computer Network   **NP 192**
The Login Process   NP 193
Launching Programs on the Network   NP 194
Using Data Files on the Network   NP 195
Using a Network Printer   NP 197

Network Configuration   **NP 198**
Network Cables   NP 198
Network Hardware   NP 200
  Network Interface Card   NP 200
  Transmitting Data   NP 201
Network Software   NP 202

Network Interactions   **NP 205**

Electronic Mail   **NP 206**

Bulletin Boards   **NP 208**

Commercial Information Services   **NP 209**

The Internet   **NP 211**
Internet Electronic Mail   NP 212

Computational Resources   NP 213
News Groups   NP 214
Library Catalogs   NP 214
Data Archives   NP 214
Telnet and FTP   NP 215

CHAPTER REVIEW   NP 218
CHAPTER QUIZ   NP 220
PROJECTS   NP 220
LAB   NP 222
  Networks Lab   NP 222
RESOURCES   NP 223

CHAPTER SEVEN

SECURITY, CONTROL, AND CONFIDENTIALITY   NP 225

Lost or Invalid Data   **NP 226**

Operator Error   **NP 226**
Erasing the Wrong File   NP 227
Formatting the Wrong Disk   NP 227
Copying an Old Version
of a File Over a New Version   NP 229

Power Problems   **NP 230**

Hardware Failure   **NP 230**

**Trojan Horses, Time Bombs, Worms, and
Logic Bombs**   **NP 232**

Computer Viruses   **NP 234**
How a Computer Virus Spreads   NP 235
Detecting a Computer Virus   NP 236
What to Do If You Detect a Computer Virus   NP 237

Computer Crime   **NP 237**

**Restricting Access to Your Computer
System**   **NP 239**
User IDs and Passwords   NP 239
Restricting User Rights   NP 240
Physical Protection   NP 241

Backup   **NP 241**
Types of Backups   NP 241
Backup Procedures   NP 243

Confidentiality   **NP 246**
Encryption   NP 247
Privacy   NP 250

CHAPTER REVIEW   NP 253
CHAPTER QUIZ   NP 253
PROJECTS   NP 254
LAB   NP 255
  Data Backup Lab   NP 255
RESOURCES   NP 255

CHAPTER EIGHT

DEVELOPING EFFECTIVE INFORMATION
SYSTEMS   NP 259
Information Systems   NP 260
Office Automation   NP 260
Transaction Processing   NP 261
Management Information Systems   NP 264
Decision Support Systems   NP 265
Expert Systems   NP 267
System Development Life Cycle   NP 268
Analyze Needs   NP 269
Define the Problem   NP 271
Study the Current System   NP 272
Determine System Requirements   NP 274
Design the New System   NP 275
Identify Potential Solutions   NP 275
Evaluate Solutions and Select the Best   NP 276
Purchase Hardware and Software   NP 277
Develop Application Specifications   NP 277
Construct the System   NP 279
Install Hardware   NP 279
Install Software   NP 279
Create Applications   NP 280
Test Applications   NP 281
Implement the New System   NP 282
Train Users   NP 282
Data Conversion   NP 283
System Conversion   NP 283
Acceptance Testing   NP 284
Maintain the System   NP 284
CHAPTER REVIEW   NP 286
CHAPTER QUIZ   NP 286
PROJECTS   NP 287
LAB   NP 289
System Testing Lab   NP 289
RESOURCES   NP 292

CHAPTER NINE

MANAGING THE DATA IN FILES
AND DATABASES   NP 295
File and Database Concepts   NP 296
Fields   NP 297
Data Types   NP 297
Records   NP 297
Flat Files   NP 299
Databases   NP 299
Approaches to File and Database
Management   NP 308
Custom Program Approach   NP 308
File Management System Approach   NP 309
Database Management System Approach   NP 310
Object-Oriented Approach   NP 312
File and Database Management Tasks   NP 313
Designing the Files or Database   NP 313
Entering Records   NP 316
Searching   NP 316
Updating Information   NP 321
Organizing Records   NP 321
Producing Output   NP 323
  Reports   NP 323
  Types of Reports   NP 324
  Graphs   NP 325
  Sonification   NP 326
  Data Visualization   NP 328
  Characteristics of Effective Output   NP 328
REVIEW   NP 329
CHAPTER QUIZ   NP 329
PROJECTS   NP 330
LABS   NP 334
  SQL Lab   NP 334
  Presenting Information Using Sound   NP 335
RESOURCES   NP 336

CHAPTER TEN

COMPUTER PROGRAMMING   **NP 339**

Software Engineering   **NP 340**

Problems and Algorithms   **NP 340**
Problem Statements   NP 340
Algorithms   NP 343
Expressing an Algorithm   NP 346

Coding Computer Programs   **NP 348**
Program Sequence and Control Structures   NP 348
Sequence Controls   NP 350
Selection Controls   NP 351
Repetition Controls   NP 351

Program Testing   **NP 352**

Program Documentation   **NP 353**
Program Remarks   NP 353
Written Documentation   NP 354

Programming Language Characteristics   **NP 354**
Procedural Languages   NP 355
Declarative Languages   NP 355
Low-Level Languages   NP 357
High-Level Languages   NP 357
Compiled Languages   NP 358
Interpreted Languages   NP 358
Object-Oriented Languages   NP 358
Event-Driven Languages   NP 361

Programming Languages   **NP 362**

CHAPTER REVIEW   **NP 365**
CHAPTER QUIZ   **NP 365**
PROJECTS   **NP 366**
LAB   **NP 367**
    Visual Programming Lab   NP 367
RESOURCES   **NP 372**

CHAPTER ELEVEN

PERSPECTIVES ON THE COMPUTER INDUSTRY   **NP 375**
Historical Threads in the Computer Industry   **NP 376**
Hardware Development   NP 376
    Calculation aids   NP 376
    Mechanical Calculating Devices   NP 377

The First Computer   NP 379
Prototype Computers   NP 379
First Generation Computers   NP 380
Second Generation Computers   NP 381
Third Generation Computers   NP 381
The Fourth Generation   NP 383
The Next Generation   NP 384
Software Evolution   NP 384
    Programming Language Evolution   NP 384
    Application Software Evolution   NP 386
    Interface Evolution   NP 387
The Companies That Shaped the Marketplace   NP 389
Computers in Popular Culture   NP 392

The Computer Marketplace   **NP 395**
Hardware Life Cycle   NP 395
    Product Announcement   NP 395
    Design and Development   NP 396
    Product Introduction   NP 396
Software Life Cycle   NP 398
    Alpha and Beta Testing   NP 399
    Product Introduction   NP 399
    Product Line   NP 400
Computer Vendors   NP 400
    Computer Retailers   NP 401
    Mail Order Suppliers   NP 401
    Value Added Resellers   NP 401
    Manufacturer Direct   NP 401
Computer Publications   NP 402
    Magazines   NP 402
    Trade Journals   NP 402
    Academic Journals   NP 403
Industry Analysts   NP 403

Buying Computer Equipment and Software   **NP 403**
Think About the Tasks You Want to Accomplish   NP 404
Select the Products That Meet Your Needs   NP 404
Collect Pricing, Service, and Support Information   NP 406
Shop a Variety of Channels   NP 406
Evaluate the Best Deal   NP 408

CHAPTER REVIEW   **NP 410**
CHAPTER QUIZ   **NP 410**
PROJECTS   **NP 411**
LAB   **NP 412**
    Computer History Lab   NP 412
RESOURCES   **NP 414**

L A B S

Computer concepts come to life with these *New Perspectives* Labs—interactive tutorials, animations, digitized images, and simulations that help instructors teach and students learn. Instructors can use them for classroom presentations and students can work with them to enhance learning. This innovative, exciting approach to learning concepts drives home the content of lectures *in a way never thought possible*.

Mouse

Practice clicking, double-clicking, and dragging with the mouse, and learn basic Windows controls.

Keyboard

Learn the parts of the keyboard and how to use modifier keys, toggle keys, and editing keys.

User Interfaces

Interact with samples of command line interfaces, menu interfaces, prompted interfaces, and graphical user interfaces.

Peripheral Devices

View animated sequences and diagrams that show how popular peripherals work.

Word Processing Tour

See animated and interactive sequences about word processing tasks, such as word wrap, entering text, editing, formatting, saving, spell checking, and printing.

Spreadsheet Tour

Learn about spreadsheet software—rows, columns, and cells; entering labels, values, and formulas; formatting cells; recalculation—through animated and interactive sequences.

Database Tour

View animated and interactive sequences that present the concepts of records, fields, files, and sorting.

Multimedia Tour

View, hear, and manipulate the components of multimedia computing—photo-quality images, vector graphics, video for Windows, synthesized speech, digitized speech, waveform audio, and MIDI music.

File Operations

Use a simulated computer system to save files, retrieve and open files, save revised files, and delete files.

Defragmentation

Learn how files become fragmented and how to use a defragmentation utility by using an animated model.

Troubleshooting

After an animation of the boot process, test and develop troubleshooting skills by determining what is wrong with a simulated computer.

Computer Architecture Tour

See an animated interactive demonstration that shows how the CPU works and how it interacts with RAM.

Data Representation

Interact with a Lab that explains the binary number system and shows how text and graphics are displayed.

Data Communications

Use a simulated modem and communications software to access a computer bulletin board and electronic mail.

Networks

See animated sequences and diagrams that show how networks connect file servers, work-stations, and peripheral devices.

Data Backup

Make backups, experience simulated hardware failures, and attempt to restore data. Develop an understanding of cyclic backups, and design appropriate backup plans.

System Testing

Use the expert system discussed in Chapter 8 to test the order-entry system at Abercrombie and Livingston Outfitters, Ltd.

SQL

Make basic SQL queries to practice using relational and logical operators.

Presenting Information Using Sound

Use an interactive simulation to see how sounds can be mapped to data and how to use sonification to report data.

Visual Programming

Construct simple programs using an object-oriented visual programming environment.

Computer History

Use a multimedia hypertext to explore the "threads" of computer history—the people, machines, software, companies, and ideas that shaped the computer industry.

PHOTOGRAPHY / ILLUSTRATION

CREDITS

CHAPTER ONE: Opener, Archive Photos, NP 2; Figure 1-8, AT&T and BO, Inc., creators of the world's fastest Personal Communicator, NP15; Figure 1-14, courtesy of the International Business Machines Corporation, NP 19; Figure 1-20, Chris Woodrow, NP 25; **CHAPTER TWO:** Opener, photo by Johnathan Barber, courtesy of *Special-Interest Autos* magazine, NP 34; Figure 2-2, Chris Woodrow, NP 37; Figure 2-5, OS/2, courtesy of the International Business Machines Corporation, NP 43; Figure 2-18, Encarta, reprinted with permission from Microsoft Corporation, Beethoven, reprinted with permission from Microsoft Corporation, Golfer, courtesy of Access Software, Inc., Space, courtesy of Compton's New Media, NP 65; Figure 2-19, The MPC certification mark is owned by the Multimedia PC Marketing Council, Inc., NP 66; Figure 2-20, courtesy of The Voyager Company, NP 67; **CHAPTER THREE**: Opener, Chris Woodrow, NP 76; Figure 3-16, courtesy of IOMEGA Corporation, NP 97; **CHAPTER FOUR**: Opener, James Kaczman, NP 112; Figure 4-3, courtesy of Intel Corporation, NP 116; Figure 4-20, courtesy of Megahertz Corporation, NP 138; Figure 4-22, courtesy of Diamond Computer Systems, Inc., NP 140; **CHAPTER FIVE**: Opener, The Granger Collection, NP 150; **CHAPTER SIX**: Opener, Dan Oja, NP 191; Figure 6-17, courtesy of America Online, NP 210; Figure 6-18, courtesy of The ImagiNation Network, NP 211; Figure 6-19, Donna Cox, Robert Patterson, NCSA, NP 212; Figure 6-26, Peter Menzel, NP 221; Figure 6-27, drawing by Peter Steiner (c) 1993 The New Yorker Magazine, Inc., all rights reserved, NP 222; **CHAPTER SEVEN**: Opener, The Granger Collection, NP 224; Figure 7-2, William McCoy/Rainbow, NP 228; Figure 7-4, U.P.S., courtesy of Tripp Lite, surge suppressor, courtesy of Curtis Manufacturing Co., Inc., Jaffrey, NH, NP 231; Figure 7-18, photo by Sarah Bendersky, text embedded by Professor Peter Wayner, NP 249; **CHAPTER EIGHT**: Opener, Minden Pictures, NP 258; Figure 8-8, courtesy of the International Business Machines Corporation, NP 270; Figure 8-12, courtesy of INTERSOLV, Inc., NP 274; **CHAPTER NINE**: Opener, D. Wells, The Image Works, NP 294; **CHAPTER TEN**: Opener, Daemmrich, The Image Works, NP 338; **CHAPTER ELEVEN**: Opener, courtesy of the International Business Machines Corporation, NP 374; Figure 11-6, courtesy of Texas Instruments, NP 382; Figure 11-7, courtesy of the International Business Machines Corporation, NP 382; Figure 11-8, courtesy of Intel Corporation, NP 383; Figure 11-14, all photos courtesy of Gateway 2000, NP 397; Figure 11-17, Seth Affoumado, NP 404.

CREDITS FOR PHOTOS USED IN COMPUTER HISTORY LAB, CHAPTER 11

ABACUS,BMP, Culver Pictures; ABC.BMP, Iowa State University, News Service, Photo Department; ADA.BMP, Charles Babbage Institute; ALTAIRMG.BMP, no credit found; BABBAGE.BMP, IBM archives; CBS.BMP, IBM archives; CENSTAB.BMP, IBM archives; DIFFENG.BMP, Culver Pictures; ENIAC.BMP, UPI/Bettman; GATES.BMP, courtesy of Microsoft Corporation; HOFF.BMP, courtesy of Intel Corporation; HOPPER.BMP, courtesy of Harvard University archives; IBMPC.BMP, courtesy of the International Business Machines Corporation; IC.BMP, courtesy of Texas Instruments; IC4004.BMP, courtesy of Intel Corporation; JLOOM.BMP, Bettmann Archive; LEIBNIZ.BMP, Culver Pictures; MAC.BMP, courtesy of Apple Computer, Inc., MARKI.BMP, IBM archives; MOTH.BMP, no credit found; NAPIERS.BMP, Culver Pictures; PASCLNE.BMP, The Computer Museum; SLIDRULE.BMP, Culver Pictures; TRANSTR.BMP, IBM archives; VISICALC.BMP, Ira Wyman; WATSON.BMP, IBM archives; WOZNJOBS.BMP, courtesy of Apple Computer, Inc.

NEW PERSPECTIVES
ON COMPUTER CONCEPTS

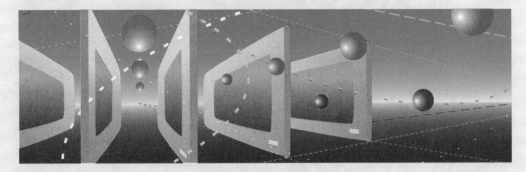

CHAPTER ONE
USING COMPUTERS: ESSENTIAL CONCEPTS

CHAPTER TWO
SOFTWARE AND MULTIMEDIA APPLICATIONS

CHAPTER THREE
COMPUTER FILES

CHAPTER FOUR
COMPUTER ARCHITECTURE

CHAPTER FIVE
DATA COMMUNICATIONS

CHAPTER SIX
COMPUTER NETWORKS AND INFORMATION SERVICES

CHAPTER SEVEN
SECURITY, CONTROL, AND CONFIDENTIALITY

CHAPTER EIGHT
DEVELOPING EFFECTIVE INFORMATION SYSTEMS

CHAPTER NINE
MANAGING THE DATA IN FILES AND DATABASES

CHAPTER TEN
COMPUTER PROGRAMMING

CHAPTER ELEVEN
PERSPECTIVES ON THE COMPUTER INDUSTRY

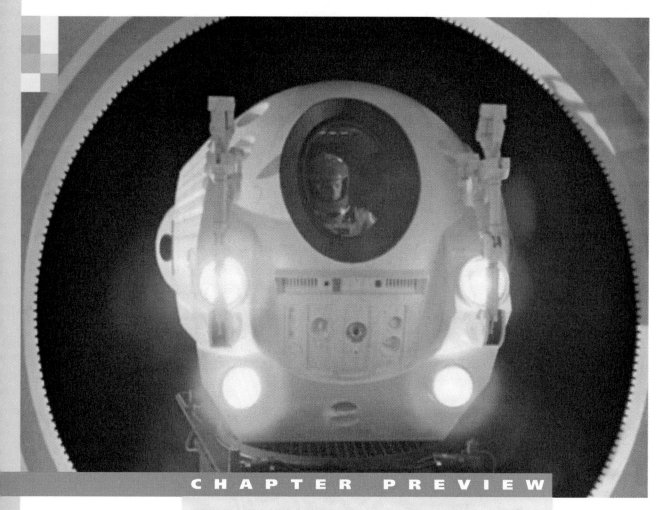

When you have completed this chapter you should be able to answer the following questions:

- What is a computer?
- What are the parts of a typical microcomputer system?
- Which peripheral devices are typically found on microcomputer systems?
- What is a user interface?
- What are the four user interface categories?
- What are the advantages and disadvantages of each type of user interface?
- What resources can you use to learn how to use computers and software?

USING COMPUTERS: ESSENTIAL CONCEPTS

I n the film *2001: A Space Odyssey,* astronaut Dave Bowman and four crew members depart on a mission to Jupiter to discover the source of a mysterious object from space. Midway through the mission, the onboard computer, named HAL, begins to exhibit strange behavior. Dave leaves the spacecraft to make some external repairs. When he is ready to reboard, he speaks to the computer, "Open the pod bay door, HAL." HAL's reply is chilling, "I'm sorry, Dave, I'm afraid I can't do that."

This dialog between a human and a computer raises some intriguing questions. How realistic is it? Can humans and computers communicate this fluently? What went wrong with the communication? Why won't the computer let Dave back into the spaceship?

To use a computer effectively, you must communicate tasks to the computer and accurately interpret the information the computer provides to you. The means by which humans and computers communicate is referred to as the *user interface*, and this is the central theme of Chapter 1. In this chapter you will learn which computer components are necessary for communication between humans and computers. Then you will learn about the user interfaces typically found on today's computer systems. The chapter concludes with a discussion about manuals, reference guides, and tutorials that will help you learn how to interact with a specific computer system or software package.

Computers: Mind Tools

Computers have been called "mind tools" because they enhance our ability to perform tasks that require mental activity. Computers are adept at performing activities such as fast calculations, sorting large lists, and searching through vast information libraries. These are all activities that humans can do, but a computer can often accomplish them much faster and more accurately. Our ability to direct a computer's activity augments or complements our mental capabilities and makes us more productive. The key to making effective use of the computer as a tool is to know what a computer is, and how to use it. That is the focus of this book.

Von Neumann's Definition

What is a computer? If you look in a dictionary printed anytime before 1940, you might be surprised to find a computer defined as a *person* who performs calculations. Although machines performed calculations too, these machines were referred to as calculators, not computers. The definition and use of the term "computer" began to change in the 1940s when the first electronic computing devices were developed.

In 1945, a team of engineers began working on a classified military project to construct EDVAC (Electronic Discrete Variable Automatic Computer). At the time, only one other functioning computer had been built in the United States. Plans for the EDVAC were described in a report by the eminent mathematician John von Neumann. Von Neumann's report was one of the earliest documents to specifically define the components of a computer and describe their functions. In the report, von Neumann used the term "automatic computing system," but popular usage has abandoned this cumbersome terminology in favor of the shorter terms "computer" or "computer system."

As von Neumann explained, a computer needs to perform basic arithmetic operations such as addition, subtraction, multiplication, and division. To **process** or carry out these arithmetic operations, von Neumann wrote that the computer must contain a "central arithmetic device," which we now call the **arithmetic logic unit**. To assist this processing, a "central control device" or **control unit** ensures that the operations are carried out in the proper sequence. Von Neumann foresaw that the arithmetic logic unit and the control unit could be regarded as one unit—what is now called the **central processing unit** or **CPU**.

The results from the intermediate stages of calculations are held temporarily in the computer **memory**. The memory holds the numbers and words that will be processed and the instructions for how to process them.

A computer communicates with humans and other machines by means of input and output devices. An **input device**, such as a keyboard, transfers into the computer memory the words and numbers that will be processed. An **output device** transfers the results of processing from the computer memory. Von Neumann used the term "outside recording medium" to describe the media used for the input and output. We now refer to the disks used with modern computers as **storage media**.

Von Neumann's definition of a **computer** can be summarized as *a device that accepts input, processes the input, stores the results of processing, and provides output.*

Study Figure 1-1 to make sure you understand the functions described by von Neumann, and see if you recognize the modern devices that help the computer accomplish each function.

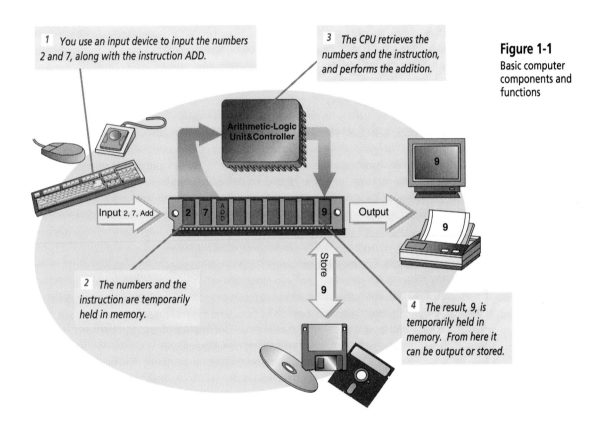

Figure 1-1
Basic computer components and functions

1   You use an input device to input the numbers 2 and 7, along with the instruction ADD.

3   The CPU retrieves the numbers and the instruction, and performs the addition.

2   The numbers and the instruction are temporarily held in memory.

4   The result, 9, is temporarily held in memory. From here it can be output or stored.

The tangible components of a computer—those you can see or touch—are referred to as **hardware**. Computer hardware in and of itself does not provide a particularly useful mind tool. To be useful, a computer requires a set of instructions, called **software** or a **computer program**, that tells the computer how to perform a particular task. The hardware and software of a computer system work together to process and store data. The term **data** refers to the words, numbers, and graphics that describe people, events, things, and ideas.

The User Interface

To effectively use the computer as a mind tool, you must communicate with it; you must tell the computer what tasks to perform and you must also accurately interpret the information the computer provides to you. The means by which humans and computers communicate is referred to as the **user interface**. Through the user interface, the computer accepts your input and presents you with output. This output provides you with the results of processing, confirms the completion of the processing, or indicates that data was stored.

The user interface is a combination of software and hardware. The software that controls the user interface defines its characteristics. For example, software controls whether you or the computer initiates the dialog—that is, whether you tell the computer what to do or whether the computer asks you what to do. The hardware controls the way you physically manipulate the computer to engage in the dialog, such as whether you use a keyboard or your voice to input commands. After you have a general understanding of user interfaces, you will be able to quickly figure out how to make the computer do what you want it to do.

The Basics of Computer Hardware

Before we turn specifically to user interfaces, it would be useful to take a brief survey of the hardware you are likely to encounter when you use computers. Familiarity with the basic components of a computer system and their function will help you understand how they are incorporated into the user interface.

Categories of Computers

Computers traditionally have been divided into five categories, based on their function, physical size, cost, and performance. Small **embedded computers** are built into microwave ovens, VCRs, and cameras as control devices. **Microcomputers** or **personal computers**—PCs for short—are the computers you typically find in homes and small businesses. **Minicomputers** are somewhat larger than microcomputers and are generally used in business and industry for specific tasks, such as processing payroll. **Mainframes** are large, fast, and fairly expensive computers, generally used by business or government. **Super computers** are the largest, fastest, and most expensive type of computer; they handle specialized information analysis, such as predicting the weather and modeling nuclear reactions.

Today the lines that divide the different computer categories are often fuzzy and tend to shift as more powerful computers become available. For example, the definition of *mini*computers in technical dictionaries published in the early 1980s specified performance features that more accurately describe today's *micro*computers. Because the characteristics of each computer category shift and change, it is difficult to categorize a particular computer unless you have up-to-date technical expertise. So, if you want to know whether a particular computer is a micro, a mini, a mainframe, or a super computer, the most practical thing to do is find out how the manufacturer classifies it.

This book focuses on microcomputers because that is the category of computers you are likely to use. Although the focus is on microcomputers, most of the concepts you will learn apply to the other categories of computers as well.

Computer System Configurations: Microcomputer Examples

The hardware components that make up a particular computer system are referred to as the **configuration** of that computer system. Because you are most likely to use microcomputers, let's take a look at some typical microcomputer configurations. Figure 1-2 explains the four most popular microcomputer configurations.

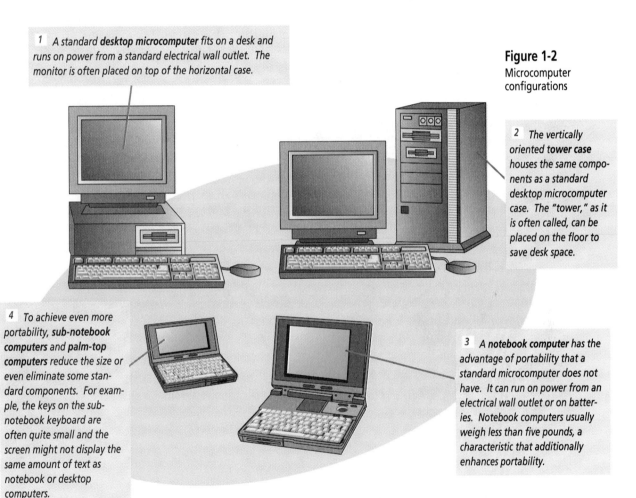

1 A standard **desktop microcomputer** fits on a desk and runs on power from a standard electrical wall outlet. The monitor is often placed on top of the horizontal case.

Figure 1-2
Microcomputer configurations

2 The vertically oriented **tower case** houses the same components as a standard desktop microcomputer case. The "tower," as it is often called, can be placed on the floor to save desk space.

4 To achieve even more portability, **sub-notebook computers** and **palm-top computers** reduce the size or even eliminate some standard components. For example, the keys on the sub-notebook keyboard are often quite small and the screen might not display the same amount of text as notebook or desktop computers.

3 A **notebook computer** has the advantage of portability that a standard microcomputer does not have. It can run on power from an electrical wall outlet or on batteries. Notebook computers usually weigh less than five pounds, a characteristic that additionally enhances portability.

Computer System Components

Microcomputers include a similar set of basic components. Most desktop microcomputers and most portable computers, such as notebooks and sub-notebooks, typically include similar components, *except* that today few portable computers have built-in CD-ROM drives, tape backup drives, or 5.25" drives. Any of these components significantly increases a computer's size and weight. Figure 1-3 diagrams the components on a typical microcomputer and explains the purpose of each component.

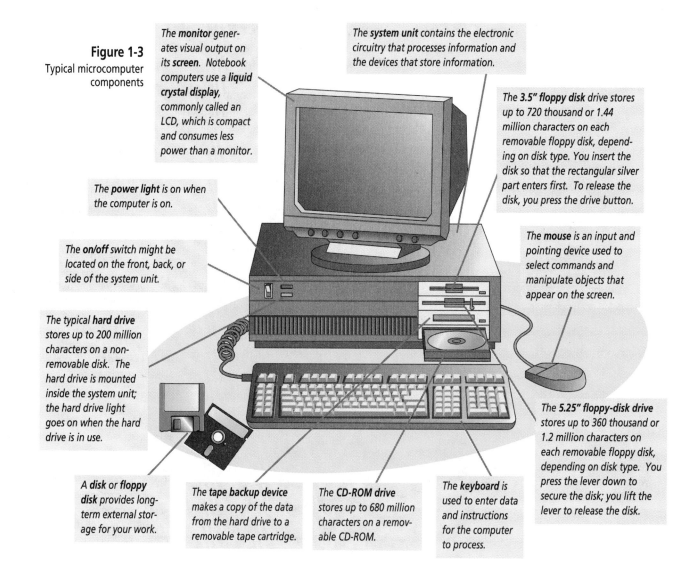

Figure 1-3
Typical microcomputer
components

The **monitor** generates visual output on its **screen**. Notebook computers use a **liquid crystal display**, commonly called an LCD, which is compact and consumes less power than a monitor.

The **system unit** contains the electronic circuitry that processes information and the devices that store information.

The **3.5" floppy disk** drive stores up to 720 thousand or 1.44 million characters on each removable floppy disk, depending on disk type. You insert the disk so that the rectangular silver part enters first. To release the disk, you press the drive button.

The **power light** is on when the computer is on.

The **on/off** switch might be located on the front, back, or side of the system unit.

The **mouse** is an input and pointing device used to select commands and manipulate objects that appear on the screen.

The typical **hard drive** stores up to 200 million characters on a non-removable disk. The hard drive is mounted inside the system unit; the hard drive light goes on when the hard drive is in use.

The **5.25" floppy-disk drive** stores up to 360 thousand or 1.2 million characters on each removable floppy disk, depending on disk type. You press the lever down to secure the disk; you lift the lever to release the disk.

A **disk** or **floppy disk** provides long-term external storage for your work.

The **tape backup device** makes a copy of the data from the hard drive to a removable tape cartridge.

The **CD-ROM drive** stores up to 680 million characters on a removable CD-ROM.

The **keyboard** is used to enter data and instructions for the computer to process.

Microcomputer Compatibility

Microcomputers are manufactured by hundreds of companies. Some of the more well known computer manufacturers are IBM, Apple, Dell, and Compaq. Despite the many manufacturers, there are only a small number of microcomputer designs or architectures, which means that many computers, manufactured by different companies, operate in essentially the same way. Computers that operate in essentially the same way are said to be **compatible**.

Today there are two major groups of compatible microcomputers: IBM-compatibles and Macintosh-compatibles. **IBM-compatible computers**, also referred to as **PC-compatibles**, are based on the architecture of the first IBM microcomputer. IBM-compatible computers are manufactured by Compaq, Dell, and hundreds of other companies. The second major group of compatibles is based on the architecture of the Macintosh computer, manufactured by Apple Computer, Inc. In the United States, Apple's copyrights and patents have made it difficult for other companies to manufacture and sell Macintosh-compatible computers, so purchasers who want to use a Macintosh computer generally buy from Apple.

The compatibility of your computer dictates the type of software you can use and the peripheral devices that will work correctly with your computer. Because about two-thirds of the microcomputers in use today are IBM-compatible, the remainder of this book will focus on this type of computer system.

The Computer Keyboard

Most computers are equipped with a keyboard as the primary input device and a monitor as the primary output device. A computer keyboard includes the same keys as a typewriter, but it also includes a number of additional keys that control computer-specific tasks. Computer keyboards also contain a number of toggle keys. A **toggle key** switches back and forth between two modes. For example, when you press the Caps Lock key, you switch or "toggle" into uppercase mode. When you are in uppercase mode, your key strokes produce all uppercase letters until you press the Caps Lock key again to toggle back into lowercase mode.

L A B

KEYBOARD

There are several types of keyboard layouts; some layouts have a few more keys than other layouts or they have the special computer control keys arranged in different locations. Figure 1-4 on the following page shows the popular 101-style keyboard containing a typing keypad, editing keypad, numeric keypad, and function key array. The figure also indicates the purpose of special keys such as Ctrl, Alt, and Esc.

The Mouse

An additional input device, called a mouse, is rapidly becoming standard equipment on most computer systems. A **mouse** is a pointing device that you use to manipulate objects displayed on the screen. As Figure 1-5 on page NP 11 shows, when you move the mouse on your desk, a **pointer**—usually shaped like an arrow—moves on the screen in a way that corresponds to how you move the mouse.

L A B

MOUSE

The **Pause** key stops the current task your computer is performing. You might need to hold down both the Ctrl key and the Pause key to stop the task.

Indicator lights show you the status of each toggle key: Num Lock, Caps Lock, and Scroll Lock.

The **Num Lock** key is a toggle key that switches the keys on the numeric keypad between number keys and cursor keys.

Page Up displays the previous screen of information.

Page Down displays the next screen of information.

Home takes you to the beginning of a line or the beginning of a document, depending on the software you are using.

The **Pause** key stops the current task your computer is performing. You might need to hold down both the Ctrl key and the Pause key to stop the task.

The function of the **Scroll Lock** key depends on the software you are using. This key is rarely used with today's software.

The **Print Screen** key prints the contents of the screen when you use some software. With other software, the Print Screen key stores a copy of your screen in memory that you can manipulate with draw or paint software.

The **Insert** key is a toggle key that switches between insert mode and type-over mode.

The **function keys** execute commands, such as centering a line of text or boldfacing text. The command associated with each function key depends on the software you are using.

Each time you press the **Backspace** key, one character to the left of the cursor is deleted. If you hold down the backspace key, multiple characters to the left are deleted one by one until you release it.

The **Esc** or "escape" key cancels an operation.

End takes you to the end of a line or the end of a document, depending on the software you are using.

The **cursor keys** move your position on the screen up, down, right, or left.

You press the **Enter** key to move down to the next line or when you finish typing a command.

The **Caps Lock** key capitalizes all the letters you type when it is engaged, but does not produce the top symbol on keys that contain two symbols. This key is a toggle key, which means that each time you press it, you switch between uppercase and lowercase modes. There is usually an indicator light on the keyboard to show which mode you are in.

You hold the **Shift** key down while you press another key. The Shift key capitalizes letters and produces the top symbol on keys that contain two symbols.

You hold the **Ctrl** key down while you press another key. The result of Ctrl key combinations depends on the software you are using.

You hold the **Alt** key down while you press another key. The result of Alt key combinations depends on the software you are using.

Numeric Keypad

Editing Keypad

Function Key Array

Typing Keypad

Figure 1-4
A computer keyboard

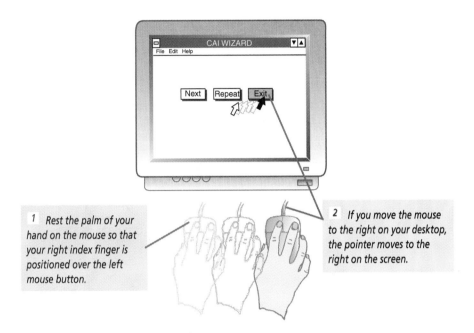

Figure 1-5
To select the Exit option, you position the pointer on the gray square labeled "Exit," then click the left mouse button.

1 Rest the palm of your hand on the mouse so that your right index finger is positioned over the left mouse button.

2 If you move the mouse to the right on your desktop, the pointer moves to the right on the screen.

The mouse was developed in the early 1970s by Douglas Engelbart to provide an input method more efficient than the keyboard. For example, when you work with word processing software, you can use the mouse instead of the cursor keys to quickly move the pointer to the next paragraph displayed on the screen. The popularity of the mouse grew slowly at first. However, in the mid-1980s, Apple Computer, Inc. began including a mouse with its popular Macintosh computer system. Now virtually every new computer system is sold with a mouse or some similar pointing device.

Peripheral Devices

The keyboard, mouse, and monitor are just three of many input and output hardware devices, referred to as **peripheral devices** or **peripherals** for short. As the name suggests, peripherals are devices that are "outside" of, or in addition to, the main computer. Figure 1-6 on the following page shows some of the more popular peripheral devices used with microcomputers.

Peripheral devices usually require that you have specially designed software to instruct the computer how to use them. When you connect peripheral devices to your computer, you should carefully follow the instructions that are packaged with the device. The instructions explain how to correctly establish the connection and how to install any necessary software on your computer. Be sure the computer is turned off before you attempt to connect a peripheral device to your computer or you might damage your computer system.

L A B

PERIPHERAL DEVICES

Figure 1-6
Peripheral devices

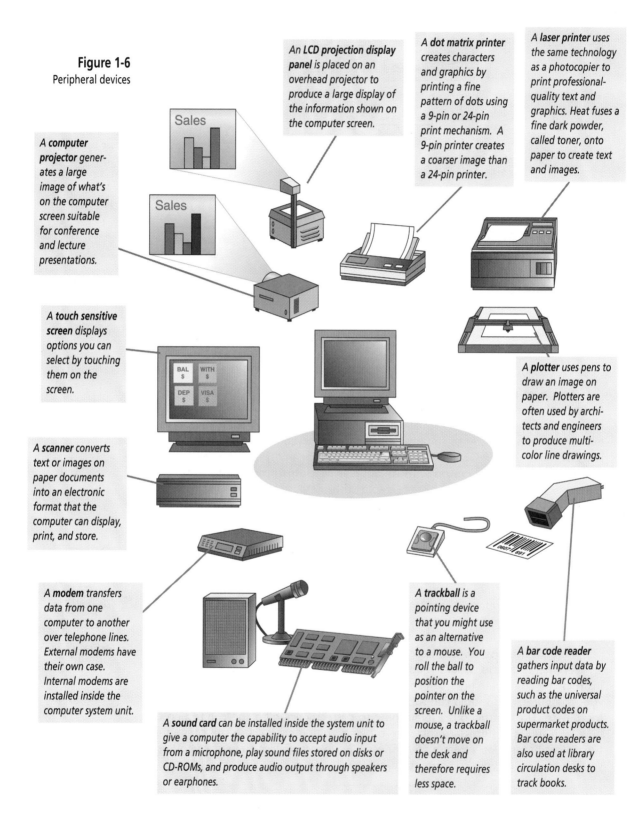

An **LCD projection display panel** is placed on an overhead projector to produce a large display of the information shown on the computer screen.

A **dot matrix printer** creates characters and graphics by printing a fine pattern of dots using a 9-pin or 24-pin print mechanism. A 9-pin printer creates a coarser image than a 24-pin printer.

A **laser printer** uses the same technology as a photocopier to print professional-quality text and graphics. Heat fuses a fine dark powder, called toner, onto paper to create text and images.

A **computer projector** generates a large image of what's on the computer screen suitable for conference and lecture presentations.

A **touch sensitive screen** displays options you can select by touching them on the screen.

A **plotter** uses pens to draw an image on paper. Plotters are often used by architects and engineers to produce multi-color line drawings.

A **scanner** converts text or images on paper documents into an electronic format that the computer can display, print, and store.

A **modem** transfers data from one computer to another over telephone lines. External modems have their own case. Internal modems are installed inside the computer system unit.

A **trackball** is a pointing device that you might use as an alternative to a mouse. You roll the ball to position the pointer on the screen. Unlike a mouse, a trackball doesn't move on the desk and therefore requires less space.

A **bar code reader** gathers input data by reading bar codes, such as the universal product codes on supermarket products. Bar code readers are also used at library circulation desks to track books.

A **sound card** can be installed inside the system unit to give a computer the capability to accept audio input from a microphone, play sound files stored on disks or CD-ROMs, and produce audio output through speakers or earphones.

Interacting with the Computer

There are four categories of user interfaces: command-line, menu-driven, prompted, and graphical. User interfaces have changed and evolved in response to the needs of a rapidly growing community of computer users. The engineering of user interfaces is, however, still in an early stage. Using computers can be enjoyable, but as with many objects in everyday life, some computer user interfaces are not well conceived. Donald Norman, a well-known cognitive scientist, wrote a delightful book called *The Psychology of Everyday Things* in which he says, "Well-designed objects are easy to interpret and understand. They contain visible clues to their operation. Poorly designed objects can be difficult and frustrating to use. They provide no clues—or sometimes false clues. They trap the user and thwart the normal process of interpretation and understanding."

As you read the user interface descriptions that follow, consider not only the characteristics of each user interface, but also consider the positive and negative aspects of each design. Which interfaces are easy to interpret and understand? Which provide clues about what to do and how to do it? If you have used computers, you should remember using some or all of these user interfaces, and you might recall your own reaction to them.

L A B

USER INTERFACES

Command-Line User Interfaces

A **command-line user interface** is based on a vocabulary of command words and rules called a **command language**. Each **command word** elicits a specific response from the computer. The command words are often English words such as *print*, *begin*, *save*, and *erase*, but command words can also be more cryptic and might even use special symbols. Some examples of cryptic command "words" include *ls*, which means list; *cls*, which means clear the screen; and *!*, which means quit. In addition to command words, command languages often feature **parameters** or **switches** that slightly modify a command word. An example is *DIR /p*, which means "show me a list of files, but *pause* after each screen of text." The command word is *DIR* and the parameter is */p*.

In addition to command words and parameters, most command languages require you to use specific punctuation—to leave spaces between command words and place quotation marks around certain parts of a command. You can combine the command words, parameters, and punctuation to create **commands** that tell the computer what you want it to do.

With a command-line user interface, you initiate the dialog with the computer by entering a command. To use a command-line user interface effectively, you must memorize the command words and know what they mean. To make the situation even more difficult, there is not a single command language that you can use for every computer and every software package. Instead, there are many different command languages.

One well-known microcomputer command language is dBASE. Figure 1-7 shows a series of commands entered using the dBASE command-line user interface. Notice the use of command words such as LIST, DEL, REPLACE, ALL, and FOR, and punctuation, such as the use of quotation marks around text and dates, and the use of periods around the word "AND."

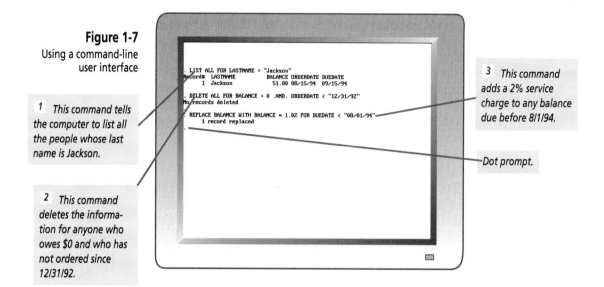

Figure 1-7
Using a command-line
user interface

1 This command tells the computer to list all the people whose last name is Jackson.

2 This command deletes the information for anyone who owes $0 and who has not ordered since 12/31/92.

3 This command adds a 2% service charge to any balance due before 8/1/94.

Dot prompt.

A command-line user interface usually displays a prompt to let you know that the computer is ready for your commands. Next to the prompt, a flashing underline or box, called the cursor, shows where your typing will appear. For example, the DOS prompt and cursor usually looks like this:

C> _

In Figure 1-7, the dBASE prompt is a period, which is usually referred to as the "dot prompt." When you see the prompt, you type a command and then press the Enter key to tell the computer to perform the command. Your command is then examined by a **command interpreter** that determines whether your command is valid. Valid commands are those that "make sense" to the computer because they conform to the syntax rules governing exactly how you can combine the language elements to form commands. The **syntax** specifies the order that the command words must be in and the punctuation that is required. Command-line user interfaces are very strict about syntax. If you misspell a command word, leave out required punctuation, or type the command words out of order, you get an **error message** or **syntax error**. If you type a command that is not *exactly* correct, few command languages have the ability to guess what you mean. When you get a syntax error, you must figure out what is wrong with the command and then retype it.

If you are not fluent in the use of a command language, you are likely to make frequent errors and then you might appreciate Dave Bowman's frustration when he couldn't get HAL to let him into the spacecraft, as depicted in *2001: A Space Odyssey*. Dave's predicament, of course, is more serious than a simple syntax error. If Dave had made a syntax error, HAL would have responded by saying he didn't understand the command. But even though Dave was using a valid command, HAL was not responding to it. Although it is unusual, computers sometimes do not respond correctly to commands. Computers make mistakes due to equipment failure or software defects.

When you use a command-line user interface, you don't generally receive many hints about how to proceed. If you forget the correct command word or punctuation, or if you find yourself using an unfamiliar command-line user interface, you should type HELP and press the Enter key. With some, but not all, command-line user interfaces, the HELP command provides you with a list of commands. If HELP doesn't work, you need to use a reference manual to find out how to proceed.

A command-line user interface typically requires only a keyboard and a monitor as input and output devices. And although the fluent interaction between Dave Bowman and HAL is not yet a reality, it is possible to equip your computer with a sound board and speech recognition software so you can speak commands into a microphone. You can also equip your computer with a sound board, a speaker, and speech synthesis software for audio output.

Another development that provides an alternative input mechanism for a command-line user interface is pen-based computing. A **pen-based computer**, such as the one in Figure 1-8, is equipped with a pointing device, usually called a **stylus**, and uses **character recognition software** to interpret commands that you write on a touch-sensitive pad that doubles as a screen.

Figure 1-8
Using a pen-based computer

Use the stylus to print a command directly on the screen.

Some people like to use command-line interfaces. They believe that once you have become fluent with a command language, the commands are easy to construct, quick to type, and have the versatility to accomplish a wide variety of tasks. However, you have probably recognized that it takes time and effort to develop fluency with a command language. The search for a user interface that is easier to learn and use led to the development of the menu-driven user interface.

Menu-Driven User Interfaces

Menu-driven user interfaces were developed as a response to the difficulties many people experienced trying to remember the command words and syntax for command-line user interfaces. With a **menu-driven user interface**, the computer initiates a dialog by displaying a list of commands called a **menu**. Each command on the menu is referred to as a **menu option** or a **menu item**. The four menu types shown in Figure 1-9 are typical menus you might find when you use menu-driven user interfaces.

Figure 1-9

Examples of four menu types

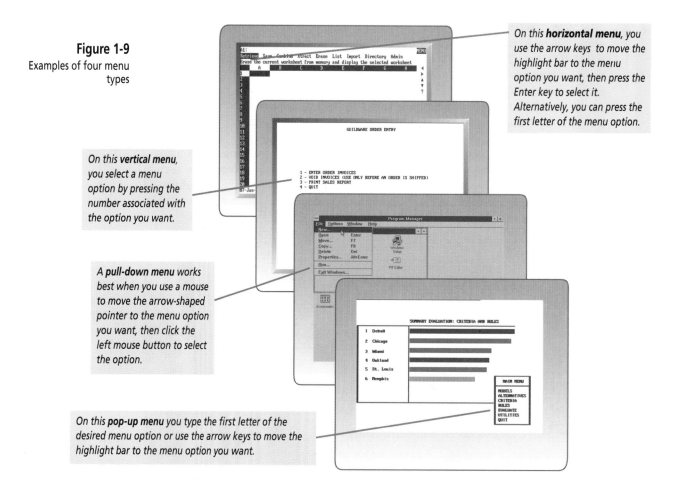

On this **horizontal menu,** you use the arrow keys to move the highlight bar to the menu option you want, then press the Enter key to select it. Alternatively, you can press the first letter of the menu option.

On this **vertical menu,** you select a menu option by pressing the number associated with the option you want.

A **pull-down menu** works best when you use a mouse to move the arrow-shaped pointer to the menu option you want, then click the left mouse button to select the option.

On this **pop-up menu** you type the first letter of the desired menu option or use the arrow keys to move the highlight bar to the menu option you want.

Menus can be arranged vertically or horizontally on the screen. **Pull-down menus** appear to drop down from a menu bar at the top of the screen. **Pop-up menus** appear in boxes in various locations on the screen. When you want to select a menu option, you can do it in different ways, again depending upon the software you are using. You might type the number associated with the menu option, type the first letter of the menu option, use the arrow keys to highlight the menu option, or use the mouse to "point" to the menu option.

Sometimes menus are not displayed unless you activate them. For example, with the popular Windows user interface, the titles of pull-down menus are displayed in a row at the top of the screen as shown in Figure 1-10. By displaying only the menu titles, the interface saves screen space until you want to view the full menu. To view the contents of a menu option, you in effect "pull down" the menu like a window shade. You can pull down a menu using a mouse, if one is available, or the keyboard. To pull down a menu using the mouse, you click the menu title or drag the mouse down from the menu title. To pull down a menu using the keyboard, you hold down the Alt key and press the underlined letter of the menu title.

The popular Windows user interface displays the titles of pull-down menus across the top of the screen.

To pull down this File menu, either you hold down the Alt key while you press the F key or you use the mouse to point to the menu title and click the left mouse button to select it.

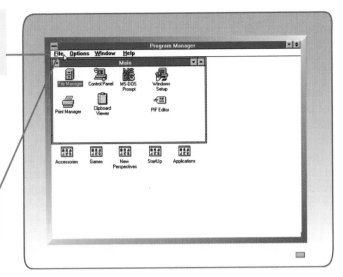

Figure 1-10
Using pull-down menus

Some menu-driven user interfaces give you fewer clues about how to access the menus than the example you just saw from the Windows software. For example, the user interface for Release 2.4 of the popular Lotus 1-2-3 software displays the menu only after you press the slash (/) key, as illustrated in Figure 1-11.

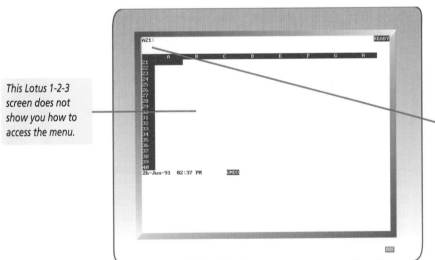

Figure 1-11
Displaying the menu on the Lotus 1-2-3 software

This Lotus 1-2-3 screen does not show you how to access the menu.

If you read the Lotus 1-2-3 reference manual, you would find out that you need to press the slash (/) key to display the menu here.

If the screen does not provide a hint about how to access menus, how can you find out what to do? When you are using a menu-driven user interface, you generally do not have access to a command-line, so typing "HELP" does not provide you with the information you need. You have to ask someone who knows how to use the package or refer to a reference manual.

Menu-driven user interfaces are popular because when you use them it is not necessary to remember command words—you just choose the command you want from a list. Also, because all the commands on the list are valid commands, it is not possible to make syntax errors.

You might wonder how a menu could present all the options you want to select—obviously there are many possibilities for combining command words, so there could be hundreds of menu options. Two methods are generally used to present a reasonably sized list of menu options; one employs a menu hierarchy and the other employs a dialog box. With the first method, the menus are arranged in a hierarchical structure. After you make a selection from one menu, a submenu appears, and you can specify further details by selecting a menu option from the submenu. In some cases, another submenu appears, and so on, until you arrive at a menu that displays the choice you want, as shown in Figure 1-12.

Figure 1-12
Menu hierarchy

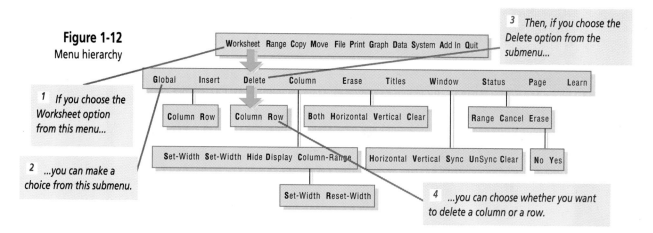

1 If you choose the Worksheet option from this menu...

2 ...you can make a choice from this submenu.

3 Then, if you choose the Delete option from the submenu...

4 ...you can choose whether you want to delete a column or a row.

With the second method, you select a menu option and the computer displays a **dialog box**, such as the one shown in Figure 1-13. You fill in the dialog box to indicate specifically how you want the command to be carried out. A dialog box is a variation of the prompted user interface, which is explained in the next section.

Figure 1-13
Using a dialog box

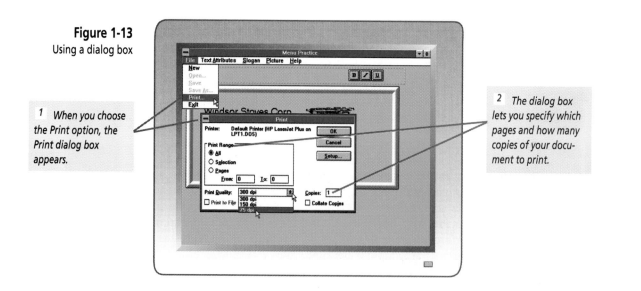

1 When you choose the Print option, the Print dialog box appears.

2 The dialog box lets you specify which pages and how many copies of your document to print.

Most menu-driven user interfaces are designed to be used with a computer system equipped with a keyboard and monitor. But, as you have seen from the descriptions here, pull-down menus work particularly well with a mouse. Pen-based computers also work well for menu-driven user interfaces; you use the stylus to point to the menu option you want. Speech recognition systems support some menu-driven user interfaces; with these systems you indicate your menu selection by speaking into a microphone. In several applications, such as information kiosks in shopping malls, museums, or hotels, a **touch-sensitive screen**, like the one shown in Figure 1-14, displays a menu and lets you make a menu selection by touching the surface of the screen.

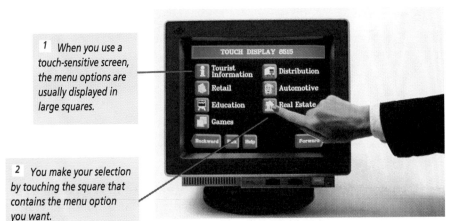

1 When you use a touch-sensitive screen, the menu options are usually displayed in large squares.

2 You make your selection by touching the square that contains the menu option you want.

Figure 1-14
Using a touch-sensitive screen

Prompted User Interfaces

As its name suggests, a **prompted user interface** is an interface in which the computer initiates the dialog by displaying a prompt. A **prompt** requests information or issues an instruction to help you proceed. In response to the computer prompt, you enter the requested information or follow the instruction. There are at least two types of prompted user interfaces: form fill-in and prompted dialog. You might also consider menu-driven interfaces to be a variety of prompted user interfaces in which the menu is the prompt and your menu selection is the response to the prompt.

When you use a **form fill-in** user interface, the computer displays the equivalent of a form, complete with captions and blank spaces, as shown in Figure 1-15. Form fill-in is rarely used by itself as a user interface. Typically, it is used in combination with elements of a menu-driven interface.

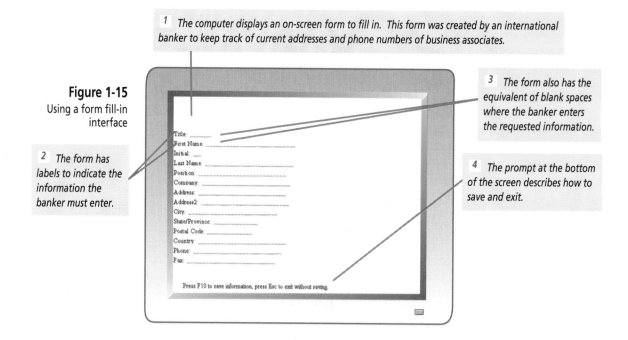

Figure 1-15
Using a form fill-in
interface

1   The computer displays an on-screen form to fill in. This form was created by an international banker to keep track of current addresses and phone numbers of business associates.

2   The form has labels to indicate the information the banker must enter.

3   The form also has the equivalent of blank spaces where the banker enters the requested information.

4   The prompt at the bottom of the screen describes how to save and exit.

The second type of prompted user interface, referred to as a **prompted conversation** or a **prompted dialog**, presents prompts one at a time and waits for a response after each one. Using a prompted dialog interface is similar to having a conversation with the computer. Here is an example of a prompted dialog that tells you how much money will accumulate in your savings account. The computer's prompts are indicated by uppercase. The user's responses are in bold.

HOW MUCH MONEY IS CURRENTLY IN YOUR ACCOUNT?
1000
HOW MUCH MONEY WILL YOU DEPOSIT EACH MONTH?
100
WHAT IS THE YEARLY INTEREST RATE PERCENT?
6
WHAT IS THE LENGTH OF THE SAVINGS PERIOD IN MONTHS?
36
O.K. AFTER 36 MONTHS YOU WILL HAVE $5149.96 IN YOUR SAVINGS ACCOUNT.

Prompted dialogs are popular with students who are learning how to program computers because these dialogs are easy to create; however, prompted dialogs are rarely found in commercial software packages. There are two reasons why. First, the process of interacting with a prompted dialog is very linear, that is, you must start at the beginning and sequentially respond to each prompt. It is difficult to back up if you make an error. The second difficulty with prompted user interfaces is the ambiguity of human language. If a prompt is not clear and you respond to it with something unexpected, the dialog will not function correctly. You can see an example of this difficulty in the dialog shown in Figure 1-16, which could occur with a computer-based library catalog system.

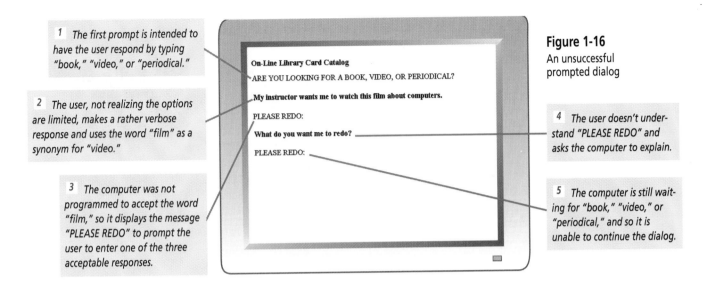

1 The first prompt is intended to have the user respond by typing "book," "video," or "periodical."

2 The user, not realizing the options are limited, makes a rather verbose response and uses the word "film" as a synonym for "video."

3 The computer was not programmed to accept the word "film," so it displays the message "PLEASE REDO" to prompt the user to enter one of the three acceptable responses.

Figure 1-16
An unsuccessful prompted dialog

4 The user doesn't understand "PLEASE REDO" and asks the computer to explain.

5 The computer is still waiting for "book," "video," or "periodical," and so it is unable to continue the dialog.

On-Line Library Card Catalog

ARE YOU LOOKING FOR A BOOK, VIDEO, OR PERIODICAL?

My instructor wants me to watch this film about computers.

PLEASE REDO:

What do you want me to redo?

PLEASE REDO:

The difficulty with the dialog in Figure 1-16 is not necessarily the fault of the user. The prompts should have provided more specific instructions, and the computer program should have been set up to accept a wider vocabulary. Unfortunately, if this were the interface on your on-line library catalog, you would need to learn how to work within its limitations.

Prompted user interfaces have traditionally used the keyboard as the primary input device and the monitor as the primary output device. However, as advances in technology improve computer-generated speech and a computer's capability to understand human speech, prompted user interfaces may use voice input and sound output devices.

Graphical User Interfaces

Graphical user interfaces or **GUIs** (pronounced "gooies") are based on the philosophy that people can use computers intuitively—that is, with minimal training—if they can manipulate on-screen objects that represent tasks or commands. A classic example of manipulating on-screen objects is the way you delete a document when you use an Apple Macintosh computer. The graphical user interface for the Apple Macintosh represents the documents you create with small pictures called **icons**. The trash can icon represents the place where you put documents you no longer want. Suppose you used your computer to write a report named "Finances," but you no longer needed the report stored on your computer system. You use the mouse to drag the Finances icon to the trash can and erase the report from your computer system, as shown in Figure 1-17.

Figure 1-17
Using the Apple
Macintosh graphical
user interface

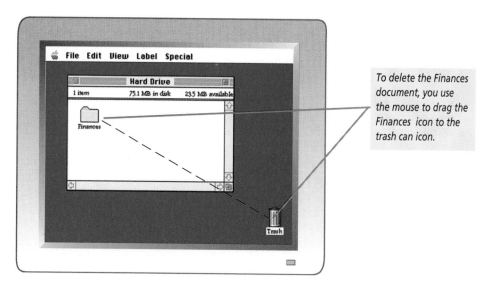

To delete the Finances
document, you use
the mouse to drag the
Finances icon to the
trash can icon.

The direct manipulation of icons is a key element of graphical user interfaces. Other key elements in a graphical user interface are **tools** or **buttons** that help you carry out tasks. A scissors tool, used to "cut" or delete unwanted sections of a document or picture, is a typical tool you might find in a graphical user interface. Figure 1-18 shows how you can use the scissors tool to cut a section of text from a document.

Figure 1-18
Using the scissors tool
to cut a section of text

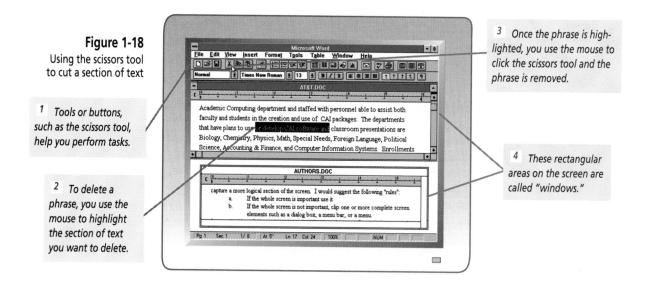

1 Tools or buttons, such as the scissors tool, help you perform tasks.

2 To delete a phrase, you use the mouse to highlight the section of text you want to delete.

3 Once the phrase is highlighted, you use the mouse to click the scissors tool and the phrase is removed.

4 These rectangular areas on the screen are called "windows."

Graphical user interfaces contain other elements, but they are not necessarily unique to this interface type. For example, most graphical user interfaces include some type of menu system because the engineers who designed the software found it difficult to assign icons and tools to all the possible tasks, commands, and options you might want to perform.

Another user interface element, called a window, has been used, not only in graphical user interfaces, but in menu-driven and command-line user interfaces as well. A **window** is a rectangular area on the screen with a border around it. You may have noticed the windows on the screen in Figure 1-18. A window usually contains a specific piece of work. For example, a window might contain a document you are typing or a picture you are drawing. You can think of windows as work areas, analogous to different documents and books that you might have open on your desk. Just as you switch between the documents and books you have on your desk, you can switch between windows on the computer screen to work on different tasks.

Most graphical user interfaces are based on a **metaphor** in which computer components are represented by real-world objects. For example, a user interface with a **desktop metaphor** might represent documents as file folders and storage as a filing cabinet. Metaphors are intended to make the tasks you perform with computers more concrete, more understandable, and more intuitive.

Graphical user interfaces were designed to be used on computer systems equipped with a pointing device, such as a mouse. Another important hardware device for graphical user interfaces is a **high-resolution monitor**. Think of your computer screen as a matrix of dots called **pixels**. Anything the computer displays on the screen must be constructed of dot patterns within the screen matrix. The more dots your screen displays in the matrix, the higher the **resolution**. A high-resolution monitor can produce more complex graphical images to represent icons and produces smoother-looking text that is easier to read.

To give you an idea of the resolutions available on computers today, let's look at the difference between CGA resolution and VGA resolution. **CGA** resolution (color graphics adapter) displays a matrix of only 320 pixels horizontally and 200 pixels vertically. **VGA** resolution (video graphics array) displays a 640 by 480 pixel matrix. Super VGA or **SVGA** resolutions range from 800 by 600 pixels to 1280 by 1024 pixels. Most graphical user interfaces require a resolution equivalent to VGA or SVGA. CGA is not sufficient, because the CGA matrix does not have enough pixels to create the detail necessary for icons and tools. You can see the difference between CGA and VGA resolution by looking at Figure 1-19.

An icon displayed using CGA resolution appears very coarse.

The same icon displayed using VGA resolution appears more precise and has more detail than its CGA counterpart.

Figure 1-19
CGA and VGA display resolutions

Learning to Use Computers

You now know that to use a computer effectively, you must become familiar with different types of user interfaces. But how do you learn to control a specific user interface? How do you learn to operate the user interface for the WordPerfect software or the Microsoft Paintbrush software?

You also know that peripheral devices are an important component of the user interface. But how do you know which peripheral devices you need? How do you install a new peripheral device and how do you operate it?

Both hardware and software generally include instructions and other information about installation and use. To use this information effectively, you need to know that it exists, you need to know where to find it, and you need to develop some strategies for applying it. Let's take a look at some of the resources you can use to do this.

Tutorials

A **tutorial** is a guided, step-by-step learning experience. Usually this learning experience teaches you the generic skills you need to use specific hardware or software. For example, suppose you purchase software to create pictures and the first thing you want to draw is your company logo. When you use a tutorial that teaches you how to create a drawing on the computer, you learn how to do such things as draw straight lines and wavy lines, use color in the drawing, and change the sizes of the pictures you draw. The tutorial does not teach you *exactly* how to draw your company logo, so while you use the tutorial, you need to think about how you can *generalize* the skills you are learning so you can apply them to other tasks.

When you use a tutorial, don't try to cover too much ground at once. Two 60-minute sessions each day are probably sufficient. As you work on a tutorial, take notes on those techniques you expect to apply to your own projects. When you have completed enough of the tutorial to do your own project, put the tutorial aside and get started on the project. You can complete the rest of the tutorial later, if you need to learn more.

Tutorials come in a variety of forms. **Printed tutorials** are very popular. To use a printed tutorial, you read how to do a step, then you try to do it on the computer. In the last few years, computer-based tutorials have become much more widespread. **Computer-based tutorials** display a simulation of the hardware or software and display tutorial instructions in boxes or windows on the screen. Computer-based tutorials have an advantage over their printed counterparts because they can demonstrate procedures using computer animation.

Audio tutorials on cassette verbally walk you through the steps of the tutorial. An advantage to this type of tutorial is that you do not have to read instructions, but you do have to stop the tutorial and rewind as necessary if you do not hear or understand the instructions. You might like audio tutorials if you easily retain information presented in lectures.

Video tutorials on videotape visually illustrate how the software or hardware works. Some video tutorials are designed so that you watch them, take notes, then try the steps on the computer later. Other video tutorials are designed to be used while you are sitting at the computer. As with audio tutorials, you can stop and rewind video tutorials if you miss something.

Aside from the printed or computer-based tutorials you might receive when you purchase software, independent publishers also provide computer-based, printed, audio, and video tutorials, as shown in Figure 1-20. It is worthwhile to consider these tutorials in addition to those included with the software, because these supplemental tutorials might have more appropriate exercises for the projects you are planning or because they might be clearer or easier to follow. You can purchase these tutorials at many bookstores and computer stores.

Microsoft supplies a reference manual and an on-line tutorial with the Windows 3.1 software.

You can also purchase reference manuals and tutorials from independent publishers.

Figure 1-20
Tutorials and reference manuals

Reference Manuals

Reference manuals are usually printed books that contain the information you need to use and install software or hardware. Reference manuals describe each feature of the software or hardware device and might also include examples of how to use these features. A reference manual is typically organized by features, rather than in the lesson format used by tutorials. A reference manual can be quite long, sometimes as long as four hundred or five hundred pages. Do not assume that you should read a reference manual from cover to cover, although you might find it useful to leaf through it to get a quick overview of all the features. You should use the reference manual if you need to find out if a feature exists or if you need to find out how to use a feature. When you use a reference manual, you should first check the table of contents or index to locate the information you need, then turn to the appropriate section and read it carefully.

Reference manuals are usually included in the box with the hardware or software that you buy. Most often, reference manuals are printed documents, but a recent trend for hardware manufacturers and software publishers is to provide computer-based reference manuals that you can read on the computer screen. Computer-based reference manuals are extensive and are often distributed on CD-ROMs. You can also usually find independent publishers who produce reference manuals for popular hardware and, particularly, for popular software. You might want to purchase one of these reference manuals if it is easier to understand or better organized than the one included with the hardware or software you purchased.

On-line Help

The term "on-line" refers to computer resources that are immediately available on request. Reference information is frequently available as **on-line Help**, accessible from a Help menu or by typing "HELP" at a command-line prompt. Figure 1-21 shows how you access the on-line help for the Microsoft Windows Paintbrush software.

Figure 1-21
Accessing on-line Help

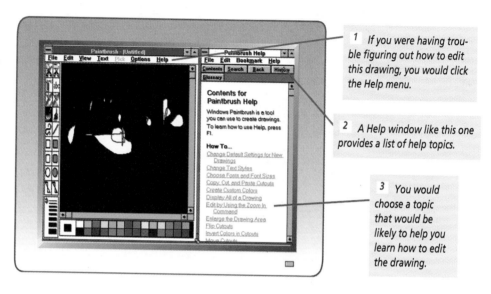

1   If you were having trouble figuring out how to edit this drawing, you would click the Help menu.

2   A Help window like this one provides a list of help topics.

3   You would choose a topic that would be likely to help you learn how to edit the drawing.

Once you have activated the on-line Help, the next step is to locate the information you need. Some on-line Help is **context sensitive**, which means that information about the task you are currently doing automatically appears when you request help. For example, if you pull down the Edit menu and then activate a context sensitive on-line Help facility, you automatically see information about how to use the Edit menu options.

Most on-line Help facilities have a table of contents menu or an index menu, so you can select a topic from a list. Many on-line Help facilities also include a search option, so you can type the name of a topic for which you want information. The search option quickly looks through the on-line Help topics and shows you a list of relevant information.

Other Sources of Information

If you like reading and easily remember the things you read in books, you will probably like using printed reference manuals and tutorials. If you are a visual learner, you will probably like video tutorials. If you are an adventurous learner, you might enjoy exploring software applications without much help from printed materials or video tutorials. Graphical and menu-driven user interfaces make this sort of exploration possible, as do interfaces that include on-line Help. Although it is okay to take this exploratory approach with software, you should probably not take this approach with hardware. You could damage equipment if you do not install it correctly, so read and follow instructions whenever you are installing hardware.

Another approach to learning about hardware and software is to take a course. Because you're reading this book, you are probably enrolled in an introductory computer course. Courses that teach you how to use software packages are available from schools and private training firms and might last from several hours to several months. Courses about software packages tend to be laboratory-based with an instructor leading you through steps. Some courses might be lecture only, however, so it is best to ask about the course format before you register. The laboratory-based course is definitely preferable if you want to have the hands-on experience necessary to learn how to be productive using computers.

Sometimes, particularly if you run into a problem and are pressed for time, the best course of action is to ask an expert. You might have a friend who knows a lot about computers or on the job you might know a computer "guru." These are both good sources of information, as long as you don't overuse them. Most software and hardware companies also have a **support line**, a telephone number you can call to talk with someone who can answer specific questions. Sometimes these support line numbers are toll-free, sometimes they are not. In addition to paying for the phone call, you might also pay a fee for the time it takes the support person to answer your question.

Learning to use computers is a challenging activity, heightened by the fact that computer hardware and software change rapidly. Just when you master one software package, a better one appears, and you face the challenge of learning something new. Happily, you will discover that many concepts you learned previously carry over to new hardware and software technologies. To maintain a good attitude about computers, it is important to view the learning process itself as an interesting challenge. Approach this challenge as if you were a detective—gather information, make hypotheses, explore and test your hypotheses, and when you've solved one case, look forward to the challenge of the next.

C H A P T E R   R E V I E W

1. Answer the questions listed in the Chapter Preview at the beginning of the chapter.
2. List each of the boldface terms used in the chapter, then *use* your *own* words to write a short definition of each term.
3. Review the labels on Figure 1-6. List each of the peripheral devices and indicate whether it is an input device, an output device, or both.
4. Create a chart like the chart below. Fill it in to summarize the key features of command-line, menu-driven, prompted, and graphical user interfaces.

	COMMAND-LINE	MENU-DRIVEN	PROMPTED	GRAPHICAL
DESCRIPTION				
ADVANTAGES				
DISADVANTAGES				
REQUIRED INPUT DEVICE(S)				
REQUIRED OUTPUT DEVICE(S)				

5. Make a list of the sources of information that might be available to learn about hardware and software. Write a one-sentence description of each source.

C H A P T E R   Q U I Z

1. Most computers are equipped with a(n) _____ as the primary input device and a(n) _____ as the primary output device.
2. An IBM computer is _____ with a Compaq computer because it operates in essentially the same way.
3. _____ rules govern exactly how you can combine command language elements to form commands.
4. A(n) _____ user interface features icons and tools.
5. A command-line user interface displays a(n) _____ to let you know that the computer is ready for your commands.
6. The flashing underline or box that marks your place on the screen is called the _____.
7. The arrow that marks your place on the screen is called the _____.
8. Graphical user interfaces generally require a(n) _____ as an output device.
9. The _____ temporarily stores the results from intermediate stages of calculations, the numbers that will be processed, and the instructions for how to process them.
10. The means by which humans and computers communicate is referred to as the _____.
11. With a prompted user interface, the dialog is initiated by _____.
12. _____ are work areas on the screen analogous to different documents and books you might have open on your desk.
13. A user interface with a desktop _____ might represent documents as file folders and storage as a file cabinet.
14. Some on-line Help is _____, so information about the task you are doing automatically appears.
15. When you use a command-line user interface and you leave out a required punctuation mark, the computer displays _____.

P R O J E C T S

1. In this chapter you learned that embedded computers are built into microwave ovens, VCRs, and cameras as control devices. List three other machines or devices that are likely to have embedded computers and describe what part the embedded computer plays in the operation of each.

2. Draw a sketch of a computer system in your computer lab, home, or office and do the following:
   a. Title the sketch appropriately, for example, "My Computer at Home."
   b. List its brand and model number, for example, "Dell 486/50."
   c. Label the following parts:

monitor	screen	keyboard
3.5" disk drive	5.25" disk drive	hard drive light
CD-ROM	power switch	power light
system unit	mouse	printer

   d. If the computer system you have sketched does not have one or more of the components listed in part c, indicate this is the case by listing the missing components at the bottom of the drawing under the heading "Components Not Available."

3. Use the resources in your library to find more information on one of the following types of computers:

   embedded computers

   minicomputers

   mainframes

   super computers

   a. Write a double-spaced, three-page report that discusses typical uses, average price ranges, and leading manufacturers.
   b. Include a sketch or photocopy of a typical system.
   c. Append a bibliography to your report.

4. In this chapter you learned that the fluent conversation between Dave Bowman and HAL, depicted in *2001: A Space Odyssey*, is not possible today, even though sound boards are available to accept your spoken input and provide audio output from the computer. The reason that such fluent conversation is not possible is because software has not yet been developed that can master human speech.

   Although this seems like a fairly simple problem at first, understanding human speech is really quite difficult for two reasons. First, language is *ambiguous,* that is, words and phrases can have more than one meaning. For example, the phrase "time flies" usually means that time goes by quickly, but it could also mean "Get out the stop watch and find out how fast flies go!" The second problem with developing software that understands human language is that much of the meaning is based on context and cultural experiences that a computer cannot access. For example, in the phrase "Terry looked at the bike in the window and wanted it" we assume that "it" refers to the bike. But "it" could also refer to the window. A computer would not be able to understand the use of "it" in this sentence, unless it truly had the ability to think intelligently and know how to assess the context of a situation.

   a. List three additional examples of ambiguous words or phrases that a computer would have difficulty interpreting.
   b. List three additional examples of situations in which a computer would need context knowledge to make an accurate interpretation.

5. You learned in this chapter that you can find four types of tutorials.
   a. List these four types and explain them briefly.
   b. Which type do you think you would prefer? Explain why.

6. Locate a software reference manual in your computer lab, home, or library, then answer the following questions:
   a. What is the title of the reference manual?
   b. How many pages does it have?

   c. What are the titles of each section of the manual? For example, there might be a "Getting Started" section or an "Installation" section, and so on.

   d. Does the reference manual include an index? If so, does it look complete? You should be suspicious of a large reference manual with a short index—it might be difficult to find the information you need.

   e. Does the reference manual contain a list of features? If so, is this list arranged alphabetically? If not, how is it arranged?

   f. Read one or two pages of the reference manual. Write one or two sentences describing what you read. Does the reference manual seem to be well written and easy to follow? Why or why not?

7. In this chapter you learned that you can take many approaches to learning how to use hardware and software.

   a. Describe the way you like to learn things in general—do you like to read about them, take a class, listen to a cassette, watch a video, think about them, do library research, or take a different approach?

   b. If you had to learn how to use a new software application, which approach would you like best: a tutorial, reference manual, explore on your own, take a class, or ask an expert? Why?

   c. How does this relate to the way you like to learn other things?

L A B S

Computer-based *New Perspectives* Labs are available for the topics in the chapter that have corresponding Lab icons. To use the *New Perspectives* Labs, the *New Perspectives* software must be installed on your computer. If you are using your school's lab computers, your instructor or technical support person should have installed the *New Perspectives* software for you. If you want to use this software on your home computer, ask your instructor for the *New Perspectives* software.

To use the *New Perspectives* software:

1. Look on your computer screen for the New Perspectives program group shown in Figure 1-22.

   Trouble? If you cannot find the New Perspectives program group, check with your technical support person.

2. Use the mouse to position the pointer here, then double-click the left mouse button. Double-click means to click twice in rapid succession.

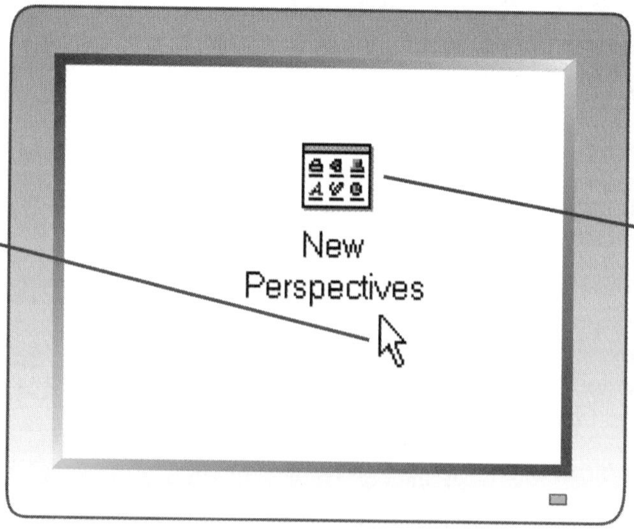

Figure 1-22
New Perspectives program group

New Perspectives program group

3. After you double-click, the New Perspectives window opens, as shown in Figure 1-23.

4. Use the mouse to position the pointer on the icon for the lab you want to use. Then double-click the left mouse button.

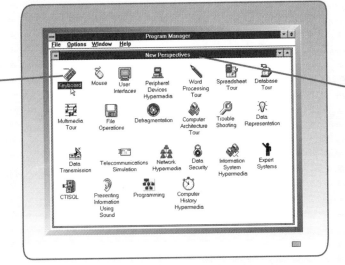

Figure 1-23
New Perspectives window

Window title is "New Perspectives"

Keyboard Lab

Use the interactive Keyboard Lab to learn the features of the computer keyboard.

1. Use a copy of Figure 1-24 or draw a sketch of your keyboard and label the following keys. If a key appears in more than one location on the keyboard, be sure you label *both* locations.

Esc	Caps Lock	Ctrl	Alt
Backspace	Insert or Ins	Delete or Del	Home
End	Page Up or PgUp	Page Down or PgDn	cursor keys (↑↓←→)
Num Lock	Enter	slash (/)	backslash (\)
Tab	Shift		

L A B

KEYBOARD

Figure 1-24

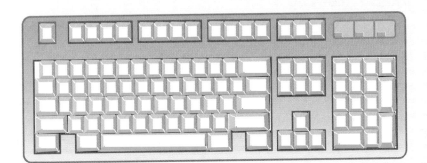

2. If the Caps Lock key is activated, what character is generated when you press the key that has % on the top and 5 on the bottom?

3. What happens when the Caps Lock key is not activated and you hold down the Shift key and press the key that displays % on the top and 5 on the bottom?

4. Write a concise explanation about the difference between the Caps Lock and the Shift keys.
5. Explain what the Num Lock key does.
6. What does a "modifier key" do? Which keys are modifier keys?
7. How does a toggle key work? Which keys are toggle keys?

Mouse Lab

L A B

MOUSE

Use the interactive Mouse Lab to find out how a mouse works.

1. What are the four mouse actions?
2. Which mouse button do you use most frequently?
3. If you move the mouse toward the back of your desk, does the pointer move up or down on the screen?
4. Draw a sketch of the mouse you use showing how many buttons it has and showing which end is attached to the cable.
5. Draw a sketch of the underside of the mouse showing the rolling ball.

User Interfaces Lab

L A B

USER INTERFACES

Use the interactive User Interfaces Lab to gain experience using different types of user interfaces.

1. Write a brief description of the different menu styles you used in this Lab. Which menu style did you like the most? Explain why.
2. Answer the two questions on Page 19 of the tutorial.
3. Answer the two questions on Page 20 of the tutorial.
4. Answer the two questions on Page 21 of the tutorial.
5. Answer the two questions on Page 22 of the tutorial.
6. Answer the two questions on the final page of the tutorial.

Peripheral Devices Lab

L A B

PERIPHERAL DEVICES

Use the Peripheral Devices Lab to learn more about how these devices work.

1. Which devices would be particularly useful for an architect who wants to input or output blueprints?
2. What are the steps you should follow to send a computer document to another computer using a modem?
3. What steps should you follow if the paper in your dot-matrix printer is not positioned at the top of a page?
4. Explain the difference in print quality between 9-pin and 24-pin dot-matrix printers.
5. Explain how a laser printer works.
6. What peripheral devices could you use if you were making a presentation to a group of people and you wanted to show them a graph from your computer screen?
7. Explain why a CD-ROM drive is more like a record player than a tape recorder.
8. Draw a sketch showing how pixels form a text or graphics image.

R E S O U R C E S

■ Clarke, A. C. *2001: A Space Odyssey.* New York: New American Library, 1968.

2001 is a science fiction classic that takes a bold perspective on how computers might develop in the future. Perhaps Clarke's writing is so powerful because of his strong background in science and research. Clarke is well known for his contribution to the invention of the communications satellite.

■ Graham, N. *The Mind Tool: Computers and Their Impact on Society*, 5th ed. St Paul, MN: West Publishing, 1989.

This well-respected text provides broad coverage of the history of computing, how computers work, and the impact computers have on society.

■ Norman, D. *The Psychology of Everyday Things.* New York: Basic Books, 1988.

Donald Norman says "This is the book I have always wanted to write, but I didn't know it." The book is an entertaining account of the predicaments caused by poor engineering of everyday objects, such as stoves and revolving doors, as well as more technological devices, such as computers and nuclear power plants.

■ Ralston, A., and E. D. Reilly, *Encyclopedia of Computer Science and Engineering,* 3rd ed. New York: Van Nostrand Reinhold, 1993.

A definitive reference work on computer concepts, this single-volume encyclopedia is arranged alphabetically by topic and is extensively indexed. You can find information on the first computers, biographies of people who made key contributions to the computer industry, and explanations of many simple and complex computer concepts. Check your library or a similar computer reference resource to find this book.

■ von Neumann, J. "First Draft of a Report on the EDVAC" [unpublished report written in 1945] in Stern, N. B. *From ENIAC to UNIVAC: An Appraisal of the Eckert-Mauchly Computers.* Bedford, MA: Digital Press, 1981.

John von Neumann's report on the EDVAC computer is printed in full as an appendix to Nancy Stern's well-researched book about the earliest efforts to build a working electronic computer. The book contains some fascinating photos of one-of-a-kind computing equipment, as well as detailed circuit diagrams showing how these machines worked.

■ *Computer Dictionary*, 2nd ed. Redmond, WA: Microsoft Press, 1994.

It is useful to have a dictionary of computer terms when you read articles in computer magazines. Microsoft Press publishes this up-to-date dictionary that will help you make sense of computer jargon.

C H A P T E R   P R E V I E W

When you have completed this chapter you should be able to answer the following questions:

- What role does the operating system play in the operation of your computer?
- What are some of the differences between the DOS, Windows, UNIX, OS/2, and Macintosh operating systems?
- What does utility software do?
- What is the difference between system software and application software?
- What are the major categories of application software?
- What restrictions do the U.S. Copyright Acts place on your use of software?
- How has the definition of multimedia changed?
- What special hardware do you need for multimedia applications?

SOFTWARE AND MULTIMEDIA APPLICATIONS

The quest for multipurpose machines has always enchanted inventors. The car-boat is, perhaps, one of the most elusive multipurpose machines. Soon after the first "horseless carriages" hit the streets, inventors schemed about ways to create a vehicle that could function on water just as well as on land. Although it is technically possible to build a carboat, the idea never really caught on. But today we have a multipurpose machine that is far more useful than a car that converts to a boat—and that machine is the computer.

The computer is the most successful and versatile machine in history. The same computer can produce professionally typeset documents, translate French into English, produce music, diagnose diseases, control machinery, keep track of airline reservations, and much more.

A computer's versatility is possible because of software. But what does software do that gives a computer such versatility? What kinds of software can you buy? How do you know what software works with your computer?

In this chapter you will learn how the computer uses software. You will learn the difference between system software and application software, and you will find out about the new trend toward multimedia computing. The chapter ends on a practical note with information about how to install new software on your computer system and what legal and ethical issues you need to consider when you buy and use software.

Computer Programs and Computer Software ▮

Computer programs and computer software determine what a computer can do, and in a sense, they transform a computer from one kind of machine to another—from a drafting station to a typesetting machine, from a flight simulator to a calculator, from a filing system to a music studio, and so on.

A **computer program** is a set of detailed, step-by-step instructions that tell a computer how to solve a problem or carry out a task. Some computer programs handle simple tasks, such as converting feet and inches to centimeters. Longer and more complex computer programs handle very complicated tasks, such as reconstructing photographs sent back from a spacecraft flyby of Jupiter. The steps in the program are written in a language that the computer can interpret or "understand." As you read through the simple computer program in Figure 2-1, which converts feet and inches to centimeters, notice the number of steps required to perform a relatively simple calculation.

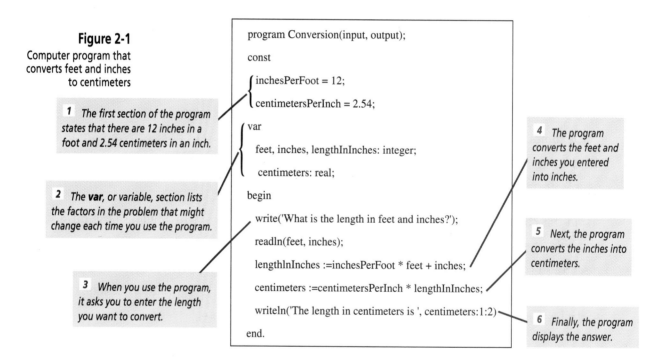

Figure 2-1
Computer program that converts feet and inches to centimeters

1 The first section of the program states that there are 12 inches in a foot and 2.54 centimeters in an inch.

2 The **var**, or variable, section lists the factors in the problem that might change each time you use the program.

3 When you use the program, it asks you to enter the length you want to convert.

4 The program converts the feet and inches you entered into inches.

5 Next, the program converts the inches into centimeters.

6 Finally, the program displays the answer.

```
program Conversion(input, output);

const

  inchesPerFoot = 12;

  centimetersPerInch = 2.54;

var

  feet, inches, lengthInInches: integer;

  centimeters: real;

begin

  write('What is the length in feet and inches?');

  readln(feet, inches);

  lengthInInches :=inchesPerFoot * feet + inches;

  centimeters :=centimetersPerInch * lengthInInches;

  writeln('The length in centimeters is ', centimeters:1:2)

end.
```

The legal definition of computer software as used in the U.S. Copyright Act of 1980 is "a set of statements or instructions to be used directly or indirectly in a computer in order to bring about a certain result." This definition implies that computer software is essentially the same as a computer program. In practice, however, the term "computer software" is frequently used in a slightly different way; it is usually used to describe a commercial product, which might include more than a single program and might also include large collections of data, as shown in Figure 2-2.

1 *Word processing software has a program to help you enter, edit, and print documents, and a program to check the spelling of the words in your documents.*

2 *The word processing software also includes collections of data, such as the words in the spelling dictionary.*

Figure 2-2
Software often includes several programs and collections of data

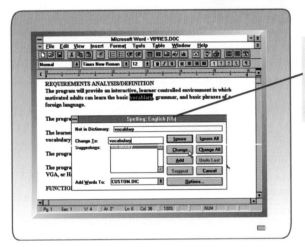

3 *To check your spelling, the spell check program compares each word in your document with the words in a dictionary of correctly spelled words.*

According to common usage, the term **computer software** is one or more computer programs and associated data that exist in electronic format on a storage medium, such as disk or CD-ROM.

Don't let this definition mislead you; not everything stored on a disk is software. Although the data that a software publisher includes on a disk is considered part of the software package, the data you *create* is generally not referred to as software. For example, suppose you write a report and store it on a disk. Your report consists of data rather than instructions for the computer to carry out. Because your report does not contain instructions, it is not software, nor is it a program.

There are many companies that publish computer software. You might be surprised to learn that some of the most productive and most successful software publishers are not the companies that design and build hardware. For example, although IBM is one of the top computer hardware vendors, Microsoft Corporation publishes the most software for IBM microcomputers. This means that when people refer to IBM software or PC software, they are talking about software that is designed to work on IBM-compatible computers, not software published by IBM.

Software publishers are continually working to produce new software and to improve their old software. When a new version of software is released, the publisher usually provides current users with an **upgrade** or **update** to the new version for a small fee. It is a good idea to use the latest software version so you can take advantage of the latest features. Figure 2-3 on the following page explains more about software upgrades.

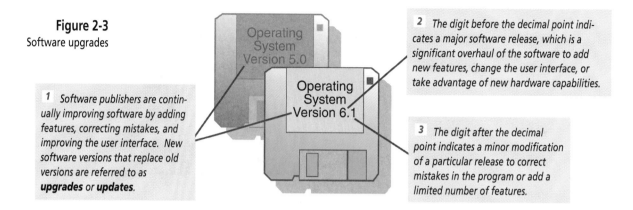

Figure 2-3
Software upgrades

1 Software publishers are continually improving software by adding features, correcting mistakes, and improving the user interface. New software versions that replace old versions are referred to as **upgrades** or **updates**.

2 The digit before the decimal point indicates a major software release, which is a significant overhaul of the software to add new features, change the user interface, or take advantage of new hardware capabilities.

3 The digit after the decimal point indicates a minor modification of a particular release to correct mistakes in the program or add a limited number of features.

To explore and understand the multifaceted nature of computer software, it is convenient to categorize it. There are two major categories of software: system software and application software. System software helps the *computer* carry out its basic operating tasks. Application software helps the *human user* carry out a task. As you continue to read this chapter, use Figure 2-4 to help you understand the distinctions between system and application software and to help you distinguish among the various types of system and application software.

Figure 2-4
Software categories

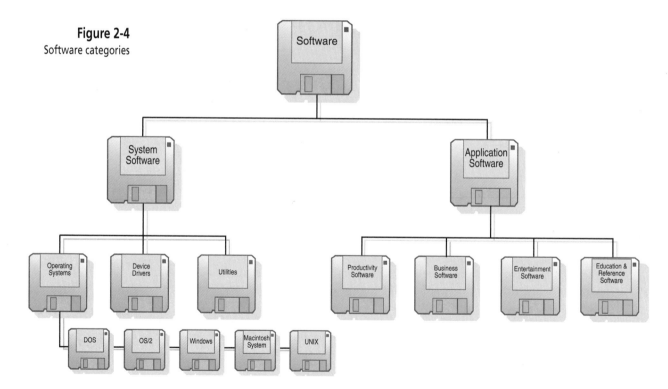

System Software

System software includes the programs that direct the fundamental operations of your computer, such as displaying information on the screen, storing data on disks, sending data to the printer, interpreting your typed commands, and communicating with peripheral devices. In addition, system software provides a foundation so that application software operates correctly and uses peripheral devices properly. For example, suppose you use application software to write a letter that you want to print. Behind the scene, the system software helps the application software communicate with your computer's printer. Although system software does not directly help you perform a particular task, it establishes a foundation of basic computer functions that is used by application software.

To clarify the purpose of system software, let's look at some of the specific functions of the three types of system software: operating systems, device drivers, and utilities.

Operating Systems

An **operating system** works like an air traffic controller to coordinate the activities within the computer. Just as an airport cannot function without air traffic controllers, a computer cannot function without an operating system. When you purchase a computer, the operating system is usually already installed on the hard disk and ready to use. When a new version of the operating system becomes available, however, you should purchase, install, and use it so you have access to all the latest features.

The operating system works "behind the scenes" most of the time to perform tasks essential to the efficient functioning of the computer system. It controls input and output, allocates system resources, manages the storage space for your programs and data, maintains security, and detects equipment failure.

Control Basic Input and Output

The operating system controls the basic input and output of data to the computer, as well as the flow of data to and from peripheral devices. It routes your input to areas of the computer where it can be processed and routes output to the screen, a printer, or any other output device you request.

Allocate System Resources

The operating system allocates system resources so programs run properly. Each program instruction takes up space inside the computer and each instruction requires a certain amount of time to complete. The operating system ensures that adequate space is available for your programs and that program instructions are completed quickly.

The operating system also manages the additional resources required for using multiple programs or for providing services to more than one user at the same time. For example, if you want to run two or more programs at the same time, a process called **multitasking**, the operating system ensures that each program has adequate space and that the computer devotes an appropriate amount of time to the tasks prescribed by each program.

To accommodate more than one user at a time, an operating system must have **multiuser** capabilities. You typically find multiuser operating systems on mainframe and minicomputer systems, where users each have their own keyboard and screen, but share a single main computer. Multiuser operating systems typically provide speedy service so users each think they are the only person using the computer.

Manage Storage Space

The operating system keeps track of the data stored on disks and CD-ROMs. Think of your disks as filing cabinets, your data as papers stored in file folders, and the operating system as a filing clerk. The filing clerk takes care of filing a folder when you finish using it. When you need something from your filing cabinet, you ask the filing clerk to get it. The filing clerk knows where to find your folder. On your computer system, the operating system stores your data at some location on a disk. Although you might not know exactly where your data is stored on the disk, when you need the data again, you only need to ask the operating system to retrieve it.

Maintain Security

The operating system also helps maintain the security of the data on the computer system. For example, the operating system might not allow you to access the computer system unless you have a user ID and password. A **user ID** is a unique set of letters and numbers, such as your name, social security number, or credit card number, that identifies a particular user. A **password** is a unique set of letters and numbers known only to the individual user and the computer. When you attempt to access information on the computer, the operating system asks for your user ID and password. Without the correct user ID and password, you cannot use the programs or data stored on the computer system.

Detect Equipment Failure

The operating system monitors the status of critical computer components to detect failures that affect processing. When you turn on your computer, the operating system checks each of the critical electronic components and takes a quick inventory of the storage devices. For example, if an electrical component inside your computer fails, the operating system displays a message identifying the problem and does not let you continue with the computing session until the problem is fixed.

Microcomputer Operating Systems

Today's popular microcomputer operating systems include DOS, Windows, OS/2, the Macintosh operating system, and UNIX. Three of these operating systems—DOS, Windows, and OS/2—are typically used on IBM-compatible systems. As you might expect, the Macintosh operating system is used on the Apple Macintosh computer. UNIX is available for both IBM-compatible and Macintosh computers. Versions of UNIX and Windows are also available for some minicomputers and mainframes.

All microcomputer operating systems perform a similar set of basic tasks. Depending on the hardware capabilities, a particular microcomputer operating system might also have additional capabilities, such as multiuser support or multitasking.

When you use a computer, you need to know which operating system your computer uses so you can enter the appropriate instructions. But how can you tell which operating system it is using? Many microcomputer users can recognize which operating system is on a particular computer by looking at the first screen that appears when they turn the computer on or by recognizing the operating system prompt. If you study Figure 2-5 on pages NP 42 and NP 43, you can identify the DOS, Macintosh, Windows, UNIX, and OS/2 operating systems when you encounter them in the future.

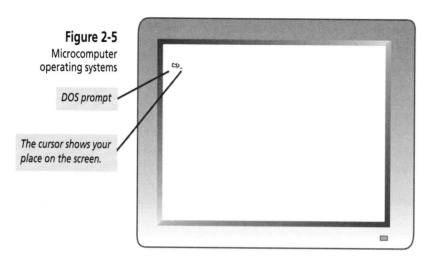

Figure 2-5
Microcomputer
operating systems

DOS prompt

The cursor shows your
place on the screen.

Initial screen of DOS operating system

DOS, which stands for Disk Operating System, is marketed under two trade names, **PC-DOS** and **MS-DOS**. Both PC-DOS and MS-DOS were developed primarily by Microsoft Corporation, and are essentially the same. DOS was introduced in 1981 with IBM's first personal computer. The first version of DOS, version 1.0, has been revised and updated through DOS 6.0, as of 1994.

Early versions of DOS provide only a command-line user interface, but more recent versions include a menu-driven user interface called the DOS Shell. The **DOS Shell** provides menu access to the most frequently used operating system features, so you do not have to memorize the DOS commands.

Following Apple's lead, Microsoft took a more graphical approach to operating systems when it designed Windows. When first introduced, Microsoft Windows could be installed only on computers that already used DOS. Microsoft Windows, in effect, "piggy-backed" on the DOS operating system. Because Microsoft Windows does not handle all operating systems tasks on its own, it is sometimes referred to as an **operating environment**, rather than an operating system. However, in 1993, Microsoft introduced Windows NT with full operating system capabilities, which no longer requires DOS.

Microsoft Windows provides icons that you can directly manipulate on the screen using a pointing device, and pull-down menus you can use to easily issue a command. The applications you use with Microsoft Windows all have a consistent look, so it is easy to learn how to use new software. Microsoft Windows also lets you run more than one program at a time in separate windows on the screen, and lets you easily transfer data between them. While using Microsoft Windows, you can still run DOS software.

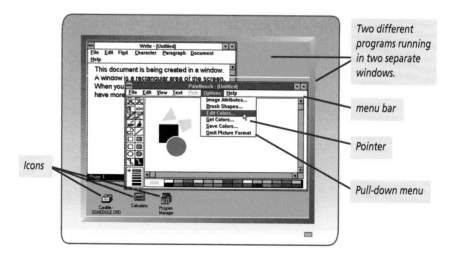

Two different
programs running
in two separate
windows.

menu bar

Pointer

Icons

Pull-down menu

Sample screen from Windows operating system

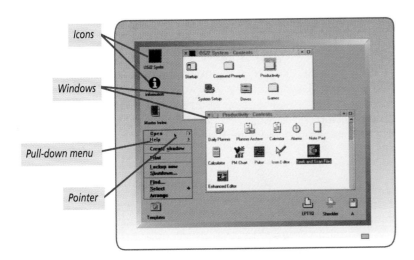

Icons

Windows

Pull-down menu

Pointer

OS/2 was designed jointly by Microsoft and IBM. Their goal was to create an operating system that would take advantage of newer, more powerful computers, plus offer a graphical user interface while retaining the ability to run DOS programs. As with other graphical user interfaces, OS/2 allows you to manipulate objects on the screen to perform tasks and select commands from menus. As with Microsoft Windows, OS/2 lets you work with more than one program at a time and easily transfer data between them. If your computer uses OS/2, you can run most DOS and Windows software, as well as software designed specifically for OS/2.

In 1984, Apple Computer, Inc. took a revolutionary step when it introduced the Apple Lisa computer with a new operating system, based on a graphical user interface featuring pull-down menus, icons, and a mouse. The Lisa computer was not a commercial success, but Apple's next product, the Macintosh computer, was very successful and defined a new direction in operating system user interfaces that became an industry standard. The **Macintosh Operating System** is usually referred to by its version number, for example, version seven is called System 7.

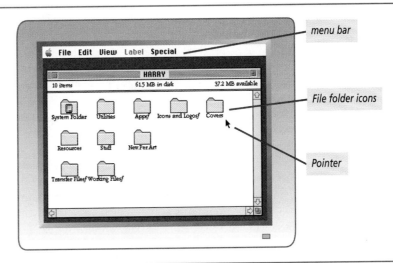

menu bar

File folder icons

Pointer

UNIX is an operating system that was developed at AT&T's Bell Laboratories in 1969. UNIX was originally designed for minicomputers, but is now also available for microcomputers and mainframes. Many versions of UNIX exist, such as AIX from IBM, XENIX from Microsoft, and ULTRIX from Digital Equipment Corporation, but these other versions are essentially the same operating system adapted for different computers. UNIX features a command-line user interface, but you can purchase add-on software that provides a graphical user interface with direct object manipulation and pull-down menus. UNIX is a **multiuser** operating system, which means that many users can run programs on a single computer at the same time. UNIX also supports **multitasking**.

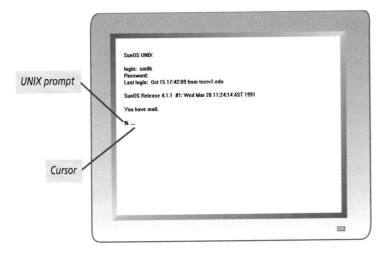

UNIX prompt

Cursor

Device Drivers

In Chapter 1, you learned that when you purchase a new peripheral device, such as a CD-ROM drive or a mouse, you often need to install software that tells your computer how to use the device. This type of system software is called a **device driver**. When you purchase a hardware device, you also receive a disk containing a device driver. Installing a device driver is usually straightforward. If you encounter problems and the device does not work, check with the manufacturer for help.

Utilities

Although an operating system usually works behind the scenes, there are times when you need **utilities**, or **utility software**, to do such things as prepare disks to store data, see what's on your disks, or copy data from one disk to another. Some utilities are included with the operating system. You can also purchase separate utilities that provide additional features.

The operating system often includes a utility that you use to format a disk. Before you can store data on a disk, you must **format** the disk. Think of formatting as creating the electronic equivalent of storage shelves. Before you can put things on the shelves, you must assemble the shelves. In a similar way, before you can store data on a disk, you must format it.

To use the format utility, you either type the name of the utility or select the format option from a menu. Study the sequence of screens in Figure 2-6 to understand how to use the format utility.

Let's return for a moment to the idea presented at the beginning of this chapter—that the computer is a multipurpose machine. System software handles internal computer functions, but it doesn't directly perform the types of tasks or problems to which the computer is applied. Instead, system software provides the foundation for basic computer capabilities. It is *application software* that enables the computer to perform many different types of tasks.

Application Software

Application software, also referred to as an **application**, is designed to help you accomplish a specific task using the computer. Application software helps you produce documents, perform calculations, manage financial resources, create graphics, compose music, play games, maintain files of information, and so on. Figure 2-7 on page NP 46 shows you an expanded view of the application software branch of the software hierarchy chart you saw in Figure 2-4.

Because there is such a vast amount of application software, it is convenient to classify it, but keep in mind that the categories are not formalized. One way to classify application software is to use four categories: productivity, business, education and reference, and entertainment.

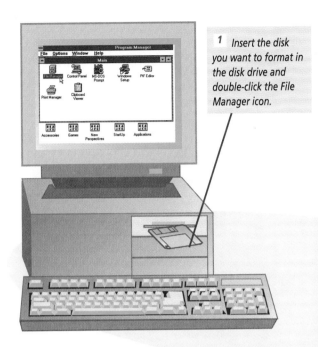

1 Insert the disk you want to format in the disk drive and double-click the File Manager icon.

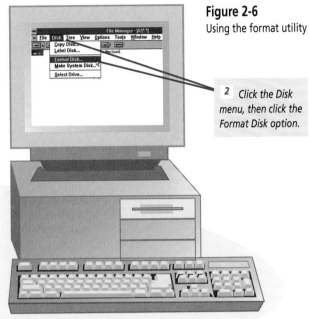

Figure 2-6
Using the format utility

2 Click the Disk menu, then click the Format Disk option.

3 Check the settings on the Format Disk dialog box and make any necessary modifications, then click the OK button.

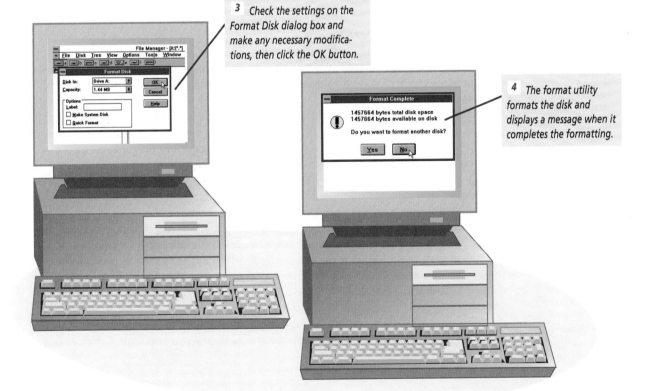

4 The format utility formats the disk and displays a message when it completes the formatting.

Figure 2-7
Applications software
hierarchy chart

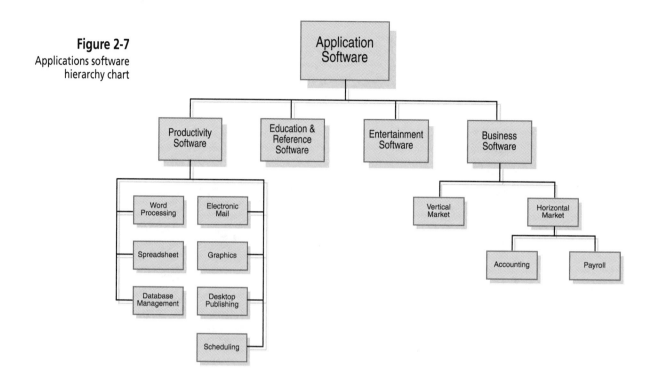

Productivity Software

**WORD
PROCESSING
TOUR**

As you might expect, **productivity software** helps you work more effectively. The most popular types of productivity software are word processing, spreadsheet, and database management.

Word processing software helps you produce documents such as reports, letters, papers, and manuscripts. To use a word processor, you type in the text of the document. As you type, you can edit your work using the insert and delete keys. You can also move text to improve the logical flow of concepts in your document.

Spreadsheet software helps you work with numbers. The software displays a grid of rows and columns on the screen. You enter numbers and formulas in the grid and the computer automatically performs the calculations.

**SPREADSHEET
TOUR**

Database management software helps you work with facts and figures, such as the customer names and addresses you might store on file cards or in a Rolodex.

Before you learn about other productivity software, let's take a closer look at the most popular productivity software: word processing (Figure 2-8), spreadsheet (Figure 2-9), and databases (Figure 2-10). If you have not used these types of software before, you can begin to develop an understanding of their basic features and functions by carefully reading and studying these figures. If you have used these types of software before, try to associate the features you remember with those described in the figures.

**DATABASE
TOUR**

Although word processing, spreadsheet, and database management software are the most popular productivity software, you are likely to encounter other types of productivity software—electronic mail, desktop publishing, graphics, and scheduling.

Electronic mail software provides you with a computerized mailbox that collects documents or "mail" you receive electronically from other computer users. You can read your electronic mail just like you can read your regular mail, you can save or throw away your electronic mail after you read it, and you can compose electronic replies to the mail you receive.

Graphics software helps you draw pictures, 3-D images, and animation. If you have limited artistic ability, you can use graphics software to retrieve pre-drawn clip art images, which you can modify.

Desktop publishing software provides you with computerized tools for page layout and design that combine text and graphics. Although many desktop publishing features are available in today's sophisticated word processing software, desktop publishing software helps you to produce professional-looking, quality output for newspapers, newsletters, and brochures.

Scheduling software helps you keep track of appointments, due dates, and special dates such as birthdays and holidays. You can use the scheduling software to print a daily, weekly, or monthly schedule.

Business Software

A second major application software category, **business software**, helps organizations efficiently accomplish routine tasks. Often, business software is divided into two categories: horizontal market software and vertical market software. **Horizontal market software** refers to generic software packages that can be used by many different kinds of businesses. Accounting and payroll applications are good examples of horizontal market software. Every business needs to maintain a set of books to track income and expenses. **Accounting software** is designed to computerize the bookkeeping tasks typically required in most businesses. Almost every business has employees and needs to maintain payroll records. **Payroll software** keeps track of employee hours and produces the reports required by the government for income tax reporting.

Vertical market software is designed for specialized tasks in a specific market or business. For example, important tasks in the construction business include estimating the cost of labor and materials for a new building and providing the customer with a bid or estimate of the price for the finished building. Estimating software designed specifically for construction businesses helps automate the task of gathering labor and materials costs and performs the calculations needed to arrive at a price estimate. Other examples of vertical market software include the software that handles billing and insurance for medical practices and software that tracks the amount of time attorneys spend on each case.

Figure 2-8

Word processing software

Word processing software helps you produce documents such as reports, letters, papers, and manuscripts. To use a word processor, you type in the text of the document. The cursor or insertion point shows where the next character you type will appear. As you type, you can **edit** your work by using the Backspace, Insert, and Delete keys. You can also highlight a block of text and delete, move, or copy it. As you write, you can use the **on-line thesaurus** to find a word with just the right meaning to convey your ideas. An **on-line spell checker** helps you proofread your document.

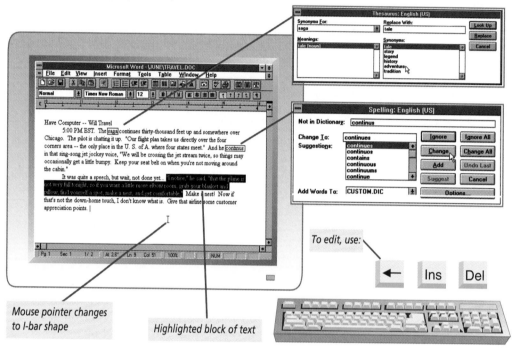

To edit, use:

Mouse pointer changes
to I-bar shape

Highlighted block of text

Word processing software has many **formatting features** to help you design the appearance of your printed document. You can use formatting features to adjust the line spacing, boldface text, italicize text, center text, change the font, and change the font size.

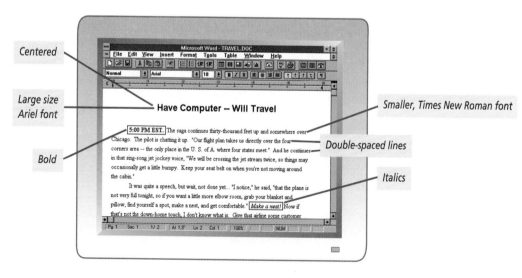

Centered

Large size
Ariel font

Bold

Smaller, Times New Roman font

Double-spaced lines

Italics

To design the page layout, word processing software helps you make borders, add headers and footers, automatically number each page, add graphics, create columns, add footnotes, and justify the margins.

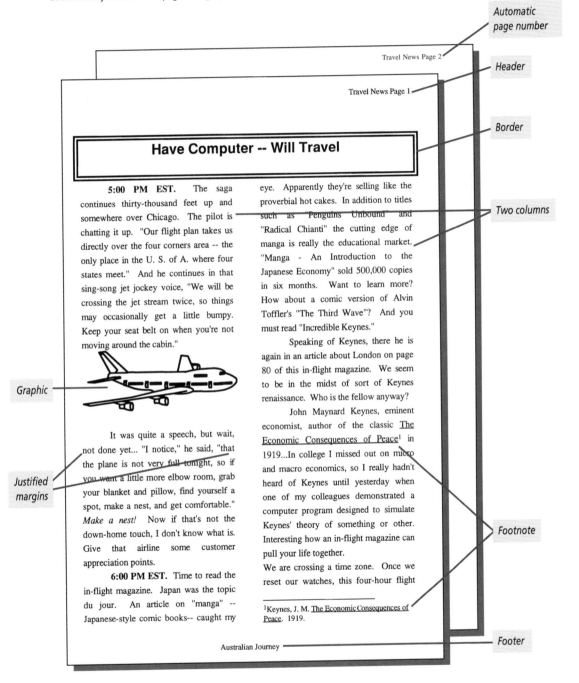

Automatic page number

Header

Border

Two columns

Graphic

Justified margins

Footnote

Footer

Travel News Page 2

Travel News Page 1

Have Computer -- Will Travel

5:00 PM EST. The saga continues thirty-thousand feet up and somewhere over Chicago. The pilot is chatting it up. "Our flight plan takes us directly over the four corners area -- the only place in the U. S. of A. where four states meet." And he continues in that sing-song jet jockey voice, "We will be crossing the jet stream twice, so things may occasionally get a little bumpy. Keep your seat belt on when you're not moving around the cabin."

It was quite a speech, but wait, not done yet... "I notice," he said, "that the plane is not very full tonight, so if you want a little more elbow room, grab your blanket and pillow, find yourself a spot, make a nest, and get comfortable." *Make a nest!* Now if that's not the down-home touch, I don't know what is. Give that airline some customer appreciation points.

6:00 PM EST. Time to read the in-flight magazine. Japan was the topic du jour. An article on "manga" -- Japanese-style comic books-- caught my

eye. Apparently they're selling like the proverbial hot cakes. In addition to titles such as "Penguins Unbound" and "Radical Chianti" the cutting edge of manga is really the educational market. "Manga - An Introduction to the Japanese Economy" sold 500,000 copies in six months. Want to learn more? How about a comic version of Alvin Toffler's "The Third Wave"? And you must read "Incredible Keynes."

Speaking of Keynes, there he is again in an article about London on page 80 of this in-flight magazine. We seem to be in the midst of sort of Keynes renaissance. Who is the fellow anyway?

John Maynard Keynes, eminent economist, author of the classic The Economic Consequences of Peace[1] in 1919...In college I missed out on micro and macro economics, so I really hadn't heard of Keynes until yesterday when one of my colleagues demonstrated a computer program designed to simulate Keynes' theory of something or other. Interesting how an in-flight magazine can pull your life together.

We are crossing a time zone. Once we reset our watches, this four-hour flight

[1]Keynes, J. M. The Economic Consequences of Peace. 1919.

Australian Journey

Figure 2-9
Spreadsheet software

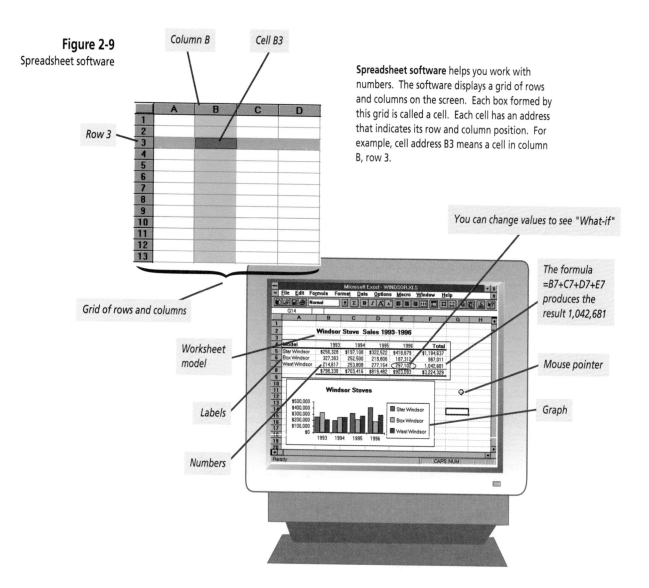

Column B

Cell B3

Row 3

Grid of rows and columns

Spreadsheet software

Spreadsheet software helps you work with numbers. The software displays a grid of rows and columns on the screen. Each box formed by this grid is called a cell. Each cell has an address that indicates its row and column position. For example, cell address B3 means a cell in column B, row 3.

You can change values to see "What-if"

The formula =B7+C7+D7+E7 produces the result 1,042,681

Worksheet model

Labels

Numbers

Mouse pointer

Graph

To use spreadsheet software, you set up a worksheet **model** by typing labels, numbers, and formulas into the cells. The **formulas** you enter are similar to mathematical equations. They tell the computer how to perform calculations. The computer automatically calculates the result of the formulas and displays them on the worksheet or as a graph.

By plugging different numbers into the formulas on your worksheet, you can examine the outcome of different **"what-if"** scenarios, such as "What if 1996 sales of the Box Windsor stoves are $300,000?" or "What if they are only $100,000?"

Spreadsheet reports can combine text and graphics. Formatting options help you automatically number pages, add headers, and position graphics.

Header

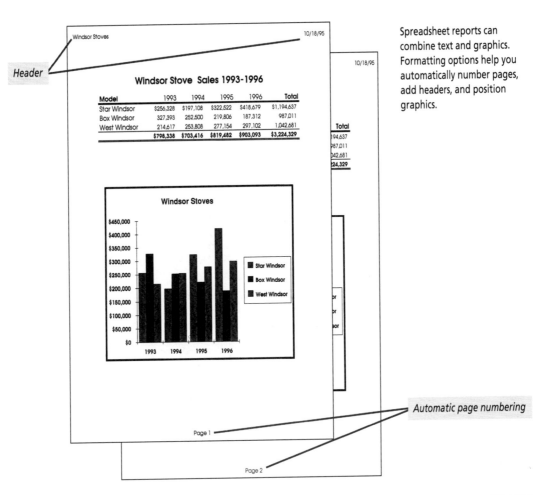

Windsor Stoves   10/18/95

Windsor Stove Sales 1993-1996

Model	1993	1994	1995	1996	Total
Star Windsor	$256,328	$197,108	$322,522	$418,679	$1,194,637
Box Windsor	327,393	252,500	219,806	187,312	987,011
West Windsor	214,617	253,808	277,154	297,102	1,042,681
	$798,338	$703,416	$819,482	$903,093	$3,224,329

Windsor Stoves

- Star Windsor
- Box Windsor
- West Windsor

Page 1

Page 2

Automatic page numbering

Windsor Stoves Cost Analysis

	Materials Costs			Labor Costs			
Model	Body	Door	Hardware	Body	Door	Surface	Total
Box Windsor	$307.00	$68.00	$31.00	$32.00	$12.00	$24.00	$474.00
Deluxe Windsor	$319.00	$72.00	$46.00	$52.00	$16.00	$28.00	$533.00
Lake Windsor	$366.00	$36.00	$24.00	$26.00	$6.00	$18.00	$476.00
Standard	$155.00	$28.00	$18.00	$14.00	$4.00	$14.00	$233.00
Star Windsor	$188.00	$42.00	$18.00	$17.00	$11.00	$22.00	$298.00
West Windsor	$218.00	$40.00	$22.00	$25.00	$12.00	$22.00	$339.00

Total Cost by Model

Box Windsor Deluxe Windsor Lake Windsor Standard Star Windsor West Windsor

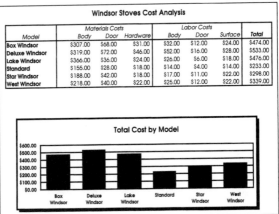

Because many spreadsheets are wider than they are long, a **landscape** print option lets you print a worksheet "sideways."

Figure 2-10
Database management
software

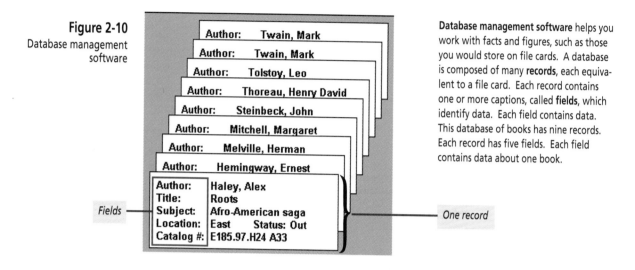

Fields

One record

Database management software helps you work with facts and figures, such as those you would store on file cards. A database is composed of many **records**, each equivalent to a file card. Each record contains one or more captions, called **fields**, which identify data. Each field contains data. This database of books has nine records. Each record has five fields. Each field contains data about one book.

One record

Another way to visualize a database is as a list or table. Each row of the table is a record. Each column of the table is a field.

One record

One field

	Author	Title	Subject	Loc.	Sts.	Catalog #
1	Haley, Alex	Roots	Afro-American saga	East	Out	E185.97.H24
2	Hemingway, Ernest	For Whom the Bell	Spanish Civil War	Main	In	PS3515.E37 F6
3	Melville, Herman	Moby Dick	whaling adventure	Main	In	AC1.672 V.48
4	Mitchell, Margaret	Gone with the Wind	Civil War	East	In	PS3525.I972 G6
5	Steinbeck, John	The Grapes of Wrath	life in the Dust Bowl	West	Out	PS3537.T3234
6	Thoreau, Henry	Walden	philosophy and nature	Main	Out	PS3042 1895
7	Tolstoy, Leo	War and Peace	Russian epic	West	In	AC1.E8 NO.525
8	Twain, Mark	Tom Sawyer	life on the Mississippi	East	Out	PS1306.A1
9	Twain, Mark	Huckleberry Finn	life on the Mississippi	Main	In	PS1305.A1

Table or list

Sorted by title

You can organize the records by **sorting** or **indexing**. Here the records are arranged in alphabetical order by title.

	Author	Title	Subject	Loc.	Sts.	Catalog #
1	Hemingway, Ernest	For Whom the Bell	Spanish Civil War	Main	In	PS3515.E37 F6
2	Mitchell, Margaret	Gone with the Wind	Civil War	East	In	PS3525.I972 G6
3	Twain, Mark	Huckleberry Finn	life on the Mississippi	Main	In	PS1305.A1
4	Melville, Herman	Moby Dick	whaling adventure	Main	In	AC1.672 V.48
5	Haley, Alex	Roots	Afro-American saga	East	Out	E185.97.H24
6	Steinbeck, John	The Grapes of Wrath	life in the Dust Bowl	West	Out	PS3537.T3234
7	Twain, Mark	Tom Sawyer	life on the Mississippi	East	Out	PS1306.A1
8	Thoreau, Henry	Walden	philosophy and nature	Main	Out	PS3042 1895
9	Tolstoy, Leo	War and Peace	Russian epic	West	In	AC1.E8 NO.525

You can make a query to find one or more records. For example, a query to "find all the books where Loc. = Main" produces four titles.

For Whom the Bell Tolls
Huckleberry Finn
Moby Dick
Walden

Grouped by status

All Books Grouped by Status

Title	Author	Catalog #
Status = In		
For Whom the Bell Tolls	Hemingway, Ernest	PS3515.E37 F6 1940
Gone with the Wind	Mitchell, Margaret	PS3525.I972 G6 1936
Huckleberry Finn	Twain, Mark	PS1305.A1 1942A
Moby Dick	Melville, Herman	AC1.672 V.48
War and Peace	Tolstoy, Leo	AC1.E8 NO.525
Books currently In = 5		
Status = Out		
Roots	Haley, Alex	E185.97.H24 A33
The Grapes of Wrath	Steinbeck, John	PS3537.T3234 G7
Tom Sawyer	Twain, Mark	PS1306.A1 1946B
Walden	Thoreau, Henry David	PS3042 1895
Books currently Out = 4		

Database management software provides sophisticated options for creating sorted or grouped **reports**. A **control-break report** groups the data by category. In this case, the data is sorted by status so that all the books that have been checked out are listed together.

Entertainment Software

Entertainment software is designed to entertain you. With entertainment software, you can fly a simulated jet, play 18 holes of golf, solve a Sherlock Holmes mystery, battle monsters, or explore new worlds. Some entertainment software is not in game format; with these "software toys" there is no competition, no score, no winner, no loser. An example is a computerized fish tank application that lets you catch, breed, and watch a collection of brilliantly realistic tropical fish inside the glass "tank" of your computer monitor. Sometimes it is hard to make this non-competitive software sound interesting, but it has a certain appeal to some computer users who are looking for low-stress diversions.

Education and Reference Software

Education and reference software is designed to help you learn more about a particular topic. One type of education software called **CAI** (computer aided instruction), or **tutorial software**, can help you learn how to do things, for example, how to type, how to fix your car, how to use your word processor, how to speak French, or how to prepare for the GMAT exam. Educational simulations let you work with a computerized model of something in the real world, manipulate it, and see what happens. For example, some colleges and universities use computerized simulations in introductory chemistry classes so students can experiment with chemical reactions without using real, and sometimes dangerous, mixtures. Reference software, such as electronic encyclopedias, can also help you look up facts on any topic.

Software Compatibility

When you purchase software, it must be **compatible** with your computer system; in other words, the software must be written for the type of computer you use and for the operating system that is installed on your computer. You must also make sure your computer meets or exceeds the minimum requirements specified for the software. The system requirements are usually listed on the outside of the software's packaging, as shown in Figure 2-11. The system requirements might also be explained in more detail in the reference manual that comes inside the box.

Suppose you want to purchase software for your IBM-compatible computer. First, you need to make sure the software is written for IBM-compatible computers, rather than for the Apple Macintosh. Sometimes, the same software title is available for more than one type of computer. For example, Microsoft Word is available for both IBM-compatible and Apple Macintosh computers, but these are two separate versions. You cannot use the Macintosh version of Microsoft Word on your IBM-compatible.

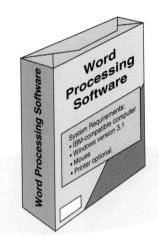

Figure 2-11
System requirements
are often listed on
the box

Once you know the software is compatible with the type of computer you use, you must make sure the software will work with your operating system. If your IBM-compatible computer uses the DOS operating system, you select DOS software, also referred to as software that "runs under DOS." If your computer uses the Microsoft Windows operating system, you can select DOS or Windows software because Windows can run software designed for both of these operating systems. If your computer uses OS/2, you can select OS/2, DOS, or Windows software because OS/2 can run software designed for all three of these operating systems.

Remember that operating systems go through numerous revisions. A higher version number indicates a more recent revision, for example, DOS 6.0 is a more recent version than DOS 5.0. Operating systems are usually **downwardly compatible**, which means that you can use software designed for earlier versions of the operating system, but not those designed for later versions. For example, you can generally use software that requires DOS version 3.3 if DOS 6.0 is installed on your computer. However, your software might not work correctly if it requires DOS 6.0 and DOS 3.3 is installed on your computer. If you want to use software that requires a newer version of your operating system, you must first purchase and install the operating system upgrade. Figure 2-12 on the following page summarizes the concept of downward compatibility.

Finally, you must be sure your computer system meets or exceeds the requirements specified for the software. It is not unusual for software to require a minimum amount of memory or storage on your hard disk. Some software requires a sound card, a high-resolution monitor, or a CD-ROM drive. If you need additional memory, storage space, or equipment, you can often add it to your computer system.

The list of software titles that are compatible with your computer is likely to be extensive. As you read through computer magazines and talk to friends or coworkers, you will undoubtedly discover that you want additional applications and utilities. After you select compatible software, you must install it on your computer system before you can use it.

Figure 2-12
Downward
compatibility

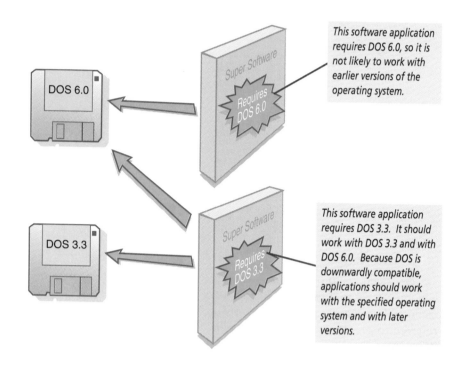

This software application
requires DOS 6.0, so it is
not likely to work with
earlier versions of the
operating system.

This software application
requires DOS 3.3. It should
work with DOS 3.3 and with
DOS 6.0. Because DOS is
downwardly compatible,
applications should work
with the specified operating
system and with later
versions.

Installing and Using Software

Computer software is usually shipped on 3.5" or 5.25" disks, called **distribution disks**, or on CD-ROMs. In the years when personal computers first appeared on the market, you could often use the software directly from the distribution disk. This is rarely possible today because the programs are so large they take up many disks. Today, instead of using software directly from the distribution disk, you usually install it on your hard disk. During the installation process, programs and data files for the software are copied to the hard disk of your computer system. Figure 2-13 summarizes the installation process that is described in the next few paragraphs.

When you install software that runs under a command-line operating system, such as DOS, you should carefully follow the installation instructions provided by the reference manual. There is not a consistent installation procedure for DOS software, so each software application might require different steps. On the other hand, for Microsoft Windows software applications, the installation process is more consistent and usually much easier. To install a Windows software application, you start the Windows operating system and place the installation disk in a disk drive. Next, pull down the File menu and select Run, then type "A:\SETUP." A **setup program** displays messages on the screen to guide you through the remaining steps of the installation process.

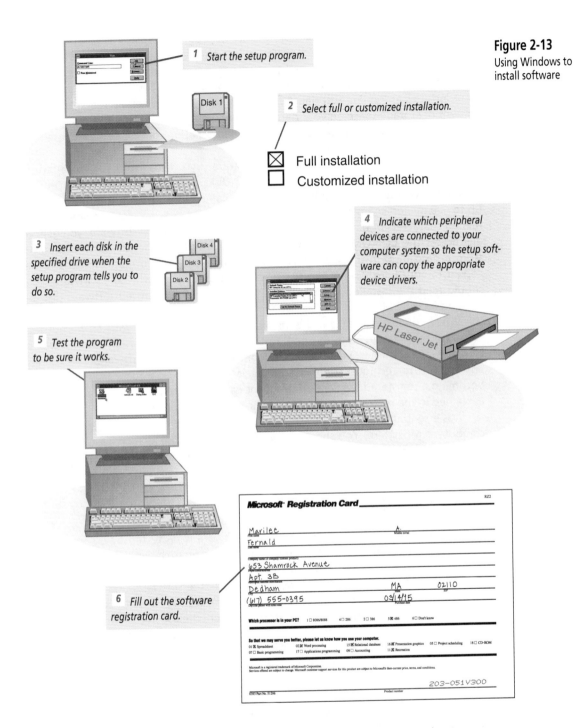

Figure 2-13
Using Windows to install software

1 Start the setup program.

2 Select full or customized installation.

☒ Full installation
☐ Customized installation

4 Indicate which peripheral devices are connected to your computer system so the setup software can copy the appropriate device drivers.

3 Insert each disk in the specified drive when the setup program tells you to do so.

5 Test the program to be sure it works.

6 Fill out the software registration card.

The number of programs and data files that the setup program copies to your hard disk depends on which features of the software you want available. For a **full installation**, the setup program copies all the files and data from the distribution disks to the hard disk of your computer system. A full installation provides you with access to all the features of the software.

During a **customized installation**, the setup program displays a list of software features for your selection. After you select the features you want, the setup program copies only the selected program and data files to your hard disk. A customized installation can save space on your hard disk. For example, some software includes an on-line tutorial. A tutorial is handy, but generally requires a large amount of storage space on your hard disk. If you already know how to use the software, you might decide to use the customized installation routine to avoid installing the large on-line tutorial.

Installing software from a CD-ROM frequently differs from the installation process for software shipped on 3.5" or 5.25" disks. Software shipped on a CD-ROM is usually too large to fit on a hard disk. As explained in Chapter 1, a CD-ROM stores up to 680 million characters of data, but a typical hard disk stores approximately 200 million characters of data. Because of the large size of CD-ROM software, you generally access the CD-ROM programs and data directly from the CD-ROM instead of from a hard disk. In this case, a very limited amount of information needs to be copied to your hard disk during the installation process. As with any software, you should read the installation instructions to find out how to install software distributed on a CD-ROM.

While you are waiting for the installation process to finish, you can fill out the **software registration card**. By sending the filled-out software registration card to the software publisher, you become a registered user of the software. This usually entitles you to technical support and special prices on upgrades. The benefits of becoming a registered user are different for each software package; they are usually explained in the reference manual or on the software registration card.

It is essential for you to know how to install software if you plan to expand your computer's repertoire. You should be aware, however, that the use of the software you install is regulated by copyright law and software licenses.

Software Copyrights

Like books and movies, most computer software is protected by a copyright. A **copyright** is a form of legal protection that grants certain exclusive rights to the author of a program or the owner of the copyright. The owner of the copyright has the exclusive right to copy the software, to distribute or sell the software, and to modify the software. If you are not the owner of the copyright, it is not legal to copy, distribute, or sell the software unless you obtain permission from the copyright owner.

When you purchase copyrighted software, you do not become the owner of the copyright. Instead, you have purchased one copy of the software distributed by the copyright owner. Because you are not the copyright owner, you may use the software on your computer, but you cannot make additional copies to give away or sell. People who illegally copy, distribute, or modify software are sometimes referred to as **software pirates**, and the illegal copies they create are referred to as **pirated software**.

Copyrights are defined by the U.S. Copyright Act. Copyrighted materials such as software must display a copyright notice that contains the word "Copyright" (or the © symbol), the year of publication, and the name of the copyright holder. When you start a computer program, the copyright notice is typically displayed on the first screen and is also usually printed in the reference manual.

Before 1976, computer software was not specifically covered by the U.S. Copyright Act, which had been in effect since 1909. The Copyright Acts of 1976 and 1980 specifically addressed software copyright issues and allow you to copy or modify software under certain circumstances. If you read the sections of the Copyright Act shown in Figure 2-14, you will discover under what circumstances you can legally copy copyrighted software.

It is legal to copy the software from the distribution disks to the hard disk of your computer system so you can access the software from the hard disk.

It is legal to make an extra copy of the software in case the copy you are using becomes damaged.

Figure 2-14
Computer Software Copyright Act of 1980

If you give away or sell the software, you cannot legally keep a copy.

You cannot legally sell or give away modified copies of the software without permission.

Section 117 - Right to Copy or Adapt Computer Programs in Limited Circumstances

Notwithstanding the provisions of section 106, it is not an infringement for the owner of a copy of a computer program to make or authorize the making of another copy or adaptation of the computer program provided:

1. that such a new copy or adaptation is created as an essential step in the utilization of the computer program in conjunction with a machine that is used in no other manner; or

2. that such new copy or adaptation is for archival purposes only and that all archival copies are destroyed in the event that continued possession of the computer program should cease to be rightful. Any exact copies prepared in accordance with the provisions of this section may be leased, sold or otherwise transferred, along with the copy from which such copies were prepared, only as part of the lease, sale, or other transfer of all rights in the program. Adaptations so prepared may be transferred only with the authorization of the copyright owner.

The restrictions stated by the Copyright Act apply only to the files and data included as part of the original software. The data you enter—the documents, files, and graphics you create—can be copied without restriction.

Copyright restrictions should not be confused with copy protection. Software publishers use **copy protection** to make it physically impossible (or nearly so) to make or use illegal copies of software. To copy protect software, the publisher might distribute the software on a special disk that cannot be copied with ordinary copy programs. Another method of copy protection requires you to attach a special hardware device to your computer: if the device is not attached, the software doesn't work.

Software Licenses

In addition to copyright protection, computer software is often protected by the terms of a software license. A **software license** is a legal contract that defines the ways in which you may use a computer program. It is important to distinguish the concept of licensing from that of purchasing a copy of software. When you pay for licensed software, you are not buying a copy of the software. Instead, you are paying for a license to use the software. Further, although you pay for the license, your legal right to use the software continues only as long as you abide by the terms of the software license. Therefore, it is important to read the terms of the software license agreement that is included with any software package you use. The software license agreement explains whether you may make copies, modify the software, or transfer it to another person.

Computer software is often packaged in plastic shrink wrapping with the software license agreement visible on the back of the package. A notification, such as the one in Figure 2-15, states that opening the wrapping signifies your agreement to the terms of the software license. With this type of software license, referred to as a **shrink-wrap license**, the software publisher avoids the lengthy process of negotiating the terms of the license and obtaining your signature. It is essentially a "take it or leave it" approach to licensing, and although the courts have yet to provide a definitive ruling on its validity, shrink-wrap licensing is one of the most frequently used methods for providing legal protection for computer software.

Figure 2-15
Shrink wrap license notification

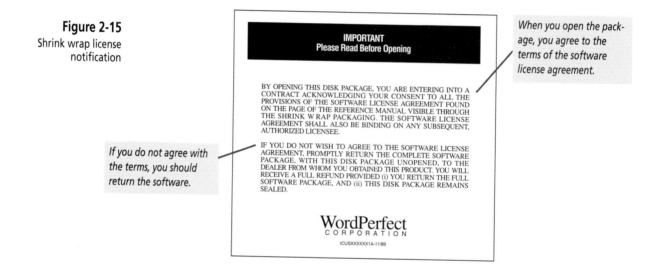

When you open the package, you agree to the terms of the software license agreement.

If you do not agree with the terms, you should return the software.

Software licenses are broadly categorized on the basis of usage. A **single-user license** limits the use of the software to one user at a time. Most commercial software is distributed under a single-user license. A **multiple-user license** allows more than one person to access a single copy of the software at the same time, generally within a multiuser environment. A **concurrent-user license** allows a certain number of copies of the software to be used at the same time. For example, if your firm has a concurrent-user license for five copies, at any one time up to five employees may use the software. A **site license** generally allows the software to be used on any and all computers at a specific location, such as within a corporate office building or on a university campus.

Although software licenses are often lengthy and make extensive use of "legalese," they are generally divided into manageable sections that you can understand by reading them carefully. To become familiar with the basic sections of a license agreement, you can read through the "No-Nonsense License Statement" used for software published by Borland International in Figure 2-16.

This section explains how you are allowed to use the software.

Figure 2-16
Borland's software
license agreement

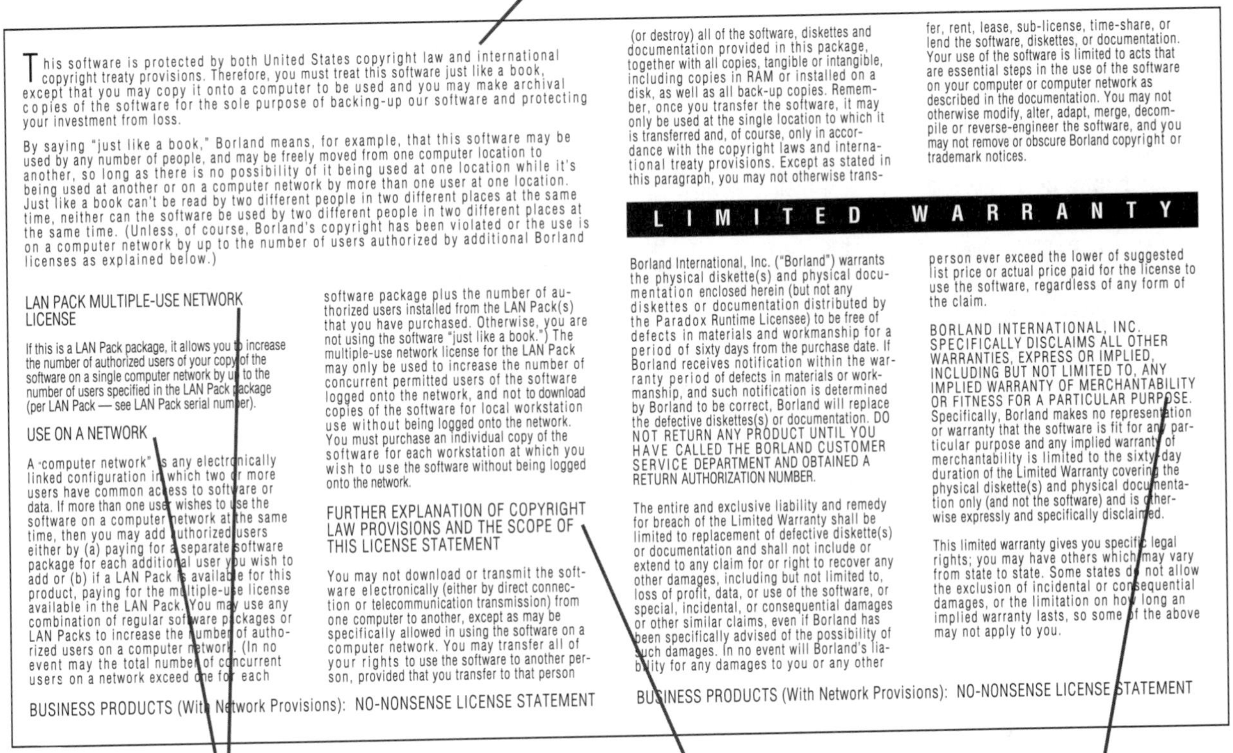

This software is protected by both United States copyright law and international copyright treaty provisions. Therefore, you must treat this software just like a book, except that you may copy it onto a computer to be used and you may make archival copies of the software for the sole purpose of backing-up our software and protecting your investment from loss.

By saying "just like a book," Borland means, for example, that this software may be used by any number of people, and may be freely moved from one computer location to another, so long as there is no possibility of it being used at one location while it's being used at another or on a computer network by more than one user at one location. Just like a book can't be read by two different people in two different places at the same time, neither can the software be used by two different people in two different places at the same time. (Unless, of course, Borland's copyright has been violated or the use is on a computer network by up to the number of users authorized by additional Borland licenses as explained below.)

LAN PACK MULTIPLE-USE NETWORK LICENSE

If this is a LAN Pack package, it allows you to increase the number of authorized users of your copy of the software on a single computer network by up to the number of users specified in the LAN Pack package (per LAN Pack — see LAN Pack serial number).

USE ON A NETWORK

A "computer network" is any electronically linked configuration in which two or more users have common access to software or data. If more than one user wishes to use the software on a computer network at the same time, then you may add authorized users either by (a) paying for a separate software package for each additional user you wish to add or (b) if a LAN Pack is available for this product, paying for the multiple-use license available in the LAN Pack. You may use any combination of regular software packages or LAN Packs to increase the number of authorized users on a computer network. (In no event may the total number of concurrent users on a network exceed one for each

software package plus the number of authorized users installed from the LAN Pack(s) that you have purchased. Otherwise, you are not using the software "just like a book.") The multiple-use network license for the LAN Pack may only be used to increase the number of concurrent permitted users of the software logged onto the network, and not to download copies of the software for local workstation use without being logged onto the network. You must purchase an individual copy of the software for each workstation at which you wish to use the software without being logged onto the network.

FURTHER EXPLANATION OF COPYRIGHT LAW PROVISIONS AND THE SCOPE OF THIS LICENSE STATEMENT

You may not download or transmit the software electronically (either by direct connection or telecommunication transmission) from one computer to another, except as may be specifically allowed in using the software on a computer network. You may transfer all of your rights to use the software to another person, provided that you transfer to that person

(or destroy) all of the software, diskettes and documentation provided in this package, together with all copies, tangible or intangible, including copies in RAM or installed on a disk, as well as all back-up copies. Remember, once you transfer the software, it may only be used at the single location to which it is transferred and, of course, only in accordance with the copyright laws and international treaty provisions. Except as stated in this paragraph, you may not otherwise transfer, rent, lease, sub-license, time-share, or lend the software, diskettes, or documentation. Your use of the software is limited to acts that are essential steps in the use of the software on your computer or computer network as described in the documentation. You may not otherwise modify, alter, adapt, merge, decompile or reverse-engineer the software, and you may not remove or obscure Borland copyright or trademark notices.

L I M I T E D   W A R R A N T Y

Borland International, Inc. ("Borland") warrants the physical diskette(s) and physical documentation enclosed herein (but not any diskettes or documentation distributed by the Paradox Runtime Licensee) to be free of defects in materials and workmanship for a period of sixty days from the purchase date. If Borland receives notification within the warranty period of defects in materials or workmanship, and such notification is determined by Borland to be correct, Borland will replace the defective diskette(s) or documentation. DO NOT RETURN ANY PRODUCT UNTIL YOU HAVE CALLED THE BORLAND CUSTOMER SERVICE DEPARTMENT AND OBTAINED A RETURN AUTHORIZATION NUMBER.

The entire and exclusive liability and remedy for breach of the Limited Warranty shall be limited to replacement of defective diskette(s) or documentation and shall not include or extend to any claim for or right to recover any other damages, including but not limited to, loss of profit, data, or use of the software, or special, incidental, or consequential damages or other similar claims, even if Borland has been specifically advised of the possibility of such damages. In no event will Borland's liability for any damages to you or any other

person ever exceed the lower of suggested list price or actual price paid for the license to use the software, regardless of any form of the claim.

BORLAND INTERNATIONAL, INC. SPECIFICALLY DISCLAIMS ALL OTHER WARRANTIES, EXPRESS OR IMPLIED, INCLUDING BUT NOT LIMITED TO, ANY IMPLIED WARRANTY OF MERCHANTABILITY OR FITNESS FOR A PARTICULAR PURPOSE. Specifically, Borland makes no representation or warranty that the software is fit for any particular purpose and any implied warranty of merchantability is limited to the sixty day duration of the Limited Warranty covering the physical diskette(s) and physical documentation only (and not the software) and is otherwise expressly and specifically disclaimed.

This limited warranty gives you specific legal rights; you may have others which may vary from state to state. Some states do not allow the exclusion of incidental or consequential damages, or the limitation on how long an implied warranty lasts, so some of the above may not apply to you.

BUSINESS PRODUCTS (With Network Provisions): NO-NONSENSE LICENSE STATEMENT

BUSINESS PRODUCTS (With Network Provisions): NO-NONSENSE LICENSE STATEMENT

These sections make provisions for multiple users.

This section restates the basic copyright restrictions about transferring software.

Here, Borland essentially says that you use this software at your own risk.

Public Domain Software

Public domain software is owned by the public rather than by an individual. Sometimes the author abandons all rights to a particular software title and places it in the public domain, making the program available for use without restriction. Public domain software may be freely copied, distributed, and even resold. The primary restriction on public domain software is that you are not allowed to apply for a copyright on it. Public domain software is fairly rare. It is frequently confused with shareware, because it is legal to copy and distribute both public domain software and shareware.

Shareware

Shareware is copyrighted software marketed under a "try before you buy" policy. Shareware usually includes a specific license that allows you to use the software for a trial period. If you want to continue to use it, you must become a registered user by sending in a registration fee. Take a look at the shareware license in Figure 2-17 and notice the rights it includes.

Figure 2-17
Shareware license agreement

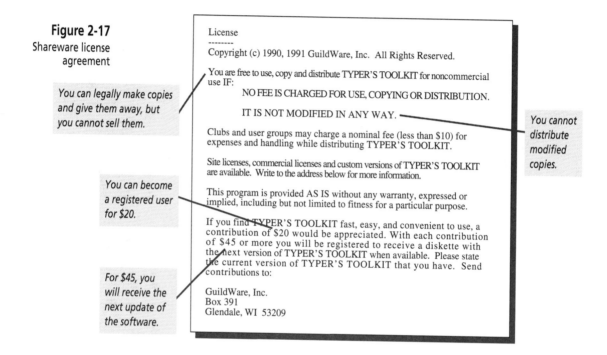

You can legally make copies and give them away, but you cannot sell them.

You can become a registered user for $20.

For $45, you will receive the next update of the software.

You cannot distribute modified copies.

License

Copyright (c) 1990, 1991 GuildWare, Inc. All Rights Reserved.

You are free to use, copy and distribute TYPER'S TOOLKIT for noncommercial use IF:

NO FEE IS CHARGED FOR USE, COPYING OR DISTRIBUTION.

IT IS NOT MODIFIED IN ANY WAY.

Clubs and user groups may charge a nominal fee (less than $10) for expenses and handling while distributing TYPER'S TOOLKIT.

Site licenses, commercial licenses and custom versions of TYPER'S TOOLKIT are available. Write to the address below for more information.

This program is provided AS IS without any warranty, expressed or implied, including but not limited to fitness for a particular purpose.

If you find TYPER'S TOOLKIT fast, easy, and convenient to use, a contribution of $20 would be appreciated. With each contribution of $45 or more you will be registered to receive a diskette with the next version of TYPER'S TOOLKIT when available. Please state the current version of TYPER'S TOOLKIT that you have. Send contributions to:

GuildWare, Inc.
Box 391
Glendale, WI 53209

When you send in the fee to become a registered shareware user, you are granted a license to use the software beyond the trial period. You might also receive a free copy of the latest version of the software or printed documentation for the program.

When you read the shareware license in Figure 2-17, you might have noticed that you are allowed to make copies of the software and distribute them to others. This is a typical shareware policy and a fairly effective marketing strategy that provides low cost advertising. Unfortunately, registration fee payment is based on the honor system, so shareware authors are likely to collect only a fraction of the payment they deserve for their programming efforts.

Ethical software use benefits everyone. Software publishers use revenues from software sales to improve current software, provide technical support, and develop new applications. By resisting the temptation to use illegal copies of software, you can help provide software publishers with the resources they need to develop more of the software that makes the computer such a versatile machine.

Multimedia Computing

In the 1960s, a group of mop-haired young musicians from England burst onto the music scene. They were called the Beatles and millions of screaming fans sent "I Want to Hold Your Hand" rocketing to the top of the charts. The Beatles formed their own record company, Apple Corps Ltd., and recorded their music under the Apple Corps label, which was protected by international trademarks and copyrights.

In 1976, two young Californians, Steve Jobs and Steve Wozniak, started a computer company in their garage. Before the decade was out, their company had one of the most successful public stock offerings in history. Both Wozniak and Jobs became instant multimillionaires. Unfortunately, they named their company Apple Computer, Inc. and that, according to the lawyers who represented Apple Corps, was a problem. The computer makers were charged with copyright infringement for using the Apple name.

In 1981, after lengthy negotiations, Apple Corps agreed to let Apple Computer use the Apple name, and Apple Computer agreed not to produce musical products. At the time, this arrangement seemed perfectly reasonable because computer technology and record companies had very little in common.

Today, however, the distinction between computer technology and record companies is not so clear. Consumer electronic inventions—radio, telephone, photography, sound recording, television, video recording, and computers—are merging and creating a new technology called multimedia.

The term "multimedia" isn't really anything new—it refers to the integrated use of multiple media, such as slides, video tapes, audio tapes, records, CD-ROMs, and photos. School children in the 1950s, for example, watched multimedia presentations that synchronized a tape-recorded sound track with a series of slides. As you can imagine, coordinating a multimedia presentation such as this was not easy. The teacher typically had difficulty getting the slides to synchronize with the sound track. If one slide was out of order or upside down, the teacher would have to stop the tape, fix the slide, and then restart the tape. Of course, the technology was too cumbersome to rewind and review segments of the presentation that students didn't understand.

Today, the computer is replacing or controlling many of the technologies and media that were previously used for multimedia presentations. Advances in computer technology have made it possible to combine text, photo images, speech, music, animated sequences, and video into a single interactive computer

L A B

MULTIMEDIA TOUR

presentation. A new definition of multimedia has emerged from this blend of technology. Today, **multimedia** is defined as an integrated collection of computer-based text, graphics, sound, animation, photo images, and video.

Consider a multimedia encyclopedia, for example. Like a regular encyclopedia, it contains articles and pictures on a wide range of topics. But there's more. If you're puzzled about the process of internal combustion, you can use your mouse to click an on-screen button to view an animated diagram of the pistons and valves in an automobile engine. If you're not sure how to pronounce a word, you can click a button to hear the word spoken by your computer. If you're reading a description of a harpsichord and you wonder what one sounds like, you can click the on-screen "play" button to hear a short harpsichord concert. If you're reading about the Apollo moon landings, you can click a button to view a video clip showing Neil Armstrong's first steps on the moon. A multimedia encyclopedia provides you with a rich selection of text, graphics, sound, animation, and video.

Multimedia Applications

Multimedia technology adds pizzazz to all types of computer applications: productivity, business, entertainment, and education and reference. You can use a multimedia scheduler to remind you of your appointments and due dates. Instead of flashing a message on your screen, the multimedia scheduler reminds you of appointments by displaying a video image of a "personal assistant" in one corner of your screen. "Excuse me," your personal assistant might say, "but I believe you have an appointment in five minutes."

You can use a multimedia presentation application to create a motivational business presentation that includes a short video message from the company president, pictures of a new product line, graphs of projected sales, sound effects of cheering crowds, and text that lists the features and benefits of the new products.

You can use multimedia entertainment applications to have an animated adventure in the far reaches of space. You control the animated instrument panel of your spacecraft from your computer keyboard, discuss tactics with video images of your crew members, and hear the sounds of your engines, instrument warnings, and weapons.

You can use multimedia computer-aided instruction to learn a foreign language. You can watch and listen to a short foreign language video segment and view a synchronized translation. Then you can practice your pronunciation by speaking into a microphone so the computer can compare your pronunciation with a native speaker's.

Figure 2-18 gives you a thumbnail sketch of some additional multimedia applications.

Figure 2-18
Multimedia applications

Microsoft's Multimedia Beethoven lets you explore Beethoven's Fifth Symphony. All you have to do is click a button to listen to the full orchestration or to select individual instruments or to read the sheet music.

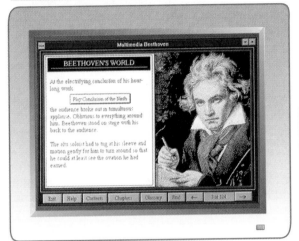

Compton's Multimedia Encyclopedia provides text and graphics on a wealth of topics. Buttons let you control graphic displays and sound.

Microsoft Encarta is a multimedia Encyclopedia that includes film clips, still photos, sound, and text. Extensive cross-referencing lets you click on subjects related to the main story and see definitions of technical terms used in the text.

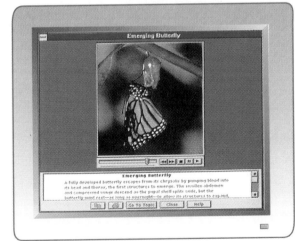

When you play multimedia golf, controls at the bottom of the screen let you pick a club and take a shot. You can hear your club contact the ball and watch the ball bounce on the fairway. More than an arcade game, Access Software Golf helps you develop strategies for improving your golf game on some of the most challenging courses in the world.

Multimedia Equipment

Today's multimedia applications require more than a basic computer system to display graphic images, run video clips, and play sounds. Most multimedia applications are shipped on a CD-ROM disk, so your computer needs to have a CD-ROM drive. Graphics, sound, animation, and video require much more storage space than text, so you need a large capacity hard drive. Your computer system must be able to quickly manipulate and transfer large amounts of data so you need a fast computer with a lot of memory. To display realistic graphical and video images, your computer system must have a high resolution monitor with the capability to display a wide range of colors. Because most computers are shipped with rudimentary sound capabilities, multimedia applications require a sound card, speakers, and a microphone.

The Multimedia PC Marketing Council publishes what is known as the MPC standards, which specify the minimum hardware requirements you need to successfully use multimedia applications on your computer system. Computers and peripheral devices that conform to the MPC standards carry a special MPC logo, shown in Figure 2-19. Many multimedia applications require your computer to meet MPC standards. These applications carry the MPC logo on their packaging. The MPC standards change every few years as technology evolves, so when you want to purchase a computer for multimedia applications, it is best to consult a computer magazine or a computer dealer to get details about the current MPC standards.

Figure 2-19
MPC logo

There are three strategies for getting a computer that meets the MPC standards. First, and easiest, is to purchase a full computer system that carries the MPC logo. Second, you can purchase an MPC upgrade kit for your current computer system, assuming that your current system meets certain requirements. Third, you can purchase the individual components that your computer needs to meet the MPC standard. This third strategy requires that you have more technical background than you'd need for the first two.

So what happened to the agreement between Apple Computer and Apple Corps?

In 1989, Apple Corps Ltd. filed a multimillion dollar lawsuit against Apple Computer, Inc., charging that the computer maker had violated the terms of the earlier agreement by manufacturing computers that were capable of synthesizing musical sounds. Obviously, the products made by both companies are more similar now than anyone imagined back in 1981 when the two companies signed their original agreement. Despite the 1989 suit, Apple Computer is very active in multimedia and produces a wide range of hardware and software products that play animation, sound, and video. In a slightly ironic turn of events, a multimedia CD-ROM recently released by Voyager Co., and shown in Figure 2-20, allows you to watch all 90 minutes of the Beatles 1964 musical movie *A Hard Day's Night*, listen to the complete sound track, and view an annotated script—on your Apple Macintosh computer.

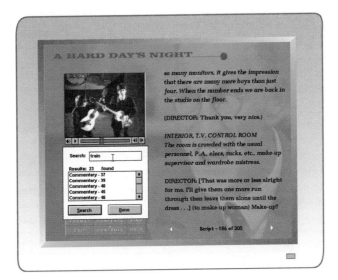

Figure 2-20
The Beatles on CD-ROM

C H A P T E R   R E V I E W

1. Use your own words to write out answers to the Chapter Preview questions.
2. List each of the boldface terms in the chapter, then use your own words to write a definition of each term.
3. Use your own words to describe the five tasks an operating system typically performs.
4. Fill in the following table by using a check mark to indicate which operating systems are available for each type of computer.

	IBM-COMPATIBLE	MACINTOSH	MINICOMPUTERS & MAINFRAMES
UNIX			
DOS			
OS/2			
WINDOWS			
SYSTEM 7			

5. Suppose you're thinking of purchasing spreadsheet software, and you read a very favorable review of Microsoft Excel for Windows. The article indicates that the software requires "an IBM-PC/AT, PS/2, or compatible; graphics compatible with Microsoft Windows version 3.0 or later; MS-DOS version 3.1 or later and Microsoft Windows version 3.0 or later; optional printer; a mouse or compatible pointing device is recommended." You have a Compaq computer with Windows 3.1, a Hewlett Packard printer, and a Microsoft mouse. Explain whether you can expect the Microsoft Excel spreadsheet software to work on your computer.
6. Review the section on software applications, then make a list of what you think are the three most important features of word processing, spreadsheet, graphics, and database software.
7. Under U.S. copyright law, what are the two major rights granted to the copyright holder? What are the three rights granted to the user of copyrighted materials?
8. For each of the following descriptions, indicate whether the software is copyrighted, copy protected, licensed, shareware, or public domain. For some descriptions, there is more than one answer.
    a. The software does not have a copyright notice.
    b. It is not possible to make a copy of the disk that contains the software.
    c. The software is shrink-wrapped and there is a notice about your rights and responsibilities.
    d. When you start the software you see a message "©1994 Course Technology, Inc."
    e. When you start the program you see a message, "Copyright 1986, 1987 SupRSoft, Inc. All Rights Reserved. You are free to use, copy, and distribute this software for noncommercial use if no fee is charged for use, copying or distribution, and if the software is not modified in any way."

C H A P T E R   Q U I Z

1. When you turn on your computer, the _____ software takes an inventory of critical computer system hardware to detect component failures that affect processing.
2. True or false: If you write a report and store it on disk, it is considered software. _____
3. Software that helps the computer carry out its basic operating tasks is _____ software.
4. True or false: DOS 6.0 is a more recent version of the operating system than DOS 5.0. _____
5. If you want to run more than one program at a time, you must use a _____ operating system.

6. _____ is a multiuser operating system.

7. _____ can be defined as one or more computer programs and associated data that exist in electronic format on a storage medium such as a disk or CD-ROM.

8. The DOS, Windows, and OS/2 operating systems are typically used on _____ computer systems.

9. Early versions of Windows were referred to as _____ because they did not handle all the operating system tasks on their own and piggy-backed on the DOS operating system.

10. _____ software helps the computer accomplish such tasks as preparing a disk for data, transferring information between storage devices, and detecting computer viruses.

11. You install a(n) _____ to tell the computer how to use the special features of a new peripheral device.

12. True or false: You can use software designed for earlier versions of an operating system that is downwardly compatible._____

13. True or false: One way to copyright software is to make it impossible to make a copy of the disk on which the software is distributed. _____

14. _____ applications frequently require a sound card and a CD-ROM drive.

15. The _____ lists the hardware requirements a computer needs to successfully run today's multimedia applications.

P R O J E C T S

1. Find out the operating system(s) used in your school computer lab. Be sure you find out the type, version, and revision. Your instructor might provide you with this information at the beginning of the project. Otherwise, you can go into the lab and obtain this information from one of the computers. If you see a command-line user interface, try typing "ver" and then pressing the Enter key. If you see a graphical user interface, try clicking the Help menu or the apple icon.

   Once you know the operating system used in your school lab, use the operating system reference manual and library resources to answer the following questions:

   a. Which operating system, version, and revision is used in your school lab?

   b. What company publishes the operating system software?

   c. When was the *original version* of your operating system introduced?

   d. Does your operating system have a command-line user interface or a graphical user interface?

   e. Does your operating system support multitasking?

   f. Do you need a password to use the computers in your school lab? Even if you do not need to use a password, does the operating system provide some way to secure access to the computers?

   g. What is the anticipated arrival date for the next version of your operating system?

   h. How much does the publisher of your operating system usually charge for upgrades if you are a registered user?

2. For each of the scenarios that follow, explain why you would recommend using word processor, spreadsheet, database, desktop publishing, graphics, or accounting software.

   a. A sales manager for a cosmetic company wants to motivate the sales force by graphically showing the increases in consumer spending in each of the past five years.

   b. The marketing specialist for a new software company wants to send out announcements to 150 computer magazines.

   c. The owners of five golf courses in Jackson County want to design a promotional flyer for tourists that can be distributed in restaurants and hotels.

   d. The owner of a small business wants to keep track of income and expenses on an on-going basis and print out monthly profit and loss statements.

e. The superintendent of a local school system wants to prepare a press release explaining why student test scores were 5% below the national average.

f. A contractor wants to calculate his cost for materials needed to build a new community center.

g. A college student wants to send out a résumé and customized letters addressed to twenty prospective employers.

h. The parents of three children want to decide whether they should invest money for their children's education in the stock market or whether they should buy into their state's pre-paid tuition plan.

i. The director of fund-raising for a large nonprofit organization wants to keep a list of prospective donors.

3. Read the IBM Program License Agreement in Figure 2-21, then answer the following questions:

Figure 2-21
IBM License
Agreement

International Business Machines Corporation   *Armonk, New York 10504*

IBM Program License Agreement

BEFORE OPENING THIS PACKAGE, YOU SHOULD CAREFULLY READ THE FOLLOWING TERMS AND CONDITIONS. OPENING THIS PACKAGE INDICATES YOUR ACCEPTANCE OF THESE TERMS AND CONDITIONS. IF YOU DO NOT AGREE WITH THEM, YOU SHOULD PROMPTLY RETURN THE PACKAGE UNOPENED AND YOUR MONEY WILL BE REFUNDED.

This is a license agreement and not an agreement for sale. IBM owns, or has licensed from the owner, copyrights in the Program. You obtain no rights other than the license granted you by this Agreement. Title to the enclosed copy of the Program, and any copy made from it, is retained by IBM. IBM licenses your use of the Program in the United States and Puerto Rico. You assume all responsibility for the selection of the Program to achieve your intended results and for the installation of, use of, and results obtained from, the Program.

The Section in the enclosed documentation entitled "License Information" contains additional information concerning the Program and any related Program Services.

LICENSE
You may:
1) use the Program on only one machine at any one time, unless permission to use it on more than one machine at any one time is granted in the License Information (Authorized Use);
2) make a copy of the Program for backup or modification purposes only in support of your Authorized Use. However, Programs marked "Copy Protected" limit copying;
3) modify the Program and/or merge it into another program only in support of your Authorized Use; and
4) transfer possession of copies of the Program to another party by transferring this copy of the IBM Program License Agreement, the License Information, and all other documentation along with at least one complete, unaltered copy of the Program. You must, at the same time, either transfer to such other party or destroy all your other copies of the Program, including modified copies or portions of the Program merged into other programs. Such transfer of possession terminates your license from IBM. Such other party shall be licensed, under the terms of this Agreement, upon acceptance of the Agreement by its initial use of the Program.

You shall reproduce and include the copyright notice(s) on all such copies of the Program, in whole or in part.

You shall not:
1) use, copy, modify, merge, or transfer copies of the program except as provided in this Agreement;
2) reverse assemble or reverse compile the Program; and/or
3) sublicense, rent, lease, or assign the Program or any copy thereof.

LIMITED WARRANTY
Warranty details and limitations are described in the Statement of Limited Warranty which is available upon request from IBM, its Authorized Dealer or its approved supplier and is also contained in the License Information. IBM provides a three-month limited warranty on the media for all Programs. For selected Programs, as indicated on the outside of the package, a limited warranty on the Program is available. The applicable Warranty Period is measured from the date of delivery to the original user as evidenced by a receipt.

Certain Programs, as indicated on the outside of the package, are not warranted and are provided "AS IS."
Z125-3301-02 4/87

SUCH WARRANTIES ARE IN LIEU OF ALL OTHER WARRANTIES, EXPRESS OR IMPLIED, INCLUDING, BUT NOT LIMITED TO, THE IMPLIED WARRANTIES OF MERCHANTABILITY AND FITNESS FOR A PARTICULAR PURPOSE.

Some states do not allow the exclusion of implied warranties, so the above exclusion may not apply to you.

LIMITATION OF REMEDIES
IBM's entire liability and your exclusive remedy shall be as follows:
1) IBM will provide the warranty described in IBM's Statement of Limited Warranty. If IBM does not replace defective media or, if applicable, make the Program operate as warranted or replace the Program with a functionally equivalent program, all as warranted, you may terminate your license and your money will be refunded upon the return of all your copies of the Program.
2) For any claim arising out of IBM's limited warranty, or for any other claim whatsoever related to the subject matter of this Agreement, IBM's liability for actual damages, regardless of the form of action, shall be limited to the greater of $5,000 or the money paid to IBM, its Authorized Dealer or its approved supplier for the license for the Program that caused the damages that is the subject matter of, or is directly related to, the cause of action. This limitation will not apply to claims for personal injury or damages to real or tangible personal property caused by IBM's negligence.
3) In no event will IBM be liable for any lost profits, lost savings, or any incidental damages or other consequential damages, even if IBM, its Authorized Dealer or its approved supplier has been advised of the possibility of such damages, or for any claim by you based on a third party claim.

Some states do not allow the limitation or exclusion of incidental or consequential damages so the above limitation or exclusion may not apply to you.

GENERAL
You may terminate your license at any time by destroying all your copies of the Program or as otherwise described in this Agreement.

IBM may terminate your license if you fail to comply with the terms and conditions of this Agreement. Upon such termination, you agree to destroy all your copies of the Program.

Any attempt to sublicense, rent, lease or assign, or, except as expressly provided herein, to transfer any copy of the Program is void.

You agree that your are responsible for payment of any taxes, including personal property taxes, resulting from this Agreement.

No action, regardless of form, arising out of this Agreement may be brought by either party more than two years after the cause of action has arisen except for the breach of the provisions in the Section entitled "License" in which event four years shall apply.

This agreement will be construed under the Uniform Commercial Code of the State of New York.

a. Is this a "shrink-wrap" license? Why or why not?

b. After you pay your computer dealer for the program this license covers, who owns the program?

c. Can you legally have one copy of the program on your computer at work and another copy of the program on your computer at home if you only use the software in one place at a time?

d. Can you legally sell the software? Why or why not?

e. Under what conditions can you legally transfer possession of the program to someone else?

f. If you were the owner of a software store, could you legally rent the program to customers if you were sure they did not keep a copy after the rental period was over?

g. Can you legally install this software on one computer, but give more than one user access to it?

h. If you use this program for an important business decision and you later find out that a mistake in the program caused you to lose $500,000, what legal recourse is provided by the license agreement?

4. Using computer magazines as your reference, find the titles of *at least two* shareware programs and *two* commercial programs for each of the categories in the table below. Expand and complete the table for the two programs you find for each category by indicating the names of the programs, the names of the retailer or vendor for each program, and the selling price. Indicate the titles of the computer magazines you used.

CATEGORY	PROGRAM NAMES	SHAREWARE/ COMMERCIAL	RETAILERS OR VENDORS	PRICES
WORD PROCESSOR				
SPREADSHEET				
DATABASE				
GRAPHICS				
UTILITY				

5. Look in recent editions of computer magazines to find at least five multimedia applications. For each application, list its title, publisher, and a short description of what it does. Also list the name of the computer magazine you used and the page on which you found the information about each multimedia application.

6. Write a two-page paper on the MPC standards using books and magazines as reference resources. Some of the questions you might try to cover in your paper include: What computer companies sponsor the Multimedia PC Council? What are the current MPC standards? How can a computer equipment manufacturer get the MPC logo for its products?

L A B S

Word Processing Tour

The Word Processing Tour demonstrates general word processing concepts and lets you try some of the basic features provided by most word processing packages. When you have completed the lab, you should be able to apply the general concepts you learned to any word processing package you use at home, at work, or in your school lab. To master a particular word processing software package, you will probably need additional instruction. You might, for example, use additional texts for this course that cover word processing software such as Microsoft Word for Windows or WordPerfect for Windows.

L A B

**WORD
PROCESSING
TOUR**

To start the Word Processing Tour, double-click the Word Processing Tour icon in the New Perspectives window. After you read the list of activities on the opening screen, click the Continue button.

As you use the Word Processing Lab, look for the answers to the following questions and write down your answers:

1. How can a word processor help you improve your writing?
2. What are the five major functions that word processing software performs?
3. What does the insertion point look like, and what does it do?
4. What does word wrap do?
5. What are some of the things word processing software can do with a block of text?
6. What does the clipboard do?
7. Why do you need to proofread your documents even after you use a spell checker?
8. Why do some people prefer to work with single-spaced text and then double-space their documents just before printing?
9. If you have stored a document on disk then later retrieve it into memory, you have two options for storing the revised version of the document. What are they?

Spreadsheet Tour

L A B

SPREADSHEET TOUR

The Spreadsheet Tour demonstrates the essential functions of spreadsheet applications. As you use the Spreadsheet Tour, look for the answers to the following questions and write out your responses:

1. What is the difference between a spreadsheet program and a worksheet?
2. Where is cell A1 located on the worksheet? What is the address of the cell to the right of cell A1? What is the address of the cell just below cell A1?
3. Cell B2 contains the number 7. Cell B3 contains the number 5. Cell B4 contains the formula =B2-B3. What number is displayed in cell B4?
4. What is a function?
5. Cells B2, B3, and B4 each contain the number 2. Cell B5 contains the function =SUM(B2:B4). What number is displayed in cell B5?
6. What is a chart? When you change a number in a worksheet, what happens to a chart that is linked to the worksheet?
7. Describe a situation in which you might use a spreadsheet program. Why would you use a spreadsheet program in this situation, rather than a word processing or database program?

Database Tour

L A B

DATABASE TOUR

The Database Tour demonstrates the essential operations of database management systems. During the tour you will use a sample database management system to perform queries and other database operations. At the end of the tour, you will have an opportunity to continue practicing database operations. After completing the Database Tour, see if you can apply what you learned by writing out your responses to the following questions about the data file in Figure 2-22.

LASTNAME	FIRSTNAME	CITY	STATE
HILL	FRANCIS	SAN FRANCISCO	CA
KOCH	GARY	MIAMI	FL
HILBERT	REGINA	CHICAGO	IL
CROWTHERS	ANNIE	SALT LAKE CITY	UT
SMITH	CHARLES	SAN FRANCISCO	CA
YU	LISA	LOS ANGELES	CA

Figure 2-22
Sample Data File

1. How many records does this file contain?
2. How many fields does each record contain?
3. Suppose you want to search for all people living in California. What entries would you make in a query by example record?
4. Suppose you want to search for all people living in San Francisco, California. What entries would you make in a query by example record?
5. Suppose you did a query by example search with H in the last name field and no other entries. How many records would be located by this search? In which cities do those people live?
6. Describe a situation in which you might use a database program. Why would you use a database program in this situation, rather than a word processing or spreadsheet program?

Multimedia Tour

The Multimedia Tour includes samples of graphics, sounds, animations, and video. As you go through the tour, write out your responses to the following questions:

L A B

MULTIMEDIA TOUR

1. Describe the components of a computer system that is suitable for use with multimedia.
2. What are the two major approaches to the use of sound and graphics on computer systems?
3. What is the difference between bitmapped and vector graphics?
4. Why do you think it is important to be aware that photographs, sounds, and video can be digitally edited to portray events that never really occurred?
5. What is the difference between synthesized speech and digitized speech?
6. How is MIDI music different from a digital recording?
7. Describe a computer application that would benefit from the use of animated sequences. Why would this application be more effective with animated sequences than with still images?
8. Describe a computer application that would benefit from the use of digital video sequences. Why would this application be more effective with video than with still images or animated sequences?
9. Suppose you were going to create a multimedia application such as an encyclopedia, game, or educational program. Write a paragraph or two to describe the application you would create, then draw a sketch of a sample screen. Be sure you show how you would incorporate sound, graphics, video, animation, text, and so forth.

R E S O U R C E S

- *A Hard Day's Night*, The Voyager Co., 1351 Pacific Coast Highway, Santa Monica, CA 90401, 310-451-1383, $39.95

  This CD-ROM contains the entire 90-minute Beatles film, *A Hard Day's Night*, along with an annotated script.
- Wodaski, R. *Multimedia Madness*. Carmel, IN: Sams Publishing, 1992.

  This 616 page book provides you with a good background in multimedia applications and hardware. The book includes a disk and CD-ROM containing hundreds of multimedia samples.

Computer Magazines

It's a good idea to become familiar with computer magazines, journals, and newsletters because they carry the most current information about the fast-moving computer industry. Although computer books are excellent for explaining computer concepts and history, computer magazines contain more up-to-date information on the latest hardware and software.

Byte

One of the oldest and most respected computer publications, *Byte*'s main focus is on computer hardware, although it also contains software reviews and a variety of regular columns. Jerry Pournelle, a science fiction writer and venerable computer columnist, provides product reviews and opinions in a column called "Chaos Manor."

Computer Shopper

If nothing else, this magazine must be the largest monthly computer publication! Each edition is about 800 pages. The articles are somewhat overshadowed by the numerous and lengthy (some up to 10 pages) computer ads. If you are going to buy a mail order computer, this is the definitive resource.

Corporate Computing

Aimed at the business market, *Corporate Computing* emphasizes applications and computer solutions to typical business problems. A case study in each issue explains how computers are deployed in real situations to improve business services and competitive advantage.

InfoWorld

This weekly publication in tabloid format reports the latest industry news and is required reading for all computer "gurus."

Macworld

Macintosh users like the hardware and software reviews they find in this monthly magazine, which is dedicated to the Apple Macintosh computer.

PC Computing

The focus of this magazine is on IBM-compatible computers and software. Featured columnist John Dvorak usually presents an interesting perspective on new developments in the computer industry.

PC World

Similar in focus to *PC Computing*, *PC World* is distinguished by its "Consumer Watch" column, which acts as an industry watchdog and consumer advocate. "Consumer Watch" answers reports on product bugs, clarifies deceptive advertising, and prints consumer complaints.

Windows Magazine

This publication is especially for Microsoft Windows users. Each issue contains hardware and software reviews, as well as hints and tips on customizing the Microsoft Windows operating environment.

CHAPTER THREE

After you have completed this chapter you should be able to answer the following questions:

- What is the difference between data and information?
- What are the differences between program files and data files?
- What are the rules for naming files under DOS and Windows?
- How do file extensions improve file access?
- What is the difference between logical and physical file storage?
- How do the directory and the FAT help you access files?
- What types of computer storage are available?
- What are typical storage capacities and access speeds for disks and CD-ROM?
- How does a typical computer user work with files?

COMPUTER FILES

A single CD-ROM has the capacity to store the equivalent of 300,000 pages of text. To give you an idea of this rather astounding storage capacity, the small CD-ROM shown here contains a collection of over 700 classic works of literature, philosophy, drama, poetry, science, and religion. The books shown in this photograph represent only a fraction of the contents. In addition, the CD-ROM contains twenty minutes of narration, over 150 high-resolution images, and a complete biography and picture of each author whose work is included.

How is it possible to store so much information in such a small area? With so many titles, how can you find the one you want? Can you change data once it is stored? What happens if you run out of space?

In this chapter you will learn how computers store data in files, and you will learn the basic operations needed to access these files. You will also learn about the speed, cost, and storage capacity of popular microcomputer storage media.

Data and Information

On the CD-ROM pictured at the beginning of the chapter, each of the 700 works of literature is stored in a file. The term "file" has several operational definitions, depending on whether you are a general computer user, a database user, or a programmer. This chapter focuses on the way files are viewed by a general computer user and defines a **file** as a named collection of data that exists on a storage medium such as a hard disk, a floppy disk, or a CD-ROM.

Files contain data. Let's take a closer look at what that means. In everyday conversation, people use the terms "data" and "information" interchangeably. However, some computer professionals make a distinction between the two terms. **Data** is the words, numbers, and graphics that describe people, events, things, and ideas. Data becomes information when you use it as the basis for initiating some action or for making a decision. **Information**, then, is defined as the words, numbers, and graphics used as the basis for actions and decisions.

To understand the distinction between data and information, consider the following: AA 4199 ORD 9:59 CID 11:09. This data, which describes an event—a flight schedule—is typical of the data stored on a computer system. As data, AA 4199 ORD 9:59 CID 11:09 exists in storage and, along with other flight schedules, it can be sorted or transmitted to other computers. Let's say that you decide to take a trip from Chicago (ORD) to Cedar Rapids, Iowa (CID). You ask your travel agent to make your reservation. Your agent requests information on flights from Chicago to Cedar Rapids and sees the following on the computer screen:

Carrier	Flight Number	From	Departs	To	Arrives
AA	4199	ORD	9:59	CID	11:09

The data stored in the computer is now considered information because your travel agent is using it to make your reservation.

The distinction between data and information might seem somewhat elusive, because "AA 4199 ORD 9:59 CID 11:09" can be both data and information at the same time. Remember that the distinction is based on usage. Usually, if it is stored, it is referred to as data. If it is being viewed or otherwise used by a person to complete an action or make a decision, it is referred to as information.

Incidentally, in Latin, the word "data" is the plural for "datum." According to this usage, it would be correct to say "The January and February rainfall data *are* stored on the disk," but "The March datum *is* not yet available." Most English dictionaries, however, accept the use of "data" as either singular or plural. The style guidelines for this text specify that "data" is used with the singular verb, as in "The data *is* stored on the disk."

Computer Files

A computer stores data in files. As shown in Figure 3-1, there are two types of files: data files and program files. Understanding the difference between these two types of files is important because you use them in different ways.

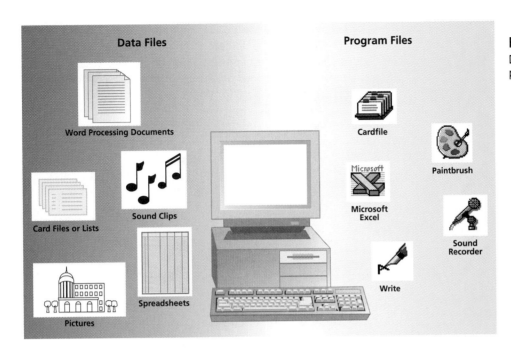

Figure 3-1
Data files and program files

Data Files

A **data file** contains words, numbers, and pictures that you can view, edit, save, send, and print. Typically, you create data files when you use application software. For example, when you store a document that you created with word processing software or when you store a picture you have drawn using a draw program, you create a data file. You also create a data file when you store the numbers for a spreadsheet, a statistical analysis, or a graph. When you store a list using database software and when you store a sound clip or a video, you also create a data file. Once you create a data file and store it on a disk, you can later view it, modify it, copy it to another disk, print it, erase it, or save it again. In the terminology used by Microsoft Windows, a data file that contains text, numbers, sounds, video, or graphics is often referred to as a **document** or **document file**.

In addition to the data files you create, you might receive data files as part of a software package you purchase. For example, as you learned in Chapter 2, word processing software often includes a dictionary data file that contains a list of words the software uses to check spelling.

You can also purchase specific data files that contain information you need. Suppose you own a business and are interested in mailing product information to prospective customers. You could purchase a data file that contains the names and addresses of people in your geographical area who fit the age and income profile of consumers who are likely to buy your product. Or suppose you want to refer to a broad collection of literature for your English Literature course. You might want to purchase *The World Literary Heritage* CD-ROM, shown at the beginning of this chapter, because it contains data files of classical literature.

Whether you create or purchase a data file, you typically use it in conjunction with an application. The application helps you manipulate the data in the file. You usually view, revise, and print a data file using the same software you used to create it. For example, if you create a data file using a word processor such as Microsoft Word for Windows, you would usually use Microsoft Word for Windows to edit the file.

If you purchase a data file, how do you know what application software to use it with? Usually, the program to manipulate the data is included with the data files. If the application that manipulates the data is not included, the package or documentation indicates which application you can use. For example, if you purchase a collection of graphical images, the documentation might indicate that you need a program such as Microsoft Paintbrush to view and modify the images.

Program Files

A **program file** contains the instructions that tell a computer how to perform a specific task. For example, the word processing program that tells your computer how to display and print text is stored on disk as a program file. Other program files on your computer system include the operating system, utilities, and the programs for application software. Program files are sometimes referred to as **executable files** because the computer performs, or executes, the instructions in the program.

You can purchase program files written by professional programmers, or you can create your own program files using a computer programming language such as BASIC, C, or COBOL. When a program file is created using most computer programming languages, the computer needs to translate the English-like program commands you enter into a set of symbols the computer can deal with directly. This translation process is called **compiling** and the program file that is created is sometimes referred to as a **compiled file**. Compiled files and executable files are essentially the same; both contain instructions that the computer carries out and both are categorized as program files.

Another type of program file is referred to as a batch file. A **batch file** is a series of operating system commands that you use to automate tasks you want the operating system to perform. Batch files are commonly used to automate DOS functions, such as starting programs or copying and printing files. A batch file found on most DOS computers is the AUTOEXEC.BAT file. When you first turn on an IBM-compatible computer, it looks for the AUTOEXEC.BAT file. If it finds this file, the computer automatically executes any instructions the file contains. You can modify the contents of the AUTOEXEC.BAT file if you want your computer to automatically perform a special task when you turn it on, such as starting Microsoft Windows.

File-naming Conventions

With so many types of files, how can you distinguish one from another? Each file has a name that identifies it. A **filename** is a unique set of letters and numbers that identifies a file and usually describes the file contents. For example, EXCEL is the name of one of the program files supplied with the Microsoft Excel spreadsheet software.

The filename might be followed by a **file extension** that further describes the file contents. For example, the file EXCEL.EXE has a .EXE extension, indicating it is an executable file. The extension is separated from the filename with a period, called a "dot." If you tell someone the name of this file, you say "EXCEL dot EXE."

As a computer user, you are not usually responsible for naming program files. These files are included with the application software you purchase, and the files are named by the programmers who write them. It is useful to know, however, that application program files generally have either a .COM (for "compiled" or "command") extension or .EXE (for "executable") extension and that batch files have a .BAT (for "batch") extension. When you look through a list of files on a disk, you can quickly identify program and batch files by their file extensions.

When you create a data file or rename an existing file, you must assign it a valid filename. A **valid filename** is created by following specific rules. The rules for creating a valid filename are referred to as **file-naming conventions**. Each operating system has a unique set of file-naming conventions. The file-naming conventions used by DOS and Microsoft Windows 3.1 are listed in Figure 3-2. Can you determine why AUX, MY FILE.DOC, and BUD93/94.TXT are not valid filenames under DOS and Windows?

A filename can contain a maximum of eight characters.
A file extension can contain a maximum of three characters.
You may use letters or numbers in a filename.
You use a period to separate a filename from the extension.
You may use uppercase or lowercase letters in a filename.
You may use symbols such as _ ^ $ ~ ! # % & - { } @ ' ( )
Do not use the following symbols: / [ ] ; = " \ : ,	* ?
Do not use blank spaces in a filename or the extension.
Do not use the following names, sometimes referred to as reserved words: AUX, COM1, COM2, COM3, COM4, CON, LPT1, LPT2, LPT3, PRN, or NUL.

Figure 3-2

File-naming conventions for DOS and Microsoft Windows 3.1 files

Using DOS or Microsoft Windows file-naming conventions, the filenames SESSION, REPORT.DOC, BUDGET1.WKS, and FORM.1 are valid. AUX is not a valid filename because it is a reserved word. MY FILE.DOC is not valid because it contains a space between MY and FILE. The filename BUD93/94.TXT is not valid because it contains a slash.

Although it is sometimes difficult to select a DOS or Windows filename that is unique and descriptive within the eight-character limit, you should choose filenames that help you remember what is in the file. When DOS was originally introduced, many computer users added a three-letter extension to each filename to further describe the file contents. For example, you might have added the extension .MEM to the data files that contained memos. Increasingly, however, the file extension is automatically assigned by the software when you create the file and is used to indicate the software application that was used to create the file. For example, when you create a file with the word processing software Microsoft Word for Windows, you can assign it any filename up to eight characters. However, instead of adding your own three-character extension, the application automatically adds a .DOC extension (to stand for "document") to every file you create. By automatically assigning an extension, the application helps you identify the files you created using that application. For example, when you want to view or edit one of the files you created using Microsoft Word, the software automatically shows you a list of filenames that have a .DOC extension, but does not show files with other extensions.

A useful computing skill is the ability to look at a file extension and understand what it tells you about the file. An .EXE extension, for example, tells you that the file is executable. A .DOC extension tells you that the file was created using Microsoft Word. Study Figure 3-3 to become familiar with the extensions typically used in DOS and Windows environments.

Figure 3-3
DOS and Windows file extensions

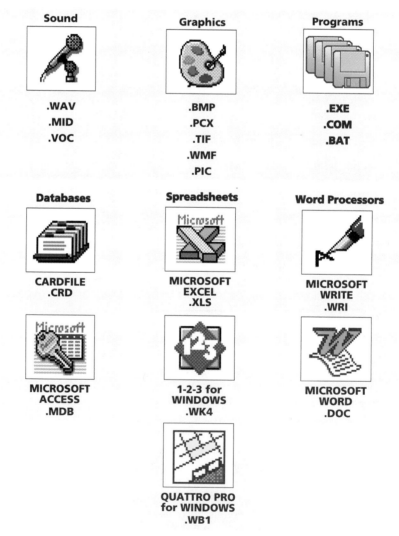

Sound
.WAV
.MID
.VOC

Graphics
.BMP
.PCX
.TIF
.WMF
.PIC

Programs
.EXE
.COM
.BAT

Databases
CARDFILE
.CRD

MICROSOFT
ACCESS
.MDB

Spreadsheets
MICROSOFT
EXCEL
.XLS

1-2-3 for
WINDOWS
.WK4

QUATTRO PRO
for WINDOWS
.WB1

Word Processors
MICROSOFT
WRITE
.WRI

MICROSOFT
WORD
.DOC

Logical File Storage

Your computer system might contain hundreds, or even thousands, of files stored on multiple disks and storage devices. To keep track of all these files, the computer has a "filing system" that is maintained by the operating system. Once you know how the operating system manages your computer's "filing system," you can use it effectively to store and retrieve files.

Most computers have more than one storage device that the operating system uses to store files. Each storage device is identified by a letter and a colon. Floppy disk drives are usually identified as A: and B:. The hard disk drive is usually identified as C:. Additional storage devices can be assigned letters from D: through Z:. Figure 3-4 shows some microcomputer configurations and the letters typically assigned to their storage devices.

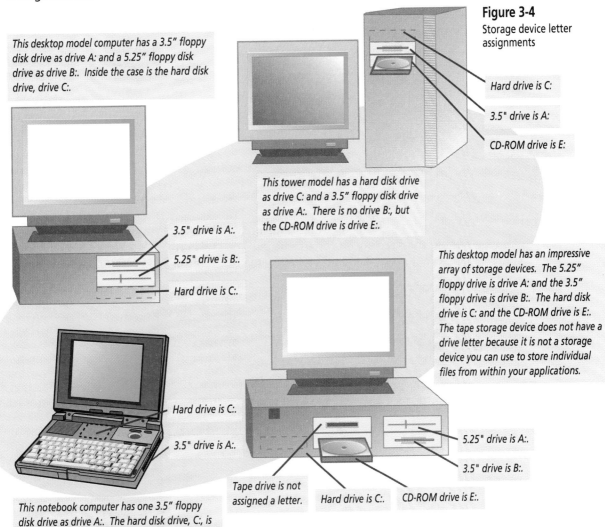

Figure 3-4
Storage device letter assignments

This desktop model computer has a 3.5" floppy disk drive as drive A: and a 5.25" floppy disk drive as drive B:. Inside the case is the hard disk drive, drive C:.

Hard drive is C:

3.5" drive is A:

CD-ROM drive is E:

3.5" drive is A:.

5.25" drive is B:.

Hard drive is C:.

This tower model has a hard disk drive as drive C: and a 3.5" floppy disk drive as drive A:. There is no drive B:, but the CD-ROM drive is drive E:.

This desktop model has an impressive array of storage devices. The 5.25" floppy drive is drive A: and the 3.5" floppy drive is drive B:. The hard disk drive is C: and the CD-ROM drive is E:. The tape storage device does not have a drive letter because it is not a storage device you can use to store individual files from within your applications.

Hard drive is C:.

3.5" drive is A:.

5.25" drive is A:.

3.5" drive is B:.

Tape drive is not assigned a letter.

Hard drive is C:.

CD-ROM drive is E:.

This notebook computer has one 3.5" floppy disk drive as drive A:. The hard disk drive, C:, is inside the case. There is no drive B:. Because of space restrictions it is difficult to fit many storage devices in a notebook computer.

The operating system maintains a list of files called a **directory** for each disk or CD-ROM. The directory contains the filename, the file extension, the date and time the file was created, and the file size for every file in the directory. The **file size** is the number of characters a file contains. You can use an operating system command to view the directory of a disk. Figure 3-5 shows the directory of a disk maintained by the DOS operating system. As you look at the directory in this figure, notice the contents of each column.

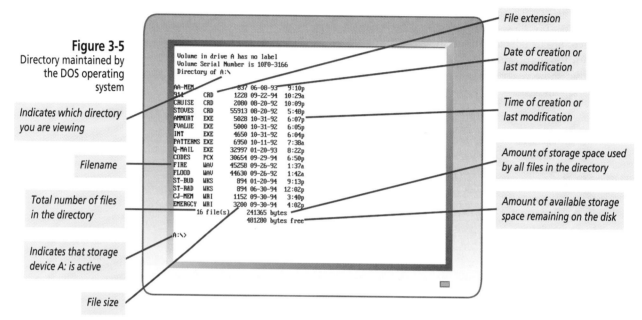

Figure 3-5
Directory maintained by the DOS operating system

Indicates which directory you are viewing

Filename

Total number of files in the directory

Indicates that storage device A: is active

File size

File extension

Date of creation or last modification

Time of creation or last modification

Amount of storage space used by all files in the directory

Amount of available storage space remaining on the disk

Figure 3-6 shows a directory maintained by the Microsoft Windows operating system. The directory is for the same disk you saw in Figure 3-5. Notice the similarities between the information displayed by the DOS directory and the Windows directory.

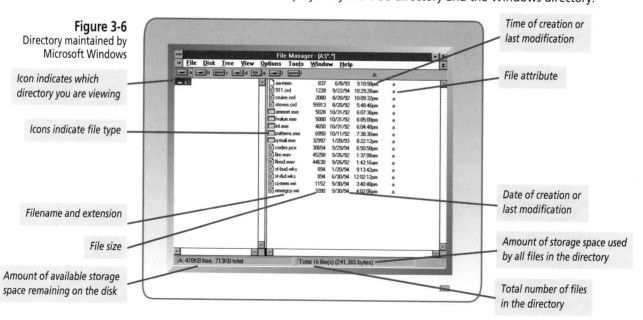

Figure 3-6
Directory maintained by Microsoft Windows

Icon indicates which directory you are viewing

Icons indicate file type

Filename and extension

File size

Amount of available storage space remaining on the disk

Time of creation or last modification

File attribute

Date of creation or last modification

Amount of storage space used by all files in the directory

Total number of files in the directory

The main directory of a disk, sometimes referred to as the **root directory**, provides a useful list of files, but it could be difficult to find a particular file if your directory contains several hundred files. To help you organize a large number of files, most operating systems allow you to divide your directory into smaller lists called **subdirectories**. For example, you can create one subdirectory to hold all your word processing documents and another subdirectory to hold all your files that contain graphical images.

A subdirectory name is separated from a drive letter and a filename by a special symbol. In DOS and Microsoft Windows, this symbol is the backslash \. (Don't confuse the backslash with the regular slash /, which slants a different way.) For example, the root directory of drive C: might have a subdirectory called BUSINESS, written as C:\BUSINESS.

A **file specification** is the drive letter, subdirectory, and filename that identifies a file. Suppose you create a subdirectory on drive A: named WORD for your word processing documents. Then suppose you want to create a list of things to do called TO-DO and put it on drive A: in the WORD subdirectory. The file specification is A:\WORD\TO-DO.

A directory name is sometimes referred to as a **pathname** because it provides a path or map to the location of a file. Figure 3-7 shows how you might envision the structure of a directory that has many subdirectories or a long path. Look at the figure and trace the path to the file A:\WORD\REPORTS\TO-DO.DOC.

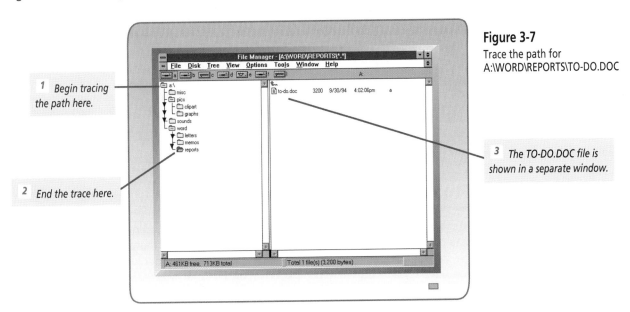

1 Begin tracing the path here.

2 End the trace here.

3 The TO-DO.DOC file is shown in a separate window.

Figure 3-7
Trace the path for A:\WORD\REPORTS\TO-DO.DOC

Many people envision a computer filing system as a tree, as shown in Figure 3-8. The root directory is the base or trunk of the tree. The subdirectories are the branches of the tree, and the files are the leaves.

Figure 3-8 represents what is sometimes called **logical storage**, not because it is the "most logical," but because it is the way you can conceptualize the organization of the files using your logical faculties, that is, your mind. This logical view of storage is a convenient mental model that helps you understand the computer's filing

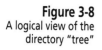

Figure 3-8
A logical view of the
directory "tree"

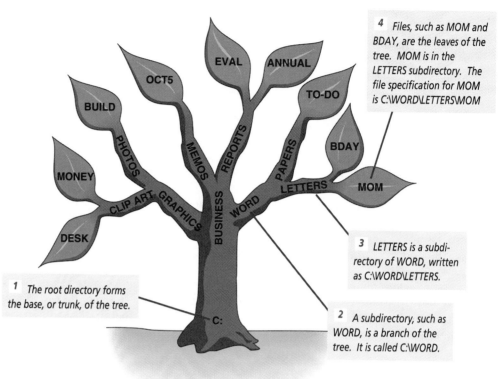

4 Files, such as MOM and BDAY, are the leaves of the tree. MOM is in the LETTERS subdirectory. The file specification for MOM is C:\WORD\LETTERS\MOM

3 LETTERS is a subdirectory of WORD, written as C:\WORD\LETTERS.

1 The root directory forms the base, or trunk, of the tree.

2 A subdirectory, such as WORD, is a branch of the tree. It is called C:\WORD.

system; however, it is not how the data is actually stored. **Physical storage** refers to how the data is actually stored on the physical disk medium. To find out more about how computers physically store data, it is useful to understand a bit about physical storage media and storage devices.

Storage Media and Devices

When it comes to computer storage, users have two main questions: How much data can I store? How fast can I access it? The answers to these questions depend on the storage medium and the storage device. A **storage medium** (the plural is "storage media") is the disk, tape, paper, or other item that contains data. A **storage device** is the mechanical apparatus that records and retrieves the data from the storage medium. The process of storing data is often referred to as **writing data** or **saving a file**, because the storage device "writes" the data on the storage medium to save it for later use. The process of retrieving data is often referred to as **reading data** or **opening a file**.

Data is stored as bytes—each **byte** usually represents one character. So, the phrase "profit margin," which contains 13 characters (including the space), requires

13 bytes of storage space. **Storage capacity** is the maximum amount of data that can be stored on a storage medium and is usually measured in kilobytes, megabytes, or gigabytes. A **kilobyte** (KB) is 1,024 bytes, but this is often rounded off to one thousand bytes. A **megabyte** (MB) is approximately one million bytes. A **gigabyte** is approximately one billion bytes. When you read that the storage capacity of a computer is 200 MB, it means the hard disk on that computer can store up to 200 million bytes of information. This is equivalent to approximately 60,000 single-spaced pages of text.

In addition to storage capacity, users are usually concerned with the access time of a computer. **Access time** is the average time it takes a computer to locate data on the storage medium and read it. Access time for microcomputer storage devices, such as a disk drive, is measured in milliseconds. One **millisecond** (ms) is a thousandth of a second. When you read, for example, that disk access time is 15 ms, it means that on average, it takes the computer fifteen thousandths of a second to locate and read data from the disk.

Magnetic Storage

The two most popular types of magnetic storage media are floppy disks and hard disks. Magnetic tape provides a third type of magnetic storage, used primarily as a backup system for disk storage on microcomputer systems.

With **magnetic storage** the computer stores data on disks and tape by magnetizing selected particles of an oxide-based surface coating. The particles retain their magnetic orientation until that orientation is changed, thereby making disks and tape fairly permanent but modifiable storage media.

You can intentionally change or erase files stored on magnetic media. If you run out of storage space on a disk, you can erase files you no longer need to make more space available.

Data stored on magnetic media can also be unintentionally altered. Magnetic media can be disrupted by magnetic fields and gradually lose their magnetic charge—and lose data. Some experts believe that the reliable life span of data stored on magnetic media is about three years and recommend that you refresh your data every two years by recopying it. Whether or not this estimated life span is correct, it is important to realize that data stored on magnetic media is subject to device and media failures, which make the data unusable. Later in this chapter you will learn some techniques to minimize data loss.

Floppy Disk Storage

A **floppy disk** (also called a **floppy** or a **diskette**) is a flexible mylar disk covered with a thin layer of magnetic oxide. Floppy disks come in several sizes. The disk sizes most commonly used on microcomputers are 3.5" and 5.25". As you can see from Figure 3-9, a 5.25" disk is sealed in a flexible square jacket, which partially protects the disk surface from contamination produced by dust, smoke, and fingerprints. A thin layer of a cloth-like substance catches any particles that might stray into the disk jacket.

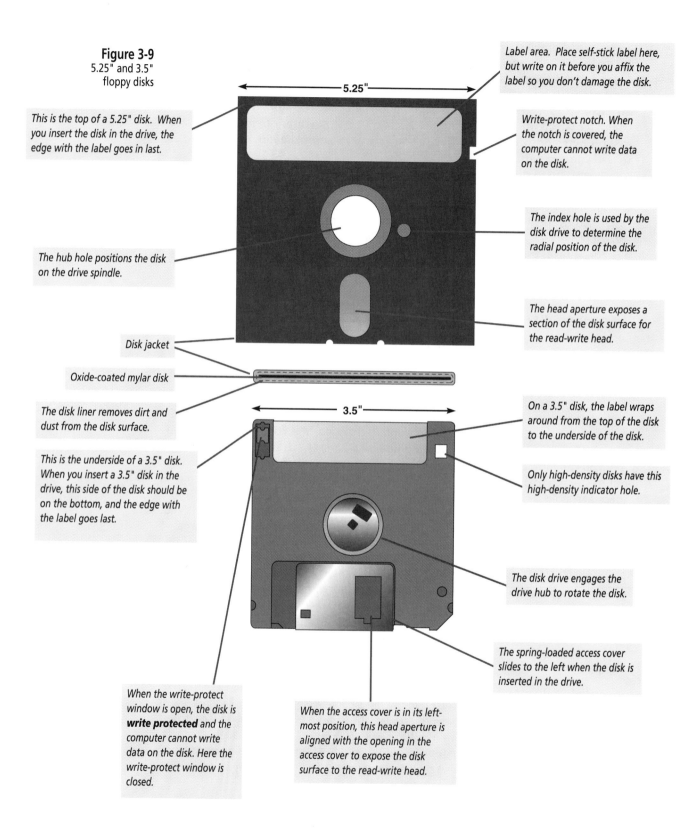

Figure 3-9
5.25" and 3.5"
floppy disks

Label area. Place self-stick label here, but write on it before you affix the label so you don't damage the disk.

This is the top of a 5.25" disk. When you insert the disk in the drive, the edge with the label goes in last.

Write-protect notch. When the notch is covered, the computer cannot write data on the disk.

The index hole is used by the disk drive to determine the radial position of the disk.

The hub hole positions the disk on the drive spindle.

The head aperture exposes a section of the disk surface for the read-write head.

Disk jacket

Oxide-coated mylar disk

The disk liner removes dirt and dust from the disk surface.

On a 3.5" disk, the label wraps around from the top of the disk to the underside of the disk.

This is the underside of a 3.5" disk. When you insert a 3.5" disk in the drive, this side of the disk should be on the bottom, and the edge with the label goes last.

Only high-density disks have this high-density indicator hole.

The disk drive engages the drive hub to rotate the disk.

The spring-loaded access cover slides to the left when the disk is inserted in the drive.

When the write-protect window is open, the disk is **write protected** and the computer cannot write data on the disk. Here the write-protect window is closed.

When the access cover is in its left-most position, this head aperture is aligned with the opening in the access cover to expose the disk surface to the read-write head.

Figure 3-9 also shows the construction of a 3.5" disk, an improvement on the 5.25" design. Like its 5.25" counterpart, a 3.5" disk is made of flexible mylar. However, the protective jacket on a 3.5" disk is rigid plastic, which provides more protection for the disk inside. In addition, the 3.5" design provides less exposure of the disk surface because the **head aperture** is covered by a spring-loaded access cover when the disk is not in the drive.

Although some floppy disks store data only on one side, today most store data on both sides. A **double-sided disk**, sometimes abbreviated as **DS**, stores twice as much data as a single-sided disk because it uses both sides of the disk.

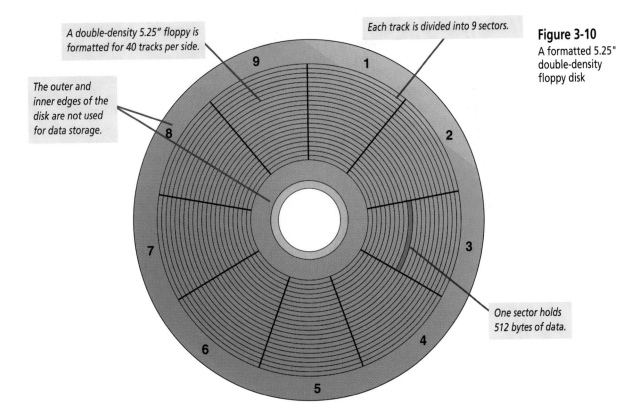

A double-density 5.25" floppy is formatted for 40 tracks per side.

Each track is divided into 9 sectors.

The outer and inner edges of the disk are not used for data storage.

One sector holds 512 bytes of data.

Figure 3-10
A formatted 5.25" double-density floppy disk

The amount of data a computer can store on each side of a disk depends on the way the disk is formatted. In Chapter 2 you learned that you must format a disk before you can store data on it. The formatting process creates a series of concentric **tracks** on the disk with each track divided into smaller segments called **sectors**, as shown in Figure 3-10. Each sector is sequentially numbered, so a disk that is formatted with 40 tracks per side and 9 sectors per track has 720 sectors. On IBM-compatible computers, each sector of a track holds 512 bytes of data, so a file that is 512 bytes or less fits in a single sector. Larger files are stored in more than one sector.

Both double-density and high-density double-sided disks are available. Disk density refers to the size of the magnetic particles on the disk surface and limits the amount of data you can reliably store on the disk. A **double-density disk**, abbreviated as **DD**, is usually formatted with 40 tracks and 9 sectors on each side of a 5.25" disk for a typical storage capacity of 360 kilobytes. A double-density 3.5" disk is usually formatted for 80 tracks per side and 9 sectors per track, and stores 720 kilobytes. Double-density disks are also referred to as "low-density" disks.

A **high-density disk**, abbreviated as **HD**, is usually formatted with 80 tracks and 15 sectors on each side of a 5.25" disk for a storage capacity of 1.2 megabytes. A high-density 3.5" disk is usually formatted for 80 tracks and 18 sectors per side for a storage capacity of 1.44 megabytes.

Other floppy disk capacities are becoming increasingly popular. For example, some 3.5" floppy disks store 2.88 megabytes on a single disk. **Floptical** disks store 21 megabytes on a special 3.5" disk that looks very similar to a regular 3.5" floppy disk.

When you purchase and use floppy disks, you must make sure the disk size and storage density match the capacity of your disk drive. You can tell the size of the disk drive by looking at the size of the opening where you insert the disk. You might need to refer to the reference manual for your computer to find out whether the drive has the capacity to read and write to high-density disks. For example, if you have a high-density 3.5" disk drive, you should purchase and use high-density 3.5" disks. You can format that high-density 3.5" disk for 720 KB or 1.44 MB, but you would usually select the higher capacity to use all of the possible storage capacity.

Computers are not very "smart" when it comes to formatting a 5.25" disk because most computers cannot tell the difference between a high-density and a low-density 5.25"disk. Your computer might let you attempt to format a low-density 5.25" disk for 1.2 MB because it can't tell the difference between the two disks. However, the data you store on an incorrectly formatted disk is not reliable, and the computer might have trouble reading the data it contains.

The storage device that records and retrieves data on a floppy disk is the floppy disk drive. Refer to Figure 3-11 to find out how the rotation of the disk, combined with the lateral movement of the read-write head, allows the drive mechanism to access any sector of the disk.

The read-write head can read or write data from any sector of the disk, in any order. This ability to move to any sector is referred to as **random access**. Random access is a handy feature of disk-based storage that provides quick access to files anywhere on a disk. Even with random access, however, a floppy disk drive is not a particularly speedy device. It takes about 0.5 seconds for the drive to spin the disk up to speed and then move the read-write head to a particular sector.

Today, floppy disk storage is used for three purposes. The most prevalent use is for software distribution. When you purchase software, the package usually includes floppy disks containing programs and data files. The second use for floppy disks is to share data with other computer users. For example, if you want to give a copy of a report to several colleagues, you can copy the report to floppy disks and give them to your colleagues. Another use for floppy disks is to make duplicate copies of your data in case something happens to the original, a process known as backup. In the past, floppy disks were the primary storage medium for microcomputer systems, but today hard disk storage has taken over that role.

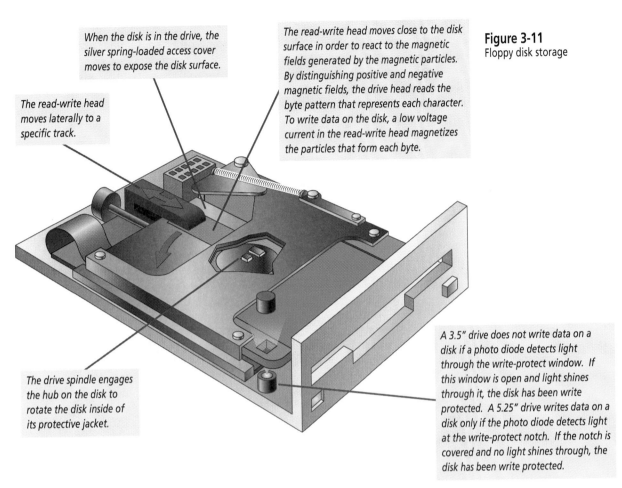

When the disk is in the drive, the silver spring-loaded access cover moves to expose the disk surface.

The read-write head moves laterally to a specific track.

The read-write head moves close to the disk surface in order to react to the magnetic fields generated by the magnetic particles. By distinguishing positive and negative magnetic fields, the drive head reads the byte pattern that represents each character. To write data on the disk, a low voltage current in the read-write head magnetizes the particles that form each byte.

Figure 3-11
Floppy disk storage

The drive spindle engages the hub on the disk to rotate the disk inside of its protective jacket.

A 3.5" drive does not write data on a disk if a photo diode detects light through the write-protect window. If this window is open and light shines through it, the disk has been write protected. A 5.25" drive writes data on a disk only if the photo diode detects light at the write-protect notch. If the notch is covered and no light shines through, the disk has been write protected.

Hard Disk Storage

A hard disk provides faster access to files than a floppy disk and is the preferred type of storage for most computer systems. A **hard disk platter** is a flat, rigid disk made of aluminum or glass and coated with a magnetic oxide. A **hard disk** is one or more platters and their associated read-write heads. This is also an operational definition for a **hard disk drive**, and you will frequently see the terms "hard disk" and "hard disk drive" used interchangeably. You might also hear the term "fixed disk" used to refer to hard disks.

Like floppy disks, hard disk platters are typically 3.5" or 5.25" in diameter, but the storage capacity of a hard disk far exceeds that of a floppy disk. Also, the access time of a hard disk is significantly faster than a floppy disk. Hard disk storage capacities of 200 MB and access speeds of 15 ms are not uncommon. How is it possible to pack so much more data on a hard disk and access it so quickly? Figure 3-12 explains.

Because 512 bytes of data are stored in each sector of each cylinder, you can determine the capacity of a hard disk using the following formula:

$$\text{capacity} = \text{cylinders} \times \text{surfaces} \times \text{sectors} \times 512$$

For example, if you have a hard disk with 615 cylinders, 4 surfaces (that is, two platters), and 17 sectors, the capacity is:

$$615 \times 4 \times 17 \times 512 = 21{,}411{,}840 \text{ bytes (about 20 megabytes)}$$

The read-write heads hover a microscopic distance above the disk surface. If a read-write head runs into a dust particle or some other contaminant on the disk, it might cause what is called a "head crash." A **head crash** damages some of the data on the disk. To help eliminate contaminants from contacting the platters and causing head crashes, a hard disk is sealed in its case. A head crash can also be triggered by jarring the hard disk while it is in use. Although hard disks have become considerably more rugged in recent years, it is best to handle and transport them with care.

Figure 3-12
Hard disk storage

The drive spindle supports one or more hard disk platters. Both sides of the platter are used for data storage. More platters mean more surface area and more data storage capacity. Hard disk platters rotate as a unit on the drive spindle to position a specific sector under the read-write heads. The platters spin continuously at 3,600 revolutions per minute.

Each data storage surface has its own read-write head. Read-write heads move in and out from the center of the disk to locate a specific track. The head hovers only five microinches above the disk surface so the magnetic field is much more compact than on a floppy disk. As a result, more data is packed into a smaller area on a hard disk platter.

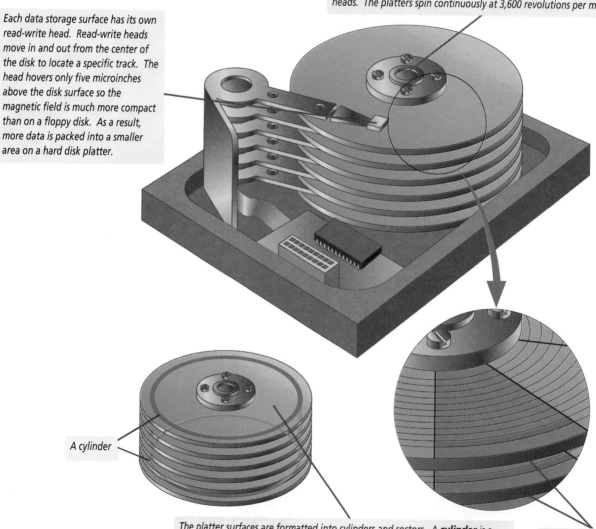

A cylinder

A sector on two platters

The platter surfaces are formatted into cylinders and sectors. A **cylinder** is a vertical stack of tracks. A hard disk could have between 312 and 2,048 cylinders. To find a file, the computer must know its cylinder, sector, and surface location.

Some hard disks are removable. **Removable hard disks** or hard disk "cartridges," such as the one pictured in Figure 3-13, contain platters and read-write heads that can be inserted and removed from the drive much like a floppy disk. Removable hard disks increase the potential storage capacity of your computer system, although the data is available on only one disk at a time. Removable hard disks also provide security for your data by making it possible for you to remove the hard disk cartridge and store it separately from the computer.

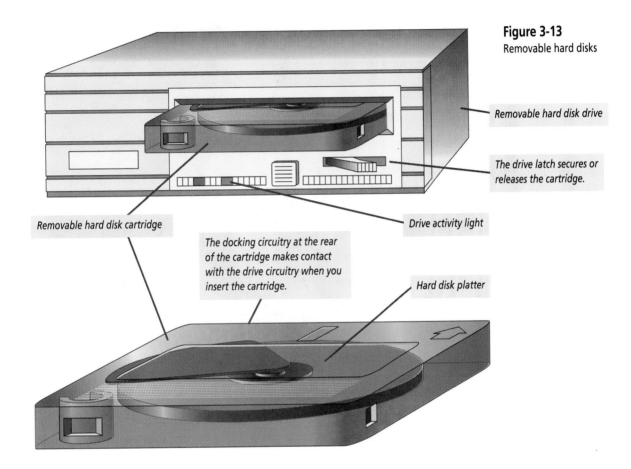

Figure 3-13
Removable hard disks

Removable hard disk drive

The drive latch secures or releases the cartridge.

Removable hard disk cartridge

Drive activity light

The docking circuitry at the rear of the cartridge makes contact with the drive circuitry when you insert the cartridge.

Hard disk platter

Like floppy disks, hard disks provide random access to files by positioning the read-write head over the sector that contains the requested data. Unlike floppy disks, which rotate only when you request data, hard disks are continually in motion, so there is no delay as the disk spins up to speed. As a result, hard disk access is faster than floppy disk access. To further increase the speed of data access, your computer might use a disk cache (pronounced "cash"). A **disk cache**, illustrated in Figure 3-14, is a special area of computer memory into which the computer transfers the data that you are likely to need from disk storage.

Figure 3-14
Disk caching

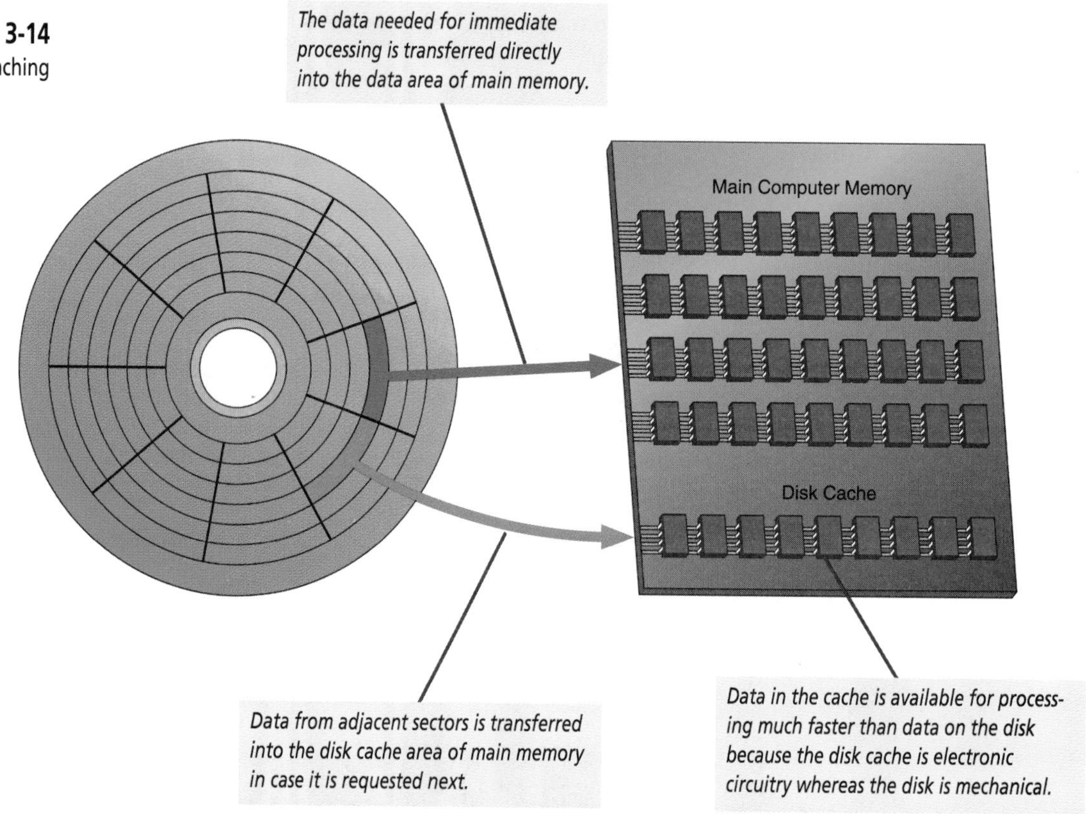

The data needed for immediate processing is transferred directly into the data area of main memory.

Main Computer Memory

Disk Cache

Data from adjacent sectors is transferred into the disk cache area of main memory in case it is requested next.

Data in the cache is available for processing much faster than data on the disk because the disk cache is electronic circuitry whereas the disk is mechanical.

How does a disk cache help speed things up? Suppose your computer retrieves the data from a particular sector of your disk. There is a high probability that the next data you need will be from an adjacent sector—the remainder of a program file, for example, or the next section of a data file. So while other processing takes place, the computer reads the data from nearby sectors and stores it in the cache. If the data you need next is already in the cache, the computer doesn't need to wait while the mechanical parts of the drive locate and read the data from the disk. Because an electrical operation, working at close to the speed of light, takes much less time than a mechanical operation, the disk cache speeds up the performance of your computer system.

Tape Storage

In the 1960s, magnetic tape was the most popular form of mainframe computer storage. When IBM introduced its first microcomputer, the legacy of tape storage persisted in the form of a cassette tape drive, similar to those used for audio recording and playback. Using tape as a primary storage device is slow and inconvenient, because tape requires sequential, rather than random, access. With sequential access, data is stored and read as a sequence of bytes along the length of the tape. To find a file stored on a microcomputer tape storage device, you advance the tape to the approximate location of the file, then wait for the computer to slowly read each byte until it finds the beginning of the file. You can see why microcomputer users abandoned tape storage for the convenience and speed of random access disk drives.

Recently, however, tape storage for microcomputers has experienced a revival—not as a principal storage device, but for making backup copies of the data stored on hard disks. As you have learned in this chapter, the data on magnetic storage can be easily destroyed, erased, or otherwise lost. Protecting the data on the hard disk is of particular concern to users because it contains so much data—data that would be difficult and time-consuming to reconstruct. Therefore, it is a good idea to have a copy of the data tucked safely away somewhere.

A **tape backup** is a copy of the data on a hard disk, transferred to tape storage media and used to restore lost data. Tape backup is relatively inexpensive and can rescue you from the overwhelming task of trying to reconstruct lost data. If you lose the data on your hard disk, you can copy the data from the tape backup onto the hard disk. Typically, you do not use the data directly from the tape backup because the sequential access is too slow to be practical.

The most popular type of tape drive for microcomputers uses a tape cartridge, but there are different tape specifications and cartridge sizes. The specifications for tape storage include tape length and width. For example, Digital Audio Tape (DAT) cartridges contain either 60 or 90 meters of four-millimeter tape. The shorter DAT tapes have a capacity of 1.3 gigabytes, the longer tapes have a capacity of 2 gigabytes. When you purchase tapes, check the tape drive manual to make sure the tapes you purchase are the correct type for your tape drive. Figure 3-15 on the following page illustrates the basic concepts of tape storage.

Bernoulli Storage

Another type of magnetic media is the Bernoulli disk. This patented technology from Iomega Corporation uses special floppy magnetic media in a rigid case and combines the advantages of floppy disks and hard disks. The Bernoulli disk drive technology was inspired by a principle of thermodynamics first explained by the Swiss mathematician Daniel Bernoulli in the 1800s. Bernoulli disks are specially designed so that air pressure lifts the disk surface when the disk is spinning. To understand a simplified version of this principle, notice what happens when you blow across the top of a small strip of paper. The paper strip rises because of the difference in air pressure between the top and the bottom of the strip.

A Bernoulli disk is made of the same flexible mylar substance as a floppy disk, but by manipulating the air pressure in the disk drive, the Bernoulli disk is raised very close to the read-write head. Because the disk is so close to the read-write head, the magnetic fields allow storage capacities more like those of a hard disk. The advantage of a Bernoulli drive is that the flexible disk is less prone to damage from head crashes—the Bernoulli disk flexes enough to prevent the head from contacting the disk surface, as shown in Figure 3-16 on page NP 97.

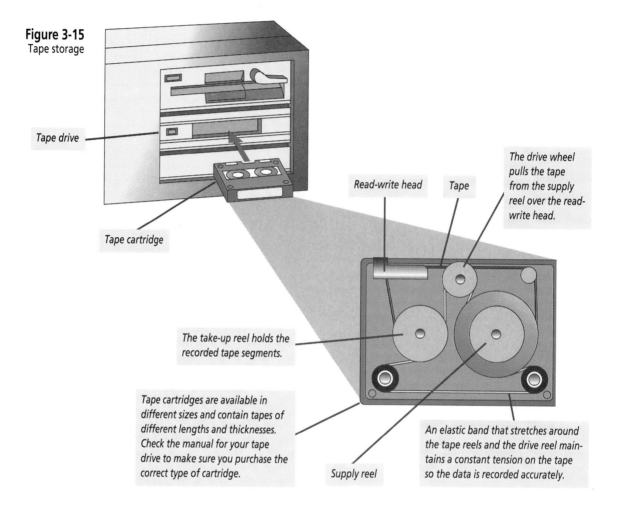

Figure 3-15
Tape storage

Tape drive

Tape cartridge

Read-write head   Tape

The drive wheel pulls the tape from the supply reel over the read-write head.

The take-up reel holds the recorded tape segments.

Tape cartridges are available in different sizes and contain tapes of different lengths and thicknesses. Check the manual for your tape drive to make sure you purchase the correct type of cartridge.

Supply reel

An elastic band that stretches around the tape reels and the drive reel maintains a constant tension on the tape so the data is recorded accurately.

Optical Storage

Another popular type of microcomputer storage uses optical media. **Optical media** store data in a form that is readable with beams of laser light. There are several types of optical storage media available for microcomputers, including CD-ROM, WORM, and rewritable optical. Each of these optical storage media uses a slightly different technology.

CD-ROM Storage

CD-ROM (Compact Disc Read Only Memory) technology is derived from the compact disc digital recording system. A computer CD-ROM disk, like its audio counterpart, contains data that has been stamped on the disk surface as a series of pits. To read the data on a CD-ROM, an optical read head distinguishes the patterns of pits that represent bytes. Figure 3-17 on page NP 98 illustrates how this works.

CD-ROMs provide tremendous storage capacity. A single CD-ROM holds up to 680 megabytes, equivalent to over 300,000 pages of text.

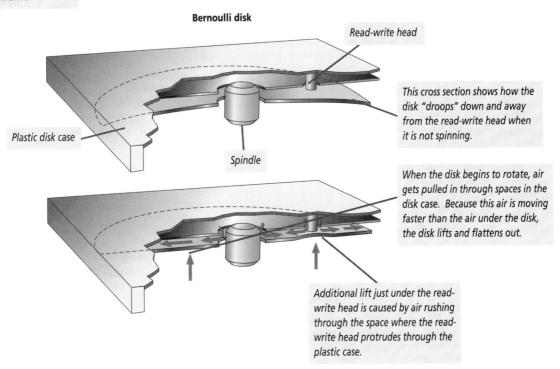

Figure 3-16
Bernoulli storage

A Bernoulli cartridge contains a flexible storage medium much like a floppy disk.

A Bernoulli drive is a separate device attached to one of the expansion slots in a computer. Other models can be installed inside the system unit like a floppy disk drive or removable hard disk drive.

Bernoulli disk

Read-write head

This cross section shows how the disk "droops" down and away from the read-write head when it is not spinning.

Plastic disk case

Spindle

When the disk begins to rotate, air gets pulled in through spaces in the disk case. Because this air is moving faster than the air under the disk, the disk lifts and flattens out.

Additional lift just under the read-write head is caused by air rushing through the space where the read-write head protrudes through the plastic case.

The CD-ROM disk surface is coated with a clear plastic, making the data permanent and unalterable. Because you can retrieve data from a CD-ROM but cannot save any new data on it, CD-ROM media is referred to as read only. In this respect, CD-ROM technology differs markedly from hard disk storage, on which you can write, erase, and read data. A CD-ROM drive does not generally serve as the sole storage device for a microcomputer. Instead, a CD-ROM drive supplements, rather than replaces, a hard disk drive.

A CD-ROM disk is relatively inexpensive to manufacture, making it an ideal way for software publishers to distribute large programs and data files. CD-ROM is the media of choice for delivery of multimedia applications because it provides the large storage capacity necessary for sound, video, and graphics files.

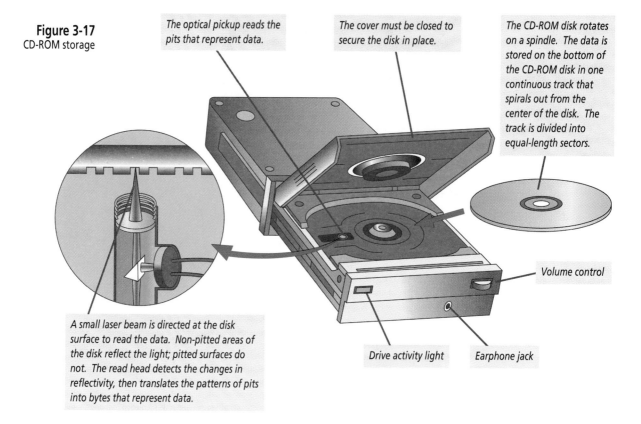

Figure 3-17
CD-ROM storage

The optical pickup reads the pits that represent data.

The cover must be closed to secure the disk in place.

The CD-ROM disk rotates on a spindle. The data is stored on the bottom of the CD-ROM disk in one continuous track that spirals out from the center of the disk. The track is divided into equal-length sectors.

A small laser beam is directed at the disk surface to read the data. Non-pitted areas of the disk reflect the light; pitted surfaces do not. The read head detects the changes in reflectivity, then translates the patterns of pits into bytes that represent data.

Volume control

Drive activity light   *Earphone jack*

Other Optical Storage

A **WORM drive** (Write Once Read Many) is an optical drive that allows you to write data once on any sector of the disk. As with a CD-ROM, you can read that data as many times a you like. You can retrieve data stored on a WORM drive and you can save new files on a WORM drive, but you cannot erase or modify the stored data. WORM drives are very useful in situations where data, such as financial or medical records, needs to be protected from erasure or modification.

Some types of optical storage media allow you to read, write, erase, and modify files. **Read/write optical drives** and **magneto optical drives** merge magnetic and optical technologies so you can read, write, erase, and modify files, as on a hard disk drive, but they offer very large storage capacity and reliable long-term storage.

Physical File Storage

Now that you have a better understanding of how a storage device records data on a storage medium, we can return to some questions about how files are stored. How does a computer's filing system know where to look for a particular file? How does the computer make the most efficient use of the storage space?

Although a disk is formatted into tracks and sectors that provide physical storage locations for data, files are actually stored in clusters. A **cluster** is a group of sectors and is the smallest storage unit the computer can access. The number of sectors that form a cluster depends on the type of computer. IBM-compatible computers form a cluster from two sectors. Each cluster is numbered, as shown in Figure 3-18, and the operating system maintains a list of which sectors correspond to each cluster.

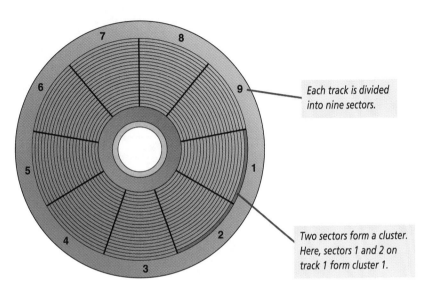

Figure 3-18
Clusters

Each track is divided into nine sectors.

Two sectors form a cluster. Here, sectors 1 and 2 on track 1 form cluster 1.

When the computer stores a file on a random-access storage medium, the operating system records the cluster number that contains the beginning of the file in a file allocation table, or FAT. The **FAT** is an operating system file that helps the computer store and retrieve files from disk storage by maintaining a list of files and their physical location on the disk. The FAT is such a crucial file that if it is damaged by a head crash or other disaster, you generally lose access to all the data stored on your disk because the list of clusters that contain files is no longer readable. This is yet another reason to have a tape backup of your hard drive.

When you want to store a file, the operating system looks at the FAT to see which clusters are empty. The operating system then records the data for the file in empty clusters. The cluster numbers and the name of the new file are recorded in the FAT so the file can be located and retrieved later.

A file that does not fit into a single cluster will spill over into the next adjacent or "contiguous" cluster unless that cluster already contains data. If the next cluster is full, the operating system stores the file in a nonadjacent cluster and sets up pointers to each piece of the file, as shown in Figure 3-19 on the following page.

When you want to retrieve a file, the operating system looks at the FAT to find where the file is stored. The operating system then moves the read-write head to the cluster that contains the beginning of the file and reads it. If the file is stored in more than one cluster, the read-write head must move to the next cluster to read more of the file. It takes longer to access a file stored in nonadjacent clusters than one stored in adjacent clusters because the disk or head must move farther to find the next section of the file.

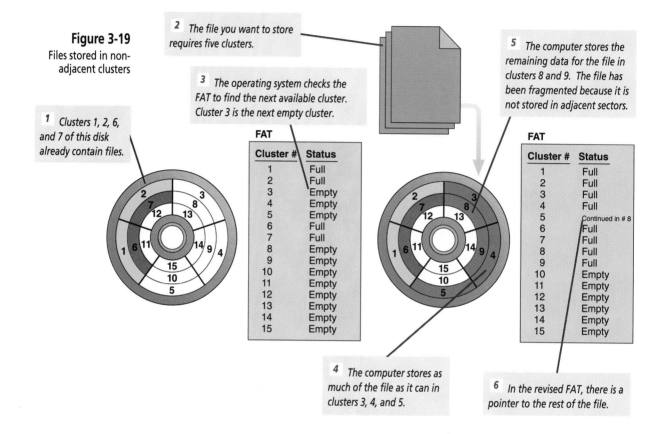

Figure 3-19
Files stored in non-adjacent clusters

1 Clusters 1, 2, 6, and 7 of this disk already contain files.

2 The file you want to store requires five clusters.

3 The operating system checks the FAT to find the next available cluster. Cluster 3 is the next empty cluster.

5 The computer stores the remaining data for the file in clusters 8 and 9. The file has been fragmented because it is not stored in adjacent sectors.

FAT

Cluster #	Status
1	Full
2	Full
3	Empty
4	Empty
5	Empty
6	Full
7	Full
8	Empty
9	Empty
10	Empty
11	Empty
12	Empty
13	Empty
14	Empty
15	Empty

FAT

Cluster #	Status
1	Full
2	Full
3	Full
4	Full
5	Continued in # 8
6	Full
7	Full
8	Full
9	Full
10	Empty
11	Empty
12	Empty
13	Empty
14	Empty
15	Empty

4 The computer stores as much of the file as it can in clusters 3, 4, and 5.

6 In the revised FAT, there is a pointer to the rest of the file.

L A B

DEFRAGMENTATION

As you use random-access storage, files tend to become **fragmented**, that is, each file is stored in many nonadjacent clusters, as shown in Figure 3-20. Drive performance generally declines as the drive works harder to locate the clusters that contain the parts of a file. To regain peak performance, you can use a **defragmentation utility** to rearrange the files on a disk so that they are stored in adjacent clusters.

When you erase a file, the operating system changes the status of the appropriate clusters in the FAT. For example, if a file is stored in clusters 1, 2, 5, and 7 and you erase it, the operating system changes the status for those four clusters to "empty." The data is not physically removed or erased from those clusters. Instead, the old data remains in the clusters until a new file is stored there. This rather interesting situation means that if you inadvertently erase a file, you might be able to "get it back" using the operating system's Undelete utility. Of course, you can only undelete a file if you haven't recorded something new over it, so it's best to discover and correct mistakes immediately.

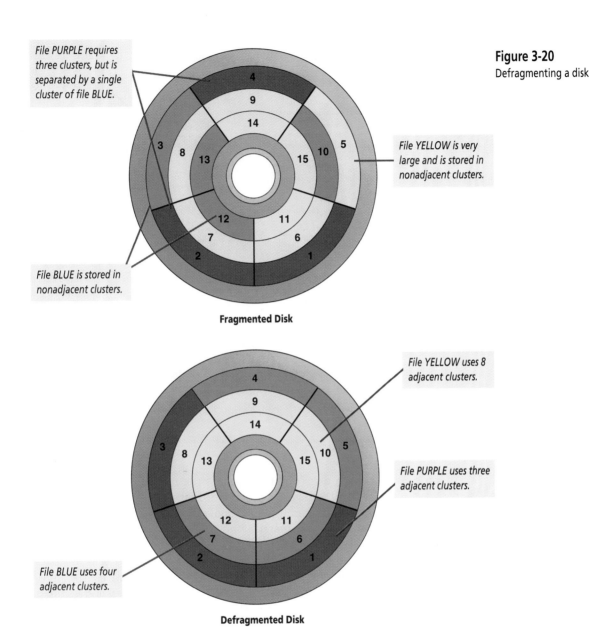

Figure 3-20
Defragmenting a disk

File PURPLE requires three clusters, but is separated by a single cluster of file BLUE.

File YELLOW is very large and is stored in nonadjacent clusters.

File BLUE is stored in nonadjacent clusters.

Fragmented Disk

File YELLOW uses 8 adjacent clusters.

File PURPLE uses three adjacent clusters.

File BLUE uses four adjacent clusters.

Defragmented Disk

Using Files

Now that you have learned about logical and physical file storage, let's apply what you've learned to how you typically use files when you work with application software. The activities involved in using a word processor to produce a document illustrate the way you use files on a computer, so let's look at the file operations for a typical word processing session. Examine Figure 3-21 on the following page to get an overview of the file activities of a typical word processing session.

L A B

FILE OPERATIONS

Figure 3-21

File activities during a
word processing session

Retrieve the data file you
want to view or edit. The
data is copied from the
disk into the main memory
of the computer and
displayed on the screen.

Launch the application you want
to use to create or modify the data
file. The application program is
copied from the disk into the main
memory of the computer, and the
computer begins to perform the
instructions.

Save the modified file.
When you issue the Save
command, the computer
copies the data in main
memory to the disk,
overwriting the previous
version of the file.

Modify the contents of the file
displayed on the screen. Your
modifications are kept in the
main memory, but are not
copied to the disk until you
issue the Save command.

Running an Application

Suppose you receive a disk containing a data file named VACATION.DOC. You
want to look at this file and modify it. You know that the easiest way to view this file
is with the application that created it. Which application was it? From the file extension, you realize that the file was created using Microsoft Word. Your first step is to
start the Microsoft Word program.

The process of starting an application is referred to as **running** or **launching** the
application. To run an application under a command-line operating system such as DOS,
you type the filename, but omit the extension. Under a graphical operating system such
as Microsoft Windows, you point to the icon for the application and double-click the
mouse button. As you learned earlier in this chapter, you can only run program files—
those with .EXE, .COM, or .BAT extensions. You cannot run data files.

Retrieving a Data File

When you want to use a data file that already exists on disk storage, you must
retrieve it. This process is also referred to as **opening** a file. As you know, the file is stored
in one or more clusters on a disk. How does the application find the one you want?

Applications have a command or menu option to open a file. You either type
the name of the file, VACATION, or select the filename from a list of files stored on
the disk. The application communicates the filename to the operating system. The

operating system looks at the FAT to find which clusters contain the file, then moves the read-write head to the appropriate disk location to read the file. The electronics on the disk drive transfer the file data into the main memory of the computer where your application software can manipulate it. Once the operating system has retrieved the file, the word processing software displays it on the screen.

Saving a Data File

When you can see the VACATION.DOC file on the screen, you can make modifications to it. Each character that you type and each change that you make is stored temporarily in the main memory of the computer, but not on the disk. The main memory retains data only as long as the computer power is on, so to store your data on a more permanent basis, you must tell the computer to copy the data from the memory of the computer to the disk.

When you create a file and save it on disk for the first time, the application or the operating system prompts you to name the file so you can later retrieve it by name. You know from earlier in the chapter that the name you give to a file must follow certain rules: it can be up to eight characters long, should not contain any spaces, and so forth.

The VACATION.DOC file is already on the disk, however, so when you are done with the modifications you have two options. Option one is to store the revised version in place of the old version. Option two is to create a new file for your revision and give it a different name, such as HOLIDAY.

If you decide to store the revised version in place of the old version, the operating system copies your revised data from the computer memory to the same clusters that contained the old file. You do not have to take a separate step to delete the old file—the operating system automatically records over it.

If you decide to create a new file for the revision, the application asks you for a filename. If you enter HOLIDAY as the filename, the application will append its own file extension. Because you are using Microsoft Word, the extension will be .DOC. After the application has a name for the new file, it notifies the operating system that it needs to store a new file. The operating system then finds some empty clusters in the FAT, stores the data, and makes the appropriate entry in the FAT.

Other File Operations: Copy and Delete

You can copy a file from one storage medium to another. When you copy a file, the original file remains intact. It is useful to make a copy of an important file as a backup, copy a file from your hard disk to a floppy disk to share with a friend, or transfer a file you receive on a floppy disk to your hard disk.

Suppose you want to copy the new HOLIDAY.DOC file from the floppy disk to your hard disk. The operating system is responsible for maintaining the list of files on your disk, so you usually use an operating system command to copy files. With a graphical operating system such as Microsoft Windows, you can drag the icon that represents HOLIDAY.DOC from its place in the directory of drive A: to the icon that represents drive C:, as shown in Figure 3-22 on the following page.

Figure 3-22
Copying a file

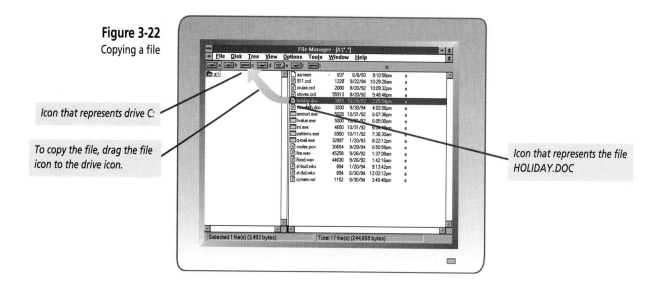

Icon that represents drive C:

To copy the file, drag the file icon to the drive icon.

Icon that represents the file HOLIDAY.DOC

With the DOS operating system, you use the COPY command. As you learned earlier, the floppy disk is either drive A: or drive B:. Let's assume that the disk containing HOLIDAY.DOC is in drive A: and your hard disk drive is drive C:. The DOS command to copy HOLIDAY.DOC from drive A: to drive C: is:

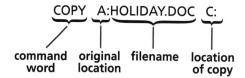

COPY   A:HOLIDAY.DOC   C:

**command   original   filename   location
word   location   of copy**

It is often necessary to eliminate files that you no longer need. If you want to eliminate a file that you have saved on disk, you **delete** or **erase** the file. As you know, when you delete a file, the operating system does not physically erase the cluster that contains the data belonging to that file. Instead, it changes the entries in the FAT to indicate that the clusters are available for storing other files. As additional files are stored on the disk, the sectors that used to contain the deleted file are gradually overwritten.

If you accidentally erase a file, you should stop using the computer immediately. Do not store anything else on the drive that contains the erased file until after you have used an Undelete utility program to restore the file.

■   ■   ■

Having access to many files stored on hard disks or CD-ROMs is a valuable advantage of today's technology. To use these files effectively, it is important to know how to interact with the computer's filing system: how to name, save, retrieve, copy, and erase files. You should now understand how storage devices, the operating system, and application software interact to help you maintain a filing system for your data.

C H A P T E R   R E V I E W

1. Answer the questions listed in the Chapter Preview at the beginning of the chapter.

2. List each of the boldface terms used in this chapter, then use your own words to write a short definition for each term.

3. Recreate the following chart. Place an X in the DATA FILES column if the feature applies to data files. Place an X in the PROGRAM FILES column if the feature applies to program files. If a feature applies to both, put an X in both columns.

FEATURE	DATA FILES	PROGRAM FILES
CREATED BY END-USERS		
CREATED BY PROGRAMMERS		
USE AN APPLICATION TO VIEW IT		
SUPPLIED WITH SOFTWARE		
HAS AN .EXE, .COM, OR .BAT EXTENSION		
CREATED USING A COMPUTER PROGRAMMING LANGUAGE		
A COMPILED FILE		
AN EXECUTABLE FILE		

4. From the following list, indicate which filenames are not valid under the operating system used in your school's computer lab, and indicate which file-naming convention each nonvalid filename violates. If you are using an operating system other than DOS or Windows 3.1, consult your instructor or the operating system's documentation to learn its file-naming conventions.

WP.EXE   PRN   WIN.EXE

AUTOEXEC.BAT   RESULTS*.WKS   MONTHLY.WK1

REPORT#1.TXT   SMITH&SMITH.DOC SEP/94.WRI

ASIA MAP.DOC   OCEAN.TIF   MN43-44.DBF

5. Suppose you need to retrieve a file from Sarah's computer. She tells you that the file is stored as C:\DATA\MONTHEND.DOC.

   a. What is the filename?

   b. What is the file extension?

   c. On which drive is the file stored?

   d. In which directory is the file stored?

6. Complete the following table to summarize floppy disk storage capacity:

SIZE	3.5"	3.5"	5.25"	5.25"
DENSITY	HIGH	LOW	HIGH	LOW
CAPACITY				
SECTORS				
TRACKS				

7. On each of the following three lines, indicate the relative position of floppy disk storage, hard disk storage, tape storage, and CD-ROM storage by placing these storage types along the line. The first one is completed for you.

a. Access time (slowest to fastest):

Tape   CD-ROM   Floppy disk   Hard disk

slow   fast

b. Capacity (smallest to largest):

small   large

c. Reliability (least reliable to most reliable):

easy to lose data   data is very secure

C H A P T E R   Q U I Z

1. The phrase "Good morning" requires _____ bytes of storage capacity.
2. A 3.5" 1.44 megabyte floppy disk can store approximately _____ times as much data as a 5.25" 360 K floppy disk.
3. A 2 gigabyte tape drive can store _____ megabytes of data.
4. A removable hard disk drive provides increased _____ by making it possible for you to remove the cartridges and store them in a secure place.
5. The three most common types of magnetic storage media are floppy disks, hard disks, and _____.
6. A floppy disk drive is a(n) _____ access device.
7. A head crash can result from jarring a(n) _____ during operation.
8. A(n) _____ can increase disk speed by reading extra data into main memory so the computer doesn't have to wait for the hard disk the next time more data is requested from the drive.

9. A(n) _____ disk combines the advantages of hard disk and floppy disk technology to provide fast, high-capacity storage without head crashes.

10. A(n) _____ is a read-only device that offers high-capacity, low-cost storage.

11. A WORM drive allows you to create and retrieve files, but does not allow you to _____ or modify files.

12. A(n) _____ file is stored in noncontiguous clusters.

13. When saving a modified version of an existing file, you can choose to save the modified file under a new name or save it under the old name, _____ the original file.

14. When you delete a file from a disk, the clusters are not actually erased. This makes it possible to _____ a deleted file if you have not stored additional files on the disk.

15. The process of storing data is often referred to as _____ data or saving a file.

P R O J E C T S

1. Use the following table to list the storage devices on the computer that you most frequently use.

LOCATION	DRIVE LETTER	DEVICE TYPE	STORAGE CAPACITY

2. Many applications use specific file extensions for data files created with that application. List ten different data file extensions and the program with which each is used.

3. Use a recent computer magazine to fill in the following "shopping list":

ITEM	BRAND	MERCHANT	PRICE
HIGH-DENSITY 3.5" FLOPPY DISK DRIVE			
210 MB 15 MS HARD DISK DRIVE			
CARTRIDGE TAPE BACKUP DEVICE			
350 MS OR FASTER CD-ROM			

4. Examine the directory listing in Figure 3-23 and answer the following questions:
   a. What is the size of the file STOVES.CRD?
   b. What date was 911.CRD last modified?
   c. How many *program* files are on the disk?
   d. Approximately how many megabytes of storage are available on the disk?
   e. What application was used to create the file CJ-MEM.WRI?
   f. How many of these files are data files?
   g. What is the largest file on the disk?
   h. Does the CODES.PCX file contain text or graphics?
   i. What type of data does the file FIRE.WAV contain?
   j. How many of the files appear to be memos?

Figure 3-23

```
Volume in drive A does not have a label
Directory of  A:\
AA-MEM              837   6-08-93   9:10p
BB-MEM              795   1-21-93   9:11p
CD-MEM    WPS       680   8-01-94  12:57p
GK-MEM    WPS      1448   8-08-94  12:20p
KM-MEM              826   3-04-93   7:06p
PATTERNS  EXE      6950  10-11-92   7:38a
ST-BUD    WKS       894   1-20-94   9:13p
ST-R&D    WKS       894   6-30-94  12:02p
ST-STATS  WKS       891   1-10-94  11:56a
STOVES    CRD     55913   8-20-92   5:48p
CRUISE    CRD      2080   8-20-92  10:09p
TB-MEM    WPS      1310   7-08-94   2:30p
CJ-MEM    WRI      1152   9-30-94   3:40p
JV-MEM    WRI      1408   7-14-94   3:42p
CODES     PCX     30654   9-29-94   6:50p
Q-MAIL    EXE     32997   1-20-93   8:22p
FIRE      WAV     45258   9-26-92   1:37a
FLOOD     WAV     44630   9-26-92   1:42a
911       CRD      1228   9-22-94  10:29a
EMERGCY   WRI      3200   9-30-94   4:02p
AMMORT    EXE      5028  10-31-92   6:07p
BRUN45    EXE     77440   9-28-88   1:43a
FVALUE    EXE      5000  10-31-92   6:05p
INT       EXE      4650  10-31-92   6:04p
        24 File(s)    1125376 bytes free
```

5. At the beginning of this chapter you learned about a CD-ROM that contained the text for more than 700 works of literature. How much storage space would your computer textbook require? To calculate approximately how many bytes of storage space the text (not pictures) of this book would require:

   a. Count the number of lines on a typical page.

   b. Count the number of characters (including blanks) in the longest line of text on the page.

   c. Multiply the number of lines by the number of characters in the longest line to calculate the average number of characters (bytes) per page.

   d. Multiply this figure by the number of pages in the book.

   e. What do you estimate is the computer storage space required for this text?

6. Suppose you need to manually defragment the files on the disk shown in Figure 3-24. Using the disk at right, show how the files are arranged after you complete the defragmentation. Use color pencils or different patterns to clearly show each file.

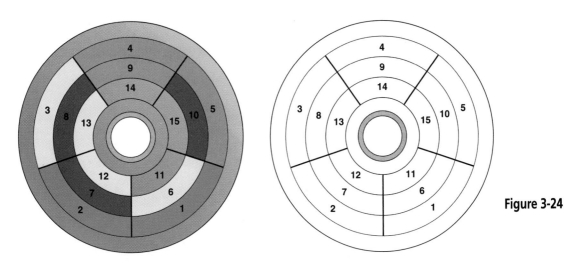

Figure 3-24

7. Read the following scenario and determine what went wrong. Then write a paragraph describing what you would do to correct the problem.

   Toni's 80 MB hard disk contained about 75 MB of files on February 18. On that day, she made a tape backup of the entire disk. On February 19, Toni moved to an office in the company's administration building one block away. The company maintenance staff moved the computer, along with Toni's paper files, in the late afternoon. The people on the maintenance crew were not computer experts so they just left the computer on the desk in the new office.

On February 20, Toni set up the computer and turned it on. Everything seemed fine. She used the computer to write a few memos using the WordPerfect for Windows application. On February 21, Toni tried to open a data file containing the names and addresses of her clients. The computer displayed a message—something about an error on drive C:. Toni turned off her computer and then turned it back on, hoping the error would go away, but the computer wouldn't let her access any data on the hard disk.

L A B S

Defragmentation Lab

DEFRAGMENTATION

The Defragmentation Lab begins with a guided tutorial that explains what happens when you format a disk, save files, and erase files. You will see how the files on your disk become fragmented and what a defragmentation utility does to reorganize the files on your disk. At the conclusion of the tutorial, you will have a chance to further explore the concepts of fragmenting and defragmenting files. When you have completed your explorations, respond to the following questions:

1. Which clusters are reserved for use by the FAT when a disk is formatted?
2. What are noncontiguous clusters?
3. What does it mean when we say a file is fragmented?
4. What is the effect of fragmentation on the performance of your computer system?
5. What is another name for a defragmentation utility?
6. Why is it necessary to use a defragmentation utility on a regular basis?
7. What happens if you try to save all the files on the disk?
8. Will files 1, 2, 3, 4, and 6 fit on the disk?
9. Format the disk, then save and erase files until the files become fragmented. Draw a picture of the disk with fragmented files. Indicate which files are in each cluster by using color, cross-hatching, or labels. List which files in your drawing are fragmented.

File Operations Lab

**FILE
OPERATIONS**

The File Operations Lab begins with a guided tour that uses a simulated computer system to show what happens when you create, save, open, and delete files. At the end of the tour, you will have a chance to use the simulator to experiment with file operations. When you have completed the File Operations Lab, respond to the following questions:

1. Where is the text stored when you start typing a new document?
2. Which file operation erases a document from the screen and main memory?
3. Which file operation erases a file from the disk?
4. Where are the contents of the file copied when you open a file?
5. What happens to the original file when you open a file, modify text in the file, then save the file with the same name?
6. Why would you open a file, modify text in the file, then save the revised file with a different name?

R E S O U R C E S

- Aspinwall, J., M. Todd, and R. Burke. *The PC Users Survival Guide*. Redwood City, CA: M & T Publishing, 1989.

  In the computer industry, "trade" books are those sold in bookstores and aimed at the general public. Trade books generally have a relatively short life span because they focus on specific computer models or software packages that are frequently updated. Published in 1989, the *PC Users Survival Guide* might be considered an "old" book by these standards, but it contains much useful information about managing the files on your hard disk as well as a collection of tips that will help you use your computer more effectively.

- Gookin, D. *Hard Disk Management with DOS*. Blue Ridge Summit, PA: Tab Books, 1990.

  Tab Books is one of the more prolific computer trade book publishers and *Hard Disk Management with DOS,* now in its second edition, is one of their classics. Although this book is aimed at DOS users, rather than those who use Windows, the concepts and tips apply to both operating systems.

- *Understanding Computers: Memory and Storage*. Alexandria, VA: Time-Life Books, 1987.

  Time-Life Books has produced a lavishly illustrated series of books on computers that provide substantial technical detail in an easy-to-understand format. One of the books in this series, *Memory and Storage*, contains an excellent section on storage devices: how they were developed and how they work.

When you have finished this chapter you should be able to answer the following questions:

- What components are on the main circuit board of a microcomputer?

- What is a microprocessor and how does it perform the instructions contained in a computer program?

- What is a computer bus and what does it do?

- What makes some microprocessors faster than others?

- What is the difference between RAM and ROM?

- Why does a computer go through the boot process every time you turn on the power?

- What components are necessary to connect a peripheral device to a computer?

COMPUTER ARCHITECTURE

R eaders of the April 1985 issue of *Scientific American* were somewhat surprised by an article about a group of archaeologists who had discovered an ancient computer constructed out of ropes and pulleys. According to the article, "archaeologists have discovered the rotting remnants of an ingenious arrangement of ropes and pulleys thought to be the first working digital computer ever constructed." The article explained in some detail how the people of an ancient culture, known as the Apraphulians, built complex devices of ropes and pulleys, housed these devices in huge black wooden boxes, and used them to perform complex mathematical computations. Some of the devices were so colossal that elephants were harnessed to pull the enormous ropes through the pulley system.

A computer constructed of ropes and pulleys? As you might have guessed, this was an April Fools' article. And yet, such a device, if it were constructed, could accurately be called a digital computer. The fact that you could build a computer out of ropes and pulleys reinforces the notion that a computer is, in many respects, a very simple device. In this chapter, we'll take a more detailed look inside the box of a modern microcomputer system. Once you understand how a computer works, you will have more success troubleshooting problems you encounter, you will understand how to expand your computer system, and you will be better equipped to understand much of the jargon you read in computer ads.

Digital Electronics

Computer architecture refers to the design and construction of a computer system. The architecture of any computer can be broadly classified by considering two characteristics: what the computer uses for power, and how the computer physically represents, processes, and moves data. The Apraphulian computer was powered by elephants but used ropes and pulleys to perform calculations. Using elephants as the source of power to operate a computer seems a bit outlandish, even though in theory it might be possible. Electricity seems a much more reasonable power source, but it is not the only potential power source for a computer. One of the first computer designs specified steam, rather than electricity, as the power source.

Sometime between 1820 and 1822, according to computer chronicler Joel Shurkin, a mathematician named Charles Babbage and an astronomer named John Herschel were checking a complex table of calculations and found many errors. Exasperated by the errors, Babbage wondered if the calculations could be performed by a device powered by a steam engine—state-of-the-art technology at the time. Herschel thought it would be possible to build such as device. By 1822, Babbage had sketched out plans for what he called a "difference engine," a steam-powered device that would perform calculations by using a complex array of interlocking gear wheels, similar to those in a Swiss watch.

Although Babbage started construction on the difference engine, he was not able to complete it, because he could not obtain gears and other parts with enough precision to accurately perform complex calculations. We can only speculate how history might have changed if Babbage had been successful—such a technological tool might have guaranteed England's preeminence as a world power well into the twenty-first century.

Most modern computers are electronic devices, that is, they are powered by electricity. Further, a modern computer uses electrical signals and circuits to represent, process, and move data. Computer designers have a choice of two methods to represent, process, and move electronic data: they can build a digital device or an analog device.

A **digital device** works with discrete numbers or digits, such as 0 and 1. An **analog device**, on the other hand, operates on continuously varying data. For example, a digital watch displays the time 12:20 for an entire minute before switching to 12:21—the 0 changes to a 1 without intermediate steps. An analog watch, on the other hand, positions its hands to show you that it is 12:01, but then moves the minute hand very slowly through the space between the minute marks. Figure 4-1 illustrates the difference between analog and digital devices.

An electronic computer represents data using electricity. How does a computer store or manipulate, say, the number 5 or the number 10? In an analog computer, the number 5 might be represented by .05 volts and the number 10 by .1 volt. In a digital computer, numbers are represented by a code and converted into electrical signals. Similar to the way that Morse code uses dashes and dots to represent letters, a digital computer represents numbers, letters, and symbols with a code that uses a series of zeros and ones. A digital computer represents the number 1 with the code 00000001. The letter A could be represented with the code 01000001. Why zeros and ones? A digital computer is an electronic device, and electricity can be

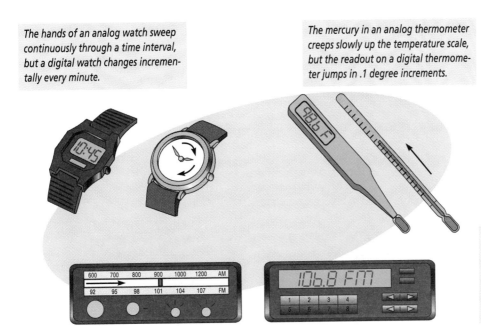

Figure 4-1
Analog and digital devices

The hands of an analog watch sweep continuously through a time interval, but a digital watch changes incrementally every minute.

The mercury in an analog thermometer creeps slowly up the temperature scale, but the readout on a digital thermometer jumps in .1 degree increments.

The dial on an analog radio tuner sweeps through a continuous range of stations, but a digital tuner jumps from one exact broadcast frequency to another.

on or off. Data that is represented by a series of ones and zeros can easily be moved or stored electronically as a series of "ons" and "offs." Each one or zero that represents data is referred to as a **bit**. Most computer coding schemes use eight bits to represent a number, a letter, or a symbol. One popular coding scheme represents the letter "A" with the code 01000001—a string of eight bits. A **byte** contains eight bits, so the string of bits that represents the letter "A" is referred to as a byte. You will learn more details about coding schemes in Chapter 5. What you need to understand for this chapter is that numbers, letters, and symbols are represented by a series of ones and zeros called bits. Figure 4-2 summarizes what you need to know about bits and bytes.

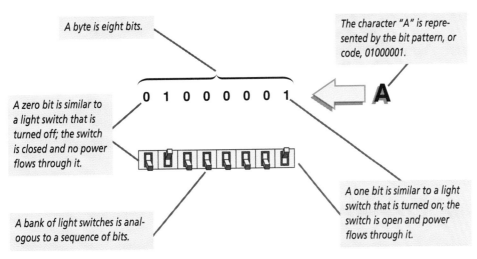

Figure 4-2
Bits and bytes

A byte is eight bits.

The character "A" is represented by the bit pattern, or code, 01000001.

A zero bit is similar to a light switch that is turned off; the switch is closed and no power flows through it.

A one bit is similar to a light switch that is turned on; the switch is open and power flows through it.

A bank of light switches is analogous to a sequence of bits.

The Main Board

The electrical components that represent, process, and move bits are housed on a circuit board called the **main board** or **motherboard**. Figure 4-3 shows the components of a typical microcomputer main board.

Figure 4-3

Microcomputer main circuit board

The main board, or motherboard, is a circuit board that contains the basic circuitry and components of a computer.

You can use an expansion slot to expand your system. The slot can hold an expansion card containing a serial port, a parallel port, a modem, a disk drive, a controller, or a video display adapter.

RAM (Random Access Memory) modules, such as these SIMMs, temporarily hold data that is waiting to be processed. The data in RAM might originate as input from the keyboard, as a copy of data that is stored on a disk, or as the result of an operation performed by the microprocessor.

A bus transports the electrical signals that represent data.

The microprocessor contains the circuitry that performs arithmetic and logic operations.

ROM (Read Only Memory) chips contain the programs that start the computer, run system diagnostics, and control low-level input and output activities.

The main board contains **integrated circuits**, sometimes called **chips**, that store or process data. If you refer back to Figure 4-3, you will see many black rectangular chips. Data moves from one chip to another along a circuit called a bus. Typically, data is moved to the main board from an input or storage device. The data is stored temporarily in the random access memory where it waits to be processed. To be processed, the data travels along a data bus to the processor. Results of the processing travel back to the random access memory, where they are temporarily stored until they are moved to an output or storage device. Let's take a closer look at the function of each of these components.

Bus

A **bus** is an electronic path that connects the main board components. The term "bus" fairly accurately describes its function. Picture a school bus that goes to a neighborhood and picks up a load of children, drops them off at school, then goes to the next neighborhood on its route to pick up a second bus load. After school, the bus transports loads of children home. Similarly, a computer bus "picks up" a load of bits that represent data from one of the components on the main board, then transfers these bits to another main board component. After dropping off this load of bits, the bus collects another load. As with the school bus that transports children to and from school, the computer bus transports bits both to and from main board components. Further, a school bus with more seats can haul more children in each load. The capacity of a computer bus depends on the number of data lines it contains—a bus with 8 lines can transport 8 bits at a time, whereas a bus with 16 lines can transport 16 bits at a time. Figure 4-4 on the following page illustrates the bus analogy and introduces the different bus types used in microcomputers.

A **system bus** transports data between the processor and other components in the system such as memory, the hard disk drive, or the video display. The system bus contains address lines and data lines. The **address lines** carry the location of data—usually a location in memory. The **data lines**, also called the **data bus**, transport the bits that represent data between the processor and other components. A computer with eight data lines has an 8-bit bus, meaning it transports 8 bits at a time. The original IBM PC had an 8-bit bus. Newer computers generally have a 16-bit or a 32-bit bus.

Figure 4-4
How a bus works

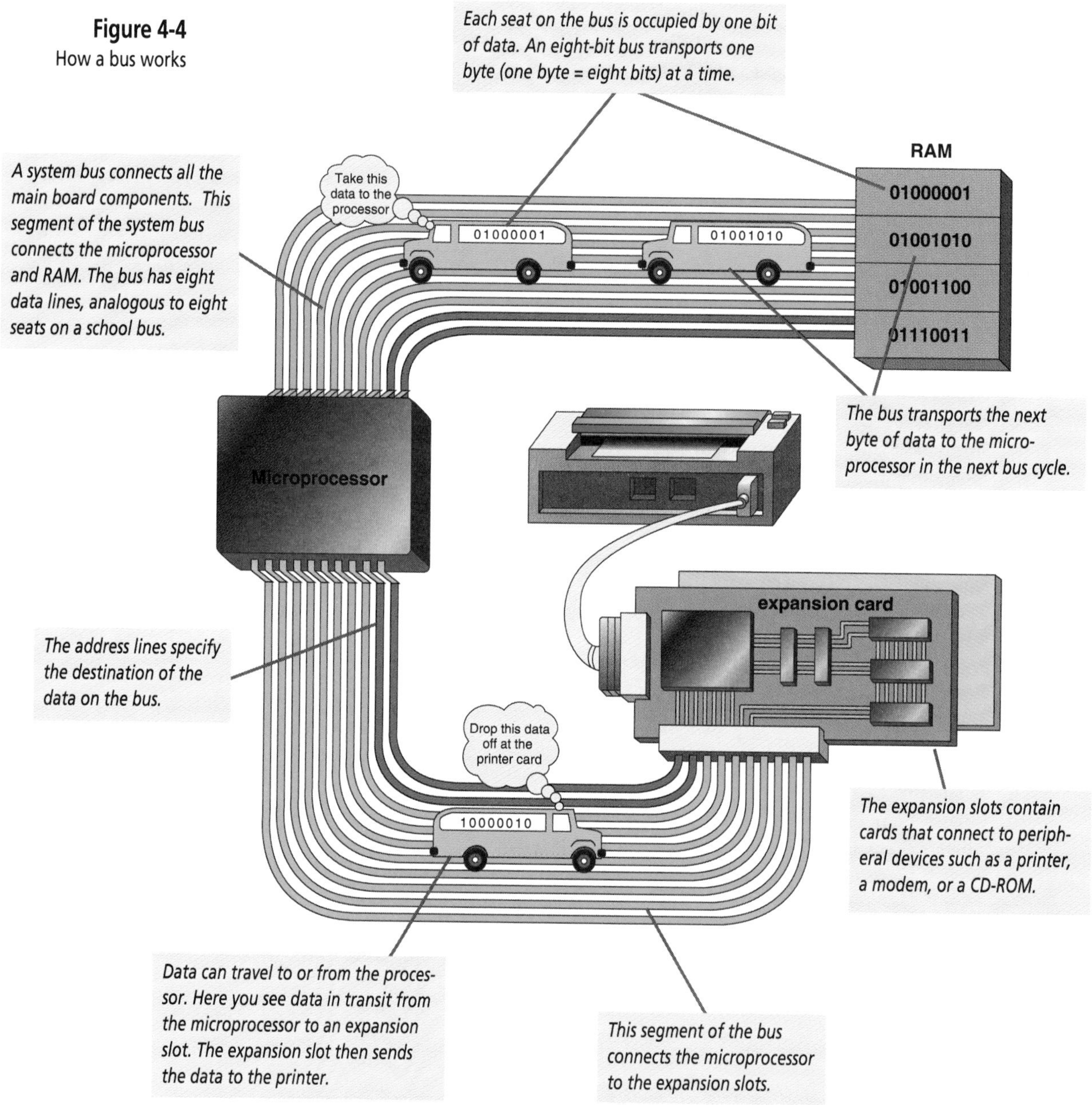

Each seat on the bus is occupied by one bit of data. An eight-bit bus transports one byte (one byte = eight bits) at a time.

A system bus connects all the main board components. This segment of the system bus connects the microprocessor and RAM. The bus has eight data lines, analogous to eight seats on a school bus.

Take this data to the processor

01000001

01001010

RAM

01000001

01001010

01001100

01110011

The bus transports the next byte of data to the micro-processor in the next bus cycle.

Microprocessor

The address lines specify the destination of the data on the bus.

Drop this data off at the printer card

10000010

expansion card

The expansion slots contain cards that connect to periph-eral devices such as a printer, a modem, or a CD-ROM.

Data can travel to or from the proces-sor. Here you see data in transit from the microprocessor to an expansion slot. The expansion slot then sends the data to the printer.

This segment of the bus connects the microprocessor to the expansion slots.

Memory

Memory is electronic circuitry that holds data and program instructions until it is their turn to be processed. A bus connects memory directly to the microprocessor. Memory is sometimes called "primary storage," but this term is easily confused with disk storage. It is preferable to use the term "memory" to refer to the circuitry that has a direct link to the processor and to use the term "storage" to refer to media, such as disks, that are not directly linked to the processor.

There are three major types of memory: random access memory, CMOS memory, and read only memory. Each type of memory is characterized by the kind of data it contains and the method it uses to maintain data.

Random Access Memory

Random Access Memory, or **RAM**, is a temporary holding area for data before and after it is processed. RAM is composed of thousands of circuits that each hold one bit of data. Although each circuit holds one bit, the smallest unit of data that a computer can access from RAM is a byte. You can think of RAM as thousands of miniature light bulbs, and each light bulb is controlled by a switch. The lights are arranged in banks of eight. The computer turns individual switches on or off in each bank to make patterns that represent numbers, letters, and symbols, as shown in Figure 4-5.

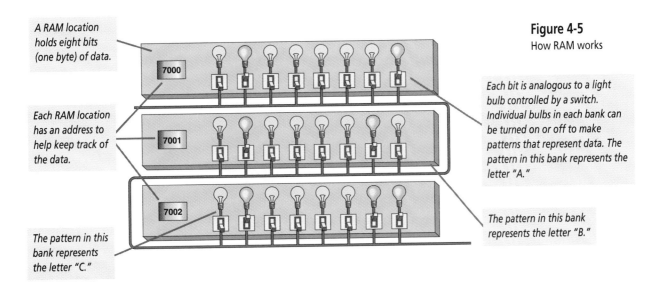

A RAM location holds eight bits (one byte) of data.

Each RAM location has an address to help keep track of the data.

The pattern in this bank represents the letter "C."

Figure 4-5
How RAM works

Each bit is analogous to a light bulb controlled by a switch. Individual bulbs in each bank can be turned on or off to make patterns that represent data. The pattern in this bank represents the letter "A."

The pattern in this bank represents the letter "B."

Each bank of eight RAM circuits has an address so the computer can locate the data each bank contains. Usually, RAM addresses are numbered using the hexadecimal number system, or base 16, in which you count 0, 1, 2, 3, 4, 5, 6, 7, 8, 9, A, B, C, D, E, F. However, in this chapter we will use decimal addresses so you don't have to deal with hexadecimal arithmetic.

The computer loads data into RAM locations, copies data from RAM locations to the processor, and copies data from the processor to RAM locations. If a RAM location contains data, and the computer places some other data in that location, the original data is replaced. Because the contents of RAM can change, it is a reusable resource. Just as you can use a chalkboard to write mathematical formulas, erase them, and then write an outline for a report, RAM can hold a series of numbers for spreadsheet calculations, then hold the text of your English essay when you use a word processor.

RAM plays a crucial role in the operation of a computer because it stores operating system instructions, program instructions, and user data. Every time you turn on your computer, a set of operating system instructions is copied from disk into RAM. These instructions, which help control basic computer functions, remain in RAM until you turn the computer off. RAM also holds program instructions. When you use a word processing program, the instructions that turn your computer into a word processor are copied from the disk into RAM. Finally, RAM holds data. When you type a document, each letter you type is held in RAM until you save it on a disk. Figure 4-6 illustrates the contents of RAM when you use a DOS word processor.

Figure 4-6
Memory contents

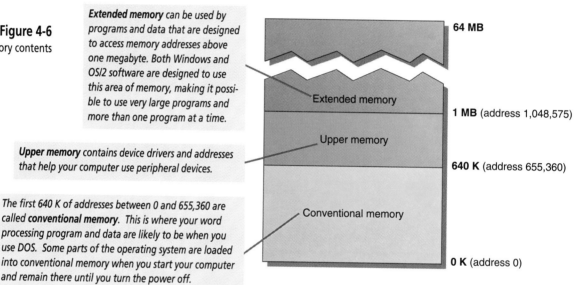

Extended memory can be used by programs and data that are designed to access memory addresses above one megabyte. Both Windows and OS/2 software are designed to use this area of memory, making it possible to use very large programs and more than one program at a time.

Upper memory contains device drivers and addresses that help your computer use peripheral devices.

The first 640 K of addresses between 0 and 655,360 are called *conventional memory*. This is where your word processing program and data are likely to be when you use DOS. Some parts of the operating system are loaded into conventional memory when you start your computer and remain there until you turn the power off.

The operating system instructions, program instructions, and data held in RAM are immediately available to the processor because the processor and RAM are linked directly by a bus. The processor continuously gets instructions from RAM, uses the data in RAM for processing, and sends the results of processing back to RAM. As you can imagine, the bus between the processor and RAM is busy.

The number of address lines in the system bus determines the amount of memory the processor can address. A processor with a 16-bit address bus can address only 64 kilobytes of memory. The 8088 processor used in the original IBM PC had a 20-bit address bus, which allowed this processor to access up to 1 megabyte of memory. A processor with a 32-bit address bus can address up to 4 gigabytes of memory.

Unlike hard disk or floppy disk storage, most RAM is **volatile**, that is, it holds data only as long as the computer power is on. If the computer is turned off or the power goes out, all data stored in RAM instantly and permanently disappears. Using our light bulb analogy, the pattern formed by a string of lights would be instantly extinguished if the power was turned off. When someone unhappily says, "I have lost all my data!" it often means that the person was entering data for a document or worksheet, and the power went out before the data was saved on disk.

RAM Capacity

The storage capacity of RAM is measured in bytes or megabytes. Microcomputers typically have between 4 and 16 megabytes of RAM, which means RAM can hold between 4 and 16 million bytes of data. With older computers that use the DOS operating system, you might occasionally get the message "out of memory" when you try to run a program. This message means that RAM doesn't have enough memory locations available to hold all the program instructions. With newer computers that use the Windows operating system, this problem rarely occurs because the computer can access significantly more memory.

RAM Technology

RAM is manufactured as chips or circuit boards called **memory modules**. If you have ever looked at the main board inside a computer, you have probably seen memory modules like those shown in Figure 4-7.

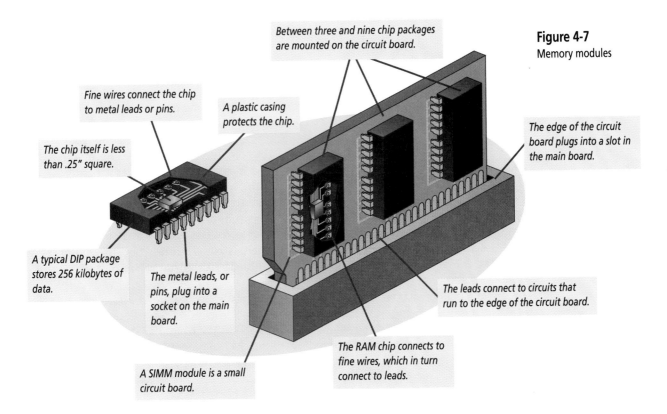

Between three and nine chip packages are mounted on the circuit board.

Fine wires connect the chip to metal leads or pins.

A plastic casing protects the chip.

The chip itself is less than .25" square.

The edge of the circuit board plugs into a slot in the main board.

A typical DIP package stores 256 kilobytes of data.

The metal leads, or pins, plug into a socket on the main board.

The leads connect to circuits that run to the edge of the circuit board.

A SIMM module is a small circuit board.

The RAM chip connects to fine wires, which in turn connect to leads.

Figure 4-7
Memory modules

A **DIP package** (Dual In-line Pin) houses a RAM chip in a rectangular case with a row of legs or "pins" along each of the long sides, as you saw in Figure 4-7. A typical DIP package holds 256 kilobytes of data. Four of these DIP packages would be required for 1 megabyte of RAM, 16 required for 4 megabytes, and 64 required for 16 megabytes. Because the typical RAM capacity of today's microcomputers is between 4 and 16 megabytes, the amount of main board space required for DIP packages would be quite large. For this reason, DIP packages are rarely used for general purpose memory in the current generation of microcomputers.

Instead of DIP packages, today's computers use SIMMs. A **SIMM** (Single In-line Memory Module), like the one shown in Figure 4-7, is a small circuit board that contains RAM chips. SIMMs are very common today because they provide large memory capacity but require very little space. SIMMs are available with different capacities: 256 kilobytes, 1 megabyte, or 4 megabytes.

SIMMs are available in several configurations. Apple Macintosh computers generally use 8-bit SIMMs, IBM-compatible computers use 9-bit SIMMs, and IBM PS/2 computers use 36-bit SIMMs. SIMMs are also available in a variety of speeds. Some computers require faster memory, and, as you might expect, faster memory is more expensive than slower memory.

Some application software might require more RAM than your computer has. You can expand the RAM capacity of your computer up to the limit set by the computer manufacturer. When you purchase additional memory for a computer system, you must make sure that the memory modules you purchase are the correct type, configuration, and speed for your computer system. The technical reference manual for your computer should contain the information you need to purchase the right memory modules.

CMOS Memory

CMOS (Complementary Metal Oxide Semiconductor) memory holds data, but requires very little power to retain its contents. Because of its low power requirements, a CMOS chip is usually powered by battery. CMOS stores vital data about your computer system configuration, even when your computer is turned off. Have you ever wondered how your computer "knows" how many floppy disk drives it has, or how it "remembers" the size of your hard disk? This information is not permanently stored or "built into" your computer, because that would make it impossible to add a disk drive or replace your hard drive with a larger one. The part of your computer that retains data about the configuration of your computer is the CMOS memory. And because battery-powered CMOS memory chips retain data when the main computer power is off, the computer "remembers" its configuration between computing sessions.

If you change your system configuration, you must also change the data in the CMOS memory. To change the CMOS data, you usually run a CMOS configuration, or setup, program by pressing a special key combination as the computer starts up. The reference manual for your computer indicates what key combination starts the setup program. The setup program allows you to change the CMOS data and save the changes in CMOS memory.

Read Only Memory

Read Only Memory, or **ROM**, is a set of chips that contains instructions to help a computer prepare for processing tasks. The instructions in ROM are permanent, and you have no way to change them, short of removing the ROM chips from the main board and replacing them with another set. You might wonder why the computer includes chips with programs permanently stored in them. Why not use the more versatile RAM?

The answer to this question is that when you turn on your computer, the processor receives electrical power and is ready to begin executing instructions. But because the computer was just turned on, RAM is empty—it doesn't contain any instructions for the processor to execute. Even though programs are available on the hard disk, the processor doesn't have any instructions to tell it how to access the hard drive and load a program.

This is when ROM plays its part. ROM contains a small set of instructions to access the disk drives and look for a more extensive program that contains the computer's operating system. When you turn on your computer, the processor performs a series of steps by following the instructions stored in ROM. This series of steps is called the "boot process." We'll look at more details about the boot process later in the chapter after you've learned more about the processor and how it works.

Processors

The Apraphulians rigged ropes and pulleys to perform arithmetic and logical operations. Charles Babbage envisioned a complex mechanism of interlocking gears. The processor of a modern computer uses microscopic electronic circuitry. Regardless of the architecture, each circuit is very simple, so each operation a computer performs is very simple.

A computer accomplishes a complex task by performing a series of very simple operations or instructions. An **instruction** tells the computer to perform a specific operation such as adding two numbers together, comparing one number to another number, or moving a number to a specific memory location. An instruction has two parts: the op code and the parameters. The **op code**, or operation code, is a command word for an arithmetic or logical operation. The **parameters** for an instruction specify the data or the address of the data for the operation. For example, in the instruction JMP 5003, the op code is JMP and the parameter is 5003. The op code JMP means "jump" or go to a different instruction. The parameter 5003 is the RAM address of the instruction to which the computer is supposed to go. Although the instruction JMP 5003 has only one parameter, some other instructions, such as ADD, can have more than one parameter.

The instructions that a processor can perform are known as its **instruction set**. As you look at the list of instructions in Figure 4-8 on the following page, consider the difficulty you'd have trying to use this set of instructions to tell the computer to balance your checkbook.

Figure 4-8
A sample
microcomputer
instruction set

OP CODE	OPERATION
MOV	Move data between memory and the microprocessor
STO	Store data to a particular memory address
ADD	Add two numbers together
SUB	Subtract one number from another
MUL	Multiply two numbers
DIV	Divide two numbers
INC	Increment a number by adding 1
DEC	Decrement a number by subtracting 1
CMP	Compare two bytes to see if they are the same
CPZ	Check if a number is equal to zero
JMP	Jump to the memory address that contains a different instruction
JPZ	Jump if a number is zero
HLT	Halt

The **processor**, or **CPU** (central processing unit), executes instructions that it gets from RAM. Within the processor, the ALU and the control unit work together to carry out each instruction. In Figure 4-9 you can see a conceptual diagram of the ALU and control unit, as well as the instructions and data in RAM.

Figure 4-9
Control unit, ALU,
and RAM

This area of RAM contains a list of instructions. The first instruction, MOV REG1 6000, is contained in RAM addresses 5000, 5001, and 5002.

The CPU contains the control unit and the ALU. The control unit holds the instruction that is being executed. The ALU performs arithmetic and logical operations.

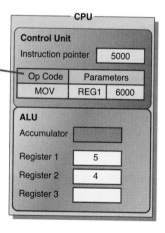

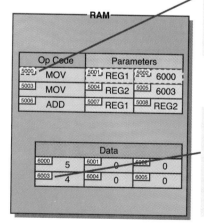

This area of RAM holds data. Address 6000 contains the value 5, and address 6003 contains the value 4.

The **ALU** (arithmetic logic unit) performs arithmetic operations such as addition and subtraction. It also performs logical operations such as comparing two numbers to see if they are the same. The ALU uses **registers** as a sort of scratch pad for its computations. The registers hold the numbers that the ALU uses for computation. The results of a computation are placed in an accumulator, as shown in Figure 4-10.

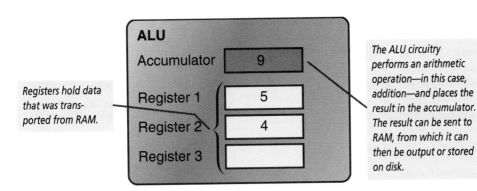

Figure 4-10
How the ALU works

Registers hold data that was transported from RAM.

The ALU circuitry performs an arithmetic operation—in this case, addition—and places the result in the accumulator. The result can be sent to RAM, from which it can then be output or stored on disk.

The processor's **control unit** directs and coordinates the operation of the entire computer system. The control unit gets or "fetches" an instruction from RAM and stores it in a special **instruction register**, as shown in Figure 4-11. The control unit then activates the circuits necessary to carry out the instruction. For example, if the instruction is "move the data from memory location 6000 to the ALU," the control unit fetches the data from RAM address 6000 and moves it to one of the ALU registers.

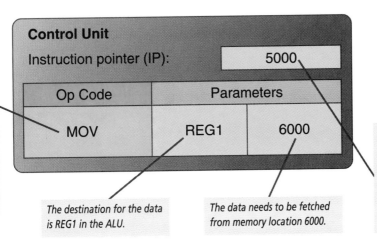

The Op Code, or operation code, for the instruction is a three-letter command word, encoded to fit into one byte. In this case, the command word is MOV, the command to move data between RAM and the microprocessor.

Figure 4-11
How the control unit works

The destination for the data is REG1 in the ALU.

The data needs to be fetched from memory location 6000.

The instruction pointer specifies an address in RAM that contains the first byte of the instruction to be executed. Each instruction is three bytes long and is stored in three consecutive memory locations.

The processor executes each instruction in two phases. During the **fetch phase**, the processor identifies the location of the next program instruction, fetches the instruction from memory, and loads it into the processor. During the **execution phase**, the processor executes the instruction by moving data from one memory location to another, then performing an arithmetic or logical operation. Together, the fetch phase and the execution phase are referred to as an **instruction execution cycle**. Study Figure 4-12 to understand the sequence of events in the instruction execution cycle.

Figure 4-12
The instruction execution cycle

CPU

Control Unit

Instruction pointer   5000

Op Code	Parameters	
MOV	REG1	6000

ALU

Accumulator

Register 1   5

Register 2

Register 3

RAM

Op Code	Parameters	
5000 MOV	5001 REG1	5002 6000
5003 MOV	5004 REG2	5005 6003
5006 ADD	5007 REG1	5008 REG2

Data		
6000 5	6001 0	6002 0
6003 4	6004 0	6005 0

1 At the beginning of the fetch phase, the instruction pointer indicates the beginning address of the next instruction to execute.

2 As the fetch phase continues, the processor fetches the program instruction from the specified memory address and loads it into the control unit.

3 During the execution phase, the instruction is executed. Here, data is moved from the RAM location specified by the instruction to a register in the ALU. The cycle begins again when the instruction pointer moves to the next instruction.

Microprocessors

L A B

COMPUTER ARCHITECTURE

In mainframe computers, the ALU and control unit circuitry exist on separate chips. In microcomputers and most minicomputers, a single chip, called a **microprocessor**, contains the circuitry for both the ALU and control unit. Since 1971, when Intel introduced the four-bit 4004 microprocessor, an explosion of research and development has spawned hundreds of new microprocessor models.

Microprocessors are usually identified by a model number, such as 4004, 6502, and 80286. Some of the longer names are abbreviated. For example, the 80286 is often referred to as the 286 (pronounced "two eighty-six"). Unfortunately, computer manufacturers have not emulated automakers' use of model names such as Electra, Regal, and Blazer, although it might make it easier to keep track of microprocessor development.

To give you some historical background on the use of the earliest microprocessor models, the Apple II computer used MOS Technology's 6502 (pronounced "sixty-five oh two") microprocessor. The original IBM PC used Intel's 8088 (pronounced "eighty eighty-eight") microprocessor, and early models of the Apple Macintosh used Motorola's 68000 (pronounced "sixty-eight thousand") microprocessor.

Today, microcomputer buyers face the difficult task of comparing systems based on many different microprocessor models. What makes one microprocessor faster than another? Is a 40 MHz 80486SX better than a 33 MHz 80486DX? How do you know? How would you decide, for example, which microprocessor should be in a computer you buy? Let's take a look at the characteristics that affect microprocessor performance: clock rate, word size, data bus width, math coprocessor, cache memory, and instruction set.

Clock Rate

A computer contains a **master clock** that emits pulses to establish the timing for all system operations. To understand how this works, think about a team of oarsmen on a Viking ship. The ship's coxswain beats on a drum to coordinate the rowers. A computer's master clock and a ship's coxswain accomplish essentially the same task— they set the pace of activity.

The **clock rate** set by the master clock determines the speed at which the microprocessor can execute an instruction and, therefore, limits the number of instructions the microprocessor can complete within a specific amount of time. The speed at which a microprocessor completes an instruction execution cycle is measured in **Megahertz** (MHz), or millions of cycles per second. Although some instructions require multiple cycles to complete, you can think of microprocessor speed as the number of instructions the microprocessor can execute in one second. The microprocessor in the original IBM PC executed 4.77 million instructions per second. Less than fifteen years later, microprocessor speeds exceeded 50 million instructions per second. If all other microprocessor specifications are identical, higher Megahertz ratings mean faster processing.

Word Size

Word size refers to the number of bits the microprocessor can manipulate at one time. A microprocessor with an 8-bit word size, referred to as an **8-bit microprocessor**, manipulates 8 bits at a time. A 16-bit microprocessor manipulates 16 bits at a time, a 32-bit microprocessor manipulates 32 bits, and so on. A microprocessor with a large word size can process more data in each instruction cycle and generally operates more quickly than a microprocessor with a small word size. Most of the early microcomputers used 8-bit or 16-bit microprocessors. Most microcomputers sold today use 32-bit or 64-bit microprocessors.

Data Bus Width

The width of a computer's data bus affects the ability of the microprocessor to move data between the microprocessor and memory. In many microprocessors, the data bus is the same size as the word size. For example, a 32-bit microprocessor with a 32-bit data bus moves an entire 32-bit word into the microprocessor in one operation. A 32-bit microprocessor with a 16-bit bus requires two operations to move the full 32-bit word into the microprocessor, as shown in Figure 4-13.

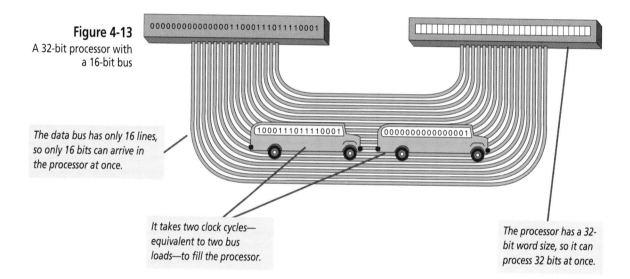

Figure 4-13
A 32-bit processor with a 16-bit bus

The data bus has only 16 lines, so only 16 bits can arrive in the processor at once.

It takes two clock cycles—equivalent to two bus loads—to fill the processor.

The processor has a 32-bit word size, so it can process 32 bits at once.

Data bus width is the primary difference between the Intel 80386DX and 80386SX microprocessors. The 80386DX has a 32-bit word size and a 32-bit data bus. The 80386SX also has a 32-bit word size, but only a 16-bit data bus. The 80386SX requires two operations to move a 32-bit word in or out of the microprocessor. This makes the less expensive 80386SX significantly slower than the 80386DX, even though they run at the same clock speed.

Math Coprocessor

A **math coprocessor** contains special circuitry to perform complex arithmetic operations much faster than the microprocessor's ALU. Math coprocessors have an extended instruction set that includes instructions not available to the main microprocessor. A math coprocessor enhances system performance when you use software written to take advantage of the coprocessor instruction set. Computation-intensive activities, such as calculating large worksheets or generating statistics for large databases, are finished faster if you have a math coprocessor and use software that takes advantage of it. However, a math coprocessor does not increase the performance of programs that use only the basic instruction set. If your computer does not have a math coprocessor, you can add one if the main board of your computer has an empty coprocessor socket. If your computer has a math coprocessor socket, it should be located next to the microprocessor. The documentation for your computer indicates whether your computer has a coprocessor socket.

A math coprocessor is not needed if your computer's microprocessor already contains an enhanced math instruction set. The enhanced math instruction set is built into the Intel 80486DX and newer Pentium microprocessors, so it is not necessary to add a math coprocessor to a computer that contains one of these microprocessors.

Cache Memory

Another factor that affects the performance of a microprocessor is cache memory. A high-speed microprocessor such as the 80486DX can process data so quickly that it often waits for data to be delivered from RAM, and this slows processing. **Cache memory**, sometimes simply called "cache" (pronounced "cash"), is special high-speed memory that gives the microprocessor more rapid access to data. As you begin a task, the computer anticipates what data you are likely to need for this task and loads or "caches" this data into cache memory. Then, when an instruction calls for data, the microprocessor first checks to see if the required data is in the cache. If the required data is there, the microprocessor takes the data from the cache, instead of fetching it from the slower RAM.

Cache memory can be built into the microprocessor chip or located elsewhere on the main board. The 80486DX microprocessor includes an 8-kilobyte cache in the microprocessor chip. An additional 256-kilobyte cache, typically located on the main board, further enhances the performance of this microprocessor.

Instruction Set

The microprocessor of a **Complex Instruction Set Computer**, or **CISC**, has a large instruction set with hundreds of instructions. John Cocke, an IBM research scientist, discovered that most of the work done by a microprocessor requires only a small subset of the available instruction set. Further research showed that only 20 percent of the instructions of a CISC computer do about 80 percent of the work. Cocke's research resulted in the development of microprocessors with streamlined instruction sets, called RISC machines.

The microprocessor of a **Reduced Instruction Set Computer**, or **RISC**, has a limited set of instructions that it can perform very quickly. Apple, IBM, and DEC have recently released microcomputers based on RISC microprocessors.

Most current microcomputers are based on either the Intel 80x86 or Motorola 680x0 family of microprocessors. Figure 4-14 lists the Intel family of microprocessors used in most IBM-compatible computers and the factors affecting their performance. Figure 4-15 lists the Motorola family of microprocessors used in most Apple Macintosh computers. Can you see any significant differences in microprocessor capability?

Figure 4-14
The Intel family of microprocessors

NAME	CLOCK SPEED	WORD SIZE	DATA BUS SIZE	MATH COPROCESSOR	CACHE
8088	4.77 MHz	16 bits	8 bits	external	none
8086	4.77-8 MHz	16 bits	16 bits	external	none
80286	8-20 MHz	16 bits	16 bits	external	none
80386SX	16-33 MHz	32 bits	16 bits	external	none
80386DX	16-40 MHz	32 bits	32 bits	external	none
80486SX	20-33 MHz	32 bits	32 bits	external	none
80486DX	33-66 MHz	32 bits	32 bits	built-in	8 K
Pentium	60-100 MHz	64 bits	64 bits	built-in	16 K

Figure 4-15
The Motorola family of microprocessors

NAME	CLOCK SPEED	WORD SIZE	DATA BUS SIZE	MATH COPROCESSOR	CACHE
68000	8-12.5 MHz	32 bits	16 bits	none	none
68020	16.67-33.33 MHz	32 bits	32 bits	external	256 bytes
68030	20-50 MHz	32 bits	32 bits	external	512 bytes
68040	25 MHz	32 bits	32 bits	built-in	8 K
68060	50-66 MHz	32 bits	32 bits	built-in	16 K

RISC microprocessors, such as those used in the Apple and IBM PowerPC computers, offer enhanced performance when running programs specifically written for the PowerPC processor. PowerPC systems must use emulation software to run programs written for the Apple Macintosh, DOS, and Windows. The use of emulation software means PowerPC computers generally run Macintosh, DOS, and Windows software somewhat slower than computers based on the fastest Intel or Motorola microprocessors.

The Boot Process

Now that you have an understanding about how RAM, ROM, and microprocessors operate, let's take a look at how they all work together to prepare your computer for accepting commands each time you turn it on. As you learned earlier, one of the most important components of the computer—RAM—is volatile, so it cannot hold any data when the power is off. Therefore, when you switch on your computer, it does not "remember" many basic functions, such as how to deal with input and communicate output to the external world.

The sequence of events that occur between the time you turn on your computer and the time it is ready for you to issue commands is referred to as the **boot process**. During the boot process, the computer system runs a series of diagnostic tests, loads the operating system, performs customized start-up instructions, and finally is ready for you to use. If you understand the boot process and your computer fails to start when you turn it on, you should be able to determine the cause of the problem and either fix it or take appropriate action.

L A B

TROUBLE-SHOOTING

The details of the boot process might vary slightly from one computer to another, depending on the instructions contained in ROM. In general, the boot process follows these steps:

1. When you turn on the power switch, the power light is illuminated and power is distributed to the internal fan and main board.
2. The microprocessor begins to execute the instructions stored in ROM.
3. The computer performs diagnostic tests of crucial system components.
4. The operating system is copied from disk to RAM.
5. The microprocessor reads and stores configuration data.
6. The microprocessor executes any customized start-up routines specified by the user.
7. The system displays a prompt indicating it is ready to receive your commands.

Let's see what happens during each step of the boot process for a typical IBM-compatible computer and what you should do when the boot process doesn't proceed smoothly. Of course, even when you know how to troubleshoot computer problems, you should always follow the guidelines provided by your school or employer when you encounter equipment problems. As you continue reading this section about the boot process, use Figure 4-16 on the following page to help you visualize what's happening inside the computer.

Power Up

The first stage in the boot process is the power-up stage. The fan in the power supply begins to spin and the power light on the case of the computer comes on. If you turn on the computer and the power light does not come on, it means the system is not getting power. There are several things you can do to fix this problem. First, you can check the power cord at the back of the computer to make sure it is firmly plugged into the wall and into the system unit. If the plugs are in place, test the wall outlet by plugging in another electrical device, such as a lamp. If the wall outlet is supplying power, the power cord is plugged in, and the power light still does not come on, then the computer's power supply might have failed. If you encounter this problem, you need to contact a technical support person for assistance.

Figure 4-16
The boot process

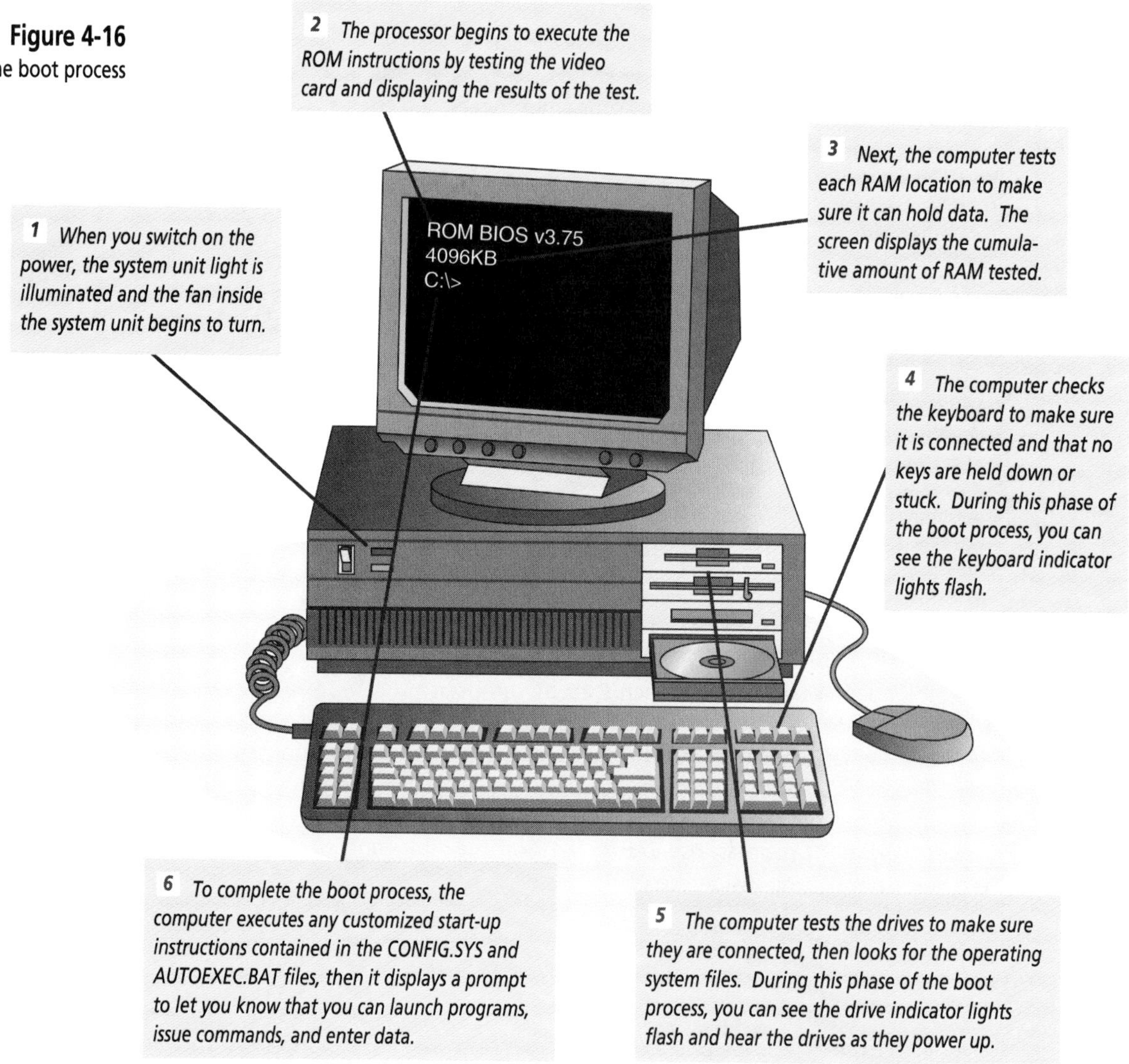

2 The processor begins to execute the ROM instructions by testing the video card and displaying the results of the test.

3 Next, the computer tests each RAM location to make sure it can hold data. The screen displays the cumulative amount of RAM tested.

1 When you switch on the power, the system unit light is illuminated and the fan inside the system unit begins to turn.

4 The computer checks the keyboard to make sure it is connected and that no keys are held down or stuck. During this phase of the boot process, you can see the keyboard indicator lights flash.

ROM BIOS v3.75
4096KB
C:\>

6 To complete the boot process, the computer executes any customized start-up instructions contained in the CONFIG.SYS and AUTOEXEC.BAT files, then it displays a prompt to let you know that you can launch programs, issue commands, and enter data.

5 The computer tests the drives to make sure they are connected, then looks for the operating system files. During this phase of the boot process, you can see the drive indicator lights flash and hear the drives as they power up.

Boot Program

When you turn on the computer, the microprocessor begins to execute the boot program stored in ROM. If the ROM chips, RAM modules, or microprocessor are malfunctioning, the microprocessor is unable to run the boot program and the computer stops or "hangs." You know you have a problem at this stage of the boot process if the power light is on and you can hear the fan, but there is no message on the screen and nothing else happens. This problem requires the assistance of a technical support person.

Diagnostic Tests

The next step in the boot process is the **POST**, or **Power On Self Test**, which diagnoses problems in the computer. The POST first checks the graphics card that connects your monitor to the computer. If the graphics card is working, a message such as "Video BIOS ver 2.1 1995" appears on the screen. Many computers beep a number of times if the graphics card fails the test. The number of beeps depends on the ROM used in your computer. If your computer beeps and does not display the graphics card message, the graphics card is probably malfunctioning. You should contact a technical support person to have the graphics card checked.

If the graphics card passes the diagnostic test, the computer tests RAM next. To make sure that all RAM locations function correctly, the microprocessor places data in each memory location, then retrieves that data to see if it is correct. As the computer tests each bank of RAM, the amount of memory tested so far is displayed on the screen. If any errors are encountered during the RAM test, the POST stops and displays a message that indicates a RAM problem.

The microprocessor then checks the keyboard. On most computers, you can see the keyboard indicator lights flash when the keyboard test is in progress. If the keyboard is not correctly attached or if a key is held down, the computer beeps and displays a keyboard error message. If a keyboard error occurs, you should turn the computer off and make sure that nothing is holding down a key on the keyboard. Next, unplug the keyboard, and carefully plug it back into the computer. Finally, turn on the computer again to repeat the boot process. If the problem recurs, you might need to have your keyboard repaired or replaced.

The next step in the boot process tests the drives. If you watch the hard disk drive and floppy disk drives during this test, you will see the drive activity lights flash on for a moment, and you will hear the drives power up. This test should only take a second or two to complete. If the computer pauses on this test, it is a signal that there might be a problem with one of your drives, which should be referred to a technical support person.

Load the Operating System

After successfully completing the POST, the computer continues to follow the instructions in ROM to load the operating system. The computer first checks drive A: to see if it contains a disk. If there is a disk in this drive, drive A: becomes the **default drive**—the drive the computer uses for the rest of the computing session unless you specify a different one. If there is no disk in drive A: but the computer has a drive C:, the computer uses drive C: as the default drive. If your computer has a hard disk, you generally want drive C: to be the default drive, so it is best not to put disks in any of the floppy-disk drives until the boot process is complete. Otherwise, the computer recognizes the floppy-disk drive as the default.

Next, the computer tries to locate and load the operating system from the default drive. First, the computer looks for two operating system files: IO.SYS and MSDOS.SYS. If these files do not exist on the disk, the boot process stops and the message "Non-system disk or disk error" or "Cannot load a file" appears on the screen. If you see this message, there is probably a disk in drive A: that doesn't belong there—remember that you want your computer to use drive C: as the default. Remove the disk from drive A: so your computer can locate MSDOS.SYS and IO.SYS on the hard drive.

The microprocessor next attempts to load another operating system file, COMMAND.COM. There are two problems you could encounter at this stage of the boot process, and both problems have the same error message: "Bad or missing command interpreter." First, the file COMMAND.COM might be missing because someone inadvertently erased it. Second, your disk might contain the wrong version of COMMAND.COM because someone inadvertently copied a different version onto the computer. If you encounter either problem, you should turn off the computer and make sure drive A: is empty, then turn the computer on again. If the "Bad or missing command interpreter" message appears when you turn the computer on again, you should turn the computer off, then find a bootable floppy disk. A **bootable floppy disk**, such as the one that came with the computer, contains operating system files. Put this floppy disk in drive A: and turn on the computer again. Even if you are successful using a floppy disk to boot your system, you need to correct the COMMAND.COM problem on your hard disk. A technical support person or experienced user can help you do this.

Check Configuration Data

In the next stage of the boot process, the computer searches the root directory of the boot disk for a file called CONFIG.SYS. **CONFIG.SYS** contains information that modifies or configures the operating system. The CONFIG.SYS file contains user-modifiable commands that customize your computing environment. For example, you can use the CONFIG.SYS file to specify the number of files that can be open simultaneously. You can also specify the device drivers required to use your sound card, tape backup drive, or CD-ROM drive. If your computer has a CONFIG.SYS file, its commands are executed in this phase of the boot process. If there is no CONFIG.SYS file, the microprocessor continues with the normal boot process.

Next, the computer searches the root directory of the default drive for a file called AUTOEXEC.BAT. Like the CONFIG.SYS file, **AUTOEXEC.BAT** is user-modifiable and provides you with a way to customize your computing environment. AUTOEXEC.BAT might contain DOS commands or the names of programs that you want the computer to execute every time you turn it on. If your system has an AUTOEXEC.BAT file, the computer performs the instructions it contains at the end of the boot process.

Display the Operating System Prompt

The boot process is complete when the computer is ready to accept your commands. Usually the computer displays the operating system prompt at the end of the boot process. On an IBM-compatible computer with drive C: as the default, the operating system prompt is typically displayed as C:>. At this prompt, you can enter commands and launch programs. If your AUTOEXEC.BAT contains a command to launch a program, such as Windows, the boot process is essentially complete when the program is loaded into RAM and ready for use.

Expanding the System

The computer industry moves at an astonishing rate. Every week, industry magazines contain announcements for hundreds of new computer products designed to make computing faster and easier. When you purchase a computer, you can be fairly certain that before its useful life is over, you will want to add equipment to expand its capabilities. Today's microcomputers are designed for easy expansion. The main board contains an expansion bus, slots, and ports to which you can connect a vast array of peripheral devices. Figure 4-17 helps you visualize how the expansion bus, slots, and ports connect peripheral devices to a computer.

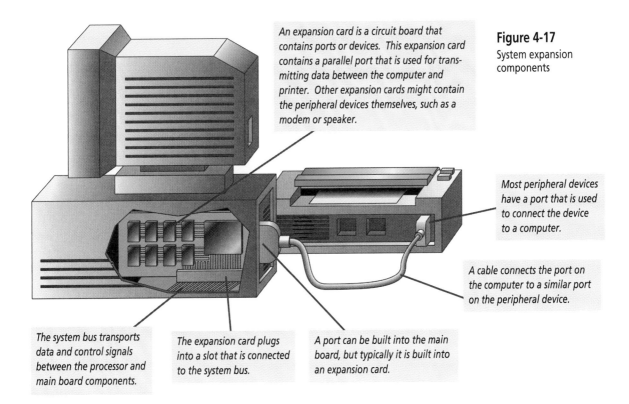

An expansion card is a circuit board that contains ports or devices. This expansion card contains a parallel port that is used for transmitting data between the computer and printer. Other expansion cards might contain the peripheral devices themselves, such as a modem or speaker.

Figure 4-17
System expansion components

Most peripheral devices have a port that is used to connect the device to a computer.

A cable connects the port on the computer to a similar port on the peripheral device.

The system bus transports data and control signals between the processor and main board components.

The expansion card plugs into a slot that is connected to the system bus.

A port can be built into the main board, but typically it is built into an expansion card.

Expansion Buses, Slots, and Cards

An **expansion bus** is a circuit that provides a path for data to travel between RAM and peripheral devices. The expansion bus connects RAM to a series of expansion slots.

An **expansion slot** is a socket into which you can plug a small circuit board called an **expansion card**. Most computers have from four to eight expansion slots, but usually some of these slots already contain expansion cards when you purchase the computer. The number of empty slots in your computer dictates its expandability.

Suppose that a few months after you purchase your computer, you decide you want to add sound capability. To find out if you have adequate expansion capability, turn your computer off, unplug it, then open the system unit case. If you have an empty expansion slot, like the one illustrated in Figure 4-18, you can insert an expansion card to add sound capability.

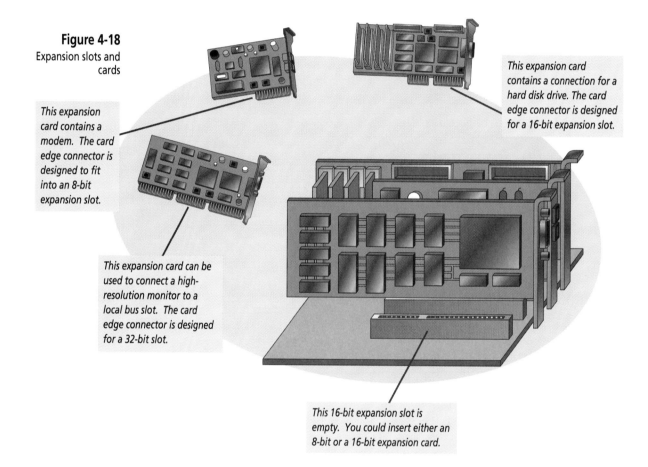

Figure 4-18
Expansion slots and cards

This expansion card contains a connection for a hard disk drive. The card edge connector is designed for a 16-bit expansion slot.

This expansion card contains a modem. The card edge connector is designed to fit into an 8-bit expansion slot.

This expansion card can be used to connect a high-resolution monitor to a local bus slot. The card edge connector is designed for a 32-bit slot.

This 16-bit expansion slot is empty. You could insert either an 8-bit or a 16-bit expansion card.

Some computers have more than one kind of expansion bus to further expand the number and type of expansion devices it can use. The types of expansion buses you might have in your computer include ISA (Industry Standard Architecture), EISA (Extended Industry Standard Architecture), VESA (Video Electronic Standards

Association), Micro Channel, and PCI (Peripheral Connect Interface). Expansion buses differ in the number of cycles they complete per second and the number of bits they transfer in each cycle. A slow bus, such as the XT bus, cycles 4.77 million times per second and carries 8 bits in each cycle. A faster bus, such as the EISA bus, cycles 8 million times per second and carries 32 bits in each cycle. Figure 4-19 shows the number of bits transferred in each cycle and the speed at which each cycle occurs for the expansion buses typically used in IBM-compatible computers.

BUS NAME	NUMBER OF BITS	SPEED
XT Bus	8 bits	4.77 MHz
ISA Bus	16 bits	8 MHz
EISA Bus	32 bits	6-8.33 MHz
Micro Channel Bus	16 or 32 bits	10 MHz
VESA Local Bus	32 bits	33-66 MHz
PCI Local Bus	32 or 64 bits	33 MHz

Figure 4-19
Microcomputer expansion buses

As with a data bus, optimal performance for an expansion bus is obtained when the expansion bus transports the same number of bits as the word size of the microprocessor, allowing an entire word to be transferred across the bus in a single operation. Recall from Figure 4-13 that if the expansion bus is narrower than the word size of the microprocessor, multiple cycles are required to transport each word.

Two special-purpose high-speed buses, the VESA Local Bus and the Intel PCI Local Bus, provide high-speed 32-bit connections that operate at the same speed as the microprocessor. Many computers provide from one to three local bus slots that can be used for video adapter cards and hard disk drive controller cards—both of which transport massive amounts of data.

PCMCIA Slots and Cards

The **PCMCIA slot** (Personal Computer Memory Card International Association) is a special type of expansion slot originally developed for use with notebook computers, which have little space in the case for regular slots and cards. A PCMCIA slot provides a small, external slot into which you can insert a PCMCIA card. PCMCIA cards are credit-card-sized circuit boards that incorporate an expansion card and a device. So, for example, some PCMCIA cards contain a modem, others contain memory expansion, and others contain a hard disk drive. Unlike traditional expansion cards, you can plug in and remove PCMCIA devices without turning the computer off, so you can switch from one PCMCIA device to another without disrupting your work. Figure 4-20 on the following page shows a PCMCIA slot and a PCMCIA card.

Figure 4-20
PCMCIA slots and cards

A PCMCIA card requires only a small slot and is an excellent way to add expansion capabilities to notebook computers.

You can insert a PCMCIA card into a slot without opening the computer case.

Floppy Disk and Hard Disk Controllers

The control circuitry for floppy disk drives and hard disk drives is sometimes incorporated into the circuitry of the main board, but more often, the drive control circuitry is housed on an expansion board called a **controller card**. The disk drive controller card usually contains circuitry to connect two hard drives and two floppy drives, as shown in Figure 4-21.

Cables run from the controllers to the floppy and hard disk drives. Most hard disk controllers are 16-bit devices with high-performance 32-bit EISA controllers, 32-bit Micro Channel controllers, VESA, and PCI Local Bus controllers available for use with particularly fast hard disk drives.

Video Display Adapters

A **video display adapter** contains the circuitry to support the display of text and graphics on the monitor. The video display adapter is sometimes built into the main board, but more typically it is a **graphics card**, or **video card**, like the one shown in Figure 4-22 on page NP 140.

Video cards connect to the expansion bus through 8-bit, 16-bit, or 32-bit connectors. The fastest video cards match the word size of the microprocessor, whether 16 or 32 bits, which allows the microprocessor to send an entire word to the video adapter in a single operation. High-speed video cards can move data between the microprocessor and the video card as fast as the microprocessor can process it.

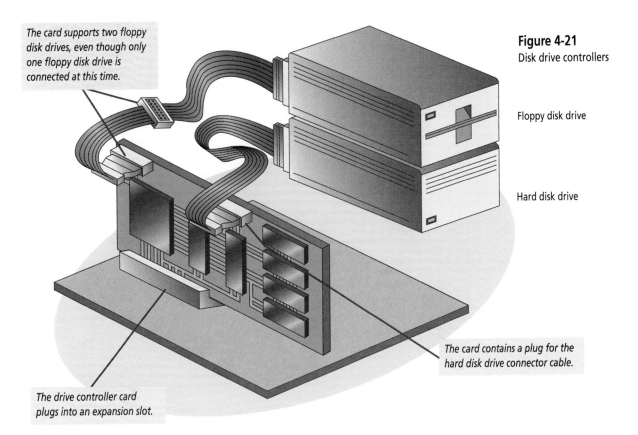

The card supports two floppy disk drives, even though only one floppy disk drive is connected at this time.

Figure 4-21
Disk drive controllers

Floppy disk drive

Hard disk drive

The card contains a plug for the hard disk drive connector cable.

The drive controller card plugs into an expansion slot.

As you learned in Chapter 1, your monitor can display graphics at a particular resolution. Display resolution depends on the number of pixels your monitor can display and the type of video display adapter you use to connect the monitor to the computer. There are many types of video display adapters. Each type of adapter has the ability to produce graphics up to a specified resolution and with a specified maximum number of colors. Figure 4-23 on the following page lists the different types of video display adapters for IBM-compatible computers, their resolutions (in pixels), and their color capabilities.

Figure 4-22
A video display adapter
or graphics card

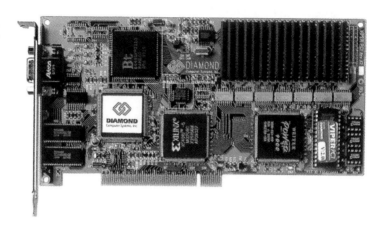

Figure 4-23
Video display adapters

ADAPTER TYPE	RESOLUTION	NUMBER OF COLORS
MDA	720x400	2
CGA	640x200 / 320x200	2 of 16 / 4 of 16
EGA	640x350	16 of 64
VGA	320x200 / 640x480	256 of 256,000 / 16 of 256,000
SVGA	800x600	16 to 16.7 million
UVGA	1024x768 / 1280x1024	16 to 16.7 million

As the resolution and the color capability increase, the amount of data required to display an image increases dramatically. To keep performance at acceptable levels, most high-resolution video display adapters use special chips to boost performance. **Accelerated video adapters** incorporate special **graphics coprocessor chips** that are designed to perform video functions at a very high speed. These accelerated video adapters can greatly increase the speed at which images are displayed.

Parallel Ports

A **parallel port** provides a connection for transmitting data eight bits at a time over a cable with eight separate data lines. Because eight bits travel simultaneously, parallel transmission is relatively fast. Parallel transmission is typically used to send data to the printer. To connect a printer to your computer, both the computer and the printer must have a parallel port. In your computer, the parallel port is either built into the main board or mounted on an expansion card. The cable that connects two parallel ports contains 25 wires; eight wires carry data and the remaining wires carry control signals that help maintain orderly transmission and reception. Figure 4-24 shows the standard connections and cable ends used to connect an IBM-compatible computer to a parallel printer.

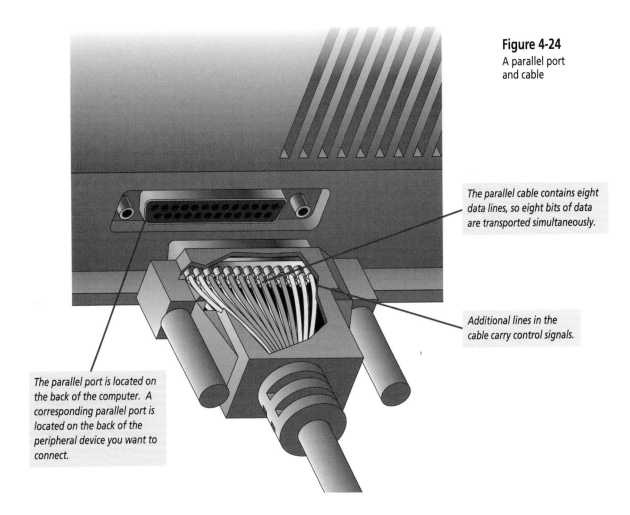

Figure 4-24
A parallel port and cable

The parallel cable contains eight data lines, so eight bits of data are transported simultaneously.

Additional lines in the cable carry control signals.

The parallel port is located on the back of the computer. A corresponding parallel port is located on the back of the peripheral device you want to connect.

Because the wires that carry data run parallel to each other for the full length of the cable, the signals in the cables tend to interfere with each other over long distances. Parallel cables can provide reliable connections for relatively short distances—from 10 to 50 feet, depending on how well the cable is shielded from electrical interference.

The parallel interface is the simplest way to connect computer components that are placed close to the main computer. IBM-compatible computers generally allow you to use up to three parallel ports, which are designated LPT1, LPT2, and LPT3. Although parallel ports most frequently connect computers and printers, some external tape drives, floppy disk drives and hard disk drives, and network adapters can be connected to a parallel port.

SCSI Ports

A **SCSI** (Small Computer System Interface) port provides a connection for one or more peripheral devices. Unlike a parallel port to which you can connect only one device, you can connect up to seven devices to a SCSI (pronounced "scuzzy") port. SCSI ports are becoming increasingly popular on IBM-compatible and Macintosh computers for attaching hard disk drives, CD-ROMs, scanners, and tape drives.

Serial Ports

A **serial port**, sometimes referred to as an **RS-232C port**, provides a connection for transmitting data one bit at a time. A serial port connects your computer to a device such as a modem, which requires two-way data transmission, or to a device such as a mouse, which requires only one-way data transmission.

To connect a peripheral device to your computer through a serial port, both the device and your computer must have a serial port. IBM-compatible computers allow you to use a maximum of four serial ports, designated COM1, COM2, COM3, and COM4. Your computer's serial ports can be built into the main board or mounted on an expansion card. IBM-compatible computers use either 9-pin or 25-pin connectors for their serial ports. The serial cable contains one data line and an assortment of control lines, as shown in Figure 4-25.

Because a serial cable requires fewer data lines, it is less susceptible to interference than a parallel cable. This makes serial connections suitable for devices that are located some distance from the computer.

Mouse Ports

A **mouse port** is a special serial port that connects a mouse to a computer. The mouse port can be built into the main board or mounted on an expansion card. Many computers include a mouse port in addition to standard serial ports.

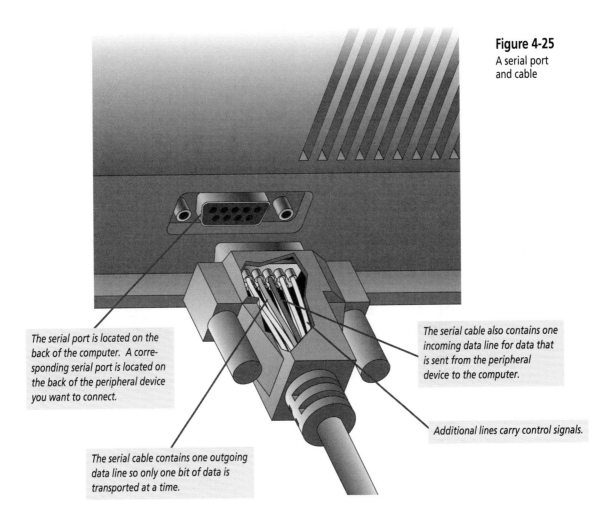

Figure 4-25
A serial port and cable

The serial port is located on the back of the computer. A corresponding serial port is located on the back of the peripheral device you want to connect.

The serial cable also contains one incoming data line for data that is sent from the peripheral device to the computer.

The serial cable contains one outgoing data line so only one bit of data is transported at a time.

Additional lines carry control signals.

In this chapter, you discovered that it would be possible, although impractical, to build a computer using ropes and pulleys. You learned that Charles Babbage attempted to build a steam-powered computer, but that this steam-powered architecture didn't catch on. Today's computers are digital electronic devices that accomplish complex tasks by performing a fairly limited set of instructions at breakneck speed. Although you might never build an electronic digital computer "from scratch," you learned that you certainly have the ability to expand and customize your computer.

C H A P T E R   R E V I E W

1. Use your own words to answer the questions in the Chapter Preview.

2. Make a list of the boldface terms in the chapter and use your own words to define each term.

3. Complete the following table to summarize the architectural characteristics of the Apraphulian computer, Babbage's computer, and a modern microcomputer.

	APRAPHULIAN	BABBAGE'S	MODERN
POWER SOURCE			
CALCULATION DEVICE			

4. Place an X in the following table to indicate which characteristics apply to each type of memory.

CHARACTERISTIC	RAM	CMOS	ROM
HOLDS DATA TEMPORARILY			
HOLDS DATA PERMANENTLY			
VOLATILE			
HOLDS USER DATA			
HOLDS PROGRAM INSTRUCTIONS			
HOLDS SYSTEM CONFIGURATION DATA			
USES BATTERY POWER			
HOLDS START-UP DATA			
HOLDS BOOT PROGRAM			

5. Draw a sketch showing the major components of a microprocessor.

6. Imagine you are a teacher. Examine Figure 4-26 and write a one- or two-page script explaining the instruction execution cycle to your class.

Figure 4-26

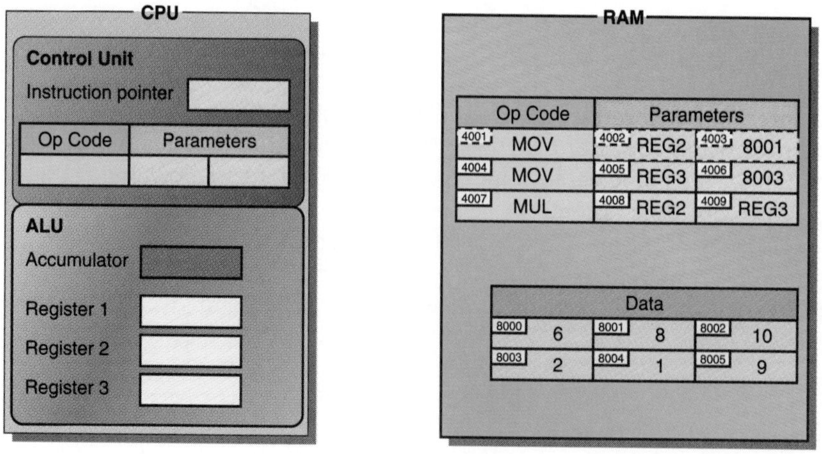

7. In Figure 4-26, after the processor executes the three instructions in RAM, what are the final values in Register 1, Register 2, Register 3, and the Accumulator?

8. Suppose you are using the Microsoft Word for DOS word processor and you are creating a document called REPORT1.DOC. Draw a sketch showing the contents of RAM.

9. List the six factors that influence the performance of a microprocessor.

10. Name three ways that you can attach additional devices to a microcomputer.

11. Label each of the computer components illustrated in Figure 4-27.

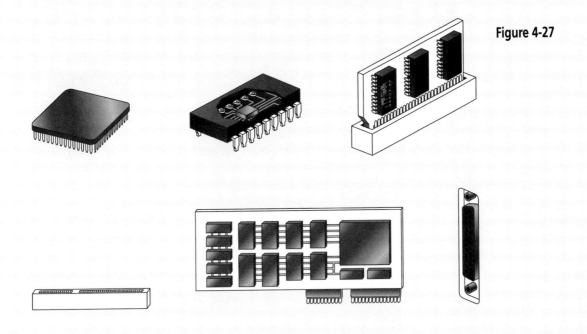

Figure 4-27

C H A P T E R   Q U I Z

1. A(n) _____ device works with discrete numbers or digits, while an analog device works with continuously varying data.

2. A one or zero that represents data is referred to as a(n) _____.

3. The word *hello* is represented by _____ bits or _____ bytes.

4. A(n) _____ is an electronic path that connects the components on a main board.

5. A computer with a 32-bit bus can transport _____ bits of information at a time.

6. _____ is electronic circuitry that holds data and programs.

7. A(n) _____ is a small circuit board containing RAM chips.

8. System configuration information, such as the types and number of hard disk drives on a computer, is stored in battery-backed _____ memory so it is retained even when the computer is turned off.

9. The series of instructions that a computer performs when it is first turned on are permanently stored in _____ .

10. The _____ in the CPU performs arithmetic and logical operations such as adding or comparing two numbers.

11. The _____ in the CPU directs and coordinates the operation of the entire computer system.

12. The instruction execution cycle consists of the _____ phase and the execution phase.

13. A(n) _____ contains the ALU and control unit on a single chip.

14. A microprocessor with a 32-bit word size but an 8-bit data bus requires _____ cycles to transport a data word from RAM to the microprocessor.

15. The _____ is the sequence of events that occurs between the time the computer is turned on and the time it is ready for user input.

P R O J E C T S

1. Browse through several computer magazines in your computer lab or library to determine which microprocessor is most popular and which microprocessor is currently state-of-the-art. Write a brief description of your findings. Include the following information:

   a. For the most popular microprocessor, include the clock speed, processor model name or number, and word size.

   b. For the state-of-the-art microprocessor, include the clock speed, processor model name or number, and word size.

   c. A brief explanation of what factors helped you determine that these particular micro-processors are the most popular and the most state-of-the-art.

   d. A bibliography of your sources.

2. Photocopy a full-page computer ad from a current issue of a computer magazine such as *Computer Shopper*. On the ad, circle any of the terms that were presented in this chapter. Make sure you watch for abbreviations; they are frequently used in computer ads. On a separate sheet of paper, or using a word processor, make a list of each term you circled and write out a definition of each.

3. For each of the following scenarios, indicate what might be wrong.

   a. You turn on the computer's power switch and nothing happens—no lights, no beep, nothing. What's the most likely problem?

   b. You turn on your computer and the computer completes the POST test. You see the light on drive A: and you hear the drive power up, but you get a message on the screen that says "Cannot load file." Explain what caused this message to appear and explain exactly what you should do to complete the boot process.

   c. You are using a word processor to compose an essay for your English composition course. You have completed eight pages, and you have periodically saved the document. Suddenly, you notice that when you press a key nothing happens. You try the mouse, but it no longer moves the pointer on the screen. What should you do next?

4. Look in computer magazines to find three peripheral devices that connect to a computer using different ports or buses. For example, you might find a printer that connects to the serial port. For each device, indicate its brand and model and the port or bus it uses. Also include the name and publication date of the magazine and the page on which you found the information.

5. Interview one of your friends who has a computer:

   a. Find out as many technical details as you can about the computer, including the type of computer, the type and speed of the microprocessor, the amount of memory, the configuration of disk drives, the capacity of the disk drives, and the resolution of the monitor.

   b. Find out how your friend might want to expand his or her computer system. For example, your friend might want to add a better printer, a sound card, more memory, or a better monitor.

   c. Look through computer magazines to find a solution for at least one of your friend's expansion plans.

   d. Write a two-page report describing your friend's computer and expansion needs, then describe the solution you found.

6. List each step in the boot process. Take your list into the computer lab and boot one of the computers. As the computer boots, read your list to make sure it is correct. For which steps in the boot process can you see or hear something actually happening?

L A B S

Computer Architecture Lab

The Computer Architecture Lab uses a simulated microprocessor to show how a computer executes program instructions. After completing the tour, answer the following questions:

L A B

COMPUTER ARCHITECTURE

1. Which operations does the CPU perform?
2. Which part of the CPU controls the execution of the program?
3. Which part of the CPU performs arithmetic and logical operations?
4. What does the Instruction Pointer do?
5. Where are the results of arithmetic and logical operations placed?
6. What are registers used for?
7. What happens when the CPU fetches an instruction?
8. REG1 contains the number 2. REG2 contains the number 3. What would happen if the CPU executed the instruction ADD REG1 REG2?
9. REG1 contains the number 7. What would happen if the CPU executed the instruction MOV REG1 6000?
10. REG3 contains the number 4. What would happen if the CPU executed the instruction DEC REG3? What would happen if it executed the instruction INC REG3?
11. The Accumulator holds the number zero. What would happen if the CPU executed the instruction JPZ 5000?

Troubleshooting Lab

In the Troubleshooting Lab you use a simulated computer system to see what happens when a computer boots normally and what happens when a problem occurs during the boot process. Each time a problem occurs you are given an opportunity to develop and test your troubleshooting skills by choosing the most likely cause of the problem. You can set the simulated computer to boot normally or to boot with a problem by clicking the appropriate button in the control panel at the top of the screen. Use the following instructions to complete this Lab:

L A B

TROUBLE-SHOOTING

To begin the first lab activity, make sure the **Boot normally** option is selected, then click the **Start Boot** button to start the normal boot process. The monitor and system unit turn on and the boot process begins. Carefully watch the sequence of steps in the boot process. Use the scroll bar to adjust the speed of the boot process.

To proceed with the second lab activity, click the **Boot With a Problem** option, then click the **Start Boot** button to boot the system with a simulated problem. The boot process begins, but a randomly selected problem stops the process from completing normally. When the boot process stops, the program displays a description of the problem and lists five possible causes.

Think about the possible cause of the problem. If you want to see the problem replayed, click the **Replay Last Boot** button. When you think you know what caused the problem, click the button in front of the cause, then click the **Check Your Answer** button.

Each time you click the **Start Boot** button, the system simulates the effects of another randomly selected problem. Continue working with the simulator until you can correctly identify the cause for the nine common boot problems, then respond to the following situations:

1. Neither the monitor nor the system unit power lights come on. What is the most likely cause of this problem? What should you do next?

2. The monitor power light comes on, but the system unit power light does not come on. What's the most likely cause of this problem? What should you do next?

3. There is no power light and no display on the monitor. The system unit power and activity lights indicate a normal boot process. What's the most likely cause of this problem? What should you do next?

4. The monitor power light is on, but nothing is displayed on the screen. The system unit power and activity lights indicate a normal boot process. What's the most likely cause of this problem? What should you do next?

5. The monitor and system unit power lights are on, but there is no display and no visible system unit activity. What's the most likely cause of this problem? What should you do next?

6. The boot process starts normally, but stops after the message "Parity error" appears. What's the most likely cause of this problem? What should you do next?

7. The boot process starts normally, but stops when the message "Keyboard error" appears. What steps should you take to resolve this problem? What should you do next?

8. The boot process starts normally, but stops when the message "Cannot load a file" appears. What's the most likely cause of this problem? What should you do next?

9. The boot process starts normally, but stops when the message "Bad or Missing Command Interpreter" appears. What's the most likely cause of this problem? What should you do next?

R E S O U R C E S

■ Dewdney, A. K. "Computer Recreations: An ancient rope-and-pulley computer is unearthed in the jungle of Apraphul." *Scientific American*, April 1985, pp. 118-121.

What begins as an April Fools' joke turns out to be an excellent explanation of the basic circuitry in a digital computer.

■ Foster, C. *Computer Architecture*. New York: Van Nostrand Reinhold, 1970.

If you really want to get into computer architecture, this is one of the classics. Be warned, it's not easy reading.

■ Kidder, T. *The Soul of a New Machine*. Boston: Little, Brown, 1981.

Kidder writes insightfully about the heady days in Silicon Valley when the computer industry was venturing into brave new worlds. This book describes a team of researchers who are consumed by a project to build the best computer.

▪ Rosch, W. L. *The Winn L. Rosch Hardware Bible*. New York: Prentice Hall, 1992.

Voted as one of the 20 all-time best microcomputer books by *Computer Magazine*, this 1,097-page book is packed with facts about personal computers.

▪ Shurkin, J. *Engines of the Mind: A History of the Computer*. New York: W. W. Norton & Company, 1984.

A lively account of the pioneers of the computer industry. The book focuses on people and personalities, rather than on machines, and provides the reader with a human perspective on the nature of creativity and invention.

▪ White, R. *How Computers Work*. Emeryville, CA: Ziff-Davis Press, 1993.

This book might be called the illustrated guide to how computers work because it contains so many great diagrams. If you are interested in what happens inside the system unit, this is the place to begin.

CHAPTER FIVE

When you have completed this chapter, you should be able to answer the following questions:

- What is Shannon's model of a communications system?
- What are some of the different coding schemes used to represent data in computers?
- How is graphical data represented?
- How is sound data represented?
- What techniques are used to compress a file?
- What is a communications protocol?
- How can computer communications recover from the disruptive effects of line noise and other interference?
- What is the difference between simplex, half duplex, and duplex transmission?
- What do you need to know if you want to set up a modem?

DATA COMMUNICATIONS

I t was April 18, 1775, the eve of the American Revolution. The Massachusetts Minutemen were huddled around a plank table planning a defense strategy against well-armed and professionally trained British troops. The deployment of the outnumbered revolutionary troops was a critical element in the Minutemen's defense plan. They needed to know the route of the British attack force. Without telephones, cellular phones, and a modern communications infrastructure, the Minutemen had a communications problem: how would they communicate to each other the British route of attack? The Minutemen solved this problem by using the plan recounted in Longfellow's poem, *Paul Revere's Ride*:

One if by land, and two if by sea;
And I on the opposite shore will be,
Ready to ride and spread the alarm
Through every Middlesex village and farm.

The Minutemen devised a simple plan. The Old North Church tower was visible for miles. As a signal for Paul Revere, either one or two lanterns would be lit in the church tower. The lanterns represented the two possible messages: one lantern meant the British were coming by land, two lanterns meant the British were coming by sea. But what if some of the British troops arrived on land and others arrived by sea? Would the Minutemen need another lantern for this third possibility? The answer to this question is clear when you understand data representation and information theory.

In this chapter you will learn how computers represent data and how different methods of data representation help solve communications problems. You will also learn how information theory could have helped the Minutemen communicate more effectively.

Transmitting and Receiving Information

Data communications is the process of transmitting and receiving data in an orderly way so the data that arrives at its destination is an accurate duplication of the data that was sent. When the data travels a short distance, such as when you send data from your computer to your printer, the communication is referred to as "local." When the data travels a long distance, the communication is referred to as **telecommunications**; the prefix "tele" is derived from a Greek word that means "far" or "far off."

The difference between a short distance and a long distance is somewhat arbitrary. For example, if your computer sends data to a printer in the next room, that transmission of data is regarded as "local" communications. However, if you phone the person in the next room, you are transmitting data over a telecommunications device. Because the same basic communications concepts apply to both local and telecommunications, in this chapter we will not further distinguish between the two.

Data communications has a profound impact on your life. Your ability to pick up a phone and talk to anyone in the world, withdraw cash from your bank account using an automatic teller machine, send an image using a fax machine, send computer data just about anywhere in the world, and watch a live news report from a different continent are all examples of how you use communications technology today. If you can gain a better understanding of data communications by reading this chapter, you will be better equipped to use this technology to succeed in your personal and career endeavors.

Encoding Information

The term "code" is used in many different ways. Just consider a few examples such as dress code, secret code, zip code, Morse code, or genetic code. In this chapter, **code** refers to the symbols that represent data and information. Transforming data into code is called **encoding**. In this chapter encoding does not refer to secret codes or encryption, in which the data that represents information is intentionally scrambled to hide its meaning. Instead, it refers to codes that are in general use.

Many codes, such as zip codes, are "public," that is, they are generally known and used. Public codes are useful because they provide effective and efficient methods for exchanging information. For example, two-letter state codes are widely used, effective, and efficient. A state code like WI uses only two letters instead of nine to represent Wisconsin. Storing a state code takes less space than storing an entire state name, and transmitting a state code takes less time than transmitting an entire state name.

In 1949, Claude Shannon, an engineer at the prestigious Bell Labs, published an article that described a communications system in terms of a simple model in which data from a source is encoded and sent over a communications channel where it is decoded by a receiver. According to Shannon, the effectiveness of communication depends on the efficiency of the coding process and the channel's resilience to interference, or "noise." Shannon's communications model is the foundation for this chapter on data communications, so study Figure 5-1 to get an overview of a communications system.

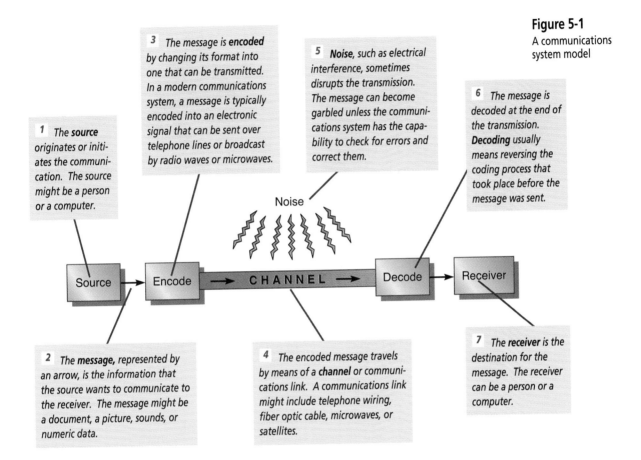

Figure 5-1
A communications system model

3 *The message is **encoded** by changing its format into one that can be transmitted. In a modern communications system, a message is typically encoded into an electronic signal that can be sent over telephone lines or broadcast by radio waves or microwaves.*

5 ***Noise**, such as electrical interference, sometimes disrupts the transmission. The message can become garbled unless the communications system has the capability to check for errors and correct them.*

6 *The message is decoded at the end of the transmission. **Decoding** usually means reversing the coding process that took place before the message was sent.*

1 *The **source** originates or initiates the communication. The source might be a person or a computer.*

2 *The **message**, represented by an arrow, is the information that the source wants to communicate to the receiver. The message might be a document, a picture, sounds, or numeric data.*

4 *The encoded message travels by means of a **channel** or communications link. A communications link might include telephone wiring, fiber optic cable, microwaves, or satellites.*

7 *The **receiver** is the destination for the message. The receiver can be a person or a computer.*

To see how Shannon's model applies to everyday communication, consider what happens when you make a phone call to a friend. You are the source of the message. Your message—the idea you have—is encoded into English words that you speak into the phone. The phone further encodes the message by converting your words into electromagnetic waves that can travel over the phone lines. The channel for your message is the phone line. If you have a "bad connection," there is noise along the channel. Your friend's phone decodes your message by converting the electromagnetic waves back into sound waves that your friend can hear. Your friend's brain performs an additional decoding step by translating the words of your message into meaning.

If we accept Longfellow's account of the historical evening in 1775, the Minutemen used a simple code in which one light meant "by land" and two lights meant "by sea," as shown in Figure 5-2.

Figure 5-2
Paul Revere's Code

One lantern in the church tower was the signal that the British were coming by land.

Two lanterns in the church tower was the signal that the British were coming by sea.

L A B

DATA REPRESENTATION

How efficient was the code used by the Minutemen? You can answer this question using information theory, an area of research that applies some of the ideas Claude Shannon developed in conjunction with his communications system model. **Information theory** describes how the amount of information you can convey depends on the way you represent or encode the information. For example, Figure 5-3 shows that with one lantern, you can convey up to two units of information; the lantern can be on or off, representing "yes" or "no," "land" or "sea," "true" or "false," and so forth.

Figure 5-3
A single lantern conveys up to two units of information

The lantern can be off, or it can be on. Therefore, a single lantern has two possible states. Each state can represent one unit of information. For example, if the lantern is off, it might mean the British decided not to come, but if the lantern is on, the British are coming!

In the on state, the lantern indicates the British are coming.

In the off state, the lantern indicates the British are not coming.

Information theory applies to computers as well as to lanterns. As you learned in Chapter 4, a computer is an electronic device that stores and manipulates electrical currents that represent bits—zeros and ones. Think of a bit as the equivalent of one lantern. A bit can be a one or a zero, just as a lantern can be on or off. The *on* state of the lantern corresponds to a *one* bit, and the *off* state of the lantern corresponds to a *zero* bit. A computer can use a single bit (one lantern) to convey up to two units of information; a *one* bit might correspond to "yes" and a *zero* bit might correspond to "no"; a *one* bit might correspond to "land" and a *zero* bit might correspond to "sea," and so forth.

Now, if you use two bits (two lanterns) or three bits (three lanterns) how many different units of information can you convey? Figure 5-4 shows that there are four ways to combine and display two bits. Figure 5-5 shows that there are eight ways to combine and display three bits.

So, information theory tells us that if the Minutemen had only two lanterns, they could have communicated up to four different messages; with three lanterns they could have communicated up to eight different messages.

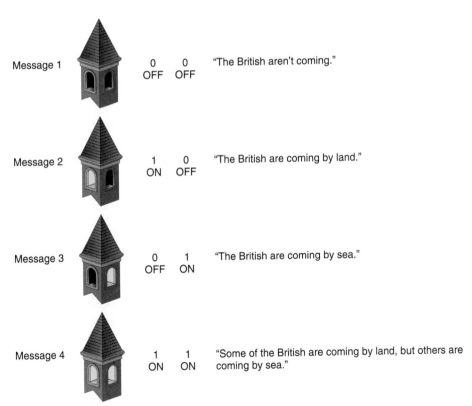

Message 1	0 OFF	0 OFF	"The British aren't coming."
Message 2	1 ON	0 OFF	"The British are coming by land."
Message 3	0 OFF	1 ON	"The British are coming by sea."
Message 4	1 ON	1 ON	"Some of the British are coming by land, but others are coming by sea."

Figure 5-4
With two lanterns, you can convey up to four different messages

Figure 5-5

With three lanterns you can convey up to eight different messages

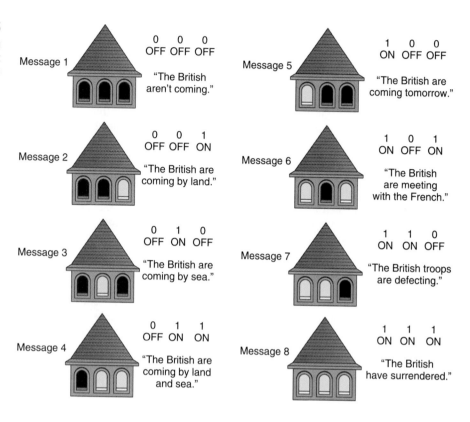

Message 1 — 0 0 0 / OFF OFF OFF — "The British aren't coming."

Message 2 — 0 0 1 / OFF OFF ON — "The British are coming by land."

Message 3 — 0 1 0 / OFF ON OFF — "The British are coming by sea."

Message 4 — 0 1 1 / OFF ON ON — "The British are coming by land and sea."

Message 5 — 1 0 0 / ON OFF OFF — "The British are coming tomorrow."

Message 6 — 1 0 1 / ON OFF ON — "The British are meeting with the French."

Message 7 — 1 1 0 / ON ON OFF — "The British troops are defecting."

Message 8 — 1 1 1 / ON ON ON — "The British have surrendered."

There is a pattern or rule about how much information you can represent, given a certain number of bits. With one bit, you can convey 2 units of information. With two bits, you can convey 4 units of information. With three bits, you can convey 8 units. The pattern is 2, 4, 8; these numbers are all powers of two:

$$2^1 = 2 \times 1 = 2$$
$$2^2 = 2 \times 2 = 4$$
$$2^3 = 2 \times 2 \times 2 = 8$$

We can state this rule as "the maximum number of different units of information you can convey within bits is 2^n." For example, if you use four bits (or four lanterns), the exponent "n" is 4. The maximum number of units you can convey is 2^4 or $2 \times 2 \times 2 \times 2$, which is 16. So, if you use four bits, you can convey a maximum of 16 different units of information. Figure 5-6 summarizes this rule.

Using this rule, you can determine how many bits you need to convey the information for different messages. For example, suppose that the Minutemen wanted to know how many British troops were in the advance force. How many bits (lanterns) would they need to convey the message that 50 British troops were about to attack? It would be convenient if they could convey this message without using 50 lanterns!

Let's see how you can use bits to represent numbers. When you know this, you can figure out how many lanterns the Minutemen would have needed, and how many bits a computer uses to represent the quantity 50.

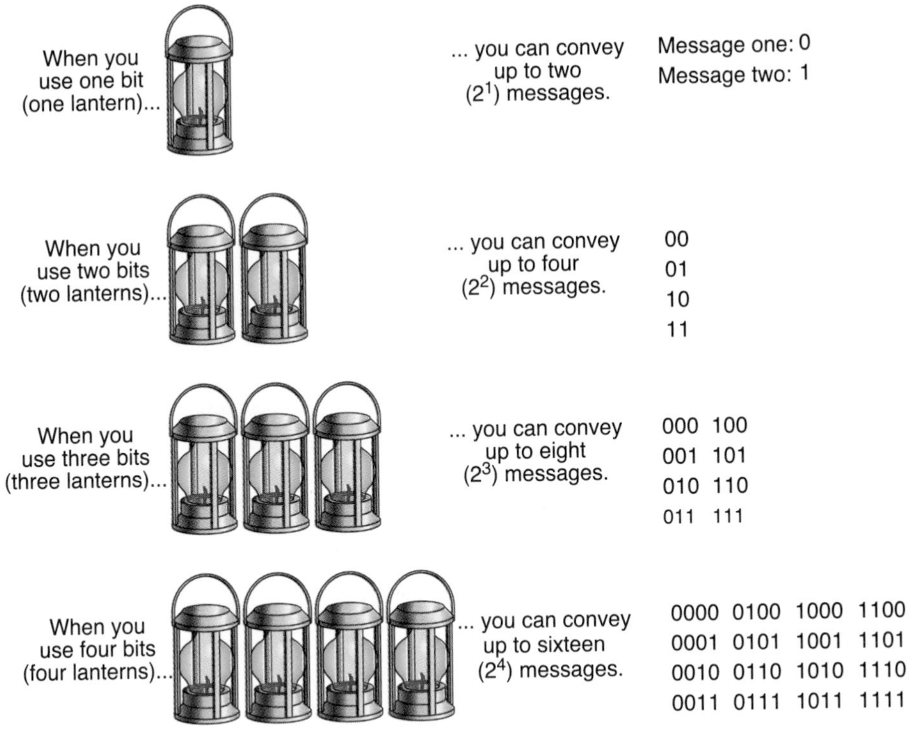

When you use one bit (one lantern)... ... you can convey up to two (2^1) messages.

Message one: 0
Message two: 1

When you use two bits (two lanterns)... ... you can convey up to four (2^2) messages.

00
01
10
11

When you use three bits (three lanterns)... ... you can convey up to eight (2^3) messages.

000 100
001 101
010 110
011 111

When you use four bits (four lanterns)... ... you can convey up to sixteen (2^4) messages.

0000 0100 1000 1100
0001 0101 1001 1101
0010 0110 1010 1110
0011 0111 1011 1111

Figure 5-6

The number of messages, or units of information, that you can convey with n bits is 2^n

Representing Numbers

The binary number system is a very convenient way to represent numbers; it uses only two digits, 0 and 1, which correspond to the off and on states of a lantern. To review how the binary number system works, let's first think about something you're more familiar with—the decimal number system. Two concepts are important: the number of digits you use and what happens when you run out of digits.

The decimal system uses ten digits: 0, 1, 2, 3, 4, 5, 6, 7, 8, and 9. Every positive whole number must be represented using only these digits. What happens when you run out of digits and want to represent the number that comes after the last digit, that is, after the digit 9? Or, asked a different way, what happens when we want to add 9+1? The rule is to write a 0 as a placeholder and "carry" the 1 to the next column to the left. In the decimal system the "ones," "tens," "hundreds," and "thousands" columns represent powers of 10: 10^0, 10^1, 10^2, 10^3, 10^4. Figure 5-7 on the following page shows how this works.

The binary number system has only two digits: 0 and 1. You follow the same rule as for the decimal system when you want to represent the number that comes after

Figure 5-7
Adding decimal numbers

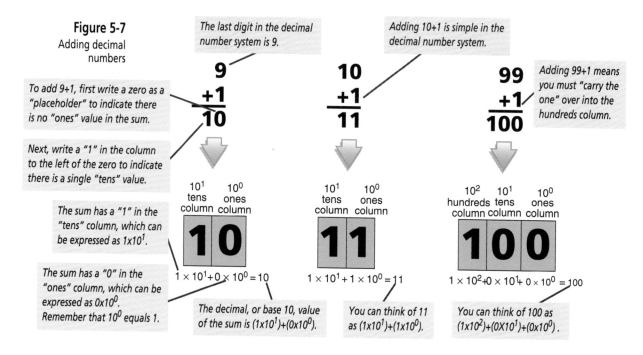

The last digit in the decimal number system is 9.

Adding 10+1 is simple in the decimal number system.

Adding 99+1 means you must "carry the one" over into the hundreds column.

To add 9+1, first write a zero as a "placeholder" to indicate there is no "ones" value in the sum.

Next, write a "1" in the column to the left of the zero to indicate there is a single "tens" value.

The sum has a "1" in the "tens" column, which can be expressed as 1×10^1.

The sum has a "0" in the "ones" column, which can be expressed as 0×10^0. Remember that 10^0 equals 1.

The decimal, or base 10, value of the sum is $(1 \times 10^1) + (0 \times 10^0)$.

You can think of 11 as $(1 \times 10^1) + (1 \times 10^0)$.

You can think of 100 as $(1 \times 10^2) + (0 \times 10^1) + (0 \times 10^0)$.

the last digit, which for the binary number system is the digit 1. You cannot count 1, 2, 3, and so on using the binary number system because symbols such as 2 and 3 are not used. In the binary number system, you count 1, 10, 11, 100, 101. A binary 1 is the same as a decimal 1. A binary 10 is equivalent to a decimal 2. The binary 11 is equivalent to a decimal 3. The binary 100 is equivalent to a decimal 4. The binary 101 is equivalent to the decimal 5. Study Figure 5-8 to understand how this works.

Figure 5-8
Adding binary numbers

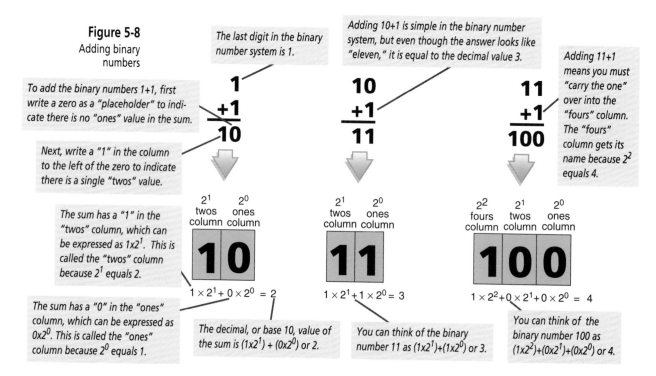

The last digit in the binary number system is 1.

Adding 10+1 is simple in the binary number system, but even though the answer looks like "eleven," it is equal to the decimal value 3.

Adding 11+1 means you must "carry the one" over into the "fours" column. The "fours" column gets its name because 2^2 equals 4.

To add the binary numbers 1+1, first write a zero as a "placeholder" to indicate there is no "ones" value in the sum.

Next, write a "1" in the column to the left of the zero to indicate there is a single "twos" value.

The sum has a "1" in the "twos" column, which can be expressed as 1×2^1. This is called the "twos" column because 2^1 equals 2.

The sum has a "0" in the "ones" column, which can be expressed as 0×2^0. This is called the "ones" column because 2^0 equals 1.

The decimal, or base 10, value of the sum is $(1 \times 2^1) + (0 \times 2^0)$ or 2.

You can think of the binary number 11 as $(1 \times 2^1) + (1 \times 2^0)$ or 3.

You can think of the binary number 100 as $(1 \times 2^2) + (0 \times 2^1) + (0 \times 2^0)$ or 4.

Now let's answer the question we asked earlier: How many bits or lanterns are required to convey the information that 50 British troops are going to attack? The binary representation of 50 is 110010, meaning that the Minutemen would arrange the lanterns as follows: on-on-off-off-on-off. As shown in Figure 5-9, six lanterns would have been needed to convey this information to Paul Revere.

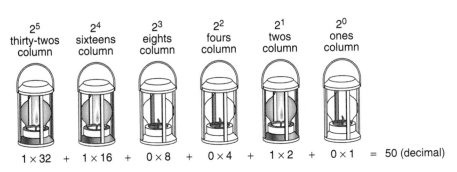

Figure 5-9

Lanterns show the binary representation for the decimal number 50

You now understand how the Minutemen could use bits to represent numbers, but suppose that they wanted to send more elaborate messages—messages that required a binary code for each letter in the alphabet.

Representing Characters

Character representation refers to the way nonnumeric information, such as letters of the alphabet and punctuation symbols, is represented by a series of bits. A **character representation scheme**, also referred to simply as a code, is a series of bits that represent a letter, symbol, or numeral. For example, suppose you need a code to represent each of the 26 characters in the alphabet. If you use four bits, you can convey 16 (2^4 or 2 x 2 x 2 x 2) different units of information, but that is not enough for all the letters in the alphabet. If you use five bits you can convey 32 (2^5 or 2 x 2 x 2 x 2 x 2) different units of information. Five bits is enough to represent the 26 characters in the alphabet, plus you could encode six additional items, such as punctuation symbols. It turns out, however, that five bits are not enough to represent the symbols typically used in written communication. Let's see why.

Written English uses uppercase and lowercase versions of each letter of the alphabet and a variety of symbols for punctuation and abbreviations, such as $ # @ & +. If you count these letters, symbols, and the numerals 0-9, there are 95 different characters that must be represented. Therefore, more than five bits are required.

As computers evolved from the primitive number crunchers of the 1940s and 1950s, several character representation schemes emerged. The three character representation schemes most widely used are ASCII, ANSI, and EBCDIC. A fourth scheme, UNICODE, has been proposed for future worldwide use.

ASCII

ASCII, or **American Standard Code for Information Interchange**, is the most widely used coding scheme for character data. The standard ASCII code uses seven bits to represent 128 symbols including uppercase and lowercase letters, special control codes, numerals, and punctuation symbols. A table or matrix is often used to provide a compact reference to the ASCII code. Figure 5-10 shows you how to use a matrix to find the ASCII code for the lowercase letter "a."

Figure 5-10
Using a matrix chart to find an ASCII code

1	1	0	0	0	0	1

Bit position	7	6	5	4	3	2	1

5 By combining bits 7, 6, and 5 from the top of the column with bits 4, 3, 2, and 1, from the beginning of the row, you can see that the ASCII code for the lowercase letter "a" is 1100001.

4 The ASCII code is a seven-bit code, so there are seven bit positions. Bit position seven is on the left; bit position one is on the right.

3 The four binary digits at the beginning of the row show you the values of bits 4, 3, 2, 1.

2 The three binary digits at the top of the column show you the values of bits 7, 6, and 5.

1 Locate the lowercase letter "a" in the matrix.

	000	001	010	011	100	101	110	111
0000	NUL	DLE	SP	0	@	P		p
0001	SOH	DCI	!	1	A	Q	a	q
0010	STX	DC2	"	2	B	R	b	q
0011	ETX	DC3	#	3	C	S	c	s
0100	EOT	DC4	$	4	D	T	d	t
0101	ENQ	NAK	%	5	E	U	e	u
0110	ACK	SYN	&	6	F	V	f	v
0111	BEL	ETB	'	7	G	W	g	w
1000	BS	CAN	(	8	H	X	h	x
1001	HT	EM	)	9	I	Y	i	y
1010	LF	SUB	*	:	J	Z	j	z
1011	VT	ESC	+	;	K	[	k	{
1100	FF	FS	,	<	L	\	L		
1101	CR	GS	-	=	M	]	m	}
1110	SO	RS	.	>	N	^	n	~
1111	SI	US	/	?	O	—	o	DEL

6 The first two columns of the matrix show "control codes." For example, LF means line feed and CR means carriage return.

ANSI

The **ANSI**, or **American National Standards Institute**, code uses eight bits to represent each character. Microsoft Windows uses the ANSI code to store the documents you create with Windows applications. The eight-bit ANSI code can convey up to 256 (2^8) units of information, so it can be used to code 256 letters and symbols.

The first 128 of the characters of the ANSI code are the same as those defined by the ASCII code, but with an additional zero as the leftmost bit. For example, the letter "a" is represented by the ASCII code 1100001 and by the ANSI code 01100001. In addition to the 128 characters represented by the ASCII code, the ANSI code represents 128 other characters such as the copyright symbol, the Japanese yen symbol ¥, and characters ß, ñ, and ç.

EBCDIC

EBCDIC, or **Extended Binary Coded Decimal Interchange Code**, is an eight-bit character representation scheme developed by IBM for its mainframe computers. EBCDIC does not use the same representation scheme as ASCII or ANSI for the initial 128 characters. For example, in EBCDIC the letter "a" is represented by 10000001. In ASCII, the letter "a" is represented by 1100001, and in ANSI, the letter "a" is represented by 01100001.

Communication between computers that use different character representation schemes can be a problem. For example, suppose you create a document on your computer using a Microsoft Windows application and you want to send it to an IBM mainframe. Your document is stored in ANSI format, but the mainframe expects documents in EBCDIC. When you send the letter "k" using the ANSI code 01101011, the mainframe decodes this as a comma using EBCDIC. To avoid this problem, one of the computers must translate the data from ASCII to EBCDIC. This task can be handled by software on either the sending or the receiving computer.

Unicode

Standard ASCII defines 128 characters, which is sufficient for the numbers, letters, and punctuation marks used in English. ANSI represents all these characters plus many of the characters used in European languages, such as the Spanish ñ, the German ß, and the French ç. EBCDIC represents the standard alphabet and an assortment of control codes. However, none of these coding schemes supports alternate character sets such as Hebrew, Cyrillic, or Arabic. These coding schemes also do not support languages such as Japanese or Chinese, which require thousands of different symbols.

Unicode is a 16-bit code that can be used to represent over 65,000 different characters. Theoretically, Unicode can represent every character in every language used today, as well as characters from languages that are no longer used. Such a code would be very helpful in international business and communications, where a document might need to contain sections of text in Japanese, English, and Chinese. Unicode also facilitates the **localization** of software, that is, the modification of software for use in specific countries. With Unicode, a software developer can modify a program to display on-screen prompts, menus, and error messages in different languages for use in specific countries or regions. Both Microsoft and Apple have announced plans to add Unicode support to their operating systems.

Representing Graphics

There are two very different approaches to encoding graphics, pictures, and images in computer systems: bitmap and vector. The differences between these two graphical coding schemes affect the image quality, the amount of space required to store the image, the amount of time required to transmit the image, and the ease with which you can modify the image.

Bitmap Graphics

A **bitmap graphic** is represented using a code that indicates the state of each individual dot or pixel displayed on the screen. The simplest bitmap graphics are monochrome, that is, they are created using only the color white on a black background. To understand how a computer codes monochrome bitmap graphics, think of a grid superimposed on a picture. The grid divides the picture into cells, each equivalent to a pixel on the computer screen. With monochrome graphics, each cell, or pixel, can be colored either black or white. If the section of the photo in a cell is black, the computer represents it with a *zero* bit. If the section of the picture in a cell is white, the computer represents it with a *one* bit. Each row of the grid is represented by a series of zeros and ones, as shown in Figure 5-11.

With monochrome graphics, the number of bits required to represent a full-screen picture is the same as the number of pixels on the screen. A monochrome graphic displayed at 640 by 480 requires 640 x 480 or 307,200 bits. With eight bits per byte, the graphic requires 38,400 bytes (307,000 ÷ 8).

Not all bitmap graphics are monochrome. **Grayscale** graphics are created using shades of gray or "gray scales," much like so-called black and white photos. The more gray shades used, the more realistic the image appears. Color images are similar in that more colors create a more realistic image. To represent grayscale and color graphics, more complex coding schemes must be used.

A computer typically represents grayscale graphics using either 16 gray shades or 256 gray shades. A computer represents color graphics using either 16, 256, or 16.7 million colors. Although 16.7 million colors might seem somewhat excessive, this recently developed color standard, called **true color graphics**, provides photographic-quality images.

Applying information theory, you can determine the number of bits required to code the information for a grayscale or color picture. For example, how many bits are required for a 16-grayscale picture? In a 16-grayscale graphic, each pixel can be white, black, or one of 14 shades of gray; a total of 16 different possibilities. How many bits are needed to convey 16 units of information? Asked another way, how many lights would the Minutemen need to convey 16 units of information from the church tower? If you answered four bits or four lights, you are correct. Therefore, a

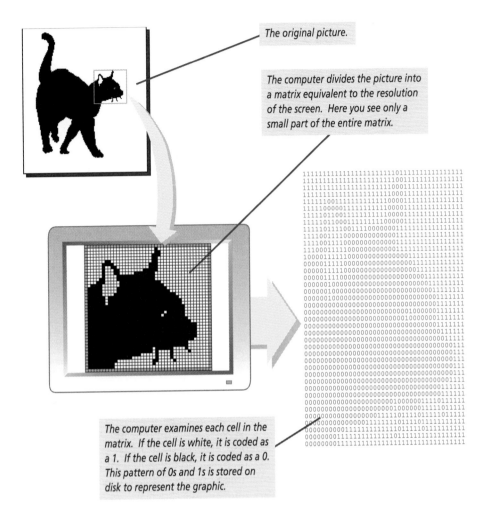

The original picture.

The computer divides the picture into a matrix equivalent to the resolution of the screen. Here you see only a small part of the entire matrix.

Figure 5-11
Encoding a picture into a monochrome bitmap graphic

The computer examines each cell in the matrix. If the cell is white, it is coded as a 1. If the cell is black, it is coded as a 0. This pattern of 0s and 1s is stored on disk to represent the graphic.

16-grayscale graphic requires four bits for each pixel. A full-screen graphic at 640 by 480 resolution requires 1,228,800 bits (153,600 bytes), as shown by the calculation in Figure 5-12 on the following page.

Although you don't generally need to calculate the size of bitmap graphics, it is useful to see how the calculation is done because it explains why bitmap graphics take up so much storage space and require lengthy transmission time. In the Projects section at the end of this chapter, you will have an opportunity to calculate the number of bytes required for 256 color graphics, so make sure you understand the calculations in Figure 5-12.

Figure 5-12

Calculating the number of bytes needed to encode a full screen graphic at 640 by 480 resolution

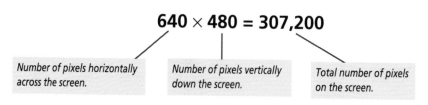

$$640 \times 480 = 307,200$$

Number of pixels horizontally across the screen.

Number of pixels vertically down the screen.

Total number of pixels on the screen.

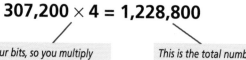

$$307,200 \times 4 = 1,228,800$$

Each pixel is represented by four bits, so you multiply the total number of pixels by four to get the total number of bits required to encode a full-screen graphic.

This is the total number of bits required to encode a full-screen graphic.

$$1,228,800 \div 8 = 153,600$$

It is more conventional to measure a graphic in bytes, rather than bits. Because there are eight bits in a byte, divide the total number of bits by eight to calculate the number of bytes required to encode a full-screen graphic.

A full-screen graphic at 640 by 480 resolution requires 153,600 bytes.

Bitmap graphics are used for realistic images such as scanned photos. The file-name extensions .BMP, .PCX, .TIF, and .GIF typically indicate files that contain bitmap images. Because bitmap graphics are coded as a series of bits that represent pixels, you can modify or edit this type of graphic by changing individual pixels.

To modify a bitmap graphic, you use bitmap graphics software such as Microsoft Paintbrush, PC Paintbrush, or Micrografx Photomagic. Such software tools let you enlarge a section of a picture so you can more easily modify individual pixels. And, because making large-scale changes pixel-by-pixel can be a tedious process, bitmap graphics software provides additional tools to cut, copy, paste, and change the color of sections of a picture. Bitmapped graphics software gives you the capability to modify photographic-quality images. For example, you can retouch or repair old photographs and design eye-catching new pictures using images you cut and paste from several photos.

Vector Graphics

Vector graphics consist of a set of instructions that recreate a picture. These instructions are converted into binary codes to store or transmit the picture. Vector graphics software performs the calculations necessary to determine which pixels must be activated to display the lines and curves. Figure 5-13 explains more about how you would use vector graphics software to create a simple picture.

When you use vector graphics software to draw a picture, you use drawing tools to create shapes or objects. For example, you can use the filled-circle tool to draw a circle that is filled with a solid color. It is easy to change the size, shape, and location of an object. The data for creating the circle is recorded as an instruction such as CIRCLE 40 Y 200 150, which means create a circle with a 40-pixel radius, color it yellow, and place the center of the circle 200 pixels from the left of the screen and 150 pixels from the top of the screen.

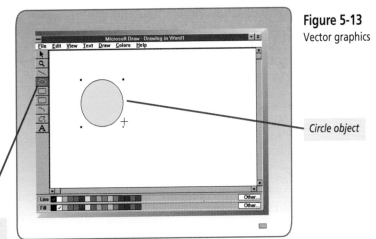

Figure 5-13
Vector graphics

Circle object

Filled circle tool

Clouds

Filled circle

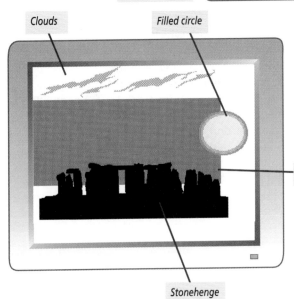

Using the drawing tools, you can create geometric objects such as filled rectangles or circles. You can also create irregular shapes by connecting points to create the outline of a shape. The clouds and Stonehenge objects in this picture were created using this technique. Irregular shapes are recorded as a list of coordinate points to indicate their position on the screen. For example, the upper-left corner of Stonehenge is at location 95,350.

Filled rectangle

Stonehenge

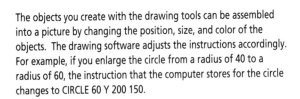

The objects you create with the drawing tools can be assembled into a picture by changing the position, size, and color of the objects. The drawing software adjusts the instructions accordingly. For example, if you enlarge the circle from a radius of 40 to a radius of 60, the instruction that the computer stores for the circle changes to CIRCLE 60 Y 200 150.

Vector graphics do not look as realistic as pictures created with bitmap graphics. Vector graphics, however, have several important advantages. First, a picture created with vector graphics software is likely to require much less storage space than a bitmap picture. The storage space required for a vector graphics picture depends on its complexity. Each instruction requires storage space, so the more lines, shapes, and fill patterns the picture contains, the more storage space it requires. The picture shown in Figure 5-13 requires only 4,894 bytes of storage.

A second advantage of vector graphics is that you can easily modify the pictures you create using vector graphics software. You can think of the parts of a vector graphics picture as separate objects that you can individually stretch, shrink, distort, color, move, or delete. For example, your vector graphics picture might contain a sun that you created with a yellow circle. You could easily move the sun to a different location in the picture, enlarge it, or change its color.

Files that contain vector graphics typically have file extensions such as .WMF, .DXF, .MGX, and .CGM.

Representing Video

A video is composed of a series of frames. Each frame is essentially a still picture, which could be represented using the same techniques as bitmap graphics. However, video captures or displays 30 frames per second, which means that digital video recording requires tremendous storage capacity.

As you have seen, a full-screen image at 640 by 480 resolution contains 307,000 pixels. If you use 256 colors, each pixel is represented by eight bits, or one byte (remember that 2^8 bits convey up to 256 units of information). So you need 307,000 bytes to represent the pixels on one screen. Multiply this number by 30 to calculate how many bytes are needed for each second of video—that's 9,216,000 bytes or about 9 megabytes for one second of video. A two-hour movie would require 66,355,200,000 bytes, more than 66 billion bytes! It would be only marginally possible to play back such a digitally recorded video, even using the most powerful super-computer. As you will learn later in this chapter, video data requires some special coding techniques to produce a video file of manageable size.

Representing Sound

Sound or audio data can be represented in two very different ways: as a waveform or as MIDI music. The difference between waveform audio and MIDI music is analogous to the difference between bitmap and vector graphics. Just as a bitmap is a digitized representation of a picture, waveform audio is a digital representation of sound. And as vector graphics is a set of instructions for recreating a picture, MIDI music is a set of instructions for recreating a sound.

Waveform Audio

Waveform audio is the digital representation of a sound. When sound is digitally recorded, samples of the waveform are collected at periodic intervals and stored as numeric data. Waveforms can be used to record music, voice, or sounds. Figure 5-14 shows how a computer digitally samples a waveform.

Sampling rate refers to the number of times per second the sound is measured during the recording process. The sampling rate is expressed in hertz (Hz). One thousand samples per second is expressed as 1000 Hz or 1 KHz (kilohertz). Higher sampling rates increase the quality of the sound recording but require more storage space than lower sampling rates.

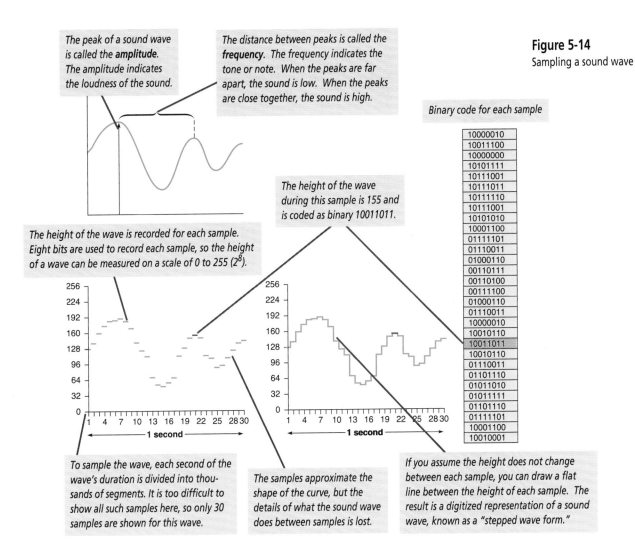

Figure 5-14

Sampling a sound wave

The peak of a sound wave is called the **amplitude**. The amplitude indicates the loudness of the sound.

The distance between peaks is called the **frequency**. The frequency indicates the tone or note. When the peaks are far apart, the sound is low. When the peaks are close together, the sound is high.

Binary code for each sample

The height of the wave during this sample is 155 and is coded as binary 10011011.

The height of the wave is recorded for each sample. Eight bits are used to record each sample, so the height of a wave can be measured on a scale of 0 to 255 (2^8).

To sample the wave, each second of the wave's duration is divided into thousands of segments. It is too difficult to show all such samples here, so only 30 samples are shown for this wave.

The samples approximate the shape of the curve, but the details of what the sound wave does between samples is lost.

If you assume the height does not change between each sample, you can draw a flat line between the height of each sample. The result is a digitized representation of a sound wave, known as a "stepped wave form."

An audio compact disc recording uses a sampling rate of 44.1 KHz, which means a sample of the sound is taken 44,100 times per second. Each sample is represented by eight bits (one byte) or by sixteen bits (two bytes). At a sampling rate of 44.1 KHz, and using two bytes for each sample, one second of music produces 88,200 bytes of data. A stereo recording produces twice as much data because you are essentially making two recordings to achieve the stereo effect. When you sample music at 44.1 KHz, you can store only eight seconds of stereo music on a 1.44 megabyte floppy disk. Forty-five minutes of music, the length of a typical rock album, requires about 240 megabytes—the entire storage capacity of a typical hard disk.

To conserve space, applications that do not require such high-quality sound use much lower sampling rates. Voice is often recorded with a sampling rate of 11 KHz or 11,000 samples per second. This results in lower-quality sound, but the file is about one-fourth the size of a file for the same sound recorded at 44.1 KHz.

The waveform files you record and store on your computer generally have .WAV, .MOD, or .VOC file extensions.

MIDI Music

MIDI, or **Musical Instrument Digital Interface**, files contain the instructions that MIDI instruments or MIDI sound cards use to recreate sounds. MIDI files are used to store and recreate musical instrument sounds, but are not used for voice.

MIDI is a music notation system that allows computers to communicate with music synthesizers. The computer codes the music as a sequence and stores it as a file with a .MID, .CMF, or .ROL extension. A **sequence** is analogous to a player-piano roll that contains punched information indicating which musical notes to play. A MIDI sequence contains instructions for when a note begins, what instrument plays the note, the volume of the note, and the duration of the note. The actual encoding scheme used for MIDI music is fairly complex, but this hasn't prevented hundreds of musicians from using computers to compose and record their music. The MIDI coding scheme produces fairly compact files. For example, three minutes of music can be stored in a 10 kilobyte (10,000 byte) file.

Data Compression

Despite the use of information theory to design effective coding schemes for representing characters, graphics, and sounds, the files that contain such data can be quite large. As you learned earlier in this chapter, a full-screen 16-grayscale bitmap graphic requires 153,600 bytes, and a forty-five minute waveform sound file might be as large as 240 megabytes. Large files can be a problem for the following reasons:

- Large files require large amounts of storage space, quickly filling up a hard disk.
- Large files are likely to become fragmented and reduce the efficiency of your disk drive.
- Opening a large file and locating a particular item of information in the file requires extra time.
- If you want to store a large file on floppy disks for safekeeping or transfer it to another computer, you need many floppy disks.
- Large files require lengthy transmission time.

If you could reduce the size of a file without losing any of the data contained in the file, you would be able to avoid the problems in this list. **File compression** is a technique that reduces the size of a large file by using fewer bits to represent the data the file contains. File compression is reversible, so the data can be returned to its original form. The process of reversing file compression is sometimes referred to as **uncompressing**, **extracting**, or **expanding** the file. File compression and uncompression are performed by compression software. Figure 5-15 will help you visualize how compression affects the size of a file.

A popular shareware compression program is PKZIP. You can obtain this program by mail from a shareware distributor or from your computer dealer. Let's see how you might use this software. Suppose you have a large 1.8 megabyte file called CLIENTS.DOC on your hard disk (drive C:). The file contains information on the customers for a mail-order business that you want to give your coworker. You want to put this file on a single 1.44 megabyte floppy disk in drive A:. Because CLIENTS.DOC requires 1.8 megabytes, it will not fit on a single floppy disk in its uncompressed state.

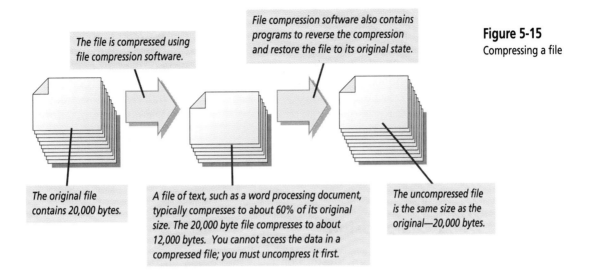

Figure 5-15
Compressing a file

The file is compressed using file compression software.

File compression software also contains programs to reverse the compression and restore the file to its original state.

The original file contains 20,000 bytes.

A file of text, such as a word processing document, typically compresses to about 60% of its original size. The 20,000 byte file compresses to about 12,000 bytes. You cannot access the data in a compressed file; you must uncompress it first.

The uncompressed file is the same size as the original—20,000 bytes.

To compress the CLIENTS.DOC file, you use the command:

PKZIP C:CLIENTS.DOC A:

As a result of your command, the computer compresses CLIENTS.DOC to make a smaller file on drive A: called CLIENTS.ZIP. The .ZIP file extension is your clue that the file is compressed.

Because it is not possible to use a compressed file directly, when your coworker gets the disk containing CLIENTS.ZIP, he or she must uncompress the file. The command:

PKUNZIP A:CLIENTS.ZIP C:CLIENTS.DOC

"unzips" or uncompresses the file and places the uncompressed version on your coworker's C: drive. Figure 5-16 summarizes how to use PKZIP and PKUNZIP.

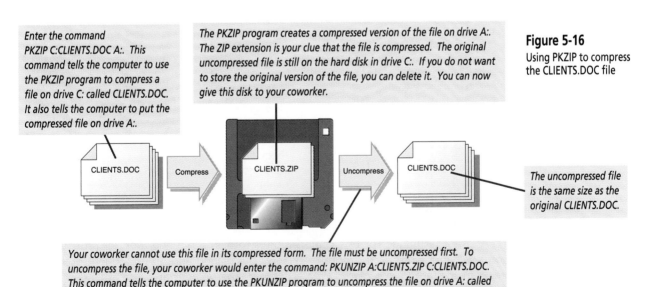

Figure 5-16
Using PKZIP to compress the CLIENTS.DOC file

Enter the command PKZIP C:CLIENTS.DOC A:. This command tells the computer to use the PKZIP program to compress a file on drive C: called CLIENTS.DOC. It also tells the computer to put the compressed file on drive A:.

The PKZIP program creates a compressed version of the file on drive A:. The ZIP extension is your clue that the file is compressed. The original uncompressed file is still on the hard disk in drive C:. If you do not want to store the original version of the file, you can delete it. You can now give this disk to your coworker.

The uncompressed file is the same size as the original CLIENTS.DOC.

Your coworker cannot use this file in its compressed form. The file must be uncompressed first. To uncompress the file, your coworker would enter the command: PKUNZIP A:CLIENTS.ZIP C:CLIENTS.DOC. This command tells the computer to use the PKUNZIP program to uncompress the file on drive A: called CLIENTS.ZIP. It also tells the computer to put the uncompressed file on drive C: and name it CLIENTS.DOC.

Many computing environments automatically compress and uncompress your files when you save and open them. If your computer provides automatic compression, you do not have to take extra steps or enter extra commands to compress a file. The same holds true for uncompression. Whenever you want to open a file, the computer automatically returns it to its original size.

Exactly how does compression software work? The basic idea behind this type of software is actually quite intuitive—using the knowledge you have of information theory and data representation, you could probably devise a workable compression scheme. You just need to think about how to take the bits, bytes, and information from a large file, look for duplicate patterns in the file, and find some way to reduce that duplication. Let's look at some simple compression techniques.

Text Compression

Adaptive pattern substitution is a compression technique designed specifically to compress text files. This compression technique scans the entire text and looks for patterns of two or more bytes. When it finds such a pattern, it substitutes a byte pattern that is not used elsewhere in the file and makes a directory entry. Let's look at a simple example.

Using adaptive pattern substitution, how much can we compress the phrase, "the rain in Spain stays mainly on the plain, but the rain in Maine falls again and again"? The uncompressed phrase is 88 bytes long, including spaces and punctuation. Look at Figure 5-17 to see how adaptive pattern substitution can compress this phrase.

Figure 5-17
Compressing a text file

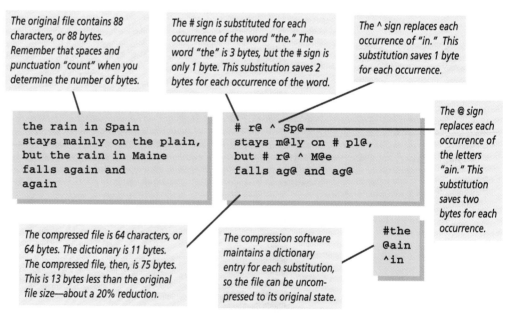

The original file contains 88 characters, or 88 bytes. Remember that spaces and punctuation "count" when you determine the number of bytes.

The # sign is substituted for each occurrence of the word "the." The word "the" is 3 bytes, but the # sign is only 1 byte. This substitution saves 2 bytes for each occurrence of the word.

The ^ sign replaces each occurrence of "in." This substitution saves 1 byte for each occurrence.

The @ sign replaces each occurrence of the letters "ain." This substitution saves two bytes for each occurrence.

```
the rain in Spain
stays mainly on the plain,
but the rain in Maine
falls again and
again
```

```
# r@ ^ Sp@
stays m@ly on # pl@,
but # r@ ^ M@e
falls ag@ and ag@
```

```
#the
@ain
^in
```

The compressed file is 64 characters, or 64 bytes. The dictionary is 11 bytes. The compressed file, then, is 75 bytes. This is 13 bytes less than the original file size—about a 20% reduction.

The compression software maintains a dictionary entry for each substitution, so the file can be uncompressed to its original state.

Another technique for text compression is to scan a file and look for repeated words. When a word occurs more than once, the second and all subsequent occurrences of the word are replaced with a number. The number acts as a "pointer" to the original occurrence of the word. Figure 5-18 shows how this works.

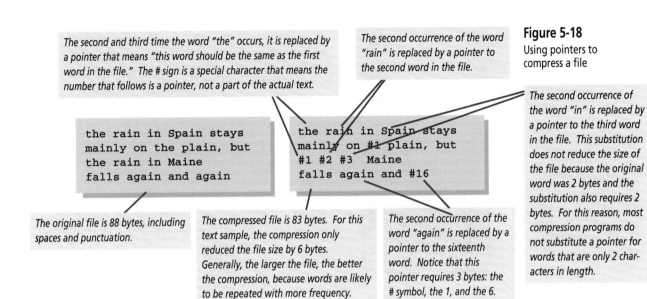

Figure 5-18
Using pointers to compress a file

The second and third time the word "the" occurs, it is replaced by a pointer that means "this word should be the same as the first word in the file." The # sign is a special character that means the number that follows is a pointer, not a part of the actual text.

The second occurrence of the word "rain" is replaced by a pointer to the second word in the file.

The second occurrence of the word "in" is replaced by a pointer to the third word in the file. This substitution does not reduce the size of the file because the original word was 2 bytes and the substitution also requires 2 bytes. For this reason, most compression programs do not substitute a pointer for words that are only 2 characters in length.

```
the rain in Spain stays
mainly on the plain, but
the rain in Maine
falls again and again
```

```
the rain in Spain stays
mainly on #1 plain, but
#1 #2 #3  Maine
falls again and #16
```

The original file is 88 bytes, including spaces and punctuation.

The compressed file is 83 bytes. For this text sample, the compression only reduced the file size by 6 bytes. Generally, the larger the file, the better the compression, because words are likely to be repeated with more frequency.

The second occurrence of the word "again" is replaced by a pointer to the sixteenth word. Notice that this pointer requires 3 bytes: the # symbol, the 1, and the 6.

Graphics Compression

Uncompressed bitmap graphics files are very large; however, they often contain repetitious data, such as large blocks of the same color, which can be compressed. **Run length encoding** is a compression technique that looks for patterns of bytes and replaces them with a message that describes the pattern. As a simple example, suppose a section of a picture had 167 consecutive white pixels and each pixel is described by one byte of data. The process of run length encoding compresses this series of 167 pixels into as few as two bytes, as shown in Figure 5-19.

Video Compression

You learned earlier in this chapter that video is composed of a series of frames, each of which is essentially a bitmap image. You also learned that storing the bitmap images for a full-length film requires more than 66 gigabytes of storage space. Clearly, this is beyond the capacity of today's personal computer systems. It is possible, however, to display video on your personal computer by reducing the number of pixels in the image, reducing the number of frames displayed per second, or coding only the changes that take place from one frame to the next.

Video for Windows and **QuickTime** are formats used to encode, compress, store, and playback video segments on computers. A **video segment** is a series of frames or individual images that are shown in quick succession. The number of frames per second directly affects the perceived smoothness of the segment. High-quality video displays 30 frames per second. Lower-quality video displays only 15 frames per second, which might appear jerky, but is acceptable for some computer applications, such as training videos or animated product catalogs.

Figure 5-19

Using run length encoding to compress a grayscale bitmap graphic

This bitmap graphic has been enlarged to show individual pixels, such as this white pixel. Each pixel is represented by eight bits (one byte). This white pixel is encoded as 11111111.

The next five pixels are black. The binary representation for black is 00000000. This section of the graphic is coded "00000101 00000000." The first byte is the binary representation of 5. The second byte is the code for black.

Without compression, the first nine rows of the graphic require 288 bytes of file space because there are 288 pixels. Using run length encoding to compress this section of the graphic, only 30 bytes are required.

The first five rows and the first seven pixels of row six are white. In the uncompressed file for this graphic, these pixels require 167 bytes. This can be compressed using the code "10100111 11111111." The first byte is the binary representation of 167. The second byte is the code for white.

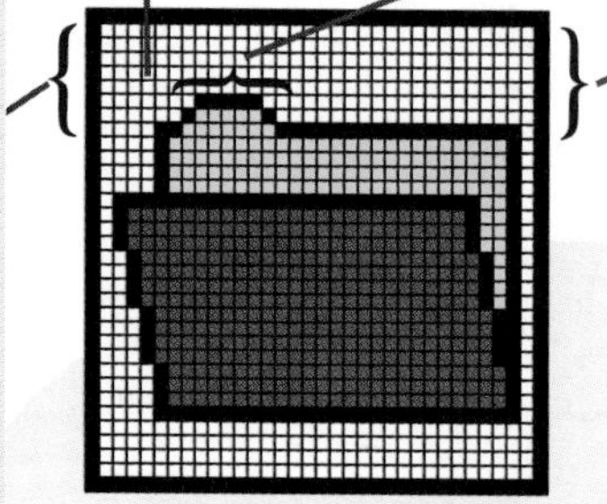

Binary representations of the number of repetitions.

Binary representation of the color white.

```
*** Repetitions*****    Data *
Decimal Binary          Binary
=====================================
 167   01010011         11111111
   5   00000101         00000000
  26   00011010         11111111
   1   00000001         00000000
   5   00000101         10100000
   1   00000001         00000000
  23   00010111         11111111
   2   00000010         00000000
   7   00000111         10100000
  18   00010010         00000000
   5   00000101         11111111
   1   00000001         00000000
  25   00011001         10100000
   1   00000001         11111111
   1   00000001         00000000
=====================================
 288
      .  .
      .  .
      .  .
```

Another technique that makes video display possible on a microcomputer is the reduction in the size of the image. Displaying an image on one-quarter of your screen requires only a fourth of the data required to display a full-screen image, so most computer video applications use only a small window on your computer screen.

There are many techniques for compressing video data, and the details of these methods are quite complex. A simple example will give you a general idea of how one video compression technique works. Suppose you have a video segment that doesn't change very much from one frame to the next. A "talking head" is a good example; the mouth and eyes change from frame to frame, but the background remains fairly stable. Instead of recording all the data for each frame, a compression program might store only the changes from one frame to the next. Storing only the changes requires far less data, saves storage space, and reduces the time required to display the data.

Now that you have an understanding of how data is encoded and compressed, you are ready to see how it is transmitted.

Communications Channels

A **communications channel** provides the means of conveying or transmitting a signal between devices, such as between two computers. Think back to Figure 5-1 and recall that in Shannon's communications model a channel connected the sender with the receiver. Channels include cables such as twisted pair, coaxial, and fiber-optic cable. Wireless transmissions use radio waves and microwaves as communications channels.

Each type of channel has unique characteristics. An important characteristic of a communications channel is the amount of data it can transport. For example, you probably know that the telephone company provides a way for more than one conversation to take place at a time. To see how this works, and how computers can use telephone lines to communicate, you need to understand bandwidth.

The signals transmitted through cables or space are electromagnetic waves. The range of frequencies that create a signal is called the **bandwidth**. For example, the human voice typically generates sound frequencies between 250 and 3,400 cycles per second, or hertz. This is equal to a bandwidth of 3,150 hertz (3,400 minus 250). The telephone company provides a bandwidth of 4,000 hertz for voice communications. The extra bandwidth acts as a sort of buffer for your voice communications and helps prevent interference from other conversations using the same cable.

If you have a channel with a bandwidth of 4,000 hertz, you can transmit a single telephone conversation. However, the telephone company would regard this as very impractical. To transmit millions of telephone conversations every day, the telephone company must use channels with more bandwidth. The telephone company makes extensive use of microwave transmission, which has a bandwidth in excess of a billion hertz. If a single voice transmission requires 4,000 hertz, a microwave link has the potential to carry 250,000 simultaneous voice transmissions. The way this works is truly a clever piece of engineering and makes worldwide voice and data communications possible.

Thinking ahead, you might expect computer communications to require a very small bandwidth—after all, a computer communicates ones and zeros instead of the range of frequencies of the human voice. However, computer communications are frequently carried out using telephone company equipment and, therefore, use the same 4,000 hertz bandwidth allocated to voice transmissions. A zero is transmitted as a 1,070 hertz wave and a one is transmitted at 1,279 hertz.

Computer communications is carried out over a variety of channels, using copper wires, optical cable, radio waves, and microwaves. Let's look at some of the more frequently used communications channels.

Twisted Pair Cable

A **twisted pair cable** consists of pairs of copper wire twisted together. Each wire is covered with a thin layer of insulating plastic. The wires are bundled together to form a cable, as shown in Figure 5-20 on the following page.

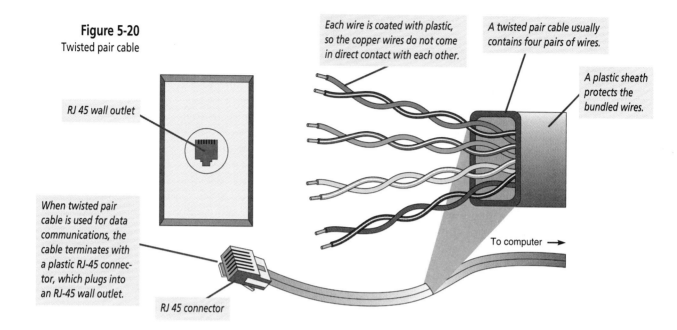

Figure 5-20
Twisted pair cable

Each wire is coated with plastic, so the copper wires do not come in direct contact with each other.

A twisted pair cable usually contains four pairs of wires.

A plastic sheath protects the bundled wires.

RJ 45 wall outlet

When twisted pair cable is used for data communications, the cable terminates with a plastic RJ-45 connector, which plugs into an RJ-45 wall outlet.

To computer →

RJ 45 connector

A twisted pair cable for data communications is generally terminated on both ends with RJ-45 plugs that look like a wide phone plug. One end of the cable plugs into a port in the back of your computer. The other end plugs into an RJ-45 outlet in the wall. The wall outlet is wired to other computers or to telephone company lines to provide your computer with a communications channel. Twisted pair cable is inexpensive and easy to install. The bandwidth of twisted pair cable is about 1,000,000 hertz.

Coaxial Cable

Coaxial cable is a high bandwidth communications cable consisting of a copper wire conductor, a nonconducting insulator, woven metal outer shielding, and a plastic outer coating. The bandwidth of coaxial cable is about 100,000,000 hertz. Coaxial cable is used for cable television where its high bandwidth allows it to simultaneously carry signals for more than 100 television channels. Coaxial cable also provides good bandwidth for data communications and is used in situations where twisted pair cable is not adequate to carry the required amount of data.

Coaxial cable is terminated with **BNC connectors**. As shown in Figure 5-21, the BNC connector plugs into a T-shaped connector at the back of the computer.

Because of its construction, coaxial cable is less susceptible to electronic interference than twisted pair cabling. Coaxial cable is also thicker and stiffer than twisted pair cable, which makes it more difficult to run through tight spaces and around corners. Coaxial cable used to be one of the most widely used cables for computer communications, but today it is being replaced by twisted pair cable, which is less expensive and easier to install. But for situations where high bandwidth is required, both coaxial cable and twisted pair cable are being replaced by fiber optic cable.

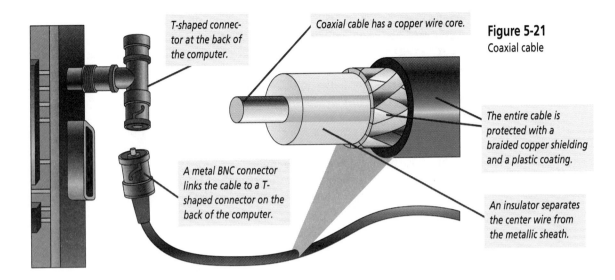

Figure 5-21
Coaxial cable

T-shaped connector at the back of the computer.

Coaxial cable has a copper wire core.

A metal BNC connector links the cable to a T-shaped connector on the back of the computer.

The entire cable is protected with a braided copper shielding and a plastic coating.

An insulator separates the center wire from the metallic sheath.

Fiber Optic Cable

Fiber optic cable is a bundle of extremely thin tubes of glass. Each tube, or **optical fibe**r, is much thinner than a human hair. A fiber optic cable usually consists of a strong inner support wire, multiple strands of optical fiber, each covered by a plastic insulator, and a tough outer covering, as shown in Figure 5-22.

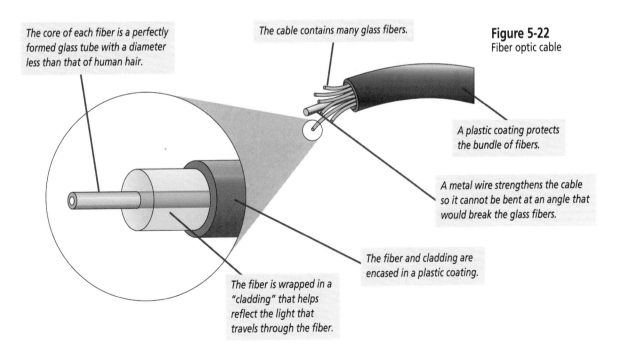

Figure 5-22
Fiber optic cable

The core of each fiber is a perfectly formed glass tube with a diameter less than that of human hair.

The cable contains many glass fibers.

A plastic coating protects the bundle of fibers.

A metal wire strengthens the cable so it cannot be bent at an angle that would break the glass fibers.

The fiber and cladding are encased in a plastic coating.

The fiber is wrapped in a "cladding" that helps reflect the light that travels through the fiber.

Fiber optic cables do not conduct or transmit electrical signals. Instead, miniature lasers or LEDs (light emitting diodes) send pulses of light through the fibers. Electronics at the receiving end of the fiber convert the light pulses back into electrical signals. Each fiber is a one-way communications channel, which means that at least two fibers are required to provide a two-way communications link. Fiber optic cable has a very high bandwidth and is capable of transmitting large amounts of data.

Fiber optic cables do not transmit electrical current, so they are not susceptible to electrical interference. However, the individual fibers are extremely thin and fragile and must be protected from damage. Because of the extra protection requirements, fiber optic cabling includes a center reinforcing wire. This makes the fiber optic cable fairly thick and difficult to run through tight places and around corners.

Wireless Communications

Wireless communications links use radio waves or microwaves to transmit data. Wireless links are used to connect mobile sites, such as cellular telephones, and in situations where it is difficult or impossible to install cabling, such as in remote, geographically rugged regions. Wireless communications channels are generally slower than cables, and they are susceptible to static and radio interference.

Microwave transmission sends data from a microwave transmitting station to a microwave receiving station. Microwave transmission is **line-of-sight transmission**, which means that no obstacles, such as mountains or buildings, can be located between the transmitting and receiving stations. Microwave transmissions can also be affected by heavy rain and snow, which block the microwaves. Microwave transmission is often used for short to medium distances where line-of-sight communication is possible and where cabling is too expensive.

Satellite transmission uses radio waves to transmit data from a ground-based transmitting station to a satellite, which then transmits the data to another ground-based station. Communications satellites are generally placed in geosynchronous orbits about 22,300 miles above the earth. A satellite in a **geosynchronous orbit** stays above the same part of the earth by orbiting around the earth at the same speed as the earth rotates. Like microwaves, satellite transmission requires a clear line of sight from the transmitting station to the satellite and from the satellite to the receiving station. Communications satellites are a powerful communications channel because they can link transmitting and receiving stations in any part of the globe visible to the satellite.

Communications Protocols

In Shannon's communications system model, noise sometimes interferes with transmission. For example, suppose that you were sending a message to a business colleague, "Let's meet at the exhibition hall at 5:00 P.M. for dinner." As the sequence of bits for the word "hall" travel across the communications channel, some interference changes a single bit. The "a," in the word "hall," which was transmitted as 01100001, arrives at its destination as 01101001, which is the ASCII code for the letter "i." When "hall" is changed to "hill," the meaning of your message has been altered. This is a fairly innocent example, but you can imagine that transmission errors that change letters or numbers—such as a digit on your paycheck—could have disastrous effects.

To ensure that the data you transmit is not altered by noise or interference, both the sending and the receiving computers must follow a set of communications protocols. **Communications protocols** are rules that ensure the orderly and accurate transmission and reception of data. A simple communications protocol that you use in everyday conversation is "only one person talks at a time." If two people are trying to hold a conversation but do not follow this protocol, it is very likely that neither person will understand what the other is trying to say.

Without protocols, data communication is impossible. As a computer user today, you should have some familiarity with communications protocols; when you set up communication between one computer and another, you frequently need to select protocols.

Parallel and Serial Communications

In Chapter 4, you learned that a parallel cable carries eight bits at a time and a serial cable carries one bit at a time. Parallel communication is the simplest type of communication because it is "standardized." In other words, after you connect two devices with a parallel cable, there is little else for you to do because parallel communication has few user-selectable options.

Serial communication is more challenging from the user perspective. Although there is a serial communication standard known as RS-232-C, this "standard" includes many user-selectable options. You usually need to make some protocol choices to establish a functional serial communication link. Let's examine some of the protocol options that affect serial communications.

Synchronous and Asynchronous Protocols

The major problem with serial communication is coordinating the transmission and the reception. The transmitting computer sends a series of bits, but how does the receiving computer know when the transmission begins and ends? If the receiving computer misses the first three bits of a serial transmission, the message would be hopelessly garbled, as shown in Figure 5-23 on the following page.

There are two ways to coordinate serial communication, referred to as synchronous and asynchronous protocols. Using **synchronous protocol**, the sender and the receiver are synchronized by a signal called a clock. The transmitting computer sends data at a fixed rate and the receiving computer expects the incoming data at the same fixed rate. Much of the communication that takes place on the main circuit board of a computer is synchronous; however, communication between two microcomputers rarely uses the synchronous protocol.

Figure 5-23
A garbled message

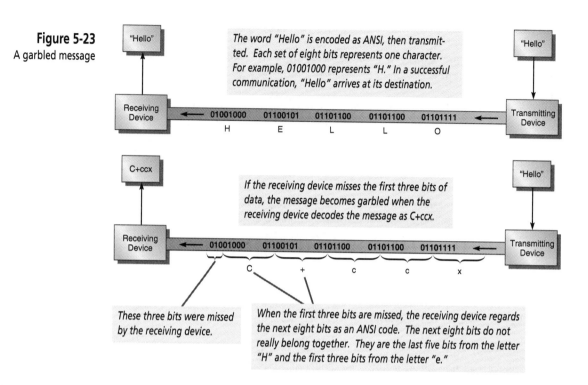

Computers typically use asynchronous protocol when they communicate using modems. Using **asynchronous protocol**, the sending computer transmits a **start bit** to indicate the beginning of the data. Next, the sending computer transmits the data as a series of bits, called a **block**. The end of each block is indicated by transmitting one or more **stop bits**, as shown in Figure 5-24.

Figure 5-24
Start bits and stop bits

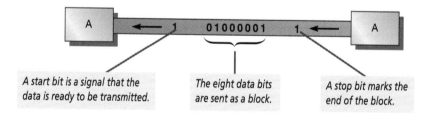

A start bit is a signal that the data is ready to be transmitted.

The eight data bits are sent as a block.

A stop bit marks the end of the block.

Parity

You already know the potentially disastrous effects of a single data bit that is changed during transmission. Computers can check for errors during transmission using a **parity bit**. The transmitting computer attaches a parity bit to a data block. The parity bit is either a 0 or a 1, depending on the protocol. With *even* parity, the number of *one* bits in a data block is an even number. With *odd* parity, the number of *one* bits in the data block is an odd number. If the protocol is for no parity, a parity bit is not attached to the data block, and the computer does not use a parity bit for error checking. Study Figure 5-25 to find out how the computer assigns parity bits.

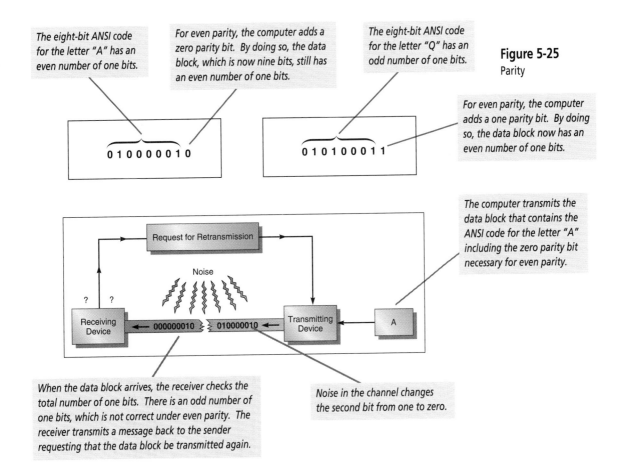

The eight-bit ANSI code for the letter "A" has an even number of one bits.

For even parity, the computer adds a zero parity bit. By doing so, the data block, which is now nine bits, still has an even number of one bits.

The eight-bit ANSI code for the letter "Q" has an odd number of one bits.

Figure 5-25
Parity

For even parity, the computer adds a one parity bit. By doing so, the data block now has an even number of one bits.

0 1 0 0 0 0 0 1 0

0 1 0 1 0 0 0 1 1

The computer transmits the data block that contains the ANSI code for the letter "A" including the zero parity bit necessary for even parity.

Request for Retransmission

Noise

Receiving Device ← 000000010 ⟨ 010000010 ← Transmitting Device ← A

When the data block arrives, the receiver checks the total number of one bits. There is an odd number of one bits, which is not correct under even parity. The receiver transmits a message back to the sender requesting that the data block be transmitted again.

Noise in the channel changes the second bit from one to zero.

From Simplex to Echoplex

Some channels support one-way communication, whereas other channels support two-way communications. For example, a CB radio can either send or receive, but it cannot send and receive simultaneously. A telephone, on the other hand, can send and receive simultaneously. You use a CB radio differently from the way you use the telephone—with the CB radio, you must press a button when you are ready to send. The protocol you use to communicate—whether you need to press a button to talk, for example—depends on the channel you are using. Let's examine how the different types of channels affect how you'd set up communications protocols.

A channel that allows a device to send only messages is referred to as a **simplex channel**. An example of simplex communication is a radio transmitter, which can transmit, but not receive signals.

A channel that allows a device to send or receive, but cannot do both at the same time, is called a **half-duplex** channel. A CB radio is an example of half-duplex transmission. The CB radio is in receive mode until you press the "talk" button.

A channel that allows a device to send and receive simultaneously is referred to as a **duplex**, or **full-duplex**, channel. A telephone line is an example of a full-duplex channel.

Some channels send information to the receiver and then echo it back to the sender as a means of checking accuracy. This type of circuit or communication is referred to as **echoplex**, or simply as an **echo**. Echoplex is useful in situations when it is important to be absolutely certain that data was transmitted accurately.

Transmission Speed

The two terms you need to know when you set transmission speeds are baud rate and bits per second. **Baud rate** refers to the number of times the state or frequency of a communications line can change per second. For example, if the transmission speed is 300 baud, the line state can change 300 times per second. Under a simple transmission protocol, each state change transmits one bit, as shown in Figure 5-26.

Figure 5-26
Baud rate

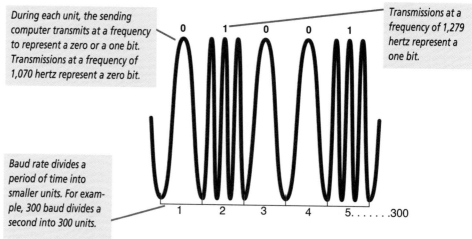

During each unit, the sending computer transmits at a frequency to represent a zero or a one bit. Transmissions at a frequency of 1,070 hertz represent a zero bit.

Transmissions at a frequency of 1,279 hertz represent a one bit.

Baud rate divides a period of time into smaller units. For example, 300 baud divides a second into 300 units.

Bits per second, or **bps**, refers to the number of bits that can be transmitted per second. In older modems, the baud rate and the bits per second were identical, because the modem transferred one bit for each unit of time. Today's high-speed modems can transmit multiple bits each time the line changes frequency; therefore, baud rate and bits per second are no longer interchangeable terms. Unfortunately, many people in the computer industry still use the two terms interchangeably, which means that the term baud rate is often used when bits per second is meant.

Transmission speed is part of the communications protocol because the sending device and the receiving device must "agree" on the same speed or else communication will not succeed. For example, suppose a device sends ten characters per second, but the receiving device is only expecting five characters during that second. The outcome of such communication is difficult to predict; the receiving device might get only every other character, or perhaps it will receive only the first five characters or the last five characters. For successful communication, the sending and receiving devices must use the same transmission rate.

Serial devices generally communicate at speeds from 300 bits per second to 19,200 bits per second. Printers and other low-speed serial devices are often connected at 1200 or 2400 bits per second, whereas modems generally operate at 1200, 2400, 9600, or 14,400 bits per second.

Modems

In Chapter 1 you were introduced to the modem as a peripheral device. A **modem** is a device that converts the digital signals used inside your computer to an analog signal that can be transmitted over the phone line. The process of converting the signals from digital to analog is known as **modulation**, while the process of converting the analog signal back to a digital signal is known as **demodulation**. The word "modem" comes from the two words MODulate and DEModulate.

There are two main types of modems—external and internal. An **external modem** is a box that is connected by cable to a serial port on a computer. An **internal modem** is a circuit board that plugs into an expansion slot inside a computer. Both internal and external modems function identically. Some people prefer external modems because they can be easily moved from one computer to another and because they have lights that can be used to diagnose communication problems. Other people prefer internal modems because they require less desk space, don't require a cable, and are generally less expensive.

When you use a modem to communicate with another computer, you need a **communications program**, which helps you select the protocols for the communication session. To connect to another computer with your modem, you must use the communications program to set the transmission speed, word size, stop bits, and parity to match the system you are calling. The communications program also helps you set up the modem so it uses the correct serial port and sends the correct dialing signal.

You might remember from Chapter 4 that IBM-compatible computers have up to four serial ports: COM1, COM2, COM3, and COM4. If your computer has a mouse, it usually uses serial port COM1. Because your modem cannot use the same port as another device, it should use COM2. If you try to use a modem and you don't hear a dialing sound when the communications program should be dialing, it is possible that the modem is connected to one serial port, while the communications program is sending its commands to another. In this case, you can use your communications software to change the COM port your modem uses.

A modem is connected to the telephone line, so when you want to communicate with another computer, the modem must "dial" the telephone number for the other computer. The modem can dial the number for you, but it must be set up for pulse or touch-tone dialing, depending on the type of telephone line you are using. Your communications software can help you specify which type of telephone line you have so the modem can use the correct dialing signals.

Configuring a Modem

L A B

DATA COMMUNICATIONS

The data communications concepts you learned in this chapter are not abstract concepts. Communicating with another computer using a modem is a very common task performed today, and to do so you must be able to correctly configure your modem and communications program.

Suppose you just purchased a new modem and want to try it out by calling a local computer bulletin board, where you can leave messages for other computer users, play games, and search for information. Suppose that the telephone number for this bulletin board is 555-9509. The information you received from the person who operates the computer bulletin board indicates the system supports 1200, 2400, and 9600 bits per second modems and requires eight data bits, no parity, and one stop bit. You have a 9600 bps external modem connected to COM2 and a touch-tone telephone line. Now that you've just about finished this chapter on communications, you should know what all this means. Let's review.

The bulletin board supports 1200, 2400, and 9600 bits per second transmission speeds. Because you have a 9600 bps modem, you set up your communications software to connect at 9600 bps for the fastest transmission rate. You know that the bits you send represent data and that the ones and zeros correspond to electrical states, such as "off" and "on."

The bulletin board requires an eight-bit word. From reading this chapter, you know that this means the system transfers data in blocks of eight bits. From your knowledge of information theory, you know that a block of eight bits can convey up to 256 different units of information. Eight bits can represent 256 different characters and symbols, 256 different colors, or a binary number up to 255. Each block of eight bits can represent a single ASCII, ANSI, or EBCDIC character. Alternatively, a block of eight bits might represent a segment of a bitmap graphic, part of an instruction to recreate a vector graphic, part of a sound sample, or part of a MIDI sequence.

The information you received about the bulletin board indicates that communications require one stop bit. You know from this chapter that a stop bit is an extra bit sent after each block to indicate that the complete block has been sent. Start bits and stop bits are used with asynchronous communication to coordinate the sending and receiving devices.

The bulletin board requires no parity. You know that a parity bit is used to check for transmission errors caused by noise in the channel. With even parity, the number of *one* bits in a data block must be an even number. With odd parity, the number of *one* bits in the data block is odd. If a communications system uses no parity, it does not use a parity bit to detect errors.

On the evening of April 18, 1775, Paul Revere saw the lantern signal in the tower of the Old North Church, mounted his horse, and sped off on his famous ride. Did the British come by land or by sea? It is interesting that most people remember the code, "one if by land, and two if by sea," but have forgotten (or never knew) if the British actually came by land or by sea. Perhaps this reflects a genuine fascination with codes and the impact of information theory in an age when computers have become an indispensable aspect of everyday life. On the other hand, it may reflect the enduring value of poetry, and remind us that technology, though indispensable, is only one aspect of our complex culture.

■   ■   ■

C H A P T E R   R E V I E W

1. Answer the questions listed in the Chapter Preview section at the beginning of the chapter.

2. List each of the boldface terms used in this chapter, then use your own words to write a short definition.

3. Complete the following chart that summarizes what you learned about information theory:

NUMBER OF BITS	NUMBER OF COMBINATIONS	MINIMUM DECIMAL VALUE	MAXIMUM DECIMAL VALUE
1	2	0	1
2	4		
3	8		
4	16		
5			
6			
7			
8			

4. Perform the calculations necessary to complete the following table:

WIDTH	HEIGHT	TYPE	NUMBER OF BITS	NUMBER OF BYTES
640	480	MONOCHROME	307,200	38,400
640	480	16 GRAYSCALE		
640	480	16 COLOR		
640	480	256 COLOR		

5. What are the decimal equivalents of the following binary numbers:

BINARY	DECIMAL
00000000	
00000001	
00000010	
10000000	
10000011	
11111111	

6. Describe each of the four character representation schemes presented in this chapter.

7. A monochrome graphic with 2 colors per pixel requires one bit to represent each pixel. A color graphic with 16 colors per pixel requires four bits to represent each pixel. How many bits per pixel are required for a color graphic with 4 colors per pixel?

8. What is the difference between bitmap graphics and vector graphics?

9. What is the difference between a waveform and MIDI music?

10. What are five problems associated with large files?

11. What are the benefits of using a parity bit in data communications?

C H A P T E R   Q U I Z

1. How many lanterns would the Minutemen have needed if they wanted to send up to eight different messages?

2. What is the decimal equivalent of the binary number 00001111?

3. The _____ code uses seven bits to represent 128 symbols including uppercase and lower-case letters, special control codes, numerals, and punctuation symbols.

4. The EBCDIC code, developed for IBM mainframe computers, uses eight bits to represent _____ symbols.

5. Unicode uses _____ bits to represent a possible 65,000 different characters.

6. The number of bits used to represent each pixel determines the number of colors available for each pixel. A monochrome system with one bit per pixel can show two colors per pixel (usually white and black), whereas a color system with four bits per pixel can show _____ colors per pixel.

7. Bitmap graphics and waveform audio are _____ of the original image or sound.

8. Vector graphics and MIDI music files require less space than bitmap graphics and waveform audio because they contain only the information necessary to _____ the original image or sound.

9. _____ refers to the number of times per second that measurements, or samples, of a sound are taken during a digital recording.

10. _____ is a compression technique that scans a text file for repeated byte sequences.

11. _____ is a compression technique commonly used with graphics that replaces repeated byte sequences with a code containing the repeated byte and the number of times the byte was repeated.

12. A(n) _____ consists of one or more transmission media, or physical links, such as twisted pair or coaxial cable, through which data flows.

13. Systems using asynchronous communication often transmit a start bit to indicate the beginning of the data, then transmit the block containing the data, and finally transmit one or more _____, indicating the end of the data block.

14. If the binary sequence 00000001 is sent with even parity, the parity bit must be set to _____.

15. A CB radio is an example of _____ communication, whereas a telephone is an example of _____ communication.

P R O J E C T S

1. In this chapter, you learned about the binary number system, which uses two digits, and the decimal number system, which uses ten digits. There are many other number systems. Computer programmers regularly use the hexadecimal number system, which uses sixteen digits: 0, 1, 2, 3, 4, 5, 6, 7, 8, 9, A, B, C, D, E, and F. In hexadecimal, A is equal to decimal 10, B is equal to decimal 11, and so on. Use this information to complete the following table:

DECIMAL NUMBER	HEXADECIMAL NUMBER
0	0
1	1
9	
10	
11	
14	
15	
16	--

2. Photocopy Figure 5-27. Fill in the pixels on the grid to reconstruct the eight pixel by eight pixel one-bit monochrome pattern from the following binary codes: 00100000, 01010000, 10001010, 10001111, 11111010, 10001000, 10001000, 10001000.

Figure 5-27

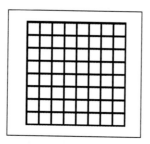

3. One way to compress text is to replace repeated occurrences of words with a pointer to the first occurrence of that word. Using a vertical bar and a number as your pointer, write out the compressed form of the following paragraph:

   A computer system is composed of a computer and peripheral devices, such as a printer. The components of a computer system that you can see and touch are referred to as hardware. Software refers to the nonphysical components of a computer system, particularly the programs, or lists of instructions, that are needed to make the computer perform a specific task.

4. Use your library resources to find more information about MIDI music and write a 2-3 page report. You might want to address questions such as: To what extent do musicians use computer-generated music today? Which modern classical and rock composers or performers make extensive use of computer-generated music? How has computer-generated music enhanced the sound quality, creativity, or appeal of modern music?

5. In this chapter, you learned about simplex, half-duplex, duplex, and echoplex communication, and you were presented with examples such as radio, CB radio, and telephone. List additional examples or analogies you can think of for simplex, half-duplex, duplex, and echoplex communications.

6. Look in current computer magazines for a modem ad, then answer the following questions:
   a. Where did you find the ad (list the magazine, issue, and page number)?
   b. Who is the manufacturer?
   c. What is the speed of the modem?
   d. Is it an internal or external modem?
   e. Does the modem come with communications software?
   f. Does the modem have additional features, such as fax capability? If so, what are the additional features?

7. In this chapter, you learned that a parity bit can be used to detect data communication errors. However, a parity bit will not work if two bits are changed. For example, if you transmit 01000001 using even parity, you would attach a zero parity bit, so the number of ones in the data block remains an even number. If you transmit this number and a one bit error changes it to 11000001, the receiver will know an error has occurred because the number of one bits is now odd.

   But what if *two* bits get changed during transmission? Suppose you transmit 01000001 under even parity, but it gets changed to 01100011? This transmission error will not be detected. Work by yourself or in a small group to devise a plan for using more than one parity bit—a plan that will catch more errors than when you use a single parity bit. Can you devise a plan that uses fewer than eight parity bits? Write a short description of your plan and include a diagram to illustrate how it works.

L A B S

Data Representation

The Data Representation Lab consists of six modules about the binary number system. As you work through this Lab, write your responses to the following questions:

L A B

DATA REPRESENTATION

1. What is the decimal equivalent of the binary number 1001?
2. What is the decimal equivalent of the binary number 11111111?
3. At the end of the Representing Text section, you have an opportunity to enter text and have the program generate the ASCII codes. Use this section of the Lab to generate the ASCII codes for the phrase **Hi there!**, then write the codes in the following table:

CHARACTER	ASCII CODE
H	
I	
(SPACE)	
T	
H	
E	
R	
E	
!	

4. Write the following words in the order they would appear when sorted according to the ANSI code value of the first letter: apple, banana, orange, Pear, Banana.
5. A series of eight pixels in a one-bit monochrome graphic are as follows: ON ON ON ON OFF OFF OFF OFF. What binary number represents this series of pixels?
6. Assuming an eight-pixel wide by eight-pixel high one-bit per pixel monochrome graphic, as shown in the Monochrome Graphics section, what pattern is represented by the decimal values 255, 0, 255, 0, 255, 0, 255, 0?
7. The size of a graphic image increases dramatically as the number of bits per pixel and the number of colors are increased. Complete the following table:

BITS PER PIXEL	# OF COLORS	MEMORY REQUIRED FOR A 640 BY 480 PIXEL DISPLAY
1	2	BYTES
4	16	BYTES
8	256	BYTES
12	32,640	BYTES
24	16.7 MILLION	BYTES

8. Consider a 16-color graphic image, eight pixels wide by eight pixels high, represented by four bits per pixel. Assuming the best case, with all pixels the same color, how many bytes would be needed to compress this file using RLE compression, as shown in the Graphics Compression section?

Data Communications

L A B

**DATA
COMMUNICATIONS**

In the Data Communications Lab you use a communications simulation to connect to a simulated electronic mail system and computer bulletin board. As you work through the Lab, write out your responses to the following questions:

1. What is a modem?

2. What is the difference between an internal modem and an external modem?

3. What happens if your modem and communications program are not correctly configured?

4. Which of the following terms is not one of the communications parameters that must be configured correctly when you use a modem and a communications program?

serial port	baud rate	stop bits
parity	access time	word size

5. You can use an electronic mail system to _____ and _____ electronic messages or mail.

6. _____ are often operated by individuals who donate their time and computer equipment.

7. Electronic mail systems and bulletin boards usually identify users by having them enter a user ID or user name, and the matching _____, before allowing them access to the system.

8. The process of transferring a file from a computer bulletin board system to your own computer is known as _____.

9. Communications protocols are used to ensure accurate transmission and reception of data. Name one of the file transfer protocols listed in the Data Communications Lab.

R E S O U R C E S

■ Asimov, I. "One, Ten, Buckle My Shoe," *Adding a Dimension*. New York: Doubleday, 1964.

If you haven't had your fill of binary numbers, you might want to read Asimov's perspective on the subject.

■ Deken, J. *The Electronic Cottage*. New York: Bantam Books, 1981.

For an alternative explanation of how computers use binary numbers, refer to Chapter 3 of *The Electronic Cottage*. In this chapter, the author uses a unique bucket and hose analogy to explain how computers communicate.

■ Longfellow, H. W. *Tales of a Wayside Inn [1863-1874], pt. 1, The Landlord's Tale: Paul Revere's Ride.*

You can find Longfellow's poem in most anthologies of American verse. You might have memorized sections of the poem in elementary school. Historians do not agree about whether it presents an accurate account of the events of April 18, 1775.

■ Shannon, C. E. and W. Weaver. *The Mathematical Theory of Communication*. Urbana, IL: University of Illinois Press, 1949.

This is a classic publication on information theory. Although the approach is rather technical, this book is required reading for serious students of data communications.

CHAPTER SIX

When you have completed this chapter you should be able to answer the following questions:

- What is a computer network?
- How do network hardware and software transmit messages over network cables?
- How do Ethernet and token-passing networks control traffic and prevent collisions?
- What are the differences between peer-to-peer and hierarchical networks?
- What is electronic mail?
- What are computer bulletin boards and commercial information services?
- What are some of the resources available on the Internet?

COMPUTER NETWORKS AND INFORMATION SERVICES

The data jack slipped smoothly into the socket just behind Kryl's ear. He flipped the switch and the universe shifted.

He stood on an infinite plane. Messages swirled and pulsed down massive conduits creating data links between heavily guarded corporate computing centers. The terrain was just what he expected. He navigated toward the crest of the hill, keeping the artificial sun at his back. After the easy climb, he looked out over a valley. The World Health Organization cube spun lazily, tipped on one of its corners. Open to the public. Lots of free data. In the distance, the towers of the Library of Congress. More free data. Interesting, but not what Kryl was after today.

He turned his attention to the golden pyramid. Rumors on the street told him this was the computing headquarters of a major drug cartel. Kryl studied it carefully. It was surrounded by a translucent security globe. Really tough to get at that data, but his job was on the line. The data was critical to the D.A.'s case.

■   ■   ■

This is a vision of cyberspace, an electronically generated mental image of a computer world, in which vast databases are represented as buildings protected by security systems, and where you travel from one building to another on computer-generated "terrain." The idea of directly connecting your brain to a computer to prowl around in cyberspace is very futuristic. It's true that nothing quite like it exists yet, but today, you can send an electronic mail message to a friend in Yokohama, read the latest issue of NASA's *Lunar and Planetary Information Bulletin*, search the Library of Congress card catalog, browse through authentic German recipes from the University of Stuttgart, play a game of Hearts with an acquaintance from Anchorage, or order gourmet chocolates from an electronic shopping mall—all from your personal computer.

In this chapter, you will learn how to use today's computer networks and information services. You'll find out what equipment you need to connect your computer to a network, and you'll learn how to navigate through a network to find information and accomplish tasks.

Using a Computer Network

A **computer network** is a collection of computers and other devices that use communications channels to share data, hardware, and software. When you physically connect your computer to a network, using a cable or other communications channel, you become a "network user," and your computer becomes a **workstation** on the network. Your workstation has all its usual resources, referred to as **local resources**, such as a local hard drive and a local printer. Your workstation can also access files stored on a file server and make use of other network resources. A **file server** is a computer connected to the network that "serves," or distributes, files to network users. **Network resources** include disk storage space, printers, and other peripheral devices available to network users. Locate the workstations, file server, and network resources in Figure 6-1.

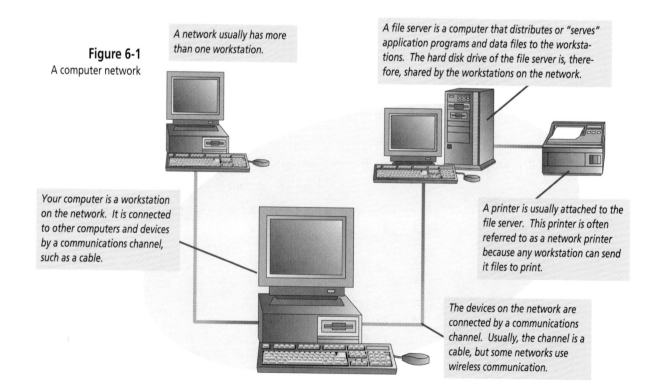

Figure 6-1
A computer network

A network usually has more than one workstation.

A file server is a computer that distributes or "serves" application programs and data files to the workstations. The hard disk drive of the file server is, therefore, shared by the workstations on the network.

Your computer is a workstation on the network. It is connected to other computers and devices by a communications channel, such as a cable.

A printer is usually attached to the file server. This printer is often referred to as a network printer because any workstation can send it files to print.

The devices on the network are connected by a communications channel. Usually, the channel is a cable, but some networks use wireless communication.

The Login Process

When your computer is physically connected to a network, you cannot use the network resources until you **log in**. When you log in, you formally identify yourself to the network as a user. First, you are prompted to enter your user ID and password. Your **user ID**, sometimes referred to as your user name, is a unique set of letters and numbers that you get from the network administrator. The **network administrator** is the person responsible for the operation and security of the network. Your **password**, a special set of symbols known only to you and the network administrator, gives you security clearance to use network resources. Entering a valid user ID and password is the beginning of the **login process**.

After you enter your user ID and password, the login process continues automatically, and your workstation gains access to the file server and its hard drive. The file server hard drive is mapped to a drive letter, just as if it were another hard drive in your workstation. **Mapping** is network terminology for assigning a drive letter to a file server disk drive. For example, on a typical workstation with a floppy drive A: and a hard drive C:, the login process maps the file server hard drive as drive F:. Once a drive letter has been mapped, you can use that drive just as you would use your local hard disk drive. You can view a directory of files, open files, and store files using the mapped network server hard disk drive. Figure 6-2 shows the drive letters available to you after you have completed the login process on a workstation in a typical network.

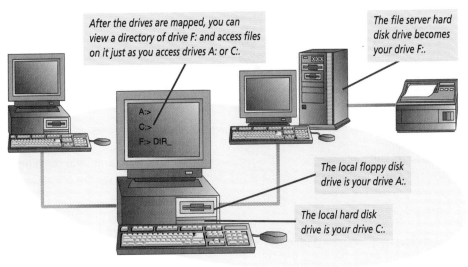

After the drives are mapped, you can view a directory of drive F: and access files on it just as you access drives A: or C:.

The file server hard disk drive becomes your drive F:.

A:>
C:>
F:> DIR_

The local floppy disk drive is your drive A:.

The local hard disk drive is your drive C:.

Figure 6-2
Your workstation drive map

After the file server hard drive is mapped to your workstation, the login process usually assigns a network printer to your workstation. Typically, each workstation on a network does not have its own printer, because it is less expensive to share a high-quality printer instead of buying a printer for each workstation. When your workstation has its own printer, most application software sends files you want to print to your workstation's parallel port. Figure 6-3 on the following page shows that when a network printer is assigned to your workstation, any data sent to your workstation's parallel port is **captured**, or **redirected**, to the network printer.

Figure 6-3
Capturing your workstation printer port

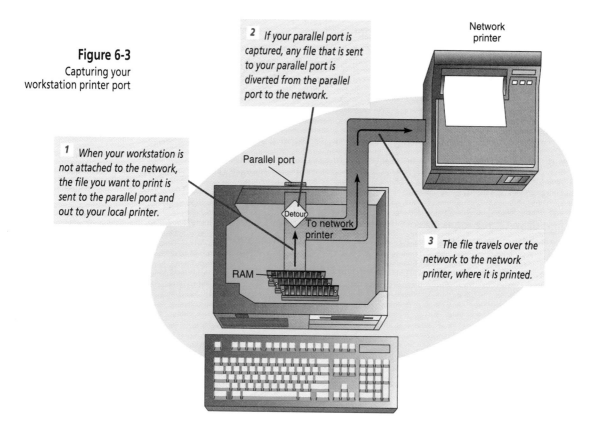

2 *If your parallel port is captured, any file that is sent to your parallel port is diverted from the parallel port to the network.*

Network printer

1 *When your workstation is not attached to the network, the file you want to print is sent to the parallel port and out to your local printer.*

Parallel port

Detour

To network printer

3 *The file travels over the network to the network printer, where it is printed.*

RAM

Once you log in to the network, you have access to network resources including application programs, files, and peripheral devices such as printers. To launch programs on the network, open data files stored on the server, and send documents to the network printer, the procedures are similar to those you use on a standalone computer.

Launching Programs on the Network

Suppose you want to use a word processing program that is stored on the hard disk of the file server. When you launch this program from your workstation, the file server sends a copy of the program to the RAM (random access memory) of your workstation. Once the program is in RAM, it runs just as if you had launched it from your workstation hard disk drive.

One advantage of a network is that more than one user can access a program at the same time. This is called **sharing** a program. While the program is running on your workstation, other users can also launch the same program. The file server sends a copy of the program to the RAM of each user's workstation, as shown in Figure 6-4.

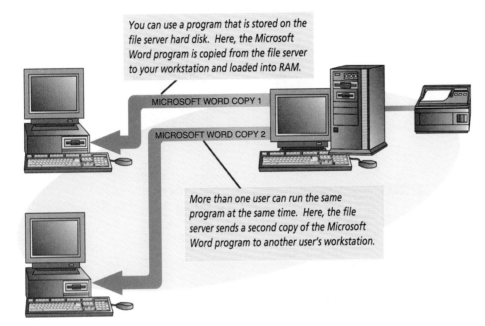

You can use a program that is stored on the file server hard disk. Here, the Microsoft Word program is copied from the file server to your workstation and loaded into RAM.

MICROSOFT WORD COPY 1

MICROSOFT WORD COPY 2

More than one user can run the same program at the same time. Here, the file server sends a second copy of the Microsoft Word program to another user's workstation.

Figure 6-4
Sharing a program

Sharing programs is effective for several reasons. First, less disk storage space is required because the program is only stored once on the file server, instead of being stored on the hard disk of multiple standalone computers. Second, when a new version of the software is released, it is easier to update one copy of the program on the file server than to update many copies stored on standalone computers. Third, it might be possible to save money by purchasing fewer copies of the software under a concurrent use license or a network license. A **concurrent use license** allows you to legally use a software program on a certain number of computers at the same time. The number of computers that can use the software at the same time varies, depending on the terms of the license. A **network license** allows you to use a software program on any number of network workstations at the same time. Note that your network administrator cannot legally purchase only a single copy of a program, load it on your file server, and give everyone access to it. To legally provide shared access to programs on a file server, your network administrator must purchase a concurrent use license, a network license, or purchase single-user licenses for each workstation.

Using Data Files on the Network

Suppose you create a document using a word processing program. You can store the document either on your local hard disk or on the file server hard disk. If you store the file on your local hard disk, you can access the file only from your workstation. However, if you store the file on the file server hard disk, you can access it from any workstation on the network, as shown in Figure 6-5.

Figure 6-5
File access

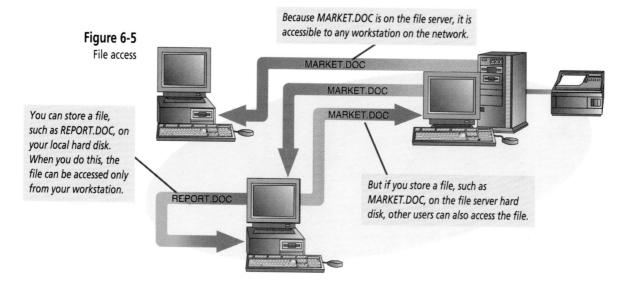

Because MARKET.DOC is on the file server, it is accessible to any workstation on the network.

MARKET.DOC

MARKET.DOC

MARKET.DOC

You can store a file, such as REPORT.DOC, on your local hard disk. When you do this, the file can be accessed only from your workstation.

REPORT.DOC

But if you store a file, such as MARKET.DOC, on the file server hard disk, other users can also access the file.

Although a *program* file on the file server can be accessed by more than one user at the same time, most of the *data* files on the server can be opened by only one user at a time. When one user has a file open, it is **locked** to other users. For example, if you are working on a document called MARKET.DOC, other users cannot open MARKET.DOC until you finish your editing and close the file. This is a sensible precaution against losing valuable data. If the network allowed two users to open and edit the same data file, both users could make changes to the file; but one user's changes might contradict the other user's changes. Whose changes would be incorporated in the final version of the file?

Suppose two users were allowed to make changes to the same file at the same time. What do you think would happen? Each user would open a copy of the original file and make changes to it. The first user to finish making changes would save the file on the file server. So far so good—the first user has replaced the original version of the file with an edited version. Remember, however, that the second user has been making revisions to the original file, but has no idea of the first user's revisions. When the second user saves her revised version of the file, the changes made by the first user are overwritten by the second user's version, as shown in Figure 6-6.

Usually, only one user at a time can access the files created with word processing, spreadsheet, and graphics applications. **Multiuser applications**, however, are specially designed so that more than one user can open and edit a file at the same time. The most popular applications of this type are multiuser databases. With a multiuser database, one user can enter data while another user searches for a particular record in the same database file.

Figure 6-6
File locking

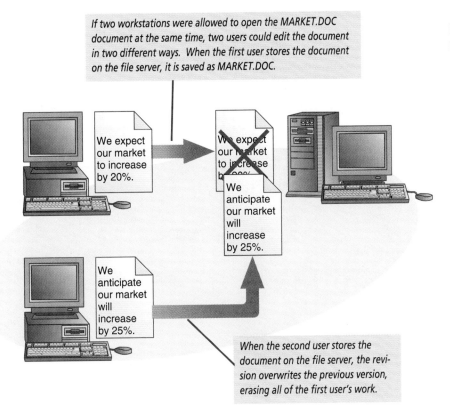

If two workstations were allowed to open the MARKET.DOC document at the same time, two users could edit the document in two different ways. When the first user stores the document on the file server, it is saved as MARKET.DOC.

When the second user stores the document on the file server, the revision overwrites the previous version, erasing all of the first user's work.

Using a Network Printer

Suppose you want to print a document on a network printer. When you log in to a network, the login process specifies that any data sent to your workstation's parallel port is redirected to a network printer. You've already seen that when you follow your regular print procedure to print a file, the file heads to the parallel port, but is captured by the network and sent to one of the network printers.

What happens if two users each send a file to a network printer at the same time? When you send a file to a network printer, the file is placed in a print queue. A **print queue** is a special holding area on the file server where files are stored until they are printed. When more than one user sends a file to the print queue, the files are added to the print queue and printed in the order in which they are received. Figure 6-7 on the following page shows what happens when one user sends a file to the printer before another user's document is finished being printed.

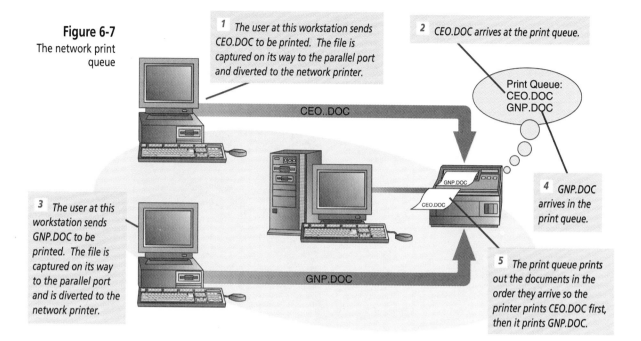

Figure 6-7
The network print queue

1 The user at this workstation sends CEO.DOC to be printed. The file is captured on its way to the parallel port and diverted to the network printer.

CEO..DOC

2 CEO.DOC arrives at the print queue.

Print Queue:
CEO.DOC
GNP.DOC

3 The user at this workstation sends GNP.DOC to be printed. The file is captured on its way to the parallel port and is diverted to the network printer.

GNP.DOC
CEO.DOC

GNP.DOC

4 GNP.DOC arrives in the print queue.

5 The print queue prints out the documents in the order they arrive so the printer prints CEO.DOC first, then it prints GNP.DOC.

Network Configuration

Now that you understand how to launch a program, use data files, and use a printer on a network, you might wonder what makes it all work. You can think of a network as a railroad system that transports cargo, or data, between destinations, or workstations. Like the railroad tracks, the **network cables** provide the physical connections between workstations. The **network hardware** directs the flow of data over the network cables, in much the same way that railroad dispatchers direct the movement of trains on the railroad tracks, prevent collisions, and make sure that each train arrives at its proper destination. **Network software** does the work of shipping companies, "packing" each shipment into acceptable containers, making sure each package is addressed to the correct destination, and verifying that each package arrives at its final destination.

Network Cables

A computer network might transfer data or messages between hundreds of devices, much like a railroad system delivers freight to hundreds of towns. In a railroad system, each town is connected to the rest of the system by a track. In a computer network, each workstation is connected to the rest of the network by a cable. Network cable is typically arranged in one of two ways. Cables can branch out to each workstation from a central device called a **concentrator,** or **hub**. Alternatively, the cable can run directly from one workstation to another, connecting them in a series.

The network cables are connected to each workstation using cable connectors and expansion cards. You can think of network cables, connectors, and expansion cards as components that fit together to form links. Study Figure 6-8 to see how the cables, connectors, and expansion cards link the network workstations.

Figure 6-8
Network cabling

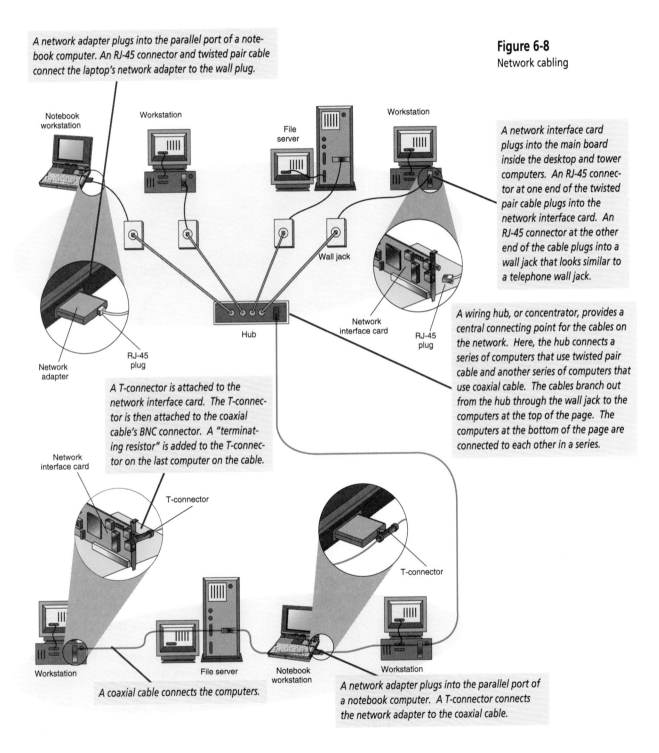

A network adapter plugs into the parallel port of a notebook computer. An RJ-45 connector and twisted pair cable connect the laptop's network adapter to the wall plug.

A network interface card plugs into the main board inside the desktop and tower computers. An RJ-45 connector at one end of the twisted pair cable plugs into the network interface card. An RJ-45 connector at the other end of the cable plugs into a wall jack that looks similar to a telephone wall jack.

A wiring hub, or concentrator, provides a central connecting point for the cables on the network. Here, the hub connects a series of computers that use twisted pair cable and another series of computers that use coaxial cable. The cables branch out from the hub through the wall jack to the computers at the top of the page. The computers at the bottom of the page are connected to each other in a series.

A T-connector is attached to the network interface card. The T-connector is then attached to the coaxial cable's BNC connector. A "terminating resistor" is added to the T-connector on the last computer on the cable.

A coaxial cable connects the computers.

A network adapter plugs into the parallel port of a notebook computer. A T-connector connects the network adapter to the coaxial cable.

Notebook workstation

Workstation

File server

Workstation

Network adapter

RJ-45 plug

Hub

Wall jack

Network interface card

RJ-45 plug

Network interface card

T-connector

T-connector

Workstation

File server

Notebook workstation

Workstation

Network Hardware

A railroad system needs dispatchers to direct trains to their appropriate destinations and make sure that trains do not collide. Network hardware, such as network interface cards and network switching devices, performs the same functions as a railroad dispatcher, directing data to the appropriate workstation and trying to prevent collisions.

Network Interface Card

Each device on a network requires a **network interface card** or **network adapter** that connects to the network cable and the electronic circuitry to send and receive network messages. You can install a network interface card in an expansion slot or connect it to a parallel port or PCMCIA slot, as shown in Figure 6-9.

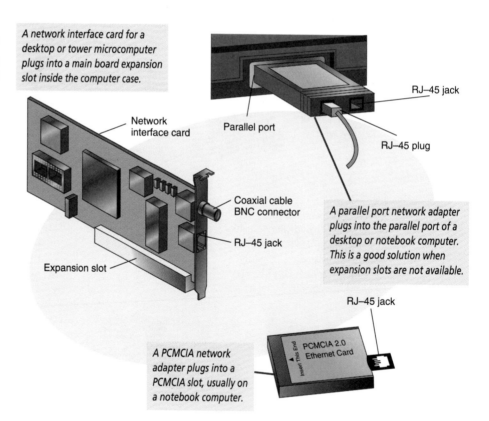

Figure 6-9
Network interface cards and adapters

A network interface card for a desktop or tower microcomputer plugs into a main board expansion slot inside the computer case.

RJ–45 jack

Network interface card

Parallel port

RJ–45 plug

Coaxial cable BNC connector

A parallel port network adapter plugs into the parallel port of a desktop or notebook computer. This is a good solution when expansion slots are not available.

RJ–45 jack

Expansion slot

RJ–45 jack

PCMCIA 2.0 Ethernet Card

Insert This End

A PCMCIA network adapter plugs into a PCMCIA slot, usually on a notebook computer.

A network interface card supports a particular network standard. A **network standard** is a set of communications protocols for orderly transmission of data. Popular network standards include Ethernet, Token Ring, and ARCnet. Every device on a network must use the same network standard or else they cannot communicate and share the network resources. One of the most important protocols specified by a network standard is the data transmission speed. The data transmission speed on a network is measured in **megabits** (one million bits) per second.

Network interface cards are designed to support a particular network standard. **Ethernet**, the most popular network standard, typically transmits data at 10 megabits per second. Ethernet network interface cards are available from many different manufacturers at very competitive prices. **Token Ring**, the next most popular network standard, transmits data at either 4 megabits or 16 megabits per second. Token Ring network interface cards are usually more expensive than Ethernet cards. **ARCnet** is a third network standard that transmits data at either 2 megabits or 20 megabits per second.

Other network standards support much higher transmission rates. **FDDI**, **ATM**, and **FastEthernet** transmit data at 100 megabits per second. These high transmission rates can be used to support high-traffic applications, such as network access to multimedia and video.

A network interface card can send messages to hundreds, or even thousands, of different devices. How does a network interface card transmit a message to a specific workstation?

Transmitting Data

Each network interface card on a network has a unique address. Data is sent as a message, addressed to a particular network interface card. As shown in Figure 6-10, each network interface card examines every message, but reads only the messages addressed to it.

L A B

NETWORKS

Figure 6-10

Network messages

That message is not for me.

That's my message; I'll read it..

To 20201

To 20201

To 20201

20001

20201

Each message on the network is addressed to a particular workstation. This message is for workstation number 20201.

When a message arrives at a workstation, the network card reads the address. If the message is not addressed to that workstation, the message is ignored.

When a network card reads the address of a message that is addressed to its workstation, the message is read and received by the workstation.

The way a network distributes messages to workstations depends on the network protocol standard. An Ethernet network distributes messages quite differently than a Token Ring network. On an Ethernet network, before a network interface card sends a message, it checks to see if the network is busy. If another network interface card is sending a message, it waits and tries again later. If the network is not busy, the network interface card broadcasts the message to every device on the network. Every device receives the message, but the message is only read by the device to which it is addressed.

Sometimes, two devices on an Ethernet network simultaneously check the network and see that it's not busy. These two devices then send messages at the same instant. When two messages are sent at the same time, it's called a **collision**. Ethernet networks use a method called **carrier sense multiple access with collision detection** or **CSMA/CD** to deal with collisions. When messages collide, both devices stop sending and wait for a random period of time before attempting to send the message again. You can probably see why it is essential that both devices wait a random period of time. If the devices were designed to wait for a specific period of time, both would wait and try again at the same time, resulting in another collision. They would continue to wait and collide, wait and collide, and never send the message. Figure 6-11 shows how messages are transmitted on an Ethernet network.

On a token-passing network, such as Token Ring or ARCnet, a special message called a **token** continuously travels around the network. The token carries a signal to indicate whether the token is busy or available to carry a message. If a device wants to send a message, it waits for the token. If the token is busy, the device must wait. If the token is available, the device attaches the message to the token, sets the signal to indicate the token is busy, and sends the token on its way. As the token passes each device, the network interface card checks the message address and reads the message if it is addressed to that device. The token and message continue traveling around the network until they return to the sending device. The sending device then removes the message, sets the signal to indicate the token is available, and sends the token on down the cable. The token prevents collisions. Figure 6-12 on page NP 204 shows how messages are transmitted on token-passing networks.

Network Software

A railroad dispatcher makes sure that a train arrives at its destination. However, the dispatcher doesn't pack the cargo on the train, address individual boxes, or unpack the cargo at the destination. These tasks are handled by a shipping company. Network software works like a shipping company to package and address messages, then unpack them at the destination workstation.

To see how the network software works, let's suppose that you are working with a data file stored on the file server. When you open or save this file, it is sent between your workstation and the file server. The network does not send the entire data file as a unit, because transmitting a long file ties up the entire network until the transmission is complete. Instead, the network transmits the file as a series of messages, called **packets**. Each packet contains the address of the destination workstation, the "return address" of the sending workstation, and a small segment of the data file.

Figure 6-11
Ethernet network protocol

One of the workstations checks the network to make sure it is not busy, then broadcasts a message over the network. The message is addressed to Workstation #21, but all the workstations receive it. Every workstation examines the address of the message, but only the workstation to which it is addressed reads it.

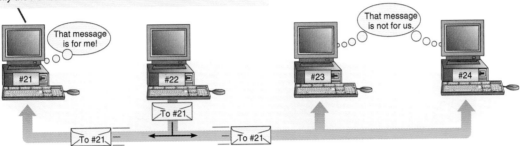

If two workstations simultaneously check the network, find it is not busy, and send messages at the same time, a collision occurs.

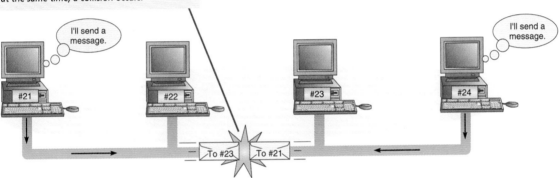

When a collision occurs, a special signal travels over the network to indicate that it is "jammed." This signal lasts a fraction of a second, then the network is again ready for traffic. The two workstations that had sent simultaneous messages each wait for a random length of time before trying to send their messages again.

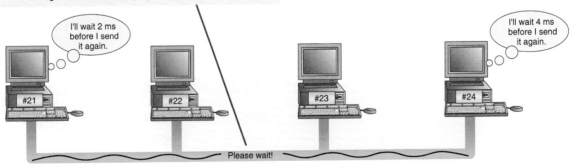

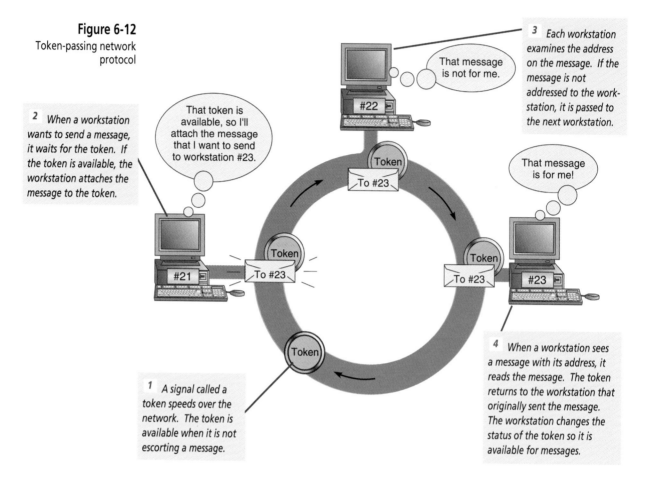

Figure 6-12
Token-passing network protocol

The network software on the sending workstation organizes the file you want to send into packets, which are then transmitted over the network. The network software on the receiving workstation reassembles the complete file from the segments that arrive in each packet. The network software uses a **network communication protocol**, which specifies the structure of the packets. To successfully send and receive packets, the sending and receiving workstations must use software with the same network communication protocol.

The most widely used network communication protocols are TCP/IP, IPX, LAT, and AFP. **TCP/IP** (transmission control protocol/Internet protocol) is used on microcomputer, minicomputer, and mainframe networks. TCP/IP is frequently used on UNIX systems and is the basis for communication on the Internet, the world's largest computer network. **IPX** (internetwork packet exchange) was developed by Novell, Inc. for use with Netware, the most popular microcomputer network software. **LAT** (local area transport), also known as DECnet, is a network protocol developed by Digital Equipment Corporation (DEC) for use with DEC minicomputers. **AFP** was developed by Apple Computer, Inc. for Appletalk networks and Apple Macintosh computers.

Network Interactions

So far, you have learned about a typical microcomputer network in which there is a file server and several workstations. This type of network is sometimes referred to as a hierarchical network. In a **hierarchical network**, the workstations generally interact with the file server, but not with each other.

In some networks, however, the workstations also act as file servers, interacting with other workstations. If some of the workstations on a network act as both workstations and file servers, the network is called a **peer-to-peer network**. If your workstation acts as a file server on a peer-to-peer network, you can allow other users to access programs and data files on your workstation. Compare the hierarchical network interactions with the peer-to-peer network interactions shown in Figure 6-13.

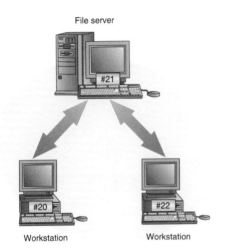 

Figure 6-13
Hierarchical and peer-to-peer network interaction

With both hierarchical and peer-to-peer networks, programs and files are typically sent to the workstations, where they are processed. Transferring large files creates heavy traffic on the network. For example, suppose you want to search for a particular record in a 10,000-record database. The file server sends you the database program and every record in the database; this process generates heavy network traffic.

To alleviate the heavy traffic caused by using large database files, a special type of software establishes a different type of interaction between network workstations and file servers. This software is called **client-server software**. It is so named because a workstation makes a request to the file server, similar to the way a client requests a lawyer or accountant to perform an information processing task. When you use client-server software, the program and data remain on the file server. Your workstation sends a command, or query, to the file server, the file server processes your query, then sends your workstation the results. Figure 6-14 shows how a client-server database reduces network traffic when you search through a 10,000-record database.

Figure 6-14
Client-server interaction

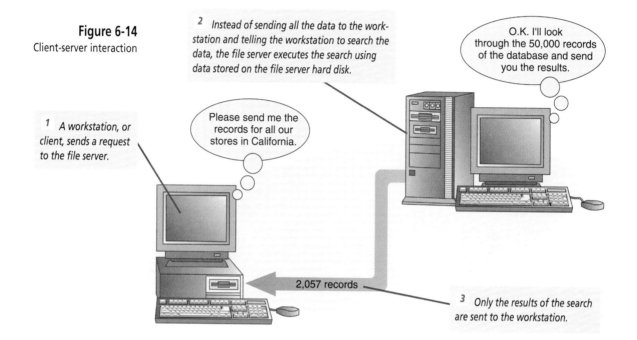

2 *Instead of sending all the data to the workstation and telling the workstation to search the data, the file server executes the search using data stored on the file server hard disk.*

O.K. I'll look through the 50,000 records of the database and send you the results.

1 *A workstation, or client, sends a request to the file server.*

Please send me the records for all our stores in California.

2,057 records

3 *Only the results of the search are sent to the workstation.*

Another type of network interaction is provided by host computers. Mainframe and minicomputers, sometimes referred to as **host computers**, were designed to interact with terminals. A **terminal** is essentially an input and output device for the host computer. A terminal has a keyboard and a screen, but does not have a local storage device and cannot run programs locally. The host and its terminals form a system similar to a network, although all the processing occurs on the host. You can access a host computer from your workstation by using terminal emulation software. **Terminal emulation software** enables a microcomputer to act as a terminal and communicate with a host computer.

Real-world networks usually combine different styles of interaction, devices, and protocols. Figure 6-15 shows a realistic, medium-sized Ethernet network with file servers, workstations, a host computer, terminals, and client-server interaction.

Electronic Mail

An **electronic mail message,** or **e-mail,** is essentially a letter or memo sent electronically from one user to another. An **electronic mail system** is the hardware and software that collects and delivers e-mail. E-mail is a more efficient means of

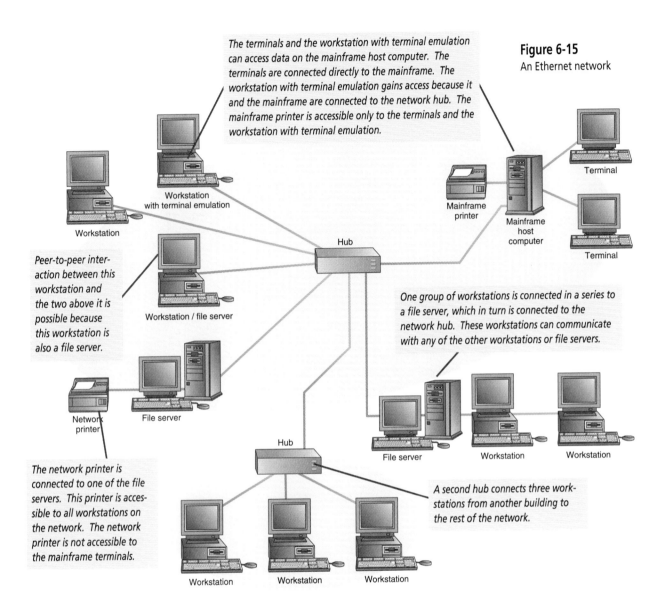

The terminals and the workstation with terminal emulation can access data on the mainframe host computer. The terminals are connected directly to the mainframe. The workstation with terminal emulation gains access because it and the mainframe are connected to the network hub. The mainframe printer is accessible only to the terminals and the workstation with terminal emulation.

Figure 6-15
An Ethernet network

Peer-to-peer interaction between this workstation and the two above it is possible because this workstation is also a file server.

One group of workstations is connected in a series to a file server, which in turn is connected to the network hub. These workstations can communicate with any of the other workstations or file servers.

The network printer is connected to one of the file servers. This printer is accessible to all workstations on the network. The network printer is not accessible to the mainframe terminals.

A second hub connects three workstations from another building to the rest of the network.

communication than ground or air mail. Rather than waiting for a piece of paper to be physically transported across the country, you can send an electronic version of a message directly to the recipient's electronic "mail box."

When e-mail is sent to you, the message is transmitted through an electronic mail system and stored on a host or file server. The next time you log in to the electronic mail system and check your mail, the message is listed as new mail. You can choose to display and read the mail on your computer screen, print it, delete it, reply to it, or save it on disk.

But what if you want to send e-mail to someone who is not connected to your computer network or host? Many e-mail systems are connected to other e-mail systems through electronic links called **gateways**. When you send an e-mail message to a user on another computer network, the message is transferred through the gateway to a larger e-mail system, which delivers the message to the recipient's network or host computer system.

Some e-mail systems allow you to send an **attachment**, which is a file such as a word processing document, worksheet, or graphic that you attach to an electronic mail message. Once received, you can save, open, or modify an attachment, just like any other file. Some electronic mail systems offer features such as **priority mail**, which immediately alerts the recipient that an important e-mail message has arrived; **return receipt**, which sends a message back to you when a recipient receives your message; **carbon copy**, which sends a copy of the message to another user; and **group addressing**, which allows you to send a copy of an e-mail message to all members of a group at the same time.

You should be aware that your e-mail might be read by someone other than the recipient. Although the U.S. justice system has not yet made a clear decision, current legal interpretations indicate that e-mail is not legally protected from snooping. You cannot assume that the e-mail you send is private. Therefore, you should not use e-mail to send any message that you want to keep confidential.

Why would an employer want to know the contents of employee e-mail? You might immediately jump to the conclusion that employers who read employee e-mail are snooping on them. This might be the case with some employers who, for example, want to discover what a union is planning. However, some employers read employee e-mail to discover if any illegal activities are taking place on the computer system. Many employers are genuinely concerned about such activities because they could, in some cases, be held responsible for the actions of their employees.

Bulletin Boards

A **bulletin board system**, or **BBS**, is a computer system connected to a modem and phone line that allows users to post electronic messages and transfer files between the bulletin board and their own computers. Many bulletin boards are run by volunteers, who do not charge for access. To access a bulletin board, you need a computer, a modem, and a communication program.

Most bulletin boards include a file area containing hundreds, or even thousands, of files that you can **download**, or transfer, to your own computer. These files usually include public domain and shareware computer programs, graphic images, sound files, and text files that contain all sorts of information and documentation.

Computer bulletin boards also have a message area that allows you to post public or private messages. Public messages can be read by anyone who connects to the bulletin board. Private messages can be read only by the person to whom the message is addressed. People can respond to messages, creating a sort of dialogue. A series of messages relating to a particular topic is called a thread. A **thread** might consist of messages from dozens of people who have participated in the dialogue over a period of weeks or even months. Figure 6-16 shows several messages from a thread discussing scanners.

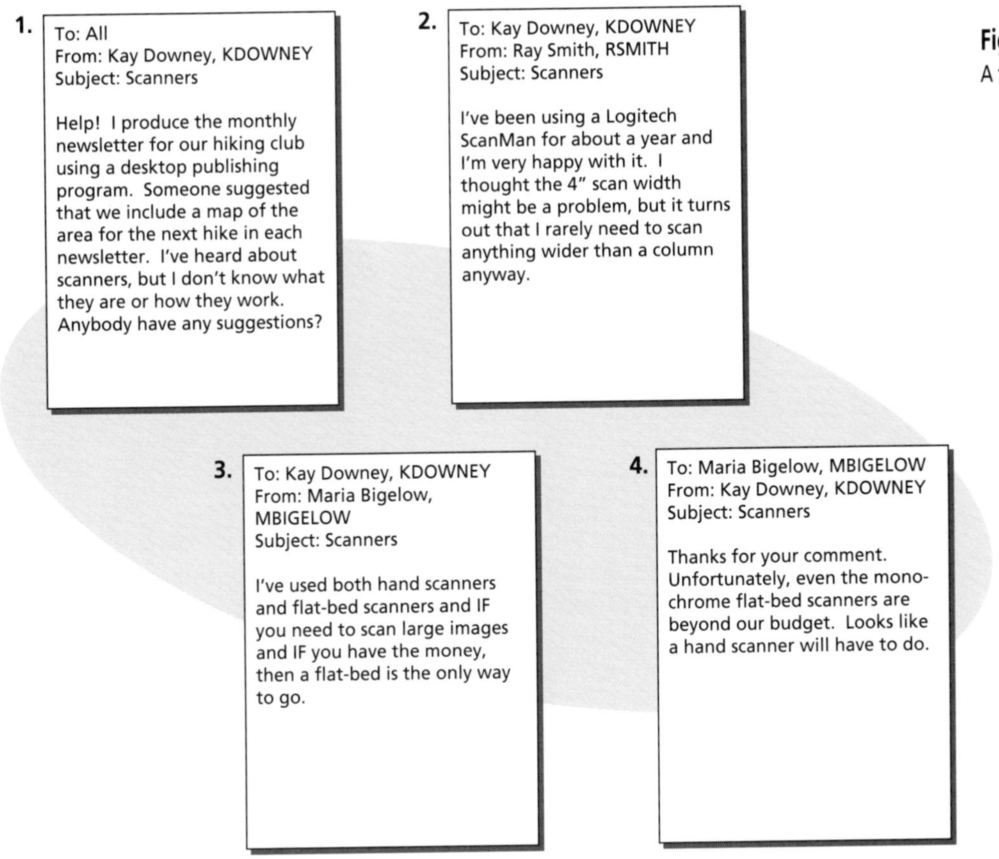

1.
To: All
From: Kay Downey, KDOWNEY
Subject: Scanners

Help! I produce the monthly newsletter for our hiking club using a desktop publishing program. Someone suggested that we include a map of the area for the next hike in each newsletter. I've heard about scanners, but I don't know what they are or how they work. Anybody have any suggestions?

2.
To: Kay Downey, KDOWNEY
From: Ray Smith, RSMITH
Subject: Scanners

I've been using a Logitech ScanMan for about a year and I'm very happy with it. I thought the 4" scan width might be a problem, but it turns out that I rarely need to scan anything wider than a column anyway.

3.
To: Kay Downey, KDOWNEY
From: Maria Bigelow, MBIGELOW
Subject: Scanners

I've used both hand scanners and flat-bed scanners and IF you need to scan large images and IF you have the money, then a flat-bed is the only way to go.

4.
To: Maria Bigelow, MBIGELOW
From: Kay Downey, KDOWNEY
Subject: Scanners

Thanks for your comment. Unfortunately, even the mono-chrome flat-bed scanners are beyond our budget. Looks like a hand scanner will have to do.

Figure 6-16
A thread about scanners

Recently, controversies over the ethical and legal use of computer bulletin boards have raised issues about what is appropriate material to post in such a public forum. The police and FBI have closed and confiscated bulletin board systems that post information that can help people commit crimes—bulletin boards, for example, that have published telephone company codes that allow you to make free long distance calls. Questionable legal and ethical bulletin board activities include posting hate messages, pornography, or confidential information.

Commercial Information Services

Commercial information services, such as CompuServe, Prodigy, and America Online, provide access to a wide range of financial, informational, and recreational services for a small monthly or per-minute charge. You can access a commercial information service using a modem and do such things as download a shareware computer game, view a current weather map, ask for help using a computer program, contribute to a continuing discussion on a special topic, play games with other subscribers, or send electronic mail to users around the world. Figure 6-17 on the following page shows the opening screen from the America Online information service.

Figure 6-17
America Online

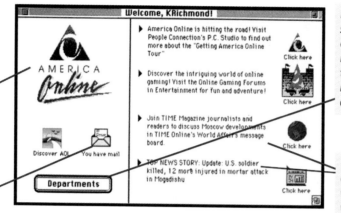

America Online is one of the fastest growing computer information services in the United States. For a monthly fee of $9.95, subscribers have access to five hours of services.

Subscribers can exchange electronic mail with other America Online subscribers as well as subscribers to other information services.

Departments provide a library of software you can download to your own computer, articles from current magazines and newspapers, access to travel reservations, educational references, and games, and a variety of other services.

You can customize your intro- ductory screen so it displays what is new about topics in which you're interested.

To subscribe to a commercial information service, you usually purchase a starter kit containing an instruction manual, list of telephone numbers, communications software, and an initial user ID and password. When you connect to the network, you select a payment plan to cover the monthly subscription fee. For a fixed fee, typically about $10 per month, you can access the basic resources of the service for a specified number of hours. Charges for the basic service, along with any additional charges, are usually billed directly to your credit card. "Basic service" usually means access to current news, some games, and several business or consumer databases. If you do not use the service at all during a particular month, your account is still charged for the basic service. Some information services charge an extra fee for special services, such as airline reservations, Dow Jones stock reports, and access to legal databases.

You connect to the service by using a modem to call the closest available informa- tion service telephone number. If you live in a major city, you can usually connect to the service with a local phone call. If you live in a smaller town, you might have to connect through an intermediate network or pay for a long distance phone call to the nearest connection. If you connect to an information service through an intermediate network, the connection fees for that network are automatically added to your bill.

One of the most innovative commercial information services is ImagiNation Network created by Sierra On-Line. ImagiNation Network is a recreational network designed to encourage social interaction. When you subscribe to ImagiNation Network, you choose from a variety of facial features, clothes, and accessories to create your own network image, or persona. You can then move your persona to different parts of the network: to towns, shops, pubs, and libraries. As you move about the network, you can see the personae belonging to other subscribers, and they can see yours. You can stop and chat with other subscribers, invite them to play a round of checkers, or arrange a meeting at a future date and time. Figure 6-18 shows a screen from the ImagiNation Network.

In many ways, ImagiNation Network is a forerunner of cyberspace, although you view the ImagiNation world on the screen instead of connecting your brain directly to a cyberspace terminal. The images of ImagiNation locations and other subscribers provide a way for you to visually navigate through the computer network, recogniz- ing services, databases, and other users by their on-screen appearance.

CasinoLand is an electronic Las Vegas with Blackjack, Roulette, Slots, and Poker. You can also drop in at Lefty's bar to converse with other ImagiNation subscribers.

The Town Hall provides access to data libraries.

The post office is the e-mail distribution center where you can pick up or send mail.

The general store provides on-line shopping services so you can purchase merchandise using a credit card.

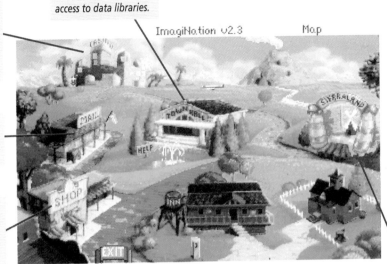

Figure 6-18
ImagiNation Network

The ImagiNation Network bills itself as a "virtual community and cyberspace theme park." The introductory screen looks like a town map. Subscribers travel from place to place by moving their personal icon.

SierraLand is an electronic amusement park with 3-D gold, stratego, a nationwide trivia contest, and many other interactive single-player and multi-player games.

The Internet

The **Internet** is the world's largest computer network. It was originally called ARPAnet and was established in 1969 by the U.S. Department of Defense as a way for military personnel and civilian researchers to communicate about defense projects. Because ARPAnet predated microcomputers, the network connected several mainframe host computers throughout the U.S. and was accessed by terminals connected to these hosts.

In 1983, ARPAnet was split into two interconnected networks, ARPAnet and MILNET, and the Internet (meaning "interconnected network") was born. Access to the Internet was first allowed only to military researchers and defense contractors. However, in 1986, the National Science Foundation network (NSFNET) connected to the Internet and provided more general access.

The NSFNET was constructed in the early 1980s to provide access to five supercomputer centers that were available to civilians for scholarly research. Providing access to the supercomputers presented a problem because researchers at organizations throughout the country, such as colleges, universities, and corporations, wanted access to the supercomputers without traveling to a supercomputer site. The most cost-effective way to connect hundreds of organizations to the network was to encourage each organization to connect to another organization somewhere nearby, forming a chain of networks that ended at a supercomputer center. It was a somewhat haphazard plan, but it worked. When NSFNET joined the Internet in 1986, the size of the Internet doubled.

Internet connections are currently available at almost every college campus in the U.S. and in almost every country of the world, from Argentina to Zimbabwe. Figure 6-19 on the following page shows a map of the extensive Internet connections in the U.S.

Figure 6-19
Internet hosts in
the U.S.

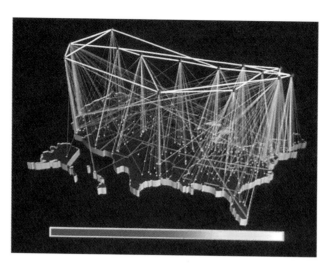

The Internet not only provides access to the NSFNET supercomputer centers but also provides a connection between computer systems operated by the government, the military, educational institutions, businesses, and other organizations. It is estimated that over 10 million people in 50 countries use the Internet, and more than a billion packets of data travel across the network each month. Why would so many people want to use the Internet? The answer to this question is related to the information and services that the Internet provides.

Internet Electronic Mail

One of the most heavily used services on the Internet is electronic mail. Internet e-mail works in much the same way as an e-mail system on a microcomputer network, except that the Internet mail system reaches to the far corners of the globe. When you want to send a message, you simply type the message, address it to the recipient, and tell the Internet e-mail system to send it. Each Internet user has a mailbox at a unique Internet address. An Internet address looks something like this:

president@whitehouse.gov

The first part of the address, *president*, is the user ID—in this case, the user ID of the president of the U.S. The @ sign separates the user ID from the machine name. In the example, the machine name is whitehouse, a computer in Washington that handles the White House Internet connection. A period separates the machine name from the "domain" or category name: com (commercial), edu (educational), gov (nonmilitary government), mil (military), org (other organizations), or net (network resources). In the address *president@whitehouse.gov*, the domain is gov, indicating it is a government agency.

The way e-mail travels over the Internet is quite interesting. Suppose you are at Stanford University in California and you want to send e-mail to the president in Washington, D.C. Your Internet mail system at Stanford sends the message to another Internet host, such as the one at the University of Michigan in Ann Arbor, Michigan. From there, the mail is forwarded to the next closest Internet host until it reaches its destination, as shown in Figure 6-20.

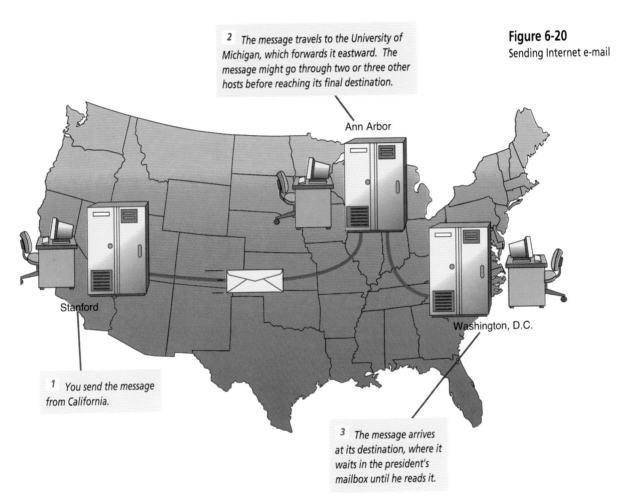

2 *The message travels to the University of Michigan, which forwards it eastward. The message might go through two or three other hosts before reaching its final destination.*

Ann Arbor

Figure 6-20
Sending Internet e-mail

Stanford

1 *You send the message from California.*

Washington, D.C.

3 *The message arrives at its destination, where it waits in the president's mailbox until he reads it.*

Computational Resources

Researchers who require complex computer-generated models, "number crunching," or simulations sometimes need more computing power than their microcomputer or even their campus mainframe can provide. Their solution is to access a supercomputer and use its capabilities. Supercomputers, such as those at the John von Neumann National Supercomputer Center, the Air Force Supercomputer Center, and the North Carolina Supercomputing Center, are accessible from the Internet. Computer resources at the National Center for Atmospheric Research, the National Magnetic Fusion Energy Computer Center, and the U.S. Army Ballistic Research Laboratory provide additional computer resources to Internet users. That is not to say that just any Internet user can connect to these computing resources and use them freely. Prospective users must apply for accounts on these systems, schedule appointments for computer time, and make arrangements to pay for the computer time used.

News Groups

Internet news groups are similar to microcomputer bulletin boards and discussion groups on information services. News groups are organized into seven major news categories: comp, news, rec, sci, soc, talk, and misc. The comp group holds discussions about computers and computer science. The news group holds discussions about Internet news and is a good source of information for new Internet users. The rec group holds discussions about a wide range of hobbies, from collecting antiques to brewing beer. The sci group holds discussions on scientific research. The soc group holds discussions on social and political issues. The talk group fosters debate and discussion on current issues, similar to a town forum. The misc group discusses everything else!

Each of the seven groups is subdivided into discussion groups on a more narrow subset of topics. For example, the comp group might have subgroups on software, IBM-compatible microcomputers, or Ethernet networks. You can join any of the ongoing discussions, read the comments that other participants have made, and then post your own contribution to the discussion.

Library Catalogs

The Internet provides access to library card catalogs at the Library of Congress and at many research universities. The Environmental Protection Agency maintains a catalog of its national library in a format available to Internet users. Some card catalogs are available to any users on the Internet. Others require local permission or a user ID on the local system.

Data Archives

A **data archive** is a collection of data, similar to a database, except that the data is not necessarily stored in a uniform record format. A data archive might contain reports, correspondence, lists of information, books in machine-readable format, and possibly software. Internet data archives contain an astonishing variety of information. Here are some samples.

Project Hermes is a data archive of recent U.S. Supreme Court decisions accessible to all Internet users. The archive is maintained by the Cleveland Free-net, which is organized as a town. When you use the Free-net, you can "walk" down main street, stop at the "courthouse," and browse through the collected court decisions.

The Minority Online Information Service maintains an archive of information about Black and Hispanic colleges and universities. Similar to a college catalog, the archive provides information on student life, degree programs, and faculty.

The Star Trek archive contains everything a "trekkie" wants to know about the original Star Trek series, the Next Generation, and the movies. The archive includes information on characters, plots, and general Star Trek trivia.

Project Gutenberg is an archive of books in machine-readable format. The text of the complete works of Shakespeare, *Alice in Wonderland*, *Paradise Lost*, *Moby Dick*, and others were entered by project volunteers and are available to all Internet users.

The Free Software Foundation (FSF) maintains an archive of public domain software that you can copy to your microcomputer. The FSF archive also contains position papers on the organization's goals and reports about software under development.

In addition to the archives listed above, you can find commodity reports compiled by the U.S. Department of Agriculture, information about Southeast Asians collected by the Anthropology Department of the Australian National University, NASA's *Lunar and Planetary Information Bulletin*, a dictionary of computer terms and jargon, abstracts of papers on education collected by the Educational Resources and Information Clearinghouses (ERIC), a mailing list of public school networks maintained by Kidsnet, U.S. Geological Survey maps of earthquake fault lines, and the text of many historical documents maintained by the University of Minnesota.

Obviously, the Internet has something for everyone, but how do you find the information you want? There are two ways to access Internet information: you can use telnet or FTP.

Telnet and FTP

Telnet is a computer program that lets you connect to a host computer anywhere on the Internet and use your computer just as if you were using a terminal directly attached to that host computer. You can use telnet to run a program on the remote computer, search through a library catalog, or "stroll" through the Cleveland Free-net. Figure 6-21 on the following page explains more about using telnet.

Figure 6-21
Using telnet

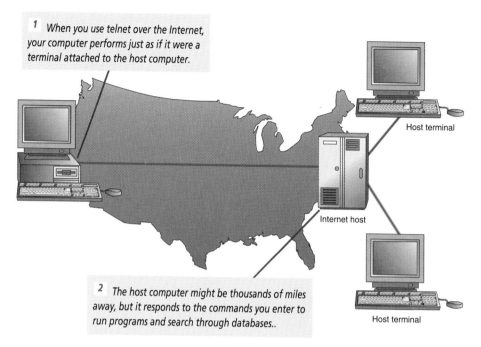

1 When you use telnet over the Internet, your computer performs just as if it were a terminal attached to the host computer.

Host terminal

Internet host

2 The host computer might be thousands of miles away, but it responds to the commands you enter to run programs and search through databases..

Host terminal

FTP is a program that moves files from one computer to another. It is similar to the MS-DOS COPY command or the copy function in Windows, except that you can use it to move files from an Internet host computer across the country to your microcomputer. Using FTP, you can log in to a host computer, view a list of files, and copy a file from the host to your local hard drive. Figure 6-22 shows a typical FTP session in which you copy the file "busweek" from an Internet host called "mola.uvi.edu" to your local hard drive.

To use FTP or telnet effectively, you generally need to know where to find the information, discussion groups, and programs you need. Finding information on the Internet is not a simple task. With over 4,000 hosts to choose from and new services appearing daily, it is not productive to just wander around. Fortunately, there are tools and reference guides to help you search. The National Science Foundation publishes a monthly newsletter and maintains a list of Internet hosts. Your local bookstore should have one or two books on the Internet that contain lists of the more popular Internet services.

Once you log in to the Internet, you have access to electronic guides to Internet services and special Internet programs, such as archie, gopher, and WAIS, that help you search for information on specific topics. More sophisticated tools are currently being developed to help you more easily navigate through the vast resources of the Internet.

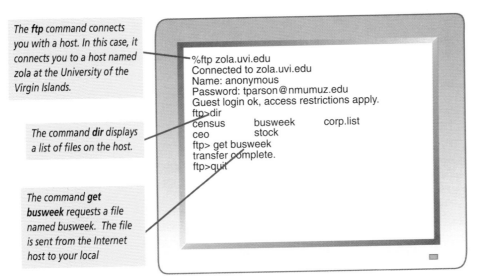

The **ftp** command connects you with a host. In this case, it connects you to a host named zola at the University of the Virgin Islands.

The command **dir** displays a list of files on the host.

The command **get busweek** requests a file named busweek. The file is sent from the Internet host to your local

```
%ftp zola.uvi.edu
Connected to zola.uvi.edu
Name: anonymous
Password: tparson@nmumuz.edu
Guest login ok, access restrictions apply.
ftp>dir
census        busweek        corp.list
ceo           stock
ftp> get busweek
transfer complete.
ftp>quit
```

Figure 6-22
Using FTP

Computers have contributed to our ability to store vast quantities of information, and networks have increased our ability to communicate and share this information. But as the amount of information stored on computer systems increases, the difficulty of finding information becomes a barrier to its use. The solution to this problem is to incorporate intuitive navigational aids in the user interface.

The possibility that cyberspace could become a user interface in the future is intriguing. At the beginning of the chapter you read a science fiction account of cyberspace in which the main character, Kryl, used a data jack to establish a direct connection between his brain and a computer network. Some of the elements for such an interface are evolving today. The Internet, with its host computers, sounds surprisingly similar to the data centers in Kryl's cyberspace world. The ImagiNation information service uses a town landscape as a navigational aid and lets subscribers design personae that move from place to place in this computer landscape. Medical science has produced devices that monitor brain activity. However, a computer's capability to transmit images directly to the brain appears to be far in the future.

An alternative possibility for future user interfaces is to build computers that understand human speech so you can interact with them essentially as you would with a human librarian. This vision of the future is also common in science fiction and is perhaps easier to achieve than cyberspace. These alternatives for future user interfaces represent two very different philosophies about the potential of computers. The cyberspace philosophy is that computers and humans might "merge" through a temporary data link. The philosophy behind the development of computers that understand human speech is that computers become a sort of intelligent entity quite apart from humans. It will be interesting to see if either of these interfaces becomes a reality.

C H A P T E R   R E V I E W

1. Answer the questions listed in the Chapter Preview section at the beginning of the chapter.
2. List each of the boldface terms used in this chapter, then use your own words to write a short definition.
3. In this chapter, a railroad analogy was used to clarify how a network functions. Use your own words to explain how a network is similar to a railroad system.
4. Draw an illustration showing how a workstation connects to a file server. Show and label the workstation, network card, network cable, cable connection, hub, and file server.
5. Complete the following table, identifying the parts of each Internet address:

ADDRESS	USER ID	COMPUTER NAME	DOMAIN
PRESIDENT@WHITEHOUSE.GOV	PRESIDENT	WHITEHOUSE	GOV
JSMITH@STUNIX.STANFORD.EDU			STANFORD.EDU
JARNOLD@FRED.CMU.EDU			
MESTIBAR@ALPHA.COM			

6. Examine the hierarchical network shown in Figure 6-23, then answer the following questions:

   a. Which workstation or workstations can edit the document REPORT?

   b. Which workstation or workstations can edit the document MEMO?

   c. Which printer or printers can be used to print the document LETTER?

   d. Which printer or printers can be used to print the document MEMO?

Figure 6-23

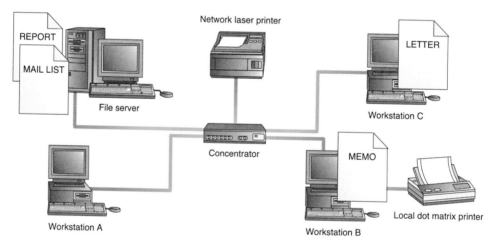

7. Figure 6-24 shows a network with a file server, workstations, a mainframe host computer, and terminals. Examine the figure, then answer the following questions:

   a. Which terminals or workstations can access the document MEMO?

   b. Which terminals or workstations can access the document LETTER?

   c. Assuming that no workstations have terminal emulation software, which terminals or workstations can access the document MAIL LIST?

   d. Assuming that terminal emulation software has been loaded on Workstation A, which terminals or workstations can access the document MAIL LIST?

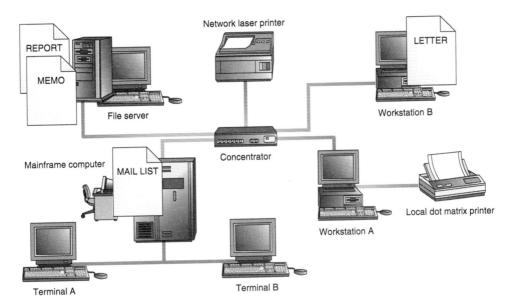

Figure 6-24

8. Examine Figure 6-25, paying close attention to the network communication protocols (TCP/IP and/or IPX) supported by each device. Answer the following questions:
   a. Which workstations or terminals can communicate with file server FS01?
   b. Which workstations or terminals can communicate with the host SMU?
   c. Can the host SMU communicate with file server FS01?

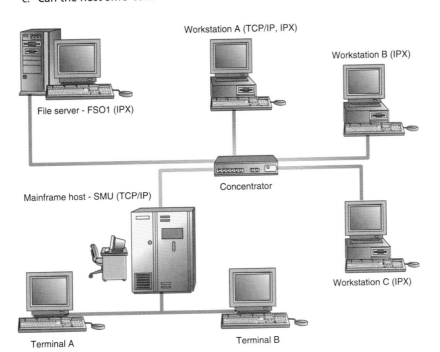

Figure 6-25

C H A P T E R   Q U I Z

1. A(n) _____ is a collection of computers and other devices that use communications channels to share data, hardware, and software.

2. Your _____ is a special identification keyword known only to you and the network administrator.

3. _____ is network terminology for assigning a drive letter to a file server hard disk drive.

4. When you _____ or redirect a parallel port on your workstation, any data sent to that port is redirected to a network printer.

5. A(n) _____ application is specially designed so that more than one user can open and edit the same file at the same time.

6. On a(n) _____ network, a workstation checks the network to see if it is busy. If the network is not busy, it transmits the message, but if it is busy, it waits and tries again later.

7. A special signal that continuously travels around the network, to which a message can be attached, is called a(n) _____.

8. A(n) _____ contains the address of the destination workstation, the address of the sending workstation, and a small segment of a file to be transmitted across the network.

9. TCP/IP and IPX are _____ .

10. A network with workstations that function as both workstations and file servers is referred to as a(n) _____ network.

11. A(n) _____ interacts with terminals or microcomputers with terminal emulation software.

12. A(n) _____ is a series of messages relating to a particular topic.

13. President@whitehouse.gov is an example of an Internet _____.

14. _____ is a computer program that lets you connect to a host computer anywhere on the Internet and use your computer just as if you were using a terminal directly attached to that host computer.

15. You can use _____ to copy files from one computer to another across the Internet.

P R O J E C T S

1. Assume that you are the network administrator at a small manufacturing company. While doing some maintenance work on the electronic mail system, you happen to view the contents of a mail message between two employees. The employees seem to be discussing a plan to steal equipment from the company. What would you do? Describe the factors that affect your decision.

2. Suppose you operate a computer bulletin board that is mostly used by members of your community. One day, while participating in some of the discussion groups, you notice a series of very obscene messages posted by a user you don't recognize. How would you deal with this problem, given the following options? Explain your response.

   a. Ignore it.

   b. Write a message to the person who posted the obscene messages telling him or her that obscene messages are not permitted on your bulletin board.

   c. Discontinue that user's access to the bulletin board immediately.

   d. Report the user to the police or FBI.

   e. Post a general notice on the bulletin board reminding everyone of your rules for bulletin board etiquette.

3. If you have a network at school, draw a diagram of how it works. Your instructor will provide you with more information, indicating the scope of the network you should include in your drawing, for example, whether you should draw only a single lab or whether you should consider other labs, residence halls, and so forth.

4. Do you have access to the Internet? If so, find out the following information:

   a. Can you send electronic mail over the Internet?

   b. What is your Internet address?

   c. Can you use telnet to run programs on remote computers?

   d. Can you use FTP to transfer files from remote computers to your own computer?

5. In this chapter, you learned how the ImagiNation Network might be a step in the direction of a future cyberspace network. Another technological advance that might make cyberspace a reality is called "virtual reality." With current virtual reality technology, you wear a specially designed set of goggles, which is essentially a stereo-optical screen, and body-motion sensors, such as gloves. What you see in the goggles appears to be real. Using the body-motion sensors, you appear to manipulate what you see, as shown in Figure 6-26. Use current books or periodicals to find more information about virtual reality, and write a two-page paper summarizing what you find.

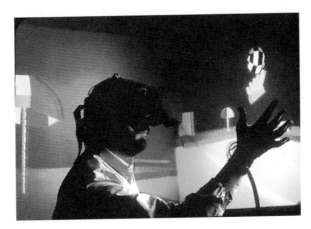

Figure 6-26

6. In a novel called *Ender's War*, two children are catapulted to national prominence because they have innovative ideas about how to solve critical social and economic issues. No one knows they are children, however, because they communicate their ideas on a public bulletin board, which is the central political arena in their society. This brings up an interesting issue, humorously alluded to in the cartoon in Figure 6-27 on the following page. Does a communication medium that depends on words, rather than on pictures or voices, reduce cultural, class, ethnic, and gender bias? According to pollsters, in 1980, many Americans voted for Ronald Reagan because they didn't like Jimmy Carter's southern accent. Would the election have been different if campaigning was carried out over the Internet? Select one of the topics from the following list, research it using library resources, then write a two- to three-page paper with bibliography:

   a. Visual communications media, such as television, encourage cultural, class, ethnic, and gender bias.

   b. Computer communications might eliminate some biases, but it is difficult for disadvantaged people to afford a computer, so they would be excluded anyway.

   d. The younger generation doesn't like to read and write so they need a communications medium like television.

   e. It is better to see and hear people than to just read what they write, but we need to become more open-minded about and tolerant of other people and cultures.

Figure 6-27

"On the Internet, nobody knows you're a dog."

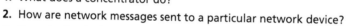

L   A   B

Networks

L A B

NETWORKS

In the Network Lab, you will explore a typical Ethernet network. Respond to the following questions as you go through the Lab:

1. What does a concentrator do?
2. How are network messages sent to a particular network device?
3. How do the devices on an Ethernet network attempt to avoid collisions that are caused when two or more devices attempt to send a message at the same time?
4. What happens when a collision occurs on an Ethernet network?
5. What is the IPX network communication protocol typically used for?
6. Terminal1 is attached directly to Host1 with an RS232-C serial cable. From Terminal1, can you access a file stored on file server1?
7. From Terminal1, can you access a file stored on Host2?
8. Assume you are using Terminal3, which is attached to a TCP/IP terminal server. Can you run a program on Host1?
9. Assume you are using WS3, which has both the IPX and TCP/IP network communication protocols loaded. Can you access a file stored on file server1?
10. Assume you are using WS3, which has both the IPX and TCP/IP network communication protocols loaded. Can you access a file stored on Host2?

R E S O U R C E S

- Card, O. *Ender's War*. New York, NY: Doubleday, 1984.

  In this science fiction adventure, also published as a short story called "Ender's Game," two gifted children use computer networks to publish political commentary. Politicians and the general public don't realize that this political commentary is from children. The children become celebrities...until someone discovers how old they are.

- Derfler, F. & L. Freed. *How Networks Work*. Emeryville, CA: Ziff-Davis Press, 1993.

  This illustrated guide to networks is the place to begin if you want to learn more about networks.

- Gibson, W. *Neuromancer*. New York, NY: Ace Books, 1984.

  This science fiction book is the mother of the cyberspace genre. Its author, William Gibson, even made a cameo appearance as the author "who started it all" in the television mini-series "Wild Palms," which depicted a world in which virtual reality was replacing conventional television.

- Hahn, H. and R. Stout. *The Internet Complete Reference*. Berkeley: Osborne McGraw-Hill, 1994.

  This is an excellent book for new Internet users as well as seasoned pros. The authors promise to guide you through the Internet, and they do.

- Kehoe, B. *Zen and the Art of the Internet: A Beginner's Guide to the Internet*. Chester, PA: Brendan P. Kehoe, 1992.

  A straightforward guide to using Internet electronic mail, FTP, telnet, and news groups, this material is distributed free by a number of organizations. You can contact the author directly on the Internet at brendan@cs.widener.edu.

- Krol, E. *The Whole Internet: User's Guide & Catalog*. Sebastopol, CA: O'Reilly & Associates, 1993.

  This is destined to be one of the classic references on the Internet. Krol's book, far from being a dry technical manual, is written in a lively, conversational style and is easy to read.

- National Science Foundation Network Service Center, 10 Moulton Street, Cambridge, MA 02138.

  This organization provides information about the Internet, such as a list of Internet hosts, a list of Internet services, and a monthly newsletter.

CHAPTER SEVEN

After you have completed this chapter you should be able to answer the following questions:

- What procedures can you establish to prevent, and recover from, typical operator errors?
- How can you protect your computer data from damage caused by power problems and hardware failures?
- How can you protect your computer system against a computer virus?
- Which passwords are the most effective deterrent to criminals who want to break into a computer system?
- What is the most effective backup procedure for your data?
- Why is encryption an effective security measure, even when other methods of data protection are in place?
- What can other people learn about your private life by legally or illegally accessing computer information maintained by government agencies and private corporations?

SECURITY, CONTROL, AND CONFIDENTIALITY

According to legend, the Trojan War began when Paris, the son of the King of Troy, kidnapped Helen, the wife of the king of the Greek state of Sparta, and took her to Troy. To rescue Helen, the Greeks sent a powerful naval expedition to Troy and laid siege to the city. But Troy, surrounded by stone walls, was well-fortified, and the siege continued for more than nine years, until one of the Greek leaders conceived a brilliant plan. He ordered his men to create a huge wooden horse. When it was completed, several Greek soldiers hid inside the horse. Under the cover of darkness, the Greeks rolled the horse up to the gates of Troy and pretended to sail away. In the morning, the Trojans awoke to see that the Greeks had gone, and a magnificent horse appeared in their stead. Believing that the horse was a gift, the Trojans pulled the horse into the city and spent the day celebrating what they thought was a great victory. Late that night, the Greek soldiers hidden inside the horse crept out and opened the city gates for the waiting Greek army. The Greeks massacred the Trojans, looted the city, and rescued Helen.

But what does the Trojan War have to do with computers? Like the city of Troy, modern computer users are under siege by **hackers**, people who, for thrills or illegal gain, attack the data of other users, whether it is stored on microcomputers, minicomputers, or mainframe computer systems. One of the techniques that hackers use to gain access to computers and cause mischief is called a "Trojan horse." A hacker writes a small computer program that deletes all the data on a computer hard disk drive or displays an irritating message every time the computer is booted. This program is then attached to a seemingly innocent program, called a Trojan horse. An unsuspecting user might purchase or download the apparently innocent program, but as soon as the program is used, it "opens the gates" to the hacker's mischief.

As a computer user, a Trojan horse might be the least of your worries. Logic bombs, time bombs, viruses, worms, trap doors, operator errors, and equipment failures are waiting to besiege your computer. In this chapter you'll learn about these and other threats to computer system security. You will also learn about the steps you can take to control access to your computer, preserve the integrity of your data, and maintain confidentiality in your data communications.

Lost or Invalid Data

The data on a computer system is important. For example, a term paper that you stored on your home computer system is important for your grade in a course and your overall grade point average. The medical records that a doctor stores on the clinic's computer are important for the correct treatment of patients. The client records that your medical insurance provider stores on its computer system ensure that you will be accurately and expediently reimbursed for your medical expenses. The payroll records stored on your employer's corporate computer system are essential for calculating accurate pay amounts. The transaction data stored on your bank's computer system keeps track of your money. The list goes on, but the point remains the same—computers are not just a convenience; our society depends on computers and the data they contain.

What happens when that data is lost or when it becomes invalid? What if a hard disk drive failure erases the term paper that you worked on for two weeks but hadn't printed? What if the data in a doctor's computer is altered and the doctor prescribes the wrong medication? Or what if you receive a paycheck that is $190 short? Such scenarios have financial and social implications for individuals, corporations, and the government.

Lost data, also referred to as **missing data**, is data that is inaccessible, usually because it was deliberately or accidentally removed. **Invalid data** is data that is not accurate because it was entered incorrectly, was deliberately or accidentally altered, or was not edited to reflect current facts.

There are many potential causes for lost and invalid data, including operator error, power problems, hardware failure, theft, and malicious destruction. Let's take a look at these causes to find out how they can be prevented or remedied.

Operator Error

The most common cause of lost data is a mistake made by a computer user, referred to as an **operator error**. At one time or another, everyone who has used a computer has accidentally copied an old file over a new file, erased an important data file, or formatted a disk containing important information. At first glance, it might seem that nothing can be done to prevent data loss due to operator error. After all, mistakes do happen. But, many of these mistakes can be prevented.

Successful computer users develop habits that significantly reduce their chances of making mistakes. These habits, when formalized and adopted by an organization, are referred to as **procedures**. Let's take a look at the most common mistakes that result in lost data and the habits or procedures that can prevent those mistakes.

Erasing the Wrong File

Suppose you want to erase a particular file, but inadvertently erase a different file containing some very important data. As you learned in Chapter 3, if you accidentally erase an important file, you might be able to recover the file if you have not attempted to store any other files on the disk and if you have an undelete utility.

But what if you don't notice your mistake right away? This makes it impossible to recover the file using an undelete utility. And that file might have been quite large. If the file was large, reconstructing and retyping the data could take days or might even be impossible.

The easiest way to avoid erasing the wrong file is to think carefully *before* you initiate any command that erases files. For example, suppose you are using a command-line user interface, such as MS-DOS, to erase a file. You should type the erase command, then read it carefully to make sure it is correct *before* you press the Enter key to initiate the command. With a graphical user interface, such as Microsoft Windows, even though you don't enter commands, mistakes can still happen. In the process of highlighting a group of files to delete, you might inadvertently include a file that should not be deleted. Usually, a graphical user interface displays a prompt telling you which files will be deleted. Whenever you see a prompt such as "Are you sure?" or "Delete file THESIS.DOC?," stop and think carefully *before* you continue. Figure 7-1 shows how Microsoft Windows requests confirmation for any commands that could potentially destroy data.

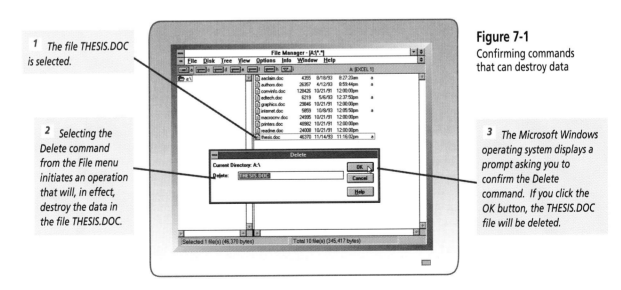

1 The file THESIS.DOC is selected.

2 Selecting the Delete command from the File menu initiates an operation that will, in effect, destroy the data in the file THESIS.DOC.

Figure 7-1
Confirming commands that can destroy data

3 The Microsoft Windows operating system displays a prompt asking you to confirm the Delete command. If you click the OK button, the THESIS.DOC file will be deleted.

Formatting the Wrong Disk

Accidentally formatting the wrong disk can be a devastating mistake, because it erases every file stored on that disk. To avoid formatting the wrong disk, you should take two steps. First, look at the directory of the disk to make sure it doesn't contain any files you want to keep. Second, always check the drive you intend to use for the format operation to make sure it contains the correct disk.

For example, suppose you need a floppy disk to store some files. You have a 3.5" disk that is unlabeled. Rather than assume the disk is blank, you should put the disk in drive A: and display the directory. If the disk contains files, they are listed in the directory, and you can determine whether it is okay to erase them. To format this disk using MS-DOS, you type FORMAT A:. The computer displays a prompt instructing you to place the disk to be formatted in drive A:. Even if you think that you have already placed the disk you want to format in drive A:, make sure you didn't inadvertently place the disk you wanted to format in drive B:, while leaving a disk with important files on it in drive A:, as shown in Figure 7-2.

Figure 7-2
Check the disk before
you format it

1   Look at the directory of the disk you want to format to make sure it does not contain important files.

2   Before you continue with the format process, make sure the disk you want to format is in the drive that will carry out the format operation.

If you accidentally format a disk containing important data, you might be able to recover the files using an **unformat program**. An unformat program attempts to restore the files that were on a disk before it was formatted. As with the undelete utility, the unformat utility is more likely to be successful if you have not stored new files on the disk. If you accidentally format a disk containing important information, stop working with that disk immediately. Carefully read the documentation about the unformat command, or find an experienced computer user to help you unformat the disk.

Copying an Old Version of a File Over a New Version

Another common user error is copying an old version of a file over a new version. When you do this, the old version of the file overwrites the new version of the file, and the new version is lost.

Suppose you have been working on a word processing document that you save on your hard disk. Each night, when you finish working on the document, you copy the file from your hard disk to a floppy disk in drive A: so you have an extra copy—just in case something happens to the original on your hard disk. One night, you work very late to finish the document. Finally, it's done. Not wanting to lose the report in case your hard disk fails, you decide to copy the document to the floppy disk. You intend to copy the latest version of the report from drive C: to drive A:, but you mistakenly copy from drive A: to drive C:, overwriting the finished version of the document, as shown in Figure 7-3.

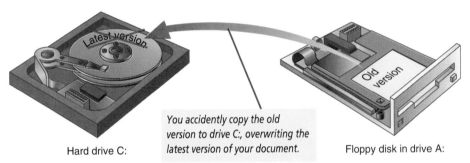

Figure 7-3
Operator error destroying the latest version of a document

Hard drive C:

You accidently copy the old version to drive C:, overwriting the latest version of your document.

Floppy disk in drive A:

To avoid such a depressing scenario, you should always double-check any command before you initiate it, especially when you are tired. If you are using MS-DOS and type COPY A:REPORT.DAT C:, stop and think before you press the Enter key. If you are using a graphical user interface such as Windows, make sure you carefully review the prompt asking if you want to replace the file on drive C: with a copy of the file from drive A:.

Power Problems

Recall from previous chapters that all data stored in RAM is lost if power is not continuously supplied to the computer system. A **power failure** is a complete loss of power to the computer system. Although you can lose power by accidentally bumping the computer on/off switch, a power failure is usually caused by something over which you have no control, such as a downed power line or a malfunction at the local power plant. The data stored in RAM can also be destroyed by a so-called **brownout**, a reduction in the flow of electrical current. Even a brief interruption in the power supply, noticeable only as a flicker of the room lights, can force your computer to reboot and lose all the data in RAM.

Power problems can also take the form of **power surges** or **power spikes**, which are sudden variations in the electrical current. Malfunctions in the local generating plant and the power distribution network can cause surges and spikes, which damage sensitive computer components. Unfortunately, there is not much you can do to increase the reliability of the local power system, but you can take steps to dramatically reduce the effect of these power problems.

An uninterruptible power supply is the best protection against power problems. An **uninterruptible power supply**, or **UPS**, is a device containing a battery and other circuitry that provides a continuous supply of power. A UPS is designed to provide enough power to keep your computer working through momentary power interruptions and to give you time to save your files and exit your programs in the event of a longer power outage. Most uninterruptible power supplies also include circuitry that shields your computer system from surges and spikes. A UPS for a personal computer system costs from $100 to $300, depending on the power requirements of your computer system. Most computer dealers can help you determine your computer's power requirements and recommend the appropriate size UPS.

If you think you'll have little need for an uninterruptible power supply, or if you have a limited budget, you might want to consider connecting your computer to an inexpensive surge suppressor. A **surge suppressor**, or **surge protector**, is a device that stops power surges and spikes from entering your computer system and damaging sensitive electronic components. A surge suppressor does not have batteries and cannot keep your computer running in the event of a power failure. Surge suppressors cost from $15 to $100, depending on the sophistication of the surge suppression features. You should not confuse the capabilities of a surge suppressor with those of an uninterruptible power supply. You can distinguish between the two by looking at them, as Figure 7-4 illustrates.

You can reduce the damage caused by power failures by activating the automatic save feature of your application programs. An **automatic save** feature periodically saves on disk the current version of the document you are editing. For example, if you set the automatic save to ten-minute intervals, your application program saves the document on disk every ten minutes. Then, if the power goes off, you can retrieve the latest version of the file that was saved. In the worst case, you lose the last ten minutes of work.

Hardware Failure

The reliability of computer components is measured as **mean time between failures**, or **MTBF**. This measurement is somewhat misleading to most consumers. For example, you might read that your hard disk drive has an MTBF of 250,000 hours, which is about 28 years. Does this mean your hard drive will work for 250,000 hours before it fails? Unfortunately, the answer is no. To understand, let's look at the typical failure pattern of computer components and how the manufacturer determines the MTBF.

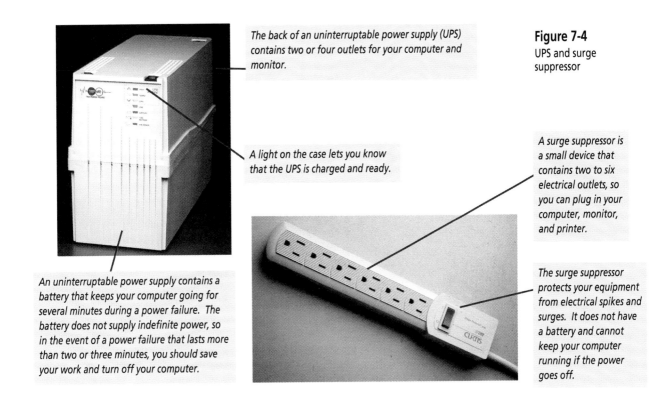

The back of an uninterruptable power supply (UPS) contains two or four outlets for your computer and monitor.

A light on the case lets you know that the UPS is charged and ready.

An uninterruptable power supply contains a battery that keeps your computer going for several minutes during a power failure. The battery does not supply indefinite power, so in the event of a power failure that lasts more than two or three minutes, you should save your work and turn off your computer.

A surge suppressor is a small device that contains two to six electrical outlets, so you can plug in your computer, monitor, and printer.

The surge suppressor protects your equipment from electrical spikes and surges. It does not have a battery and cannot keep your computer running if the power goes off.

Figure 7-4
UPS and surge suppressor

The failure rate of computer components can be illustrated by the graph in Figure 7-5. Much of the equipment that fails does so within the first hours or days of operation, but after that it can be expected to work fairly reliably until it nears the end of its useful life cycle.

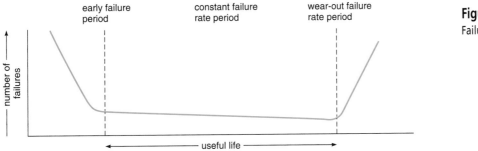

Figure 7-5
Failure rate curve

You should be aware, however, that the graph in Figure 7-5 and the MTBF are summaries or estimates for *every* component of this type that is manufactured. Further, the failure data is obtained in regulated laboratory environments where power problems, failure of other components, and regular wear and tear do not exist. A 250,000 hour MTBF means that, on average, a hard disk drive like yours is likely to function for 250,000 hours without failing. The fact remains, however, that *your* hard disk drive might work only for 100 hours before it fails. With this in mind, it is important to plan for hardware failures, rather than hope they won't happen.

The effect of a hardware failure depends on the component that fails. Most hardware failures are simply an inconvenience. For example, if your monitor fails, you can obtain a replacement monitor, plug it in, and get back to work. On the other hand, a hard disk drive failure can be a disaster, because your computer system will be out of order, and you might lose all the data stored on the hard disk drive.

A hard disk drive failure might occur because of damage to the disk platter or because of one or more malfunctioning electronic circuits. When your hard disk drive fails, an experienced computer technician might be able to recover some of the files on the hard disk and transfer them to another hard disk. But it is more often the case that all the program and data files stored on the hard disk are permanently lost.

The impact of a hard disk drive failure is considerably less if you have complete, up-to-date backups of the programs and data files on your hard disk. If you have backups, you can simply purchase a new hard drive and copy your backup data to it.

If you don't have up-to-date backups, however, you must reconstruct the contents of your hard disk. You have to install all your computer programs again, which might take hours, assuming you can locate all of the original program disks. Then, you must recreate your data files. If you have printed copies of your files, you can type them in again. If you have access to a scanner, you might be able to scan your printed documents, edit them, and store them as new files. Depending on the amount of data that was lost, it might take days, weeks, or months to reconstruct the lost files. For example, if you are using an accounting system and your hard disk drive fails in November and you don't have any backups, you might have to re-enter every transaction from January through November. As you can see, backups are insurance against disaster. You'll learn more about backups later in this chapter.

Trojan Horses, Time Bombs, Worms, and Logic Bombs

At the beginning of this chapter, you learned about the legendary Trojan horse and the modern software version that waits to surprise unwary computer users. But in addition to Trojan horses, other dangers, such as time bombs, worms, and logic bombs, lurk on disks and bulletin boards waiting to destroy data and cause inconvenient mischief to your computer system.

A **Trojan horse** is a computer program that appears to perform one function while actually doing something else. For example, suppose a hacker writes a program to format hard disk drives, and embeds this program in a file called SCHED.EXE. The hacker then distributes disks containing this Trojan horse and posts it on computer bulletin boards where other users are likely to assume it is a free scheduling program. Any users who download and run SCHED.EXE will discover that the program has erased all the files on their hard disk. Figure 7-6 shows how this type of Trojan horse program works.

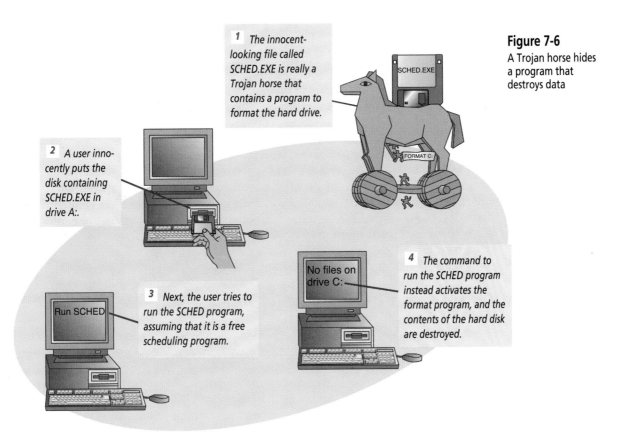

1 The innocent-looking file called *SCHED.EXE* is really a Trojan horse that contains a program to format the hard drive.

SCHED.EXE

FORMAT C:

Figure 7-6
A Trojan horse hides a program that destroys data

2 A user innocently puts the disk containing *SCHED.EXE* in drive A:.

3 Next, the user tries to run the SCHED program, assuming that it is a free scheduling program.

Run SCHED

No files on drive C:

4 The command to run the SCHED program instead activates the format program, and the contents of the hard disk are destroyed.

A **time bomb** is a program that is triggered when the computer system clock reaches a certain date and time. A time bomb is sometimes legitimately placed in software that is rented or leased for a particular period of time. For example, when a customer leases software for a one-year period, a time bomb is set with a date one year in the future. Each day, the time bomb checks the date. When the current date exceeds the date in the time bomb, the leased software stops working. If the customer renews the lease before the end of the lease period, he or she receives a series of commands that resets the time bomb for the new expiration date.

Hackers use time bombs too, but generally they are not polite enough to supply users with a way to reset or defuse them. An example of a widespread time bomb is the Michelangelo virus, designed to damage files on your hard disk. Hackers seem to favor dates such as Halloween, Friday the 13th, and April Fool's Day for time bomb attacks.

A **logic bomb** is a program that is triggered by the appearance or disappearance of specific data. For example, suppose a programmer in a large corporation believes that she is on the list of employees to be terminated during the next cost-cutting campaign. Her hostility overcomes her ethical judgment, and she creates a logic bomb program that checks the payroll file every day to make sure her employment status is still active. If the programmer's status changes to "terminated," her logic bomb activates a program that destroys data on the computer.

You learned in Chapter 4 that a WORM drive is a computer storage device that writes data once, but can read that data many times. A **software worm** has little relationship to a WORM drive. Instead, a software worm is a program designed to enter a computer system through security "holes." For example, an e-mail system offers a potential hole for a worm to enter with legitimate mail messages.

In 1988, a software worm attacked the Internet. It entered Internet computers through a security hole in the electronic mail, then used data stored on the computer to, in effect, mail itself to other computers. The worm spread rapidly, eventually attacking an estimated 6,000 computers. On the positive side, the worm was not designed to destroy data. Instead, it filled up storage space and dramatically slowed computer performance. On the negative side, the only way to eradicate the Internet worm from a computer was to shut down the electronic mail system on the Internet hosts, then comb through hundreds of programs to find and destroy the worm, a process that took each user up to eight hours. A NASA spokesperson claimed that researchers lost 142 person-years of work because of the Internet worm.

Computer Viruses

A **computer virus** is a program designed to reproduce itself and spread from one computer to another. Computer jargon borrows from medical jargon when describing a virus, how it spreads, and how you should treat it. Your computer is a "host," and it can become "infected" with a virus that might destroy data, display an irritating message, or otherwise disrupt computer operations. A virus can spread from one computer to another, but you can "inoculate" your computer against many viruses. If your computer has not been inoculated and catches a virus, you can use special virus removal software to "cure" it. Study Figure 7-7 to get an overview of a computer virus.

Figure 7-7
Overview of a
computer virus

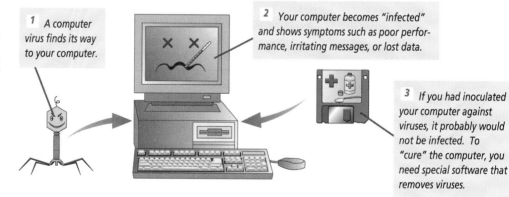

1   A computer virus finds its way to your computer.

2   Your computer becomes "infected" and shows symptoms such as poor performance, irritating messages, or lost data.

3   If you had inoculated your computer against viruses, it probably would not be infected. To "cure" the computer, you need special software that removes viruses.

A computer virus generally infects the executable files on your computer system, not the data files. When you run an infected file, it triggers the virus, which might display an irritating message, damage files on your computer system, or infect other programs. A computer virus might be a time bomb or a logic bomb. However, a virus requires another program as a host or carrier to help it enter a computer system. A Trojan horse typically harbors a virus, but once a virus exists in a computer system, it can often reproduce itself and use other programs as hosts. A virus is different from a worm, because a worm is an independent program that does not require a host or carrier.

How a Computer Virus Spreads

Computer viruses typically lurk on disks containing public domain software or shareware, and on disks containing illegal copies of computer programs downloaded from bulletin boards. Disks and programs from these sources should be regarded as having a "high risk" of infection. The incidence of infected programs circulated in high schools is particularly high, because students frequently exchange software, seem to enjoy pranks, and might not be as responsible as more mature computer users. Figure 7-8 shows how quickly a computer virus can spread.

You can generally avoid a computer virus if you do not use "high-risk" disks or programs. If you need to use a disk that you suspect might be infected, you can use a virus detection program to check for viruses before you run any programs from the disk.

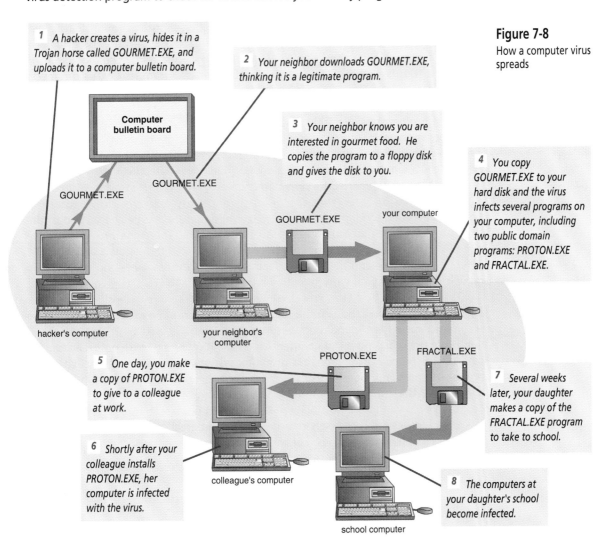

Figure 7-8
How a computer virus spreads

1 A hacker creates a virus, hides it in a Trojan horse called GOURMET.EXE, and uploads it to a computer bulletin board.

2 Your neighbor downloads GOURMET.EXE, thinking it is a legitimate program.

3 Your neighbor knows you are interested in gourmet food. He copies the program to a floppy disk and gives the disk to you.

4 You copy GOURMET.EXE to your hard disk and the virus infects several programs on your computer, including two public domain programs: PROTON.EXE and FRACTAL.EXE.

5 One day, you make a copy of PROTON.EXE to give to a colleague at work.

6 Shortly after your colleague installs PROTON.EXE, her computer is infected with the virus.

7 Several weeks later, your daughter makes a copy of the FRACTAL.EXE program to take to school.

8 The computers at your daughter's school become infected.

Detecting a Computer Virus

A **virus detection program**, or **virus scan program**, is a program that examines the files stored on a disk to determine if they are infected with a virus. You can purchase these programs from your local computer dealer or by mail order. Shareware virus detection programs are also available from reputable bulletin boards and shareware dealers.

Virus detection programs work in various ways. As mentioned earlier, a virus attaches itself to an existing program, often increasing the length of the original program. The earliest virus detection programs simply examined the files on your computer and recorded the length of each. Each time you turned on your computer, the virus detection program checked the actual length of the programs against the original length recorded in the file and alerted you if any program had become longer.

In response to the early virus detection programs, the people who create viruses became more clever. They created viruses that insert themselves into unused portions of an original program file, but do not to change its length. They also created viruses that fooled the detection programs by making the infected program appear to be the regular length.

Of course, the people who designed virus detection programs fought back. They designed programs that examine the bits in an uninfected application program and calculate a checksum. A **checksum** is a value that is calculated by combining all the bytes in a file. Each time you run the application program, the virus detection program recalculates the checksum and compares it to the original. If any byte in the application program has been changed, the checksum will be different, and the virus detection program assumes that a virus changed the application program file. The checksum approach requires that you start with a copy of the program that is not infected with a virus. If you start with an infected copy, the virus is included in the original checksum and the virus detection program never detects it.

Another technique used by virus detection programs is to search for a **signature**, or unique series of bytes, that can be used to identify a known virus, much as a fingerprint is used to identify an individual. The signature is usually a section of the virus program—such as a unique series of instructions. The signature search technique is fairly quick, but can identify only those viruses with a known signature. To detect new viruses—and new viruses seem to appear every week—you must obtain regular updates for your virus detection program.

The virus detection programs presented so far work more or less like a periodic physical examination. You run the virus detection program periodically to check to see if any viruses have found their way into your computer system. Other virus detection programs work more like an intensive care unit monitor. These programs continually run in the background of your computer system; they monitor the activity of all other programs and look for signs of virus-like activity. If any program attempts to change another program or modify the operating system, the virus detection program alerts you to the possibility of a virus infection.

Some viruses are specifically designed to avoid detection by one or more of the above virus detection methods. For this reason, the most sophisticated virus protection schemes combine elements from each of these methods.

What to Do If You Detect a Computer Virus

If you detect a computer virus on your computer system, you must take steps to stop the virus from spreading. If you are connected to a network, alert the network administrator that you found a virus on your workstation. The network administrator can then take action to prevent the virus from spreading throughout the network.

If you are using your own computer system and you detect a virus, you must remove it. There are two ways to remove a virus. **Virus removal programs** attempt to restore a program to its original condition by deleting the virus instructions from the program. However, depending on how the virus attached itself to the program, it might not be possible to remove the virus without destroying the program. If the virus cannot be removed successfully, you must erase the infected program, test the system again to make sure the virus has been eliminated, then install the program again from the original disks. In cases where the virus has infected most of the programs on the system, it's often best to make a backup of your data files (which should not be infected), reformat the hard disk, and install all the programs again from backup copies of the original disks.

You must also test and, if necessary, remove the virus from every floppy disk and backup used on your computer system. If you don't remove every copy of the virus, your system will become infected again the next time you use an infected disk or restore data from an infected backup. You should also alert your colleagues, and anyone with whom you shared disks, that a virus might have traveled on those disks and infected their computer system.

Computer Crime

The accounting firm of Ernst & Young estimates that computer crime costs individuals and organizations in the U.S. between $3 billion and $5 billion a year. **Computer crime** includes a wide variety of activities in which people steal proprietary information stored on computers, maliciously destroy computer data, or use computers to commit "old fashioned" crimes, such as embezzlement and theft.

"Old fashioned" crimes that are carried out with the aid of a computer are often prosecuted using traditional laws. For example, a person who attempts to destroy computer data by setting fire to a computer might be tried under traditional arson laws. However, traditional laws do not cover the range of possibilities for computer crimes. If a person unlawfully enters a computer facility, that person might be prosecuted for breaking and entering or charged with burglary. But would the breaking and entering laws apply to a person who uses an off-site terminal to "enter" a computer system without authorization? Another example is larceny, which means taking away another person's property without consent. Laws against larceny clearly cover the case in which a thief steals your computer and printer. But what about the situation in which a person copies a file that contains a new product design from a corporate computer and sells it to the competition? Is the data personal property?

The answers to these questions about computer crime are different for each state. In 1978, Florida was the first state to enact a computer crime law. Since that time, most other states have also enacted computer crime laws. One of the most important aspects of these laws is that they define computer data and software as personal property. Another important aspect of computer crime laws is that they define as a crime the unauthorized access, use, modification, or disabling of a computer system or data. Under most state laws, intentionally circulating a destructive virus is a crime. Study the excerpt from a typical computer crime law in Figure 7-9 to see what is specifically defined as illegal.

Figure 7-9

Excerpt from a state computer crime law

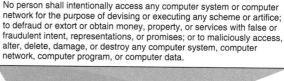

No person shall intentionally access any computer system or computer network for the purpose of devising or executing any scheme or artifice; to defraud or extort or obtain money, property, or services with false or fraudulent intent, representations, or promises; or to maliciously access, alter, delete, damage, or destroy any computer system, computer network, computer program, or computer data.

State authorities have jurisdiction over computer crimes committed in one state, but crimes that occur in more than one state or across state boundaries are under federal jurisdiction. The Computer Fraud and Abuse Act of 1986 makes it illegal to access a computer across state lines for fraudulent purposes. This act also specifically outlaws the sale of entry pass codes, passwords, and access codes that belong to others. In a well-publicized espionage case, dramatized in a documentary called *Computers, the KGB, and Me*, hackers used an unclassified military network and the Internet to piece together details on current military research in the United States, which they then sold to the KGB. The hackers, based in Germany, used stolen passwords and telephone access codes to set up communications links from Europe to Virginia, and on to California. Because the communications crossed state lines, the case was under federal jurisdiction, and the FBI became involved. With FBI assistance, the case was ultimately cracked by a computer operator of an Internet host computer at Lawrence Berkeley Labs in California.

In addition to federal and state law, many organizations have policies about the use and misuse of computers. These policies generally apply to employees, or in the case of a college or university, to students. Typically, these policies provide penalties, such as suspension or dismissal, for students or employees who make illegal copies of software, copy or alter data without authorization, or use company or school computers to commit crimes.

Restricting Access to Your Computer System ▬▬▬

One of the best ways to prevent people from damaging or stealing data is to restrict access to your computer system. If potential criminals cannot gain access, they cannot steal or damage your data.

User IDs and Passwords

The most common way to restrict access to a computer system is with user IDs and passwords. As you know from previous chapters, when you work on a multi-user system or network, you generally must have a user ID and password. Some stand-alone or single-user computers also have a password function built into the boot program. After you activate the boot program password protection on your personal computer, you must enter your password every time you boot your computer. Boot program passwords provide only limited protection, because a moderately experienced user can wipe out the password by resetting the startup settings in CMOS memory.

The security of the data on a computer system that is guarded by user IDs and passwords depends on the secrecy of the passwords. To preserve the secrecy of a password-protected computer, you must never tell anyone your password. If other people learn your password, they can log in to the computer, perform activities, and access data, just as if they were you. If they do anything wrong, such as erase important files, make copies of sensitive files, or change important information, it appears as if you had done it. Never write down your password, and *never* stick it on a little note taped to your monitor or the bottom of your keyboard—this would be the modern day equivalent of hiding your house key under the doormat.

You should not use a password that can be easily guessed, such as your middle name, your best friend's name, or the name of your dog. Also, you should not use any word that can be found in a dictionary. One brute force method that hackers use to break into computer systems is to write a program that tries to log in with a particular password. Each time the computer system displays the password prompt, the program tries the next word from a dictionary. It might take thousands of attempts, but sooner or later, the program will find the password if it exists in the dictionary. To ensure security, you should use a "safe" password.

One method of generating a safe password is to combine two or more words with no space or punctuation mark between them. For example, a potentially safe password is THISISIT, a combination of the words "this is it." Another technique is to use the first letters from a line of poetry or nursery rhyme. HDDTMRUTC, for example, is from "Hickory dickory dock, the mouse ran up the clock." Mixing words and numbers is another effective technique, but don't combine your name and birth date—it's too easy to guess.

If you ever have reason to believe that an "intruder" has learned your password, follow your school or workplace procedure to change your password as soon as possible. Once you change your password, the old password stops working and the intruder cannot access the system.

Restricting User Rights

Another way to restrict access to computer data is to restrict user rights. **User rights** are rules that limit the directories and files that each user can access. When you receive a user ID and password for a password-protected system, the system administrator gives you specific rights to particular directories and files on the host computer or file server. Most networks and host computers allow the system administrator to assign user rights, such as those shown in Figure 7-10.

Figure 7-10
User rights

RIGHTS	FUNCTIONS
File find rights	allow you to list files with a directory command
Read rights	allow you to open files and read information
Write rights	allow you to save information in existing files
Create rights	allow you to create new files
Erase rights	allow you to erase files

You typically have *file find* and *file read* rights to programs stored on a file server or host computer. With these rights, you can locate and run programs, but you cannot erase or modify them. *Write*, *create*, and *erase* rights are granted only to users who need to save data or erase files on the file server.

Granting users only the rights they need helps prevent both accidental and deliberate damage to data. If users are granted limited rights, a criminal who steals someone's password has only those rights granted to the person from whom the password was stolen.

Another way people gain unauthorized access to computer systems is through a trap door. A **trap door** is a special set of instructions that allows a user to bypass the normal security precautions and enter the system. Trap doors are often created during development and testing and should be removed before the system becomes operational. If a trap door is not removed, it becomes a possible means of entry for any hacker who discovers it.

In the 1983 film *WarGames*, a trap door was the key to preventing widespread nuclear destruction. A young hacker breaks into a secret military computer that has been programmed to deal with enemy nuclear attacks. The hacker begins to play what he thinks is a detailed computer game. The computer, however, thinks it is an actual attack. Soon the computer passes the stage at which it can be stopped from launching nuclear missiles, except by a trap door designed by the reclusive programmer who created the original program. The trap door provides a way for the programmer to bypass official military channels and access the computer's fail-safe program. A special password is required to enter the trap door, and in the exciting climax of the film, the hacker races against time to get the password and gain access to the computer deep within the military installation in Cheyenne Mountain.

A trap door can be as simple as a default user ID and password, set up by the software manufacturer so the system administrator can initially get into the system and set up the rest of the users. For example, when network software is installed, the default user ID and password are often named something like "supervisor," "system," or "access." These defaults must be changed as soon as the system is installed, because anyone who has ever set up a similar system knows the default password. If the default password is not changed, it leaves a trap door open that computer criminals might use.

Physical Protection

Not all data is protected by passwords and restricted rights. For example, the data stored on the local hard disk of a network workstation or on a floppy disk is not protected by the network password system and might not be protected by a boot program password. Anyone with physical access to that workstation or floppy disk can access the data if additional protection has not been provided.

Some computer manufacturers provide a lock on the front of the computer case. The computer cannot be used when the system is locked. To protect data on floppy disks, removable hard disks, or Bernoulli cartridges, you can store them in a secure place such as a locked drawer, a locking file cabinet, or a safe. Some users even lock their keyboard in a drawer when they are not using their computer.

Backup

One of the most distressing computing experiences is to lose all your data. It might be the result of a hardware failure or a virus, but whatever the cause, most users experience only a moment of surprise and disbelief before the depressing realization that they might have to recreate all their data and reinstall all their programs. A backup can pull you through such trying times, making them a minor inconvenience, rather than a major disaster. A **backup** is a duplicate copy of a file or the contents of a disk drive. If the original file is lost or damaged, you can use the backup copy to restore the data to its original working condition.

L A B

DATA BACKUP

You can also use a printout of your data for backup purposes. To restore the data from a printout, you can use a scanner or you can retype it; however, with either method, you can easily introduce errors, so it is preferable to make backups to one or more floppy disks, a tape drive, or another hard drive. Most operating systems include software to help you back up and restore your data. Backup software usually gives you a choice of three types of backup: a full backup, a differential backup, and an incremental backup.

Types of Backups

A **full backup** is a copy of all the files on a disk—usually a hard disk. A full backup is very safe because it ensures that you have a copy of every file on the disk—every program and every data file. Because a full backup includes a copy of every file on your computer, it can take a long time to make one, but some users consider it worth the time because this type of backup is easy to restore. You simply have the computer copy the files from your backup to the hard disk, as shown in Figure 7-11 on the following page.

Figure 7-11
Full backup and restore

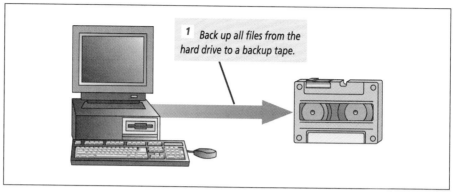

1 Back up all files from the hard drive to a backup tape.

Backup

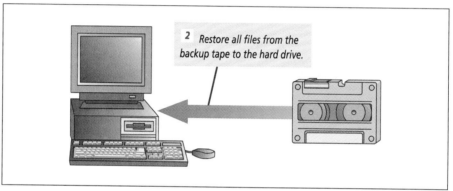

2 Restore all files from the backup tape to the hard drive.

Restore

A **differential backup** is a copy of all the files that have changed since the last full backup. You must, therefore, maintain two sets of backups—a full backup that you make infrequently, say once a month, and a differential backup that you make more frequently, say once a week. To restore your data after a differential backup, you first restore data from the last full backup, then restore the data from the latest differential backup, as shown in Figure 7-12.

An **incremental backup** is a copy of the files that have changed since the last backup. When you use incremental backups, you must have a full backup, and you must maintain a series of incremental backups. The incremental backup procedure sounds like the differential backup procedure, but there is a subtle difference. With a differential backup, you maintain one full backup and one differential backup. The differential backup contains any files that were changed since the last full backup. With an incremental backup procedure, you maintain a full backup and a *series* of incremental backups. Each incremental backup contains only those files that changed since the last incremental backup. To restore the data from a series of incremental backups, you restore the last full backup, then sequentially restore each incremental backup. Incremental backups take the least time to make, since they contain only the files that have been changed since the last backup, but incremental backups take the most time to restore, as shown in Figure 7-13 on page NP 244.

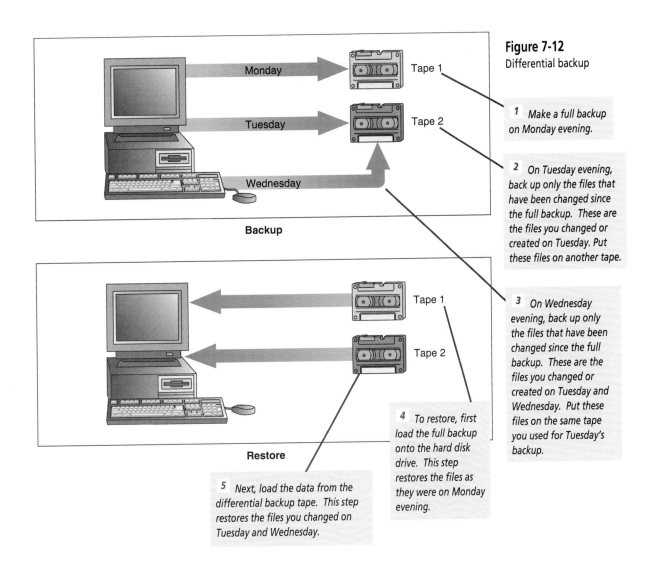

Figure 7-12
Differential backup

1 *Make a full backup on Monday evening.*

2 *On Tuesday evening, back up only the files that have been changed since the full backup. These are the files you changed or created on Tuesday. Put these files on another tape.*

3 *On Wednesday evening, back up only the files that have been changed since the full backup. These are the files you changed or created on Tuesday and Wednesday. Put these files on the same tape you used for Tuesday's backup.*

4 *To restore, first load the full backup onto the hard disk drive. This step restores the files as they were on Monday evening.*

5 *Next, load the data from the differential backup tape. This step restores the files you changed on Tuesday and Wednesday.*

Backup Procedures

A **backup procedure** is the process and schedule you use to make backups. Any backup procedure is a compromise between the level of protection and the amount of time devoted to backup. To be absolutely safe, you would need to back up your system every time you did anything, which would seriously reduce the amount of work you could complete in a day. The alternative is periodic backups. With periodic backups, you must decide how frequently to make backups and how much of your data you want to back up.

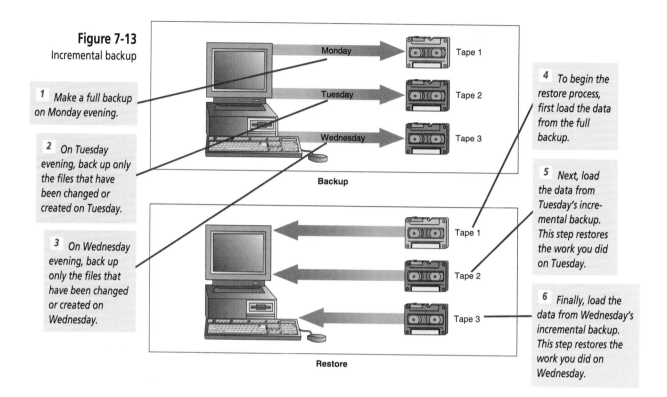

Figure 7-13
Incremental backup

1 Make a full backup on Monday evening.

2 On Tuesday evening, back up only the files that have been changed or created on Tuesday.

3 On Wednesday evening, back up only the files that have been changed or created on Wednesday.

Monday — Tape 1
Tuesday — Tape 2
Wednesday — Tape 3

Backup

4 To begin the restore process, first load the data from the full backup.

5 Next, load the data from Tuesday's incremental backup. This step restores the work you did on Tuesday.

Tape 1
Tape 2
Tape 3

6 Finally, load the data from Wednesday's incremental backup. This step restores the work you did on Wednesday.

Restore

A typical backup procedure combines full backups with differential or incremental backups of modified files. At specific intervals, you make a full backup containing all files stored on the system. The full backup is followed by a series of incremental backups, each of which contains copies of the files that have been modified since the last backup. Periodically, another full backup is performed, and the cycle starts over again. Many computer systems are backed up on a weekly cycle, as shown in Figure 7-14.

A one-week backup cycle might not be sufficient for applications that operate on longer cycles, in which certain problems might not become apparent until the end of the month or year. In an accounting system, for example, you might not discover a problem such as a virus or disk error until you attempt to close the month or close the books at the end of the year.

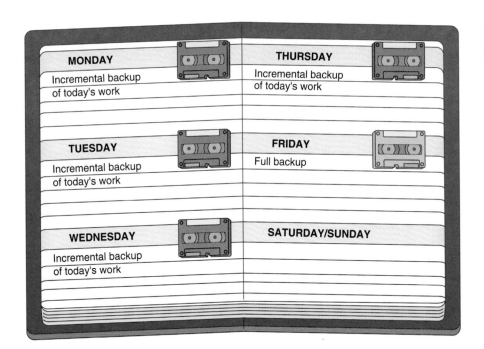

Figure 7-14
Weekly backup cycle

Accounting systems require a more sophisticated backup procedure with backups made at various points in the accounting cycle. One method uses daily, weekly, and monthly backups. The daily backups are incremental backups, one performed each day of the week, except for the day during which the weekly backups are performed. The weekly backups are a series of three *full* backups, one for each week of the month, except the week when you make the monthly backup. The monthly backups are a series of twelve full backups, each performed just before month-end closing. This backup procedure for an accounting application is illustrated in Figure 7-15.

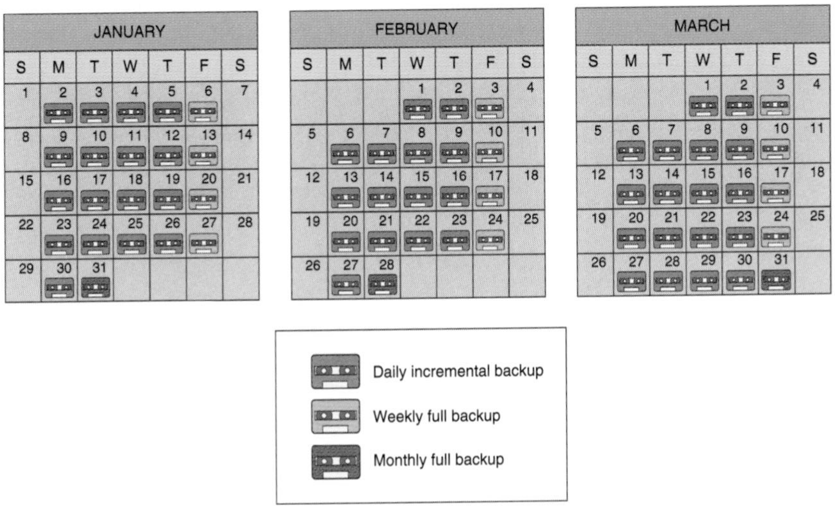

Figure 7-15
An accounting system backup schedule

A backup procedure such as the one in Figure 7-15 provides multiple levels of protection. The backups, performed at different times during the cycle, make it possible to restore the data to a point just before a problem occurred. This backup procedure provides very good protection for the current week and moderate protection for previous weeks of the current month. Remember, you can only restore data up to the point at which the problem occurred, so if you discover a problem with last month's data, you can restore last month's data, but you must re-enter all the transactions that occurred since that time.

To help you understand the level of protection provided by this backup procedure, let's examine some of the possible situations that could arise. Assume you have been using the procedure shown in Figure 7-15 to back up an accounting system that is used Monday through Friday. You perform a full backup every Friday, and that backup is stored at an off-site location. Monday through Thursday evenings, you perform an incremental backup of the files that have changed that day, and store the backups in a file drawer next to the computer.

What if the hard drive fails on Thursday afternoon? To recover, you restore the full backup from the preceding Friday, then restore the incremental backups performed on Monday, Tuesday, and Wednesday evenings. You need to re-enter all the transactions made on Thursday.

What if the entire computer room is destroyed by fire on Thursday afternoon? To recover, you need to purchase replacement computer equipment, reload the off-site backup from the previous Friday, then re-enter the data for Monday, Tuesday, Wednesday, and Thursday.

Suppose that during the third week of the month, your computer gets a virus that corrupts some of the data stored in the system, but the error is not detected, and you continue with the normal backup cycle. Then, when you attempt to close the books at the end of the month, you discover that you cannot access any data from the third or fourth weeks of the month. To recover, you first use a virus detection program to identify and eliminate the virus from your computer. Next, you restore the full backup performed at the end of the second week. You then have to re-enter every transaction for the last two weeks of the month.

Now suppose that during the month of November, a head crash damages some of the data for the month of October. You do not detect the damage immediately because you have no need to access the data for October. At the end of December, however, when you attempt to close the books for the year, you discover that the data for October is damaged. What do you do? To recover, you restore the full backup performed at the end of September, then re-enter every transaction for October, November, and December.

As you can see, a backup procedure does not guarantee that you will not have to re-enter large amounts of data. However, it provides a good level of protection for the problems that are most likely to damage data.

Confidentiality

When an unauthorized person reads data, the data is no longer confidential. Even though password protection and physical security measures are taken to limit access to computer data, hackers and criminals can still acquire access to data, as you have seen in this chapter. Data encryption provides a last line of defense against the unauthorized use of data. If data is encrypted, unauthorized users obtain only scrambled gibberish instead of meaningful information.

Encryption

Edgar Allan Poe, the American writer famous for his tales of horror, was quite interested in secret codes and ciphers. He was convinced that it was impossible to design an unbreakable method of encryption. Was he right?, You will find out in this section.

Data can be **encrypted**, or scrambled, so it cannot be used until it is **decrypted**, or **deciphered**, to change it back to its original form. You might be familiar with simple encryption and decryption techniques. For example, can you figure out this encrypted message?

17 21 15 20 8 20 8 5 18 1 22 5 14 14 5 22 5 18 13 15 18 5

This message was encrypted using a simple substitution technique in which the number of each letter's position in the alphabet represents the letter, like this:

A	B	C	D	E	F	G	H	I	J	K	L	M	N	O	P	Q	R	S	T	U	V	W	X	Y	Z
1	2	3	4	5	6	7	8	9	10	11	12	13	14	15	16	17	18	19	20	21	22	23	24	25	26

The 17 in the encrypted message is the letter "Q," the 21 is the letter "U," and so forth. This is a very simple encryption technique. Using this technique, you can the decipher the message to see that it is the famous quote from Edgar Allan Poe's poem "The Raven":

...Quoth the Raven "Nevermore."

In the jargon of cryptographers—people who study codes—a **key** specifies the procedure for encrypting and decrypting a message. Even if you didn't have the key to the encrypted message shown above, you could probably figure it out using a **frequency analysis**, that is, by looking at the frequencies of letter occurrences. Historians believe that Arab linguists were the first to use frequency analysis, sometime around 1300 A.D. In most languages, some letters occur much more frequently than others in messages, text, and documents. For example, in English, the letter "E" is the most frequently used letter, appearing 13% of the time, as shown in the frequency table in Figure 7-16.

LETTER	PERCENTAGE	RANK		LETTER	PERCENTAGE	RANK
A	8	3		N	7	5
B	1.5	18		O	8	4
C	3	12		P	2	16
D	4	10		Q	.25	25
E	13	1		R	6.5	7
F	2	15		S	6	9
G	1.5	19		T	9	2
H	6	8		U	3	14
I	6.5	6		V	1	23
J	.5	21		W	1.5	20
K	.5	22		X	.5	24
L	3.5	11		Y	2	17
M	3	13		Z	.25	26

Figure 7-16
A frequency analysis table

In the encrypted line from "The Raven," the number "5" appears most frequently, and sure enough, it is an "E" in the unencrypted text. Obviously, using an easily deciphered substitution code to encrypt computer data would not be very effective. A slightly more effective encryption technique might be to use a number to represent each letter of the original message, but add three to each number. Using this technique, for the letter "a," you would substitute the number 4 (1 + 3) and for the letter E, you would substitute the number 8 (5 + 3). Still too easy? You could use 3-5-9 as your substitution key by adding three to the number that represents the first letter, 5 to the number that represents the second letter, and 9 to the number that represents the third letter, as shown in Figure 7-17.

Figure 7-17
3-5-9 encryption

ORIGINAL TEXT	Q	U	O	T	H	T	H	E
SIMPLE SUBSTITUTION	17	21	15	20	8	20	8	5
USE 3-5-9 KEY	3	5	9	3	5	9	3	5
FINAL ENCRYPTED MESSAGE	20	26	24	23	13	29	11	10

1 *Using the 3-5-9 key, the letter "T" is first encrypted as a "23," but the next occurrence of the letter "T" is encrypted as "29."*

A three-digit substitution key is not unbreakable, although even a high-speed computer would need to work at it for a while. To create an unbreakable code, you could use a different digit for each character in the message. If your message was 50 characters long, your key would also be 50 characters long. This method of encryption is called a *one time pad*, because to use it, both the sender and the receiver have an identical book or "pad" of keys. To encrypt the first message, the sender uses the key on page 1 of the pad, then tears it off and destroys it. The receiver deciphers the message using the key on page 1 of the pad, then tears it off and destroys it. The one time pad technique is unbreakable, but not entirely secure because someone could photocopy the pad and have access to all the keys in the pad. Modern computer systems use other methods of encryption such as manipulating bits, hiding data, and combining more than one encryption technique.

Because computers work with bits and because letters are represented by ASCII, ANSI, or EBCDIC codes, it is possible to encrypt messages at the bit level. For example, you could exchange the first four bits and the last four bits of each character. The letter "g," represented by the ANSI code 01100111 would be encrypted as 01110110, which when printed or displayed would appear to be the letter "v." This encrytion technique would still be an easy code to decipher using frequency analysis, because the code for the letter "e" would still appear most frequently. You might decide, however, to use the bit exchange scheme for every other letter in the original message and, thereby, make the code less easy to decipher.

Another encryption technique is to hide data among other non-related data. For example, you could hide 307,200 bits of data in a single 256 grayscale image by changing a single bit for each pixel. Figure 7-18 shows how this tricky encryption technique works.

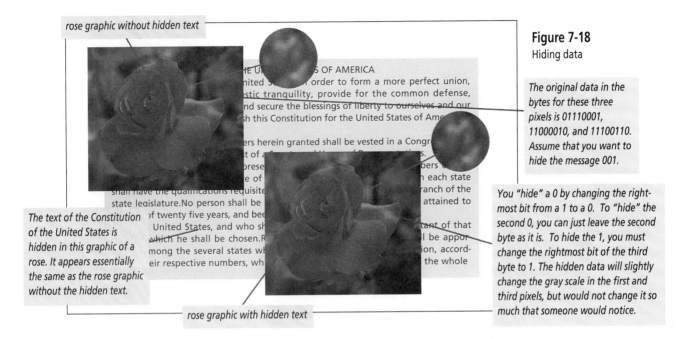

rose graphic without hidden text

Figure 7-18
Hiding data

The original data in the bytes for these three pixels is 01110001, 11000010, and 11100110. Assume that you want to hide the message 001.

You "hide" a 0 by changing the rightmost bit from a 1 to a 0. To "hide" the second 0, you can just leave the second byte as it is. To hide the 1, you must change the rightmost bit of the third byte to 1. The hidden data will slightly change the gray scale in the first and third pixels, but would not change it so much that someone would notice.

The text of the Constitution of the United States is hidden in this graphic of a rose. It appears essentially the same as the rose graphic without the hidden text.

rose graphic with hidden text

To secure computer data, sophisticated cryptographers combine several encryption techniques. For example, the **Data Encryption Standard (DES)**, the most widely used computer data encryption technique, uses an eight-digit key to scramble the data at least 16 different ways. To decipher a DES message, the receiver must know the original key used to encrypt the message. To decipher the original message without the key, you must test each of the 70 quadrillion possible keys—a task estimated to take approximately 1,142 years with a relatively speedy computer system.

There are many effective encryption techniques that virtually guarantee the security of computer data, and this worries law enforcement agencies in the U.S. government. Recently, the National Security Agency (NSA) proposed that the **Clipper Chip** encryption scheme become a standard for all public, private, and government encryption. The Clipper Chip was designed to provide secure transmission of voice and data communications while providing a back door that law enforcement agencies could use to decipher messages. If a law enforcement agency obtained a court order allowing it to tap into encrypted voice or data communications, it could then obtain and use the key to decipher the messages.

Understandably, a controversy has arisen over the Clipper Chip. Law enforcement agencies say they must have a way to decipher messages; it's not very useful to obtain a search warrant if criminals have encrypted their data with a scheme that could take over 1,000 years to decipher. But opponents of the Clipper Chip maintain that the government has no right to require citizens to use a specific encryption method just so the government can break it. Some people believe that the Clipper Chip is equivalent to the government requiring citizens to use a certain type of lock on their house or business, a lock to which the government holds the master key.

Privacy

Does it matter whether government agencies and private businesses encrypt data and take other steps to keep it confidential? It should matter to you, because you are the subject of some of that data, although you might not realize the extent to which the use of this data could be an invasion of your privacy.

In 1898, Michigan State Supreme Court Judge Cooley defined privacy as "the constitutional right to be let alone." Although privacy rights are not specifically stipulated in the U.S. Constitution, amendments to the Constitution imply that citizens have such rights: the Third Amendment prohibits the government from lodging soldiers in private homes without the owner's consent, the Fourth Amendment protects citizens from unwarranted searches, and the Fifth Amendment provides protection against self-incrimination. It was not until Congress passed the Privacy Act of 1974, however, that legislation formally defined the individual's right to be "let alone."

Information about you is stored everywhere. The telephone company has records of who you call and where you live. Your credit card company has records of the kinds of merchandise you purchase: the books and magazines you buy, the clothes you purchase, and your clothing size! Your bank and independent credit bureaus have information about how you manage your money: how much money is in your checking account, how much money you have saved, whether you pay your bills on time, how many bad checks you write, and whether you have ever declared bankruptcy. The government has records of how much you earn, whether you contribute to charities, whether you have children or support your parents, and whether you have been arrested. The Department of Motor Vehicles in your state has information on the type of car you drive, your age, your height, your weight, and your driving record. Your insurance company has information on the size of your home, the type of car you drive, and the medical history of you and your family. Your employer might have records of your job performance, drug test results, or psychological test results. Your college has records on your academic performance and might have detailed information on your family finances if you applied for financial aid.

If it were possible to merge all this data, it would be easy to compile a fairly accurate and very personal profile of you—a profile that would be very valuable to sales representatives, fund-raisers, police, and criminals. Sales representatives would know if you are likely to buy their products. Fund-raisers would be able to discover if you are likely to agree with their cause. Police would be able to look for patterns of aberrant activity. Criminals would be able to determine if you are their kind of target.

In 1985, a *Boston Globe* reporter showed just how easy it is to uncover information about someone. The reporter, posing as an ordinary citizen, looked through government records for information about a Massachusetts resident named Joseph Brown and found:

> Joseph Brown is 58 years old and is married to a woman named Mary, works as an engineer, drives a Cadillac, owns a motor boat, holds a hunting license and a fresh water fishing license, and is an officer in a corporation. His wife, Mary, is a 56-year-old physical therapist who drives a Chevrolet. Their son, David Brown, lives in Boston in a condominium with a mortgage rate of 13.5 percent. He works as an accountant, owns a snowmobile, drives a Volvo, and donated money to the 1984 campaign of Governor Dukakis.

Before computers were used to store data, it was difficult to locate information for even one person. In an uncomputerized world, government agencies such as the Department of Motor Vehicles (DMV) had enough to do just to create, find, and file records. "Selling" a list of automobile owners to a direct-mail advertising company would have been very time consuming, if not next to impossible: someone would need to retype all the names, license numbers, and so on found at the DMV or would need to photocopy all the records. Then, someone would have to carry crates of paper records from the DMV to the direct-mail advertising company. What a lot of work! Paper records are just too difficult to manipulate.

Computerized records are another story. In computerized format, data can be stored in a small space and can be copied or printed quickly. These factors make it easy to electronically transfer files containing client lists, customer mailing lists, and personnel records from one organization to another.

Is there anything you can do to protect your privacy? Yes, but it is not easy. Under the Privacy Act of 1974, you are entitled to examine information about you that is maintained by any federal government agency, except when national security interests prohibit the release of information. You must, however, request this information directly from each agency by letter, and you might be charged a fee for searching and mailing costs. You can find a list of government agencies and their addresses in the *United States Government Manual*, available in most libraries.

The Privacy Act only applies to federal government agencies, and not all states have enacted legislation that provides you with the right to examine the information the state government maintains about you. You can contact your representative to the state legislature if you would like to know the status of privacy legislation in your state.

What about private organizations that maintain information about you—credit bureaus, credit card companies, and banks? Three federal acts provide you with some protection: the Fair Credit Reporting Act, the Fair Credit Billing Act, and the Equal Credit Opportunity Act. The Fair Credit Reporting Act is the most important in providing you with the clout to examine and correct the information that private organizations maintain about you. If you submit a written request, an organization is required to provide you with all the information it maintains about you, except medical records. Credit bureaus are required to also furnish you with the sources for the information it has collected about you. If you find errors in the information, you may request that they be corrected.

The amount of data stored on computer systems, combined with the vulnerability of those systems, creates a potentially volatile situation. As you have learned, a surprising amount of personal data is maintained about you. All of it might not be accurate. It can be accessed and altered by criminals. It can be destroyed by hardware failure, human sabotage, or natural disaster. The same can be said for national security data or for the data that keeps the world financial market running smoothly. One of the main issues that has emerged in the computer age concerns the security and ethical use of computer data.

In the story about the Trojan War, the Trojans seemed so naive. Who would be so foolish as to pull such a suspicious horse into the city? But you have learned that modern computer users are often just as naive about modern technology. They install programs on their computers without checking for viruses, they store massive amounts of data without backups, and they transmit sensitive data without first encrypting it. The Trojans fell for the wooden horse trick the first time, but they wouldn't have again. Will modern computer users repeat their mistakes or learn to take precautions? Now that you've read this chapter, what will you do?

C H A P T E R　　R E V I E W

1. Answer the questions listed in the Chapter Preview section at the beginning of the chapter.
2. List each of the boldface terms used in this chapter, then use your own words to write a short definition of each term.
3. Make a list of the ways computer data can become altered or destroyed.
4. Complete the following chart to summarize what you have learned about Trojan horses, time bombs, logic bombs, and software worms.

	STANDALONE:	VIRUS/STANDALONE:	TRIGGERED BY:
TROJAN HORSE		STANDALONE (MIGHT CONTAIN A VIRUS)	INSTALLATION
TIME BOMB			A DATE ON THE SYSTEM CLOCK
LOGIC BOMB		BOTH	
SOFTWARE WORM			

5. Make a list of the encryption methods mentioned in the chapter and write a one- or two-sentence description of each.
6. Make a list of procedures that prevent data loss.

C H A P T E R　　Q U I Z

1. Formalized habits or _____ can significantly reduce the chances of mistakes and operator errors.
2. If you accidentally erase a file, you can use a(n) _____ to search for the clusters previously used by the erased file and combine them into a new file.
3. You can avoid many mistakes if you stop and _____ before you press the Enter key to execute any command that erases a file, copies a file, or formats a disk.
4. A(n) _____ contains a battery and other circuitry that provides a continuous supply of power to keep your computer operating during a brownout or brief blackout; a(n) _____ protects your computer from electrical spikes and surges, but does not keep your computer operating if the power fails.
5. A(n) _____ feature periodically saves the current version of your document on disk. Then, if the power goes off, you can retrieve the last version of the file that was saved.
6. A(n) _____ is a program designed to activate when the computer system clock reaches a certain date or time.
7. A(n) _____ is a program designed to spread from one computer to another by attaching itself to other programs.
8. A(n) _____ is a unique series of bytes that can be used to identify a known virus.
9. A(n) _____ allows a user to bypass the normal security precautions and access a computer system.
10. If you have file find and _____ rights to a subdirectory on a file server, you can locate and run the programs in that subdirectory, but you cannot create or erase files.

11. A(n) _____ backup is a copy of all files on a hard disk drive.

12. A(n) _____ backup is a copy of the files that have changed since the last backup of any type.

13. An important aspect of state computer crime laws is defining computer data as _____ .

14. The Data Encryption Standard or DES encryption method uses a single eight-digit _____ to scramble data at least 16 different times, producing an encrypted file that is extremely difficult to decipher.

15. The _____ is an encryption method designed to provide secure transmission of voice and data while providing a back door that allows law enforcement agencies to decipher messages.

P R O J E C T S

1. Describe a situation in which you or someone you know lost data stored on a computer. What caused the data loss? What steps could have been taken to prevent the loss? What steps could you have taken to recover the lost data?

2. Think about the programs and data files stored on the hard disk drive of your computer. Describe what you would need to do to reconstruct these files if the hard disk drive failed and you did not have any backups.

3. Describe the backup method and virus protection on your computer system. Why do you think your current protection is or is not sufficient?

4. Assume that your hard disk drive fails on a Friday afternoon. Explain how you would restore your data if you had been using each of the following backup systems:

   a. A full backup every Friday evening

   b. A full backup every Friday evening with a differential backup on Wednesday night

   c. A full backup every Friday evening with an incremental backup Monday through Thursday evenings

5. Discuss the concerns raised by the plans for the Clipper Chip encryption method. Do you think the Clipper Chip is a good idea? Can you think of any alternative methods that would protect the privacy of individual citizens while providing a way for law enforcement agencies to effectively perform their job?

6. Use the frequency table in Figure 7-16 to decode this message:

   GJXXNGGOTZNUCOTWMOHYJTKTAMTXOB

   YNFGOGINUGJFNZVQHYNGNEAJFHYOTW

   GOTHYNAFZNFTUINZANFGNLNFUTXNXU

   FNEJCINHYAZGAEUTUCQGOGOTHJOHOA

   TCJXK

7. The Internet virus created concern about the security of data on military and research computer systems, and it raised ethical questions about the rights and responsibilities of computer users. Select one of the following statements and write a two-page paper that argues for or against it. You might want to use library resources to learn more about each viewpoint. Be sure you include your resources in a bibliography.

   a. People have the "right" to hone their computing skills by breaking into computers. A computer scientist once said, "The right to hack is held higher than the right of someone to tell you not to. It's an inalienable right."

   b. If problems exist, it is acceptable to use any means to point them out. The computer science student who created the Internet virus claimed at his trial that he was just trying to point out that security holes exist in large, connected computer networks.

   c. Computer crimes are no different than other crimes, and computer criminals should be held responsible for the damage they cause. The student who created the Internet virus received a suspended sentence, because his actions were viewed more as a prank than as a deliberate attempt to damage information that would take time and money to restore. But others have said that computer criminals should be held responsible for the time and cost of replacing or restoring data.

8. Obtain a copy of your school's student code and/or computer use policy, then answer the following questions:

   a. To whom does the policy apply: students, faculty, staff, community members, others?

   b. What types of activities does the policy specifically prohibit?

   c. If a computer crime is committed, would the crime be dealt with by campus authorities or by state law enforcement agents?

   d. Does the policy state the penalties for computer crimes? If so, what are they?

L A B

Data Backup

The Data Backup Lab gives you an opportunity to make tape backups on a simulated computer system. Periodically, the hard disk on the simulated computer will fail, which gives you a chance to assess the convenience and efficiency of different backup procedures. To complete this lab, perform the following procedure:

L A B

DATA BACKUP

1. Create a full backup every Friday using only Tape 1. Indicate the date of the hard disk failure on your simulation. After you try to restore your files, list the files that you lost using this backup procedure.

2. Create a full backup every Friday on Tape 1 and an incremental backup every Wednesday on Tape 2. Indicate the date of the hard disk failure on your simulation. Describe the procedure you used to restore your files. How many files did you lose?

3. Create a full backup on Tape 1 every Monday. Make incremental backups on Tapes 2, 3, 4, and 5 each day for the rest of the week. Indicate the date of the hard disk failure on your simulation. Describe the procedure you used to restore your files. How many files did you lose?

4. Experiment with this simulation to determine if the backup procedure you used in question #3 above is the optimal way to back up your data. Write two paragraphs describing what you found.

R E S O U R C E S

■ Kahn, D. *The Codebreakers*. New York: Macmillan, 1976.

   This is one of the classic books on the history of cryptography. The book is huge—over 1,000 pages—and extensively referenced. But don't let that discourage you from checking this book out from your library. It is written in a captivating style, and you can dip in anywhere and sample tales of intrigue—such as how the Greeks established the first system of military cryptography, how the English broke the "unbreakable" German enigma code during World War II, and how to interpret messages from outer space.

Linowes, D. *Privacy in America*. Chicago: University of Illinois Press, 1989.

This well-researched book is sure to motivate you to think about the kind of data that government and private computer systems are accumulating about you. The book concludes with a series of guidelines for protecting your personal privacy.

Stoll, C. *The Cuckoo's Egg*. New York: Doubleday, 1987.

While monitoring user accounts on a large research computer system, the author of this book noticed a $0.75 discrepancy that mushroomed into an international hunt for hackers who were selling U.S. military data to the KGB. This book has all the elements of an espionage thriller, but the story is true and contains a wealth of factual information on computer security.

Understanding Computers: Computer Security. Alexandria, VA: Time-Life Books, 1986.

A lavishly illustrated, in-depth look at computer security, the methods that hackers use to avoid it, and the improved methods used to foil them.

CHAPTER EIGHT

CHAPTER PREVIEW

When you have completed this chapter you should be able to answer the following questions:

- What are the phases of the systems development life cycle?
- How do you use PIECES to identify problems in a computer information system?
- What are the advantages and disadvantages of purchasing commercial software applications?
- What role does a systems analyst have in developing a new information system?
- What role does a programmer have in developing a new information system?
- What is the role of the user in developing an information system?

DEVELOPING EFFECTIVE INFORMATION SYSTEMS

The three men sat around a kitchen table in Oslo, Norway. "So we'll try it!" one said, and the rest agreed. It was the beginning of a daring attempt to cross 413 nautical miles of shifting ice, snow drifts, and frigid water between Canada and the North Pole without assistance from sled dogs, snowmobiles, or resupply flights. Each man would pull a specially designed Kevlar and fiberglass sled containing food, water, and fuel. Each sled would weigh 265 pounds fully loaded. The expedition would begin March 9.

The expedition members knew that their success depended on having the appropriate gear and provisions, so they turned to Abercrombie & Livingston Outfitters, Ltd. of London for assistance. Outfitters to generations of explorers, A&L provides expertise on appropriate gear for any terrain or climate and has an extensive network of suppliers and manufacturers willing to customize equipment. A&L has branch outlets in Telluride, Colorado; Katmandu, Nepal; Geneva, Switzerland; Lima, Peru; Guatemala City, Guatemala; and Dar es Salaam, Tanzania, as well as 12 field agents who can be dispatched to any location in the world.

A&L Outfitters relies on computers to conduct business efficiently and effectively. Customer satisfaction and the success of expeditions, such as the Norwegians' attempt to reach the North Pole, depend on A&L's ability to deliver equipment to the right place at the specified time. A&L's ability to provide expertise on local conditions depends on access to information from diverse sources. In this chapter, you will learn how computer systems like the one at A&L Outfitters help businesses and organizations function effectively.

Information Systems

An **information system** collects, maintains, and provides information to people. Today, many information systems are computerized. These **computerized information systems** can be defined as the computers, peripheral devices, programs, data, people, and procedures that work together to record, store, process, and distribute information. In this chapter, the terms "information system" and "computer information system" are used interchangeably to refer to information systems that are computerized.

It is important to recognize that an information system includes people and procedures as well as computer hardware, programs, and data. An information system is designed to provide information to people and is maintained by people, so it is important to consider the needs of human users and operators, as well as hardware and software, when designing an information system.

The purpose of an information system is usually to improve the effectiveness of a business or organization by providing useful, accurate, and timely information. For example, a computerized information system helps A&L Outfitters improve the effectiveness of its operations by improving communications among outlets, tracking orders from customers, scheduling shipments to expedition base camps, and tracking inventory at each branch outlet.

An information system might have one or more of the following components or subsystems: an office automation system, a transaction processing system, a management information system, a decision support system, and an expert system.

Office Automation

As its name suggests, an **office automation system** "automates," or computerizes, routine office tasks, such as producing documents, tracking schedules, making routine calculations, and facilitating interoffice voice and written communication. Word processors, spreadsheets, scheduling software, and electronic mail are integral parts of most office automation systems. Study Figure 8-1 to learn how computers automate routine tasks in a typical office.

The office automation system at A&L uses electronic mail to overcome the problem of communicating between outlets in seven time zones. Word processing software helps with routine correspondence, such as responses to inquiries from potential customers, congratulatory messages to successful expeditions, and letters to suppliers. Desktop publishing software provides a cost-effective way to prepare A&L's quarterly newsletter. In the London office, scheduling software maintains appointment calendars for A&L sales agents and executives.

A new trend in office automation is groupware. **Groupware** is software that is designed to help people collaborate on projects. In organizations, many projects or procedures are not completed by only one person. Reports, for example, are often the product of more than one person's efforts—many people might participate by contributing sections of a report, by reviewing a draft document and suggesting changes, or by approving a final version of the report. A groupware word processor facilitates this process by providing a way for a group of people to work on the document; it allows more than one person to access the report file, it records the

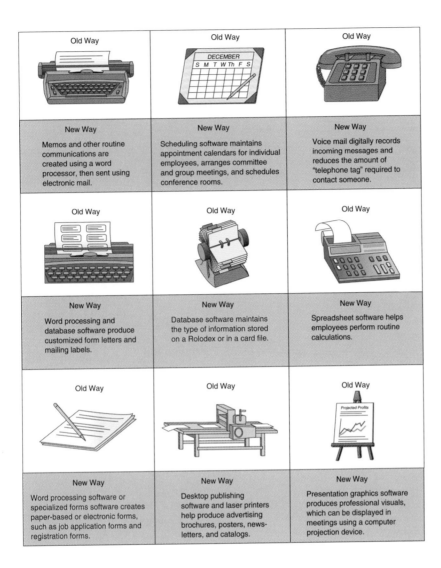

Figure 8-1
Office automation software automates routine office tasks

changes and comments made by each person, and it contains a routing mechanism for approvals. In addition to word processing, groupware is available for scheduling, project planning, and decision making.

Transaction Processing

In an information system context, a **transaction** is an event that requires a manual or computer-based activity. When you order a product by mail or when you buy merchandise in a store, you are involved in a transaction. When you make a phone call or when you pay your phone bill, you are also involved in a transaction. Most transactions require a sequence of steps. For example, to pay your phone bill, you must receive the bill, write a check for the amount due, and place the check in the mail. Then, the post office must deliver your payment to the phone company, and the phone company must record the payment. For the transaction to be successful, all the steps of the transaction must be completed. If even one step fails, the entire transaction has failed.

A **transaction processing system** keeps track of all the transactions for a business or organization by providing a way to collect, display, modify, and cancel transactions. The transaction data is stored in one or more files. Usually, a transaction processing system cannot produce elaborate reports, but it can produce basic reports, such as those that list the transactions contained in the file. Figure 8-2 diagrams the processes that take place in a typical transaction processing system.

Figure 8-2

Basic functions of a transaction processing system

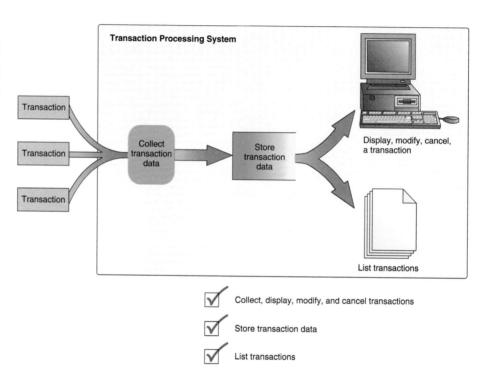

Some examples of transaction processing systems that are commonly found in businesses today are:

- Order-entry/invoice system. This system provides a way to input, view, modify, and delete customer orders. It also helps track the status of each order, and it creates invoices.
- Point-of-sale system (POS). This type of system records items purchased at a cash register and calculates the total amount due for each sale. Some POS systems automatically verify credit cards, calculate change, and identify customers who have previously written bad checks.
- Inventory control system. This system records the sale of inventory items and increases the quantity recorded for inventory items when new inventory arrives.
- General accounting system. This system records the financial status of a business by keeping track of income, expenses, and assets.

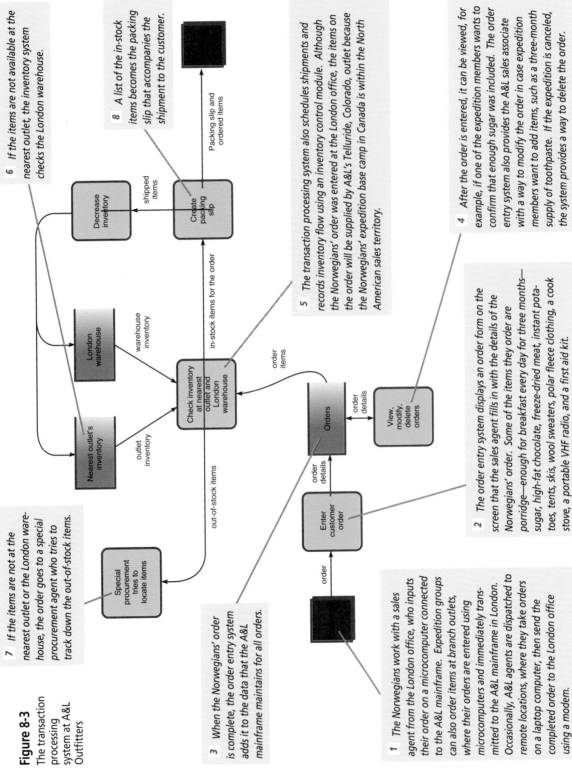

Figure 8-3
The transaction processing system at A&L Outfitters

1 The Norwegians work with a sales agent from the London office, who inputs their order on a microcomputer connected to the A&L mainframe in London. Expedition groups can also order items at branch outlets, where their orders are entered using microcomputers and immediately transmitted to the A&L mainframe in London. Occasionally, A&L agents are dispatched to remote locations, where they take orders on a laptop computer, then send the completed order to the London office using a modem.

2 The order entry system displays an order form on the screen that the sales agent fills in with the details of the Norwegians' order. Some of the items they order are porridge—enough for breakfast every day for three months—sugar, high-fat chocolate, freeze-dried meat, instant potatoes, tents, skis, wool sweaters, polar fleece clothing, a cook stove, a portable VHF radio, and a first aid kit.

3 When the Norwegians' order is complete, the order entry system adds it to the data that the A&L mainframe maintains for all orders.

4 After the order is entered, it can be viewed, for example, if one of the expedition members wants to confirm that enough sugar was included. The order entry system also provides the A&L sales associate with a way to modify the order in case expedition members want to add items, such as a three-month supply of toothpaste. If the expedition is canceled, the system provides a way to delete the order.

5 The transaction processing system also schedules shipments and records inventory flow using an inventory control module. Although the Norwegians' order was entered at the London office, the items on the order will be supplied by A&L's Telluride, Colorado, outlet because the Norwegians' expedition base camp in Canada is within the North American sales territory.

6 If the items are not available at the nearest outlet, the inventory system checks the London warehouse.

7 If the items are not at the nearest outlet or the London warehouse, the order goes to a special procurement agent who tries to track down the out-of-stock items.

8 A list of the in-stock items becomes the packing slip that accompanies the shipment to the customer.

Decrease inventory

Create packing slip

London warehouse

Nearest outlet's inventory

Check inventory at nearest outlet and London warehouse

Orders

View, modify, delete orders

Enter customer order

Special procurement tries to locate items

shipped items

warehouse inventory

outlet inventory

in-stock items for the order

order items

order details

order details

out-of-stock items

order

Packing slip and ordered items

The transaction processing system at A&L Outfitters computerizes order entry, invoicing, inventory control, and general accounting. Study Figure 8-3 to learn how A&L's order entry system processes transactions, such as the order for the Norwegians' North Pole expedition.

A transaction processing system is designed mainly for use by clerical personnel to record transactions. Most transaction processing systems generate a limited number of reports, which provide a basic record of completed transactions. However, managers need more sophisticated reports to help them understand and analyze data. These reports are usually created by a management information system.

Management Information Systems

A **management information system**, or **MIS**, generally uses the data collected by a transaction processing system but manipulates that data to create reports that inform managers of the current status of operations, thereby helping managers make routine and structured decisions. A **routine decision** is one that is made regularly and repeatedly, for example, a monthly decision about what to order to restock inventory. A **structured decision** is one that has a clear and replicable method for reaching a solution. An example of a structured decision is figuring out which customers should receive overdue notices. The method for reaching a solution is to find the records that have an outstanding balance, then check whether the due date for their payment falls before today's date. As Figure 8-4 shows, an MIS is characterized by the production of routine reports that managers use for routine and structured decisions.

Figure 8-4
Functions of a management information system

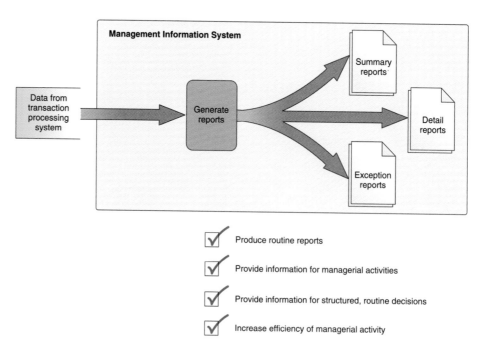

The goal of an MIS is to increase the efficiency of managerial activity. Different levels of management have different information needs, so a management information system produces several different types of reports. A **detail report** is an organized list, for example, a report of inventory items alphabetized by product name. A **summary report** combines or groups data and often shows totals. A summary report might show the total annual sales for the past five years. An **exception report** contains information that is outside of normal or acceptable ranges, such as a reorder report showing low-stock items in inventory.

The MIS at A&L provides the managers of the branch outlets and main office with many reports that are produced on a daily, weekly, or monthly basis. Once a day, the managers at each branch outlet receive a summary report showing the number of orders filled, the total amount due for the orders, the number of payments received, and the total amount of all the payments. On a weekly basis, the inventory manager of each branch outlet receives a report that lists inventory that needs to be reordered. Every month, each branch outlet manager receives a summary report of total income and expenses for the branch. Also on a monthly basis, the Vice President of Sales in the London office receives a summary report showing income and expenses for all the branches, along with the total profit for the entire company.

To create these reports, the MIS sorts, extracts, and totals the data from the transaction processing system. The specifications for most of these reports were created by personnel in A&L's information systems department when the MIS system was designed. A manager at A&L can request an additional customized report if the current reports do not meet his or her needs, but as is the case in many businesses, the information system personnel at A&L have many projects that are behind schedule, and they would not be able to find the time to add a new report to the processing routine for several months.

Because managers cannot quickly obtain customized reports, A&L's MIS system is not very flexible. For example, it does not provide a way for a manager to quickly request a customized report that compares sales at the Katmandu outlet with those at the Geneva outlet. However, A&L managers can create customized reports on demand using the corporate decision support system.

Decision Support Systems

A **decision support system**, or **DSS**, allows users to manipulate data directly and produce customized reports. A DSS is designed to help managers and other personnel make nonroutine decisions, even for **semi-structured problems**, where the decision might be based on imprecise data or might require "guesstimates." Decision makers use a DSS to design decision models and make queries. A **decision model** is a numerical representation of a realistic situation, such as a cash flow model of a business that shows how income adds to cash accounts and how expenses deplete those accounts. A **decision query** is a question or set of instructions that describes the data that needs to be gathered to make a decision.

A decision support system derives its name from the fact that it "supports" the decision maker, that is, it provides the tools the decision maker needs to examine the data. However, a DSS does not make decisions—that remains the role of the human decision maker.

A DSS typically includes modeling tools, such as spreadsheets, so managers can create a numerical representation of a situation and explore "what-if" alternatives. A DSS also typically includes statistical tools so managers can study trends before making a decision. A DSS usually includes data from the organization's transaction processing system, but it might also include or access external data such as stock market reports, as shown in Figure 8-5.

Figure 8-5

Functions of a decision support system

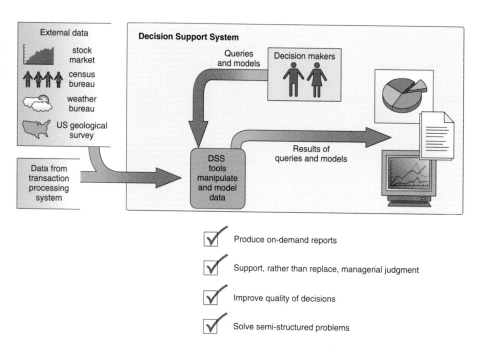

The managers at Abercrombie & Livingston Outfitters, Ltd. use their DSS to tackle diverse problems because it contains a good selection of decision support tools. For example, one A&L branch outlet manager is using the DSS to project next year's sales of cold-weather camping equipment. To make this projection, he first retrieves from the A&L transaction processing system the data on the past two years' sales of each item of cold-weather camping equipment. He then transfers the data into a spreadsheet so he can manipulate it and examine several "what-if" scenarios. He uses the DSS link to a commercial information service to filter through articles about camping, recreation, and weather. For example, the manager discovers that weather systems last year were especially intense. Because of the bad weather, expeditions to cold climates were not advisable and sales of cold-weather equipment declined.

Next, the manager uses the DSS to search through an A&L database that contains information on all the expeditions of the past five years. The DSS helps him create a graph showing that expeditions to cold regions declined last year after a steady increase for the previous three years. Should he gamble and assume that last year was an unusual deviation in a steadily increasing cold-weather equipment market? By manipulating the data in the spreadsheet, the manager looks at best- and worse-case scenarios and decides that it is not too risky to order 5% more cold-weather camping equipment.

Expert Systems

You've just seen how a DSS helps a manager manipulate the data necessary to make a decision, but it is up to the manager to analyze the data and reach a decision. The DSS does not substitute for the judgment of the manager, and this system is appropriate in situations where trained professionals are making decisions. However, in many organizations, it would be useful if every decision did not need to be made by a highly paid expert.

For example, A&L customer service would be improved if order clerks could decide whether to extend credit to customers. If the clerks could make this decision, they would not need to take the time to consult with a manager and then get back to customers with an answer. Customers would probably be pleased if clerks could make this decision, because they would not have to wait for an answer about whether credit will be extended to them. However, uninformed credit decisions by order clerks could result in a high number of uncollectible accounts. What if the computer could examine a customer's credit history, determine the credit risk using the same criteria as an experienced credit analyst, then make a credit decision and provide the result to a clerk? This process would be like having a credit analyst working with every order clerk. Customer service would improve with minimal risk.

An **expert system**, or **knowledge-based system**, is a computer system designed to analyze data and produce a recommendation or decision. As the name implies, an expert system is a computerized expert. To create an expert system, the knowledge of an expert about a particular type of decision is "cloned," or captured, in a set of rules called a **knowledge base**. The knowledge base is stored in a computer file and then manipulated by software called an **inference engine**. When it is time to make a decision, the inference engine begins analyzing the available data by following the rules in the knowledge base. If the expert system needs additional data, the expert system checks external databases, looks for the data in a transaction processing system, or asks the user to answer questions, as shown in Figure 8-6.

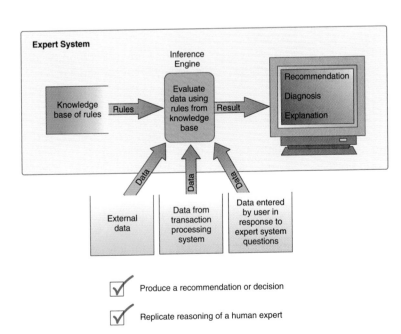

Figure 8-6
Functions of an expert system

An expert system is not a general-purpose problem solver or decision maker. Each expert system is designed to make decisions in a particular area or "domain." For example, an expert system created for the Campbell Soup Company captured the knowledge of an expert cooking-vat operator to help less experienced employees troubleshoot problems that might arise as the soup cooks. Other expert systems have been developed to locate mineral deposits, diagnose blood diseases, evaluate corporate financial statements, underwrite complex insurance policies, and recommend stock purchases.

Expert systems are sometimes created using a computer programming language, but more often, they are created using an expert system shell. An **expert system shell** is a software tool used for developing expert system applications. An expert system shell is an expert system without any rules to solve a particular problem. The shell contains the inference engine and a method for entering the rules for the knowledge base. To create an expert system, you use the shell to enter rules, then use the inference engine to test the rules and make certain the decisions they produce are correct.

A&L Outfitters does not currently have an expert system, but the special procurement agent is trying to convince management to explore the possibility of using an expert system to fill orders more efficiently. Now let's see how an organization can successfully develop an expert system and integrate it with an existing information system.

System Development Life Cycle

The computer industry abounds with tales of information systems, developed at great expense, that didn't meet expectations: they didn't work correctly, were too complex to use, or weren't flexible enough to meet changing business needs. As Frederick Brooks observes in his book, *The Mythical Man-Month*, "One can expect the human race to continue attempting systems just within or just beyond our reach, and software systems are perhaps the most intricate and complex of all man's handiwork."

Whether you are part of a team to develop a complex corporate information system or you are developing a small information system for your own use, you are more likely to succeed if you analyze the purpose of the information system, carefully design the system, test it thoroughly, and document its features.

A **system development life cycle**, or **SDLC**, is an outline of a process that helps develop successful information systems. Several variations of the SDLC exist, but most of them are similar to, or variations of, the one shown in Figure 8-7.

Computer professionals called **systems analysts** are often responsible for analyzing information requirements, designing a new information system, and supervising the new system implementation. Systems analysts also create specifications for application software for the new system, then give those specifications to computer **programmers** who create computer programs to meet those specifications.

Increasingly, managerial and clerical employees initiate and participate in the development of information systems, as is the case at A&L Outfitters. That's why no one was surprised when the special procurement agent at A&L Outfitters suggested that it was time to automate part of her job. The special procurement agent and a systems analyst from A&L's information systems department formed a project team to work on the new system.

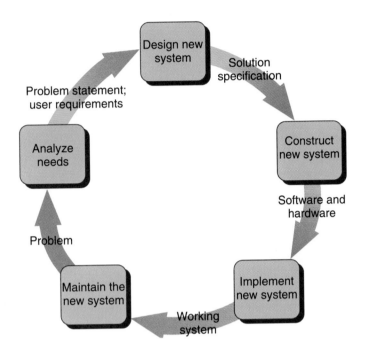

Figure 8-7
Systems development life cycle

A **system development project team**, or "project team" for short, is a group of people who are assigned to analyze and develop an information system. The composition of the project team depends on the scope of the project. Large and fairly complex projects have big project teams, and a high percentage of the team is composed of systems analysts or other computer professionals. Small projects have fewer members on the project team, and a high percentage of the team members are likely to be users rather than computer professionals. Figure 8-8 on the following page contains some excerpts from the first meeting of the special procurement project team as the special procurement agent explains what she calls the "cross-shipping problem."

Analyze Needs

Instead of jumping to a solution and forging ahead, it is important to clearly define the problem that the information system will solve, learn how the current system functions, and define the requirements for a successful solution. The major activities in the analysis phase are listed in Figure 8-9 on page NP271.

Figure 8-8
Excerpts from the
special procurement
project team meeting

Systems Analyst (SA): I'm not very familiar with your job. Would you fill me in?

Special Procurement Agent (SPA): As you probably know, when a customer places an order, it is usually shipped from the A&L outlet nearest the expedition base camp or departure point. However, if that outlet is out of stock on an ordered item, the computer checks to see if it is available in the London warehouse.

SA: Yes, I know how that works. And if the item is in stock in London, we ship it from London to the outlet.

SPA: Right. But if the item is not in the outlet or the London warehouse, the order comes to me. I try to locate the item by using the DSS system. If I find the item at another outlet, I usually ask them to "cross-ship" the item to the outlet nearest the base camp or departure point.

SA: By cross-ship, do you mean that one outlet ships the item to another outlet?

SPA: Exactly.

SA: That sounds like you're making effective use of the system. What's the problem?

SPA: The problem is that it takes time for me to check the inventories and decide which outlet can supply the item fastest and least expensively. I usually don't receive notification for 24 hours; then, with my work load, it might be another day or two before I can tackle it.

SA: I see.

SPA: It's costing the company a lot of money to deliver some of these items, considering the time I spend and the possible delay to the customer.

SA: So I assume you would like to automate the cross-shipping decision, if possible?

SPA: Yes, I think it would be cost effective.

Define the Problem

The first activity in the analysis phase is to define the problem. The analyst tries to write a sentence that identifies what needs to be improved or fixed. Here are some examples of well-defined problems for information systems:

- In a garden supply store: The price tags frequently fall off items, especially the plants, so customers have to wait at the registers while an employee checks the price.
- In a casino: Croupiers are not allowed to extend additional credit to a gambler, so everyone at the table must wait while a manager goes to the cashier cage to check the customer's credit.
- In a police car: Officers do not have access to out-of-state arrest warrants, so they might stop a motorist for a minor violation, but fail to make an arrest on a more serious charge.

Figure 8-9
Analysis activities

A common pitfall in the analysis phase is to state a solution rather than a problem. Solutions are not appropriate at this stage of the SDLC because you should not consider solutions until you understand more about the problem with the current system. Although the following statements might sound reasonable, they are solutions, not problems:

- The garden supply store needs a bar-code reader so cashiers can determine the price of an item even if it doesn't have a price tag.
- The casino should provide floor managers with cellular phones so they can call the cashier's cage for a credit check.
- The police car should be equipped with a computer that can access a national database of outstanding arrest warrants.

James Wetherbe developed the PIECES framework to help identify problems that exist in an information system. Each letter of PIECES stands for a potential problem, as shown in Figure 8-10.

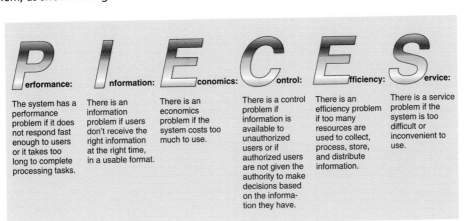

Figure 8-10
PIECES helps identify problems

Performance:	Information:	Economics:	Control:	Efficiency:	Service:
The system has a performance problem if it does not respond fast enough to users or it takes too long to complete processing tasks.	There is an information problem if users don't receive the right information at the right time, in a usable format.	There is an economics problem if the system costs too much to use.	There is a control problem if information is available to unauthorized users or if authorized users are not given the authority to make decisions based on the information they have.	There is an efficiency problem if too many resources are used to collect, process, store, and distribute information.	There is a service problem if the system is too difficult or inconvenient to use.

At A&L Outfitters, the special procurement agent classified the procurement problem as an efficiency problem. Too many resources, that is, too many hours of her time, are devoted to choosing the best location from which to cross-ship items. The special procurement agent and systems analyst at A&L Outfitters created the following problem statement:

> *If a customer orders an item that is out of stock in London and at the outlet closest to the expedition departure point, the current procedures are not efficient for finding out whether other outlets have the item in stock and from which outlet the item can be cross-shipped cost effectively.*

Study the Current System

In an organization, employees don't always have a clear idea how the entire information system works. Sometimes this is because their knowledge about the system is limited to the procedure or process for their particular job. Although it is not realistic for every employee to become an expert on the entire information system, if you use part of an information system, it is useful to know how that piece fits into the larger system. Systems analysts use *data flow diagrams (DFDs)*, *data dictionaries*, and *structured English* to document the way a system, or a part of a system, works. Study Figure 8-11 to see how this documentation gives you a better idea of the information system at A&L and the nature of the cross-ship problem.

Data flow diagrams, data dictionaries, and structured English are valuable tools for analyzing information systems. These tools help produce documentation that is also useful in the design and maintenance phases. However, it can be difficult to keep the diagrams, dictionaries, and structured English specifications for an information system up to date. For example, if the information systems department at A&L decided to rename Qty to QtyOrdered, several revisions would need to be made in the data dictionary and the process specification. It might be easy to miss one of the changes, which could lead to errors and bugs in the information system.

To make it easier to maintain data flow diagrams, data dictionaries, and process specifications, systems analysts use CASE tools. CASE stands for Computer Aided Software Engineering. A **CASE tool** is software that is designed for drawing diagrams of information systems, writing process specifications, and maintaining data dictionaries. A CASE tool keeps track of the labels on data flow diagrams, data dictionaries, and process specifications. If you change a label in one place, the CASE tool makes the appropriate revisions everywhere else. Figure 8-12 on page NP 274 shows a screen from a CASE tool called Excelerator.

Figure 8-11
System documentation

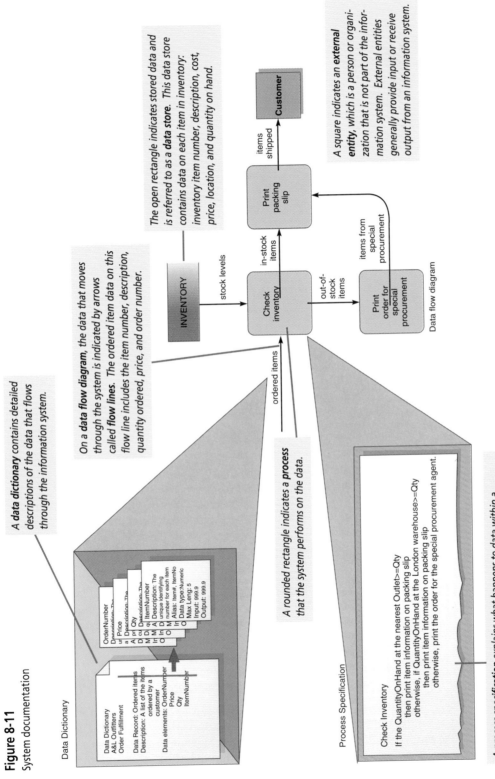

A **data dictionary** contains detailed descriptions of the data that flows through the information system.

Data Dictionary

Data Dictionary
A&L Outfitters
Order Fulfillment

Data Record: Ordered items
Description: A list of the items ordered by a customer
Data elements: OrderNumber
Price
Qty
ItemNumber

OrderNumber
Description: The
Price
A Description: The
D Description: The
M ItemNumber
In A Description: The
O In unique identifying
In number for each item
O Alias: Item#, ItemNo
Data type:Numeric
Max Leng: 5
Input: 999.9
Output: 999.9

On a **data flow diagram**, the data that moves through the system is indicated by arrows called **flow lines**. The ordered item data on this flow line includes the item number, description, quantity ordered, price, and order number.

The open rectangle indicates stored data and is referred to as a **data store**. This data store contains data on each item in inventory: inventory item number, description, cost, price, location, and quantity on hand.

A square indicates an **external entity**, which is a person or organization that is not part of the information system. External entities generally provide input or receive output from an information system.

INVENTORY

stock levels

Check inventory

in-stock items

Print packing slip

items shipped

Customer

ordered items

out-of-stock items

Print order for special procurement

items from special procurement

Data flow diagram

A rounded rectangle indicates a **process** that the system performs on the data.

Process Specification

Check Inventory
If the QuantityOnHand at the nearest Outlet>=Qty
then print item information on packing slip
otherwise, if QuantityOnHand at the London warehouse>=Qty
then print item information on packing slip
otherwise, print the order for the special procurement agent.

A **process specification** explains what happens to data within a process. Often, process specifications are written in structured English to concisely and unambiguously explain the logic of the process.

Figure 8-12

A screen from the Excelerator CASE tool

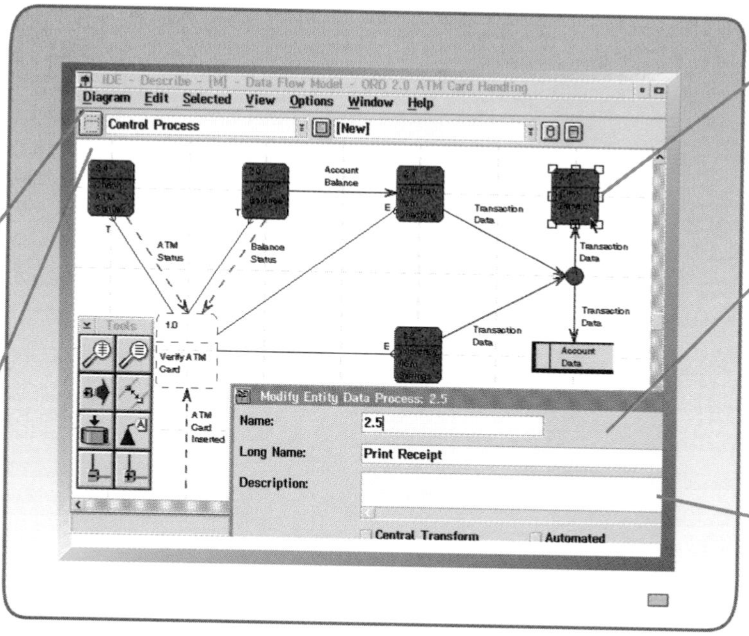

This is the process currently being added to the DFD.

Menus help the analyst modify the diagram and edit the data dictionary.

The analyst adds the name of the process using the Modify Entity Data Process window.

The analyst uses the rounded rectangle tool to draw the process symbols on the DFD.

Additional information about the process can be added, including a description of a process specification.

Determine System Requirements

System requirements are the criteria for successfully solving the problem or problems you have identified. The requirements guide you as you design and plan the new information system. Requirements also serve as an evaluation checklist at the end of the project, so they are sometimes called **success factors**. The information system you create should meet the requirements or success factors you defined.

Requirements are determined by interviewing users and studying successful information systems that solve problems similar to those defined in the earlier stages of analysis. The special procurement agent at A&L Outfitters created the following list of requirements:

- When the current information system fills an order, it should check stock in all outlets, then correctly determine which outlets have the item in stock and from which outlet the item can be shipped most efficiently and cost effectively.
- Without any human intervention, the system should be able to determine the best outlet from which to ship.
- The system should be easy to maintain. When shipping rates or shipping times change, it should be easy to change that information in the system.

Another way to determine requirements is to construct a prototype. A **prototype** is an experimental or trial version of an information system that is under development. Often the prototype is not a fully functioning system because it is designed only to demonstrate selected features that might be incorporated into a new information system. The prototype is demonstrated to users who evaluate which features of the prototype are important for the new information system.

Design the New System

In the design phase, alternate solutions are identified and evaluated, hardware and software are selected, and the specifications for constructing the system are developed, as noted in Figure 8-13.

Identify Potential Solutions

There might be more than one way to solve the problem you identified and meet the requirements you specified in earlier phases of the SDLC. Some potential solutions might be better than others: more effective, less costly, or less complex. Therefore, it is not a good idea to proceed with the first solution that comes to mind. Instead, you should identify several potential solutions and compare the advantages and disadvantages of each. Finally, select the solution that provides you with the most benefits for the least cost.

Remember that information systems include people, procedures, data, hardware, and software. When you

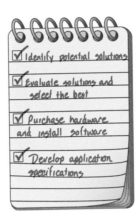

Figure 8-13
Design activities

identify a potential solution, consider whether there are alternatives in any of these areas. As an example, there are often several potential software solutions. An organization could create a custom-built information system using a computer programming language or application development tool, or it could purchase commercial software.

An **application development tool**, sometimes called a **4GL** for Fourth Generation Language, is essentially a type of software construction kit that contains building blocks that can be assembled into an application. Application development tools usually produce applications faster than traditional programming languages. As an analogy, consider baking a cake. You can sift the flour with the salt, mix the sugar, eggs, shortening, and milk, then combine the dry and wet ingredients, and so forth to create a cake "from scratch." This is analogous to creating an application using a programming language. Another way to bake a cake is with a cake mix. You just add water and eggs, mix, and bake. An application development tool is the programmer's "cake mix" and provides a quicker, easier way to construct an application.

Creating an information system using a programming language takes many months (or years) and is very costly. Using an application development tool reduces the time and cost somewhat, but application development is still a major effort. Another possibility is to purchase a commercial software application and customize it, where possible, to fit with the way the organization works. In summary, there are often three potential software solutions: (1) create the application using a programming language, (2) build the application using an application development tool, or (3) buy a commercial software application.

The project team at A&L Outfitters considered all three of these software options. They could use a programming language to write a custom module to determine when and where to cross-ship. The advantage of this solution is that a custom program can be designed to meet the procurement agent's requirements exactly. The disadvantage of this solution is that it requires the services of one or more programmers. Considering the backlog in the information systems department, the module would probably not be available for 18 months.

Another potential solution for A&L is to purchase a commercial software application that already includes the ability to determine when and where to cross-ship. The advantage of this solution is that commercial applications have already been well tested and could be installed very quickly. But it might be difficult to locate a commercial application that would work with the current transaction processing system. Many commercial applications are designed to interact only with other modules purchased from the same vendor. Aside from the cross-shipping problem, A&L is happy with the current transaction processing system and doesn't intend to switch to an entirely new system just to add cross-shipping capability.

Another possible solution is for A&L to use an application development tool, such as an expert system shell, to design an expert system module that determines the feasibility of cross-shipping. An advantage of this solution is that the special procurement agent can play an active role in the development process by feeding knowledge into the expert system shell. Disadvantages of this solution include the time the special procurement agent must spend developing the system and the possible trouble she and the systems analyst might have integrating the expert system with the rest of the transaction processing system.

Evaluate Solutions and Select the Best

To evaluate the three potential solutions, the special procurement agent creates a list of evaluation criteria:

- The solution must run on A&L's current hardware.
- The software application for the solution must integrate with the current transaction processing system.
- The solution must be in place within six months.
- The solution must meet the requirements delineated in the analysis phase.
- Support for the solution must be available from a vendor, software publisher, manufacturer, or the A&L information systems department.

After evaluating the alternatives, the project team decides that the best solution is to use an expert system shell to create an expert system that would work with the current transaction processing system. Custom programming would take too long, and the team was unable to locate an appropriate commercial application that would work with A&L's current system.

The project team takes its proposal to management. In most organizations, management approval is necessary for modifications or additions to the current information system. Management approval is also necessary for equipment purchases, software purchases, and time commitments for personnel resources, such as the time it takes to design, create, test, and maintain an information system.

Purchase Hardware and Software

Once a solution has been selected and management has approved the project, the next activity is to purchase the hardware and software necessary to implement the solution. Typically, more than one vendor sells the necessary hardware and software, so an organization often has a choice of vendors. The method used to select the hardware, software, and vendor depends on the project team's understanding of the hardware and software that is required for the solution. If the team members do not know exactly what hardware and software are needed, they can describe the problem and ask vendors how they would resolve it. If they know exactly what they want, they just need to find a reputable vendor who sells the equipment at a reasonable price.

A **request for proposal**, or RFP, is a document you send to vendors that describes the problem you are trying to solve and the requirements for the solution. An RFP essentially asks vendors to recommend a solution and describe their qualifications to implement the solution. You usually use an RFP when you have not yet selected the equipment or software that meets your needs.

A **request for quotation**, or RFQ, is a request for a formal price quotation on a list of hardware and software. You submit an RFQ when you know the make and model of the equipment, as well as the software packages you need, and you want to compare prices among vendors. Figure 8-14 on the following page shows the difference between an RFP and an RFQ.

The special procurement agent and systems analyst at A&L Outfitters explore a variety of expert system development tools. Eventually, they select a product called ExSys. It is an expert system shell that has been used successfully in many companies in Europe and North America. They select ExSys because it runs on their current hardware, it will integrate with their current transaction processing system, and it appears to provide the capabilities they need. Because the special procurement agent knows exactly what she wants, she asks the A&L purchasing department to send RFQs to vendors who sell ExSys. When the vendors return the RFQs, the purchasing agent at A&L looks for the vendor that offers the most competitive price and then orders ExSys from that vendor.

Develop Application Specifications

Application specifications describe the way an application should interface with the user and how it should store data, process data, and format reports. The specifications are similar to an architectural blueprint that shows the detailed plan for constructing a building. For large information systems, a systems analyst develops the specifications after interviewing users to determine their information needs. The specifications are then given to a programmer or application developer, who creates the application. On a small information systems project, you as the user might develop your own specifications. Then you might give the specifications to a programmer, or if you have the expertise, you might create the application yourself.

Figure 8-14
An RFP and an RFQ

Abercrombie & Livingston Outfitters, Ltd.
23 Baker Street, London, PL2 3BB England
Telephone (0752) 506102/Fax (0752) 506398

RFP describes the problem and asks the vendor to suggest a solution.

Request for Proposal

Abercrombie & Livingston Outfitters, Ltd. is an international supplier of expedition equipment. Inventory and order fulfillment are performed using the Summit order entry and inventory control system running on a DEC VAX 4000-600 computer system.

The current Summit order entry and inventory control system does not allow for automated cross-shipment of goods that are out of stock at the local outlet. Orders for items that are out-of-stock locally are sent to the special procurement agent, who checks to see if the item is in stock in any other A&L outlet. If the item is in stock elsewhere, the special procurement agent determines the most efficient location from which to ship the item and requests a cross-shipment to the required location.

We would like to automate this process. If your company has previous experience with projects of this sort, we invite you to prepare a proposal as outlined below:

1. Company information
2. Similar project experience: include information on similar projects undertaken by your company, with names and telephone numbers of contacts on those projects
3. Proposal summary: briefly explain how you would resolve the problem
4. Materials listing: list the materials required to implement your proposal
5. Projected project cost: provide estimated costs for labor and materials, as well as the total estimated cost for the project
6. Projected timetable

Please dir
Procureme

All propos
addressed
in our offi

Abercrombie & Livingston Outfitters, Ltd.
23 Baker Street, London, PL2 3BB England
Telephone (0752) 506102/Fax (0752) 506398

Request for Quotation

Please return this form showing your current price for the following item(s) by 30 June.

RFQ asks vendor for a price on specific items.

Item	Description	Quantity	Price	Delivery Date
1.	ExSys development system with manuals	1		

Whether a large or small system is under development, it requires detailed specifications so that the final system solves the problem that was defined during the analysis phase. At A&L, the specifications for the expert system define the rules for the knowledge base. The project team develops the following rules for the cross-shipping expert system:

- If the ordered item is in stock at the outlet nearest the destination of the order, then deliver the item from that outlet.
- If the ordered item is not in stock in any outlet, then send the order to the special procurement agent.
- If the ordered item is in stock at only one outlet, then cross-ship the item from that outlet to the outlet nearest the destination of the order. That outlet will then deliver the item to the customer.
- If the ordered item is in stock in more than one outlet, then cross-ship it from the outlet with the lowest shipping cost and fastest delivery time.

Construct the System

In the construction phase, new hardware and software are installed, applications are created to meet the specifications developed during the design phase, and the new applications are tested, as noted in Figure 8-15.

Figure 8-15
Construction activities

Install Hardware

The expert system for A&L Outfitters does not require any new hardware. However, many development projects do require new hardware, which is typically installed during the construction phase. New hardware can either replace old equipment or it can be connected to existing equipment. In either case, new hardware must be tested to make sure it operates correctly. Problems with the hardware or the connections to other equipment must be corrected during the construction phase so they do not disrupt the implementation phase.

Install Software

Many new information systems require new software, such as a commercial application, a programming language, or an application development tool, such as an expert system shell. Before it is used, software must be installed and tested to make sure it works correctly. Software testing can reveal problems that result from incompatibilities with the existing hardware or an incorrect installation of the software. These problems must be corrected before continuing with system construction activities. Other problems might result from **bugs**, or errors, in the software and must be corrected by the organization that originally wrote the software.

The A&L project team installs and tests the expert system shell, ExSys. At this stage, the project team is testing *only the shell* to make sure it runs on the computer without generating error messages—the rules for the expert system have not yet been entered, so the team is not yet testing the cross-shipping rules. When the team members are sure that the expert system shell operates correctly, they continue with the construction of the cross-shipping system.

Create Applications

So far, you have seen that information systems can be constructed using tools such as a programming language, commercial software, or an application development ment tool, such as an expert system shell. As Figure 8-16 shows, the construction techniques depend on the construction tool used.

Figure 8-16
Construction techniques
depend on the tool

CONSTRUCTION TOOL	CONSTRUCTION TECHNIQUES
Programming language	Install programming language. Write application modules using the programming language. Test application modules separately and as a whole to make sure there are no errors.
Application development tool	Install the application development tool. Use the tool's building blocks to construct application. Test application modules separately and as a whole to make sure there are no errors.
Commercial software	Install the commercial software. Customize software to meet specifications, if possible. Test the software to make sure the customization reflects the specifications.
Expert system shell	Install the expert system shell. Enter rules in the knowledge base. Test the expert system to make sure the rules are correct.

When the applications, or programs, for an information system are created using a programming language or application development tool, the process is referred to as software engineering. You will learn more about **software engineering** in Chapter 10.

When an information system is constructed using a commercial application, the application has been written and tested by the software publisher. However, the application sometimes needs to be customized. **Software customization** is the process of modifying a commercial application to reflect the needs of users. Customization might include changing the appearance of the user interface, enabling or disabling the mouse, selecting which menus should appear, and designing forms or reports. The extent to which a commercial application can be customized depends on the options available in the application. For example, some commercial applications provide options for customizing report formats whereas other commercial applications do not.

When an information system requires the construction of an expert system, the rules for the knowledge base must be entered and tested. The process of designing, entering, and testing the rules in an expert system is referred to as **knowledge engineering**. Because the members of the A&L project team have decided to use an expert system shell to construct the cross-shipping application, their major construction activities are to enter and test the rules for the expert system. As with any application, the A&L expert system must meet the design specifications and go through a rigorous testing process to ensure that the rules produce the expected results.

Test Applications

Application testing is the process of trying out various sequences of input values and checking the results to make sure the application works correctly. During the construction phase, testing is performed in three ways: unit testing, integration testing, and system testing.

As each application unit, or component, is completed, it is **unit tested** to make sure that it operates reliably and correctly. Then, when all units are complete and tested, **integration testing** is performed to ensure that the units operate correctly together.

Unit testing and integration testing are usually performed in a test area. A **test area** is a place where software testing can occur without disrupting the organization's regular information system. A test area might be an isolated section of storage on the computer system that runs the organization's regular information system, or it might be on an entirely separate computer system. When problems are discovered during unit testing or integration testing, the cause of the problem is determined and the problem is corrected. Unit testing and integration testing are then repeated to make sure that the problem is corrected and to make sure that no new problems were introduced when the original problem was fixed.

After the unit and integration testing are complete, **system testing** ensures that all the hardware and software components work together. When an existing information system is modified, system testing is performed when the new or modified units are combined with the rest of the existing system. In a completely new information system, system testing is performed to simulate daily work loads and make sure that processing speed and accuracy meet the specifications. System testing is ideally performed in a test area; however, an organization might not have the hardware resources to duplicate its existing information system for testing purposes. In this case, system testing must be performed on the "live" system, and this process can potentially cause some disruption in the normal functions of the organization.

L A B

**SYSTEM
TESTING**

The A&L project team has one application unit to test: the expert system. To perform the test, the project team places a series of sample orders. The results of the test are examined to see if the expert system completes the orders as expected. In most cases, the expert system works, but the team discovers that two orders are not processed correctly. On examining these two orders, the A&L team notices that in both cases, the item was in stock in two locations that had the same shipping cost and the same shipping time. No rule had been entered that told the system which location to select when an item is available in more than one location that has the same shipping time and the same shipping cost. The A&L team then added the following rule and retested the system.

■ If more than one outlet has the item in stock, and the shipping cost and the shipping time are the same, then ship from the outlet that has more of the items in stock.

After the team adds this rule, they test the expert system again, and this time all the test orders are processed correctly.

The A&L project has only one module, so integration testing is not necessary. For system testing, the project team loads the expert system and a copy of the order system into a test area. The purpose of this testing session is to make sure the order data is correctly communicated between the existing order entry system and the new expert system. The system test goes smoothly, so it is time for the project team to schedule implementation of the new system.

Implement the New System

Figure 8-17
Implementation
activities

In the implementation phase, the information system is placed into operation. This phase requires careful planning and preparation. The activities that occur in the implementation phase are shown in Figure 8-17.

Train Users

The expert system for A&L Outfitters works behind the scenes, so it doesn't require any user interaction or training. However, in many new information systems, users need extensive training on system operation, data entry, and additional procedures. If user training is required, the organization schedules training sessions. Training sessions are sometimes conducted by systems analysts, but might also be conducted by professional trainers or by users from the project team. During the training sessions, users learn how to interact with the interface, how to perform tasks using the new system, and how to find additional information in user manuals or procedure handbooks. **Procedure handbooks** contain step-by-step instructions for performing specific job tasks. A procedure manual takes the place of a complete user manual, because in large organizations, employees in a particular department usually perform specific tasks and do not need to know how all the features of the system work.

Data Conversion

The data used by the A&L expert system is taken directly from the transaction processing system, so it is not necessary to convert any data before implementing the new system. However, implementation of many new information systems requires data to be converted to the new system from a manual system or from a previous computer system.

When converting data from a manual system to a computer system, the data can either be typed or scanned electronically into the appropriate storage media. Some organizations have a lot of data that must be converted, and the conversion process can take a long time, require extra personnel, and be quite costly. When converting data from a previous computer system to a new system, a programmer writes **conversion software** that reads the old data and converts it into a format that is usable by the new system.

System Conversion

System conversion refers to the process of deactivating the old system and activating the new one. Don't confuse system conversion and data conversion—data conversion changes data from one format to another, whereas system conversion converts a site from one information system to another. System conversion is also referred to as "cutover" or "go live." There are several strategies for converting to a new system.

A **direct conversion** means that the old system is completely deactivated and the new system is immediately activated. Direct conversion usually takes place during nonpeak hours to minimize disruption in normal business routines. Direct conversion is risky, however, because if the new system does not work correctly, it might need to be deactivated and tested further. In the meantime, the old system must be reactivated, and the transactions that were entered into the new system need to be reentered into the old system so business can continue.

A **parallel conversion** avoids some of the risk of direct conversion, because the old system remains in service while some or all of the new system is activated. Both the old and the new systems operate "in parallel" until the team members determine that the new system is performing correctly. Parallel conversion often requires that all entries are made in both the new and old systems, which is costly in terms of time, computer resources, and personnel. Parallel conversion is fairly safe, but it is often not practical because of the cost and duplication of effort.

Phased conversion works well with large information systems that are modularized. In a **phased conversion**, one module of the new information system is activated at a time. After the team members determine that a module is working correctly, the next module is activated until the entire new system is operating. In a phased conversion, each module of the new system must work with both the old system and the new system, greatly increasing the complexity and cost of the conversion.

A **pilot conversion** works well in organizations with several branches that have independent information processing systems. The new information system is activated at one branch. After the team members determine that the system works correctly at one branch, it is activated at the next branch. During a pilot conversion, the systems analyst must develop a method to integrate information from branches using the new system with information from branches that are still using the old system.

A&L Outfitters has decided to implement a direct conversion for the following reasons:

- The added expense of a parallel conversion is probably unnecessary because the expert system has been extensively tested and is likely to work correctly.
- Phased conversion would not be feasible because there is only one module.
- A pilot conversion is not possible because all the branch outlets access the same information system.

Acceptance Testing

After the conversion, an information system undergoes a final test called acceptance testing. **Acceptance testing** is designed to assure the purchaser or user of the new system that the system does what it is supposed to do. The procedures for acceptance testing are usually designed by the users and systems analysts and often include the use of real data to make sure that the system operates correctly under normal and peak data loads.

At A&L Outfitters, the special procurement agent has allotted a week's time to observe the expert system to make sure it is working acceptably. If the week passes and no major problems appear with the system, the project team will consider the implementation phase complete.

Maintain the System

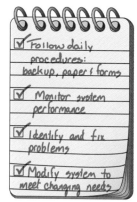

Figure 8-18
Maintenance activities

After a system is implemented, it remains in operation for a period of time. During this time, maintenance activities ensure that the system functions as well as possible. Figure 8-18 shows the major maintenance activities for a typical information system.

The A&L expert system will be maintained along with the rest of the transaction processing system. Information systems personnel will make sure that it is backed up regularly. They will also monitor system performance to make sure the expert system does not create a bottleneck and slow down the rest of the system. The special procurement agent has a copy of the expert system that she can use to make modifications in response to changing conditions, for example, if Federal Express changes its shipping rates.

Some organizations spend as much as 80% or more of their information systems budget on software maintenance. Maintenance tasks come from many sources and follow a U-shaped curve, as shown in Figure 8-19.

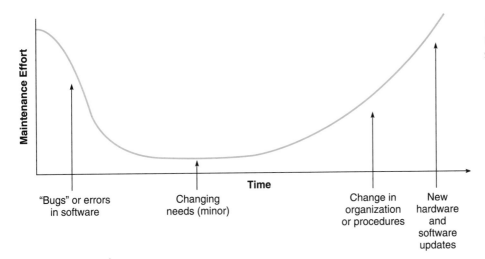

Figure 8-19
Factors that require system maintenance

The maintenance phase continues until the information system is no longer cost effective or until changes in the organization make the information system obsolete. It is not unusual for an information system to remain in operation for 20 years, but eventually, its useful or cost-effective life nears a close, and then it is time to begin the systems development life cycle again.

The Norwegian expedition members carefully checked their gear in Resolute, Canada, before their departure. Everything had arrived, including the ski poles that the A&L expert system cross-shipped from the Geneva outlet. "You're the best-prepared expedition I've ever seen!" exclaimed the pilot, who flew the Norwegians to their departure point on Ellesmere Island.

The trek was not uneventful. Just six days out, one expedition member injured his back when his sled slipped into a crevasse. They radioed for help and a rescue plane ferried him back to Resolute. Weeks later, an attack by a hungry polar bear proved almost fatal, but the two remaining expedition members trudged northward and, finally, reached the North Pole on May 4. The next day, a U.S. Navy research plane established contact with the expedition. "Who are you?" the pilot radioed. "Is there an emergency?" "No," was the reply. "We are just two Norwegians who skied here from Canada."

C H A P T E R   R E V I E W

1. Answer the questions listed in the Chapter Preview section at the beginning of the chapter.
2. List each of the boldface terms used in this chapter, then use your own words to write a short definition of each term.
3. What is the purpose of an information system?
4. Describe three possible uses of an office automation system.
5. List three examples of transaction processing systems.
6. Discuss the difference between an MIS and a DSS.
7. Discuss the difference between an expert system and a DSS.
8. Draw a diagram similar to the one in Figure 8-7, but add the next level of detailed tasks for each phase of the SDLC. For example, the detailed tasks for the analysis phase are define the problem, study the current system, and determine requirements.
9. Create a table that shows the differences among unit testing, integration testing, system testing, and acceptance testing. Your table should show the purpose of the testing, what is tested, and in which phase of the SDLC it is tested.
10. Create a table that lists the advantages and disadvantages of each type of system conversion strategy.

C H A P T E R   Q U I Z

1. The purpose of a(n) _____ is usually to improve the effectiveness of a business or organization by providing useful, accurate, and timely information.
2. Word processing software is likely to be a part of a(n) _____ system.
3. A system used to register students for classes would be an example of a(n) _____.
4. A(n) _____ is characterized by the production of routine reports that managers use for structured and routine tasks.
5. A(n) _____ report contains information that is outside of normal, or acceptable, ranges, such as a reorder report showing low-stock items in inventory.
6. A(n) _____ provides users with the ability to directly manipulate data and produce on-demand reports.
7. A(n) _____ is a computer system designed to analyze data and produce a recommended decision.
8. A(n) _____ is software that contains an inference engine and a method for entering rules, but it does not contain any rules.
9. A(n) _____ is a set of rules that is manipulated by an inference engine to reach decisions.
10. A(n) _____ is responsible for analyzing information requirements, designing a new information system, and supervising the new system implementation.
11. A(n) _____ is a document that you send to potential suppliers that describes your needs and requests information regarding the supplier and the equipment that the supplier would recommend to meet those needs.
12. _____ is modification of software to meet the requirements of a specific situation.

13. Unit testing is the testing of each component of software to make sure it operates reliably and correctly. _____ is testing that ensures that the units operate correctly together.

14. In a(n)_____ conversion, the old system remains in service until it can be determined if the new system is performing correctly.

15. As part of _____, a system is regularly backed up, performance is monitored, and minor changes are made to keep the system current.

P R O J E C T S

1. Complete the following table, indicating the type of computer system represented by each example. The first one is filled in for you.

	EXAMPLE	TYPE
A.	SYSTEM USED TO WRITE REPORTS AND SCHEDULE MEETINGS IN A LAW OFFICE	OFFICE AUTOMATION
B.	SYSTEM USED TO SELL AIRLINE TICKETS AT A TRAVEL AGENCY	
C.	SYSTEM USED TO ANALYZE AUTOMOBILE PROBLEMS AND DETERMINE THE MOST LIKELY CAUSE, AND SOLUTION, TO THE PROBLEM	
D.	SYSTEM THAT PRODUCES DAILY REPORTS SHOWING PERCENTAGE OF SEATS FILLED ON ALL FLIGHTS FROM A SPECIFIC AIRLINE	
E.	SYSTEM USED BY AN EXECUTIVE WHO WANTS TO FIND OUT HOW MANY TOASTERS THE WICHITA STORE SOLD IN OCTOBER	

2. Some of the following statements describe a problem, and others describe a solution. Complete the table, indicating if each statement is a problem or a solution:

	STATEMENT	PROBLEM OR SOLUTION
A	THE DESK CLERKS AREN'T QUICKLY INFORMED OF CANCELLATIONS AND SOMETIMES TELL PEOPLE THE HOTEL IS FULL, EVEN WHEN ROOMS ARE AVAILABLE DUE TO CANCELLATIONS.	
B.	NOTEBOOK COMPUTERS SHOULD BE PURCHASED FOR THE SALES PEOPLE SO THEY CAN PREPARE QUOTATIONS WITHOUT RETURNING TO THE MAIN OFFICE.	
C.	WHEN A CUSTOMER CALLS AND ORDERS AN ITEM THAT IS NOT IN STOCK, THE ORDER CLERKS CANNOT FIND OUT WHEN THE ITEM IS EXPECTED TO BE BACK IN STOCK.	
D.	THE CLERK IN ACCOUNTING NEEDS A FASTER LASER PRINTER.	
E.	IT TAKES TOO LONG TO PRINT THE CURRENT DAILY REPORTS.	
F.	WHEN THE PUBLIC RELATIONS DEPARTMENT SENDS ALL ADS TO A TYPESETTER, IT IS VERY EXPENSIVE AND TAKES AT LEAST TWO DAYS TO MAKE A CHANGE.	

3. For each of the problem descriptions, use the PIECES framework to indicate if each problem is caused by Performance, Information, Economics, Control, Efficiency, or Service.

		PROBLEM DESCRIPTION	PROBLEM TYPE
	A.	EMPLOYEES ARE USING COMPANY COMPUTERS TO PRINT BANNERS FOR SPECIAL OCCASIONS, USING UP TRACTOR-FEED PAPER AND RIBBONS.	
	B.	CUSTOMERS AT THE DEPARTMENT OF MOTOR VEHICLES MUST WAIT WHILE CLERKS WALK TO COMPUTER TERMINALS LOCATED IN THE BACK OF THE OFFICE, CHECK RECORDS, THEN RETURN.	
	C.	WHEN ORDER ENTRY CLERKS COMPLETE AN ORDER, THEY MUST WAIT 10 SECONDS WHILE THE COMPUTER STORES THE ORDER. DURING THIS TIME, THEY CANNOT ENTER OTHER ORDERS.	
	D.	WHEN CUSTOMERS CALL TO CHECK THE STATUS OF THEIR ORDERS, A CUSTOMER SERVICE REPRESENTATIVE CAN TELL THEM IF AN ORDER WAS SHIPPED, BUT NOT THE DATE ON WHICH IT WAS SHIPPED.	
	E.	WHEN PATIENTS ARE ADMITTED TO A HOSPITAL, THE ADMITTING CLERK WRITES INFORMATION ON A PAPER FORM. THIS INFORMATION IS THEN SENT TO THE DATA ENTRY DEPARTMENT WHERE IT IS ENTERED INTO THE HOSPITAL COMPUTER. THE DATA ENTRY CLERKS ARE BACKLOGGED, SO PATIENT DATA IS NOT AVAILABLE IN THE COMPUTER SYSTEM FOR AT LEAST 24 HOURS.	

4. Rodney Watson is a system analyst for U-Fix-It hardware stores. U-Fix-It installed bar-code readers at each register to speed checkouts and improve inventory control. Unfortunately, the clerks are complaining that the bar-code labels are falling off many of the items. When this happens, the clerk must call for someone to go back and check the price of the item, which causes a long delay in the checkout line. Rodney has identified four possible solutions:

a. Switch to a bar-code label that has better adhesive on the back so the labels are less likely to fall off.

b. Modify the system so that clerks can check the current price of an item on a computer price list from their terminals.

c. Print weekly price lists and place them at each register so the clerks can check the price on any item.

d. Hire additional workers to check the prices so customers don't have to wait so long for a price check.

Explain which of these solutions you would select and why you would select that solution. If you need additional information before making a final decision, describe the information that you need.

5. Jennifer Aho works in the circulation department of *Cycle*, a magazine dedicated to bicycle and triathlon enthusiasts. The MIS department prints a monthly report showing the current number of *Cycle* subscribers in each zip code. Jennifer calculates the total number of subscribers for the current month and enters this total on a worksheet. She then creates a line chart showing the increase or decrease in total subscribers for the current year. It takes Jennifer four hours each month to calculate the number of total subscribers, enter the total on her worksheet, and print the latest copy of the chart.

a. What is the problem?

b. Think of two possible solutions to this problem. Describe each solution.

c. Which solution do you think is better? Why?

L   A   B

System Testing Lab

In the System Testing Lab, you are responsible for testing the expert system designed for A&L Outfitters. Study the data flow diagram in Figure 8-20 to understand how the newly modified system should work.

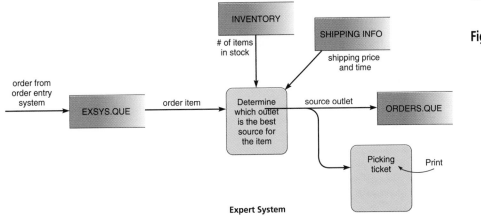

Figure 8-20

To test the system, you can adjust the sample inventory at each A&L outlet and place sample orders. The system processes your orders based on the sample inventory and produces a "picking ticket," like the one in Figure 8-21.

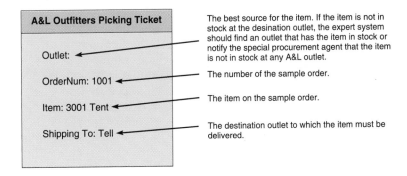

Figure 8-21

By examining the contents of EXSYS.QUE and ORDERS.QUE, and by studying the information on the picking tickets, you can determine if the system is operating correctly.

The A&L project team has identified seven tests that you should perform on the system. If you discover a problem, explain what is wrong and how the system should work.

Test One

When you start the System Testing Lab, the quantity of the inventory items has been set to zero for you, as if there are no items in inventory at any A&L outlet. When an item on an order is not in stock at any location, the system should address the picking ticket to the special procurement agent.

To complete Test One:

1. Click the **Place Order on Queue** button. Make sure Telluride is selected as the outlet to which the item should be shipped. Make sure the item to order is 3001 Tent 2 Psn. Note the order number at the top of the dialog box.

2. Click the **Order** button to place the order on the queue. The order data should appear in the file EXSYS.QUE. Make sure the item number is 3001, the destination is Tell, and the order number is 1001. This is the data that the expert system will process.

3. Click the **Process Order** button to process the order. The expert system processes the order by checking to see which outlets have the item in inventory. The name of the outlet from which the item should be shipped is added to the order data, placed in the file ORDERS.QUE, and shown on the picking ticket.

4. Look at the contents of ORDERS.QUE. The "From" column shows "Unav," which means unavailable. This indicates that the item on the order is not at any of the A&L outlets.

5. Look at the picking ticket. Because the item on the order is not available at any A&L outlet, this order must go to special procurement.

6. Write a summary of the results of Test One. Does the system correctly process an order for item 3001 if it is not in stock at any outlet? If not, explain what the system does wrong and how it should work.

Test Two

The system must correctly handle orders for any item from the test inventory.

To complete Test Two:

1. Repeat Test One, but place the order for item 3002. Complete the order by clicking the **Process Order** button. Make sure the correct information appears on ORDERS.QUE and the picking ticket.

2. Repeat this process for each of the items in the test inventory to make sure the system correctly processes orders for every item in the test inventory.

3. Does the system correctly process orders for each item in the test inventory? If not, explain what the system does wrong and how it should work.

Test Three

When an item is in stock at the outlet to which it will be shipped, the system should address the picking ticket to that outlet.

To complete Test Three:

1. Click the **View/Edit Inventory** button to display the View/Edit Inventory dialog box.

2. Click the **Telluride** button to display the Telluride inventory.

3. Click the box in front of item 3001 and type 1 to indicate that one unit of item 3001 is in stock at Telluride.

4. Click the **Continue** button to return to the main screen.

5. Place an order on the queue for item 3001 to be shipped to Telluride.

6. Click the **Process Order** button, then make sure that the system places the correct order on ORDERS.QUE and prints the correct picking ticket. Because the item is in stock at Telluride, the picking ticket should show "Outlet: Tell."

7. Repeat this process for a variety of orders. Test different items and different outlets. Because of the number of items and outlets, it may not be possible to test every item from every outlet. Repeat the testing until you discover a problem or until you are reasonably sure that the system works correctly.

8. Does the system appear to correctly process orders for an item that is in stock at the destination outlet? If not, explain what the system does wrong and how it should work.

Test Four

When an item is not in stock at the destination outlet, but is in stock at another outlet, the system should address the picking ticket to the outlet that has the item in stock.

To complete Test Four:

1. Use the **View/Edit Inventory** dialog box to make sure item 3002 is in stock at only the Geneva outlet.

2. Place an order on the queue for item 3002 to be shipped to Katmandu.

3. Process the order. The item is not in stock at the destination outlet, Katmandu, so the expert system should search the inventory of other outlets and find the item in Geneva. The picking ticket should show "Outlet: Genv" and "Ship to: Katm."

4. Repeat this test until you discover a problem or until you are reasonably sure that the system works correctly.

5. Does the system correctly process orders for an item that is not in stock at the destination outlet, but is in stock at one of the other A&L outlets? If not, explain what the system does wrong and how it should work.

Test Five

When an item is not in stock at the destination outlet, but is in stock at two or more other outlets, the system should address the picking ticket to the outlet with the lowest shipping cost.

To complete Test Five:

1. Use the **View/Edit Inventory** dialog box to make sure item 3002 is in stock only in Geneva and Telluride.

2. Place an order for item 3002 to be shipped to Katmandu.

3. Process the order. This item is not in stock at the destination outlet, Katmandu, but it is available in Geneva and Telluride. The expert system should select the outlet with the lowest shipping cost.

4. Click the **View Shipping Info** button to check the shipping information. Click **Katmandu**, the destination to which the item will be shipped, to view the cost per pound and the time in days it takes to ship an item to that outlet from each of the other outlets. Of the two outlets where this item is available (Geneva and Telluride), Geneva's shipping cost is lowest. The picking ticket should show "Outlet: Genv."

5. Repeat this test using different items and destinations until you discover a problem or until you are reasonably sure that the system works correctly.

6. Does the system correctly process an order for an item that is not in stock at the destination outlet, but is in stock at two or more other outlets? If not, explain what the system does wrong and how it should work.

Test Six

When an item is in stock at two outlets with the same shipping cost, the system should address the picking ticket to the outlet with the fastest shipping time.

To complete Test Six:

1. Click the **View Shipping Info** button, then click the outlet **Guatemala City**. Notice that items shipped to Guatemala City from Lima and Geneva have the same shipping cost. Also notice that items shipped from Lima will arrive faster—shipping takes two days from Lima, but three days from Geneva. Therefore, if an item is needed in Guatemala City, but is in stock in Geneva and Lima, the expert system should select Lima. Let's test this.

2. Make sure item 3004 is in stock only in Lima and Geneva, then order item 3004 from Guatemala City.

3. Process the order. Because the shipping cost is the same from Lima and Geneva, the expert system should select the outlet with the fastest shipping time. The picking ticket should show "Outlet: Lima."

4. Shipping rates are also the same from Telluride and Guatemala City to Geneva. Set up a test in which item 3005 needs to be shipped to Geneva, but is in stock only at Telluride and Guatemala City.

5. Does the system correctly process an order for an item that is in stock at two outlets with the same shipping cost? If not, explain what the system does wrong and how it should work.

Test Seven

If an item is not in stock in the destination outlet, but is in stock at two other outlets with the same shipping cost and the same shipping time, the system should address the picking ticket to the outlet that has the highest number of the item in stock.

To complete Test Seven:

1. There is one situation in the test system in which an item can be in stock in two outlets and have the same shipping cost and the same shipping time. This situation arises if an item is in stock in Telluride and Guatemala City and is to be shipped to Katmandu. Make sure two of item 3005 are in stock in Telluride and five of item 3005 are in stock in Guatemala City. Also make sure item 3005 is not in stock in any other outlets.

2. Place an order on the queue for item 3005 to be shipped to Katmandu.

3. Process the order. Because there are more of item 3005 in stock in Guatemala City, the picking ticket should show "Outlet: Guatemala City."

4. Does the system correctly process an order for an item that is in stock in two outlets and has the same shipping cost and shipping time? If not, explain what the system does wrong and how it should work.

R E S O U R C E S

■ Brooks, F. *The Mythical Man-Month: Essays on Software Engineering*. Reading, MA: Addison-Wesley, 1982.

This classic book contains a series of essays that examine the problems encountered during the construction of complex information systems. One of the central problems identified by Brooks is the need to develop a conceptual vision of the product.

■ Davis, G., and M. Olson. *Management Information Systems: Conceptual Foundations, Structure, and Development*, 2nd ed. New York: McGraw-Hill, 1985.

This book is the most widely cited concepts text on MIS.

■ Martin, J., and C. McClure. *Diagramming Techniques for Analysts and Programmers*. Englewood Cliffs, NJ: Prentice-Hall, 1985.

This book provides an excellent introduction to a variety of charts and diagrams that can be used to document information systems.

■ Turban, E. *Decision Support and Expert Systems*. New York: Macmillan, 1988.

This is an excellent text on computer applications for management support. The explanations are clear, and there are many examples provided to illustrate concepts.

■ Wetherbe, J. *Systems Analysis and Design*, 3rd ed. St. Paul, MN: West Publishing, 1988.

James Wetherbe developed the PIECES framework to help systems analysts identify problems in information systems. A section of this text describes the PIECES framework in detail.

■ Yourdon, E. *Managing the Systems Life Cycle*, 2nd ed. Englewood Cliffs, NJ: Yourdon Press, 1988.

Yourdon, a well-respected authority on information systems, describes a structured approach to creating successful computer information systems.

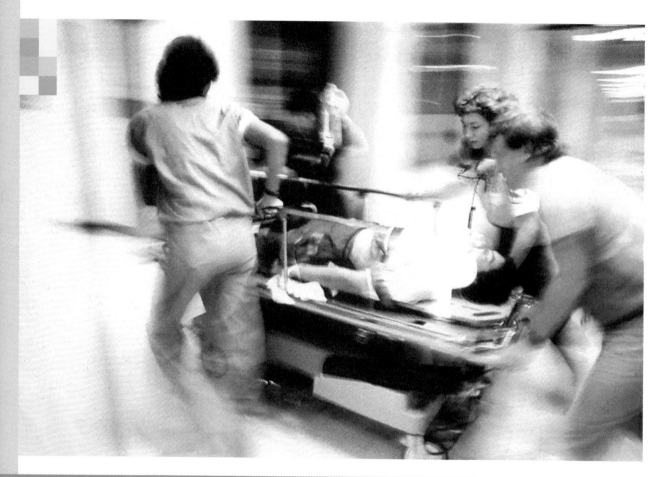

When you have completed this chapter you should be able to answer the following questions:

- What is the difference between a database and a file?
- How do file management systems and database management systems promote data independence?
- What is the difference between the structure of a record and an occurrence of a record?
- What are the four major database models?
- What are the four approaches to managing data?
- How can you avoid data redundancy?
- What are the six main database management activities?
- What is the difference between sorting and indexing?
- What are the options for presenting the information stored in a data file?
- What are relational operators and logical operators?
- How can you create effective reports?

MANAGING THE DATA IN FILES AND DATABASES

Midtown General Hospital was operating at capacity. The staff was bustling to provide patient services. The hospital-wide computer system was churning out admission reports, order requests, and schedules. The loudspeakers were constantly paging doctors, nurses, and other staff members. Amidst all this activity, the director of human resources was gazing at his computer display and smiling. Curiously, the screen displayed a brilliantly colored landscape of flowers in a garden. Why was the human resources director smiling, and what does the garden have to do with human resources?

Computers are used extensively to collect and maintain large collections of data. In this chapter, you will learn how data can be gathered and stored effectively; then you will find out how this data can be transformed into information that is useful for decision making. Along the way, you will discover how the garden relates to data collections and why it is useful information for the human resources director at Midtown General Hospital.

File and Database Concepts

In Chapter 3, you learned the difference between program files and data files. Now you will focus on a specific type of data file—the type that contains information that is organized in a uniform format. An example of this type of file is a telephone directory. All the information is in a uniform format: last name, first name, address, phone number. Other examples of files that are organized in a uniform format are an inventory list, a library card catalog, and a schedule of university courses.

A file that is organized in a uniform format is formally referred to as a **structured data file** or a **database file**; but more commonly, it is referred to as a "data file" or just a "file." Unfortunately, the terms "data file" and "file" do not distinguish between files that are organized in a uniform format and those that are in a more free-form format, such as word processor, spreadsheet, graphics, and sound files. Therefore, when you see the term "data file" or "file" in a computer magazine or in documentation, you might have to use clues from the context of the article to decide whether "file" means a file organized in a uniform format or a free-form file. In this chapter, the term "data file" refers to a file that is organized in a uniform format, and the concepts you learn in this chapter apply specifically to this type of data file.

The tasks associated with maintaining and accessing the data stored in a data file are often referred to as **data management**. In this chapter, you will learn about data management concepts using data about the employees who work at Midtown General Hospital. Typically, this data would be used by the Midtown human resources department to maintain information about employees, track absenteeism, examine gender equity, and make staffing projections. Much of the same data would be used by the payroll department to generate employee paychecks. The Midtown data is stored in a series of **data files**. Each data file has a file structure that describes the way the data is stored in the file. Figure 9-1 shows some of the data in a file named "Personnel" and provides a conceptual overview of file structure terminology.

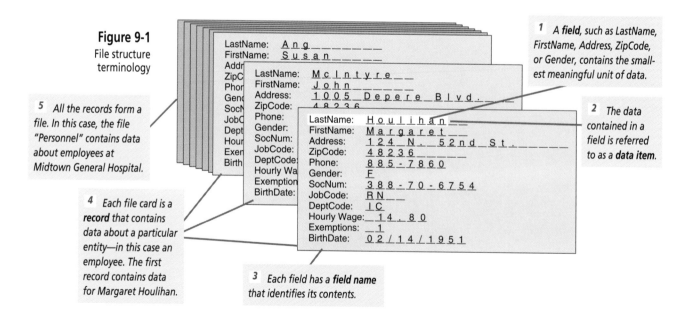

Figure 9-1
File structure terminology

1 A **field**, such as LastName, FirstName, Address, ZipCode, or Gender, contains the smallest meaningful unit of data.

2 The data contained in a field is referred to as a **data item**.

3 Each field has a **field name** that identifies its contents.

4 Each file card is a **record** that contains data about a particular entity—in this case an employee. The first record contains data for Margaret Houlihan.

5 All the records form a file. In this case, the file "Personnel" contains data about employees at Midtown General Hospital.

LastName: A n g
FirstName: S u s a n

LastName: M c I n t y r e
FirstName: J o h n
Address: 1 0 0 5   D e p e r e   B l v d .

LastName: H o u l i h a n
FirstName: M a r g a r e t
Address: 1 2 4   N .   5 2 n d   S t .
ZipCode: 4 8 2 3 6
Phone: 8 8 5 - 7 8 6 0
Gender: F
SocNum: 3 8 8 - 7 0 - 6 7 5 4
JobCode: R N
DeptCode: I C
Hourly Wage: 1 4 . 8 0
Exemptions: 1
BirthDate: 0 2 / 1 4 / 1 9 5 1

Fields

As you can see in Figure 9-1, a **field** contains the smallest unit of meaningful data. Each field has a **field name** that describes the contents of the field. For example, the field name BirthDate might describe a field containing employee birth dates. A field is usually a fixed length, which is allocated in characters or bytes. In Figure 9-1 the BirthDate field is allocated a length of 10 characters. The data that you enter in a field cannot exceed the allocated, or fixed, field length. If the data in a field is shorter than the allocated length, blank spaces are automatically added to fill the field.

Data Types

Each field is assigned a **data type**, which from a technical perspective specifies the way the data is represented on the disk and in RAM. From a user perspective, the data type determines the way you can manipulate the data.

The two most common data types are numeric and character. A **numeric data type** is assigned to fields containing numbers that you might want to manipulate mathematically by adding, averaging, multiplying, and so forth. As an example, the HourlyWage field in Figure 9-1 is a numeric field, so the data in this field can be multiplied by the number of hours worked to calculate gross pay. There are two main numeric data types: real and integer. The data in the HourlyWage field is a **real number** because it contains a decimal point. The data in the Exemptions field is an **integer**, or whole number.

The **character data type**, also referred to as the **string data type**, is assigned to fields containing data that does not need to be mathematically manipulated. Some examples of character data include names, descriptions, cities, and state abbreviations.

Some of the data we call "numbers" does not require a numeric data type. A Social Security "number" is an example of data that looks numeric, but would not be mathematically manipulated. Social Security numbers, therefore, are usually stored as character data. Other examples of "numbers" that are generally stored as character data include phone numbers and zip codes.

Records

An **entity** is a person, place, thing, or event about which you want to store data. A **record** contains fields of data about one entity. For example, one of the records in Figure 9-1 contains fields of data about the entity Houlihan, Margaret. In a medical office, a patient record contains the data for one patient, such as medical history, insurance carrier, and current address. In a retail business, an inventory record contains the data for one inventory item, such as part number, description, cost, price, and quantity in stock.

When the structure of a data file specifies fixed-length fields, the records are also fixed length, that is, each record takes up the same amount of storage space. You might wonder how this is possible if the data in each field is different for each record. What if an employee has a very long last name—shouldn't that record be longer than the record for an employee with a short last name? The answer is no. Recall that blanks are added to fields that contain data with less than the maximum allocated bytes, so including the blanks, each record contains the same number of bytes.

Calculating record length is important, because it helps determine storage needs. For example, if you want to store a data file on a high-density 3.5" floppy disk, there are approximately 1,440,000 bytes of storage space available. Could you fit 10,000 of the Midtown employee records on this disk? To answer this question, you need to calculate the size of one employee record by summing the field sizes. Figure 9-2 shows how to calculate the size of one employee record and then from that calculation how to determine the number of records that will fit on a disk.

Figure 9-2

Calculating the size of one employee record

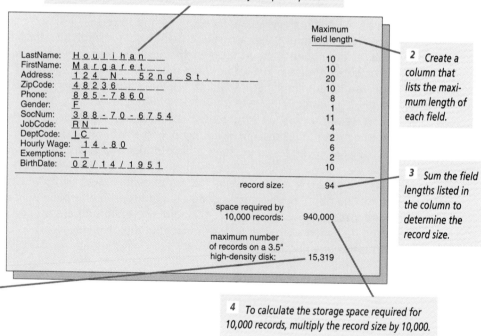

1   Each field has a fixed or maximum length. For example, the LastName field can hold up to 10 characters, so it has a maximum length of 10. In this case, the last name is 8 characters. If the last name was "Stephanopolous," the field would hold only "Stephanopo."

2   Create a column that lists the maximum length of each field.

3   Sum the field lengths listed in the column to determine the record size.

4   To calculate the storage space required for 10,000 records, multiply the record size by 10,000.

5   To calculate how many records would fit on a 3.5" high-density disk, divide the total disk capacity by the size of one record. A 3.5" high-density disk holds 1,440,000 bytes, and each record is 94 bytes. The calculation is: 1,440,000÷94 =15,319.15. A maximum of 15,319 records will fit on a 3.5" high-density disk.

A record contains the data collected for a particular person, place, thing, or event. Midtown has a record for an employee named Margaret Houlihan and another record for John McIntyre. A record for a specific entity is sometimes referred to as a **record occurrence** to distinguish it from the general record format, which is called a **record type**. This is an important distinction to grasp, so examine Figure 9-3 to be certain you understand the difference.

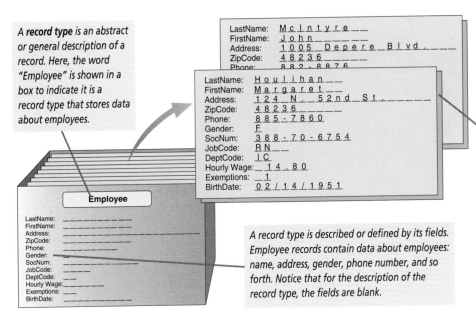

Figure 9-3
Record types and record occurrences

A **record type** is an abstract or general description of a record. Here, the word "Employee" is shown in a box to indicate it is a record type that stores data about employees.

A completed record is a **record occurrence**. Here is a record occurrence for Houlihan, and another record occurrence for McIntyre.

A record type is described or defined by its fields. Employee records contain data about employees: name, address, gender, phone number, and so forth. Notice that for the description of the record type, the fields are blank.

Flat Files

The term **flat file** is sometimes used to refer to a data file in which all the records have the same **record format**, that is, the same field names, field lengths, and data types. You could also say that a flat file is a single **record type**. People use the term flat file primarily when they want to distinguish between a single file and a database. The file "Personnel" shown in Figure 9-1 is a flat file, because all the records have the same format.

Flat files are not particularly efficient for complex data management tasks, and they are increasingly being replaced by databases. To find out why, you need to understand what a database is and how it stores data.

Databases

"Database" is one of those terms that has no single definition. It is sometimes loosely used to describe any data file made up of records and fields. However, this usage does not distinguish between a flat file and a database, so it is not completely accurate from a technical perspective. It is more accurate to define a **database** as a variety of different record types that are treated as a single unit. This definition implies that several flat files or record types can be consolidated or related in such a way that they can be used essentially as one unit—a database. Let's see how this works. In addition to the Employee record type, Midtown stores the following data:

- Job classifications are stored using a record type called Job.
- Department descriptions are stored with a record type called Department.
- Payroll history is stored using a record type called Timecard.

Look at Figure 9-4 on the following page to get a general idea of the data that Midtown stores.

Figure 9-4
Midtown record types

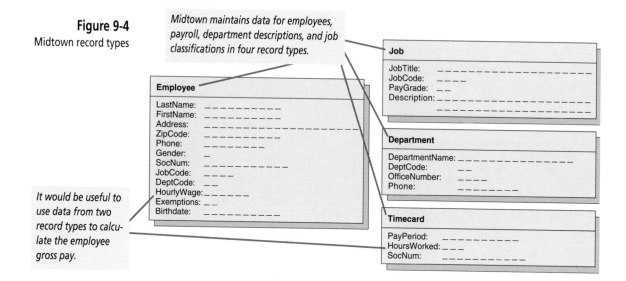

Midtown maintains data for employees, payroll, department descriptions, and job classifications in four record types.

Job
JobTitle:
JobCode:
PayGrade:
Description:

Employee
LastName:
FirstName:
Address:
ZipCode:
Phone:
Gender:
SocNum:
JobCode:
DeptCode:
HourlyWage:
Exemptions:
Birthdate:

Department
DepartmentName:
DeptCode:
OfficeNumber:
Phone:

It would be useful to use data from two record types to calculate the employee gross pay.

Timecard
PayPeriod:
HoursWorked:
SocNum:

To use these four record types as essentially one unit, you need to consolidate them into a database. After you create this database, you can combine the data from more than one record type. For example, you could use the HoursWorked data from the Timecard and the HourlyWage data from the Employee record type to calculate an employee's gross pay.

To use data from more than one record type, a database maintains relationships between record types. A **relationship** is an association between the entities in a file. For example, in the Midtown files there is a relationship between the employee entity and a timecard. You could describe this relationship by saying "an employee has a timecard." A database lets you define relationships between record types, which provides you with more flexibility for manipulating data than by using a single flat file or a group of unrelated flat files. For example, if the Employee record type is a flat file and the Timecard file is another flat file, the procedure to calculate Margaret Houlihan's pay is somewhat complex, as shown in Figure 9-5.

Figure 9-5
Using two flat files to calculate gross pay

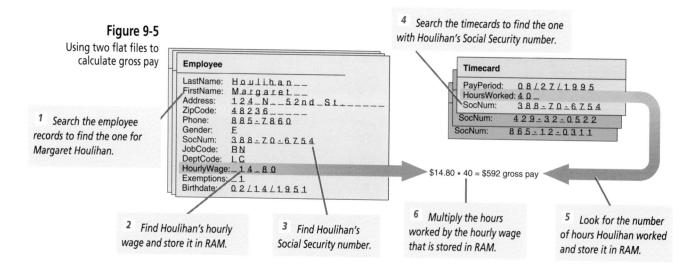

4   Search the timecards to find the one with Houlihan's Social Security number.

Employee
LastName: Houlihan
FirstName: Margaret
Address: 124 N 52nd St
ZipCode: 48236
Phone: 885-7860
Gender: F
SocNum: 388-70-6754
JobCode: RN
DeptCode: LC
HourlyWage: 14.80
Exemptions: 1
Birthdate: 02/14/1951

Timecard
PayPeriod: 08/27/1995
HoursWorked: 40
SocNum: 388-70-6754
SocNum: 429-32-0522
SocNum: 865-12-0311

1   Search the employee records to find the one for Margaret Houlihan.

$14.80 * 40 = $592 gross pay

2   Find Houlihan's hourly wage and store it in RAM.

3   Find Houlihan's Social Security number.

6   Multiply the hours worked by the hourly wage that is stored in RAM.

5   Look for the number of hours Houlihan worked and store it in RAM.

This calculation is easier if you have defined a relationship between the Employee record type and the Timecard record type, as shown in Figure 9-6.

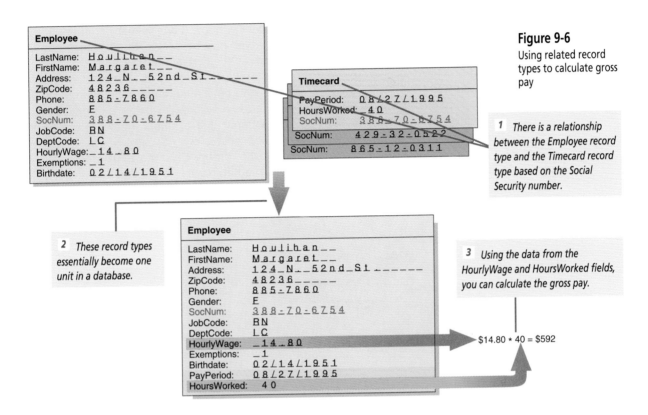

Figure 9-6
Using related record types to calculate gross pay

1 There is a relationship between the Employee record type and the Timecard record type based on the Social Security number.

2 These record types essentially become one unit in a database.

3 Using the data from the HourlyWage and HoursWorked fields, you can calculate the gross pay.

$14.80 * 40 = $592

A **data structure diagram**, also called an **entity relationship diagram**, shows the relationships between record types. It is a general outline or plan for the way the actual records are related. A data structure diagram helps you visualize the data relationships and design better databases. On a data structure diagram, each record type is shown as a box. There are three possible relationships: one-to-one, one-to-many, and many-to-many. Figure 9-7 shows how these relationships are drawn on a data structure diagram.

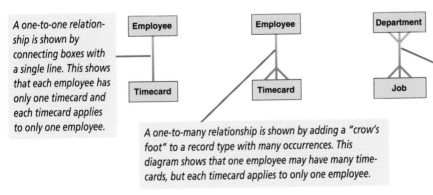

Figure 9-7
Diagramming relationships

A one-to-one relationship is shown by connecting boxes with a single line. This shows that each employee has only one timecard and each timecard applies to only one employee.

A one-to-many relationship is shown by adding a "crow's foot" to a record type with many occurrences. This diagram shows that one employee may have many timecards, but each timecard applies to only one employee.

A many-to-many relationship is shown by adding a "crow's foot" to both ends of the line that connects boxes. This diagram shows that each department might require personnel with different jobs; for example, the emergency room might require nurses, doctors, and clerks. It also shows that a particular job might be required by many different departments; for example, a clerk might be required in the emergency room, in the admissions department, and in the billing department.

A one-to-one relationship means that one record in a particular record type is related to only one record of another record type. This would be true at Midtown if each employee had only one timecard. This is not the case, however, because employees have a timecard for each pay period, so the relationship between the Employee record type and the Timecard record type is one-to-many. A one-to-many relationship means that one record in a particular record type may be related to more than one record of another record type. Finally, a many-to-many relationship means that one record in a particular record type can be related to many records in another record type and vice versa. For example, a department might require personnel with many job descriptions such as nurses, technicians, and physicians. Further, a particular job might be required in more than one department. For example, nurses might be required in the intensive care department and in obstetrics.

How can we show the relationships in the Midtown database? The database structure for Midtown can be represented by a data structure diagram like the one in Figure 9-8. Figure 9-9 shows a single occurrence of the database structure so you can see a specific example of the relationships.

Figure 9-8

Data structure diagram for Midtown General Hospital

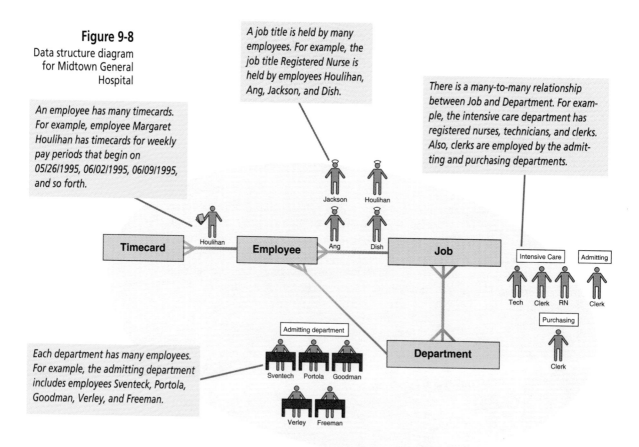

A job title is held by many employees. For example, the job title Registered Nurse is held by employees Houlihan, Ang, Jackson, and Dish.

An employee has many timecards. For example, employee Margaret Houlihan has timecards for weekly pay periods that begin on 05/26/1995, 06/02/1995, 06/09/1995, and so forth.

There is a many-to-many relationship between Job and Department. For example, the intensive care department has registered nurses, technicians, and clerks. Also, clerks are employed by the admitting and purchasing departments.

Each department has many employees. For example, the admitting department includes employees Sventeck, Portola, Goodman, Verley, and Freeman.

There are four major **database models**: the hierarchical model, the network model, the relational model, and the object-oriented model. Each model has a different way of representing relationships between record types. Also, each database model is described using slightly different terminology, but the concepts of record types, fields, and relationships are useful for understanding all of the models. Study Figure 9-10 on page NP 304, Figure 9-11 on page NP 305, Figure 9-12 on page NP 306, and Figure 9-13 on page NP 307 to learn the basic characteristics of each database model.

The decision of which database model to use is usually made by a **database administrator**, who is responsible for designing and supervising the database. In the past, mainframe databases often followed the hierarchical or network model. During the 1980s, the databases maintained on microcomputers by companies and individuals typically followed the relational model, primarily because most database management software for microcomputers supported the relational database model. The new trend is toward the object-oriented model, although the commercial tools for developing and maintaining object-oriented databases have emerged only recently.

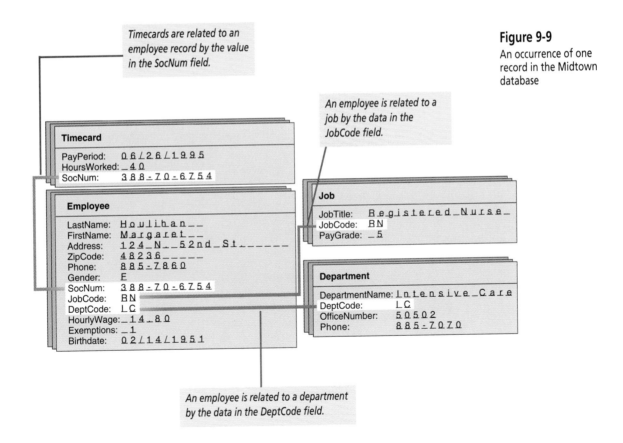

Figure 9-9

An occurrence of one record in the Midtown database

Figure 9-10

The hierarchical model

In a **hierarchical database**, a "parent" record type can be linked to one or more "child" record types, but a child record type can have only one parent. The relationships between records are established by creating physical links between the stored records. A **physical link** means that the records are stored on the disk medium in such a way that the computer can trace the links from one record to another.

A hierarchical database is effective for data that has fairly simple relationships, and it is useful when data access is routine and predictable. Hierarchical databases are less effective for data with complex relationships and in situations that require flexible or "on the fly" data access, because the relationships are physical links defined at the time the database is created. Also, because links between records are established when the database is created, if you want to add a record type or define a new relationship, it is necessary to redefine the database and then store it in its new form.

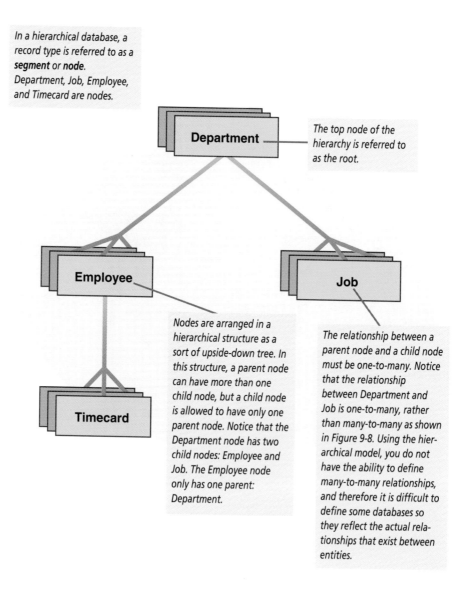

In a hierarchical database, a record type is referred to as a *segment* or *node*. Department, Job, Employee, and Timecard are nodes.

The top node of the hierarchy is referred to as the root.

Nodes are arranged in a hierarchical structure as a sort of upside-down tree. In this structure, a parent node can have more than one child node, but a child node is allowed to have only one parent node. Notice that the Department node has two child nodes: Employee and Job. The Employee node only has one parent: Department.

The relationship between a parent node and a child node must be one-to-many. Notice that the relationship between Department and Job is one-to-many, rather than many-to-many as shown in Figure 9-8. Using the hierarchical model, you do not have the ability to define many-to-many relationships, and therefore it is difficult to define some databases so they reflect the actual relationships that exist between entities.

The **network database** model resembles the hierarchical model in many respects. For example, as with the hierarchical model, the network model is a collection of physically linked record types in one-to-many relationships. The physical link is created when the data is stored on tape or disk. There are differences between the two models, however. In a network database, related record types are referred to as a **set**. A set contains an **owner**, which is similar to a parent record in a hierarchical database. A set also includes one or more **members**, roughly equivalent to child records in a hierarchical database. A network database provides more flexibility than a hierarchical database because it allows child records to have more than one parent record type.

Figure 9-11
The network model

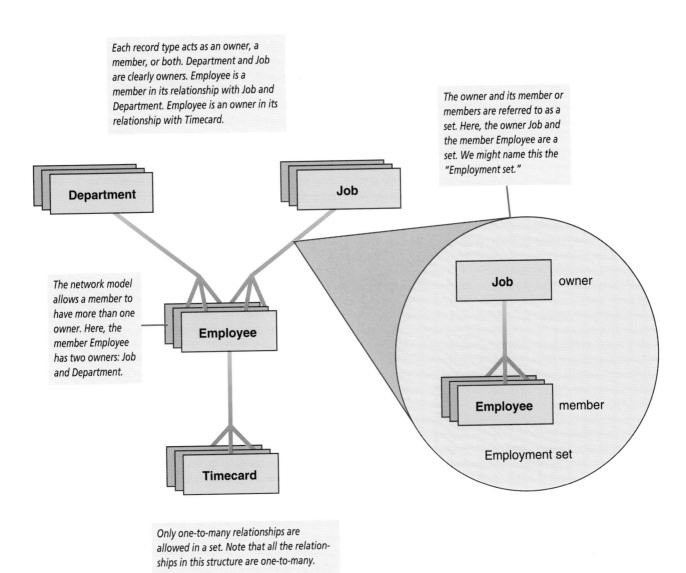

Each record type acts as an owner, a member, or both. Department and Job are clearly owners. Employee is a member in its relationship with Job and Department. Employee is an owner in its relationship with Timecard.

The owner and its member or members are referred to as a set. Here, the owner Job and the member Employee are a set. We might name this the "Employment set."

The network model allows a member to have more than one owner. Here, the member Employee has two owners: Job and Department.

Only one-to-many relationships are allowed in a set. Note that all the relationships in this structure are one-to-many.

Department

Job

Employee

Timecard

Job   owner

Employee   member

Employment set

Figure 9-12
The relational model

The **relational database** model is the most prevalent one in use on microcomputers. A **relational database** is perceived by its users to be a collection of **tables** roughly equivalent to a collection of record types.

The strategy for defining relationships in the relational model is fundamentally different from the relationships in the hierarchical or network models. In the relational model, records are related by the data stored jointly in fields of the records in two files. For example, Margaret Houlihan's employee record is related to her timecards because the data in the SocNum fields is the same. The significance of this plan is that the tables seem to be essentially independent, but they can be related in many flexible ways. Further, because the table structure is a perceptual aid, you do not need to deal with a physical storage plan for the data on the disk.

*The data for each record type is stored in a table, also called a **relation**. A relational database for Midtown General Hospital would have four tables: Employee, Timecard, Job, and Department.*

*The columns in the table are called **attributes** and are equivalent to fields.*

Data from one relation can be combined with the data from another by matching the data in two attributes, or fields. For example, the data in the Employee and the Timecard tables can be joined by matching the data in the SocNum field.

Table: Employee

*A row of the table is called a **tuple** and is equivalent to a record.*

LastName	FirstName	Address	SocNum
Ang	Susan	99 Lake Shore Dr.	453-78-2311
Houlihan	Margaret	124 N. 52nd St.	388-70-6754
McIntyre	John	1005 Depere Blvd.	475-66-6245

Table: Timecard

PayPeriod	HoursWorked	SocNum
05/26/1995	45	453-78-2311
05/26/1995	40	388-70-6754
05/26/1995	49	475-66-6245
06/02/1995	40	453-78-2311
06/02/1995	40	388-70-6754
06/02/1995	43	475-66-6245

Table: Job

JobTitle	JobCode	PayGrade	Description
Registered Nurse	RN	5	A registered...
Staff Physician	SMD	9	A staff...

Table: Department

DepartmentName	DeptCode	OfficeNumber	Phone
Intensive Care	IC	S0502	885-7070
Emergency Room	ER	B100	885-1222
Obstetrics	OB	SO301	885-1344
Accounting	AC	AD230	885-4536
Human Resources	HR	AD260	885-1908

Databases have become more complex in response to expanded organizational needs and the inclusion of graphics, video, and sound. Object-oriented databases provide a structure capable of defining complex data relationships. As with a relational database, an **object-oriented database** presents conceptual data relationships so the designer and users do not need to be concerned with how to physically link records.

An object-oriented database provides the flexibility to create variations of a single record type. For example, in the hierarchical, network, and relational models, all the employee records have the same record structure that includes a field for hourly wage. What if the staff physicians were not paid by the hour, but were paid according to salary? An object-oriented database allows you to define a variation of the Employee record that provides a field called AnnualSalary instead of HourlyWage. With the hierarchical, network, and relational models, you would need to design a new record type such as SalaryEmployee. With the object-oriented database, the record type for salaried employees is only a variation of Employee and does not require a separate series of commands.

The contents of an object-oriented database are significantly different from the contents of a hierarchical, network, or relational database. In addition to passive data items, such as employee names and Social Security numbers, an object-oriented database also stores operations called **methods** that perform actions on the data.

Figure 9-13
The object-oriented model

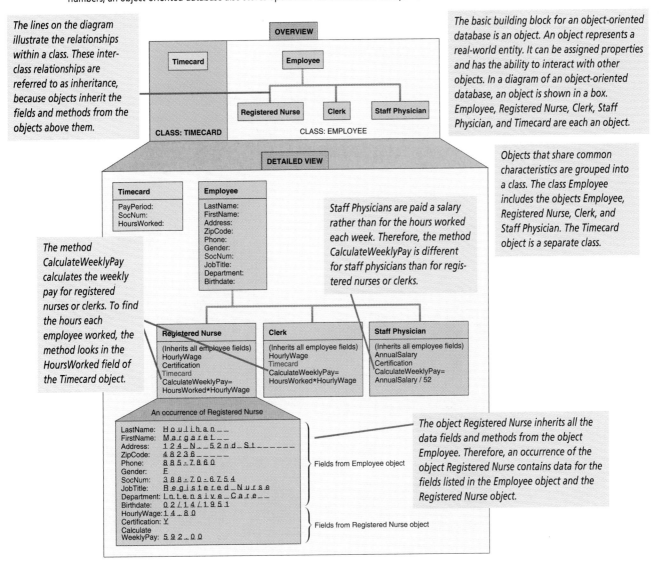

The lines on the diagram illustrate the relationships within a class. These inter-class relationships are referred to as inheritance, because objects inherit the fields and methods from the objects above them.

The basic building block for an object-oriented database is an object. An object represents a real-world entity. It can be assigned properties and has the ability to interact with other objects. In a diagram of an object-oriented database, an object is shown in a box. Employee, Registered Nurse, Clerk, Staff Physician, and Timecard are each an object.

Objects that share common characteristics are grouped into a class. The class Employee includes the objects Employee, Registered Nurse, Clerk, and Staff Physician. The Timecard object is a separate class.

Staff Physicians are paid a salary rather than for the hours worked each week. Therefore, the method CalculateWeeklyPay is different for staff physicians than for registered nurses or clerks.

The method CalculateWeeklyPay calculates the weekly pay for registered nurses or clerks. To find the hours each employee worked, the method looks in the HoursWorked field of the Timecard object.

The object Registered Nurse inherits all the data fields and methods from the object Employee. Therefore, an occurrence of the object Registered Nurse contains data for the fields listed in the Employee object and the Registered Nurse object.

Approaches to File and Database Management ■

Many data management tasks are common to both flat files and databases:

- You must design the structure for the file or database.
- Once you define the structure, you must enter the data.
- You must perform updates by adding, changing, or deleting data.
- To organize the data so it is easier to use and understand, you must be able to sort the data.
- To find a specific record or group of records, you must be able to search through the data.
- You must obtain on-screen or printed output.

There are four approaches to manipulating or managing data: the custom program approach, the file management approach, the database management approach, and the object-oriented approach.

Custom Program Approach

The first approach to managing data, called the custom program approach, involves writing a program to directly manipulate the data in a file. The program usually provides a way to enter records, sort records, search for one or more records, and print records. With the custom program approach, each file requires its own set of programs. An organization with many different data files requires many custom programs to manipulate the data in those files, as shown in Figure 9-14.

Figure 9-14
The custom program approach

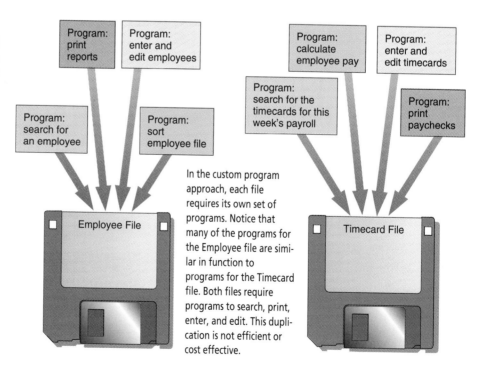

Program:
print
reports

Program:
enter and
edit employees

Program:
calculate
employee pay

Program:
enter and
edit timecards

Program:
search for the
timecards for this
week's payroll

Program:
print
paychecks

Program:
search for
an employee

Program:
sort
employee file

Employee File

Timecard File

In the custom program approach, each file requires its own set of programs. Notice that many of the programs for the Employee file are similar in function to programs for the Timecard file. Both files require programs to search, print, enter, and edit. This duplication is not efficient or cost effective.

A significant amount of time must be devoted to writing each of the programs to manage a file, and this approach usually requires the services of professional programmers. As a result, the custom program approach generally is not cost effective.

The programs that manipulate data files are very similar; any program that manipulates a data file must provide some way to enter, edit, organize, display, and print the data. The obvious problem with the custom program approach to file management is that expensive programmer time is spent "reinventing the wheel" by writing essentially the same file management programs for each data file. For this reason, the custom file approach is being phased out in favor of file management and database management system approaches.

File Management System Approach

The second approach to file management avoids the necessity of writing a file management program for each data file. Instead, a single program, referred to as **file management software**, is used for the data management tasks common to all the data files. The file management software handles the tasks required by any data file—tasks such as entering, changing, organizing, displaying, locating, and printing data. Figure 9-15 illustrates how file management software handles the data management tasks common to a number of data files.

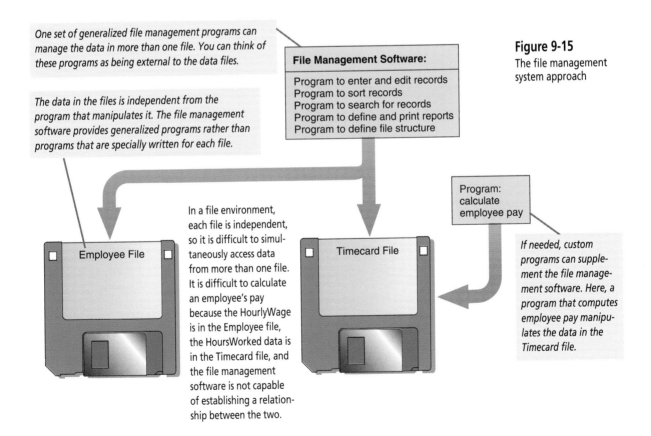

One set of generalized file management programs can manage the data in more than one file. You can think of these programs as being external to the data files.

The data in the files is independent from the program that manipulates it. The file management software provides generalized programs rather than programs that are specially written for each file.

File Management Software:

Program to enter and edit records
Program to sort records
Program to search for records
Program to define and print reports
Program to define file structure

Program: calculate employee pay

In a file environment, each file is independent, so it is difficult to simultaneously access data from more than one file. It is difficult to calculate an employee's pay because the HourlyWage is in the Employee file, the HoursWorked data is in the Timecard file, and the file management software is not capable of establishing a relationship between the two.

Employee File

Timecard File

If needed, custom programs can supplement the file management software. Here, a program that computes employee pay manipulates the data in the Timecard file.

Figure 9-15
The file management system approach

The separation of data from the programs that manipulate that data is referred to as **data independence**. This means that if you change the data file structure, for example, by adding a field, the programs that manipulate the data will still function. File management software promotes data independence because the file management software is not tied to a particular data file.

With the file management approach, the file management software is not part of the database, and therefore you might say that it is **external** to the data. In fact, if you found that you didn't like the file management software you used to create your data files, it is usually possible to change to different file management software and use it with your existing data files.

File management software can either be purchased or created using a programming language. In some situations, the basic file management features provided by commercial file management software are not sufficient for the needs of an organization—perhaps the software does not allow enough flexibility in designing reports or it does not provide a way to graph the data. If the basic features provided by file management software are not sufficient, a customized program might be required, but it would typically be used in addition to the commercial file management software.

Although file management software manages the data in different files, it works with only one file at a time and, therefore, does not recognize any relationships that exist between entities. File management software only creates and manipulates flat files. For example, the file management software in Figure 9-15 cannot find the names of the employees who worked more than 40 hours in the pay period beginning 5/16/94 because the employee names are in one file and the timecard data is in another file.

Database Management System Approach

A **database management system** (DBMS) is application software that helps you manage the data in a database. A DBMS performs the same functions as a file management system, but in addition, a DBMS allows you to work with more than one file and define the relationships among record types, as shown in Figure 9-16.

A DBMS supports either a hierarchical, network, or relational database model. It provides a way to define a database structure, define and modify relationships, and manipulate data.

A DBMS typically provides a way to save, as customized programs, the procedures for the tasks you frequently perform. For example, you might want the database to find all the timecards for the current pay period, then find the hourly wages from each employee's Employee record, and finally calculate the gross pay. You could save the series of commands to accomplish this task as a custom program.

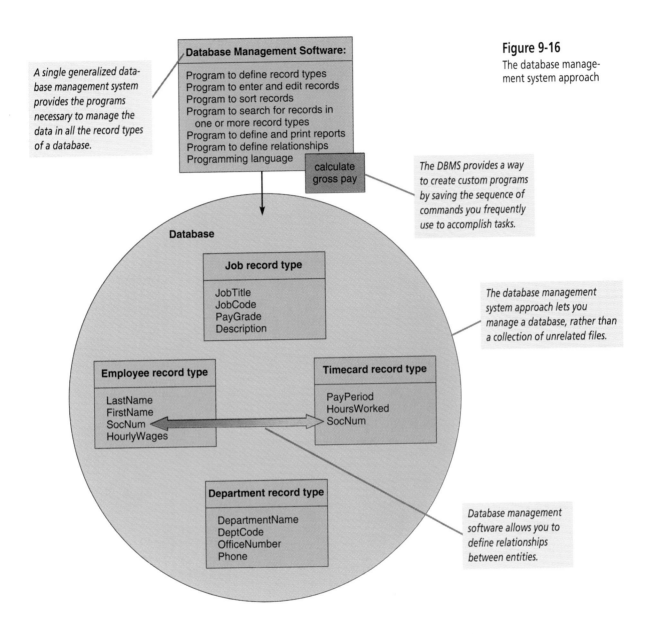

Figure 9-16
The database management system approach

A single generalized database management system provides the programs necessary to manage the data in all the record types of a database.

Database Management Software:

Program to define record types
Program to enter and edit records
Program to sort records
Program to search for records in one or more record types
Program to define and print reports
Program to define relationships
Programming language

calculate gross pay

The DBMS provides a way to create custom programs by saving the sequence of commands you frequently use to accomplish tasks.

Database

Job record type

JobTitle
JobCode
PayGrade
Description

The database management system approach lets you manage a database, rather than a collection of unrelated files.

Employee record type

LastName
FirstName
SocNum
HourlyWages

Timecard record type

PayPeriod
HoursWorked
SocNum

Department record type

DepartmentName
DeptCode
OfficeNumber
Phone

Database management software allows you to define relationships between entities.

Although it would be possible to create a database management system using a programming language, a DBMS is quite complex; most users elect to purchase a commercial package. The cost of a database management system can be a worthwhile investment, especially for an organization with a number of databases to maintain.

Object-Oriented Approach

The custom program, file management, and database management approaches operate on a passive data set—in other words, the data simply waits for a program to process it. The object-oriented database model, however, does not have a passive data set, because the objects that form the database include methods for performing actions on the data. Therefore, the object-oriented model requires an approach that provides a way to define and manipulate objects with their associated methods. Figure 9-17 illustrates the concept of the object-oriented approach.

Figure 9-17
Peripheral devices

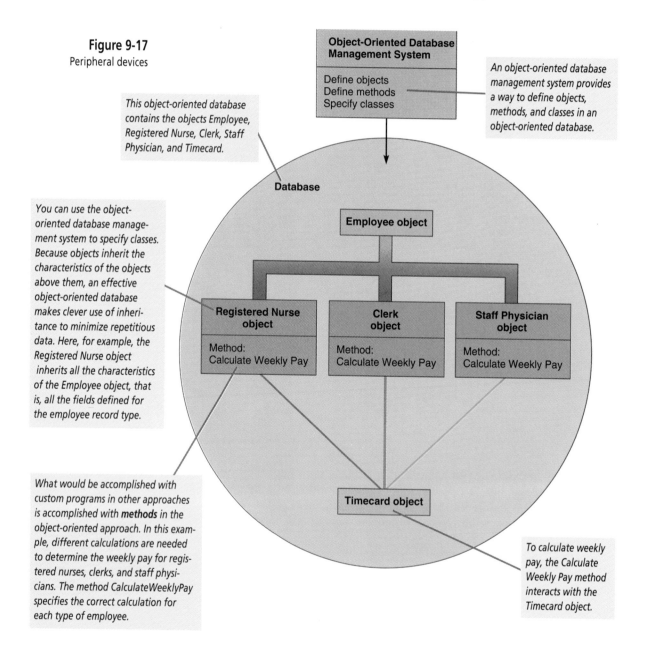

This object-oriented database contains the objects Employee, Registered Nurse, Clerk, Staff Physician, and Timecard.

Object-Oriented Database Management System
Define objects
Define methods
Specify classes

An object-oriented database management system provides a way to define objects, methods, and classes in an object-oriented database.

Database

You can use the object-oriented database management system to specify classes. Because objects inherit the characteristics of the objects above them, an effective object-oriented database makes clever use of inheritance to minimize repetitious data. Here, for example, the Registered Nurse object inherits all the characteristics of the Employee object, that is, all the fields defined for the employee record type.

Employee object

Registered Nurse object
Method:
Calculate Weekly Pay

Clerk object
Method:
Calculate Weekly Pay

Staff Physician object
Method:
Calculate Weekly Pay

Timecard object

What would be accomplished with custom programs in other approaches is accomplished with **methods** in the object-oriented approach. In this example, different calculations are needed to determine the weekly pay for registered nurses, clerks, and staff physicians. The method CalculateWeeklyPay specifies the correct calculation for each type of employee.

To calculate weekly pay, the Calculate Weekly Pay method interacts with the Timecard object.

With the object-oriented approach, the only program that operates external to the database is the program you use to define the objects, methods, and classes of the database structure. This definitional program is usually included in the object-oriented database software, although it does not become part of the database itself. Compare this to the external programs required for the custom program approach, the file management system approach, and the database management system approach. You should review Figures 9-14, 9-15, 9-16, and 9-17 to identify additional differences between the four data management approaches. As you study these figures, ask yourself the following questions: (1) Is the data treated as active or passive? (2) Is the data organized as a file, record type, or object?

File and Database Management Tasks

Regardless of the approach an organization takes to manage its data—whether it uses the custom program, file management, database management, or object-oriented approach—many of the data management tasks are the same. In this section, you will learn more about specific data management tasks. To generalize our discussion and encompass all the database models and approaches we have looked at, let's use the term **data management environment** to refer to the software or program you use to design and manage data, whether that data is in a file or a database.

Designing the File or Database

The key to an effective file or database is the initial design of its structure. With a well-designed structure, the data can be flexibly manipulated to provide meaningful, accurate, and timely information for decision-making. Suppose that you are a database administrator faced with the task of designing an effective way to store and manage your organization's data. How do you proceed?

The first step is to determine what data must be collected and stored. In other words, you must decide what fields to include. To do this, you might begin by listing the information that is available as well as any additional information that is necessary to produce the screen output or printed reports that your organization requires. Each piece of information on your list is a candidate for a data field. For example, if you are designing a file or database for the human resources department, you would probably recognize the need for information such as employee name, address, phone number, job code, and birth date. Each of these might become a data field.

The next step in the design process is to decide how to organize the information into fields so it can be used flexibly. For example, would it be better to store an employee name as one field or to have separate fields for the first name and the last name? If you want to print mailing labels with the name in the format "Margaret Houlihan" and also print an employee list with the names in the format "Houlihan, Margaret" you would need to have separate fields for the first and the last names. If you do not use separate fields for first and last names, "Margaret Houlihan" would be entered into a single field. It would then be very difficult to devise a way to separate the first name from the last name and reverse them if you wanted to output the name as "Houlihan, Margaret."

Next, you must decide on the data type for each field. As you learned earlier in the chapter, the most common data types are character and numeric. Some file and database management systems provide additional data types such as date, logical, and memo. The **date data type** is used to store dates, particularly when you want to manipulate dates, such as when you want to store 10/15/95, but display it as "October 15, 1995." The **logical data type** is used to store true/false or yes/no data using minimal storage space. For example, you might want to store data in a field that indicates whether an employee has a CPR certificate. You could use a logical field called "CPRCert" in which you would enter either Y or N. A **memo data type** is also called a **memo field** and usually provides a variable-length text field into which you can enter comments. For example, a manager might use a memo field to make notes about an employee's outstanding job performance.

After you define the data types, you should decide on the format and valid range for each field. The field format provides a template for the way data is displayed on the screen and printed. For example, if you specify a field format of XX/XX/XXXX, when you enter 10151995, it appears as 10/15/1995. On the other hand, if you specify the format XX-XX-XXXX, the entry 10151995 appears as 10-15-1995. In addition to dates, other commonly used fields and their formats include:

FIELD DESCRIPTION	FIELD FORMAT
Currency	$9,999.99
Social security number	XXX-XX-XXXX
Telephone number	(XXX)XXX-XXXX
Zip code	XXXXX-XXXX

Notice that to specify the field format, a series of 9s is used when the field type is numeric, but a series of Xs is used when the field type is character.

Many data management environments allow you to use a **range check** to specify what constitutes the range of valid entries in each field and, thereby, decrease errors. For example, you might specify that the HourlyWage field can contain values from $0.00 to $20.00. If a user enters $150 in this field instead of $15, the database will not accept the entry. Your ability to define field formats and range checks depends on the particular data management environment you use. The programming languages used to create custom file management programs generally provide the commands necessary to create a section of your program that displays and prints fields in the format you specify. With the object-oriented approach, you define formats and range checks as methods. Not all file and database management systems provide a way to define field formats and range checks. To find out if a particular environment supports these two features, you need to refer to the documentation.

The next consideration in database design is how to group the fields. Each group you create becomes a record type, or, if you are using an object-oriented model, each group becomes an object and the objects may further be grouped into classes. You should structure the field groups to reduce storage space requirements and provide the level of access-flexibility required by the people who use the data.

In an object-oriented environment, you can also define the methods that process the data in each object. Careful consideration of which objects inherit each method will help you produce an efficient object-oriented database.

When you group fields into record types, you essentially make the choice between using a flat file and a database. If you arrange all the fields in a single record type, you are using a flat file structure. If you arrange the fields into more than one record type, you are using a database structure. Let's look at an example.

Suppose the information systems manager of Midtown wants to keep track of computer equipment in case it must be replaced or repaired. Should he maintain a flat file or a database? Figure 9-18 shows six records from a large flat file, which would keep track of computer equipment and provide the information necessary to send it to a repair center.

ITEM	SERIAL NUMBER	DATE PURCHASED	REPAIR CENTER	REPAIR CENTER PHONE	REPAIR CENTER ADDRESS
computer	458876	02/12/1995	Epson	415-0786-9988	93 Torrance Blvd.
computer	433877	03/03/1994	IBM	913-559-5877	2 Bradhook Ave.
printer	6855200	03/03/1994	Epson	415-786-9988	93 Torrance Blvd.
computer	884411	01/21/1993	Epson	415-786-9988	93 Torrance Blvd.
modem	B7654D	01/21/1993	High Tech	509-776-7865	4109 Highway 56
computer	5544998	01/21/1993	IBM	913-559-5877	2 Bradhook Ave.

Figure 9-18
Equipment flat file

Using a flat file, such as the one in Figure 9-18, is not very efficient for this data. The problem with this flat file structure becomes evident when you look at the repair center data. The Epson repair center name, address, and phone number are repeated on many records. If the repair center moves to a different location, a data entry clerk would have to change the address in many records.

Repetition of data is referred to as **data redundancy** and is undesirable because it makes inefficient use of storage space and makes updating cumbersome. In a well-structured database, the data is stored nonredundantly.

The process of analyzing data to create the most efficient database structure is referred to as **normalization**. There are five normalization procedures, the first of which is to eliminate data redundancy. The remaining normalization procedures are somewhat technical and are best left to more advanced students of database management. To eliminate data redundancy, you remove the repeating fields and group them as a new record type, as shown in Figure 9-19.

When the specifications for the database structure are complete, it is then possible to enter the data for each record.

Figure 9-19
Eliminating data
redundancy

2 *If you are using a relational model, leave the Repair Center column in the Equipment record type, but duplicate it in the RepairCenter record type. This field establishes the relationship between the tables.*

1 *To reduce data redundancy, move the repair center data to a new record type called RepairCenter.*

Record type: Equipment

Item	Serial Number	Date Purchased	Repair Center
Computer	458876	02/12/1995	Epson
Computer	433877	03/03/1994	IBM
Printer	6855200	03/30/1994	Epson
Computer	884411	01/21/1993	Epson
Modem	B7654D	01/21/1993	High Tech
Computer	5544998	01/21/1993	IBM

Record type: RepairCenter

Repair Center	Repair Center Phone	Repair Center Address
Epson	415-786-9988	93 Torrance Blvd.
IBM	913-559-5877	2 Bradhook Ave.
High Tech	509-776-7865	4109 Highway 56

3 *The RepairCenter record type only needs one record for each repair center. Compare this new structure with the flat file structure in Figure 9-18, and notice that the flat file structure has more data redundancy because the Epson phone and address information repeats three times.*

4 *The Equipment and Repair Center record types are related by the Repair Center fields.*

Entering Records

When you specify a database structure, you essentially design a blank form that will hold data. After the form design is complete, you can enter data. As you enter each record, the data management environment assigns it a **record number**. The first record you enter becomes record #1, the second record you enter becomes record #2, and so forth. In an object-oriented database, each object receives a unique **object ID** number, which is similar to a record number in some respects. Record numbers and object IDs are used by the computer to keep track of the data you enter.

Consistency is important for data entry because it affects the efficiency of your searches. Suppose you're entering employee data and you enter "RN," for registered nurse, as the job code for some employees, but you enter "NURS" for other employees who hold the same position. If you later want the database software to print a list of all nurses and you ask for all the RNs, the employees you identified as NURS will not be included on the list.

Another issue related to entering consistent data is case sensitivity. **Case sensitivity** means that uppercase letters are not equivalent to their lowercase counterparts. If you enter the state abbreviation MI, it is not the same as the abbreviation Mi, with its lowercase "i." Not all data management environments are case sensitive. You must read the documentation to determine whether a particular data management environment is case sensitive.

Searching

A realistic file or database contains hundreds or thousands of records. If you want to find a particular record or a particular group of records, it is too cumbersome for you to scroll through every record; however, the computer can quickly locate the records that meet specific search criteria of a **query**. For example, if you want a list of everyone who has "Jones" as a last name, you would use a query to tell the computer to look for all the records with "Jones" in the LastName field.

Most DBMS have a special query language that you use to state the search criteria. A **query language** provides a set of commands you can use to locate and manipulate data. A popular query language for both mainframes and microcomputers is **Structured Query Language**, more commonly called **SQL**. As an alternative to a query language, many DBMSs allow you to query by example. **Query by example** provides you with a blank record into which you enter examples or specifications of the records you want to find. Figure 9-20 shows how you might use query by example on a form for the Midtown employee records.

L A B

SQL

When you begin a query, the field names are displayed on a blank form.

You specify the query by typing in examples of the records you want to find. Here, the query specifies all female RNs who make more than $10.00 per hour.

Figure 9-20
Query by example

Simple queries are usually accomplished using a command word such as FIND and an expression such as LastName = 'Houlihan.' A simple **expression** usually has a field name on the left and the specific item you want to find on the right. The query you use to locate the record for an employee with the last name Houlihan is *FIND LastName = 'Houlihan'*. You can create expressions using any of the following **relational operators**: =, >, <, >=, <=, and <>. You can review the meanings of these operators in Figure 9-21.

OPERATOR	DESCRIPTION
=	equal to
>	greater than
<	less than
>=	greater than or equal to
<=	less than or equal to
<>	not equal to

Figure 9-21
Relational operators

A complex query, such as one to find only those female employees who are registered nurses and have Houlihan for their last name, requires the use of **logical operators** such as NOT, AND, and OR. Let's use a sample set of employees from Midtown General Hospital to find out more about complex queries. Study Figure 9-22 to refresh your memory about set theory and logical operators, then continue reading about how you can apply these operators to complex queries.

Figure 9-22
Logical operators

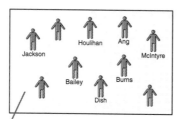

1 A rectangle represents what is called the universe, which contains all the entities under consideration. Here, the universe consists of all employees at Midtown General Hospital. To keep things simple, we'll focus on the seven named employees: Houlihan, Ang, Dish, Bailey, McIntyre, Burns, and Jackson.

2 A set, or group, of employees may be represented by a shaded circle. This diagram shows the set of all registered nurses. As an alternative to the diagram, we could write out the elements of this set and place them in curly brackets like this:
registered nurse = {Houlihan, Ang, Dish, Bailey}

3 The employees who are not registered nurses are shown by the shaded area outside the circle. The group of employees who are not registered nurses can also be described by either of the following notations:
NOT{registered nurse}
~{registered nurse}

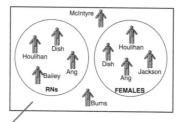

4 Let's use another circle to represent the group of all female employees. Now we have two sets:
registered nurse = {Houlihan, Ang, Dish, Bailey}
female = {Houlihan, Ang, Dish, Jackson}

5 Since some of the employees are in both sets, a more accurate diagram shows the two circles overlapping. Employees who are in the overlapped area belong to both sets.

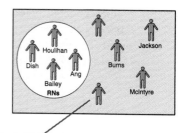

6 To write an expression describing who is in both groups, use the logical operator AND. Any one of the following notations describes the employees who are both registered nurses and females:
registered nurse AND female
registered nurse & female
registered nurse ∩ female

7 To write an expression describing who is in either group, use the logical operator OR. Any one of the following notations describes the employees who are either registered nurses or females:
registered nurse OR female
registered nurse | female
registered nurse ∪ female

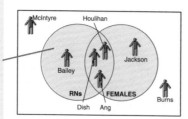

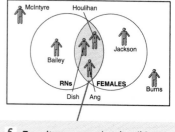

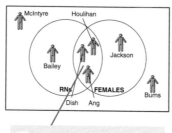

When used in a query, the logical operator AND connects two expressions, both of which must be true to match the search criteria. For example, the search criteria JobCode = 'RN' AND Gender = 'F' requests the records for female registered nurses. If Margaret Houlihan is a female and a registered nurse, her record would match the search criteria.

The logical operator OR connects two expressions, but only one of them must be true to match the search criteria. The search criteria JobCode = 'RN' OR Gender = 'F' produces all the records for females, regardless of their job code; the search also produces all the records for registered nurses of either gender. All of the following records match the search criteria:

Houlihan	Margaret	RN	F
Jackson	Tony	SMD	F
Bailey	Rick	RN	M
Dish	Betty	RN	F
Ang	Susan	RN	F

The logical operator NOT precedes a simple or complex expression and, in a search specification, produces the records that do not match the expression. For example, the expression NOT JobCode = 'RN' produces records for all employees who are not registered nurses. What about the search criteria NOT(JobCode = 'RN' AND Gender = 'F')? Think of it this way, the computer locates the records for all employees who are registered nurses and female (like Margaret Houlihan, who is a female registered nurse), but it does not produce these records. Instead, it produces all the other records. So, will the search NOT(JobCode = 'RN' AND Gender = 'F') produce Rick Bailey? Yes it will, and Figure 9-23 shows why.

The area where the circles overlap represents JobCode='RN' AND Gender = 'F,' but the search specifies the records NOT in this area.

Rick Bailey is not in the area where the circles overlap, so he matches the search criteria NOT(JobCode = 'RN' AND Gender = 'F'). Jackson, Burns, and McIntyre also match the search criteria.

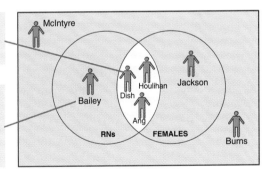

Figure 9-23
NOT(JobCode = 'RN' AND Gender = 'F')

What about using NOT and OR in the same query, as in the search criteria NOT(JobCode = 'RN' OR Gender = 'F')? This time, the computer eliminates any records for registered nurses; it also eliminates any records for female employees. Figure 9-24 shows a conceptual diagram for this query. You should compare

Figure 9-23 and Figure 9-24 to make sure you understand the difference between the queries NOT(JobCode = 'RN' AND Gender = 'F') and NOT(JobCode = 'RN' OR Gender = 'F').

Figure 9-24

NOT(JobCode = 'RN' OR Gender = 'F')

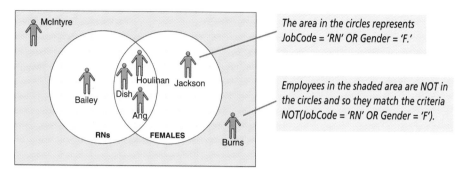

Search criteria can become quite complex. Look at the Employee table in Figure 9-25; let's use it to learn how to use a complex query.

Figure 9-25

Employee table

LASTNAME	FIRSTNAME	GENDER	STARTDATE	JOBCODE
Ang	Susan	F	08/10/1988	RN
Bailey	Rick	M	02/03/1992	RN
Burns	Frank	M	05/04/1990	SMD
Dish	Betty	F	01/16/1992	RN
Houlihan	Margaret	F	10/05/1985	RN
Jackson	Tony	F	12/04/1989	SMD
McIntyre	Jon	M	04/14/1986	SMD

Suppose you want to find the salaries of only those female employees who started working after August 1, 1988, but before August 1, 1990, and who are registered nurses or staff physicians (SMD). The search criteria would be Gender = 'F' AND (StartDate>08/01/1988 AND StartDate<08/01/1990) AND (JobCode = 'RN' OR JobCode= 'SMD'). The parentheses in this search criteria indicate the order in which the expressions should be evaluated by the DBMS. The expressions in parentheses should be evaluated first.

When you need to do a complex search, you might want to experiment with parts of the search first to be certain the parts produce what you expect. For example, in the complex search above, you might first test the expression

(StartDate>08/01/1988 AND StartDate<08/01/1990)

to be certain it retrieves records with start dates during the correct time period. Once you have tested parts of your query, you can combine them to create your complete query.

Updating Information

Often the reason you search for a particular record is to **update** it, that is, to change it or delete it. The typical process is to first enter a query so the computer finds and displays the record you want to update. Next, you make the changes and, if necessary, indicate that you want to save the record in its changed format.

Different data management environments have different ways of saving updated records. With many environments, changes are automatically saved as soon as you move to the next record. With other environments, you must issue a command to save the changes you make. To learn the specific procedures for the data management environment you use, you should refer to the software documentation or Help facility.

In addition to individual changes, computers make it easy to perform **global updates** to change the data in more than one record at a time. Consider the Employee file in the Midtown General Hospital database. A number of employees are working at $4.35 per hour, the minimum wage set by the government. Suppose that the minimum wage increases to $5.65 per hour. Instead of searching for each employee with an hourly wage of $4.35 and manually changing the numbers to $5.65, you could enter a command such as:

UPDATE EMPWAGE SET HourlyWage = 5.65 WHERE HourlyWage < 5.65.

Let's see how this command performs a global update. The UPDATE command means you want to change the data in some or all of the records. EMPWAGE is the name of the file that contains the data you want to change. SET HourlyWage = 5.65 tells the DBMS to change the data in the HourlyWage field to 5.65. WHERE HourlyWage < 5.65 tells the DBMS to change only those records in which the current hourly wage is less than $5.65.

Organizing Records

It is easier to use information if it is presented in a sequence related to how the information is going to be used. For example, if you want to view a list of employees and you are looking for a specific employee by name, it is handy to have the employee records alphabetized by last name. On the other hand, if you want to view a list of employees to compare hourly wages, it is useful to have the records in numeric order according to the number in the HourlyWage field.

A **sort key** is a field used to arrange records in order. Suppose you want the Personnel file records arranged alphabetically by last name. The sort key would be LastName. Alternatively, if you want the records arranged by hourly wage, the sort key would be HourlyWage.

There are two ways to organize records in a file; you can sort them or you can index them. If you change the order of the file itself, essentially by rearranging the sequence of the records on the disk, you are **sorting**. Because the records are rearranged, each record receives a new record number to indicate its new position in the file. So, for example, in a file sorted by last name, the record with the name that appears first in the alphabet becomes record #1.

Sorting is an acceptable procedure for small files, in which the time to sort the records is minimal, or for files that you don't want sorted multiple ways. However, if you sometimes need to view a file in alphabetical order by last name but at other times you need to view the file sorted in order by salary, sorting is not very efficient because it takes time and uses valuable system resources every time you sort the file.

An alternative way to organize records is by indexing. **Indexing** leaves the file in its original order and retains the original record numbers, but creates additional files, called **index files**, that allow you to display the information in alphabetical or numeric order. Think of an index file as being similar to the index of a book. The index of a book contains topics in alphabetical order, which allows you to easily find the topic in the index list. Next to the topic is a page number that points to the location of the actual information about the topic. Figure 9-26 shows how an index file lists the contents of the LastName field in alphabetical order, then uses the record number as a pointer to indicate the corresponding record number in the original file.

Figure 9-26
Indexing

1 Records are typically numbered in the order in which they are entered, so the employee record with the earliest start date is record 1.

Record #	LastName	FirstName	Gender	StartDate	JobCode
1	Houlihan	Margaret	F	10/05/1985	RN
2	McIntyre	John	M	04/14/1986	SMD
3	Ang	Susan	F	08/10/1988	RN
4	Jackson	Tony	F	12/04/1989	SMD
5	Burns	Frank	M	05/04/1990	SMD
6	Dish	Betty	F	01/16/1992	RN
7	Bailey	Rick	M	02/03/1992	RN

Database table

2 To make an index file, the computer arranges only the data in the LastName field in order by last name.

3 The only other field in the index file contains the original record number for each record. Notice that in the table, the record for Susan Ang is record 3. In the index file, Susan's record is listed first because her name is first in the alphabet, but her record number remains 3.

LastName	Record #
Ang	3
Bailey	7
Burns	5
Dish	6
Houlihan	1
Jackson	4
McIntyre	2

Index file

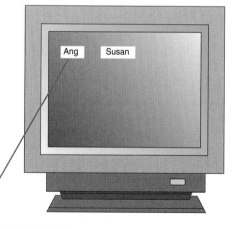

4 Because the index file contains only some of the information for each employee, the computer only uses the index file to look up information from the original database table. To display the first and last names in alphabetical order, the computer looks at the first item in the index file and displays the contents of the LastName field, Ang. To find Ang's first name, the computer looks at record 3 in the table. It finds Susan in the FirstName field and displays it.

In database management systems, such as dBASE IV, the distinction between sorting and indexing helps you more effectively utilize the DBMS to organize your data. However, you should be aware that other data management environments do not provide these options. Further, some data management environments do not differentiate between the terms "sort" and "index." For example, Microsoft Access uses the term "sort" for procedures that organize data without rearranging records.

Producing Output

The reason you produce output is so that you can present information in a format that facilitates making a decision, preparing an analysis, or taking some action. Traditionally, output is presented as words and numbers in reports, but output can assume other formats such as graphs, graphics, and sound. How can you determine the best way to present information? It is useful to know what types of output options are available and the advantages of each type.

Reports

A simple list of data from a file or database might display the information you need, but might not provide it in the optimal format. The list might include some unnecessary fields, it might not include a title or page numbers, it might not display subtotals or totals, and the column headings might not be as descriptive as you would like them to be. If a list is not adequate, you can design a report on the screen or as a printed document to convey information more effectively. A **database report** is the formatted output of some or all of the data from a database.

The part of a data management environment that provides you with the ability to design reports is called a **report generator**. Usually a report generator helps you create a template for a report. A **report template** does not contain any data. Instead, it contains the outline or general specifications for a report, including such things as what to title the report, which fields should be included, which fields you want to subtotal or total, and how the report should be formatted. Typically, reports are designed in columnar format, as shown in Figure 9-27.

After you use a report generator to design a template for a report, you can produce the report at any time. When you produce the actual report, it is based on the data currently contained in the file. Suppose you create a report template called EMPLOYEE.RPT, which specifies the following information:

- The title of the report is Midtown General Hospital Employees.
- The report contains six columns for data from these fields: LastName, FirstName, SocNum, Gender, StartDate, and JobCode.
- The headings for the columns are Last Name, First Name, Social Security #, Gender, Start Date, and Job Code.
- The report is arranged alphabetically by last name.

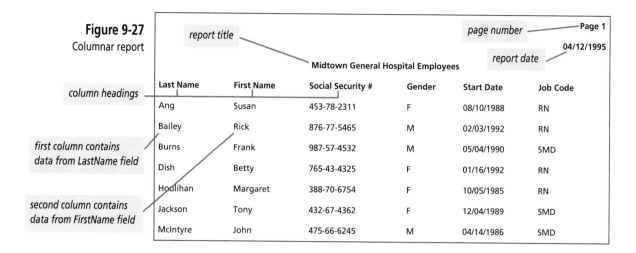

Figure 9-27
Columnar report

Now suppose you use the EMPLOYEE.RPT report template to print the report on August 1, 1995. The report includes employees who are listed in the database as of August 1. On September 1, your organization hires several new employees who are added to the database. When you use the EMPLOYEE.RPT report template to print a report on September 2, the report follows the same format as the previous report, but the new employees are included because the report uses the data in the database at the time the report is printed.

An organization uses several different types of reports, depending on specific information needs. Some types of reports provide data that is appropriate for decision making, whereas other types of reports provide a simple historical record of events and transactions.

Types of Reports

A **detail report** lists transactions, usually in chronological order. A detail report of daily cash register transactions, for example, contains each item sold at each cash register. This report is likely to be fairly long, and not particularly useful, unless a checkout clerk needs to trace back through the day's transactions to reconcile an error.

A **summary report** is a condensed version of a detail report, and it is usually produced for managers. A summary report might show total sales by department, providing a manager with information useful to make a decision about which departments are meeting their sales goals for a specific period of time. A detail report, showing each of the items sold in every department, would not be as useful as a summary report for this decision for two reasons. First, a detail report requires manual effort to total the sales for each department. Second, the detail report is information on specific items sold and is not relevant to analyzing whether a department met sales goals.

A **control-break report** is a specific type of summary report in which subtotals are created by category. To produce a control-break report, you must make sure the records are sorted or indexed to reflect the groups on the report. A report that is grouped by department should be sorted or indexed using DeptCode as the key field. Figure 9-28 illustrates the characteristics of a control-break report.

Midtown Department Payroll

Last Name	First Name	Social Security	Hourly Wage	Hours Worked	Gross Pay
Bailey	Rick	876-77-5465	$14.80	42.00	$621.60
Brown	Karen	372-17-2227	$10.50	40.00	$420.00
McIntyre	John	475-66-6245	$90.00	55.00	$4,950.00
Nardi	Susan	371-28-1882	$8.50	36.00	$306.00
Peterson	Angela	578-02-0092	$9.50	38.00	$361.00
Smith	Tracy	421-88-1384	$8.45	40.00	$338.00
St. Aubin	Harold	461-28-1228	$9.25	40.00	$370.00
DEPARTMENT CODE: ER			SUBTOTAL:	291.00	$7,366.60
Burns	Frank	987-57-4532	$90.00	63.00	$5,670.00
Choi	Lisa	398-13-1883	$8.85	45.00	$398.25
Houlihan	Margaret	388-70-6754	$14.80	45.00	$666.00
Kaefer	Kathryn	387-18-1882	$110.00	44.00	$4840.00
Matsuzaki	Akiko	443-28-1998	$9.75	44.00	$429.00
Smith	Ralph	538-18-1888	$10.75	42.00	$451.50
DEPARTMENT CODE: IC			SUBTOTAL:	283.00	$12,454.75
Ang	Susan	453-78-2311	$14.80	52.00	$769.60
Dish	Betty	765-43-4325	$14.80	42.00	$621.60
Jackson	Tony	432-67-4362	$90.00	58.00	$5,220.00
Nunez	Maria	377-13-1773	$10.60	40.00	$424.00
DEPARTMENT CODE: OB			SUBTOTAL:	238.00	$7,702.20
			TOTAL:		$27,523.55

Figure 9-28
Control-break report

1 In a control-break report, records are grouped. Here, the records are grouped by DeptCode; all the employees in the ER (emergency room) are listed in one group, all the IC (intensive care) staff are in one group, and so forth.

2 At the end of each group, the report displays subtotals for gross pay.

An **exception report** provides a list of records that match a condition outside of the usual range or limits. For example, a report that lists customers who have overdue balances would be an exception report—the data in the DatePaid field for these records is outside the time limit set for payment.

Graphs

In many cases, character-based reports, such as detail, summary, control-break, and exception reports, are most appropriate to meet an organization's information needs. In other cases, a graph is more appropriate. A **graph** visually presents data in a way that can be quickly assimilated and understood. Graphs are appropriate for presenting a summary of data when detailed data is not relevant to the decision process. However, graphs can be misleading when details should be considered to make the decision. For example, consider the graph in Figure 9-29. It shows annual sales increasing slightly over four years, but it does not reveal the fact that sales for only one "star" product have significantly increased while sales of other products have decreased. If the managers at this organization use this graph to conclude that business is going well and that they have nothing to worry about, they could face a disaster when sales of the "star" product begin to decrease.

Figure 9-29
A potentially misleading graph

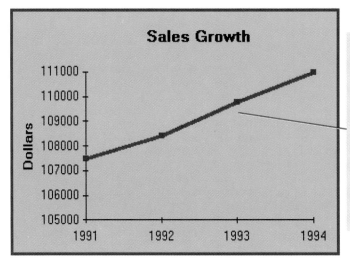

Sales appear to be steadily increasing, but the graph does not show the composition of sales. It is possible that only one "star" product is doing well, but that sales of all other products are declining. A sales manager who assumes from this graph that sales are healthy could be making a mistake and, as a result, make a bad decision.

A well-designed graph should convey your point within a few seconds. A graph with too much data might not be a great improvement over a detailed report. To check whether a graph you create is meaningful, try to write one sentence explaining what the graph shows: for example, "U.S. sales have increased, but foreign sales have decreased" or "Most people support tax reform." If you have trouble writing a descriptive sentence, your graph may not be effective.

Although there are many types of graphs, four types are used most often for business and the social sciences: a **bar graph** for showing comparisons, a **line graph** for showing trends over time, a **pie chart** for showing percentages, and a **scatter plot** for showing data pairs, as shown in Figure 9-30.

Sonification

Sonification, or **audio mapping**, uses audio cues to present data. As an example, consider a laboratory that routinely performs a series of tests on water samples. Each test measures the amount of a particular contaminant. A water sample is of acceptable quality if the contaminants it contains are within a specified normal range.

L A B

PRESENTING INFORMATION USING SOUND

The laboratory technicians use sonification to represent the data for contaminant amounts. The data points for normal ranges are represented by the notes of a tune, while data points outside the normal ranges are represented by discordant notes. A technician can easily determine which water samples are normal just by listening to the audio playback of the test results. Any sample that sounds wrong can be checked more closely to determine exactly which contaminant is outside its normal range.

Although it might seem plausible that sonification was developed for people with visual problems, this is not the case. Sonification was originally developed for situations in which there are conflicting demands on a decision maker's visual attention, but demand for auditory attention is low. In such situations, presenting information in auditory format enables the decision maker to process more information than would be possible from a single input source.

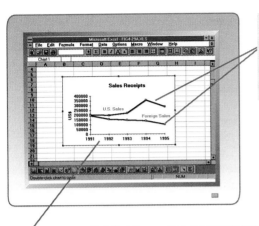

2 Line graphs can represent more than one set of data. Here, one line represents a set of data for U.S. sales. The other line represents a set of data for foreign sales. On graphs that display more than one data set, it is important to label the lines or use a legend.

Figure 9-30
Graph types

1 A line graph shows trends over time. Typically, the horizontal axis shows days, months, or years.

3 Bar graphs show comparisons rather than trends. If you find that you have created a bar graph with dates on the horizontal axis, consider using a line graph instead.

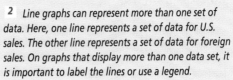
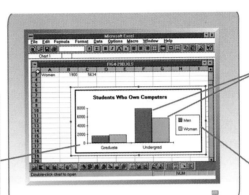

4 Bar graphs can represent more than one data set. Here, male computer-users are one set of data and female computer-users are another set.

5 As with any graph that shows more than one data set, it is important to use a legend that identifies the sets.

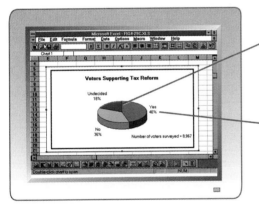

6 A pie chart is best used to show parts of a whole or percentages. The data for a pie chart comes from only one data set.

7 It is useful to show the actual percentages on each slice of the pie.

8 An x-y chart shows the location of data pairs. It is also referred to as a scatter plot. This chart shows data pairs representing age and pounds of sugar consumed per year. Each data pair represents one person of age x who eats y amount of sugar. This data point represents a five-year-old who eats four pounds of sugar a year.

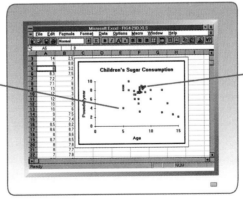

9 On a scatter plot, a cluster of data points indicates a trend. Here, we see that many of the people surveyed were about eight years old and ate about seven pounds of sugar per year.

Data Visualization

Data visualization is based on the human ability to determine patterns at a glance and is used in situations where spotting trends in data is a major requirement. Consider the example presented at the beginning of the chapter. The human resources manager at Midtown General Hospital is interested in the continuing health of the employees, and he wants to monitor trends in employee absences. The usual approach to supplying information on employee absences is to create a character-based report showing the number of employees out sick in each department for each day of the month. Spotting trends from these numbers would take some mental effort. A better route might be to provide a series of line graphs, but consolidating the series to get a picture of the overall organization would be tough.

The human resources manager could use data visualization to represent employee data with an animated graphic of a garden in which each employee is represented by a plant. The plants would be grouped by department in particular areas of the garden. Healthy employees would be represented by healthy plants, but as their absences increased, their plants would begin to appear less healthy by wilting and turning brown. The human resources director can get a fairly good overview of accumulated sick days by looking at the garden.

Data visualization techniques have potential uses for presenting dynamic information such as buying patterns, investment returns, stock prices, and demographic data.

Characteristics of Effective Output

Whether you use reports, graphs, sonification, or visualization, you can present information effectively by observing the following guidelines:

- Present only the information that is necessary to make a decision or to take appropriate action. Too much information makes it difficult to identify and interpret the essential information, and it is time consuming to assemble and to understand.
- Present information in a usable format. If subtotals and totals are necessary for making a decision, present them. The reader should not have to make additional manual calculations.
- Information should be timely. Reports must arrive in time to be used for effective decision making. Some decisions require information periodically, for example, monthly sales reports. Other decisions require ongoing information that will be best satisfied by a continuous display, for example, changing stock prices.
- Information should be presented in a clear and unambiguous format. On a report, the report title, page numbers, date, and column headings help decision makers identify the information.
- Present the information in the format most appropriate for the decision and the decision maker. In many cases, a traditional report organized in rows and columns is most appropriate. In other cases, alternative formats such as sonification, graphs, or visualization might be more effective.

R E V I E W

1. Answer the questions listed in the Chapter Preview section at the beginning of the chapter.
2. List each of the boldface terms used in this chapter, then use your own words to write a short definition of each term.
3. Complete the following table to summarize the terminology used to describe the elements of hierarchical, network, relational, and object-oriented databases:

	RELATIONAL	HIERARCHICAL	NETWORK	OBJECT-ORIENTED
RECORD TYPE				
RECORD				
FIELD				

4. Complete the following table to summarize the characteristics of the four approaches to managing data files:

	CUSTOM PROGRAM	FILE MANAGEMENT	DATABASE MANAGEMENT	OBJECT-ORIENTED
FILES MANIPULATED WITH:	A CUSTOM PROGRAM	FILE MANAGEMENT SOFTWARE		
PROMOTES DATA INDEPENDENCE:	NO			
FILE SUPPORT:	ONE AT A TIME			
MANIPULATES RELATIONSHIPS:		NO		

5. List the steps you should follow to design a file or database.
6. Create a topic outline for the material presented in the section "Producing Output" that begins on page NP 323.
7. Describe the difference between a record and a record type.
8. Draw a hierarchy diagram showing the relationships among the following items: file, program file, data file, free-form data file, structured data file, flat file, database, relational database, hierarchical database, network database, object-oriented database.

C H A P T E R   Q U I Z

1. What data type should you use for a field that contains Social Security numbers?
2. All records have the same format in a(n) _____ file.
3. If you want your database to include methods, you should use the _____ approach to data management.
4. A(n) _____ is a diagram that shows the relationships between record types in a database.
5. A(n) _____ database does not use pointers or physical links, but instead finds related records by examining the contents of fields.
6. The _____ approach to managing data is the least effective method for promoting data independence.
7. If you are defining a record type and you have a field that contains pay rates, you can use a(n) _____ to specify that the field can only contain values between 0.00 and 15.00.
8. If your database management software is _____, a last name entry of "McArthur" is not the same as "Mcarthur."

9. When used in a query, the logical operator _____ connects two expressions, both of which must be true to match the search criteria.

10. To find the records for all people aged 21, regardless of education, and all college graduates, regardless of age, you use the search criteria AGE = 21 _____ Education = "College Graduate."

11. If you want to sort records alphabetically by state, you specify State as the _____.

12. If you have personnel records that you want alphabetized by last name, ordered numerically by age, and organized by date hired, you should _____ the records.

13. When you want to group data on a report and show subtotals for each group, you should create a(n) _____ report.

14. In addition to reporting and graphing, you can present output using _____ or _____.

15. Managers seldom use _____ reports for decision making.

P R O J E C T S

1. Suppose you are the database administrator for a large retail department store. You are working with the inventory manager to define an effective record format for a file containing data about the merchandise. The inventory manager gives you a sample of the index cards now being used to keep track of the inventory (see Figure 9-31). Use this card and the following instructions to design an effective record format for the inventory data file.

Figure 9-31

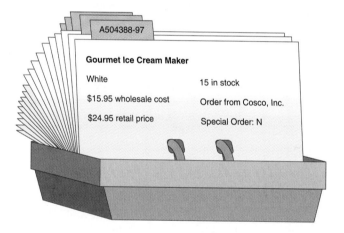

A504388-97

Gourmet Ice Cream Maker

White   15 in stock

$15.95 wholesale cost   Order from Cosco, Inc.

$24.95 retail price   Special Order: N

a. List each field the inventory record should contain. Your field names should be descriptive, contain no more than ten characters, and be only one word; for example, use "ItemName," not "IN." Remember to think about how the data might be used for output—the fields you define might not be exactly the same as the fields on the index card.

b. Assign a data type to each field. You can use the following data types: character, numeric, date, and logical.

c. Define the length of each field. You might have to make some intelligent guesses about field length, since you do not know what all the data looks like. You can see from the part number on the tab that some part numbers are at least 10 characters long, but you might guess that some part numbers will be longer—use your judgment. Be careful about the length of fields that contain dollar values. You should not leave a space for the $ sign, but you should leave a space for the decimal point.

d. Where appropriate, indicate the input or output format for a field; for example, you use $9999.99 for currency fields.

2. Suppose that you work on the staff at Central State University and you have the following data:

   The Management Department (phone: 455-9800) has three graduate faculty: Professor Sharon Smith (office: BA 502, phone: 455-9897), Associate Professor Rico Gomez (office: BA 510, phone: 455-9888), and Associate Professor Ariel Headly (office: BA 402, phone: 455-9776). S. Smith teaches Quantitative Analysis (course ID: MM525) on Tuesday and Thursday, 7-9 p.m., in room BA 10. She also teaches the Graduate Seminar (course ID: MM698) on Monday, 7-10 p.m., in room BA 21. R. Gomez teaches Personnel Management (course ID: MM560) on Monday and Wednesday, 7-9 p.m., in room BA 20. A. Headly teaches Leadership in Organizations (course ID: MM610) on Thursday evenings, 6-9 p.m., in room BA 20.

   a. Draw a data structure diagram showing how you would arrange this data in a hierarchical database, then draw the specific occurrence of the data that was described above.

   b. R. Gomez decides to help A. Headly teach the Leadership in Organizations course. Now this course has two instructors. Redraw your data structure diagram using a network model to show this relationship. Also redraw your diagram showing an occurrence of the data.

   c. Create the tables you would use if you were to structure this data as a relational database.

3. Use the printout on page NP 332 of the inventory data for a small toy store to determine the results of the queries in questions a through k, then write out the queries you would use to find the data indicated in questions l through t.

   How many records match each of the following queries?

   a. Quantity < 50

   b. Wholesale > 2.50 and Wholesale < 4.00

   c. Ordered < '7/1/89'

   d. Brand = 'Nature's Kids' OR Brand = 'Plastic Pets'

   e. Brand = 'Galaxy Toys' AND Brand = 'Flying Fun'

   f. (Brand = 'Flying Fun' OR Brand = 'Nature's Kids') AND Retail < 5.00

   g. Brand = 'Flying Fun' OR (Brand = 'Nature's Kids' AND Retail < 5.00)

   h. (Color = 'Brown' OR Color = 'Purple') AND Retail = 4.99

   i. Color = 'Brown' OR (Color = 'Purple' AND Retail = 4.99)

   j. Stock > 10 OR Stock < 50 AND Ordered By = 'J. Mathers' OR Retail > 10.00

   k. NOT(Supplier = 'Toy Barn' OR Supplier = 'GraphInc')

   Write out the query you would use to find:

   l. All the toys ordered between July 1 and July 7

   m. Any toys with a wholesale cost more than $4.99 that were not ordered by J. Mathers

   n. All the brown toys that retail for more than $10.00

   o. Any toys made by Zen Toys or Rich Folks for which there are fewer than 10 in stock

   p. Any toys that were ordered by T. Livingston or A. Hayes before 7/1/89

   q. The names of any toys from the Toy Barn that retail between $4.00 and $8.00

   r. Any purple toys that retail for less than $5.00 or any green toys of which the store has less than 10 in stock

   s. Any toys that the store ordered in quantities of 50 that do not have a wholesale cost of $4.99

   t. Any toys that are pink or red or magenta but have a retail price less than $10.00

Toy	Brand	Supplier	Color	Ordered	Ordered By	Quantity	Wholesale	Retail	Stock
Fortran Learner	Computer Fun	Fun Factory	Yellow	7/1/89	A. Hayes	50	$3.99	$5.39	32
Rocket Racer	Flying Fun	Fun Factory	Red/Blue	7/14/89	A. Hayes	50	$2.50	$3.38	32
Day-Glo Frisbees	Flying Fun	Fun Factory	Lime/Pink	7/1/89	A. Hayes	50	$2.50	$3.38	45
Model Cessna	Flying Fun	Fun Factory	Black	7/1/89	A. Hayes	50	$8.99	$12.14	0
Model Satellite	Flying Fun	Fun Factory	Red/White	6/25/89	A. Hayes	50	$5.50	$7.43	12
Satellite Launcher	Flying Fun	Toy Barn	Silver/Taupe	6/24/89	A. Hayes	50	$12.50	$16.88	10
Kaleidoscope	Galaxy Toys	Toy Barn	Purple	7/14/89	T. Livingston	50	$3.99	$5.39	10
Warp 10 U.F.O.	Galaxy Toys	Toy Barn	Silver/Blue	7/1/89	T. Livingston	50	$2.50	$3.38	40
Space Station	Galaxy Toys	Toy Barn	N/A	7/1/89	T. Livingston	25	$12.50	$16.88	50
Orbitron	Galaxy Toys	Toy Barn	Magenta	6/23/89	T. Livingston	25	$13.99	$18.89	3
Brontosaurus Bruce	Nature's Kids	GraphInc	Olive	7/14/89	T. Livingston	25	$4.99	$6.74	6
Ferdie Frog	Nature's Kids	Toy Barn	Green	7/1/89	T. Livingston	25	$2.50	$3.38	70
Stegosaurus Sam	Nature's Kids	Toy Barn	Brown/Olive	7/1/89	T. Livingston	25	$2.50	$3.38	84
Agatha Alligator	Nature's Kids	Toy Barn	Green	7/1/89	T. Livingston	25	$4.99	$6.74	54
Eight-color Paintset	Non-Toxic Toys	Toy Barn	N/A	7/14/89	J.Mathers	25	$2.99	$4.04	75
Wooden Tugboat	Non-Toxic Toys	Toy Barn	Brown	6/25/89	J.Mathers	50	$6.50	$8.78	23
Wooden Train Set	Non-Toxic Toys	Toy Barn	Brown	6/25/89	J.Mathers	25	$8.50	$11.48	1
Inflatable Crab	Plastic Pets	Toy Barn	Red	7/5/89	J.Mathers	50	$4.99	$6.74	1
Inflatable Lobster	Plastic Pets	Toy Barn	Pink	7/5/89	J.Mathers	50	$4.99	$6.74	18
Inflatable Snails	Plastic Pets	Toy Barn	Green/Olive	7/5/89	J.Mathers	50	$4.99	$6.74	20
Plastic Penguin	Plastic Pets	Toy Barn	Black/White	7/5/89	J.Mathers	50	$4.99	$6.74	20
Micro Mice	Plastic Pets	Toy Barn	White	7/5/89	J.Mathers	50	$4.99	$6.74	21
Vampire Fangs	Plastic Pets	Toy Barn	Pink	7/5/89	J.Mathers	50	$4.99	$6.74	22
Thinking Trees	Plastic Pets	Toy Barn	Brown	7/5/89	J.Mathers	50	$4.99	$6.74	13
Model Mercedes	Rich Folks	GraphInc	Blue/Tan	7/5/89	J.Mathers	50	$4.99	$6.74	4
Model Ferrari	Rich Folks	GraphInc	Red/Blue	7/5/89	J.Mathers	50	$4.99	$6.74	25
Plastic Sushi	Rich Folks	GraphInc	Yellow/Green	7/5/89	J.Mathers	50	$4.99	$6.74	33
Expanding Espresso	Rich Folks	GraphInc	Brown	7/5/89	J.Mathers	50	$4.99	$6.74	27
Rock n' Roll Ron	Zap Toys	Toy Barn	Magenta/Red	7/5/89	J.Mathers	50	$4.99	$6.74	28
Singing Slugs	Zap Toys	Toy Barn	Green/Olive	7/5/89	J.Mathers	50	$4.99	$6.74	2
Piano Pete	Zap Toys	Toy Barn	Brown	7/5/89	J.Mathers	50	$4.99	$6.74	30
Dan the Drummer	Zap Toys	Toy Barn	Brown	7/5/89	J.Mathers	50	$4.99	$6.74	1
Bronco Buster	Zen Toys	GraphInc	N/A	7/5/89	J.Mathers	50	$4.99	$6.74	23
The Entertainer	Zen Toys	GraphInc	N/A	7/5/89	J.Mathers	50	$4.99	$6.74	33
Flower Child	Zen Toys	GraphInc	N/A	7/5/89	J.Mathers	50	$4.99	$6.74	14

TOY STORE INVENTORY*

*This data file is included in the Microsoft Works for Windows on-line tutorial.

4. Suppose you have a small file with the following records about computer books:

Record Number	Author	Title	Publication Date
1	Norton, Peter	Programmer's Guide to the IBM PC	1985
2	Craig, John Clark	Visual Basic Workshop	1991
3	Minsky, Marvin	Society of Mind	1986
4	Nelson, Theodore	Literary Machines	1987
5	Wodasky, Ron	Multimedia Madness	1992
6	Waite, Mitchell	UNIX Primer Plus	1983

a. Complete the following table to create an index that will organize the records in alphabetical order according to the author's last name:

AUTHOR NAME	RECORD NUMBER
CRAIG, JOHN CLARK	2
MINSKY, MARVIN	3

b. Create an index table to organize the records by publication date.

5. Describe a situation in which data visualization or sonification might be the most effective way to present information. In your description, include a list of the data, indicate how you would use visualization or sonification to represent it, and indicate the type of decisions that the output would be used to make.

6. Take the first step in the normalization process by eliminating the data redundancy in the file below. If necessary, create new record types. Assume you are working with a relational database model.

Invoice file

Invoice Number	Customer Name	Address	Date	Item Number	Item	Price	Number Purchased
0010	Jack Wei	503 S. HWY 7	09/01/1994	56887	B&D Hammer	17.69	1
0010	Jack Wei	503 S. HWY 7	09/01/1994	67433	Sand Paper - Fine	4.98	2
0010	Jack Wei	503 S. HWY 7	09/01/1994	2230B	CTR Sink	2.49	1
0011	Sally Zachman	834 N. Front St.	09/01/1994	56887	B&D Hammer	17.69	1
0012	Brad Koski	2910 52nd St.	09/02/1994	56887	B&D Hammer	17.69	2
0012	Brad Koski	2910 52nd St.	09/02/1994	4311A	9-inch Brush	7.89	1

L   A   B   S

SQL Lab

L A B

SQL

Double-click the SQL Lab icon in the New Perspectives window to launch the SQL Lab. After you read the list of activities on the preview screen, click the Continue button. Look at the labels in Figure 9-32 to familiarize yourself with the parts of the SQL Lab window.

Figure 9-32

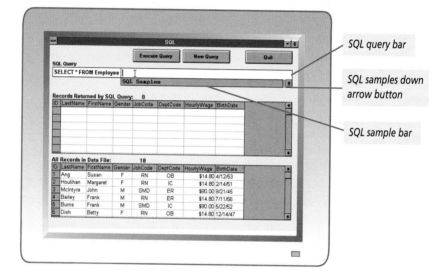

In the first part of the Lab, you will use some sample queries to locate data in the Midtown General Hospital database. As you use the sample queries, see if you can figure out the syntax for typing in SQL queries. In Part 2 of the Lab, you will type in your own queries.

SQL Lab Part 1. To complete Part 1 of the SQL Lab, carefully follow these steps:

1. Notice that the partial SQL command in the SQL Query bar reads "SELECT * FROM Employee." This part of the command means that you want to select certain records from a database called Employee. This will be the first part of every command you use, so it appears permanently on the command bar in this Lab to save you typing time. The words SELECT and FROM are capitalized to show you they are SQL command words; however, SQL is not case sensitive, so it will accept commands in either uppercase or lowercase. Suppose you want to know the names of all the employees who work as RNs.

2. Click the down arrow button on the SQL Samples bar to see a list of sample SQL queries. The first query on the list asks for all the records with RN as the job code. Notice that RN is enclosed in single quotes because it is text, not a value.

3. Click the sample, **WHERE JobCode = 'RN'** to select it. Let's see what happens when you execute this query.

4. Click the **Execute Query** button. The query locates, or "returns," five records. Ang, Houlihan, Bailey, Dish, and Jackson are the RNs in the database.

5. Now suppose you want to know the gender of all the employees who make less than $9.50 per hour. Click the down arrow button on the sample query bar to display the list of sample queries.

6. Click the sample **WHERE HourlyWage < 9.50** to select it. Next, click the **Execute Query** button. The query returns four records: three are females and one is a male.

Use the sample queries to answer questions 7 through 10:

7. How many employees make between $10 and $15 per hour?

8. What are the names of the RNs who work in the OB (obstetrics) department?

9. If you use the ORDER command from the list of sample queries to arrange the employee records alphabetically by last name, who is the last employee on the list and how much does he or she make per hour?

10. If you arrange the RNs by department and by last name, who is the first employee on the list?

SQL Lab Part 2. Follow these steps to complete Part 2 of the SQL Lab:

1. Click the **New Query** button to erase the query displayed on the white query line.

2. Click inside the white query line to position the insertion point.

3. What query would you use to find out which departments have male nurses? You want to find all the male nurses, so type the query **WHERE JobCode = 'RN' AND Gender = 'M'**, then click the **Execute Query** button.

   Why don't you need to include DeptCode in your query? Because when the query returns with a list of the male RNs, you can look at the DeptCode field to find out their departments. As it turns out, there is only one male nurse and he works in ER, the emergency room.

For the questions that follow, indicate the answer and the query you used to find the answer:

4. What are the names of the staff physicians? (*Hint*: The staff physician JobCode is SMD.)

5. Who is the youngest licensed practical nurse (LPN)?

6. How many LPNs are males?

7. How many females earn more than $20 per hour?

8. Who is the oldest member of the nursing staff? (*Hint*: Be sure you check both RNs and LPNs.)

9. How many employees work either in intensive care (IC) or in the emergency room (ER)?

10. What is the job code of the highest-paid employee?

11. What are the last names of the female employees who make between $10 and $15 per hour?

Presenting Information Using Sound Lab

L A B

PRESENTING INFORMATION USING SOUND

This Lab shows you how information can be presented using sound. Imagine that you work in a water-quality lab that processes many water samples each day. You have a machine that analyzes the level of 14 chemical elements, compounds, or bacteria for each sample, including the level of acidity (pH), iron (Fe), and lead (Pb). The machine shows you the levels for each sample, but you must determine which samples have acceptable levels and which do not. Is there an easy way for you to tell without looking at the data for each sample? Let's try the Lab and find out.

To complete this Lab, carefully follow each of the numbered steps.

1. Double-click the icon for the Presenting Information Using Sound Lab, then click the **Continue** button.

2. Notice that the first item on the Location list is "Normal Results."

3. Click **Normal Results** to highlight it. This data represents a water-quality sample with acceptable levels on each of the 14 tests.

4. Click the **Play Data** button to hear the test results. Each note in the song represents the data from a test of a particular element, a compound, or bacteria. If the song sounds "right," the water sample is entirely within acceptable ranges.

5. Click **Dead River** from the Location list. To find out if this sample is within acceptable limits, click the **Play Data** button. It sounds like Dead River is within acceptable limits.

6. Next, click **Deer Lake**, then click the **Play Data** button. This sample sounds "wrong," so it is not within acceptable limits for water quality.

7. To see which test results are not within the acceptable limits, click the **View Data** button. A table of data appears. The first column of the table lists the chemical elements that were tested. The second column lists the test results. The third and fourth columns show you the acceptable range. For example, the first test determines the pH, or acidity, of the water. An acceptable pH falls between the minimum value of 6.5 and the maximum value of 8.5. If any result is not within the acceptable range, it appears in red in the table and results in "sour" notes.

8. Listen to the data for Yellow Dog River, Lake Beaufort, and Perch Lake, then answer the following questions:

   a. Is the water from the Yellow Dog River acceptable according to these water quality standards? If not, which elements are not within acceptable limits?

   b. Is the water from Lake Beaufort acceptable according to these water quality standards? If not, which elements are not within acceptable limits?

   c. Is the water from Perch Lake acceptable according to these water quality standards? If not, which elements are not within acceptable limits?

R E S O U R C E S

■ Codd, E. F. "A Relational Model of Data for Large Shared Data Banks." *Communications of the ACM* 13(6), June 1970.

Codd developed the relational database model in 1970 and described it in this article. Although the relational database model was thought to be impractical during the 1970s, modern computer architecture now provides the power necessary for its implementation.

■ Date, C. J. *An Introduction to Database Systems*, 5th ed. Reading, MA: Addison-Wesley, 1990.

Date's book is a classic on database management. Date has worked extensively on many database-related theories, including a set of standards for the SQL query language.

■ Rob, P., and C. Coronel, *Database Systems: Design, Implementation, and Management*. Belmont, CA: Wadsworth, 1993.

This textbook provides a basic introduction to files and databases, with good coverage of object-oriented methodology appropriate for students who are planning to become computer information systems professionals.

■ Stix, G. "Earcons: 'Audification' may add a new dimension to computers." *Scientific American*, July 1993.

If you are interested in more information about the emerging field of sonification, or audification, you will find an interesting discussion in this article.

C H A P T E R   P R E V I E W

When you have completed this chapter you should be able to answer the following questions:

- How do I begin the process of writing a computer program?
- What are the characteristics of a well-composed problem statement?
- What is an algorithm, and how does it relate to computer programming?
- What is the difference between pseudocode and structured English?
- What are control structures, and how are they typically used in computer programs?
- Why do good programmers avoid the GOTO command?
- How can you test a program to be sure it works?
- Why do you need to document the programs you write?
- What general characteristics help computer scientists classify computer languages?

COMPUTER PROGRAMMING

It's Tuesday night. You and a group of friends are studying late when the munchies strike. Pizza sounds really good, but when you and your friends pool all your money, you have a grand total of $24.63—not much to feed eight hungry students. You all agree to call several pizza places to compare prices. One of your friends, looking up from her financial management text, says, "Maximize pizza, minimize cost!"

You call VanGo's Pizzeria first and find out that they have a 14" round pizza with two toppings for $12.00. Next, you call a pizza place named The Venice and discover that they have a 12" square pizza for $10.99. Which one is the better deal? You search for a calculator but can't find one. Your friend with the pocket protector offers to let you use his notebook computer so you can write a program to compare pizza prices. Now what?

In this chapter, you'll learn about computer programming and find out how to write a program that compares pizza prices. You can apply what you learn about the pizza program to many different problems that a computer can help you solve. You will also pick up the thread on software engineering introduced in Chapter 8 and learn about the methodology programmers use to specify, code, and test computer programs. Your understanding of this methodology will be useful if you become involved in software development as a programmer or as a computer user.

Software Engineering

Software engineering is the systematic approach to the development, operation, maintenance, and retirement of software. As you learned in Chapter 8, software engineering takes place as part of the system development life cycle (SDLC). The jobs of the systems analyst and the software engineer overlap, but they are not the same. A systems analyst plans an entire information system, including hardware, software, procedures, personnel, and data. A **software engineer** focuses on the software component of an information system: on software design, coding, and testing. Let's look at the process of software engineering, beginning with problem statements and algorithms, which form the foundation for software design.

Problems and Algorithms

In Chapter 2, you learned that a **computer program** is a set of detailed, step-by-step instructions that tell a computer how to solve a problem or carry out a task. You also briefly studied a short program, written in the Pascal programming language, designed to convert feet and inches into centimeters. Where do these instructions come from? Although we speak of "writing a computer program," it is not exactly the same process as writing a letter. When you write a letter, you usually compose it "on the fly"; you are not particularly concerned about the structure, nor are you particularly concerned with efficiency, as long as you communicate your message.

People can tolerate some degree of ambiguity when they communicate. Suppose you write your friend a letter that includes the following statement: "Remember to water my plants and lock the doors. Oh, and don't forget to feed the fish."

You assume your friend knows which plants to water and how much water to use, you hope your friend remembers what to feed the fish, and you assume your friend will feed the fish before leaving the house and locking the door.

Computers don't deal with ambiguity as well as people. So, when you give the computer a set of instructions, you need to be more explicit than you would be with a person. Consequently, you must think of computer programming as a process that is more structured than writing a casual letter to a friend. Computer programming begins with a problem statement, which is the basis for an algorithm. An algorithm, in turn, is the basis for program instructions. Let's take a closer look at what we mean by problem statement, algorithm, and program instructions.

Problem Statements

Problems that you might try to solve using a computer often begin as questions. For example: "Which pizza place has the best deal?" But this question is not stated in a way that helps you devise a way for the computer to arrive at an answer. The question is vague. It doesn't tell you what information is available for determining the best deal. Do you know the price of several pizzas at different pizza places? Do you know the size of the pizzas? Do you know how many toppings are included in the price? The question "Which pizza place has the best deal?" does not explain what "best deal" means: Is it merely the cheapest pizza? Is it the pizza that gives you the most toppings for the dollar? Is it the biggest pizza you can get for the $24.63 that you and your friends managed to scrape together? Study Figure 10-1 and see if you can pose a problem statement that is better than the initial vague question, "Which pizza place has the best deal?"

Figure 10-1
The pizza problem

A well-posed problem statement has three characteristics:

- It specifies any assumptions that define the scope of the problem.
- It clearly specifies the known information.
- It specifies when the problem has been solved.

In a problem statement, an **assumption** is something that you accept as true in order to proceed with the program design. For example, in the pizza problem, you can make the assumption that there are two pizzas you want to compare. Further, you can assume that some pizzas are round and others are square. To simplify the problem, you might make the additional assumption that none of the pizzas are rectangular, that is, none will have one side longer than the other. This simplifies the problem because you only need to deal with the "size" of a pizza, rather than the "length" and "width" of a pizza. A fourth assumption for the pizza problem is that the pizzas you compare have the same toppings. Finally, you assume that the pizza with the lowest cost per square inch is the best buy.

The **known information** in a problem statement is the information you supply the computer to help solve a problem. For the pizza problem, the known information includes the prices, the shapes, and the sizes of pizzas from two pizza places. The known information is often included in the problem statement as "givens"; for example, a problem statement might include the phrase, "given the prices, the shapes, and the sizes of two pizzas. . . ."

After you specify the known information in a problem statement, you specify how you will determine when the problem has been solved. Usually this means specifying the output you expect. Of course, you cannot specify the answer in the problem statement—you won't know, for example, whether VanGo's Pizzeria or The Venice has the best deal before you run the program. But you can specify that the computer should output which pizza is the best deal. Suppose you and your friends decide that the best deal means getting the biggest pizza at the lowest price; in other words, the best deal is the pizza that has the cheapest price per square inch. In this case, a 10" square cheese pizza for $5.00 ($.05 per inch) is a better deal than an 8" round pizza for $4.50 ($.07 per square inch). The problem is solved, therefore, when the computer has calculated the price per square inch for both pizzas, compared the prices, and printed a message indicating which one has the lowest price per square inch. You could write this part of the problem statement as "The computer will calculate the price per square inch of each pizza, then print a message indicating whether Pizza 1 or Pizza 2 has the lowest price per square inch."

So after you have thought carefully about the problem, you have a list of assumptions, a list of known information, and a description of what you expect as output. The complete problem statement is:

> Assuming that there are two pizzas to compare, that both pizzas contain the same toppings, and that the pizzas could be round or square, and given the prices, the shapes, and the sizes of the two pizzas, the computer will calculate the price per square inch of each pizza, then print a message indicating which pizza has the lowest price per square inch.

This problem statement is rather lengthy. The following format for the problem statement is easier to understand:

ASSUMPTIONS:

There are two pizzas to compare, Pizza 1 and Pizza 2
The pizzas have the same toppings
The pizzas could be round or square
Neither of the pizzas is rectangular
The pizza with the lowest cost per square inch is the "best buy"

GIVEN:

The prices of two pizzas in dollars
The shape of each pizza (round or square)
The size of each pizza

COMPUTE:

The price per square inch of each pizza

DISPLAY:

"Pizza 1 is the best buy" if Pizza 1 has the lowest price per square inch
"Pizza 2 is the best buy" if Pizza 2 has the lowest price per square inch
"Neither is the best buy" if both pizzas have the same price per square inch

Now that you have learned how to write a problem statement, we can move to the next step in the programming process—creating an algorithm.

Algorithms

An **algorithm** is a set of steps for carrying out a task. An algorithm is an abstract idea, but it can be written down and it can be implemented. For example, the algorithm for cooking up a batch of macaroni and cheese is a set of steps that includes boiling water, cooking the macaroni in the water, and adding cheese. The algorithm is written down, or expressed, in the form of instructions in a recipe. You can implement the algorithm by following the instructions.

An important characteristic of a correctly formulated algorithm is that by carefully following the steps, you are guaranteed to accomplish the task for which the algorithm was designed. So, if you carefully follow the recipe on the macaroni package, you should be guaranteed of a successful batch of macaroni and cheese.

An algorithm for a computer program is the set of steps that explains how to begin with the known information that is specified in a problem statement and manipulate that information to arrive at a solution. An algorithm for a computer program is typically first written in a format that is not specific to a particular computer or programming language. This way, the software engineer focuses on formulating a correct algorithm, rather than on expressing the algorithm using the commands of a computer programming language. In a later phase of the software development process, the programmer translates the algorithm into instructions written in a computer programming language so the algorithm can be implemented by a computer.

When you are just beginning to work with computer programming, it might seem difficult to determine the amount of detail required to express an algorithm. For example, you might wonder if your algorithm needs to specify the steps necessary to do addition—do you need to explain how to "carry"? The detail necessary for the algorithm depends on the computer language you intend to use to write the program. As you become familiar with a particular computer language—the commands that the language contains and what each command does—you will gain an understanding of the level of detail required. For the pizza problem, let's suppose that you will use the BASIC computer language. Study Figure 10-2 to understand the level of instructions that are appropriate for algorithms that are the basis for BASIC programs.

ALGORITHM TASK	PIZZA PROBLEM ALGORITHM EXAMPLE
Assign a value to a variable	Size = 12
Evaluate an expression or "solve an equation"	SquareInchPrice = Price / SquareInches
Ask for information (input) from the user	Enter the Price of a pizza
Display or print the results of calculations	Display the SquareInchPrice
Make decisions	If the pizza is square, calculate SquareInches by multiplying the Size * Size
Repeat some instructions	Repeat the price calculations for as many pizzas as the user wants

Figure 10-2

A sample of the kinds of tasks an algorithm for a BASIC program can specify

To design an algorithm, you might begin by solving the problem yourself and recording the steps you take. If you take this route, remember that to solve the pizza problem you have to obtain initial information on the cost, the size, and the shape of the pizzas. The computer also needs this initial information, so part of your algorithm must specify how the computer gets it. When the pizza program runs, it should request the user to enter the initial information needed to solve the problem. Your algorithm might begin like this:

Ask the user for the shape of the first pizza and hold it in RAM as Shape1.
Ask the user for the price of the first pizza and hold it in RAM as Price1.
Ask the user for the size of the first pizza and hold it in RAM as Size1.

Next, your algorithm should specify how to manipulate this information. You want to calculate the price per square inch, but an instruction like "Calculate the price per square inch" neither specifies how to do the calculation nor does it deal with the fact that you must perform different calculations for square and round pizzas. A more appropriate set of instructions is shown in Figure 10-3:

Figure 10-3
Algorithm for calculating the price per square inch

To calculate the area of a square pizza, multiply the length of one side by the length of the other side. The sides are the same size in a square, so you can use the formula $Size1 * Size1$.

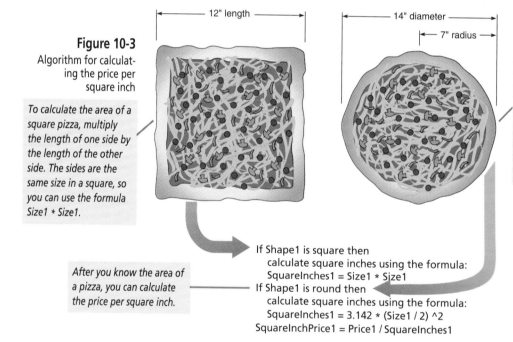

— 12" length —

— 14" diameter —
— 7" radius —

The area of a circle is calculated using the formula πr^2. π is approximately 3.142. r^2 is the square of the radius of the circle. The size of a pizza is its diameter, so you need to divide the diameter by 2 to get the radius, using $Size1 / 2$. Then you need to square the radius. ^{2} is the notation you use on a computer to indicate the exponent 2.

After you know the area of a pizza, you can calculate the price per square inch.

If Shape1 is square then
    calculate square inches using the formula:
    SquareInches1 = Size1 * Size1
If Shape1 is round then
    calculate square inches using the formula:
    SquareInches1 = 3.142 * (Size1 / 2) ^2
SquareInchPrice1 = Price1 / SquareInches1

The algorithm you have designed so far calculates the price per square inch of one pizza. The algorithm should specify a similar process for calculating the price per square inch of the second pizza:

Ask the user for the shape of the second pizza and hold it in RAM as Shape2.
Ask the user for the price of the second pizza and hold it in RAM as Price2.
Ask the user for the size of the second pizza and hold it in RAM as Size2.

If Shape2 is square then
    calculate the square inches using the formula:
    *SquareInches2 = Size2 * Size2*

If Shape2 is round then
  calculate the square inches using the formula:
  *SquareInches2 = 3.142 * (Size2 / 2) ^2*

SquareInchPrice2 = Price2 / SquareInches2

Finally, the algorithm should specify how the computer decides what to display as the solution. You want the computer to display a message telling you which pizza has the lowest square inch cost, so your algorithm should include something like this:

If SquareInchPrice1< SquareInchPrice2 then
  display the message "Pizza 1 is the best deal."

If SquareInchPrice2 < SquareInchPrice1 then
  display the message "Pizza 2 is the best deal."

But don't forget to indicate what you want the program to do if the price per square inch of both pizzas is the same:

If SquareInchPrice1 = SquareInchPrice2 then
  display the message "Both pizzas are the same deal."

The complete algorithm for the pizza problem is shown in Figure 10-4.

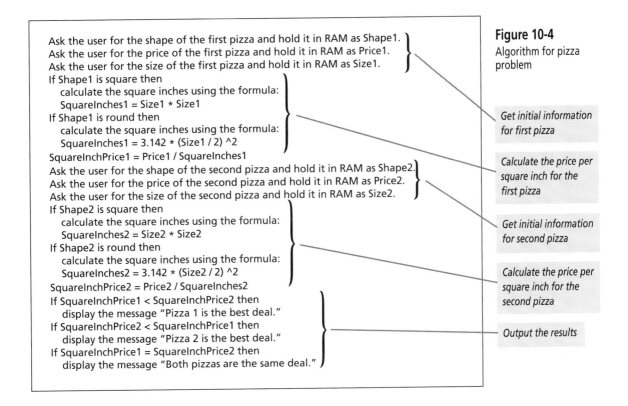

Ask the user for the shape of the first pizza and hold it in RAM as Shape1.
Ask the user for the price of the first pizza and hold it in RAM as Price1.
Ask the user for the size of the first pizza and hold it in RAM as Size1.
If Shape1 is square then
  calculate the square inches using the formula:
  SquareInches1 = Size1 * Size1
If Shape1 is round then
  calculate the square inches using the formula:
  SquareInches1 = 3.142 * (Size1 / 2) ^2
SquareInchPrice1 = Price1 / SquareInches1
Ask the user for the shape of the second pizza and hold it in RAM as Shape2.
Ask the user for the price of the second pizza and hold it in RAM as Price2.
Ask the user for the size of the second pizza and hold it in RAM as Size2.
If Shape2 is square then
  calculate the square inches using the formula:
  SquareInches2 = Size2 * Size2
If Shape2 is round then
  calculate the square inches using the formula:
  SquareInches2 = 3.142 * (Size2 / 2) ^2
SquareInchPrice2 = Price2 / SquareInches2
If SquareInchPrice1 < SquareInchPrice2 then
  display the message "Pizza 1 is the best deal."
If SquareInchPrice2 < SquareInchPrice1 then
  display the message "Pizza 2 is the best deal."
If SquareInchPrice1 = SquareInchPrice2 then
  display the message "Both pizzas are the same deal."

Figure 10-4
Algorithm for pizza problem

Get initial information for first pizza

Calculate the price per square inch for the first pizza

Get initial information for second pizza

Calculate the price per square inch for the second pizza

Output the results

Expressing an Algorithm

You can express an algorithm in several different ways. In Figure 10-4, the algorithm for the pizza problem is expressed in structured English. You should remember from Chapter 8 that **structured English** uses a specific subset of English words to describe a process.

Another way to express an algorithm is with pseudocode. **Pseudocode** is a notational system for algorithms that has been described as "a mixture of English and your favorite programming language." Compare the pseudocode for the pizza problem in Figure 10-5 with the structured English in Figure 10-4 to understand some of the differences between these two ways of expressing an algorithm.

Figure 10-5

Pseudocode for
pizza program

```
display prompts for entering shape, price, and size
input Shape1, Price1, Size1
if Shape1 = square then
    SquareInches1←Size1 * Size1
if Shape1 = round then
    SquareInches1←3.142 * (Size1 / 2) ^2
SquareInchPrice1←Price1 / SquareInches1

display prompts for entering shape, price, and size
input Shape2, Price2, Size2
if Shape2 = square then
    SquareInches2←Size2 * Size2
if Shape2 = round then
    SquareInches2←3.142 * (Size2 / 2) ^2
SquareInchPrice2←Price2 / SquareInches2

if SquareInchPrice1 < SquareInchPrice2 then
    output "Pizza1 is the best deal."
if SquareInchPrice2 < SquareInchPrice1 then
    output "Pizza2 is the best deal."
if SquareInchPrice1 = SquareInchPrice2 then
    output "Both pizzas are the same deal."
```

A third way to express an algorithm is to use a flow chart. A **flow chart** is a graphical representation of the way a computer should progress from one instruction to the next when it performs a task. The flow chart for the pizza problem is shown in Figure 10-6.

Another way to express an algorithm is to define the objects that the computer must manipulate, then specify the method for manipulating each object. This way of expressing an algorithm is useful for designing object-oriented programs, which you will learn more about later in this chapter. Figure 10-7 shows a description of one of the objects for the pizza program.

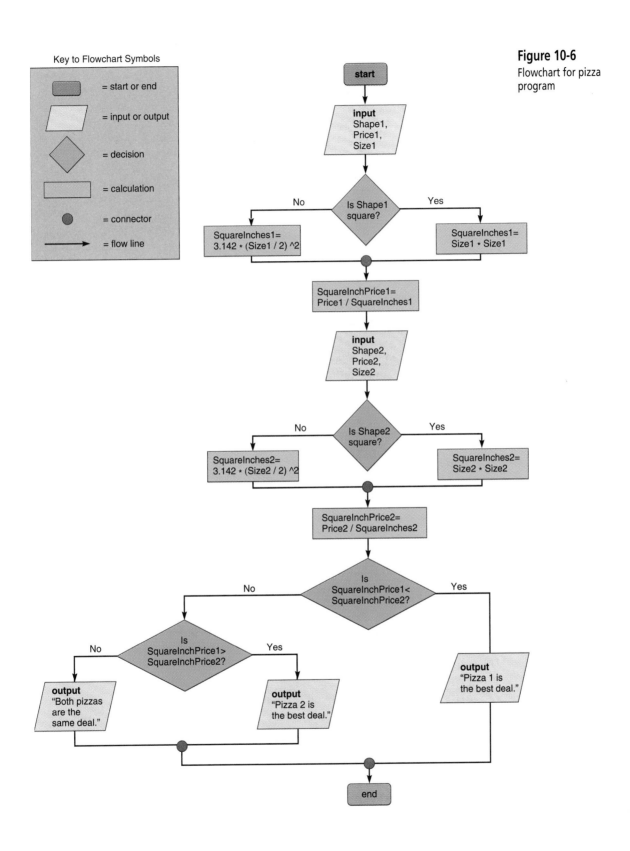

Figure 10-6
Flowchart for pizza program

Key to Flowchart Symbols

= start or end
= input or output
= decision
= calculation
= connector
= flow line

start

input
Shape1,
Price1,
Size1

Is Shape1 square?
No — SquareInches1= 3.142 * (Size1 / 2) ^2
Yes — SquareInches1= Size1 * Size1

SquareInchPrice1= Price1 / SquareInches1

input
Shape2,
Price2,
Size2

Is Shape2 square?
No — SquareInches2= 3.142 * (Size2 / 2) ^2
Yes — SquareInches2= Size2 * Size2

SquareInchPrice2= Price2 / SquareInches2

Is SquareInchPrice1< SquareInchPrice2?
No — Is SquareInchPrice1> SquareInchPrice2?
Yes — **output** "Pizza 1 is the best deal."

Is SquareInchPrice1> SquareInchPrice2?
No — **output** "Both pizzas are the same deal."
Yes — **output** "Pizza 2 is the best deal."

end

Figure 10-7

Object descriptions for the pizza program

Object: Calculate Best Deal
Type: Button
Appearance:

Calculate Best Deal

Method:
IF Shape1 = "square" **THEN** SquareInches1 = Size1 * Size1
IF Shape1 = "round" **THEN** SquareInches1 = 3.142 * (Size1 / 2) ^2
SquareInchPrice1 = Price1 / SquareInches1
IF Shape2 = "square" **THEN** SquareInches2 = Size2 * Size2
IF Shape2 = "round" **THEN** SquareInches2 = 3.142 * (Size2 / 2) ^2
SquareInchPrice2 = Price2 / SquareInches2
IF SquareInchPrice1 < SquareInchPrice2 **THEN** BestDeal = "Pizza 1 is the best deal."
IF SquareInchPrice2 < SquareInchPrice1 **THEN** BestDeal = "Pizza 2 is the best deal."
IF SquareInchPrice1 = SquareInchPrice2 **THEN** BestDeal = "Both pizzas are the same deal."

Coding Computer Programs

L A B

VISUAL PROGRAMMING

A problem statement and an algorithm are often combined into a document called the **program specification**, which is essentially a blueprint for a computer program. When the program specification is complete, you can begin coding the program. **Coding** is the process of using a computer language to express an algorithm. With many computer programming languages, the coding process means entering commands. With other computer programming languages, you enter or select the characteristics of objects or you enter descriptive statements about the objects.

To code the pizza algorithm using the BASIC computer language, you type a list of commands. Look at the completed program in Figure 10-8 and study the callouts to get a general understanding of the elements of a computer program. After you study the figure, we'll take a closer look at the details.

Program Sequence and Control Structures

The normal pattern of program execution is for a computer to perform each instruction in sequence. The first instruction in the program is executed first, then the second instruction, and so on through the rest of the instructions in the program. Here is a simple program written in the QBASIC computer language that outputs "This is the first line," then outputs "This is the second line."

```
PRINT "This is the first line."
PRINT "This is the second line."
END
```

Although most modern programming languages do not use line numbers, older programming languages, such as the original version of BASIC, required programmers to number each instruction like this:

```
100 PRINT "This is the first line."
200 PRINT "This is the second line."
300 END
```

If line numbers are used, a computer begins executing the instruction with the lowest number, then proceeds to the instruction with the next highest number, and so on.

Figure 10-8
BASIC code for the
pizza program

The program is written as a list of steps. The computer executes the steps starting at the top of the list.

Command words are boldface

Remarks that begin with REM explain each section of the program.

Data is stored in variables, or memory locations, in RAM. The variable Shape1$ stores text, such as the word "round." The $ indicates a text variable. Other variables, such as Price1, store numbers, and the variable name does not include a $.

```
REM  The Pizza Program
REM  This program tells you which of two pizzas is the best deal
REM  by calculating the price per square inch of each pizza.

REM  Collect initial information for first pizza.
INPUT "Enter the shape of pizza one:"; Shape1$
INPUT "Enter the price of pizza one:"; Price1
INPUT "Enter the size of pizza one:"; Size1

REM  Calculate price per square inch for first pizza.

REM  If the first pizza is square, calculate the square inches by multiplying one side by
the other.
IF Shape1$ = "square" THEN SquareInches1 = Size1 * Size1

REM  If the first pizza is round, calculate the number of square inches where
REM  pi = 3.142, size / 2 = radius, and (size / 2) ^2 = radius squared:
IF Shape1$ = "round" THEN SquareInches1 = 3.142 * (Size1 / 2) ^2
SquareInchPrice1 = Price1 / SquareInches1

REM  Collect initial information for second pizza.
INPUT "Enter the shape of pizza two:"; Shape2$
INPUT "Enter the price of pizza two:"; Price2
INPUT "Enter the size of pizza two:"; Size2

REM  Calculate price per square inch for second pizza.
IF Shape2$ = "square" THEN SquareInches2 = Size2 * Size2
IF Shape2$ = "round" THEN SquareInches2 = 3.142 * (Size2 / 2) ^2
SquareInchPrice2 = Price2 / SquareInches2

REM  Decide which pizza is the best deal and display results.
IF SquareInchPrice1 < SquareInchPrice2 THEN Message$ = "Pizza 1 is the best deal."
IF SquareInchPrice2 < SquareInchPrice1 THEN Message$ = "Pizza 2 is the best deal."
IF SquareInchPrice1 = SquareInchPrice2 THEN Message$ = "Both pizzas are the same
deal."
PRINT Message$
END
```

Some algorithms specify that a program execute instructions in an order different from the sequence in which they are listed, skip some instructions under certain circumstances, or repeat instructions. **Control structures** are instructions that specify the sequence in which a program is executed. There are three types of control structures: sequence controls, selection controls, and repetition controls.

Sequence Controls

A **sequence control structure** changes the sequence, or order, in which instructions are executed by directing the computer to execute an instruction elsewhere in the program. In the following simple QBASIC program, the GOTO command tells the computer to jump directly to the instruction labeled "Finish." The program will never execute the command PRINT "This is the second line."

```
PRINT "This is the first line."
GOTO Finish
PRINT "This is the second line."
Finish: PRINT "All done!"
END
```

Although it is the simplest control structure, GOTO and its equivalents are rarely used by skilled programmers because these statements can lead to programs that are difficult to understand and maintain. In 1968, the journal *Communications of the ACM* published a now famous letter from Edsger Dijkstra, called "Goto Statement Considered Harmful." In his letter, Dijkstra explained that injudicious use of the GOTO statement in programs makes it difficult for other programmers to understand the underlying algorithm, which in turn means that such programs are difficult to correct, improve, or revise. You might think that a few GOTOs in a program are hardly harmful, but just take a look at Figure 10-9 and try to determine the output of the program when a user responds to the first question with "black" and to the next question with "Yes."

Figure 10-9
Too many GOTOs

```
100     PRINT "What color is Napoleon's white horse?"
200     INPUT Color$
300     IF Color$ = "White" THEN GOTO 500
400     IF Color$ <> "White" THEN GOTO 800
500     PRINT "How did you know the answer?"
600     INPUT Response$
700     GOTO 1200
800     PRINT "No, that's not right. Do you want to try again?"
900     INPUT Response$
1000    IF Response$ = "Yes" THEN GOTO 100
1100    IF Response$ = "No" THEN GOTO 1300
1200    PRINT "You did very well."
1300    END
```

Experienced programmers prefer to use sequence controls other than GOTO to transfer program execution to a subroutine, procedure, module, or function. **Subroutines**, **procedures**, **modules**, and **functions** are sections of code that are part of a program, but are not included in the sequential execution path. Figure 10-10 shows the execution path of a program that uses the GOSUB command to transfer execution to a subroutine.

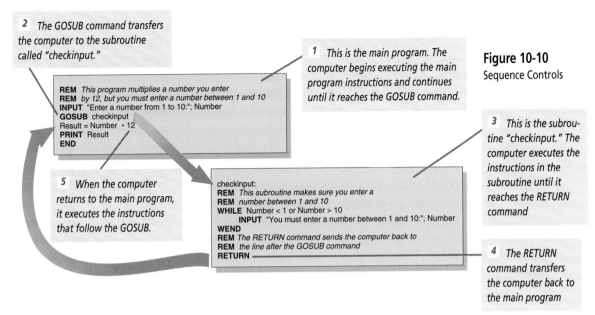

Figure 10-10
Sequence Controls

2 The GOSUB command transfers the computer to the subroutine called "checkinput."

1 This is the main program. The computer begins executing the main program instructions and continues until it reaches the GOSUB command.

```
REM  This program multiplies a number you enter
REM  by 12, but you must enter a number between 1 and 10
INPUT "Enter a number from 1 to 10:"; Number
GOSUB checkinput
Result = Number * 12
PRINT  Result
END
```

3 This is the subroutine "checkinput." The computer executes the instructions in the subroutine until it reaches the RETURN command

5 When the computer returns to the main program, it executes the instructions that follow the GOSUB.

```
checkinput:
  REM  This subroutine makes sure you enter a
  REM  number between 1 and 10
  WHILE Number < 1 or Number > 10
    INPUT "You must enter a number between 1 and 10:"; Number
  WEND
  REM The RETURN command sends the computer back to
  REM the line after the GOSUB command
  RETURN
```

4 The RETURN command transfers the computer back to the main program

Selection Controls

A **selection control structure**, also referred to as a **decision structure** or **branching structure**, tells a computer what to do based on whether a condition is true or false. A simple example of a selection control structure is the IF..THEN command. The following program uses the IF..THEN command to decide whether a number entered is greater than 10. If the number is greater than 10, the computer prints "That number is greater than 10!" If the number is not greater than 10, the program does not print this message.

```
INPUT "Enter a number from 1 to 10:"; Number
IF Number > 10 THEN PRINT "That number is greater than 10!"
END
```

Repetition Controls

A **repetition control**, also referred to as a **loop** or **iteration**, repeats one or more instructions until a certain condition is met. In QBASIC, one of the most commonly used loop commands is FOR..NEXT. The following simple QBASIC program uses the FOR..NEXT command to print a message three times.

```
FOR N = 1 TO 3
  PRINT "There's no place like home"
NEXT N
END
```

The FOR..NEXT command is used to repeat a series of instructions a specified number of times. To see how this works, pretend that you are the computer executing this FOR..NEXT loop. The variable N is a RAM location in the computer. You can use the box labeled N in the margin. As the computer, you would also have a screen on which to display output. Use a piece of note paper to represent the screen.

As the computer, the first time you see the instruction FOR N = 1 TO 3, you set N equal to 1. To do this, write the number 1 in the box in the margin. You would then execute the next instruction, PRINT "There's no place like home." To do this, write the phrase "There's no place like home" on the sheet of paper that represents your output screen.

N

The instruction NEXT sends you back to the command FOR N = 1 TO 3. Because this is the second time you have executed this statement, put a 2 in the box in the margin (you can erase the 1 that was there previously). You need to check if the value in box N is greater than 3. Why do this? Because the command FOR N = 1 TO 3 means you can only continue to loop if N is 3 or less. Well, N is only 2, so you can proceed.

Go to the next instruction, which is PRINT "There's no place like home." So, write this again on the paper you're using for your output screen.

Moving on, you reach the NEXT statement again, and this sends you back to the FOR statement. Continue by changing the value in the N box to 3. Check the N box to make sure it does not contain a value greater than 3. It doesn't, so continue.

The next line instructs you to PRINT "There's no place like home," so write this again on your output screen. The NEXT statement sends you back to the FOR statement. Increase the value in the N box to 4. This time when you check if the value in N is greater than 3, it is. That means the loop is complete and you should jump to the statement past the end of the loop.

Program Testing

A computer program must be tested to ensure that it works correctly. Testing often consists of entering test data to see if the program produces correct results. If the module does not produce correct results, the programmer must examine the program for errors, correct the errors, and test the program again.

For example, to test the pizza program, you could run the program and enter data for which you have already calculated the results. Suppose you use a calculator to determine that the price per square inch of an $18.50, 15" square pizza is about $.08. One way to test the program is to run it and enter $18.50 for the price, 15 for the size, and square for the shape. The program should produce the result $.08 for the price per square inch of this pizza. If it doesn't, you know that you made an error when you wrote the program, and so you must correct the error.

But testing a single set of values is not enough. At minimum, you should test every statement at least once, and you should test every decision branch. The pizza program has two possible decision branches for calculating the price per square inch. One branch is for square pizzas, the other branch is for round pizzas. Even if you enter a set of test data for a square pizza and the program provides the correct result, you cannot assume the program is working correctly until you test it with data for a round pizza.

When you find an error, or **bug**, in a program, it might be a syntax error or it might be a run-time error. A **syntax error** is caused when an instruction does not follow the syntax rules, or grammar, of the programming language. For example, when you want to print a message, you need to use the PRINT command. The command IF AGE = 16 THEN "You can drive" will produce a syntax error because the command word PRINT is missing. The correct version of the command would be IF AGE = 16 THEN PRINT "You can drive."

Syntax errors are very common, but they are easy to detect and correct. Syntax errors can be caused by omitting a command word, misspelling a command word, or using incorrect punctuation, such as a colon (:) where a semicolon (;) is required. Many modern programming languages detect and point out syntax errors when you are in the process of coding each instruction. Because these languages show you syntax errors when you type in each line, you typically will have corrected syntax errors before you test programs written with these languages.

The other type of program bug is a run-time error. A **run-time error** is an error that shows up when you run the program. Run-time errors can be caused by an instruction that has the correct syntax, but that doesn't make any sense, or by a **logic error**, which is an error in the logic or design of the program. For example, suppose you erroneously use the < symbol and include the following command in the pizza problem:

```
IF SquareInchPrice1 < SquareInchPrice2
THEN PRINT "Pizza 2 is a better deal than Pizza 1."
```

The command produces the wrong output as a result of the logic error you introduced when you erroneously used the < sign instead of the > sign.

Logic errors can be caused by an inadequate definition of the problem or by an incorrect or incomplete solution specified by the flowchart or pseudocode. Logic errors are usually more difficult and time-consuming to identify than syntax errors.

Program Documentation

A computer program inevitably must be modified because needs change. Modifying a program is much easier if the program has been well documented. For example, suppose VanGo's Pizzeria and The Venice have both added a new rectangular pizza to their menu. In that case, you want to modify the pizza program so you can enter the dimensions of a rectangular pizza. First, you need to understand how the current program works. Although this might seem like a fairly easy task for the short pizza program, imagine trying to understand a 5000-line program that calculates income tax, especially if you weren't the person who wrote the original program. You might want some additional information to explain the logic behind the program and the formulas that the programmer devised to perform calculations.

In these situations, program documentation can help. **Program documentation** explains how a program works and how to use it. The explanation of how a program works is closely linked to the program's algorithm and the way the programmer coded the algorithm into program commands. The explanation of how to use a program includes information on how to start it, what options are available, and what data should be entered. Typically, program documentation takes two forms: remarks inserted into the program code and "written" documentation.

Program Remarks

To revise a computer program, a programmer reads through the original program to find out how it works, then makes revisions to the appropriate sections of code. It is easier to understand the original program if the person who writes it places explanatory comments in the program. These explanatory comments are referred to as **remarks** or **comments**. These remarks are ignored by the computer when it executes the program; but for programmers who must modify the program, these remarks are very handy.

A well-documented program contains initial remarks that explain the purpose of the program. These remarks contain essentially the same information as the problem statement. For example, the pizza program contains the following initial remarks:

```
REM The Pizza Program
REM This program tells you which of two pizzas is the better deal
REM by calculating the price per square inch of each pizza.
```

Remarks should also be added to the sections of a program in which the purpose of the code is not immediately clear. For example, in the pizza program, the purpose of the expression 3.142 * (size / 2) ^2 might not be immediately obvious to a programmer reading the code. Therefore, it would be helpful to have a remark preceding the expression, like this:

```
REM Calculate the number of square inches in a round pizza where
REM pi = 3.142, size / 2 = radius, and (size / 2 )^2 = radius squared:
SquareInches = 3.142 * (size / 2)^2
```

There is no hard and fast rule about when you should include a remark in a program. However, if you were to work with a group of other programmers on a project, your group might develop guidelines to ensure that remarks are used consistently throughout the code for the project. As you gain experience writing programs, you will develop a sense for appropriate use of remarks.

Written Documentation

Written documentation is external to a program and contains information about the program that is useful to both programmers and the people who use the program. Written documentation can be paper-based or in electronic format. Because documentation serves two audiences—the programmers and the users—so there are two broad categories of written documentation for computer programs: program manuals and user references.

A **program manual** contains any information about the program that might be useful to programmers, including the problem statement and algorithm. Because a program manual is a software development and maintenance tool, it is used by programmers, not users. The **user reference**, or **reference manual**, as explained in Chapter 1, contains information that helps users learn and use a computer program. Figure 10-11 lists the types of information that might be included in a program manual and a user reference.

Programming Language Characteristics

Hundreds of programming languages have been developed over the last 30 years. Some languages were developed to make the programming process more efficient and less error-prone. Some languages were developed to provide an effective command set for specific types of programs, such as business programs or scientific programs. Other languages were created specifically as teaching tools.

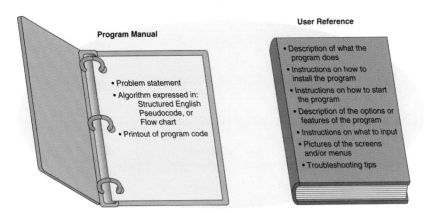

Figure 10-11
Program documentation

Programming languages have characteristics that describe how they work and provide information about the types of computing tasks for which they are appropriate. For example, PASCAL can be described as a high-level, procedural, compiled language. When you need to select a language to use for a program, it is useful to understand some of the general characteristics of programming languages and the advantages or disadvantages of these characteristics.

Procedural Languages

Languages with procedural characteristics are referred to as **procedural languages**. In a procedural language, programs are composed of a series of statements that tell the computer *how* to perform the processes for a specific task. BASIC, the language that you used for the pizza program, is a procedural language. The instructions tell the computer exactly what to do: display a message on the screen asking the user to enter the shape of the pizza; display a message asking for the size of the pizza; display a message asking for the price of the pizza; if the shape is square, calculate the square inch price with the formula SquareInchPrice = Price/Square Inches, and so forth.

As you might guess, procedural languages are well-suited for programs that follow a step-by-step algorithm. Programs created with procedural languages have a starting point and an ending point. The flow of execution from the start to the end is essentially linear; that is, the computer begins at the beginning and executes the prescribed series of instructions until it reaches the end, as shown in Figure 10-12 on the following page.

Declarative Languages

A **declarative language** lets a programmer write a program by specifying a set of statements and rules that define the conditions for resolving a problem. The language has a built-in method for considering the rules and determining a solution.

Figure 10-12
Procedural language

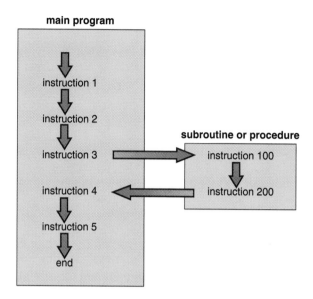

Unlike programs that are created using a procedural language, programs created with a declarative language do not tell the computer how to solve a problem. Instead, a program created with a declarative language describes what the problem is. For example, Figure 10-13 contains a short program written in the Prolog language that describes several people and determines which of these people have a sister in the list.

Figure 10-13
Prolog program

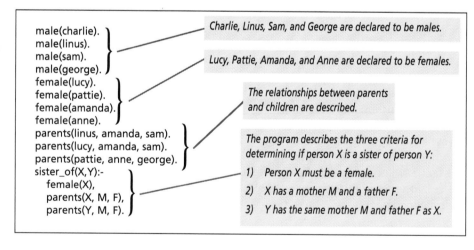

Describing a problem and the rules that lead to a solution places an emphasis on words rather than on mathematical formulas. For this reason, declarative languages are useful for programs that manipulate ideas and concepts, rather than numbers.

Low-Level Languages

A **low-level language** requires a programmer to write instructions for the lowest level of the computer system, that is, for specific hardware elements such as the processor, registers, and RAM locations. A low-level language is useful in situations when a programmer needs to directly manipulate what happens at the hardware level. Low-level languages are typically used to write system software such as compilers, operating systems, and device drivers.

Each instruction in a low-level language usually corresponds to a single instruction for the processor. Recall that in Chapter 4 you saw how an assembly language instruction, such as MOV REG1 6000, tells a computer to move a number from a RAM location into a register. When a low-level language is used, several instructions are necessary to tell the computer how to do even simple operations, such as add two numbers together. Figure 10-14 shows a section of a program, written in a low-level language, that adds two numbers together.

ASSEMBLY LANGUAGE INSTRUCTIONS	EXPLANATION OF INSTRUCTIONS	COMPUTER ACTION
LDA 5	Load 5 in the accumulator	Accumulator 5
STA NUM1	Store the 5 in a memory location called NUM1	Accumulator 5 → NUM1 5
LDA 4	Load 4 in the accumulator	Accumulator 4
ADD NUM1	Add the contents of memory location NUM1 to the number in the accumulator	Accumulator 9
STA TOTAL	Store the sum in a memory location called TOTAL	Accumulator 9 → TOTAL 9
END	Stop program execution	

Figure 10-14
Assembly language program

A **machine language** is a low-level language in binary code that the computer can execute directly. Machine languages are very difficult for humans to understand and manipulate. They were primarily used in the earliest days of computer development when other programming languages were not available.

High-Level Languages

A **high-level language** allows a programmer to use instructions that are more like human language, such as the BASIC command, PRINT "Please wait. . . ." When high-level languages were originally conceived in the 1950s, computer scientists thought that they would eliminate programming errors. This was not to be the case—syntax and logical errors are possible even with high-level languages. However, high-level languages significantly reduce programming errors and make it possible to write programs in less time than when using low-level languages.

Compiled Languages

A **compiled language** uses a compiler to translate a program written in a high-level language into low-level instructions before the program is executed. When you use a compiled language, the commands you write are referred to as **source code**. The low-level instructions that result from compiling the source code are referred to as **object code**. Figure 10-15 explains more about the compiling process.

When you use a compiled language, you must compile your program to produce executable program code. Therefore, if you write, compile, and run a program, but then discover that it contains a bug, you must fix your program, then recompile it before you test it again. Once you have compiled your bug-free final version, however, you can run the program without recompiling it.

Interpreted Languages

An **interpreted language** uses a translator instead of a compiler to create code that the computer can execute. When you run a program that is written in an interpreted language, the language's **interpreter** reads one instruction and converts it into a machine language instruction, which the computer executes. After the instruction is executed, the interpreter reads the next instruction, converts it into machine language so it can be executed, and so forth. Programs written in interpreted languages take longer to execute because the computer must translate every instruction as it is executed. A program with many loops is especially inefficient in an interpreted language, because the instructions contained in the loop are translated multiple times, once for each time the loop is executed.

What is the advantage of an interpreted language over a compiled language? With an interpreted language, you do not need to wait for your program to compile, so the testing process seems to take less time. Figure 10-16 on page NP 360 illustrates the concept of a language interpreter.

Object-Oriented Languages

Object-oriented languages are based on a new approach to programming that uses objects. An **object** is an entity or "thing" that a program manipulates. For example, a button—a rectangular icon on the screen—is an object. You are familiar with the way you can click a button using the mouse. A programmer can use an object-oriented language to define a button object in a program and display the button when the program runs.

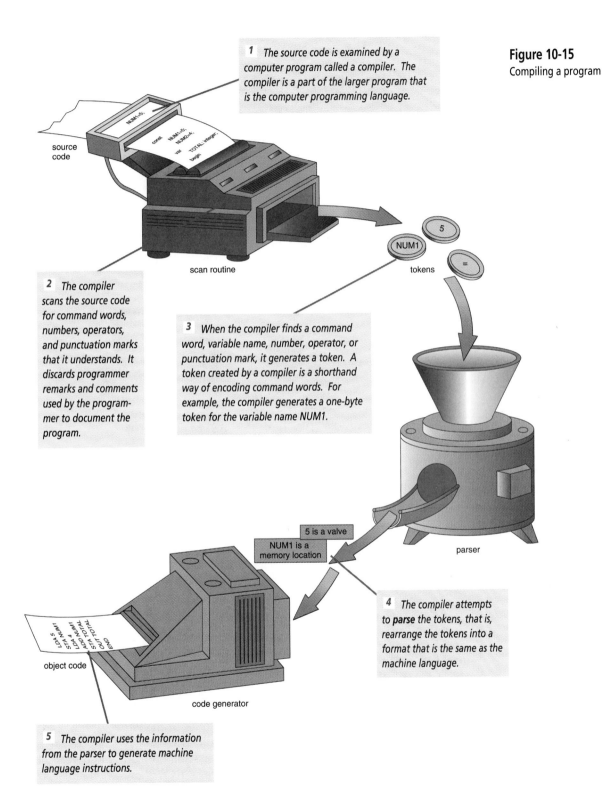

Figure 10-15
Compiling a program

1 The source code is examined by a computer program called a compiler. The compiler is a part of the larger program that is the computer programming language.

source code

scan routine

tokens

2 The compiler scans the source code for command words, numbers, operators, and punctuation marks that it understands. It discards programmer remarks and comments used by the programmer to document the program.

3 When the compiler finds a command word, variable name, number, operator, or punctuation mark, it generates a token. A token created by a compiler is a shorthand way of encoding command words. For example, the compiler generates a one-byte token for the variable name NUM1.

parser

5 is a valve
NUM1 is a memory location

4 The compiler attempts to **parse** the tokens, that is, rearrange the tokens into a format that is the same as the machine language.

object code

code generator

5 The compiler uses the information from the parser to generate machine language instructions.

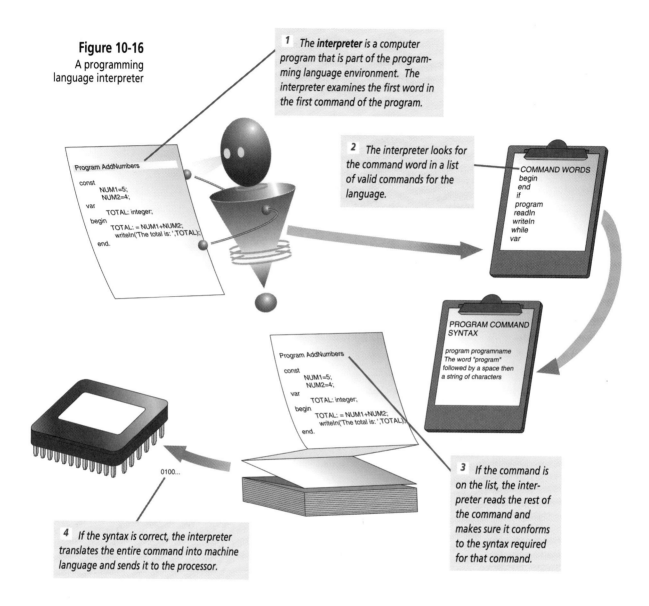

Figure 10-16
A programming
language interpreter

1 The **interpreter** is a computer program that is part of the programming language environment. The interpreter examines the first word in the first command of the program.

2 The interpreter looks for the command word in a list of valid commands for the language.

Program AddNumbers

const
NUM1=5;
NUM2=4;
var
TOTAL: integer;
begin
TOTAL: = NUM1+NUM2;
writeln('The total is: ',TOTAL);
end.

COMMAND WORDS
begin
end
if
program
readln
writeln
while
var

PROGRAM COMMAND SYNTAX

program programname
The word "program"
followed by a space then
a string of characters

Program AddNumbers

const
NUM1=5;
NUM2=4;
var
TOTAL: integer;
begin
TOTAL: = NUM1+NUM2;
writeln('The total is: ',TOTAL);
end.

3 If the command is on the list, the interpreter reads the rest of the command and makes sure it conforms to the syntax required for that command.

0100...

4 If the syntax is correct, the interpreter translates the entire command into machine language and sends it to the processor.

An object belongs to a **class**, or group, that has specific characteristics. A common example is the object class *window*. All window objects, including application windows, belong to the class window and share certain characteristics, such as a title bar and a control-menu box. When a programmer creates a new window object, it acquires, or **inherits**, the characteristics and capabilities of the *window* class. Each specific instance of a window object may also have its own unique characteristics, such as a particular series of characters in a title, specific horizontal and vertical dimensions, or a particular location on the screen. Figure 10-17 shows several objects from a related object class.

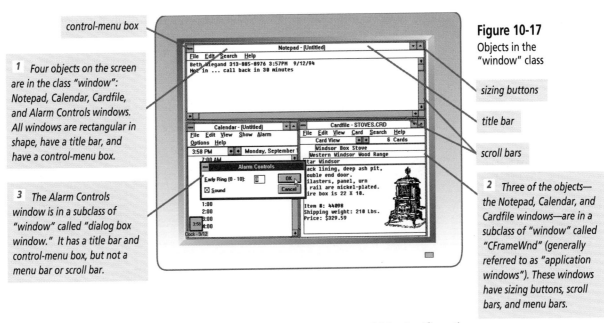

control-menu box

Figure 10-17
Objects in the "window" class

sizing buttons

title bar

scroll bars

1 *Four objects on the screen are in the class "window": Notepad, Calendar, Cardfile, and Alarm Controls windows. All windows are rectangular in shape, have a title bar, and have a control-menu box.*

3 *The Alarm Controls window is in a subclass of "window" called "dialog box window." It has a title bar and control-menu box, but not a menu bar or scroll bar.*

2 *Three of the objects—the Notepad, Calendar, and Cardfile windows—are in a subclass of "window" called "CFrameWnd" (generally referred to as "application windows"). These windows have sizing buttons, scroll bars, and menu bars.*

The same object can be used in many different programs, which significantly enhances programmer productivity. For example, let's say you are writing a program and want to include an object that handles the common situations in which a user must interact with the program to save, select, or name a file. You can make the object versatile enough so it could be used to save a file, save a file under a new name, open a file, or print a file. This object would be very handy, because anytime you wrote a program that needed to do these tasks, you could simply use this object and avoid "recreating the wheel."

In fact, this object is such an obviously good idea that it already exists. Version 3.1 of Microsoft Windows includes a file called COMMDLG.DLL (for COMMon DiaLoG) that contains the menu and dialog box objects for opening, saving, and printing files. Programmers writing programs for Windows don't have to create these menus and dialog boxes from scratch; they can simply include commands in their programs that tell COMMDLG.DLL to activate a menu or dialog box. This also explains why the File menu in most Windows programs looks the same. Actually, file menus are identical because they all use the COMMDLG.DLL object.

Event-Driven Languages

An **event-driven language** helps programmers easily create programs that must constantly check for and respond to a set of events, such as key presses or mouse actions. Most programs that use graphical user interfaces are event-driven—they display controls, such as menus, on the screen and take action when the user activates one of the controls. To create an event-driven program, code segments are attached to graphical objects, such as command buttons and icons. Users manipulate an object to generate an event, for example, clicking a button labeled "Continue." The event causes the instructions attached to that object to be executed. Figure 10-18 shows a screen from an event-driven program and the program code attached to one of the events.

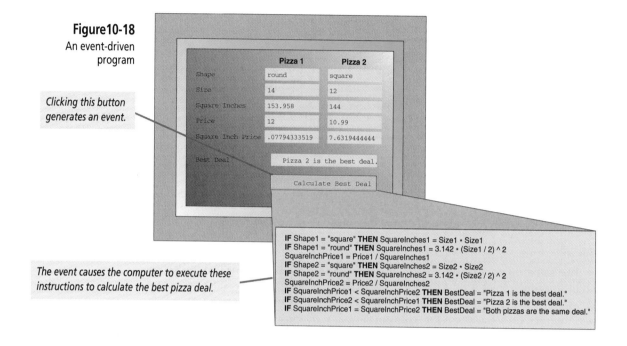

Figure10-18
An event-driven program

Clicking this button generates an event.

The event causes the computer to execute these instructions to calculate the best pizza deal.

Event-driven languages are useful for creating programs that feature graphical user interfaces, such as those that run on the Macintosh computer or under the Windows operating system. Although other languages can be used to develop such programs, an event-driven language simplifies the development process.

Programming Languages

BASIC (Beginner's All-purpose Symbolic Instruction Code) was designed as a language for beginning programmers. Since its introduction in 1964, many popular versions of BASIC have been created, including GW-BASIC shipped with the original IBM PCs and Microsoft's QBASIC. BASIC has become one of the most popular and widely used programming languages, because it is easy to use and is available for almost every type of computer system. BASIC is a high-level, procedural language. Most versions of BASIC are interpreted languages, although some versions provide compiling capabilities.

Early versions of BASIC were too limited for the development of sophisticated commercial programs, but newer versions, such as Microsoft's Visual Basic, are comprehensive and powerful programming languages suitable for use in professional programming projects. Visual Basic is especially useful for creating event-driven programs that have a graphical user interface.

Cobol (COmmon Business-Oriented Language) is the language most typically used for transaction processing on mainframe computer systems. Developed in 1960, Cobol is a high-level, procedural, compiled language used by thousands of professional programmers to develop and maintain complex programs in large organizations and businesses. Cobol programs tend to be rather long, but they are easy to understand, debug, and maintain. This functionality is particularly important in large organizations where critical programs must be maintained and modified by a variety of programmers over a period of years.

Fortran (FORmula TRANslator), developed in 1954, is the oldest high-level computer language still in use, although it has undergone many changes since its creation. Fortran was designed by scientists and is often used to create scientific, mathematical, and engineering programs on mainframe and minicomputers.

Pascal was designed in 1971 as a teaching language that helps students learn how to program computers. Pascal is a highly structured high-level, procedural, compiled language. The design of the language encourages a structured approach to programming. Despite its structured design, Pascal has gained only moderate popularity as a programming language for professional and commercial applications.

C is the most popular language for developing professional and commercial programs for microcomputer systems. Most major application programs and operating systems, such as Lotus 1-2-3 and Microsoft Windows, are written in C. C is a compiled procedural language that provides both high-level commands and low-level access to hardware. This gives the programmer significant flexibility in writing programs. Because of this flexibility, experienced C programmers can take steps to make their programs very fast and efficient. However, this flexibility can make C programs difficult to understand, debug, and maintain.

C++ is an object-oriented version of C. Many people believe that the object-oriented nature of C++ will make programmers more productive. However, object-oriented programming requires a significantly different mental perspective from that of procedural programming. Therefore, many programmers experience difficulty using the object-oriented features of C++.

Lisp (LISt Processor) and **Prolog** are declarative languages, often used to develop expert systems. These languages, developed in 1960 and 1971 respectively, have not gained as much popularity as procedural languages, probably because early computer applications were designed to handle tasks that required simple and repetitious calculations—tasks that procedural languages could handle effectively. Tasks that require a computer to perform complex logical operations on character data are better handled by declarative languages.

SQL (Structured Query Language) was developed to provide a standard language for defining and manipulating a database. SQL is a high-level declarative language that allows programmers and users to describe the relationship between the data elements in a database and the type of information they want to derive from the database. Although a database can also be manipulated by a procedural language such as Cobol, SQL is generally regarded as more effective because SQL commands are tailored to database activities.

8086 assembly language is a low-level language that uses short mnemonic commands that can be easily translated by the computer into machine language. The instructions in the 8086 assembly language instruction set are specific to the Intel 8086 microprocessor, and, therefore, programs written in this language can execute only on computers with microprocessors from the 8086 family. Today, 8086 assembly language is used primarily for programs, or segments of programs, that must be made as short as possible or that must run as quickly as possible. Professional programmers use 8086 assembly language for the sections of application programs that need to execute quickly and for system software that controls computer hardware.

■   ■   ■

The pizza program used as an example in this chapter is a relatively "tiny" program. The commercial programs you use—word processing or spreadsheet programs, for example—are much larger. By the Department of Defense standards, a "small" program is one with less than 100,000 lines of code. A "medium-size" program is one that has between 100,000 and one million lines of code. A "large" program is one with more than one million lines of code.

Research has shown that on average, one programmer creates 20 lines of code per day, including coding, testing, and documenting. It is not surprising, then, that most commercial programs are written by a team of programmers and take many months, or years, to complete.

But what is the point of learning about computer programming if you are not planning to become a programmer? There are several reasons. First, you are likely to use many computer programs during your career, and when you realize that your word processing program contains 750,000 lines of code, you will understand how a few bugs might exist. You will also understand that you, individually, would not want to undertake the task of writing a word processing program; that is a project best left to professional programming teams. Finally, although you would not typically write the productivity software you use, it is possible that you might have the opportunity to develop or participate in the development of software applications that are specific to your needs. Your understanding of computer programming and software engineering will help you plan constructively and participate productively in the development process.

C H A P T E R   R E V I E W

1. Answer the questions listed in the Chapter Preview section at the beginning of the chapter.
2. List each of the boldface terms used in this chapter; then use your own words to write a short definition of each term.
3. Describe how the job of a systems analyst differs from the job of a software engineer.
4. Is there a difference between an algorithm and a computer program? Why or why not?
5. Give an example of a sequence control structure, a selection control structure, and a repetition control structure.
6. Explain the difference between a syntax error and a logic error.
7. Explain the difference between program remarks and written documentation.
8. Make a list of the characteristics of programming languages and provide one or two examples of a specific computer language that has each characteristic.

C H A P T E R   Q U I Z

1. A(n) _____ is a set of steps for carrying out a task or solving a problem.
2. A(n) _____ is a graphical representation of the way a computer should progress from one instruction to the next when it performs a task.
3. _____ is the process of using a computer language to express an algorithm.
4. A(n) _____ changes the sequence, or order, in which instructions are executed by transferring program execution to instructions elsewhere in the program.
5. A(n) _____ tells a computer what to do, depending on whether a condition is true or false.
6. A(n) _____ repeats one or more instructions until a certain condition is met.
7. Entering known data to see if a program produces the correct results is part of the _____ process.
8. A(n) _____ error is caused by an incorrectly typed instruction.
9. _____ explains how a program works and how to use it.
10. A(n) _____ language creates programs that are composed of a series of statements that tell a computer how to perform the processes for a specific task.
11. A(n) _____ language lets a programmer construct a program by specifying a set of rules that define the conditions for resolving a problem.
12. A(n) _____ language requires a programmer to write instructions for the lowest level of the computer system, that is, for the specific hardware elements, such as the processor, registers, and RAM locations.
13. In a compiled language, _____ is compiled, or translated, into object code, which the computer can execute.
14. _____ is the language most typically used for transaction processing on mainframe computers in businesses.
15. In a(n) _____ language, program code is attached to objects and executed when something happens to that object.

P R O J E C T S

1. List the known information required to solve the following problems:

	PROBLEM	KNOWN INFORMATION REQUIRED
A.	Calculate the square footage of a rectangular room.	
B.	Calculate the amount of gasoline required to drive your car from Chicago to Miami.	
C.	Calculate how much it costs to ship a box of books from Columbus to Dallas.	
D.	Calculate how much it costs to purchase new carpeting for your living room.	

2. Examine the following BASIC program. Indicate the value of X and Y after each instruction is executed. At the beginning of the program, X and Y are each assigned a value of 0.

INSTRUCTION		VALUE AFTER THIS INSTRUCTION IS EXECUTED	
		X	Y
REM SAMPLE PROGRAM		0	0
X = 10			
Y = X*2			
X = X*Y			
END			

3. A friend has written a BASIC program to calculate the number of tanks of gas her car will require to go a specified number of miles. Unfortunately, the program doesn't work correctly. She shows you a printout of the program and asks for your help.

REM This program calculates the number of tanks of gas

REM required to drive my car a specified number of miles.

MilesPerGallon = 22.5

GallonsPerTank = 12

INPUT "Enter the number of miles to drive:"; MilesToDrive

GallonsRequired = MilesToDrive / MilesPerGallon

TanksRequired = GallonsRequired / GallonsPerTank

PRNT "This trip will require:"

PRINT MilesPerGallon

PRINT "tanks of gas."

END

There is a syntax error and a logic error that prevent the program from working correctly. Examine the program code carefully to locate the two errors; then write what the corrected lines should be.

Corrected Line

_____

_____

4. Describe the documentation for a computer program that you have used. Discuss what you liked or did not like about the documentation, and indicate how you think the documentation can be improved.

5. Select a computer language. Research the language, then answer the following questions:

   a. Is this a procedural or a declarative language?

   b. Is this a high-level or a low-level language?

   c. Is this a compiled language or an interpreted language?

   d. Is this an object-oriented language?

   e. Is this an event-driven language?

   f. When was the language developed?

   g. For what purpose was the language developed?

6. A baseball player's batting average is calculated by dividing the number of times the player hit the ball by the number of times the player was at bat, minus the number of times the player "walked," as in the formula, Hits / (TimesAtBat – Walks). Write the specifications for a program that calculates a baseball player's batting average. Be sure to include the assumptions, known information, formula for calculation, and output description. Use a flowchart to express the algorithm.

7. Assume your school has a computer literacy exam that students must pass before they can graduate. Scores on the exams can be between 0 and 100. A student must score at least 70 to pass the test. Marsha Murray in the testing office has a list of students and scores for the exam that was given in December. Write the specification for a program that would allow Marsha to input student names and scores, analyze each score to see if the student passed, and print out a list of student names, scores, and "Passed" or "Failed." Use pseudocode to express the algorithm.

8. Assume you are talking to a friend on the phone. You know your friend has three cards and they are all in the same suit. For example, your friend might have the two of clubs, the five of clubs, and the eight of clubs. Further, assume that the cards are shuffled so they are in no particular order. You need to tell your friend how to sort the cards so the lowest numbered card is first and the highest numbered card is last. However, you cannot see the cards and your friend cannot communicate with you except to say OK. You need to give your friend general instructions, such as "Take the first two cards and compare the numbers on them." Write out the instructions, or algorithm, for sorting the three cards.

L A B

Visual Programming Lab

In the Visual Programming Lab, you use an event-driven, object-oriented programming environment to create simple programs. These programs incorporate three different types of objects.

L A B

VISUAL PROGRAMMING

▪ Buttons contain program code that is executed when the button is clicked by the user.

▪ Labels identify text boxes and provide the user with additional information.

▪ Text boxes are used to obtain input from the user or display output.

Program One

You will use the Visual Programming Lab to create a program to calculate the area of a square pizza. Here are the specifications for the program:

ASSUMPTIONS:

The pizza is square, so both sides are the same length

KNOWN INFORMATION

The length of one side of the pizza

CALCULATE

Area = Side * Side

DISPLAY

The area of the pizza

To calculate the area of a square pizza, your program needs to use two variables, or storage locations. One variable holds the length of one side of the pizza after the person using the program enters it. The other variable holds the area of the pizza after the computer calculates it. Each of these variables will be represented on the screen by a text box.

To create the variables for a program that calculates the area of a pizza:

1. Double-click the Visual Programming Lab icon in the New Perspectives window to start the Lab. Read the introductory screen, then click the **Continue** button.

2. Position the pointer over the Text Box icon on the toolbar. Press the left mouse button and hold it down while you drag a new text box down into the programming window. Position the text box near the top of the programming window. Release the mouse button.

   TROUBLE? If you want to reposition the text box, place the pointer over the text box, press the left mouse button, then drag the text box to the desired location.

3. Position the pointer over the new text box and click the right mouse button (we'll call this "right click" in subsequent steps) to display the Edit Properties dialog box.

4. Double-click the Variable Name edit box to highlight the text it contains, then type **Side** as the variable name.

   This variable holds the length of one side of the pizza after a user enters it. Because this variable holds a number, make sure the Variable Type box has "Number" selected.

   When the program begins, this variable does not contain a value, so make sure the Initial Value box is blank.

   Now that the Side variable is defined, click the **Continue** button to return to the programming window.

5. Drag a second text box into the programming window and place it below the first text box.

6. Right click the new text box, as you did in Step 3, to display the Edit Properties dialog box. Double-click the Variable Name box, then type **Area** as the variable name.

   This variable holds the area of the pizza after the computer calculates it. Make sure the Variable Type is Number and the Initial Value is blank, then click the **Continue** button to return to the programming window.

Next, you will create a button that the person using the program can click to calculate the area of the pizza.

To create a button:

1. Drag the Button icon from the toolbar to an empty area in the programming window.
2. Right click the button to display the Edit Properties dialog box.
3. Double-click the Object Caption edit box and type **Calculate** as the caption.
4. Click the Code edit box and type the following instruction that the computer will perform when the button is clicked:

   Area = Side * Side

   Make sure you use exactly the same capitalization and spelling in the instruction as you used for the variable names.
5. Click the **Continue** button to return to the programming window.

   Now your program is complete, so you can run it and test it with some sample data.

To run and test your program:

1. Click **Run** on the menu bar, then click **Start** to run your program.
2. Click the top text box and type **10** as the length of a side.
3. Click the **Calculate** button to calculate the Area. The number 100 should be displayed in the Area text box.
4. Test your program by entering different numbers in the Side text box, then clicking the Calculate button to calculate the Area. Your program should calculate the correct area for any length side.

   TROUBLE? If you need to change your program, click **Run**, then click **End** to stop the program. You can then drag any object to a new location or right click any object to edit it.
5. When you are satisfied that your program is operating correctly, click **Run**, then **End** to end your program.
6. Click **File**, then click **Print** to print your program. Enter your name when prompted, then click the **OK** button to print your program documentation.

You will need Program 1 to complete Program 2. If you are continuing directly to the next part of the Lab, it is not necessary to save your program. However, if you are going to take a break, you should save the program you have just completed.

To save your program:

1. Insert a formatted disk in drive A: of your computer.
2. Click **File**, then click **Save As** to display the Save As dialog box.
3. Select drive A: in the Drives list box.
4. Double-click the File Name box to highlight the text it contains, then type **PROGONE**.
5. Click the **OK** button.

Program 2

Now you will enhance Program 1 by adding the capability to calculate the price per square inch of the pizza. This capability requires two new variables. One of these variables holds the price of the pizza, and the other variable holds the price per square inch after the computer calculates it. As with the variables in Program 1, these two new variables will be represented by text boxes on the screen.

You will also add an additional instruction to the Calculate button to calculate the price per square inch. To make the program easier to use, you will add labels to indicate the contents of each text box.

To load Program 1:

1. Perform this set of steps only if Program 1 is not currently on your screen. Start the Visual Programming Lab.
2. Put your disk in drive A:.
3. Click **File**, then click **Open** to display the Open dialog box.
4. Select drive A: in the Drives list box.
5. Double-click PROGONE.VPG.

To create the variables for Price and PricePerSquareInch:

1. Drag a text box into the programming window and place it below the first two text boxes.
2. Right click the new text box, then enter **Price** as the variable name.
3. Click the **Continue** button.
4. Drag another text box into the programming window and place it below the first three text boxes.
5. Right click the new text box, then enter **PricePerSquareInch** (all one word) as the variable name. Click the **Continue** button.

Next, you will change the program that is attached to the **Calculate** button so the computer will also calculate the price per square inch:

1. Drag the **Calculate** button to position it below the bottom text box.
2. Right click the **Calculate** button to display the Edit Properties dialog box.
3. Click the Code edit box, then click the end of the first line to move the flashing insertion point there.
4. Press the Enter key to move to the next line.
5. Type the following instruction that the computer will perform after it calculates the area of a pizza:

   PricePerSquareInch = Price / Area

   Once again, you must use the exact spelling and capitalization as you used when you named the text boxes.
6. Click the **Continue** button to return to the programming window.

In the next set of steps you will create labels for the text boxes.

To create labels:

1. Drag the Label icon from the toolbar into the programming window and place it to the left of the top text box.
2. Right click the label to display the Edit Properties dialog box.
3. Change the contents of the Object Caption box to **Side**, then click the **Continue** button.
4. Add labels for the remaining text boxes: Area, Price, and Sq Inch Price.

   TROUBLE? If a label does not fit in its box, use the "click to change size" option on the Edit Properties box.

Now, you are ready to run and test Program 2.

To test Program 2:

1. Click **Run**, then click **Start** to start your program.
2. Click the first text box (the one for side) and type **10**.
3. Click the third text box (the one for price) and type **10**.
4. Click the **Calculate** button to calculate the area and the price per square inch. The Area should be displayed as 100 and the Sq Inch Price should be displayed as .1 dollars.
5. Test your program by entering different numbers in the Side and Price text boxes and then clicking the **Calculate** button to calculate the area and price per square inch. If you need to change your program, click **Run**, then click **End** to stop the program. You can then drag any object to a new location or right click any object to edit it.

    TROUBLE: If your program does not work correctly, go back and make sure that all the variable names are spelled correctly.

6. When you are satisfied that your program is operating correctly, click **Run**, then click **End** to stop the program. Click **File**, then click **Print** to print your program. Enter your name when prompted, then click the **OK** button to print your program documentation.
7. Save your program as PROGTWO if you are going to take a break.

Program 3

Program 3 is a further enhancement of the pizza program that calculates the area and price per square inch for both round and square pizzas.

To begin Program 3:

1. Make sure the Visual Programming Lab window is open on your screen.
2. If Program 2 is not currently on your screen, click **File**, then click **Open** and load PROGTWO.VPG.

You will need to add a text box to the program into which users can type "round" or "square." Data such as "round" and "square" is referred to as character data, or a **string**, and when you define the variable to hold this data, you need to indicate that the variable will hold text, rather than a number.

To create a variable to hold a string:

1. Drag a new text box to an empty area on the screen.
2. Click the right mouse button over the text box to display the Edit Properties dialog box and enter **Shape** as the Variable Name.
3. While the Edit Properties dialog box is still open, select the **String** option in the Variable Type box.
4. Click the **Continue** button to return to the programming window.
5. Drag a label into the programming window and place it to the left of the text box you just created.
6. Right click the label to open the Edit Properties dialog box and enter **Shape** as the Object Caption, then click the **Continue** button.

Now you need to add an instruction to the Calculate button that will check the Shape variable to see if it contains "round" or "square" and then make the appropriate calculation.

1. Right click the **Calculate** button to display the Edit Properties dialog box. Click the left side of the instruction "Area = Side * Side" to position the flashing insertion point at the beginning of the line.

2. Press the Delete key repeatedly to delete this line.

3. Type the following instruction:

   IF Shape = "square" THEN Area = Side ∗ Side

   Make sure you use the correct spelling and capitalization for the variable names. This IF..THEN statement checks the value of the string variable Shape. If Shape holds the string "square," then it will calculate Area as Side ∗ Side. If Shape does not hold the string "square," it will not do anything.

4. Press the Enter key, then type the following instruction:

   IF Shape = "round" THEN Area = 3.142 ∗ ((Side / 2) ^2)

   TROUBLE? To type the ^ symbol, hold down the Shift key and press 6.

   In this IF..THEN statement, if the variable Shape holds the string "round," then Area is calculated as 3.142 (an approximate value of pi) times ((Side / 2) ^2). Since Side is equal to the diameter, Side / 2 is equal to the radius of the pizza. The expression ((Side / 2) ^2) is equivalent to the radius squared. If Shape does not hold the string "round," then this statement will not do anything.

5. Click the **Continue** button to return to the programming window.

The revision to the program is complete, so you can now run and test the program.

To test the program:

1. Click **Run**, then click **Start** to start your program.

2. Click the Shape text box and then type **round**. Make sure the Side box contains 10 and the Price box contains 10.

3. Click the **Calculate** button to run the program. The Area should be calculated as 78.55 square inches and the Sq Inch Price should be calculated as approximately .127 dollars.

4. Click the Shape text box and type **square**.

5. Click the **Calculate** button to run the program. The Area should be calculated as 100 and the Sq Inch Price should be calculated as .1 dollars.

6. Test your program for both square and round pizzas with different sizes and prices.

7. When your program is operating correctly, click **Run**, then click **End** to stop the program. Click **File**, then click **Print** to print your program. Enter your name when prompted, then click the **OK** button to print your program documentation.

8. Save your program on your disk as PROGTHR.VPG.

R E S O U R C E S

Clocksin, W., and C. Mellish. *Programming in Prolog*, 3rd. ed. New York: Springer-Verlag, 1987.

This is the classic textbook on programming with the Prolog computer language. If you are interesting in learning more about declarative languages and expert systems, this book is excellent.

Dijkstra, E. "Goto Statement Considered Harmful," *Communications of the ACM*, 11, 3.

Dijkstra's original letter about GOTO statements was published in the *Communications of the ACM*, a prestigious journal of the Association of Computing Machinery.

- Lammers, S. *Programmers at Work*. Redmond, WA: Microsoft Press, 1986.

  In this book you will find fascinating interviews with the star programmers of the early microcomputer era, including Bill Gates, Gary Kildall, and Dan Bricklin. The programmers give their views on issues such as "Is programming an art or a science?," "How did you develop your programming skills?," and "What is your programming style?" You will also find some original examples of programs, flowcharts, and program specifications.

- McConnel, S. *Code Complete: A Practical Handbook of Software Construction*. Redmond, WA: Microsoft Press, 1993.

  A realistic guide to computer programming, written by experienced programmers. This book is well researched and contains abundant references and hard data, yet is easy to read. We think *Code Complete* is destined to become a classic.

- Pattis, R. E. *Karel the Robot: A Gentle Introduction to the Art of Programming*. New York: Wiley, 1981.

  In this book the author uses a robot named Karel to teach students intuitively about programming, particularly Pascal. Pattis wrote this book when he was a graduate student at Stanford University. It is entertaining and very easy to understand.

- Payne, J. *Structured Programming with QuickBasic*. Boston: PWS-Kent, 1991.

  This introduction to the QuickBasic programming language is written for students with little or no programming background. QuickBasic and QBasic are essentially the same language. QBasic is included with recent versions of DOS, so most computer users have it. If you want to learn more about programming, this book could be your next step.

- Sigwart, C., G. Van Meer, and J. Hansen. *Software Engineering: A Project-Oriented Approach*. Irvine, CA: Franklin, Beedle, & Associates, 1990.

  This book presents a good basic foundation in software engineering. It is well referenced, and the glossary contains relevant definitions selected from the *IEEE Standard Glossary of Software Engineering Terminology*.

CHAPTER ELEVEN

CHAPTER PREVIEW

When you have completed this chapter you should be able to answer the following questions:

- How can I evaluate new computer industry developments and trends in light of previous events?

- How can I critically evaluate the importance of new computer products?

- What is the best way for me to make informed hardware and software purchasing decisions?

PERSPECTIVES ON THE COMPUTER INDUSTRY

To many people, IBM is synonymous with computers. However, IBM did not invent computers. It did not even produce the first commercial computer or the first microcomputer. Certainly, IBM has had dynamic leadership, particularly Thomas Watson, Sr., whose slogan, THINK, we suppose might have been directed to both employees and computers. And one cannot dispute that with more than 400,000 employees, offices in almost every country in the world, and annual sales of over $50 billion, IBM is one of the largest corporations in the world. But the computer industry is much larger than even the mammoth IBM. In this chapter, you will find out more about the computer industry: the corporations that are its major players, the people whose ideas and inventions have contributed to the blazing progress of technology, and the ever-changing selection of products that this young industry produces.

You are almost certain to interact with computers for the rest of your life. One thing, perhaps the only thing, we know for certain about the computer systems you will use in the future is that they will be very different from those you use today. In this chapter, we will try to provide you with perspectives that help you understand, evaluate, and use the remarkable advances in computer technology that you're sure to see in the coming years.

Historical Threads in the Computer Industry

L A B

COMPUTER HISTORY

The **computer industry** consists of the corporations and individuals that supply goods and services to the people and organizations that use computers. The history of the computer industry makes sense when you view it as a series of "threads" that connect events. Some of the most important threads are hardware development, software evolution, the corporations that shaped the computer marketplace, and the image of computers in popular culture.

Hardware Development

The ancestors of the computer were simple calculating devices. Progress from the early abacus to today's microcomputer has been logarithmic. In other words, things happened slowly at first, but innovations occurred faster and faster, to the point that new developments occur at a blinding pace. Figure 11-1 summarizes the time frame of hardware development relative to the history of all calculating devices.

Figure 11-1
Computer hardware development

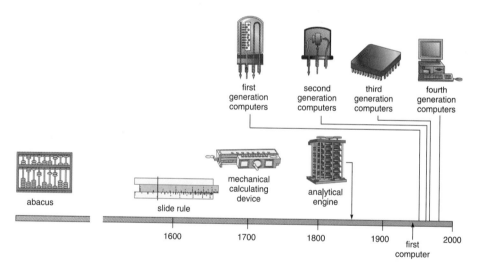

Calculation Aids

From earliest times, people used their fingers to help them count and calculate. Using pebbles and marks carved on sticks was an early but somewhat crude innovation. More sophisticated devices, such as the abacus, were used as early as 500 B.C. The next major steps in calculating technology came in the early 1600s when John

Napier invented a device to do multiplication and William Oughtred invented the slide rule, an essential aid for scientists and engineers through the 1960s.

Mechanical Calculating Devices

The computer industry is built upon a foundation of calculating devices that date back to 1623, when a German named Wilhelm Schickard built a mechanical adding machine. In 1642, a mathematician named Blaise Pascal invented an adding machine that he tried to sell to accountants and tax officials.

These early calculators were experimental. Some did not work reliably. Others could add, but not subtract, multiply, or divide. Some required a human operator to use clever manual algorithms to supplement the calculator's processing.

In 1822, Charles Babbage drew up plans for a steam-powered calculating device, which he called the "analytical engine." His plans for the analytical engine included the major elements of a modern computer. It was automatic, that is, it could perform most calculations without intervention from a human operator; it included a processing unit, which could add, subtract, multiply, and divide; it used an input mechanism to read instructions and data; it featured an output mechanism to display the result of calculations; and it had a very simple memory device for storing the intermediate results of a complex calculation. Babbage also planned for the analytical engine to be programmable. As work on the machine progressed, a mathematician named Augusta Ada, the Countess of Lovelace, collaborated with Babbage to devise a method to input data and instructions using a series of punched cards.

Babbage persuaded the British government to subsidize the development of the analytical engine. Some historians believe that this was the first government subsidy for a computing device. As is the case with many government contracts, Babbage's ran late and over budget. Eventually, the funds ran out and Babbage abandoned the project. Work on constructing computers would not resume for another century.

Although Babbage did not complete the analytical engine, he laid a remarkably robust foundation of computer theory that included the characteristics of a basic computer system and the rudiments of programming it. To understand how Babbage's ideas affected modern computer development, you can review von Neumann's description of the ENIAC computer that was presented in Chapter 1 and compare it to the description of Babbage's computer in the paragraph above.

Calculating devices reached new levels of sophistication in 1890, when Herman Hollerith developed a punched card tabulating device for the 1890 census. Hollerith founded the Tabulating Machine Company, which later became IBM.

The theory of computing took another major step forward in 1936 when Alan Turing wrote a scholarly article describing a device that is now known as the Turing Machine. The Turing Machine is an abstract device that represents a theoretical computer. Using only a pencil and a strip of paper that moves left and right, a Turing Machine can simulate any real computing device. The Turing Machine so well represents the capability of real computers that any problem that cannot be computed on a Turing Machine cannot be computed on a real computer. The Turing Machine shows that there are some apparently unsolvable problems, and this is valuable information for computer scientists. Figure 11-2 on the following page illustrates how a Turing Machine works.

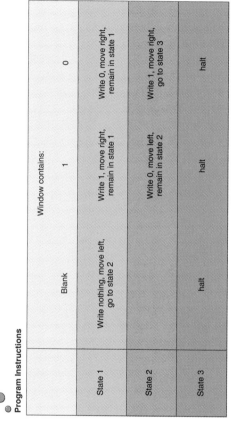

Figure 11-2
A Turing Machine that adds 1 to a binary number

The First Computer

Some historians consider the Harvard MARK I, a device built in 1939 and based on electronic relays, to be the first computer. Other historians regard the ABC computer, developed by John Atanasoff in 1937, as the first electronic computer. Still others maintain that ENIAC, a gigantic computer completed in 1945 by a team led by John W. Mauchley and J. Presper Eckert, or the Manchester Mark I, built in Manchester, England, in 1946, should be considered the first computer.

In truth, it is difficult to identify the device that should be called the "first computer." Instead, computer history provides us with a series of "firsts": the first "electronic" computer, the first electronic "digital" computer, the first "stored program" computer, the first "commercial" electronic digital computer, and so forth.

One way to make sense of developments in the computer industry is to divide it into "generations." The beginning of each new generation is marked by a significant change in the fundamental nature of computer architecture.

Prototype Computers

In the period between 1930 and 1950, engineers in the United States, England, and Germany pieced together the technology that eventually produced the first generation of computers. The machines these engineers constructed can be referred to as "prototype computers." A **prototype** is a preliminary version or a trial model of a device. A prototype computer is usually built as an experiment to determine if its design has merits. Prototypes such as Konrad Zuse's Z-series, built in Germany beginning in 1938, and the IBM Automatic Sequence Controlled Calculator, also called Harvard MARK I, built in 1939, were essentially experiments to find out if electromagnetic relays, shown in Figure 11-3, were practical for performing arithmetic electronically.

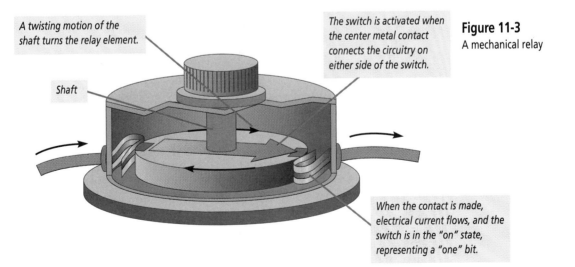

A twisting motion of the shaft turns the relay element.

The switch is activated when the center metal contact connects the circuitry on either side of the switch.

Shaft

When the contact is made, electrical current flows, and the switch is in the "on" state, representing a "one" bit.

Figure 11-3
A mechanical relay

Other prototypes, such as the ABC, the ENIAC, and the Manchester Mark I, were experiments in the use of vacuum tubes as a replacement for electromagnetic relays. Prototype computers showed how technologies such as electromagnetic relays and vacuum tubes could be applied to the construction of computers. Therefore, they were an essential bridge between earlier mechanical devices, such as the IBM tabulating machines, and first generation electronic computers.

First Generation Computers

The computer industry began in earnest in the early 1950s and progressed like no other industry in history. To make a point of the phenomenal increase in computer speed, efficiency, and economy, one industry analyst wrote: "If the aircraft industry had evolved as spectacularly as the computer industry over the past 25 years, a Boeing 767 would cost $500 today, and it would circle the globe in 20 minutes on five gallons of gas!"

First generation computers are defined as computers that use vacuum tubes, like the one shown in Figure 11-4, rather than electromagnetic or mechanical switches to store data and perform calculations.

Figure 11-4
A vacuum tube

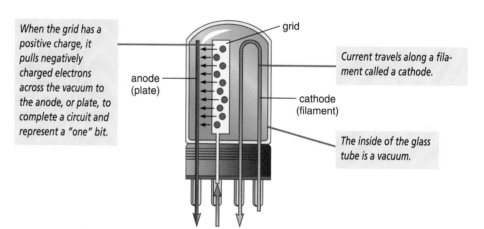

When the grid has a positive charge, it pulls negatively charged electrons across the vacuum to the anode, or plate, to complete a circuit and represent a "one" bit.

anode (plate)

grid

Current travels along a filament called a cathode.

cathode (filament)

The inside of the glass tube is a vacuum.

The vacuum tubes used in first generation computers required a large amount of power, and they failed frequently, making the computers somewhat unreliable. The size and number of the vacuum tubes plus their associated wiring resulted in a computer that filled a large room and weighed several tons. Despite their size, first generation computers were not very powerful by today's standards. Processing speeds, measured by the system clock, ranged from 1 MHz to 2 MHz, impressive for the 1950s, but slower than any personal computer used today. Memory capacity of first generation computers was small, about 12 thousand bytes, considerably less than the 4 to 8 million bytes in today's typical microcomputer.

First generation computers were also expensive. The UNIVAC (Universal

Automatic Computer) had a retail price of $500,000 in 1950, equivalent to $2,400,000 of today's inflated dollars. Today, for less than $100 you can buy a hand-held programmable calculator that is more powerful than the UNIVAC. First generation computers became obsolete in the late 1950s, when second generation computers became available.

Second Generation Computers

Second generation computers, built between 1957 and 1965, used transistors, instead of vacuum tubes. Figure 11-5 shows how a transistor works. Second generation computers were smaller in size, used less power, were more reliable, and were less expensive than their first generation counterparts. However, second generation computers also became obsolete when third generation computers became available in the mid-1960s.

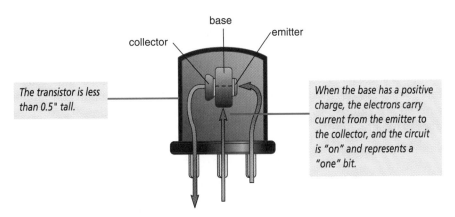

The transistor is less than 0.5" tall.

When the base has a positive charge, the electrons carry current from the emitter to the collector, and the circuit is "on" and represents a "one" bit.

Figure 11-5
A transistor

Third Generation Computers

In 1952 G.W.A. Dummer addressed the Royal Radar Establishment in England and said, "It seems now possible to envisage electronics equipment in a solid block with no connecting wires. The block may consist of layers of insulating, conducting, rectifying, and amplifying materials, the electrical functions being connected directly by cutting out areas of the various layers." Such a circuit, now called an "integrated circuit," was developed in 1958 by Jack Kilby. An **integrated circuit** packages transistors and other components on a small wafer of silicon and is very cost effective to manufacture because the components do not have to be individually wired to a circuit board. Kilby's first integrated circuit, shown in Figure 11-6, was very primitive. It took seven additional years of development before integrated circuits were incorporated in commercial computers.

Figure 11-6
Kilby's first integrated
circuit

Beginning in 1965, third generation computers built using integrated circuits were smaller, faster, more reliable, and less expensive than computers from previous generations. Figure 11-7 shows the evolution of computer circuitry from vacuum tubes to integrated circuits.

Figure 11-7
Evolution of computer
circuitry

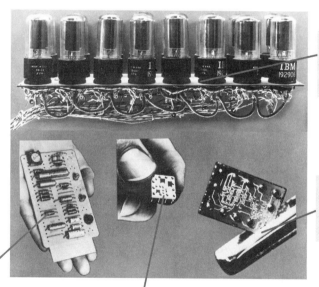

First generation computers contained thousands of vacuum tubes wired to circuit boards.

Integrated circuits technology evolved smaller, more efficient circuitry, shown here being held by tweezers.

Second generation computer circuit boards featured transistors instead of vacuum tubes.

In third generation computers, ceramic circuit modules and integrated circuits plugged into circuit boards.

While IBM developed powerful and expensive third generation mainframe computers, some other manufacturers produced smaller, special-purpose computers they called "minicomputers." Minicomputers, such as the DEC PDP-8, priced at $18,000, challenged the dominance of mainframes, which were far more expensive. Soon minicomputers had taken over some of the processing tasks that previously had been handled by mainframes. Minicomputers also provided cost-effective automation of some processes that would have been prohibitively expensive for a mainframe.

The Fourth Generation

In 1971, Ted Hoff, an employee of a Silicon Valley integrated circuit maker named Intel, produced the design for an entire computer on a chip. This "microprocessor," as it was called, was an all-purpose logic circuit. The circuitry in a microprocessor such as the Pentium shown in Figure 11-8 contains all the elements of a computer.

The microprocessor had significant impact on computer miniaturization and price reduction. A microprocessor is tiny—less than .25" on a side—and it can be mass produced. Hobbyists began using the microprocessor to create their own computers, and in 1975, the MITS Altair—the first commercial microcomputer—was released. And so the the fourth generation was born and the age of the microcomputer began.

The control unit directs the flow of processing by fetching data and instructions.

The arithmetic logic unit carries out the instructions.

Figure 11-8
A microprocessor

Temporary memory stores 16K of data.

The clock coordinates the flow of data.

The input/output circuitry helps the microprocessor communicate with external devices.

The Next Generation

Future computer historians might one day mark a new generation with the advent of optical computers that store and process instructions and data as pulses of light. A team of researchers at the University of Colorado demonstrated a working prototype of an optical computer in 1993, but members of the team estimate that optical computers will not be commercially available until the year 2000.

Software Evolution

Now let's take a look at a second thread of the history of the computer industry—the evolution of computer software—and see how it has affected computer programming languages, application software, and user interfaces. Figure 11-9 summarizes software developments.

Figure 11-9
Software evolution

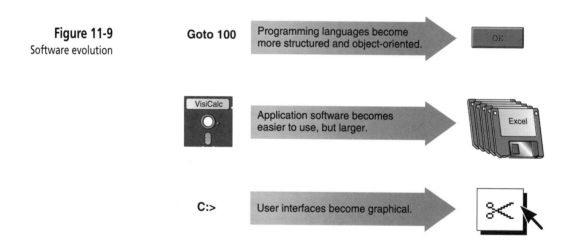

Programming Language Evolution

The first computer programming languages were low-level machine languages that required programmers to translate their instructions into patterns of ones and zeros. The translation process required hours upon hours of tedious concentration. It was easy to make mistakes and difficult to locate them in the rows of repetitious digits. Although it seems obvious now that an alternative to this error-prone and tedious programming process was needed, the Manchester engineering group that worked on the Mark I advocated that programming should be in a form as close as possible to the computer's internal representation of commands and data, that is, in machine language. The Cambridge engineering group working on the ESDAC (Electronic Storage Delay Automatic Computer) opposed this view and developed a rudimentary assembly language to shift some of the burden of translation to the computer. They believed that this would simplify the programming process and eliminate many errors.

Following the lead of the Cambridge group, assembly language became the preferred alternative to programming in machine language in the early 1950s. Using assembly language, a programmer enters mnemonic op codes such as MOV for "move" and LDA for "load accumulator." Programs can be developed more rapidly than with machine language, and errors can be located more quickly.

Despite the advantages of assembly language, programmers soon recognized that assembly language was not the perfect programming environment. Because each assembly language instruction represented a machine language instruction, each model of processor required its own unique assembly language. Programmers were forced to learn a different assembly language for each type of computer, and the assembly language programs for one type of computer had to be rewritten if they were to be used on a different type of computer. So although assembly language was an improvement over machine language, neither language created programs that were "portable" from one type of computer to another.

High-level languages, such as Cobol, Pascal, and BASIC, provide programmers with portable tools. Versions of BASIC, for example, are available for every major type of computer, and it is possible to transport BASIC programs from one type of computer to another with only slight modification. Fortran, developed in 1956, was the first widely used high-level language. Cobol followed close on its heels in 1960, and both are still in widespread use today. The trend to more structured languages was set in motion by Edsger Dijkstra's condemnation of the GOTO statement and the "spaghetti code" that resulted when programmers made injudicious use of it.

Today, a trend in computer programming languages is toward improving the interface that a programmer uses to specify program instructions. Instead of typing long lists of commands, today's programming languages provide a graphical programming environment in which programmers point and click the objects they want to assemble into programs. Developed in the early 1990s, these so-called "visual" programming environments, such as Visual Basic and Visual C++, provide programmers with graphical tools for creating screen layouts, designing graphical user interfaces, and editing commands. With these tools, programmers can design program screens interactively, creating visually appealing and effective programs in less time than with traditional languages.

Another trend in programming is object-oriented languages, which enable programmers to create and manipulate data objects. Smalltalk, developed in 1971, was one of the first languages to support the use of objects. The use of objects tends to encourage **component programming**, that is, building new programs by assembling prewritten, fully tested program components. Object-oriented programming and a component approach to software design can dramatically increase programmer productivity; instead of writing program code for every task the computer must perform, a programmer just uses a prewritten object or component that contains the code for the task.

As in other areas of the computer industry, programming languages are likely to continue to evolve. One current programming bottleneck appears to be accurate specification of the logic needed to code an algorithm. A few programming environments, such as Matrix Layout, have been developed to provide programmers with tools for constructing an on-screen flowchart that is then automatically compiled into object code. Such a programming environment would seem to be a likely step forward in the evolution of computer programming languages. In any event, it appears likely that programming languages will continue to evolve to provide programmers with better methods of creating more sophisticated, reliable programs in less time and with less effort.

Application Software Evolution

Before the introduction of microcomputers in the late 1970s, most computer applications were custom-built for a specific task within a particular corporation. Essentially every corporation that acquired a mainframe computer had a programming staff to hand-tailor its software. Now, even in the mainframe market, commercial software is available and is used whenever possible because it eliminates the time and expense required to design, write, and test software.

Commercial software has been vital to the success of the microcomputer since the introduction of VisiCalc. VisiCalc was the first electronic spreadsheet software and was largely responsible for the success of the Apple II computer. Commercial software has continued to become more sophisticated, each generation building on the features of previous programs. For example, Lotus 1-2-3, the successor to VisiCalc in the spreadsheet market, provides improved graphing features such as pie charts, line graphs, bar graphs, and XY graphs, in addition to sophisticated functions for data manipulation, statistical analysis, and financial calculations.

As features increased, microcomputer software ballooned in size. Today's software requires disk storage space that would have been unbelievable only a few years ago. In 1979, the VisiCalc spreadsheet software was shipped on a single-sided 160K disk. In 1983, the original Lotus 1-2-3 spreadsheet software was shipped on five 360K disks. The most recent version of the Microsoft Excel for Windows spreadsheet software is shipped on nine 1.44 megabyte disks containing compressed files. The uncompressed files require 29 megabytes of storage space—more than the entire hard-drive capacity of a typical microcomputer in 1983. The trend toward graphical user interfaces, an increased number of features, and the inclusion of extensive on-line help and tutorials have all contributed to the growing size of software applications.

Microcomputer software has also become more diversified. From the "big three"—word processing, spreadsheets, and databases—the scope of microcomputer software has expanded to include games, educational programs, presentation graphics programs, paint programs, desktop publishing, computer-aided design, utility programs, schedulers, financial management programs, tax programs, and more. Specialty programs are available for every topic from gardening, to bridge, to kitchen design. Multimedia applications have added new dimensions to computer games and have popularized computer reference applications such as multimedia encyclopedias.

Future evolution of microcomputer software is likely to result from the integration of the communications, computer, and entertainment industries. Some possibilities include interactive television, movies on demand, the integration of electronic and voice mail, and further enhancements of the Internet, on-line shopping, and other on-line services.

Interface Evolution

In an attempt to simplify human-computer interaction, user interfaces have evolved from the command-line interfaces of the 1960s and 1970s, to the menu-driven interfaces of the 1980s, and then to the graphical user interfaces of today. This evolution has been made possible by advances in computer hardware, such as increased memory, large hard-disk capacity, enhanced processor speed, and the high-resolution monitors necessary to process and display the large amount of data required for graphics.

The current trend in user interfaces appears to be heading toward continued development of graphical user interfaces. However, the computer industry can change direction very quickly, and we should expect development of alternative user interfaces. There is persistent grumbling among computer users that graphical interfaces are, if not a step backward, a detour from the path of progress. Why would users say this? To get an understanding of the fundamental problem with graphical user interfaces, take the icon identification quiz in Figure 11-10.

As you probably discovered from the quiz, icons can be very ambiguous. A picture (or icon) might be "worth a thousand words" as the saying goes, but many computer functions and actions are difficult to clearly represent with an icon. Human languages are very sophisticated—they have many words that can't be adequately represented with pictures. That's why hieroglyphics proved somewhat inadequate as the basis for a writing system.

A more modern example of the difficulty using pictographs is the development of computerized word processing in Japan. Written Japanese is based on thousands of pictographs called kanji, each representing a word. For example, a single symbol represents the concept "beautiful." How would a user enter such a symbol?

Figure 11-10
Icon identification quiz

Icon Quiz

Can you correctly guess the meaning of the following icons?

1. Save a document

2. Open a document

3. Disk operations

4. Format a disk

1. Add a new page

2. Open a document

3. Copy to clipboard

4. Copy a document

1. Lighten colors

2. Activate TipWizard

3. Turn on cell protection

4. Create light source

1. Undo

2. Create diagonal background lines

3. Electronic white-out

4. Paintbrush

1. Change to uppercase letters

2. Sort in alphabetical order

3. Accept letters only

4. Check spelling

See page NP 417 for answers.

Obviously, it would be impractical to have a keyboard with thousands of keys and each key representing one word. Fortunately, the Japanese also have a set of symbols that are used to phonetically represent the vowel and consonant sounds in a word. The keyboard on a Japanese word processor contains these phonetic symbols. To use a Japanese word processor, you type the keys that represent the sound of the word. The word processing software looks for the single kanji symbol that represents the word and displays that symbol on the screen. If more than one kanji has the same sound, the word processing software displays the possibilities and asks you to select the correct one. Although word processing is now possible in Japanese, it is not as straightforward as in English.

The problem with graphical user interfaces is virtually the same problem the Japanese encountered with word processing. A user interface is essentially a language that people and computers use to communicate. If the communication is limited to a few, say 10, tasks, it should be fairly easy to represent those tasks with icons. However, as the number of tasks and variations on those tasks expand, the number of icons required to represent them also expands. Displaying a large number of icons becomes a problem for the software designer, and remembering the function of each icon becomes a problem for the user. Just as you were once required to memorize commands with command-line interfaces, you must now memorize the meaning of dozens of icons.

Critics also point out that use of a metaphor, such as the desktop metaphor in Windows and Macintosh software, adds another layer of complexity to the interface. You need to translate the command you want to issue into its metaphorical representation, which adds a superfluous cognitive task to the process.

If a graphical user interface is not the best way for people and computers to communicate, what is? In Chapter 6, you read about two possibilities for future user interfaces: speech and cyberspace. The ability of computers to speak and understand human speech is still in the developmental stages, and the concept of communicating with computers by some sort of direct mental link is still relatively fresh on the pages of science fiction; it has a long way to go before it becomes science fact. So although we might speculate about the perfect user interface, for now, we can only use our GUIs and wait patiently to see what software designers will provide for us in the future.

The Companies That Shaped the Marketplace

A third thread in the history of the computer industry is the way companies shaped the market for computer products. As the computer age dawned, there were four established contenders in the office-machine business who were financially prepared to pursue the development of computers. Hollerith's Tabulating Machine Company had emerged as International Business Machines in 1924. The rest of the lineup included Remington Rand, National Cash Register, and Burroughs. Some of the major events in the progress of computer companies are shown in Figure 11-11 on the following page.

Figure 11-11

Major events for
computer companies

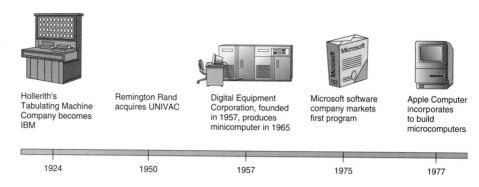

Hollerith's
Tabulating Machine
Company becomes
IBM

Remington Rand
acquires UNIVAC

Digital Equipment
Corporation, founded
in 1957, produces
minicomputer in 1965

Microsoft software
company markets
first program

Apple Computer
incorporates
to build
microcomputers

1924   1950   1957   1975   1977

In 1950, Remington Rand seemed to have made a shrewd business decision when it bought Eckert and Mauchly's computer company and outstanding contracts for six UNIVAC computers. From 1950 until 1955, when Remington Rand merged with the Sperry Corporation, 30 UNIVACs had been delivered, and it appeared that Sperry Rand, as it was now called, was headed for dominance in the computer marketplace. The Sperry Rand balloon burst, however, when IBM unleashed its experienced business machine sales force. By 1956, IBM had installed 76 computers compared to Sperry Rand's 46.

IBM's star rose quickly. By 1961, 71% of the total $1.8 billion in computers had been built by IBM. Sperry Rand had only about 10% of the market. Although IBM seemed to have captured the computer market, technology marched on, and IBM executives recognized that the company could not survive if it continued to offer its lineup of transistorized computers. So, in 1960, IBM executives "gambled the company," as one analyst put it, and decided to abandon its transistorized architecture and replace it with a single all-purpose computer built with integrated circuit technology. The development effort cost IBM $5 billion over four years and left the company financially vulnerable. The new computer, called the System/360, was introduced on April 7, 1964, and it attracted orders at the high rate of 1,000 per month placing IBM once again in a strong financial position.

Another challenge to IBM's industry leadership was the appearance of the minicomputer in 1965. The premier minicomputer company was Digital Equipment Corporation (DEC), founded in 1957. Soon, additional competitors for the minicomputer market emerged, including Hewlett-Packard and Data General. Minicomputers, with their small size and low cost, were eating into the mainframe market. In response, IBM developed its own line of minicomputers.

IBM also experienced erosion in the high-end market for the fastest, most powerful computers when Control Data Corporation and Cray Research developed and marketed supercomputers. For about 10 years the computer industry maintained something of an equilibrium, with IBM the uncontested giant and a bevy of companies such as DEC, Hewlett-Packard, Control Data, Data General, and Cray Research nibbling for the crumbs of specialized minicomputer and supercomputer markets.

In 1977, the computer market was on the brink of a major upheaval, although the big players were unaware of it. In that year, three companies, Radio Shack, Commodore, and Apple, began marketing microcomputers. At first, sales faltered. Businesses, as well as the general public, were not certain how they could use these machines. Very little commercial software had been written for microcomputers, and most people did not have the time or the ability to write their own. In 1978, the first electronic spreadsheet program, called VisiCalc, was released for the Apple II computer. Sales of the computer and the software soared. Apple Computers, incorporated in 1977, had the most profitable public stock offering in Wall Street history only three years later and quickly became one of the best-known computer companies in the world.

In the early microcomputer market, four companies vied for market share: Apple, Commodore, Atari, and Radio Shack. VisiCalc had given Apple a boost in the business market. Atari developed a reputation for computers with excellent graphics and arcade games. Commodore, with its inexpensive Vic 20 and Commodore 64, was recognized as selling some of the least expensive computers the world had ever seen. The craze for inexpensive computers attracted additional contenders. A British firm, under the guidance of inventor Clive Sinclair, produced a $499 computer, and Texas Instruments dropped prices to a new low when they sold their TI 99/4A computers in a $99 clearance sale.

Fearful of cannibalizing its mainframe sales, IBM was hesitant to enter the microcomputer market. However, even IBM was soon forced to face the inevitable: microcomputers were the wave of the future. In 1981, IBM began marketing a microcomputer called the IBM PC. More of a marketing experiment than a major product rollout, the phenomenal sales of the IBM PC caught IBM executives by surprise. A critical factor in the IBM PC design was the use of standard off-the-shelf circuitry. As a result, virtually any computer company could assemble a computer that would look and function like the IBM PC. Most important of all, these IBM-compatible machines, or "clones" as they came to be called, could use software developed for the IBM PC.

The operating system for the IBM PC, called the Microsoft Disk Operating System, or MS-DOS, had been developed by a Harvard University student barely out of his teens who founded a company called Microsoft. Although IBM called the operating system PC-DOS, clone makers could license essentially the same operating system from Microsoft. The ability to use the same operating system as IBM helped ensure that IBM-compatibles could run the same software as the IBM PC. The royalties that Microsoft earned from sales of PC-DOS and MS-DOS helped Microsoft Corporation become the most successful software company in the world.

Since 1981, hundreds of companies have produced IBM PC clones. Some, such as Compaq, were successful, while many others failed. The list of IBM PC clone makers included new startups as well as venerable corporations, such as AT&T, Xerox, Sperry, Data General, Texas Instruments, DEC, and National Cash Register. Companies from Taiwan, Korea, and Japan produced many of the integrated circuits, circuit boards, and peripheral devices for IBM-compatible PCs, and many even manufactured their own computers.

In 1983, Apple released the Lisa computer, a sophisticated computer system featuring a graphical user interface and a mouse. The Lisa's $10,000 price tag discouraged buyers in a market where the average price of other computer systems was less than $5,000. Apple's sales sagged until the release of the Macintosh computer in 1984. The Macintosh featured a graphical user interface and a mouse at a competitive price and sold well against the more difficult to use IBM compatibles.

In 1987, Microsoft released Windows 1.0, a graphical user interface for IBM-compatible computers. Initial sales were slow, but Microsoft kept improving Windows and eventually released the highly successful Windows 3.0 and 3.1. As new high-speed Intel processors boosted performance and fierce competition kept prices low, IBM-compatible computers came to dominate the computer industry.

Computers in Popular Culture

A fourth theme in the history of the computer industry is the role of computers in popular culture. The way computers are depicted in books, in films, and on television is an indication of society's attitudes about computers. Today, U.S. society seems to be in the process of adapting to technology and computers, and this trend is reflected by the media events shown in Figure 11-12.

Figure 11-12

Technology and computers in popular culture

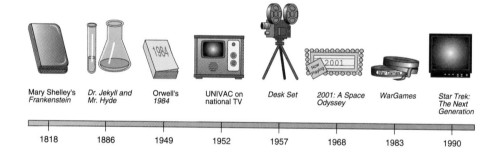

A recurring theme in literature is the relationship between people and technology. This theme spawned its own style of literature called science fiction. Many scholars consider Mary Shelley's *Frankenstein*, published in 1818, the first science fiction novel. *Frankenstein* tells a tale of how a scientist set out with a noble mission to create life, but instead created a monster. Another tale of technology run amok is Robert Louis Stevenson's *Dr. Jekyll and Mr. Hyde*, published in 1886. George Orwell's *1984*, written in 1949, could be viewed as a more contemporary extension of this genre. In Orwell's *1984*, "Big Brother" uses technology to spy on people and pressure them into conforming to the government ideological line.

Computers did not make much of an impact on U.S. culture until 1952, but when they did, the public seemed immediately ready to believe that science had created another monster that would, like Frankenstein and Hyde, produce more harm than good.

In 1952, Dwight D. Eisenhower and Adlai Stevenson were in a close presidential race. CBS news beefed up its election-night coverage by using the newly completed UNIVAC computer to predict the outcome of the election. With only 7% of the vote tabulated at 9 P.M. Eastern Standard Time, the UNIVAC awarded the election to Eisenhower in a landslide. The pollsters, however, had predicted a close race, so the programmers altered UNIVAC's software to predict an Eisenhower win by a slight margin. CBS announced this prediction, but as the evening progressed it turned out that UNIVAC's original prediction had been accurate. CBS sheepishly admitted that it had mistrusted the UNIVAC's original prediction.

This incident captured the attention of Americans, but the publicity was not positive. Most misinterpreted CBS newsman Edward R. Murrow's observation that "The trouble with machines is people." The headlines instead took up the theme of "Giant Mechanical Brains" that would soon outsmart and replace people.

Alan Turing, a British mathematician, fired the first rounds in an ongoing debate about whether computers have the ability to think. In an article published in a 1950 issue of the journal *Mind*, Turing considered the question "Can machines think?" and suggested, as an answer, a game that is now referred to as the Turing Test. In the Turing Test, there is a man (A), a woman (B), and an interrogator, who cannot see or directly communicate with either A or B. The object of the game is for the interrogator to determine the gender of A and B either by asking questions through an intermediary or by using a keyboard. There are two "twists" to this game. The first is that A tries to mislead the interrogator. The second is that A might be a computer. So, the real test is not whether the interrogator can determine the gender of A or B, but whether a computer, substituted for A, can deceive the interrogator by making the interrogator think the computer is a human. Turing appeared to believe that someday a computer would pass the test; although Turing died in 1954, the Turing Test lives on as an annual contest in which computer and software designers attempt to produce a computer that can pass the test.

Opposed to Turing's apparent belief in the potential of computers are John Searle, a prestigious philosopher who created the Chinese-Room Thought Experiment (1980), and John Dreyfuss, who authored the book *What Computers Can't Do* (1979). Scholars are still engaged in the battle that rages over the question "Can computers think?"

The American public of the 1950s lacked either the sophistication or the inclination to enter into debate about a computer's potential to think. Influenced by the "Giant Brain" headlines after the Eisenhower election, popular culture regarded people and computers in constant struggle. Headlines aside, the fact that computers were controlled by government and big business left many people feeling discouraged about their ability to control technology. Representative of this attitude is the film *Desk Set*, a 1957 comedy featuring the legendary actors Spencer Tracy and Katharine Hepburn. The firm where Hepburn works hires Tracy as an "efficiency expert," what we would now call a systems analyst. Tracy installs a computer, which employees view with suspicion. Events take a turn for the worse when, on Christmas Eve, the computer places termination notices in all the paycheck envelopes. In one memorable scene, the computer runs amok and spews out reams of paper, reducing the prim computer operator to tears.

2001:A Space Odyssey was a landmark film directed by Stanley Kubrick and released in 1968. The film won awards for special effects, cinematography, best sound, and best art direction, but the message of the film was standard fare: technology vs. humanity. A synopsis of the story was provided in Chapter 1. The computer, HAL, played a major role in the film and might be considered a sophisticated big brother to creatures of the Frankenstein genre. HAL is supposed to be man's perfect companion, but as events progress, some fatal flaws in the computer's design are revealed. HAL is disconnected, but not before all but one member of the crew is dead and the mission is in shambles. HAL's final words as he is disconnected bring us to the frontiers of computer technology and the debate about whether computers can think, "Dave, I can feel it . . . my mind is going."

WarGames, a 1983 film, depicts technology in a more pragmatic way. In the film, a soulless technology was harnessed under the influence of an evil military establishment. Perhaps there was a message in this film that, in the end, human compassion and cleverness will triumph over evil. In the popular culture of the 1980s, the computer was an arcade game, a toy, and a tool, but not a technology to consider deeply as a growing part of the social fabric.

In the 1990s we can look back over almost 50 years to assess the impact of computers in our society. In addition, personal computers have existed for more than 15 years; this fact has dissipated much of the tendency to view computers as a tool that empowers governments and corporations, but not individuals. Computers have become a part of our daily lives. Computers now appear in films and on television as background props. There are factual weekly computer programs such as "Computer Chronicles." And your local newspaper might carry a regular computer column. But what indication do we have about the way people view computers today?

One of the most popular television series featuring computers is *Star Trek: The Next Generation*, which depicts two types of computers: an onboard computer and an android. The onboard computer helps control ship-wide systems. The crew can interact verbally with it: "Computer, what is your analysis of the alien's biological structure?" However, more often, the crew requests and receives data from the computer by means of a graphical display. This vision of computers, although on a futuristic spaceship, seems not too far advanced from today's technology.

Commander Data, the android with a powerful computer "brain," presents us with a more thought-provoking viewpoint on the potential of computers. One of the subthemes of the *Next Generation* examines Data's humanness—his ability to feel emotions. This poses an interesting question: what ethical responsibility would we have if computers could think and feel? Can we disconnect them? Can we own them? Can we control them? These questions represent a more mature perspective on technology in our society—that as technology evolves, we need to be prepared to consider some remarkable issues.

The Computer Marketplace

The computer marketplace is in a continual state of change as new products appear and old products are discontinued; as corporations form, merge, and die; as corporate leadership shifts; as consumers' buying habits evolve; and as prices steadily continue to decrease. Having some background on hardware and software life cycles, vendors, computer publications, and industry analysts will help you understand many of the reasons for the rapid changes in the computer marketplace.

Hardware Life Cycle

Automobile manufacturers introduce new models every year. The new models serve two purposes: they allow the manufacturers to incorporate new features, and they provide customers with incentive to purchase a new and improved model. Computer manufacturers also introduce new models—and for the same reasons as their counterparts in the automotive industry. Unfortunately, the computer industry is not on an annual cycle, so the computer marketplace seems rather chaotic with new product announcements, preannouncements, ship dates, and availability dates all coming at irregular intervals. To make some sense out of this apparent chaos, let's look at a typical hardware product life cycle.

Product Announcement

Ideas for new products are everywhere; users express their needs for improved features, engineers produce more efficient designs, scholars publish new theories, and competitors announce new products. Periodically, hardware manufacturers evaluate ideas for new products. As part of the evaluation process, a manufacturer considers how many people might be interested in buying the product, the costs required to produce the product, the time it will take to bring the product to market, and its effect on the competition.

Sometimes a manufacturer cannot assess customer interest without a product announcement. A **product announcement**, such as the one in Figure 11-13, declares a company's intention of producing a particular product.

A product announcement is not necessarily a declaration that a product has been completed and is available if you want to buy it. Often a product announcement is a "trial balloon," designed to assess customer interest and to see what countermoves the competition might make. Therefore, a product announcement often means, "We're thinking of making this product; what would happen if we did?"

Figure 11-13
A product announcement for Intel's 80486 100MHz microprocessor

COMPUTER RESELLER NEWS JANUARY 10, 1994

Intel DX4 to crown 486 line

BY FRED GARDNER
Santa Clara, Calif.
....

Intel Corp. will release its fastest 486 microprocessor early this quarter, a 100MHz 3.3/5-volt version that will be designated the DX4, according to Hans G. Geyer, general manager of the 486 microprocessor division.

In addition to clock tripling, the chip will include other unspecified features that will avoid bus saturation, to which clock-tripled chips are prone, Geyer said. The chip will be appropriate for notebooks as well as desktop PCs, Geyer said.

Santa Clara-based Intel's DX4 will impact the market by bringing added performance to the existing system price point, Geyer said. While exact price has yet to be determined, he said the chip's price will fall between the DX2 66MHz and Pentium, which would put it in the $450-to-$600 price range.

A product announcement can precede the actual product by several years. Sometimes, products are announced but are never made or marketed. These products are sometimes referred to as **vaporware**.

Design and Development

When a manufacturer decides to build and market a hardware product, the engineers and marketing divisions usually make a series of design compromises. The engineers propose a design that is modified by cost and development restrictions. A critical design decision concerns which components should be custom-manufactured and which should be assembled from off-the-shelf parts. Custom components often offer enhanced features and allow a company to distinguish its products from others in the market, but custom components can also increase the price of the device and make it more difficult and expensive for the consumer to obtain replacement components.

Once a design is finalized, engineers create a prototype, which is usually tested in a laboratory. When the prototype functions according to the design specifications, the company prepares for production by converting a factory, changing equipment, or contracting with a manufacturer. The design and development phase might last for several months or several years.

Product Introduction

When a hardware product is first introduced, the hardware manufacturer usually prices it slightly higher than its previous generation of products. Initial supplies of the product are generally low while manufacturing capacity increases to meet demand; consumers who want the scarce product must pay a higher price. As supply and demand reach an equilibrium, the price of the product decreases slightly. Usually the price decrease is due to discounting by dealers, rather than a change in the manufacturer's list price. Manufacturers tend to maintain a slightly high list price; this practice gives their dealers room to provide customer discounts.

When a new product becomes available, it is usually added to the current product line, as shown in Figure 11-14. The prices of the older products are reduced to keep them attractive to buyers. Gradually, the oldest products are discontinued as demand for them declines.

Figure 11-14
Computer product line

P5-90: Intel 90 MHz Pentium CPU, 16 MB RAM, 256 KB cache, 540 MB 13 ms IDE hard drive, PCI Local Bus graphics with 2 MB, double-speed CD-ROM, 3.5" diskette drive, 4 ISA, 2 PCI & 1 PCI/ISA slots, 17" color monitor. **$3995**

P5-60: Intel 60 MHz Pentium CPU, 8 MB RAM, 256 KB cache, 540 MB 13 ms IDE hard drive, PCI Local Bus graphics with 1 MB, double-speed CD-ROM, 3.5" diskette drive, 4 ISA, 2 PCI & 1 PCI/ISA slots, 15" color monitor. **$2495**

P4D-66: Intel 66 MHz 486 DX2 CPU, 8 MB RAM, 128 KB cache, 540 MB 13 ms IDE hard drive, PCI Local Bus graphics with 1 MB, double-speed CD-ROM, 3.5" diskette drive, 5 ISA & 2 PCI slots, 15" color monitor. **$2295**

4DX2-50V: Intel 50 MHz DX2 CPU, 8 MB RAM, 128 KB cache, 424 MB 13 ms IDE hard drive, Vesa Local Bus graphics with 1 MB, 3.5" drive, 5 ISA slots, 14" color monitor, 5 ISA & 2 VESA/ISA slots. **$1995**

4SX-33V: Intel 33 MHz 486SX CPU, 4 MB RAM, 340 MB 13 ms IDE hard drive, Vesa Local Bus graphics with 1 MB, 3.5" drive, 5 ISA slots, 14" color monitor. **$1295**

New products offer the latest features and usually sell for a premium price. Older products don't include the latest features and must be sold at a discounted price. Very old products are usually available at super-low, close-out prices. For the consumer, this means that the latest generation of products are the most expensive, while products from a previous generation are less expensive and might offer good performance for the price.

The price and performance of the computers in a typical microcomputer product line can be depicted by a curve, as shown in Figure 11-15. The products in the middle of a typical microcomputer product line—those that are 8 to 18 months old—tend to offer the best performance for the price.

Figure 11-15

Hardware price performance curve

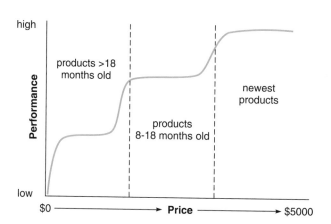

Software Life Cycle

Software, like hardware, begins with an idea that is then shaped by a design team and marketing experts. Product announcements are information-gathering tools for software publishers, just as they are for hardware manufacturers, and the software industry also has its share of vaporware. The software life cycle, however, is somewhat different from the hardware life cycle, and the guidelines for buying software are also different.

As you learned in Chapter 2, a new software product can be an entirely new product, a new version with significant enhancements, or a revision designed to add minor enhancements and eliminate bugs found in the current version. New products are usually released with a major advertising campaign. New versions of an existing product are also often released with much fanfare as companies tout the latest features and advantages the new version has over competitors' products. New versions of software are often offered at discounted prices to owners of the older versions to encourage them to switch to the new version and to discourage them from switching to a competing product.

Revisions are often made available to current owners of the software at little or no cost. However, revisions are often released with little publicity because software companies can't afford to have every owner of the product request the new revision. Sometimes customers don't know a revision is available until they call the publisher's technical support line with a problem. If the problem turns out to be a result of a bug in the version they are using, the technical support person then informs the customers of the existence of the revision.

Alpha and Beta Testing

Once a software publisher begins serious development of a new software product or a new version of a current product, programming teams code the program according to the design specifications. The program code is tested by programmers and software testers employed by the publisher, a process known as **alpha testing**. However, modern programs are so large that it is virtually impossible to test every logical branch of the program or to find out how the program interacts with the many programs and hardware devices that might be found on the computer systems of typical users. Therefore, the publisher sends the software to selected users for testing under realistic conditions. This phase of testing is referred to as **beta testing**, and the users who test the software are referred to as **beta testers**.

Beta testers use the beta software and report any problems to the publisher, who then tries to fix the problems before shipping the final version of the software. Beta testers usually do not get paid for their work, but often receive a complimentary copy of the finished product. Sometimes a software product undergoes several rounds of beta testing before it is ready for market. Generally, even after extensive alpha and beta testing, the software still contains some bugs that will be corrected in subsequent revisions and versions.

Product Introduction

When a new software product first becomes available, it often appears on the market at a special introductory price to entice customers. Several software products that carry a list price of $495 have been introduced at a special $99 price. Another type of introductory offer might be called "switch and save." The way this works is that customers can switch to a new software product for a special price—often $129—if they own a competitor's product. Microsoft ran an aggressive switch and save campaign in 1992, hoping to convince WordPerfect users to switch to Microsoft Word for Windows. Microsoft ran full-page ads with the headline, "No wonder WordPerfect users prefer Word for Windows. It has 'easy' written all over it." The ads offered a special $129 price on Word for Windows to people with current licenses for competing word processing software, such as WordPerfect, MultiMate, WordStar, and DisplayWrite.

Product Line

Soon after a new version of a product is released, the software publisher usually stops selling earlier versions. For example, when WordPerfect Corporation released version 5.0 of its word processing software, version 4.2 was discontinued soon afterward. However, when a new product is released for a different operating system or computer type, other versions of the software are still maintained in the product line. For example, WordPerfect for DOS was first produced for IBM-compatible computers. A short time later, a new product, WordPerfect for the Macintosh, was produced. Both products remained in the product line.

Computer Vendors

If you are planning to buy computer products or work in the computer industry, it is useful to know how the industry is structured. Figure 11-16 diagrams the relationship among the marketing outlets or "channels" in the computer industry.

Figure 11-16
Computer market channels

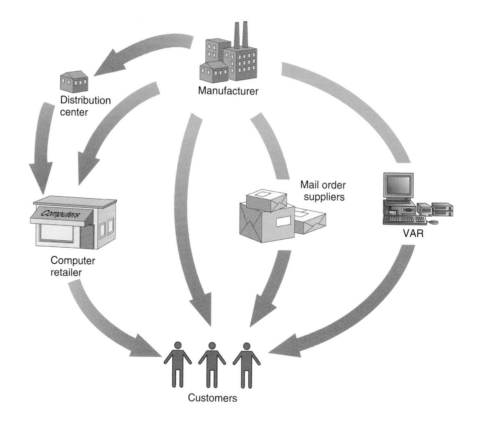

Computer Retailers

A **computer retail store** is usually a local shop that purchases computer products from a manufacturer or distribution center and then sells the products to customers. Computer retail stores specialize in the sales of microcomputer software and hardware. The employees at computer retail stores are often knowledgeable about a variety of computer products and can help you select a hardware or software product to fit your needs. Many computer retail stores also offer classes and training sessions, answer questions, provide technical support, and repair hardware products. Computer retail stores are often the most expensive channel for hardware and software, reflecting the cost of purchasing merchandise from a distributor, maintaining a retail storefront, and hiring technically qualified staff. A computer retail store is often the best source of supply for buyers who are likely to need assistance after the sale, such as beginning computer users or those with complex computer systems such as networks.

Mail Order Suppliers

Mail order suppliers take orders by mail or telephone and ship the product directly to customers. Mail order suppliers generally offer low prices but provide limited service and support. A mail order supplier is often the best source of products for buyers who are unlikely to need support. Experienced computer users who can install components, set up their software, and do their own troubleshooting are often happy with mail order suppliers. Inexperienced computer users might not be satisfied with the support and assistance they receive from mail order suppliers.

Value Added Resellers

A **VAR (Value Added Reseller)** combines commercially available products with special hardware or software to create a computer system designed to meet the needs of a specific industry. Although VARs charge for their expertise, they are often the only source for a system that actually works for your specific industry. For example, if you own a video rental store and want to automate your store, the best type of vendor might be a VAR. The VAR can offer you a complete hardware and software package, which means that you do not need to find the individual computer, scanner, printer, and software components that integrate effectively to keep track of video rentals.

Manufacturer Direct

Many hardware manufacturers sell their products directly to the public using a direct sales force or mail order. This is often referred to as **manufacturer direct** selling. A manufacturer's direct sales force usually targets large corporate or educational customers where large volume sales can cover the cost and commissions of the sales force. In the personal computer market, manufacturers usually choose to use mail order for direct sales. Manufacturers can sell their products directly for a lower price than when they sell them through dealers, but cannot generally offer the same level of support and assistance as a local retailer. However, in an effort to improve customer support, some manufacturers have established customer support lines and provide repair services at the customer's place of business.

Computer Publications

Computer publications provide information on computers, computing, and the computer industry. The type of computer publication you need depends on the kind of information you are trying to obtain.

Magazines

One of the earliest computer magazines, *Byte*, began publication in August 1975 and still remains one of the most widely read sources of information for computers and computing. The success of *Byte* might be attributed to its wide coverage of computers and computing topics. Many magazines that featured only a single type of computer, such as the Apple II, had staying power only as long as the computer maintained good sales. Nevertheless, some magazines for specific computers, such as *MacWorld*, maintain a healthy subscription list.

Computer magazines generally target users of both personal and business computers. Articles often focus on product evaluations, product comparisons, and practical tips for installing hardware and using software. These magazines are fairly well saturated with product advertisements, which are useful if you want to keep informed about the latest products available for your computer. Computer magazines can be found on virtually any newsstand, and discounted subscriptions are often available from the magazine's publisher.

Trade Journals

Computer trade journals have a different focus than computer magazines. **Trade journals** are publications for the people who design, build, sell, and market computer products. Computer trade journals, such as *InfoWorld* and *Computer Reseller News*, tend to focus on company profiles, product announcements, and sales techniques. Often corporate decision makers are provided with free subscriptions to trade journals because advertisers want them to be aware of their products. Trade journals are not always available on newsstands, and subscriptions are not always available to the general public.

Academic Journals

Academic journals offer a different perspective from either trade journals or computer magazines. **Academic journals** focus on research in computing, with articles on such topics as the most efficient sorting technique to use in a database management system, the implication of copyright law for educational institutions, or the prevalence of spreadsheet use by executives in Fortune 500 companies.

An article in an academic journal is usually "refereed," which means that it is evaluated by a committee of experts who determine if the article is original and based on sound research techniques. The best place to find academic journals is in a university library. Some of the most respected journals in the computing field include *Communications of the ACM* (Association for Computing Machinery), *Communications of the IEEE* (Institute of Electrical and Electronics Engineers), *SIAM* (Society of Industrial and Applied Mathematics) *Journal on Computing*, and *Journal of Information Science*.

Industry Analysts

As with most industries, the computer industry has a bevy of **industry analysts** who monitor industry trends, evaluate industry events, and make predictions about what the trends seem to indicate. Computer industry analysts range from professional financial analysts, who report on the computer industry for the *Wall Street Journal* and *Forbes* magazine, to the "rumor-central" analysts who spark up the back pages of trade journals and computer magazines with the latest gossip about new products. For people who are interested in investing in the stock of a computer corporation, the financial analysts might offer some good insights. For those people who are interested in investing in a personal computer, the rumor-central columns are the place to get the scoop about product shortages, hardware glitches, software bugs, and impending customer service problems. Figure 11-17 on the following page describes some of the better-known industry analysts.

Buying Computer Equipment and Software

Chances are that you will purchase a computer more than once in your lifetime. And, because the computer industry changes so rapidly, the computer you might buy in a few years will certainly be quite different from the one you would buy today. Therefore, instead of telling you which computer you should purchase, we'll provide you with a set of guidelines to help you make an informed purchasing decision, no matter when you buy.

Figure 11-17
Computer market analysts and commentators

Portia Isaacson is a well-respected industry analyst who has a good track record predicting trends and who provides balanced insight into many of the issues facing the computer industry.

Spencer F. Katt runs Rumor Central from his column on the back pages of PCWeek. Katt issues a weekly collection of inside tips on people, companies, and products.

Laurie Flynn writes a feature column for the Computing section of the San Jose Mercury News. She focuses on new products that make computers effective and easy to use.

A science fiction writer and long-time computer columnist, Jerry Pournelle writes about a potpourri of hardware and software products.

John Dvorak has had long-running columns in several computer publications and now makes appearances in PC Computing magazine as well as on a syndicated radio program.

Robert X. Cringely's weekly column in Infoworld is filled with gossip about the executives, finances, and products of the leading computer industry companies.

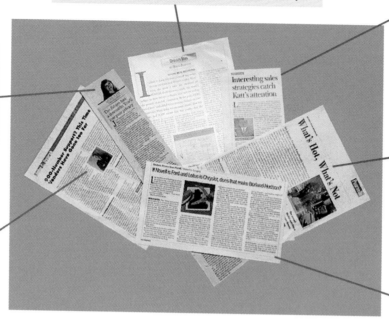

Think About the Tasks You Want to Accomplish

First, make a list of the tasks you want to accomplish. Word processing is the most popular computer application, but as you have learned, you can use a computer for many different things. Individuals are finding computers increasingly useful for managing their money, figuring out taxes, planning trips, learning, accessing reference information, and entertainment. A good way to find more information about the many uses of computers is to browse through the current issues of several computer magazines. The advertisements cover a good cross section of computer applications.

Select the Products That Meet Your Needs

Once you know what you want to do, you can try to locate specific hardware and software products that will meet your needs. Your software research should reveal the answers to three questions:

1. Is software available to effectively accomplish the tasks you want to accomplish?
2. What is the price of the software?
3. Which hardware is required to run the software?

You can find answers to these questions from a number of sources, including computer magazines, software publishers, hardware manufacturers, software vendors, user groups, bulletin boards, information services, and the Internet.

Computer magazines carry ads that describe product features. Many advertisers have 800 numbers so you can call toll-free to get more information or place an order. Some software publishers offer demos of their programs for free or for a minimal shipping charge. A **demo** is a demonstration copy of a software product, usually limited in some way so you can't use it for real tasks, but complete enough so that you can use it to explore the program's features, evaluate the user interface, and decide if you want to purchase the full version of the product.

Computer magazines often contain reviews of specific products and comparative evaluations of several similar products. For example, if you're interested in purchasing a database program, you can be certain that one or more of the major computer magazines has featured a comparative review of database programs within the last six months or so. You might have to look through back issues of several computer magazines to locate the review, but you'll be rewarded with a comprehensive evaluation of the latest products in that category. In general, don't pay too much attention to reviews that are more than a year old because they won't include information on the latest products.

If you cannot get information from a manufacturer or a magazine review, you might be able to get some information from your local computer retail store. However, remember that there are thousands of computer products on the market, and the sales people at your local store are usually familiar with only a few of the best-selling products.

Computer user groups are an excellent source of information on computer products. A **computer user group** is an organization of people who use, and usually own, computers. Most user groups meet periodically and also provide information through printed newsletters, networks, or computer bulletin boards. Almost every user group has some very experienced members who can give you firsthand accounts of a product's strengths and weaknesses and who can help you resolve specific problems. Just remember that the strength of a person's opinion is not always directly related to their knowledge.

Information services such as CompuServe, Prodigy, and America Online have discussion groups devoted to particular hardware and software products. If the product you are considering has a discussion group, you should be able to get valuable information by reading through a transcript of previous discussions and posting your own questions. You can also post questions about a product to a Usenet news group on the Internet. A master list of current news groups is posted on the Internet as *news.lists*. You can look through the master list for a news group for a particular product or general application area.

Collect Pricing, Service, and Support Information

When your software research is complete, the specifications for running the software will have provided you with an idea of the computer configuration you need. You can then begin to look at computer hardware and compare prices. The price alone is not sufficient information for making a purchasing decision. The fact that one computer costs $1299 and another costs $1999 is not useful until you know what is included in the price. In addition, you must look beyond the hardware configuration to consider the warranty and the vendor's reputation, service policy, and quality of technical support. You might use a form like the one in Figure 11-18 to record the information for each computer system you are considering.

Shop a Variety of Channels

To gather pricing, service, and support information, you should shop more than one channel, that is, you should shop computer retail stores, mail order outlets, manufacturers, and possibly value added resellers. You are likely to find some significant price differences among the channels, but the different service and support policies are likely to account for some of the price differences.

Service refers to a vendor's ability to repair hardware when it breaks. A vendor's ability to quickly service your product depends on the expertise of the vendor's technical staff and the vendor's parts inventory. Some vendors offer to repair your computer at your home or business. This is often referred to as **on-site service**. Other vendors require you to bring your defective equipment in to the nearest store. Still other vendors might require you to mail the computer to a repair depot.

Support refers to a vendor's ability to answer your questions after the sale. A vendor's ability to provide you with effective support depends on the quality of the vendor's support staff and on its support policies. Some vendors provide free support to their customers. Other vendors charge customers for support contracts or bill customers by the minute for the support technician's time.

Most of the time, when someone has trouble with a computer product, the product isn't broken; the user just does not know how to get the computer to perform a particular task. What this means is that computer users need a lot of assistance and have a lot of questions that they need answered, but don't actually need their equipment repaired very often. Support is often far more important than the product warranty or service contract that covers only broken products.

Computer brand, model, and manufacturer: _____

Processor type: _____

Processor speed: _____ MHz

RAM capacity: _____ megabytes

Type of bus: ❏ EISA ❏ ISA ❏ MicroChannel ❏ Local Bus ❏ PCI

Number and size of floppy disk drives: _____

Capacity of hard drive: _____ megabytes

Speed of hard drive: _____ ms

Speed of CD-ROM drive: _____

Capacity and speed of tape drive: _____

Amount of cache memory: _____ kilobytes

Monitor screen size: _____ inches

Monitor resolution: _____ by _____

Type of video adapter: ❏ VGA ❏ SVGA

Amount of video memory: _____ megabytes

Number of parallel ports: _____

Number of serial ports: _____

Number of SCSI ports: _____

Number of expansion slots: _____

Operating system: _____

Mouse included: ❏ Yes ❏ No

Sound card and speakers included: ❏ Yes ❏ No

Value of bundled application software: $ _____

Does it have good expansion capabilities? ❏ Yes ❏ No

Does it have an upgrade path for new technologies, such as new processors?
❏ Yes ❏ No

Does the vendor have a support team in place that will meet my needs?
❏ Yes ❏ No

Are the technical support hours sufficient? ❏ Yes ❏ No

Is it inexpensive to get support? ❏ Yes ❏ No

Can I contact technical support personnel without being put on hold for an extended time? ❏ Yes ❏ No

Are technical support people knowledgeable? ❏ Yes ❏ No

Can I get my computer fixed in an acceptable time period? ❏ Yes ❏ No

Are the costs and procedures for fixing the computer acceptable? ❏ Yes ❏ No

What is the warranty period? _____ years

Does the warranty cover parts and labor? ❏ Yes ❏ No

Are other users satisfied with this computer? ❏ Yes ❏ No

Is the manufacturer a well-financed and stable company? ❏ Yes ❏ No

Are the computer parts and components standard? ❏ Yes ❏ No

Price: _____

Figure 11-18
Hardware
comparison worksheet

Evaluate the Best Deal

Evaluate your best deal by considering price, availability, service, support, and warranty. You could set up a decision support worksheet like the one in Figure 11-19 to help you decide which computer is the best deal.

Figure 11-19
Decision support worksheet for evaluating product choices

1 List at least two possible options. This worksheet is designed to help you choose between Computer #1 and Computer #2.

3 Assign a "weighting factor" to each criterion using a scale of 1 to 10. Give the most important criteria the highest weighting factors.

4 After you research the options, assign a raw score for each factor.

2 List the factors that are important criteria for making your selection.

5 Add a formula in the spreadsheet to multiply the raw score by the weighting factor to produce a weighted score.

6 Add a formula in the spreadsheet to total the weighted scores for each option. The option that has the highest total is the best system for you to purchase.

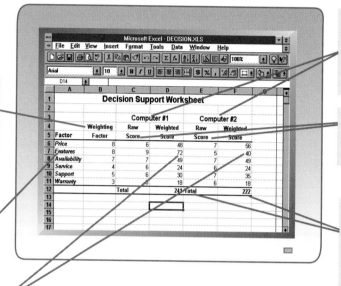

At the beginning of this text we introduced computers as "mind tools" that enhance your ability to perform tasks that require mental activities. We also suggested that the key to making effective use of a computer as a tool is to know what a computer is and how to use it.

In Chapter 11 we introduced IBM's THINK slogan. We hope you recognize some of the many ways in which that slogan is tied to computers and to the study of computers. While reading the text, we hope you have had a chance to THINK about how computers can help you become more productive: how you can use software to accomplish specific tasks, how networks broaden your access to information, how multimedia provides a rich environment for research and learning, and how you can use the Internet as a highway to vast landscapes of information. We also hope you have been challenged to THINK about some of the issues and controversies that swirl through the computer industry: how computers impact your privacy, the ethics of legal software use, and the implications of computers that might someday be intelligent. Finally, we hope you will THINK about how you can build, extend, and apply the knowledge you gained from this text to your own personal and career development.

C H A P T E R   R E V I E W

1. Answer the questions listed in the Chapter Preview section at the beginning of the chapter.
2. List each of the boldface terms in this chapter, then use your own words to write a short definition of each term.
3. What was the analytical engine and how does it relate to a modern microcomputer?
4. Look back at the Turing Machine in Figure 11-2. If you start with the window on the leftmost 1 in the binary number 101 (which is a decimal 5), will the Turing Machine accurately add 1 and produce 110 (which is a decimal 6)?
5. Describe the significant features of the first, second, and third generation computer systems.
6. Describe the development of computer programming languages.
7. Discuss some of the ways computers have been viewed in popular culture.
8. Describe each of the marketing channels in the computer industry.
9. List the sources of information you can use to find out about a particular computer product.
10. What are the advantages and disadvantages of purchasing computer equipment from mail order vendors as opposed to local dealers?

C H A P T E R   Q U I Z

1. The _____ consists of the corporations and individuals that supply goods and services for the people and organizations that use computers.
2. First generation computers used _____ as the device that carried out arithmetic operations.
3. Second generation computer circuitry used _____, which were faster, smaller, less expensive, more reliable, and used less power than the devices used in first generation computers.
4. The architecture of third generation computers was based on _____, which were faster, smaller, more reliable, and less expensive than the devices used in second generation computers.
5. The _____, essentially a computer on a chip, led to the development of the microcomputer.
6. In the early days, computer users had to write their own software. The development of commercial software such as _____, the first electronic spreadsheet program, made it possible to use a computer without writing a program.
7. A computer will have passed the _____ when a person communicating with a computer cannot tell if he or she is communicating with a computer or a person.
8. A(n) _____ is a trial balloon that computer companies and software publishers use to assess customer interest and see what countermoves the competition might make.
9. A graph of the _____ for computer products indicates that the best deal on computer equipment can often be found on products that have just been replaced by a new product.

10. During _____ testing, a software developer sends preliminary copies of a program to selected users who work with the program and report any problems or bugs that they find in the program.

11. A(n) _____ often provides the best support and assistance, but charges the highest prices for their products.

12. A(n)_____ usually offers the lowest prices, but offers limited support and assistance.

13. A(n) _____ specializes in solutions to meet the needs of a specific industry.

14. Many software publishers provide _____ that allow you to explore the features of a software product before deciding whether to purchase the full program.

15. A(n) _____, an organization of people who use and own computers, can be an excellent source of information and assistance with specific problems.

P R O J E C T S

1. Collect advertisements featuring similar computer systems from three different manufacturers and complete the following table:

	System 1	System 2	System 3
Processor type/speed			
RAM			
Hard-disk capacity			
Video adapter type and memory			
Monitor size and resolution			
Expansion slots			
Bus type			
Value of bundled software			
Value of bundled hardware			
Warranty			
Technical support			
Price			

2. After examining the table you completed in Project 1, explain which computer is the best deal and why.

3. Locate and read one issue of a computer magazine, trade journal, or academic journal related to computing. Describe the magazine and the type of articles and advertisements included in it.

4. Locate two issues of a popular computer magazine, one current issue and one from at least one year ago. Look through the ads and articles to locate a topic or product that underwent significant change during that time period. Describe the topic or product and the changes that occurred during that time period.

5. Select an individual, company, event, or device that played an important role in the development of computers. Write a one-page description of that individual, company, event, or device and explain its significance in computer history.

L   A   B

Computer History Lab

L A B

**COMPUTER
HISTORY**

The Computer History Lab contains information about the inventions, people, and events that shaped the computer industry. It has a user interface similar to a multimedia encyclopedia; by using the Lab, you will learn how to use multimedia reference software.

The information in the Computer History Lab is arranged much like an encyclopedia, that is, there are many topics, and the topics are presented in a specific order. And, just as you would not sit down and read an encyclopedia from cover to cover, you will not begin with the first computer history topic and then continue to read the rest of the information in sequential order.

The topics in the Computer History Lab are indexed and cross-referenced so you can easily jump from one topic to another related topic. Let's see how this works before you begin your own research to answer the questions posed later in the Lab:

1. Open the Computer History Lab and read the introductory screen. Click the **Continue** button when you are ready to proceed.

2. The first screen is the Table of Contents, which lists the major milestones in the development of computers. You can jump to any one of these milestones. Let's jump to the information on second generation computers.

3. Move the pointer to **Second generation computers: transistors** and notice that the pointer changes to a pointing hand.

4. Click the left mouse button. You should see the screen titled "Transistorized Computers 1957."

5. You can return to the Table of Contents at any time. Do it now by clicking the **Contents** button on the toolbar.

The Computer History Lab provides you with a way to jump to related topics and follow your own "threads" of research:

1. In the Table of Contents, click **Third generation computers: integrated circuits** to jump to a screen titled "The Integrated Circuit 1959."

2. Take a moment to read about the development of the integrated circuit. As you do, notice that some of the information is underlined.

3. Now suppose you want to find out more about Robert Noyce. Because his name is underlined, you can jump directly to information about him. Click **Robert Noyce** to jump to the screen titled "Intel 1969."

4. Now suppose you want to find out more about the IBM PC. Click **IBM PC** to display the screen "IBM PC 1981."

The Computer History Lab also contains photos that relate to the topics. When a photo is available, you will see a camera icon on the screen. Let's look at a photo of the original IBM PC:

1. Click the **camera icon** to display a photo of the IBM PC. You might have to wait a few seconds for the photo to appear, depending on the speed of your computer.

2. After you have seen the photo, you must close the photo window or the photo will remain on the screen as you go to other topics. To close the photo window, look for the word "File" in the photo window. Click **File**, then click **Exit**.

Sometimes after you have jumped from topic to topic, you might want to back up and view a previous topic. Let's go back to the screen containing information on Intel.

1. Click the **Back** button and you should see the topic titled "Intel 1969."

You also might want to search for a particular topic that is not listed in the Table of Contents. Suppose you want to find out more about Ethernet networks. To search for information about Ethernet:

1. Click the **Search** button, located on the toolbar. The Search dialog box appears. There are two ways to search: you can scroll through the topics using the scroll bar, or you can type the name of the topic you want. We'll use the typing method. You can experiment with the scroll bar later.

2. Type **et** and notice that Ethernet appears in the topic box. (You usually only need to type the first few letters of the topic you are searching for.)

3. Click the **Show Topics** button to look at a list of topics that include information about Ethernet. The two related topics are displayed in the lower box: Ethernet and Xerox PARC. Let's look at Xerox PARC:

4. Click **Xerox PARC**, then click the **Go To** button. The topic titled "Xerox PARC 1974" appears.

5. Now let's return to the Table of Contents, so you can continue with the Lab activities. Click the **Contents** button on the tool bar.

Now that you know how to navigate through the topics in the Computer History Lab, do the following activities:

1. Several mechanical calculating devices were produced between the early 1600s and the middle 1800s. Select one of these devices and explain why you think this device was particularly significant or interesting.

2. Complete the following chart:

Computer	Estimated Cost	Instructions/Second	RAM or Internal Storage Capacity
ENIAC	_____	_____	_____
UNIVAC	_____	_____	_____
The computer you usually use	_____	_____	_____

3. Complete the following table:

Event	Date	Device
First automatic adding machine	_____	_____
First electronic computer	_____	_____
First fully electronic stored program computer	_____	_____
First widely used high-level programming language	_____	_____
First microprocessor	_____	_____
First microcomputer	_____	_____
First word processing program	_____	_____
First spreadsheet program	_____	_____

4. Describe Grace Hopper's contributions to the development of the computer industry.

5. Describe some of the individuals and events critical to the development of hypertext.

6. List three products that played an important role in the development of the company now known as IBM, and explain why you think those products were particularly significant.

7. Discuss the companies, people, and events that have played an important role in the development of the graphical user interface.

8. Explain who you would credit with the development of the stored program concept if you were writing a history of the computer industry.

9. Explain how you would respond to the question "Who invented the computer?"

10. Explain how events in 1971 affected the development of the computer and software industry.

R E S O U R C E S

■ Augarten, Stan. *BIT by BIT, An Illustrated History of Computers*. New York: Ticknor & Fields, 1984.

This book is an outstanding illustrated history of the computer industry, covering everything from the abacus to the release of the IBM PC. Extensive background material and descriptions bring to life the many brilliant and eccentric characters who played important roles in the development of the modern computer system.

■ Freiberger, P. and M. Swaine. *Fire in the Valley. The Making of the Personal Computer*. Berkeley: Osborne/McGraw Hill, 1984.

This book provides energetic coverage of the development of the microcomputer from the first microprocessor through the Altair, CP/M, IMSAI, Microsoft, Apple, and the IBM PC. The authors include many photos and anecdotes about the colorful figures who played prominent roles in the early days of the microcomputer industry.

■ Rodgers, W. *THINK: Biography of the Watsons and IBM*. New York: Stein and Day, 1969.

Rodgers wrote an unauthorized but lively account of IBM and its leadership. Published in 1969, this book ends before the advent of the microcomputer and is therefore an account of the "glory days" of mainframe computing.

■ Rogers, E. and J. Larsen. *Silicon Valley Fever: Growth of High-Technology Culture*. New York: Basic Books, 1982.

Rogers, a professor of International Communication at Stanford University, and Larson, a Silicon Valley research scientist, teamed up to create a very readable account of the impact of technology on the businesses and people of Silicon Valley. The legends are all here: the multimillion-dollar companies that started in a garage, the teenagers who became corporate magnates, the most successful public stock offering in the history of Wall Street, and the spreadsheet empire that went from rags to riches and back to rags.

■ Searle, John. *Minds, Brains, and Science*. Cambridge, MA: Harvard University Press, 1984.

In 1984, Searle presented his views on artificial intelligence as the BBC Reith Lecturer. In this book, Searle argues with Turing's position on the possibility of computer intelligence by posing his now-famous Chinese Room analogy.

■ Shurkin, Joel. *Engines of the Mind, A History of the Computer*. New York, London: W.W. Norton & Company, 1984.

This comprehensive book includes extensive coverage of Babbage, Hollerith, and computer pioneers through the early 1980s.

- Turing, A. "Computing Machinery and Intelligence," *Mind* 59, 1950.

  In this article Turing proposes the Turing Test as a means of answering the question "Can machines think?".

  The Machine That Changed the World (video). A production of WGBH Science Unit and the BBC. PBS, 1988.

  First aired on PBS as five one-hour segments, parts two and three examine issues in the development of modern computers. The entire series is definitely worth watching and can be purchased from Films for the Humanities, Inc., P.O. Box 2053, Princeton, NJ 08543-2053, 800-257-5126.

ANSWERS TO CHAPTER QUIZZES

CHAPTER 1

1. keyboard, monitor
2. compatible
3. Syntax
4. graphical
5. prompt
6. cursor
7. pointer
8. high-resolution monitor
9. memory (or random access memory)
10. user interface
11. the computer
12. Windows
13. metaphor
14. context sensitive
15. an error message (or a syntax error)

CHAPTER 2

1. operating system
2. false
3. system
4. true
5. multitasking
6. UNIX
7. Software
8. micro
9. operating environments
10. Utility
11. device driver
12. true
13. false
14. Multimedia
15. MPC standard

CHAPTER 3

1. 12
2. 4
3. 2,000
4. security
5. tapes (or magnetic tapes)
6. random
7. hard disk drive
8. disk cache
9. Bernoulli
10. CD-ROM drive
11. erase (or delete)
12. fragmented
13. overwriting
14. undelete
15. writing

CHAPTER 4

1. digital
2. bit
3. 40 bits or 5 bytes
4. bus
5. 32
6. RAM (or random access memory)
7. SIMM
8. CMOS
9. ROM (or read only memory)
10. ALU (or arithmetic logic unit)
11. control unit
12. fetch
13. microprocessor
14. 4
15. boot process

CHAPTER 5

1. 3
2. 255
3. ASCII
4. 256
5. 16
6. 16
7. digital representations
8. reconstruct (or recreate)
9. Sampling rate
10. Adaptive pattern substitution
11. Run length encoding
12. communications channel
13. stop bits
14. 1
15. simplex, duplex

CHAPTER 6

1. network
2. password
3. Mapping
4. capture
5. multiuser
6. Ethernet
7. token
8. packet
9. network communication protocols
10. peer-to-peer
11. host
12. thread
13. address
14. telnet
15. FTP

CHAPTER 7

1. procedures
2. undelete utility
3. think
4. uninterruptible power supply (UPS), surge suppressor
5. automatic save
6. time bomb
7. virus
8. signature
9. trap door
10. read
11. full
12. incremental
13. personal property
14. key
15. Clipper Chip

CHAPTER 8

1. information system
2. office automation
3. transaction processing system
4. management information system
5. exception report
6. decision support system
7. expert system
8. expert system shell
9. knowledge base
10. systems analyst
11. request for proposal (RFP)
12. Customization
13. Integration
14. parallel
15. maintenance

CHAPTER 9

1. Character
2. flat
3. object-oriented
4. data structure diagram
5. relational database
6. custom program
7. range check
8. case sensitive
9. and
10. or
11. sort key
12. index
13. control-break
14. sonification or graphics (data visualization techniques)
15. detail

CHAPTER 10

1. algorithm
2. flow chart
3. Coding (or programming)
4. sequence control structure
5. selection control
6. repetition control (or loop)
7. testing
8. syntax
9. documentation
10. procedural
11. declarative
12. low-level language
13. source code
14. Cobol
15. event-driven

CHAPTER 11

1. computer history
2. vacuum tubes
3. transistors
4. integrated circuits
5. microprocessor
6. VisiCalc
7. Turing Test
8. product announcement
9. price performance
10. beta
11. computer retail store
12. mail order supplier
13. value-added retailer (or VAR)
14. demos
15. user group

ICON IDENTIFICATION QUIZ

icon 1: 1. Save a document (Microsoft Windows)
icon 2: 3. Copy to Clipboard (Microsoft Windows)
icon 3: 2. Activate Tip Wizard ((Microsoft Excel 5.0)
icon 4: 1. Undo (Microsoft Word 2.0)
icon 5: 4. Check spelling (Microsoft Word 2.0 and 6.0)

GLOSSARY / INDEX

A

abacus, NP 376-377

ABC computer, NP 379, NP 380

academic journal A publication that focuses on research in computing, NP 403

accelerated video adapter A type of video card that uses graphics coprocessor chips designed to perform video functions at very high speed, NP 140

acceptance testing The final test of an information system in which the purchaser or user of the new system verifies the new system is operating correctly, NP 284

access cover, floppy disks, NP 88

Access Software Golf, NP 65

access time The average time it takes for a computer to locate data on the storage medium and read it, NP 87

accounting software, NP 47

Ada, Augusta, NP 377

adaptive pattern substitution A compression technique designed to compress text files by scanning the entire text and looking for patterns of two or more bytes, NP 170

adding machines, mechanical, NP 401

address
    cell, spreadsheet software, NP 50
    RAM, NP 119
    workstation, NP 201, NP 212

address lines The part of the bus that carries the memory location of the data, NP 117, NP 118, NP 120

AFP A network protocol developed by Apple Computer, Inc. for Appletalk networks and Apple Macintosh computers, NP 204

AIX, NP 43

algorithm A set of steps for carrying out a task, NP 343-348
    expressing, NP 346-348

alpha testing The software testing phase when a computer program is tested by programmers and software testers employed by the publisher of a software product, NP 399

Alt key, NP 10

ALU. *See* arithmetic logic unit (ALU)

America Online, NP 209-210, NP 405

analog device A device that operates on continuously varying data, NP 114-115

analysis of needs, NP 269, NP 271-274
    current system, NP 272-274
    problem definition, NP 271-272
    system requirements, NP 274

analytical engine, NP 377

AND operator, NP 318-320

ANSI (American National Standards Institute) code An eight-bit code used by Microsoft Windows for representing letters, numerals, punctuation, and control codes, NP 161

Apple Computer, Inc., NP 63, NP 67, NP 391, NP 392. *See also* Apple II computer; Macintosh computer

Apple Corps Ltd., NP 63, NP 67

Apple II computer, NP 386, NP 391

application development tool a programming environment containing building blocks that can be assembled into an application, NP 275, NP 276, NP 280

application software A type of software you use to accomplish a specific task using the computer. Categories of application software include productivity, business, education and reference, and entertainment, NP 17, NP 38, NP 44-54
    creating, NP 280-281
    creating data files, NP 79
    evolution, NP 386-387
    file extensions, NP 82
    hierarchy, NP 46
    launching, NP 102
    Microsoft Windows, NP 42

application specification A document that describes the way an application should interface with the user and how it should store data, process data, and format reports, NP 277, NP 279

application testing The process of trying out various sequences of input values and checking the results to make sure an application works correctly, NP 281-282

ARCnet A popular network standard that transmits data at either 2 or 20 megabits per second, NP 200, NP 201, NP 202

arithmetic logic unit (ALU) The part of the CPU that performs arithmetic operations such as addition and subtraction, and logical operations such as comparing two numbers. Also called ALU, NP 4, NP 124, NP 125, NP 126, NP 383

ARPAnet, NP 211

ASCII (American Standard Code for Information Interchange) A widely used seven-bit code for representing letters, numerals, punctuation, and control codes, NP 160

assembly languages, NP 357, NP 363-364, NP 385

assumption The part of a problem statement that you accept as true in order to proceed with the program design, NP 341

asynchronous protocol A communications protocol in which the sending computer transmits a start bit to indicate the beginning of a data block and a stop bit to indicate the end of a data block, NP 178

Atanasoff, John, NP 379

Atari, NP 391

ATM A high speed network standard capable of transmitting data at 100 megabits per second, NP 201

AT&T, NP 391

attachment A file such as a word processing document that can be attached to an electronic mail message, NP 208

attributes, tables, NP 306

audio mapping, NP 326

audio output, NP 15

audio tutorial A type of cassette-based tutorial that contains spoken directions telling you how to perform a task, NP 24

AUTOEXEC.BAT A file loaded into memory during the boot process that contains DOS commands or the names of programs that you want the computer to automatically execute every time you turn it on, NP 80, NP 134

automatic save feature A feature of an application program that periodically saves on disk the current version of the document you are editing to minimize potential data loss, NP 230, NP 231

B

Babbage, Charles, NP 114, NP 377

Backspace key, NP 10

backup A duplicate copy of a file or the contents of a disk that you can use to restore data to its original working condition, NP 232, NP 241-246
    copying files, NP 103-104
    differential, NP 242, NP 243, NP 244
    floppy disks, NP 90

full, NP 241-242, NP 244

incremental, NP 242, NP 244

tape storage, NP 8, NP 83, NP 94-95, NP 96

backup procedure The process and schedule you use to make backups, NP 243-246

"bad or missing command interpreter" message, NP 134

bandwidth A range of frequencies; the difference between the highest and lowest frequencies in a channel, NP 173

bar code reader, NP 12

bar graph Type of graph you use to show comparisons, NP 326, NP 327

base 16, NP 119

BASIC A high-level computer language introduced in 1964 as a language for beginning programmers, NP 355, NP 357, NP 362, NP 385

batch file A series of operating system commands that you use to automate tasks you want the operating system to perform, NP 80, NP 81, NP 134

baud rate The number of times the state or frequency of a communications line can change per second, NP 180

BBS. See bulletin board system

Bernoulli disk, NP 95, NP 97

beta tester A user who performs beta testing on a software product, NP 399

beta testing The software testing phase when selected users test a computer program and report bugs to the publisher, NP 399

binary number system, NP 157-159

bit Each one or zero that represents data, NP 115

data communications, NP 155-157

parity, NP 178-179, NP 182

start, NP 178

stop, NP 178, NP 182

bitmap graphic A picture that is represented using a code that indicates the state of each individual dot or pixel displayed on the screen, NP 162-164

bits per second (bps) The number of bits that can be transmitted in one second, NP 180-181, NP 182

block A series of bits that contains the data to be transmitted in asynchronous communication, NP 178

BNC connector Used to connect coaxial cable to the T-shaped connector on a network interface card, NP 174

boot process The sequence of events that occur between the time you turn on your computer and the time it is ready for you to issue commands, NP 130-135

boot program, NP 132

checking configuration data, NP 134

diagnostic tests, NP 133

displaying operating system prompt, NP 134-135

loading operating system, NP 133-134

power up, NP 131-132

bootable floppy disk A floppy disk that contains the files needed to load the operating system into memory. The files IO.SYS, MSDOS.SYS, and COMMAND.COM are required on a DOS bootable disk, NP 134

bps. See bits per second

Brooks, Frederick, NP 268

brownout A temporary reduction in the flow of electrical current to the computer that can result in the destruction of data stored in RAM, NP 229

bug An error in a program, NP 279, NP 350, NP 399

program testing, NP 352-353

bulletin board system (BBS) A computer system connected to a modem and phone line that allows users to post electronic messages and transfer files between the

bulletin board and their own computer, NP 182, NP 208-209

Burroughs, NP 389-390

bus An electronic path that connects the mainboard components, NP 116, NP 117-118, NP 120

address lines, NP 117, NP 118, NP 120

data, NP 117, NP 128

EISA, NP 136, NP 137, NP 138

expansion, NP 135-137

ISA, NP 136, NP 137

Micro channel, NP 137

PCI, NP 136, NP 137, NP 138

system, NP 117, NP 118, NP 135

VESA, NP 136-137

width, NP 128

XT, NP 137

business software Application software that helps organizations efficiently accomplish routine tasks, NP 47

buttons, NP 22

byte Eight bits, or one character of data, NP 86-87, NP 115, NP 119, NP 121

Byte magazine, NP 402

C

C++ programming language An object-oriented version of the C language, NP 363, NP 385

C programming language The most popular computer language for developing professional and commercial programs for microcomputer systems, NP 363

cables, NP 135, NP 138

coaxial, NP 174-175

fiber optic, NP 175-176

networks, NP 198-199

twisted pair, NP 173-174

cache Special high-speed memory used to give the CPU more rapid access to data, NP 94, NP 129

CAI. *See* Computer-aided instruction (CAI)

calculation aids, NP 376-377

Cambridge engineering group, NP 385

Campbell Soup Company, NP 268

"cannot load a file" message, NP 133-134

Caps Lock key, NP 10

capture Redirecting the output from your workstation's parallel port to a network printer, NP 194

carbon copy, NP 208

carrier sense multiple access with collision detection. *See* CSMA/CD (carrier sense multiple access with collision detection)

CASE (Computer Aided Software Engineering) tool Software that is designed for drawing diagrams of information systems, writing process descriptions, and maintaining data dictionaries, NP 272, NP 274

case sensitivity Uppercase letters are not equivalent to their lowercase counterparts; MI is not the same as Mi, NP 316

CD-ROM (compact disc read only memory) A computer storage medium that uses technology derived from the compact disc digital recording system to store data on a disk as a series of pits that are read using a laser beam, NP 8, NP 56, NP 96-98

capacity, NP 77

drive, NP 66

drive identification, NP 83

files, NP 78
  installing software, NP 58
cell The intersection of a row and column in a spreadsheet, NP 50
  address, spreadsheet software, NP 50
central processing unit (CPU) The circuitry in a computer that performs arithmetic and logic operations and executes instructions. Also called the CPU or processor, NP 4, NP 5, NP 123-130. *See also* microprocessor
CGA. *See* color graphics adapter (CGA)
channel. *See* Communications channel
character data type Data that does not need to be mathematically manipulated, NP 297
character recognition software A computer program that scans handwritten or printed characters and accepts them as input, NP 15
character representation The way that non-numeric information is represented by a series of bits, NP 159-162
character representation scheme. *See* code
checksum A technique used by virus detection programs in which a value is calculated by combining all the bytes in a file each time a program is run and comparing the result to the original sum of the bytes, NP 236
child node, hierarchical model, NP 304
chip. *See* integrated circuit
CISC. *See* complex instruction set computer (CISC)
class, object A collection of objects that share a common structure and methods, NP 307, NP 312, NP 360-361
client-server software A type of software that helps workstations access data stored on a file server. When your workstation makes a request to the file server, the server processes your request and sends your workstation the results, NP 205-206
Clipper Chip A chip designed to provide secure transmission of voice and data communications while providing a back door that law enforcement agencies could use to decipher messages, NP 249
clock, NP 383
  synchronous communications protocol, NP 177
clock rate The speed of the master clock in a computer system, NP 127
clones, NP 391, NP 392
cluster A group of sectors and the smallest storage unit the computer can access, NP 99, NP 100
CMOS Battery-powered Complementary Metal Oxide Semiconductor memory that stores vital information about your computer system configuration even when your computer power is off, NP 122
coaxial cable A high bandwidth communications cable consisting of a copper wire conductor, a nonconducting insulator, woven metal outer shielding, and a plastic outer coating, NP 174-175
Cobol The most common computer language used for transaction processing on large mainframe computer systems, NP 363, NP 385
code A set of symbols that represent data and information, NP 152, NP 159-162. *See also* coding; encoding
  ANSI, NP 161
  ASCII, NP 160
  EBCDIC, NP 161
  op code, NP 123, NP 124
  Unicode, NP 161-162
coding The process of using a computer language to express an algorithm, NP 348-352

control structures, NP 349-352
  program sequence, NP 348-352
collision An event that occurs when two devices attempt to transmit on the network at the same time, NP 202, NP 203
color graphics adapter (CGA) A circuit board that connects a monitor to a computer and displays graphics in a matrix of 320 pixels horizontally and 200 pixels vertically, NP 23
column, spreadsheet software, NP 50
columnar format, NP 323, NP 324
command A combination of words, parameters, and punctuation that tells the computer what you want it to do, NP 13
  confirming, NP 227
  COPY, NP 104
  dBASE, NP 13, NP 14
  GOSUB, NP 350-351
  GOTO, NP 350, NP 385
  HELP, NP 14-15, NP 26
  IF..THEN, NP 351
  mnemonic, NP 363-364
  RETURN, NP 351
  syntax errors, NP 14, NP 18
  valid, NP 14
command files, NP 81
command interpreter Part of the command language that examines a command and determines whether it is valid, NP 14
  bad or missing, NP 134
command language A vocabulary of words and rules that allow the user to communicate with the computer, NP 13
command word, NP 13
COMMAND.COM file, NP 134
command-line user interface A user initiated dialog based on a vocabulary of command words and rules called a command language, NP 13-15
  installing software, NP 56
COMMDLG.DLL file, NP 361
comment. *See* remark
commercial information service A for-profit computer network such as CompuServe, Prodigy, or America Online that provides access to a wide range of financial, informational, and recreational services for a monthly or per-minute charge, NP 209-211
commercial software
  creating applications, NP 280
  database management systems, NP 311
  evolution, NP 386-387
  file management software, NP 310
  system design, NP 276
Commodore, NP 391
Commodore 64, NP 391
communication program Software that enables your computer to communicate with other computers, NP 181
communications. *See* data communications
communications channel The communication link used to carry a signal between devices, NP 153, NP 172-176
  coaxial cable, NP 174-175
  fiber optic cable, NP 175-176
  full-duplex, half-duplex, and simplex, NP 180
  twisted pair cable, NP 173-174
  wireless communications, NP 176
Communications of the ACM, NP 403
Communications of the IEEE, NP 403

communications protocol The rules that ensure the orderly and accurate transmission and reception of data, NP 176-181, NP 204
    channel types, NP 179-180
    network standard, NP 200-201, NP 202, NP 203
    parallel and serial communications, NP 177
    parity, NP 178-179
    synchronous and asynchronous, NP 177-178
    transmission speed, NP 180-181
communications system model, NP 153
Compaq, NP 391
compatible A term used to describe computers that operate in essentially the same way and can use the same software
    microcomputer compatibility, NP 8-9
    software compatibility, NP 55, NP 56
compile The process of translating English-like program commands (source code) into a set of instructions the computer can deal with directly (object code), NP 80
compiled file The program file that is created when a program is translated from English-like statements into machine language, NP 80, NP 81
compiled language A characteristic of computer languages that use a compiler to translate a program written in a high-level language into low-level instructions before the program is executed, NP 358, NP 359, NP 363
compiler, NP 359
complex instruction set computer (CISC) A microcomputer with a large assembly language instruction set, NP 129
complex queries, NP 318-320
compression. *See* file compression
Compton's Multimedia Encyclopedia, NP 65
CompuServe, NP 209, NP 405
computer An electronic device that accepts input, processes the input, stores the results of processing, and provides output, NP 4-5
    booting. *See* boot process
    categories, NP 6, NP 7
    CISC and RISC, NP 129-130
    embedded, NP 6
    expanding system, NP 135-143
    host, NP 206
    IBM-compatible. *See* IBM-compatible computer
    learning to use, NP 23-27
    Macintosh. *See* Macintosh computer
    notebook, NP 7, NP 83, NP 137-138
    palm-top, NP 7
    pen-based, NP 15
    physical protection, NP 241
    PS/2, NP 122
    restricting access. *See* security
    storage device identification, NP 83
    sub-notebook, NP 7
    tower, NP 83
    upgrades, NP 66
computer architecture The design, construction, or structure of a computer system, NP 113-114
    compatibility, NP 8-9
computer crime A wide variety of activities in which people steal information stored on computers, maliciously destroy computer data, or use computers to commit embezzlement and theft, NP 237-238
Computer Fraud and Abuse Act, NP 238
computer "guru," NP 27

computer hardware The tangible parts of a computer that you can see or touch, NP 5, NP 6-12
    buying, NP 403-409
    categories of computers, NP 6, NP 7
    comparison worksheet, NP 407
    configuration. *See* configuration
    development, NP 376-384
    failure, NP 14, NP 41, NP 230-232
    installing, NP 279
    life cycle, NP 395-399
    microcomputer compatibility, NP 8-9
    multimedia, NP 66
    network. *See* network hardware
    peripheral devices. *See* keyboard; monitor; mouse; peripheral device; printer; storage device; stylus
    purchasing, NP 277
    system components, NP 7-8
computer industry The corporations and individuals that supply goods and services to the people and organizations that use computers, NP 375-409
    buying hardware and software, NP 403-409
    history, NP 376-395
    marketplace, NP 395-403
computer magazine A publication that targets users of both personal and business computers, NP 402, NP 403, NP 405
computer network A collection of computers and peripheral devices that use communications channels to share data, hardware, and software, NP 192-198
    bulletin boards, NP 208-209
    cables, NP 198-199
    commercial information services, NP 209-211
    communication protocols, NP 200-201, NP 202, NP 203, NP 204
    configuration, NP 198-204
    data files, NP 195-197
    electronic mail, NP 206-208
    hardware, NP 199, NP 200-202, NP 203, NP 204
    hierarchical, NP 205
    interactions, NP 205-206
    Internet, NP 211-216
    launching programs, NP 194-195
    login process, NP 193-194
    peer-to-peer, NP 205
    printers, NP 193-194, NP 197-198, NP 207
    software, NP 195, NP 199, NP 202, NP 204
computer program A set of detailed, step-by-step instructions that tell a computer how to solve a problem or carry out a task, NP 5, NP 340. *See also* computer software; program file
    definition, NP 36
    Trojan horse, NP 232-233
    viruses, NP 233, NP 234-237
computer projector, NP 12
Computer Reseller News, NP 402
computer retail store A local retail business that purchases computer products from a manufacturer or distribution center and then sells the products to customers, NP 377, NP 405
computer software One or more computer programs and associated data that exist in electronic form on a storage medium, NP 5, NP 37. *See also* application software; computer network; Microsoft Windows; operating system; program file; shareware; software license; user interface; software headings

alpha and beta testing, NP 399
buying, NP 403-409
categories, NP 38
character recognition, NP 15
client-server, NP 205-206
communication program, NP 181
compatibility, NP 54-56
computer-aided instruction, NP 54, NP 64
controlling user interface, NP 6
copyrights, NP 58-59
data *versus*, NP 37
defects, NP 14
electronic mail, NP 47, NP 206-208, NP 212-213
evolution, NP 384-389
file management, NP 309-310
floppy disks, NP 90
installation, NP 56-58
installing, NP 279-280
life cycle, NP 398-400
localization, NP 161-162
maintenance, NP 284
multimedia, NP 64-65
network, NP 199, NP 202, NP 204
pirated, NP 58
public domain, NP 61, NP 215, NP 235
reference manual, NP 15, NP 25
shareware, NP 62
speech recognition, NP 15
technical support, NP 27, NP 58
terminal emulation, NP 206, NP 207
tutorial, NP 54
upgrades, NP 37-38, NP 58
utility, NP 44
version numbers, NP 38
computer vendors, NP 400-402
computer virus A program designed to reproduce itself and spread from one computer to another, NP 234-237
detecting, NP 236
Michelangelo, NP 233
removing, NP 237
spread, NP 235
computer-aided instruction (CAI) Education software that helps you learn how to do something, NP 54, NP 64
computer-based reference manual, NP 25
computer-based tutorial A type of tutorial that displays a simulation of hardware or software, and displays the tutorial instructions in boxes or windows on the screen, NP 24, NP 58
computer-generated speech, NP 21
computerized information system The computers, peripheral devices, programs, data, people, and procedures that work together to record, store, process, and distribute information, NP 260
concentrator A device that provides a central connecting point for the cables on the network, NP 198, NP 199
concurrent user license A software license that allows a certain number of copies of a software package to be used at the same time, NP 60, NP 195
confidentiality, NP 246-251
electronic mail, NP 208
encryption, NP 247-249
CONFIG.SYS A file loaded into memory during the boot process that customizes your computing environment by

loading device drivers and specifying the number of open files, NP 134
configuration The hardware components that make up a computer system, NP 7
checking, NP 134
CMOS memory, NP 122
modems, NP 182
network, NP 198-204
construction phase. *See* system construction
context sensitive help On-line help that displays information about the current task, NP 26
Control Data Corporation, NP 390
control structure Instructions that specify the sequence in which a program is executed, NP 349-352
control unit, NP 383
control unit The part of the CPU that directs and coordinates the operation of the entire computer system by fetching an instruction from RAM and storing it in an instruction register, NP 4, NP 124, NP 125, NP 126
control-break report 1. A method of producing a report with database software that groups the data by category; 2. A type of summary report in which data is grouped and subtotals are created for each group, NP 53, NP 324-325
controller card An expansion board that contains the circuitry needed to connect hard disk drives and floppy disk drives to a computer system, NP 138, NP 139
conventional memory The first 640K of memory, containing addresses between 0 and 655,360, NP 120
conversion software, NP 283
COPY command, NP 104
copy protection, NP 59
copying a file Creating a duplicate of a file. To copy a file in MS-DOS, use the COPY command, NP 86, NP 103-104
copyrighted software, NP 58-59
old version over new version, NP 229
public domain software, NP 61
shareware, NP 62
copyright A form of legal protection that grants certain exclusive rights to the author of a program or the owner of the copyright, NP 58-59
Copyright Act, NP 58-59
cost-effective life, NP 285
courses, NP 27
CPU. *See* central processing unit (CPU); microprocessor
Cray Research, NP 390
creating applications, NP 280-281
CSMA/CD (carrier sense multiple access with collision detection) Ethernet protocol that handles collisions, NP 202
Ctrl key, NP 10
cursor
DOS, NP 42
UNIX, NP 43
cursor keys, NP 10
custom installation A method of installing software in which you select the features of the software you want to install, NP 58
custom program approach, file and database management, NP 308-309
cyberspace, NP 210, NP 217, NP 389
cylinder A vertical stack of tracks on a hard disk, NP 92

DAT (Digital Audio Tape), NP 95

data The words, numbers, and graphics that describe people, events, things, and ideas, NP 78
  communications. *See* communications channel; communications protocol; data communications; modem
  compression. *See* file compression
  information *versus,* NP 78
  invalid, NP 226
  lost, NP 226
  reading, NP 86, NP 99, NP 102-103
  security, NP 40-41
  software *versus,* NP 37
  storage. *See* memory; storage
  transmission, network hardware, NP 201-202, NP 203, NP 204
  writing, NP 86, NP 102, NP 103, NP 230, NP 231

data archive A collection of data, similar to a database, except that the data is not necessarily stored in a uniform record format, NP 214-215

data bus. *See* bus

data communications The process of transmitting and receiving data in an orderly way so that the data that arrives at its destination is an accurate duplication of the data that was sent, NP 150-183
  channel. *See* communications channel
  communications system model, NP 153
  data compression, NP 168-172
  distance, NP 152
  encoding information, NP 152-168
  modem. *See* modem
  parallel and serial, NP 177
  protocol. *See* communications protocol
  software, NP 181

data conversion, NP 283

data dictionary A detailed, alphabetical listing of the data elements, data flows, data stores, and processes in an information system, NP 272-273

Data Encryption Standard (DES) The encryption technique used by the U.S. Government that is based on an eight-digit key that scrambles the data. To decipher a message, the receiver must know the series of numbers used to scramble the message, NP 249

*data file 1. A file that contains data created by using application software; 2. A computer file that contains data that is stored in a structured or uniform format, NP 78, NP 79-80, NP 296-299

data file 1. A file that contains data created by using application software; 2. A computer file that contains data that is stored in a structured or uniform format
  creating and purchasing, NP 79-80
  flat files, NP 299, NP 315
  networks, NP 195-197
  retrieving, NP 102-103
  saving, NP 103
  structure, NP 296-299
  structured, NP 296

data flow diagram A graphical representation of the way data moves through an information system, NP 272-274

Data General, NP 390, NP 391

data independence In a database, the separation of data and the programs that manipulate the data, NP 310

data item An individual unit of data, NP 296

data lines The part of the bus that transports the bits that represent data, NP 117

data management environment Software or program used to design and manage data files, NP 313

data management The tasks associated with maintaining and accessing the data stored in a data file, NP 296, NP 308-328
  custom program approach, NP 308-309
  data visualization, NP 328
  database management system approach, NP 310-311
  designing file or database, NP 313-316
  effective output, NP 328
  entering records, NP 316
  file management system approach, NP 309-310
  graphs, NP 325-326, NP 327
  object-oriented approach, NP 312-313
  organizing records, NP 321-323
  reports, NP 323-325
  searching, NP 316-320
  sonification, NP 326
  updating information, NP 321

data redundancy The undesirable repetition of data in a data file, NP 315, NP 316

data store The open rectangle symbol used in a data flow diagram to indicate stored data, NP 273

data structure diagram A diagram that shows the relationships between record types, NP 301, NP 302

data type Describes the way data is represented on a disk; data types include numeric, character, and logical, NP 297, NP 314

data visualization A method of displaying data as a graphical analog; showing employee absentee rates as a flower garden, NP 328

database A variety of different record types that are treated as a single unit, NP 299-307, NP 315
  management. *See* data management
  relational, NP 306
  relationships, NP 300-302
  Structured Query Language, NP 363

database administrator The person responsible for designing and supervising the database, NP 303

database file A file that is organized in a uniform format and may contain more than one record type, NP 296-299

database management software A type of productivity software that helps you work with facts and figures comparable to those that might be stored on file cards or in a rolodex, NP 46, NP 52-53

database management system approach, file and database management, NP 310-311

database management system (DBMS) Application software that helps you manage the data in a database, NP 310-311

database model A method used to represent relationships between record types, NP 303-307

database report The formatted output of some or all of the data from a database, NP 323

date data type In a database, the type of field used to store dates, NP 314

dBASE commands, NP 13, NP 14

dBASE IV, NP 323

DBMS (database management system), NP 310-311

DD disk. *See* double-density (DD) disk

DEC PDP-8, NP 383

decimal system, NP 157

deciphered data. See decrypted data

decision model A numerical representation of a realistic situation, NP 265

decision query A question or set of instructions that describes the data that is required to make a decision, NP 265

decision structure. See selection control structure

decision support system (DSS) A system that provides data and modeling tools that managers use to make structured and semi-structured decisions, NP 265-266

decision support worksheet, NP 408

decisions
      routine, NP 264
      structured, NP 264

declarative language A characteristic of computer languages that lets you write a program by specifying a set of statements and rules that define the conditions for resolving a problem, NP 355-356, NP 363

DECnet A network protocol developed by Digital Equipment Corporation (DEC) for use with DEC minicomputers, NP 204

decoding The reversal of the coding process that took place before the message was sent, NP 153

decrypted data Data that has been changed back to its original form from an encrypted state, NP 247

default drive The drive the computer uses to load a program or data file into memory. Also called current drive, NP 133

definitional program, NP 313

defragmentation utility A program that rearranges the files on a disk so that they are stored in adjacent clusters, NP 100, NP 101

deleting a file Removing a file from a disk. In MS-DOS, delete files using either the DEL or ERASE command, NP 87, NP 100, NP 104, NP 227

demo A demonstration copy of a software product, usually limited in some way but complete enough to explore its features so you can decide if you want to purchase the full version of the product, NP 405

demodulation, NP 181

design phase. See system design

Desk Set (film), NP 394

desktop computer, storage device identification, NP 83

desktop metaphor, NP 23, NP 389

desktop publishing software Application software that provides you with computerized tools for page layout and design, NP 47

detail report 1. A complete list of transactions, usually in chronological order; 2. A list of transactions or data items, such as a list of inventory items alphabetized by product name, NP 265, NP 324

device driver A type of system software that tells the computer how to use a hardware device, NP 44

diagnostic tests, NP 133

dialog box A message or input area displayed by the computer in response to a menu selection. You fill in the dialog box to indicate how you want the command carried out, NP 18

difference engine, NP 114

differential backup A copy of all the files that have changed since the last full backup, NP 242, NP 243, NP 244

Digital Audio Tape (DAT), NP 95

digital device A device that works with discrete numbers or digits, such as 0 and 1, NP 114-115

Digital Equipment Corporation (DEC), NP 390, NP 391

Dijkstra, Edsger, NP 350, NP 385

DIP package A Dual In-line Pin Package is a RAM chip in a rectangular case with a row of pins along each of the long sides, NP 122

direct conversion, NP 283, NP 284

direct conversion A type of information system conversion in which the old system is completely deactivated and the new system is immediately activated, NP 284

directory A list of files maintained by the operating system. A directory usually contains the filename, file extension, the date and time the file was created, and the file size for every file in the directory, NP 84-85

directory tree, NP 85, NP 86

disk. See also disk drive; floppy disk; hard disk drive
      CD-ROM. See CD-ROM (compact disc read only memory)
      deleting files, NP 87, NP 100, NP 104, NP 227
      distribution, NP 56
      floptical, NP 90
      formatting, NP 44, NP 45, NP 89-90
      high-density, NP 90
      low-density, NP 90

disk cache A special area of computer memory into which the computer transfers the data that you are likely to need from disk storage, NP 94, NP 129

disk drive. See also floppy disk; hard disk drive
      indicator light, NP 93, NP 132, NP 133
      mapping, NP 193
      spindle, NP 91, NP 92
      testing, NP 132, NP 133

"disk error" message, NP 133-134

disk operating system. See DOS (disk operating system)

diskette. See floppy disk

DisplayWrite, NP 399

distribution disks, NP 56

document A file consisting of text, numbers, sounds, video, or graphics. Also called document file, NP 79, NP 82

document file. See document

documentation
      programs, NP 353-354. See program documentation
      system, NP 272-273

domain, Internet addresses, NP 212

DOS (disk operating system), NP 41, NP 42
      batch file commands, NP 80
      copying files, NP 104
      deleting files, NP 227
      directory, NP 84
      error messages, NP 121
      file-naming conventions, NP 81
      MS-DOS and PC-DOS, NP 42, NP 391
      prompt, NP 42
      running applications, NP 102
      software compatibility, NP 55

dot matrix printer, NP 12

dot prompt, NP 14

double-density (DD) disk A 3.5 inch disk that has been formatted with 80 tracks per side and 9 sectors per track and stores 720 kilobytes. A 5.25 inch disk that has been formatted with 40 tracks and 9 sectors per side and stores 360 kilobytes, NP 89-90

double-sided (DS) disk A disk that stores data on both sides of the disk, NP 89

download The process of transferring a file from a bulletin board system or host computer to your own computer, NP 208

downwardly compatible A feature of operating systems that allow you to use software designed for earlier versions of the operating system, NP 55, NP 56

Dr. Jekyll and Mr. Hyde (Stevenson), NP 392

drawing tools, NP 165

Dreyfuss, John, NP 393

drive. *See* disk drive; floppy disk; hard disk drive

DS disk. *See* double-sided (DS) disk

DSS. *See* decision support system

Dummer, G.W.A., NP 381

duplex. *See* full-duplex channel

EBCDIC (Extended Binary Coded Decimal Interchange Code) An eight-bit code developed by IBM for representing letters, numerals, punctuation, and control codes, NP 161

echo. *See* echoplex

echoplex A communication protocol in which information sent from the source to the receiver is then sent back to the source as a means of checking accuracy, NP 180

Eckert, J. Presper, NP 379

editing, word processing software, NP 48

editing keypad, NP 10

education and reference software Application software designed to help you learn more about a particular topic, NP 54

EDVAC (Electronic Discrete Variable Automatic Computer), NP 4

8086 assembly language A low-level computer language written for the Intel 8086 microprocessor family, NP 363-364

8086 microprocessor, programming languages, NP 363-364

8-bit microprocessor, NP 127

EISA (extended industry standard architecture) bus, NP 136, NP 137, NP 138

Eisenhower, Dwight D., NP 393

electrical/electronic interference. *See also* brownout; noise; power failure
    coaxial cable, NP 174
    fiber optic cable, NP 176
    parallel cables, NP 141
    twisted pair cable, NP 174

electromagnetic relays, NP 379-380

electronic mail software Software that maintains electronic mailboxes and sends messages from one computer to another, NP 47, NP 206-208
    Internet, NP 212-213

electronic mail system The hardware and software that collects and delivers e-mail, NP 206-207

electronic spreadsheets, NP 17, NP 363, NP 386

e-mail A letter or memo sent electronically from one user to another, NP 47, NP 206-208, NP 212-214

embedded computers The smallest category of computers, embedded computers are often built into electronic devices to control the device, NP 6

encoding The process of transforming data into code, NP 152-168
    characters, NP 159-162
    graphics, NP 162-166

    numbers, NP 157-159
    run length, NP 171
    sound, NP 166-168
    video, NP 166

encrypted data Data that has been scrambled so it cannot be used until it is changed back to its original form, NP 247-249

End key, NP 10

Engelbart, Douglas, NP 11

English, structured, NP 272-273, NP 346

ENIAC, NP 379, NP 380

Enter key, NP 10

entertainment software Application software designed to entertain or amuse you, NP 54, NP 64

entity A person, place, thing, or event about which you want to store data, NP 297
    external, NP 273

entity relationship diagram. *See* data structure diagram

Equal Credit Opportunity Act, NP 251

equal to operator (=), NP 317

equipment failure, NP 14, NP 41, NP 230-232

erasing a file. *See* deleting a file

error messages, NP 14
    "bad or missing command interpreter," NP 134
    "cannot load a file," NP 133-134
    "disk error," NP 133-134
    "non-system disk," NP 133-134
    "out of memory," NP 121

errors. *See* bugs

Esc (escape) key, NP 10

ESDAC (Electronic Storage Delay Automatic Computer), NP 385

estimating software, NP 47

Ethernet The most popular network standard. Typically transmits data at 10 megabits per second, NP 200, NP 201, NP 202, NP 203, NP 207

ethics
    bulletin boards, NP 209
    electronic mail, NP 208

even parity, NP 178-179

event-driven language A characteristic of computer languages that help programmers create programs that constantly check for and respond to a set of events, NP 361-362

Excel for Windows, NP 387

Excelerator, NP 272, NP 274

exception report A list of records that match a condition outside of the usual range or limits, NP 265, NP 325

executable file. *See* program file

execution phase The part of the instruction cycle in which the processor executes the instruction by moving data from one memory location to another and performing an arithmetic or logical operation, NP 126

expanding. *See* uncompressing

expansion bus A circuit that connects RAM to a series of expansion slots, NP 135-137

expansion card A small circuit board that you can plug into an expansion slot to add a capability or connect a device to your computer, NP 135, NP 136, NP 199

expansion slot A socket on the mainboard that enables you to plug in a small circuit board called an expansion board, NP 116, NP 118, NP 135-136, NP 137-138

expert system A computer system designed to analyze data and produce a recommendation or decision, NP 267-268, NP 276

knowledge engineering, NP 281
maintenance, NP 284
programming languages, NP 363
testing, NP 282
expert system shell Software that contains the inference engine and a method for entering the rules for the knowledge base but not the rules to solve a particular problem, NP 268, NP 276
creating applications, NP 280
expression In a database query, usually a field name, relational operator, and value that the computer evaluates on the basis of the stored data, NP 317
extended instruction set, NP 128-129
extended memory Any memory above the first megabyte of memory, NP 120
external entity The square shaped data flow diagram symbol that indicates a person or organization that provides input to or receives output from an information system, NP 273
external modem A modem in a box that is connected by cable to a serial port on a computer, NP 181
external programs File management software that is not part of the database, NP 310
extracting. *See* uncompressing

F

Fair Credit Billing Act, NP 251
Fair Credit Reporting Act, NP 251
FastEthernet A high speed network standard capable of transmitting data at 100 megabits per second, NP 201
FAT. *See* file allocation table (FAT)
FDDI A high speed network standard capable of transmitting data at 100 megabits per second, NP 201
fetch phase The part of the instruction execution cycle in which the processor identifies the location of the next instruction, fetches the instruction from memory, and loads it into the processor, NP 126
fiber optic cable A high bandwidth communications cable that consists of a bundle of extremely thin tubes of glass, NP 175-176
field A group of characters that identify data, NP 52
field A location in a record in which a particular type of data is stored, NP 296, NP 297
determining, NP 313
grouping, NP 314-315
size, NP 298
field format, NP 314
field name A unique identifier that describes the contents of a field, NP 296
file A collection of data that is stored on a storage device such as a hard disk, floppy disk, or CD-ROM, NP 78-86
batch, NP 80, NP 81, NP 134
command, NP 81
compiled, NP 80, NP 81
copying, NP 58-59, NP 61, NP 62, NP 86, NP 103-104, NP 229
data. *See* data file
deleting, NP 87, NP 100, NP 104, NP 227
directory, NP 84-85
document, NP 79, NP 82
downloading, NP 208
fragmented, NP 100, NP 101

locked, NP 196
modifying, NP 102
opening, NP 86, NP 99, NP 102-103
program, NP 78, NP 80, NP 81, NP 82
running applications, NP 102
size, NP 84
specification, NP 85
storage, NP 83-86, NP 98-101. *See also* memory; storage
writing, NP 86, NP 102, NP 103, NP 230, NP 231
file allocation table (FAT) An operating system file that helps the computer store and retrieve files from disk storage by maintaining a list of files and their physical location on the disk, NP 99, NP 100, NP 104
file compression A technique that reduces the size of a large file by using fewer bits to represent the data the file contains, NP 168-172
graphics, NP 171
text, NP 170-171
video, NP 171-172
file extension A set of characters, separated from the filename by a period, that further describes the file contents, NP 81, NP 82
bitmap graphics, NP 164
MIDI music, NP 168
vector graphics, NP 166
waveform audio, NP 167
file find rights, NP 240
file management software A computer program used to manipulate the data in a flat file, NP 309-310
file management system approach, file and database management, NP 309-310
file-naming conventions The rules for creating a valid filename, NP 80-82
file read rights, NP 240
file servers, NP 192, NP 205, NP 207
file size The number of bytes, or characters, a file contains, NP 84
file specification The drive letter, directory, and filename that identifies a file, i.e., C:\TMP\LETTER.DOC, NP 85
filename A unique set of letters and numbers that identifies a file and usually describes the file contents, NP 80
conventions, NP 80-82
extension. *See* file extension
valid, NP 81
files
database. *See* data file
flat, NP 299
free-form, NP 296
index, NP 322
management. *See* data management
first generation computers Computers that used vacuum tubes rather than electromagnetic or mechanical switches to store data and perform calculations, NP 380-381
fixed disk. *See* hard disk drive
flat file A data file in which all records have the same record format, NP 299, NP 315
floppy disk A flexible mylar disk covered with a thin layer of magnetic oxide. The most common microcomputer storage media are 3.5 inch and 5.25 inch floppy disks. Also called a "floppy" or a diskette, NP 8, NP 83, NP 87-91
bootable, NP 134
controller, NP 138, NP 139

double-density, NP 89-90
double-sided, 89
files. *See* file
formatting, NP 228
sizes, NP 87, NP 90
floptical disk A special 3.5 inch disk that stores 21 megabytes of data, NP 90
flow chart A graphical representation of the way a computer should progress from one instruction to the next when it performs a task, NP 347
Forbes magazine, NP 403
form fill-in A type of user interface in which the computer displays the equivalent of a form on the screen for you to fill in, NP 19, NP 20
format
columnar, NP 323, NP 324
records, NP 299
formatting disks, NP 44, NP 45, NP 89-90, NP 228
formatting feature A feature of word processing software that helps you design the appearance of your printed document, NP 48
formula A mathematical equation entered in a spreadsheet cell that tells the computer how to perform a calculation, NP 50
FOR..NEXT command, NP 351-352
Fortran The oldest high-level computer language still in use, designed for solving scientific type problems, NP 363, NP 385
4GL (Fourth Generation Language), NP 275, NP 276. *See also* application development tool
fourth generation computers Computers built using a microprocessor, NP 383
Fourth Generation Language (4GL), NP 275, NP 276. *See also* application development tool
fragmented files Files that are stored in nonadjacent clusters, NP 100, NP 101
Frankenstein (Shelley), NP 392
Free Software Foundation (FSF), NP 215
free-form file, NP 296
frequency analysis A technique for breaking codes by examining frequency of letter occurrences in an encrypted message, NP 247-248
FSF (Free Software Foundation), NP 215
FTP A program that moves files from one computer to another on the Internet, NP 216-217
full backup A copy of all the files on a disk, NP 241-242, NP 244
full installation A method of installing software so all features of the software are available for use, NP 57
full-duplex channel A communication channel that allows a device to simultaneously send and receive data, NP 180
function A section of code that is part of a program but not executed in the sequential execution path, NP 350
function keys, NP 10

G

gateway An electronic link that connects e-mail systems, NP 208
general accounting system, NP 262
geosynchronous orbit The orbit used by communications satellites to maintain a constant position above the earth, NP 176

gigabyte One thousand megabytes, or approximately one billion bytes, NP 87
global update To change the data in multiple records at one time, NP 321
GOSUB command, NP 350-351
GOTO command, NP 350, NP 385
graphical user interface (GUI) A type of user interface in which you manipulate on-screen objects to activate commands, NP 21-23, NP 387, NP 389, NP 392
copying files, NP 103-104
graphics, NP 162-166
bitmap, NP 162-164
compression, NP 171
grayscale, NP 162
true color, NP 162
vector, NP 164-166
graphics card A small circuit board that contains the video display adapter. Also called a video card, NP 132, NP 133, NP 138-140
graphics coprocessor chip Integrated circuits used on accelerated video adapters designed to perform video functions at very high speed, NP 140
graphics software Application software that helps you draw pictures, 3-D images, and animation, NP 47
graphs, NP 325-326
misleading, NP 325-326
types, NP 326, NP 327
graphs, spreadsheet software, NP 50
grayscale A bitmap graphic created by using shades of gray to produce images, NP 162
greater than operator (>), NP 317
greater than or equal to operator (>=), NP 317
group addressing, NP 208
groupware Software that is designed to help people collaborate on projects, NP 260-261
GUI. *See* graphical user interface (GUI)
GW-BASIC, NP 362

hacker A person who for thrills or illegal gain attacks the data of others, NP 225, NP 232-234, NP 237-238, NP 240-241
HAL, NP 394
half-duplex channel A communication channel that allows a device to send or receive but not both at the same time, NP 180
hard disk. *See* hard disk drive
hard disk drive One or more hard disk platters and their associated read-write heads. A hard disk drive is capable of storing large amounts of data. Also called a hard disk or a fixed disk, NP 8, NP 91-94
cartridges, NP 93
controller, NP 138, NP 139
default drive, NP 133
failure, NP 232
files. *See* file
identification, NP 83, NP 91
installing software, NP 56-58
multimedia applications, NP 66
removable, NP 93
saving space, NP 58
hard disk platter A storage medium that is a flat, rigid disk

made of aluminum or glass and coated with a magnetic oxide, NP 91, NP 93

hardware. *See* computer hardware

Harvard MARK I, NP 379

HD disk. *See* high-density (HD) disk

head aperture The opening on a floppy disk that enables the read-write head of the disk drive to access the disk surface, NP 88, NP 89

head crash Occurs when a read-write head runs into a dust particle or some other contaminant on a disk, damaging some of the data on the disk, NP 92, NP 99

help, on-line, NP 26

HELP command, NP 14-15, NP 26

Herschel, John, NP 114

Hewlett-Packard, NP 390

hexadecimal number system, NP 119

hierarchical database A database model in which a parent record type can be linked to one or more child record types, and in which a child record can have only one parent, NP 303, NP 304

hierarchical network A type of network in which workstations interact with the file server but not with each other, NP 205

high-resolution monitor Type of monitor that produces high quality output by displaying many pixels on the computer screen, NP 23, NP 66

high-density (HD) disk A 3.5 inch disk that has been formatted with 80 tracks per side and 18 sectors per track and stores 1.44 megabytes. A 5.25 inch disk that has been formatted with 80 tracks and 15 sectors per side and stores 1.2 megabytes, NP 90

high-level language A characteristic of computer languages that allow you to use instructions that are more like human language, NP 357-358, NP 363, NP 385

Hoff, Ted, NP 383

Hollerith, Herman, NP 377

Home key, NP 10

horizontal market software Generic business software, such as accounting software, that can be used by many different kinds of businesses, NP 47

host computer Usually refers to a mainframe or minicomputer that is the central computer in a system of connected computers, NP 206

hub. *See* concentrator

hub hole, floppy disks, NP 88

IBM, NP 375, NP 377, NP 389-390, NP 390, NP 391

IBM Automatic Sequence Controlled Calculator, NP 379

IBM PC, NP 362, NP 391

IBM System/360 computer, NP 382, NP 390

IBM-compatible computer Computer systems based on the architecture of the first IBM microcomputers. Also called PC-compatibles, NP 9, NP 391, NP 392

    boot process, NP 131-135

    displaying prompt, NP 134-135

    microprocessors, NP 127, NP 130

    operating systems, NP 41

    parallel ports, NP 142

    physical file storage, NP 99

    serial ports, NP 181

    SIMMs, NP 122

software, NP 37

    video display adapters, NP 139-140

icon A picture used by a graphical user interface to represent a task or command, NP 21-22, NP 42, NP 43, NP 387-389

IF..THEN command, NP 351

ImagiNation Network, NP 210-211, NP 217

implementation phase. *See* system implementation

incremental backup A copy of the files that have changed since the last backup, NP 242, NP 244

index file A file that contains a list of data in order (alphabetical or numeric) and pointers to the complete records in a data file, NP 322

index hole, NP 88

index menu, NP 26

indexing A method of organizing data that leaves a data file in its original order but creates an index file to display the information in a specified order, NP 53, NP 322-323

indicator lights, NP 10

    disk drives, NP 93, NP 132, NP 133

    keyboard, NP 132, NP 133

    system unit, NP 8, NP 132

industry analyst A person who monitors computer industry trends, evaluates computer events, and makes predictions about what the trends seem to indicate, NP 403, NP 404

inference engine The part of an expert system that analyzes the data in the knowledge base, NP 267, NP 268

information services, NP 405

information system A system that collects, maintains, and provides information to people, NP 260-268

    analysis phase. *See* analysis of needs

    computerized, NP 260

    construction phase. *See* system construction

    cost-effective life, NP 285

    decision support systems, NP 265-266

    design phase. *See* system design

    expert systems, NP 267-268

    implementation phase. *See* system implementation

    maintenance phase, NP 284-285

    management information systems, NP 264-265

    office automation, NP 260-261

    transaction processing, NP 261-264

information The words, numbers, and graphics used as the basis for actions and decisions, NP 78

    data *versus*, NP 78

    sources, NP 26-27

information theory A theory that describes how the amount of information you can convey depends on the way you represent or encode the information, NP 154-157

InfoWorld, NP 402

inheritance, object-oriented model, NP 307

input, basic, control, NP 39

input device Transfers into the computer memory the words and numbers to be processed. The keyboard and the mouse are the most commonly used input devices, NP 4, NP 5. *See also* keyboard; mouse; stylus

input/output circuitry, NP 383

Insert key, NP 10

installation

    device drivers, NP 44

    hardware, NP 279

    software, NP 56-58, NP 279-280

instruction A command that tells the computer to perform a specific operation, NP 123

instruction execution cycle The process of executing one instruction by fetching and executing an instruction, NP 126

instruction pointer, NP 125

instruction register A special holding area of the CPU that contains the instruction that is to be executed by the ALU, NP 125

instruction set The list of assembly or machine language instructions that a processor can perform, NP 123-124, NP 129-130

integer A whole number, NP 297

integrated circuit A thin wafer of silicon that contains miniaturized circuitry. Also called a chip, NP 117, NP 381-383. *See also* microprocessor

    Clipper Chip, NP 249

    graphics coprocessor, NP 140

    math coprocessor, NP 128-129

    ROM, NP 116, NP 123

integration testing The type of testing to ensure that the individual units of a new information system operate correctly together, NP 281

Intel microprocessors, NP 130, NP 383

    programming languages, NP 363-364

interfaces, evolution, NP 387-389

interference. *See* electrical/electronic interference; noise

internal modem A modem on a circuit board that plugs into an expansion slot inside a computer, NP 181

International Business Machines. *See* IBM

Internet The world's largest computer network, established in 1969 by the U.S. Defense Department, NP 211-216, NP 405

    computational resources, NP 213-214

    computer crime, NP 238

    data archives, NP 214-215

    electronic mail, NP 212-213

    FTP, NP 216-217

    library catalogs, NP 214

    news groups, NP 214

    software worm, NP 234

    Telnet, NP 215-216

interpreted language A characteristic of computer languages that use a translator instead of a compiler to create code that the computer can understand, NP 358, NP 362

interpreter The part of an interpreted language that reads and executes one instruction at a time, NP 358, NP 360

invalid data Data that is not accurate because it was entered incorrectly, was deliberately or accidentally altered, or was not edited to reflect current facts, NP 226

inventory control system, NP 262

IO.SYS file, NP 133, NP 134

IPX (Internetwork packet exchange) A popular microcomputer network protocol developed by Novell for use with the Netware local area network software, NP 204

ISA (Industry Standard Architecture) bus, NP 136, NP 137

iteration. *See* repetition control

Jobs, Steve, NP 63

Journal of Information Science, NP 403

kanji, NP 387, NP 389

KB. *See* kilobyte (KB)

key

    encryption, NP 247-249

    sort, NP 321

keyboard, NP 8, NP 9, NP 10

    connector, NP 116

    indicator lights, NP 132, NP 133

    testing, NP 132, NP 133

    toggle keys, NP 9, NP 10

    user interfaces, NP 15, NP 19, NP 21

    word processing software, NP 48

Kilby, Jack, NP 381

kilobyte (KB) A kilobyte equals exactly 1,024 bytes, but is often rounded off to one thousand bytes, NP 87

knowledge base The part of an expert system that contains a set of rules and data for producing a decision, NP 267

knowledge engineering The process of designing, entering, and testing the rules in an expert system, NP 281

knowledge-based system. *See* expert system

known information The information you supply the computer so it can solve a problem, NP 341

labels, spreadsheet software, NP 50

landscape A spreadsheet print option that prints a worksheet or graph sideways, with the width of the page greater than the length, NP 51

language

    ambiguity, NP 20-21

    programming, NP 80

languages

    application development tools, NP 275

    programming. *See* programming languages

    query, NP 317

laser printer, NP 12

LAT. *See* DECnet

launching an application. *See* running an application

LCD (liquid crystal display), NP 8, NP 12

less than operator (<), NP 317

less than or equal to operator (<=), NP 317

library catalogs, Internet, NP 214

life cycle

    hardware, NP 395-399

    software, NP 398-400

line graph The type of graph you use to show trends over time, NP 326, 327

line-of-sight transmission Signals sent between two devices that are not separated by hills, mountains, or the earth's curvature, NP 176

link, physical, NP 304

liquid crystal display (LCD), NP 8, NP 12

Lisa computers, NP 392

Lisp One of the first declarative computer languages, NP 363

list, database management software, NP 52

loading, operating system, NP 133-134

local resources, NP 192

localization The modification of software for use in specific countries, NP 161-162

locked file, NP 196

logic bomb A program that is triggered by the appearance or disappearance of specific data, NP 233, NP 234

logic errors, NP 353, NP 358

logical data type, NP 314

logical operator A keyword such as NOT, AND, and OR used to perform a complex query, NP 318-320

logical storage A mental model that helps you to understand the computer's filing system, NP 85-86

login process The process you use to access network resources, including entering your user ID and password, NP 193-194

loop. *See* repetition control

lost data Data that is inaccessible due to deliberate or accidental removal, NP 226

Lotus 1-2-3, NP 363
    menus, NP 17

low-density disks, NP 90

low-level language A characteristic of computer languages that require you to write instructions for specific hardware elements of a computer system, such as the processor, registers, and RAM locations, NP 357, NP 363-364, NP 384-385

M

machine language A low-level language expressed in binary code that the computer can understand, NP 357, NP 384-385
    language, generating instructions, NP 359

Macintosh computer, NP 9, NP 11
    AFP protocol, NP 204
    microprocessor, NP 127, NP 130
    operating systems, NP 41, NP 43
    SIMMs, NP 122
    user interface, NP 21-22

Macintosh operating system An operating system created for Apple Macintosh computers, based on a graphical user interface featuring pull-down menus, icons, and a mouse, NP 41, NP 43

MacWorld magazine, NP 402

magazine. *See* computer magazine

magnetic fields, disruption of magnetic media, NP 87

magnetic storage The technology with which the computer stores data on disks and tapes by magnetizing selected particles of an oxide-based surface coating, NP 87-96
    Bernoulli disk, NP 95, NP 97
    floppy disk. *See* floppy disk
    hard disk. *See* hard disk
    tape, NP 8, NP 94-95, NP 96, NP 99

magneto optical drive. *See* read/write optical drive

mail order supplier A business that takes orders by mail or telephone and ships the products directly to customers, generally offering low prices with limited customer support, NP 400-402

mainboard A circuit board that contains the basic circuitry and electronics of a computer. Also called motherboard, NP 116-117

mainframe computers Large, fast, and fairly expensive computers generally used by business and government, NP 6, NP 40
    history, NP 380-383
    market, NP 390
    programming languages, NP 363

mainframe Large, fast, and fairly expensive computers

generally used by business and government, NP 206

maintenance phase, NP 284-285

management information system (MIS) A system that uses the data collected by a transaction processing system but manipulates the data to create reports that help managers make routine and structured decisions, NP 264-265

Manchester engineering group, NP 384-385

Manchester Mark I, NP 379, NP 380, NP 384-385

manuals, NP 354

manufacturer direct A hardware manufacturer that sells its products directly to the public using a direct sales force or mail order, NP 401-402

many-to-many relationship, NP 301, NP 302

mapping Network terminology for assigning a drive letter to a file server disk drive, NP 193

market, NP 389-392

marketing channels, NP 400-402, NP 406, NP 407

marketplace, NP 395-403

master clock A computer component that emits pulses to establish the timing for all system operations, NP 127

math coprocessor A chip that contains special circuitry used to perform complex arithmetic operations faster than the main microprocessor, NP 128-129

Matrix Layout, NP 386

Mauchley, John W., NP 379

MB. *See* megabyte (MB)

mean time between failures (MTBF) Term used to measure the reliability of computer components, measured in hours, NP 230-232

mechanical calculating devices, NP 377-378

mechanical relays, NP 379

megabits per second (mps) One million bits per second. Used to measure the data transmission speed on a network, NP 201

megabyte (MB) One thousand kilobytes, or approximately one million bytes, NP 87, NP 121

megahertz (MHz) One million cycles per second, NP 127

member In a network database model a member is a dependent (child) record type, NP 305

memo data type In a database, data that has a variable length, NP 314

memo field A field that holds memo data, NP 314

memory Electronic circuity that holds data and program instructions until it is their turn to be processed. Also called primary storage, NP 4, NP 5, NP 118-123. *See also* storage
    cache, NP 129
    CMOS, NP 122
    conventional, NP 120
    extended, NP 120
    random access. *See* random access memory (RAM)
    read only, NP 116, NP 123, NP 383. *See also* CD-ROM (compact disc read only memory)
    software compatibility, NP 55
    temporary, NP 383
    upper, NP 120

memory module A circuit board that contains memory. A SIMM module is the most common type of memory module, NP 116, NP 121, NP 122

menu List of commands, or options, that can be selected by the user, NP 15, NP 16, NP 17
    graphical user interface, NP 22
    hierarchy, NP 18
    item, NP 15

on-line help, NP 26

menu option An individual item on a menu, NP 15, NP 16

menu-driven user interface Type of user interface in which the computer initiates a dialog by displaying a list of commands called menus, NP 15-19

message The information that the source wants to communicate to the receiver, NP 153
  bulletin boards, NP 208-209
  collision, NP 202, NP 203
  network, NP 201-202, NP 203

metaphor A means of graphically representing computer components and tasks by real-world objects that make the tasks more concrete, more understandable, and more intuitive, NP 23, NP 389

method An operation or process specification stored by object-oriented database, NP 312
  object-oriented environment, NP 315
  object-oriented model, NP 307

MHz. *See* megahertz (MHz)

Michelangelo virus, NP 233

Micro channel bus, NP 137, NP 138

microcomputer A category of computers that are usually found in homes and small businesses. Also called personal computer, NP 6, NP 7. *See also* IBM-compatible computer; Macintosh computer
  compatibility, NP 8-9
  history, NP 383
  market, NP 391
  operating systems, NP 41-43
  programming languages, NP 363
  software evolution, NP 387

microprocessor A single integrated circuit that contains the circuitry for both the arithmetic logic unit and the control unit, NP 116, NP 126-130, NP 383
  cache memory, NP 129
  clock rate, NP 127
  data bus width, NP 128
  8-bit, NP 127
  instruction set, NP 129-130
  math coprocessor, NP 128-129
  model numbers, NP 127
  word size, NP 127-128

Microsoft Corporation, NP 37, NP 391, NP 399. *See also* Microsoft Windows
  Encarta, NP 65
  Windows NT, NP 42

Microsoft Disk Operating System (MS-DOS), NP 391

Microsoft Windows An operating environment with a graphical user interface that allows you to run multiple programs in separate windows on the screen at the same time, NP 41, NP 42, NP 361, NP 362, NP 363, NP 392
  copying files, NP 103-104
  directory, NP 84
  erasing files, NP 227
  file-naming conventions, NP 81
  installing software, NP 56-57
  running applications, NP 102
  software compatibility, NP 55
  user interface, NP 16, NP 17

microwave transmission Signals sent over a short to medium distance from a microwave transmitting station to a microwave receiving station, NP 173, NP 176

MIDI (Musical Instrument Digital Interface) A music notation system that allows computers to communicate with music synthesizers, NP 168

millisecond (ms) One one-thousandth of a second, NP 87

MILNET, NP 211

minicomputer A category of computers that are somewhat larger than microcomputers and generally used in business and industry for specific tasks, NP 6, NP 40, NP 206
  history, NP 383
  market, NP 390

Minority Online Information Service, NP 215

MIS. *See* management information system

missing data, NP 226

MITS Altair, NP 383

mnemonic commands, NP 363-364

mnemonic op codes, NP 385

modeling tools, decision support systems, NP 266

modem A peripheral device that converts the digital signals used inside your computer to an analog or voice signal that can be transmitted over the phone lines, NP 12, NP 181-182
  baud rate, NP 180
  bps, NP 180-181
  bulletin board systems, NP 182, NP 208-209
  commercial information services, NP 209-211
  communications protocol. *See* communications protocol
  configuring, NP 182

modifying files, NP 102

modulation, NP 181

module A section of a computer program that performs a particular task, NP 350

monitor, NP 9
  graphical user interface, NP 23
  high-resolution, NP 23, NP 66
  multimedia applications, NP 66
  resolution, NP 23, NP 139-140
  touch-sensitive screen, NP 12, NP 19
  user interfaces, NP 15, NP 19, NP 21

monochrome bitmap graphics, NP 162

motherboard. *See* mainboard

Motorola microprocessors, NP 130

mouse A pointing device used to manipulate objects displayed on the screen, NP 8, NP 9, NP 10, NP 392
  spreadsheet software, NP 50
  user interfaces, NP 19

mouse port A special serial port that connects a mouse to a computer, NP 142

MPC standard The minimum hardware requirements needed to successfully use certain multimedia applications, NP 66

mps. *See* megabits per second (mps)

ms. *See* millisecond (ms)

MS-DOS Microsoft Disk Operating System. An operating system for IBM and compatible microcomputers, NP 42. *See also* DOS (disk operating system)

MSDOS.SYS file, NP 133, NP 134

MultiMate, NP 399

multimedia An integrated collection of computer-based text, graphics, sound, animation, photo images, and video, NP 63-67
  applications, NP 64-65, NP 387
  computer-aided instruction, NP 64
  equipment, NP 66

Multimedia PC Marketing Council (MPC) standards, NP 66

multiple-user license A software license that allows more than one person to access a single copy of a software package at the same time, NP 60

multitasking A feature of an operating system that allows a user to run two or more programs at the same time, NP 40, NP 43

multiuser application An application specially designed so that more than one user can open and edit a file at the same time, NP 196

multiuser operating system An operating system that accommodates more than one user at a time, NP 40, NP 43

Murrow, Edward R., NP 393

Napier, John, NP 377

National Cash Register, NP 389-390

National Science Foundation network (NSFNET), NP 211

needs, analyzing. *See* analysis of needs

network. *See* computer network

network adapter. *See* network interface card

network address A unique number assigned to each device on a network, NP 201

network administrator The person responsible for the operation and security of a computer network, NP 193

network cable A communication cable that provides a physical connection between workstations, NP 198-199

network communication protocol The rules that specify the structure of packets transmitted over the network, NP 200-201, NP 202, NP 203, NP 204

network hardware The network cards, hubs, concentrators, and cables that direct the flow of data over the network, NP 199, NP 200-202

    data transmission, NP 201-202, NP 203, NP 204

    network interface card, NP 199, NP 200-201

network interface card A circuit board that plugs into the main board of the computer and is used to connect the computer to a network, NP 199, NP 200-201

network license A software license that allows you to use a program on any number of network workstations at the same time, NP 195

network model, NP 303, NP 305

network printer A printer that is attached to a network, NP 193-194, NP 197-198, NP 207

network resource Any device connected to a network that is available to network users, such as a disk drive or printer, NP 192

network software The part of a computer network that ensures that packets of data are addressed to the correct destination and verifies that the data packets arrive at the proper destination, NP 199, NP 202, NP 204

network standard A set of communications protocols that provides for the orderly transmission of data on a network, NP 200-201, NP 202, NP 203

news groups, NP 405

    Internet, NP 214

news lists, NP 405

1984 (Orwell), NP 392

no parity, NP 179

node. *See* segment

noise Any interference that disrupts the communication process, NP 153, NP 177. *See also* electrical/electronic interference

"non-system disk" message, NP 133-134

normalization The process of creating the most efficient database structure by reducing data redundancy, NP 315

Norman, Donald, NP 13

not equal to operator (<>), NP 317

NOT operator, NP 318-320

notebook computers, NP 7, NP 83, NP 137-138

NSFNET (National Science Foundation network), NP 211

Num Lock key, NP 10

numbers, encoding, NP 157-159

numbers, real, NP 297

numeric data type The data type assigned to data that contains numbers to be manipulated mathematically, NP 297

numeric keypad, NP 10

object An abstract representation of a real-world entity that has a unique identity, properties, and the ability to interact with other objects, NP 307, NP 358

    classes, NP 360-361

    descriptions, NP 348

    object-oriented approach, NP 312

object code The low-level instructions that result from compiling your source code, NP 358

object ID number, NP 316

object-oriented database A type of database that deals with data as objects, NP 303, NP 307, NP 312-313

    program design, NP 346

object-oriented language Computer languages that are based on a new approach to programming that uses objects, NP 358, NP 360-361, NP 363, NP 385-386

odd parity, NP 179

office automation system A system that automates or computerizes routine office tasks such as producing documents, tracking schedules, making calculations, and facilitating voice and written communication, NP 260-261

one time pad, NP 248

one-to-many relationship, NP 301, NP 302

    hierarchical model, NP 304

    network model, NP 305

one-to-one relationship, NP 301, NP 302

on-line help Computer-based help that you can access on screen while using a program, NP 26

on-line spell checker A feature of word processing software that helps proofread documents by notifying you of misspelled words, NP 48

on-line thesaurus A feature of word processing software that helps you find the right words to convey your ideas, NP 48

on-line tutorial, NP 58

on/off switch, NP 8

on-site service The offer of a vendor to repair your computer at your home or business, NP 406, NP 407

op code The part of an assembly language instruction that contains a command word for an arithmetic or logical operation. Also called operation code, NP 123, NP 124

opening a file The process of retrieving data from a storage medium into the computer's memory. Also called reading data, NP 86, NP 99, NP 102-103

operating environment, NP 42

operating system A set of programs that manages the resources of a computer, including controlling input and output, allocating system resources, managing storage space, maintaining security, and detecting equipment failure, NP 39-43, NP 391. *See also* DOS (disk operating system)

    basic input and basic output control, NP 39
    batch file commands, NP 80, NP 134
    copying files, NP 103-104
    directories, NP 84-85
    equipment failure detection, NP 41
    loading, NP 133-134
    microcomputers, NP 41-43
    multiuser, NP 40, NP 43
    prompt, NP 42, NP 43, NP 134-135
    security maintenance, NP 40-41
    software compatibility, NP 55, NP 56
    storage space management, NP 40
    system resource allocation, NP 40
    versions, NP 55

operator error A cause of lost data in which a computer user makes a mistake, NP 226-229
    copying files, NP 229
    erasing files, NP 227
    formatting disks, NP 228

operators
    logical, NP 318-320
    relational, NP 317

optical computers, NP 384

optical fiber A single glass tube, thinner than a human hair, in a fiber optic cable, NP 175

optical media The storage media on which data is stored in a form that is readable with beams of laser light, NP 96-98
    CD-ROM. *See* CD-ROM (compact disc read only memory)
    magneto optical drives, NP 98
    read/write optical drives, NP 98
    WORM drive, NP 98

OR operator, NP 318-320

order-entry/invoice system, NP 262

Orwell, George, NP 392

OS/2 An operating system created by IBM and Microsoft that offers a graphical user interface and retains the ability to run DOS and Windows programs, NP 41, NP 43

Oughtred, William, NP 377

"out of memory" message, NP 121

output
    audio, NP 15
    basic, control, NP 39

output device Transfers the results of processing from the computer memory. Printers and monitors are the most commonly used output devices, NP 4, NP 9. *See also* monitor; plotter; printer

owner In a network database, the portion of a set equivalent to a parent record in a hierarchical database, NP 305

P

packet A small section of a large file that is transmitted on a network. A packet consists of the address of the destination workstation, the address of the sending workstation, and a small segment of a data file, NP 202, NP 204

Page Down key, NP 10
Page Up key, NP 10
palm-top computers, NP 7
parallel communications, NP 177

parallel conversion A type of information system conversion in which the old system remains in service along with the new system until it is determined that the new system operates according to specifications, NP 283

parallel port A socket that provides a connection for transmitting data eight bits at a time over a cable with eight separate data lines, NP 140-142, NP 197

parameter The part of a computer programming language instruction that specifies the data or address of the data to be used by an instruction, NP 13, NP 123

parent node, hierarchical model, NP 304

parity bit An additional bit added to a data block by the transmitting computer that enables computers to check for errors, NP 178-179, NP 182

parsing tokens, NP 359

Pascal, Blaise, NP 377

Pascal A structured high-level computer language designed to help students learn how to program computers, NP 355, NP 363, NP 385

password A special set of symbols, known only to you and the network administrator, that gives you security clearance to use network resources, NP 40-41, NP 193, NP 239

pathname The directories that lead from the current directory to the location of a file, i.e., \WORD\REPORTS\MEMO.TXT. Also called directory name, NP 85

Pause key, NP 10

payroll software, NP 47

PC-compatible computer. *See* IBM-compatible computer

PC-DOS, NP 42, NP 391

PCI (peripheral connect interface) bus, NP 136, NP 137, NP 138

PCMCIA slot A special type of expansion slot developed for notebook computers that allows you to plug in a credit-card-sized circuit board, NP 137-138

peer-to-peer network A type of computer network in which the workstations act as both workstations and file servers, NP 205

pen-based computer A computer equipped with a pointing device called a stylus that uses character recognition software to interpret commands written on a touch-sensitive pad that doubles as a screen, NP 15, NP 19

peripheral device An input, output, or storage device that is outside of the main computer, NP 11, NP 12, NP 39, NP 312. *See also* keyboard; monitor; mouse; storage device; stylus

personal computer. *See* IBM-compatible computer; Macintosh computer; microcomputer

phased conversion A type of information system conversion in which the new information system is activated one module at a time, NP 283

physical link A method of linking records in which the links are related to the physical position of the data on the storage medium, NP 304

physical storage The way data is actually stored on the physical disk medium, NP 86, NP 98-101

pie chart The type of graph you use to show percentages, NP 326, 327

PIECES framework, NP 271

pilot conversion A type of information system conversion in which the new information system is activated at one business location at a time, NP 283-284

pirated software, NP 58

pixel An individual point of light on the computer screen, NP 23 plotter, NP 12

pointer An arrow-shaped symbol on the screen, controlled by a mouse or other input device, NP 9

 graphical user interface, NP 23

 Macintosh operating system, NP 43

 Microsoft Windows, NP 42

 mouse, NP 9, NP 10

 OS/2, NP 43

 spreadsheet software, NP 50

 stylus, NP 15

point-of-sale system (POS), NP 262

popular culture, NP 392-395

pop-up menu A menu that appears in a box located in an unused area of the screen, NP 16

port, NP 135

 mouse, NP 142

 parallel, NP 140-142, NP 197

 SCSI, NP 142

 serial, NP 142, NP 143, NP 181

POST. *See* power on self test (POST)

power brownout. *See* brownout

power failure A complete loss of power to the computer system, NP 121, NP 229-230

power light, NP 8, NP 132

power on self test (POST), The part of the boot process that diagnoses problems in the computer, NP 133

power spikes/surges, NP 230

power up, NP 131-132

presentation application, multimedia, NP 64

prices

 collecting information, NP 406, NP 407

 hardware, NP 396-397, NP 398

 software, NP 399

primary storage. *See* memory

print queue A special holding area on the file server where files are stored until they are printed, NP 197-198

Print Screen key, NP 10

printed tutorial A type of tutorial in which the directions are printed on paper. You read a step and then try to do it on the computer, NP 24

printer, NP 12

 bps, NP 181

 computer network, NP 193-194

 network, NP 197-198, NP 207

 parallel transmission, NP 141-142

priority mail, NP 208

privacy, NP 250-251

Privacy Act, NP 250, NP 251

problem statement A description of the problem or problems in an information system, NP 340-342

problems. *See also* solutions

 defining, NP 271-272

 semi-structured, NP 265

procedural language A characteristic of computer languages that require the programmer to specify how the computer must perform a task, NP 355, NP 362, NP 363

procedure A section of a computer program to which control is transferred to perform a specific task, NP 227, NP 350

procedure handbook A manual that contains step-by-step instructions for performing specific job tasks, NP 282

process A rounded rectangle symbol on a data flow diagram that indicates the processing or manipulation of data by the system, NP 4, NP 273

process specification A detailed description of how data

should be manipulated by an information system, NP 273

processor. *See* central processing unit (CPU); graphics coprocessor chip; microprocessor

Prodigy, NP 209, NP 405

product announcement A declaration by a company that they intend to produce a particular product

 hardware, NP 395-396

 software, NP 398

product introduction, NP 396-398

 software, NP 399

product line, software, NP 400

productivity software A category of application software that helps you work more effectively. Types of productivity software include word processing, spreadsheet, and database management, NP 46-53

program

 definitional, NP 313

 size, NP 354

program documentation Written or on-screen information that explains how a program works and how to use it, NP 353-354, NP 355

 program remarks, NP 353-354

 written, NP 354

program file A file that contains the instructions that tell a computer how to perform a specific task. Also called an executable file, NP 78, NP 80, NP 81, NP 82

 viruses, NP 233, NP 234-237

program manual Written documentation that contains information such as the problem statement and algorithm that might be useful to programmers, NP 354

program specification A document that includes a problem statement and algorithm, and serves as a blueprint for a computer program, NP 348

program testing, NP 352-353

programmer A person who creates and modifies computer programs, NP 268

 custom program approach, NP 308-309

programming, NP 339-365. *See also* programming languages

 algorithms, NP 343-348

 coding, NP 348-352

 problem statements, NP 340-342

 program documentation, NP 353-354

 program testing, NP 352-353

 software engineering, NP 340

programming language, NP 80

programming languages, NP 80, NP 275-276, NP 280, NP 354-364

 characteristics, NP 354-362

 creating applications, NP 280

 database management systems, NP 311

 evolution, NP 384-386

 file management software, NP 310

Project Gutenberg, NP 215

Project Hermes, NP 215

project team, NP 269, NP 270

Prolog A declarative computer language, NP 356, NP 363

prompt A message displayed by the computer to request information or help you proceed, NP 14, NP 19

 displaying, NP 134-135

 DOS, NP 42

 dot, NP 14

 UNIX, NP 43

prompted dialog A type of user interface in which the

computer presents prompts one at a time and waits for a response after each one. Also called prompted conversation, NP 20

prompted user interface A method of human-computer communication in which the computer initiates a dialog by displaying a prompt, NP 19-21

prototype 1. An experimental or trial version of an information system that is under development; 2. A preliminary version or a trial model of a device, NP 274, NP 379-380
    hardware, NP 396

PS/2 computers, SIMMs, NP 122

pseudocode A notational system that uses a mixture of English and computer language commands to express an algorithm, NP 346

public codes, NP 152

public domain software Software that is available for use without restriction and may be freely copied, distributed, and even resold, NP 61, NP 215
    viruses, NP 235
    publications, NP 402-403

pull-down menu A menu that appears to drop down from a menu bar located at the top of the screen, NP 16, NP 17, NP 42, NP 43

punched cards, NP 377

punctuation, command languages, NP 13

purchasing
    hardware, NP 277
    software, NP 277

Q

QBASIC, NP 362

query A request you make to the database for records that meet specific criteria, NP 53, NP 317-320
    decision, NP 265

query by example The process of filling in a blank record with a sample of the data you want to find, NP 317

query language A set of commands that you can use to locate and manipulate data, NP 317

QuickTime A format used to encode, compress, store, and playback video segments on computers, NP 171

R

Radio Shack, NP 391

RAM. *See* random access memory (RAM)

RAM address A unique identifier assigned to each location within memory, NP 119

random access The ability of a disk-based storage device to go directly to any location on the storage medium, NP 90, NP 93, NP 99, NP 100

random access memory (RAM) A temporary holding area for data before and after it is processed, NP 116, NP 117, NP 119-121, NP 124
    addresses, NP 119
    capacity, NP 121
    power problems, NP 229
    technology, NP 121-122
    testing, NP 132, NP 133
    variables, NP 349

range check, NP 314

read only memory (ROM) A set of chips that contain permanent instructions that help a computer prepare for processing tasks, NP 116, NP 123, NP 383. *See also* CD-ROM (compact disc read only memory)

reading data. *See* opening a file

read-write head, NP 88, NP 90, NP 91, NP 92, NP 96, NP 97

read/write optical drive An optical storage device that merges magnetic and optical technologies. Also called magneto-optical drive, NP 98

real number Numeric data that contains a decimal point, NP 297

receiver The destination for the message, NP 153

record A group of fields containing information about a single person, place, or thing. A record in a database is equivalent to a card in a card file, NP 52, NP 296, NP 297-299
    entering, NP 316
    indexing, NP 322-323
    saving, NP 321
    size, NP 298
    sorting, NP 321-322, NP 323
    updating, NP 321

record format The field names, field lengths, and data types that specify a data record, NP 299

record number Unique identifier used to identify the records in a database, NP 316

record occurrence, NP 298, NP 299

record type An abstract or general description of a record, NP 298, NP 299

redirected data, NP 194

reduced instruction set computer (RISC) A microcomputer with a limited set of assembly language instructions, NP 129-130

reference. *See* reference manual

reference manual A printed book that contains the information about installing and using software or hardware, NP 15, NP 25, NP 354

register A special holding area of the CPU for the numbers the ALU uses for computation, NP 125

relation, NP 306

relational database A database model that represents data as a collection of tables, NP 300-302, NP 303, NP 306

relational operator A symbol (=, >, <, >=, <=, <>) used to create an expression, NP 317

relationship An association between the entities in a file, databases, NP 300-302, NP 304, NP 305

remark An explanatory comment that helps describe what a program or instruction is supposed to do, NP 353-354

Remington Rand, NP 389-390

removable hard disk Platters and read-write heads that can be inserted and removed from a removable hard disk drive much like a floppy disk, NP 93

repetition control A control structure that repeats one or more instructions until a certain condition is met, NP 351-352

repetition control structure, NP 351-352

report generator The part of a database or file management system that provides you with the ability to design reports, NP 323

report template A document that contains the outline or general specifications for a report, but does not contain the data for the report, NP 323-324

reports, NP 323-325
    database management software, NP 53

detail, NP 265
    exception, NP 265
    spreadsheet software, NP 51
request for proposal (RFP) A document you send to vendors that describes the problem you are trying to solve and the requirements for the solution, and requests that vendors recommend a solution for the problem, NP 277, NP 278
request for quotation (RFQ) A request for a formal price quotation on a specified list of hardware and software, NP 277, NP 278
resolution The maximum number of pixels that can be displayed on the screen at one time, NP 23, NP 139-140
retrieving a file. *See* opening a file
RETURN command, NP 351
return receipt, NP 208
reviews, NP 405
revisions, software, NP 398-399
RFP. *See* request for proposal
RFQ. *See* request for quotation
RISC. *See* reduced instruction set computer (RISC)
ROM. *See* read only memory (ROM)
root directory The main directory of a disk. In MS-DOS, the root directory is created when the disk is formatted, NP 85
routine decision A decision that is made regularly and repeatedly, NP 264
row, spreadsheet software, NP 50
RS-232C port. *See* serial port
rumor-central columns, NP 403
run length encoding A compression technique that looks for patterns of bytes and replaces them with a code that describes the pattern, NP 171
running an application The process of starting an application program. Also called launching an application, NP 102, NP 194-195
run-time errors, NP 353

S

sampling rate The number of times per second that sound is measured during the recording process, NP 166-167
satellite transmission Signals that are sent from a ground-based transmitting station to a satellite, which then transmits the data to other ground-based stations, NP 176
saving, updated records, NP 321
saving a file. *See* writing data
scanner, NP 12
scatter plot The type of graph you use to show data pairs, NP 326, 327
scheduling software Application software that helps you keep track of appointments, due dates, and special events, NP 47, NP 64
Schickard, Wilhelm, NP 377
science fiction, NP 392
Scroll Lock key, NP 10
SCSI port (Small Computer System Interface) A socket designed to provide a connection for between one and seven peripheral devices, NP 142
SDLC. *See* system development life cycle
search option, on-line help, NP 26
searching databases, NP 316-320

Searle, John, NP 393
second generation computers, NP 381
sector A portion of a track that holds 512 bytes of data, NP 89
security
    maintenance, NP 40-41
    passwords, NP 40-41, NP 193, NP 239
    user IDs, NP 40, NP 41, NP 193, NP 212, NP 239
See system requirements, success factors
segment A record type in a hierarchical database, NP 304
selection control structure A control structure that tells the computer what to do based on whether a condition is true or false, NP 351
semi-structured problems, NP 265
sequence control structure A control structure that changes the order in which instructions are executed by directing the computer to execute an instruction elsewhere in the program, NP 350-351
sequence, music A set of instructions used for MIDI music that contains instructions for when a note begins, what instrument plays the note, the volume of the note, and the duration of the note, NP 168
sequential access The method used to access data that has been stored on tape as a sequence of bytes along the length of the tape, NP 95
serial communications, NP 177
serial port A socket that provides a connection for transmitting data one bit at a time. Also called an RS-232C port, NP 142, NP 143, NP 181
service A vendor's ability to repair hardware when it breaks or fails to work properly, NP 406, NP 407
set Related record types in a network database model, NP 305
setup program, NP 56, NP 58, NP 122
Shannon, Claude, NP 153
shareware Copyrighted software marketed under a try-before-you-buy policy that allows you to use a software package for a trial period. After the trial period, you should send in a registration fee, NP 62, NP 236
    viruses, NP 235
sharing programs, NP 194-195
Shift key, NP 10
shrink-wrap license A software license that is visible in the back of a software product shrink-wrapped in plastic. Opening the wrapping indicates the user agrees to the terms of the software license, NP 60
SIAM Journal on Computing, NP 403
signature A unique series of bytes in program code that can be used by virus detection programs to identify a virus, NP 236
SIMM (Single In-line Memory Module) A circuit board that contains RAM chips, NP 116, NP 122
Simple queries, NP 317
simplex channel A communication channel that allows a device to send only messages, NP 180
Sinclair, Clive, NP 391
single-user license A software license that limits the use of software to one user at a time, NP 60
site license A software license that allows a software package to be used on any and all computers at a specific location, NP 60
slide rule, NP 377
Smalltalk, NP 385
software. *See* computer software

conversion, NP 283
purchasing, NP 277
software customization The process of modifying a commercial application to reflect the needs of the users
software engineer A person who focuses on the design, coding, and testing of software for an information system, NP 340
software engineering The systematic approach to the development, operation, maintenance, and retirement of software, NP 280, NP 340
software license A legal contract that defines the ways in which a user may use a computer program, NP 59-61, NP 62
software pirates, NP 58
software registration card A card the purchaser of the software package fills out and returns to the software publisher to become a registered user, NP 58
software testing, NP 279
software worm A program designed to enter a computer system through a security hole, NP 234
solutions
evaluating and selecting, NP 276
potential, identifying, NP 275-276
sonification The use of audio cues to represent data, NP 326
sort key A field used to arrange records in order, NP 321
sorting The process of rearranging the sequence of the records on a disk, NP 53, NP 321-322, NP 323
sound board, NP 15
sound card, NP 12
sound representation, NP 166-168
MIDI music, NP 168
waveform audio, NP 166-167
source code The text of a computer program written in a high-level language, NP 358, NP 359
source The originator of a communication, NP 153
spaghetti code, NP 385
speaker, NP 15
speech
computer-generated, NP 21
interfaces, NP 389
speech recognition, NP 15, NP 19, NP 217
spell checker, on-line, NP 48
Sperry Corporation, NP 390, NP 391
Sperry Rand, NP 390
spreadsheet software A type of productivity software that helps you do calculations by entering numbers and formulas in a grid of rows and columns, NP 17, NP 46, NP 50-51, NP 363, NP 386
SQL (Structured Query Language) A declarative language that was developed to provide a standard method for defining and manipulating a database, NP 317, NP 363
Star Trek: The Next Generation (television series), NP 394-395
Star Trek archive, NP 215
start bit Used in asynchronous protocol to indicate the beginning of data, NP 178
Stevenson, Adlai, NP 393
stop bit Used in the asynchronous protocol to indicate the end of a block of data, NP 178, NP 182
storage, NP 4, NP 83-86. *See also* memory
logical, NP 85-86
magnetic, NP 87-96, NP 97. *See also* floppy disk; hard disk drive; tape backup
management, NP 40
optical, NP 96-98

physical, NP 86, NP 98-101
primary. *See* memory
storage capacity The maximum amount of data that can be stored on a storage medium. Usually measured in kilobytes, megabytes, or gigabytes, NP 87
storage device The mechanical apparatus that records and retrieves data from a storage medium, NP 86
identification, NP 83
storage medium The disk, tape, paper, or other item that contains data, NP 4, NP 86, NP 87
string data type. *See* character data type
structured data file A data file in which the data is stored as records, NP 296
structured decision A decision that has a clear and replicable method for reaching a solution, NP 264
structured English A method of expressing an algorithm using a specific subset of English words, NP 272-273, NP 346
Structured Query Language (SQL) A popular query language for both mainframes and microcomputers, NP 317, NP 363
stylus A pointing device used to enter data into a pen-based computer system, NP 15, NP 19
subdirectory A directory that contains a set of files divided off of the root directory. In MS-DOS, the MD or MKDIR command creates a subdirectory, NP 85
submenu, NP 18
sub-notebook computers, NP 7
subroutine A section of a computer program to which control is transferred to perform a specific task, NP 350
summary report A report which shows summary information about the items in a system, NP 324-325
super computer The largest, fastest, and most expensive type of computer, used to handle specialized information analysis, NP 6, NP 213-214, NP 390
Super VGA (SVGA) A circuit board that connects a computer and monitor and displays graphics in a range from 800 by 600 pixels to 1280 by 1024 pixels, NP 23
supercomputers, NP 390
support A vendor's ability to answer your questions after the sale, NP 406, NP 407
support line A telephone number maintained by a software or hardware company that users can call to get assistance, NP 27, NP 58
surge protector. *See* surge suppressor
surge suppressor A device that stops power surges and spikes from entering your computer system and damaging sensitive electronic components, NP 230, NP 231
switch. *See* parameter
synchronous protocol A communications protocol in which the sender and receiver are synchronized by a signal called a clock. The transmitting computer sends data at a fixed rate, and the receiving computer expects the incoming data at the same rate, NP 177
syntax The rules of a command language that specify the order of the command words and parameters and the punctuation that is required for valid commands, NP 14
syntax error An error caused by misspelling a command word, leaving out required punctuation, or typing the command words out of order, NP 14, NP 18, NP 358
program testing, NP 352-353
system bus, NP 117, NP 118, NP 135
system construction, NP 279-282
application testing, NP 281-282

creating applications, NP 280-281
hardware installation, NP 279
software installation, NP 279-280
system conversion The process of deactivating an old information system and activating a new system, NP 283-284
system design, NP 275-279
application specifications, NP 277, NP 279
evaluating and selecting solutions, NP 276
identifying potential solutions, NP 275-276
purchasing hardware and software, NP 277, NP 278
system development life cycle (SDLC) An outline of the process that helps develop successful information systems, NP 268-269
system development project team A group of people who are assigned to analyze and develop an information system, NP 269, NP 270
system documentation, NP 272-273
system implementation, NP 282-284
acceptance testing, NP 284
data conversion, NP 283
system conversion, NP 283-284
training users, NP 282
system maintenance, NP 284-285
system requirements The criteria for successfully solving the problems in an information system, NP 274
software, NP 54, NP 55
system resources, allocation, NP 40
System 7, NP 43
system software Programs that direct fundamental operations of a computer, such as displaying information, storing data, printing, interpreting typed commands, and communicating with peripheral devices, NP 38, NP 39-44. *See also* operating system
system testing The process of testing an information system to ensure that all the hardware and software components work together, NP 281-282
system unit, NP 8
light, NP 8, NP 132
systems analyst A computer professional responsible for analyzing information requirements, designing a new information system, and supervising the new system implementation, NP 268

table A two-dimensional structure used to store data in the relational database model. A row is called a tuple and is equivalent to a record. A column is called an attribute and is equivalent to a field, NP 52, NP 306
table of contents menu, NP 26
Tabulating Machine Company, NP 377, NP 389-390
tape backup A copy of the data on a hard disk, transferred to tape storage media and used to restore lost data, NP 8, NP 83, NP 94-95, NP 96, NP 99
TCP/IP (Transmission control protocol/Internet protocol) A widely used network communication protocol on microcomputer, minicomputer, and mainframe networks, NP 204
technical support, NP 27, NP 58
telecommunications Transmitting and receiving data over a long distance, NP 152
Telnet A computer program that lets you connect to a host

computer anywhere on the Internet and use your computer just as if you were using a terminal directly attached to that host computer, NP 215-216
template, report, NP 323-324
temporary memory, NP 383
terminal An input and output device for a host computer, NP 206, NP 207
terminal emulation software Software that enables a microcomputer to act as a terminal and communicate with a host computer, NP 206, NP 207
test area A computer system that can be used for software testing without disrupting the information system of an organization, NP 281
testing. *See also* program testing
acceptance, NP 284
applications, NP 281-282
software, NP 279
systems, NP 281-282
Texas Instruments, NP 391
text compression, NP 170-171
thesaurus, on-line, NP 48
third generation computers Computers based on an architecture that uses integrated circuits, NP 381-383
thread A series of messages relating to a particular topic on a bulletin board system, NP 208-209
TI 99/4A, NP 391
time bomb, NP 233, NP 234
toggle key A key on the computer keyboard that is used to switch back and forth between two modes, NP 9, NP 10
token, NP 359
token An electronic signal that circulates on a token passing network to indicate when a device can send a message, NP 202, NP 204, NP 359
Token Ring A popular network standard developed by IBM that uses a token to regulate the flow of data, NP 200, NP 201, NP 202
tool A graphical object used to carry out a specific task, NP 22, NP 165
touch sensitive screen An input and output device designed to be used with a menu driven user interface. You make menu selections by touching the surface of the screen, NP 12, NP 19
tower case, NP 7
tower computer, storage device identification, NP 83
track One of a series of concentric circles in a disk that holds data, NP 89
trackball, NP 12
trade journal A publication designed for people who design, build, sell, and market computer products, NP 402
training, users, NP 282
transaction An event that requires a manual or computer-based activity, NP 261-262
transaction processing system A system that keeps track of all the transactions for a business by providing a way to collect, display, modify, and cancel transactions, NP 261-264
transistors, NP 381
translator, NP 358
trap door A special set of instructions that allows a user to bypass the normal security precautions and enter a computer system, NP 240-241
Trojan horse A computer program that appears to perform

one function while actually doing something else, NP 232-233, NP 234-235

true color graphics A color graphics standard that uses 16.7 million colors to produce photographic-quality images, NP 162

tuple, NP 306

Turing, Alan, NP 377, NP 393

Turing Machine, NP 377-378

Turing Test, NP 393

tutorial A guided, step-by-step learning experience that helps you develop the skills needed to use hardware or software, NP 24-25, NP 54, NP 58

twisted pair cable A communications link that consists of pairs of copper wire twisted together and covered with a thin layer of insulating plastic, NP 173-174

2001: A Space Odyssey (film), NP 394

typing keypad, NP 10

ULTRIX, NP 43

uncompressing The process of reversing file compression, NP 168

Undelete facility, NP 100

unformat program A program that attempts to restore the files that were on a disk before it was formatted, NP 228

Unicode A 16-bit code that can represent over 65,000 different characters proposed as an international standard for data representation, NP 161-162

uniform format. *See* data file

uninterruptible power supply (UPS) A device containing a battery and other circuitry that provides enough power to keep a computer working through momentary power interruptions or to allow you to save your files and exit your programs, NP 230, NP 231

unit testing The process of testing a single component of a software package to ensure that it operates reliably and correctly, NP 281

UNIVAC computers, NP 381, NP 390, NP 393

UNIX Command line multiuser, multitasking operating system developed by AT&T's Bell Laboratories, NP 41, NP 43

update To change or delete a record in a database, NP 321

upgrade A new release or enhanced version of a product computers, NP 66
software, NP 37-38, NP 58

upper memory The last 348K of the first megabyte of memory, NP 120

UPS. *See* uninterruptible power supply (UPS)

Usenet news group, NP 405

user groups, NP 405

user ID A unique set of letters and numbers that identifies a particular user of a computer system, NP 40, NP 41, NP 193, NP 212, NP 239

user interface The hardware and software that provide a means by which humans and computers communicate, NP 3, NP 5-6, NP 13-23
command-line, NP 13-15
graphical, NP 21-23
menu-driven, NP 15-19
navigational aids, NP 217
prompted, NP 19-21

user reference, NP 354

user rights Rules that limit the directories and files that each user can access, NP 240-241

users, training, NP 282

utility software A type of system software that helps you perform maintenance work on the system, such as backing up a hard drive or checking for viruses, NP 44

vacuum tubes, NP 380-381

valid commands, NP 14

valid filename A filename that conforms to the rules for naming files, NP 81

value added reseller (VAR) A vendor that combines commercially available products with special hardware or software to create a package designed to meet the needs of a specific industry, NP 400-402

vaporware A product that is announced but never made or marketed
hardware, NP 396
software, NP 398

VAR (Value Added Reseller), NP 400-402

variables, NP 349

vector graphics Graphics that recreate an image from a set of instructions, NP 164-166

vertical market software Business software designed for specialized tasks in a specific market or business, NP 47

VESA (video electronic standards association) bus, NP 136-137, NP 137, NP 138

VGA. *See* video graphics array (VGA)

Vic 20, NP 391

video card. *See* graphics card

video compression, NP 171-172

video display adapter The circuitry needed to display text and graphics on the monitor. The video display adapter can be built into the mainboard or onto an expansion card, NP 138-140

Video for Windows A format used to encode, compress, store, and playback video segments on computers, NP 171

video graphics array (VGA) A circuit board that connects a computer to a monitor and displays graphics in a 640 by 480 pixel matrix, NP 23

video representation, NP 166

video segment, NP 171

video tutorial A type of tutorial using videotape to visually illustrate how a specific piece of software or hardware works, NP 24

virus. *See* computer virus

virus detection program A program that examines the files stored on a disk to determine if they are infected with a virus, NP 235, NP 236

virus removal programs, NP 237

virus scan program. *See* virus detection program

VisiCalc, NP 386, NP 391

Visual Basic, NP 362, NP 385

Visual C++, NP 385

voice input, NP 21

volatile A term used to refer to memory that holds data only as long as the computer power is on, NP 120-121

von Neumann, John, NP 4

Wall Street Journal, NP 403

WarGames (film), NP 394

Watson, Thomas Sr., NP 375

waveform audio The digital representation of a sound, NP 166-167

what-if analysis, spreadsheet software, NP 50

window A rectangular area on the screen that contains a document, program, or message, NP 23, NP 43

window object class, NP 360-361

Windows. *See* Microsoft Windows

wireless communication link A communication channel that uses radio waves or microwave transmission to transmit data in mobile sites and in remote geographical regions, NP 176

wiring hub, NP 198, NP 199

Word for Windows, NP 399

word processing software A type of productivity software that you use to produce text-based documents such as reports, letters, and papers, NP 37, NP 46, NP 48-49

word size The number of bits the microprocessor can manipulate at one time, NP 127-128

WordPerfect, NP 399

WordPerfect Corporation, NP 400

WordStar, NP 399

worksheet model A spreadsheet in which numbers and formulas have been entered to perform specific calculations, NP 50

workstation A personal computer connected to a computer network, NP 192, NP 205, NP 207

workstation address, NP 201, NP 212

WORM drive A Write Once Read Many optical storage device that allows you to write data once on any sector of the disk, NP 98

Wozniak, Steve, NP 63

write-protected disk A disk that cannot have data written on it by the computer. A 3.5 inch disk is write protected when the write-protect window is open. A 5.25 inch disk is write protected when the write-protect notch is covered, NP 88

write-protect notch, NP 88

writing data The process of storing data on a storage medium. Also called saving a file, NP 86, NP 102, NP 103, NP 230, NP 231, NP 321

written documentation Paper-based or electronic external documentation that contains information about a program, NP 354

XENIX, NP 43

Xerox, NP 391

XT bus, NP 137

x-y chart, NP 327

Z-series computers, NP 379

Zuse, Konrad, NP 379